Acknowledgements

CW01502396

This book has been a long time coming and presents itself as one of the more esoteric by-products of the Covid pandemic of 2020. This provided the time and space to re-visit research and writing originally completed in the 1970s and early 1980s. At the heart of the text lies a PhD thesis completed in 1984 at the University of Manchester and an earlier article submitted for inclusion in James Epstein and Dorothy Thompson's *The Chartist Experience* collection of essays. Though well received, this proposed contribution was bumped by Gareth Stedman Jones' pivotal chapter on 'The Language of Chartism', which, in Andrew Messner's phrase, is 'widely credited as the progenitor of the much discussed "linguistic turn"'. The rest, as they say, is history.

The book, in keeping with many of its protagonists, was originally very much the product of an academic out-worker, happily operating on the margins of the vast and powerful knowledge factories, and originally using traditional methods – index cards, micro-fiches and reams of hand transcriptions of primary sources. It has, though, been suitably updated by drawing on subsequent research and new sources and search techniques. My present status as an unaffiliated 'independent scholar' and the impact of the pandemic, however, mean that the revised book was completed without full access to the paraphernalia of academic scaffolding (particularly university library resources). I am therefore particularly thankful for the joys of JSTOR, and to authors and their institutions who have made their material 'open access'. In regard to less publicly accessible work by fellow researchers I unreservedly apologise for any inadvertent omissions or oversights. Any errors of fact or interpretation, however, are mine alone.

I am also grateful to a number of historians who I contacted 'out of the blue' to explore the possibility of renovating and updating my original work: notably Keith Laybourn, Matthew Roberts, John Baxter, and Alan Brooke. Their response was uniformly positive and collegial. Subsequent correspondence with Mark Crail of the Chartist Ancestors website, and with John Hargreaves and David Glover of the Halifax Antiquarian Society, was similarly illuminating and supportive. It would also be remiss not to acknowledge the annual polite but persistent, Thanksgiving reminders of Dr Bruce Leslie of the State University of New York Brockport encouraging me to 'get back to doing a bit of history'. The resultant book would not have seen the light of day without the patient support and diligent copy editing of Paul Mangan at Breviary Stuff Publications.

Admittedly rather belatedly, I would like to express my thanks to the staff of the many libraries and record offices in which I laboured during the 1970s and to the fellow researchers of that period who were generous in their advice and sharing of information. Special mention should also be made to the practical support and typing skills provided during this period by my late sister-in-law Sue Edwards. Equally, I would not have completed my original thesis without the backing and active connivance of my esteemed colleague and boss in the early 80s, the late Aubrey Black; and the rigour and patience of my supervisor, Dr Iori Prothero. His generous support, encouragement and subsequent friendship continue to be much appreciated.

Finally, neither the original thesis nor its new iteration would have been possible without the forbearance, positivity and unstinting support of my wife, Madeleine Edwards. In family lore the original thesis, written in 1983-4 while two toddlers (Paul and David) slept, was our missing mythical third child. That gap was filled with the arrival of Katharine, a budding historian, the following spring. Fittingly the new book has been completed shortly after the birth of Katharine's third child, Alice. This book is dedicated to her and to her two siblings, Daniel and Joseph.

WORKERS OF THEIR OWN EMANCIPATION

John Sanders

Workers of Their Own Emancipation

Working-class leadership and organisation in the West Riding textile district, 1829-1839

BREVIARY STUFF PUBLICATIONS
2024

Breviary Stuff Publications,
BCM Breviary Stuff, London WC1N 3XX
breviarystuff.org.uk
Copyright © John Sanders 2024
The centipede device copyright © Breviary Stuff Publications

A CIP record for this book is available from
The British Library

ISBN: 978-1-9161586-7-2

Contents

Abbreviations

BC	*Bradford Courier*
BLPFCF	*The British Labourer's Protector and Factory Child's Friend*
BO	*Bradford Observer*
BPL	Bradford Public Library
BPP	British Parliamentary Papers
BS	*Boot and Shoemaker*
BWC	*Bradford and Wakefield Chronicle*
CC	Co-operative Congress
CN	*Co-operative News*
EHR	*English Historical Review*
GNCTU	Grand National Consolidated Trades' Union
GNU	Great Northern Union
HC	*Halifax Courier*
HCC	*Halifax Commercial Chronicle*
HCH	*Huddersfield Chronicle*
HDCMA	Halifax District Co-operative Manufacturing Association
HDE	*Huddersfield Daily Examiner*
HG	*Halifax Guardian*
HHE	*Halifax and Huddersfield Express*
IRSH	*International Review of Social History*
LDA	London Democratic Association
LI	*Leeds Intelligencer*
LM	*Leeds Mercury*
LP	*Leeds Patriot*
LT	*Leeds Times*
LWMA	London Working Men's Association
LYC	*Lancashire and Yorkshire Co-operator*
NAPL	National Association for the Protection of Labour

NS	*Northern Star*
NU	Northern Union
NUWC	National Union of the Working-Classes
NWC	*Newcastle Weekly Chronicle*
Oastler Coll.	Goldsmiths Library, Senate House Library, University of London, Oastler Collection
OC	Owen Correspondence, Co-operative Union Library, Manchester
PMA	*Poor Man's Advocate*
PMG	*Poor Man's Guardian*
PP	British Museum, Place Papers
PU	Political Union
RA	Radical Association
RPU	Radical Political Union
RRA	Radical Reform Association
SSLH	Society for the Study of Labour History
STC	Short Time Committee
TN	*Trades' Newspaper*
TNA: HO	The National Archives: Public Record Office, Kew, Home Office papers
UPCI	*Union Pilot and Co-operative Intelligencer*
VP	*Voice of the People*
VWR	*Voice of the West-Riding*
Webb Coll.	Webb Collection of Trade Union Manuscripts, London School of Economics
WFP	*Weekly Free Press*
WMA	Working Men's Association

About the author

During a varied career in adult, further, and higher education, John Sanders pioneered strategies to extend student access and enhance progression and produced reports and commentaries on different aspects of adult learning, widening participation, and teaching excellence. Since retiring he has returned to his earlier historical research and authored a series of articles on popular radicalism and trade unionism in the 1820s and 1830s.

Introduction

> People who have not shared in the hopes of the Chartists, who have no personal knowledge of the deep and intense feelings which animated them, can have little conception of the difference between our own times and those of thirty and forty years ago. The whole governing classes – Whigs even more than Tories – were not only disliked; they were positively hated by the working population.[1]

Nowhere was this truer than in the West Riding of Yorkshire. Here in the towns, out-townships and outlying villages, flourished advanced political and social ideas; and here also in the 1830s, the wide range of interrelated campaigns and agitations, which culminated in Chartism, found their most consistent support. As J. F. C. Harrison pointed out many years ago: 'these movements were not so much rivals competing for support, nor even complementary parts of a greater national movement, as different expressions of a discontent on the part of the people with their lot under the new conditions of industrialism, and a reaching out to a more just and equitable organisation of society'.[2]

The study which follows deals with one area of the West Riding, the 'textile district', taking in the towns of Leeds, Bradford, Huddersfield, Halifax, Keighley and Dewsbury and their environs. Although extremely varied, the sub-region, with its 'wool textiles' focus, undoubtedly had a distinctive identity and character. Localism remained strong and many of the small industrial villages of the area were highly cohesive communities with strong internal links of kinship, bolstered by keen local pride and a suspicion of outsiders. Nevertheless, it is clear from the developments of the late 1820s and the 1830s that insularity was being broken down. New means of

---

1   *NWC*, 4 Jan 1879. (Letter from 'Ironside').
2   J. F. C. Harrison, *Living and Learning, 1790-1960: A study in the History of the English Adult Education Movement* (London: Routledge and Kegan Paul, 1961), p. 95.

Localism (handwritten annotation in left margin)

communication were a key driver of this process, as the first edition of unstamped *Voice of the West-Riding* in June 1833 proclaimed:

> The present Era is truly encouraging, the Press is rapidly becoming democratic, new papers are springing forth, almost every large town is possessed of a paper, or is seeking to establish one wherein popular rights are advocated. Every achievement of this sort is strength, it is like a new rail-road laid across a barren tract, connecting the distant and familiarizing the unacquainted...'[3]

Although firmly based in their respective communities, leaders increasingly operated, and organised their agitations, within a regional structure. Thus the area sent five West Riding, not individual town, delegates to the Chartist Convention in 1839. Despite the diversity of the district's economy and the continuing pull of parochialism, this focus on common interests and shared identity helped to shape the distinctive political response of the era: early Chartism – a strong national movement with vigorous local roots. Taking a regional focus enables us to link these two features and to study the diverse campaigns and agitational endeavours which came together in Chartism in a wider context, and to isolate some of their key features and interconnections. Such an approach provides sufficient breadth to enable comparisons between the different centres and overcome some of the drawbacks of purely local studies.

The chronological limits of the book also require some explanation. The prime focus is on the years between 1829 and 1839. The study begins in 1829 with the coincidence of a more fluid political atmosphere at the centre and the recurrence of extreme economic depression in the localities. This gave rise, via the 'Distress' meetings and the early co-operative endeavours of 1829, to renewed attempts in a number of the working communities of the textile district to address the effects of, and suggest alternatives to, an unregulated competitive economy and an unrepresentative parliament. Looking back in the late 1830s contemporaries recognised this change of atmosphere and gear in the late 1820s; and historians ever since have generally accepted the distinctiveness of the decade after 1829.[4]

The 1829-34 period, bookended by local campaigns to highlight distress and the decisive defeat of Yorkshire trades' unionism, was particularly crucial. It witnessed a fundamental shift in the national political landscape, the establishment of a robust agitational infrastructure and the emergence of a new generation of local leaders. As Malcolm Chase has noted, 'Politically ... [these years] constitute one of the most eventful episodes in modern British history, perhaps the only one about which it can legitimately be asked how close the country came to revolution'.[5]

---

3   *VWR* 1 June 1833. On the impact of the communication revolution in print in one (Lancashire) community see, Robert G. Hall, 'At the Dawn of the Information Age: Reading and the Working Classes in Ashton–under–Lyne, 1830–1850', in J. J. Connolly *et al.*, (eds.), *Print Culture Histories Beyond the Metropolis* (Toronto: University of Toronto Press, 2016), pp. 243–67.

4   See, for example, Gwyn A. Williams' introduction to Dorothy Thompson (ed.), *The Early Chartists* (London: Macmillan, 1971), pp x-xi.

5   Malcolm Chase, *Early Trade Unionism: Fraternity, Skill and the Politics of Labour* (London: Breviary Stuff, 2010 edn.), p. 110.

That is not to say that 1829 saw a complete break, and the chronological limits of the study are not applied too rigidly. The movements of the 1830s did not emerge out of a vacuum. They and their local leaders were firmly rooted in a rich community-based radical culture. There was much continuity in terms of ideas and traditions, meeting places and organisational forms, and some in terms of local leadership, between the radical political movements of the post-Napoleonic War period and those of the late 1820s and 1830s. The lessons and legacy of the flowering of trade unionism, the defeats of 1825 and the depression of 1826 were also highly influential.

More generally the 'strangely quiet' 1820s were a period of reflection and the gradual dissemination of oppositional ideas.[6] Traditional radical icons and propositions were not forgotten. Thomas Paine's birthday continued to be celebrated, Cobbett and Hunt retained sizeable overlapping followings, and Carlile's individualistic freethinking radicalism resonated in many West Riding localities.[7] Although the poor man's press had largely collapsed, literature remained cheap and the gradual diffusion of the texts and ideas of Thomas Hodgskin, Robert Owen and William Thompson offered fresh insights into the predicament in which large numbers of working people found themselves. The ideas which underpinned an alternative way of seeing things, incorporating traditional radical tenets, aspects of a deep-rooted 'moral economy', and more recent anti-capitalist texts were hammered into shape in these years. The cohesiveness and strength of feeling evident in the upsurge of working-class activity after 1829 owed much to the aggregate store of ideas and frustration accumulated during the 'decade of "the silent insurrection"'.[8] Like a vast spring pushed back to its limits, the early working-class movements unleashed themselves after 1829 with a ferocity and latent energy built up in the preceding years of hardship and uncertainty.

The breadth, variety and ubiquity of these movements, and the speed of development – from the poorly printed, scarcely legible, first edition of the *Voice of the West-Riding*, selling a few hundred copies in June 1833, to the stamped, highly professional and innovative *Northern Star*, selling many thousands nearly five years later – justifies the detailed and special attention paid to the 1829 to 1839 period. Nor did these movements or the *Star* fade in 1839. Many of the ideas, leaders and organisations which flourished in the 1830s remained influential and important into the 1840s and well beyond. Nevertheless 1839, with the calling off of the 'Sacred Month' in August and the failure of the risings of winter 1839-40, can be taken as a convenient finishing date: the end of the first, 'early' phase of the Chartist movement. A number of important local leaders dropped out of prominence in the late 1830s and early 1840s and new leaders, almost exclusively drawn from the ranks of the workers, emerged. Just as importantly, the sense of imminent change, crisis and possible conflict which had been so evident at key times during the previous decade – notably 1831-2,

---

6   E. P. Thompson, *The Making of the English Working Class* (Harmondsworth: Penguin, 1968 edn.), p. 781.

7   John Halstead 'The Huddersfield Short Time Committee and its radical associations, c.1820-1876' in John A. Hargreaves and E. A. Hilary Haigh (eds) *Slavery in Yorkshire: Richard Oastler and the Campaign against Child Labour in the Industrial Revolution* (Huddersfield: University of Huddersfield Press, 2012), pp. 107-8.

8   Williams, introduction, p. x.

1833-4, and 1838-9 – was largely absent in the years which followed.[9] Leaders now operated on a timescale of years rather than months.

On the surface the places and period under consideration would appear to have been well covered in a series of groundbreaking works produced during the second half of the twentieth century. E. P. Thompson's enormously influential *The Making of the English Working Class* drew heavily on West Riding evidence. J. T. Ward, in his studies of the factory, anti-poor law and Chartist movements, wrote extensively about the region and added substantially to our knowledge of local leaders and campaigns. Derek Fraser's exhaustive studies of Leeds politics, though concentrating on the rival middle-class elites, gave due weight and consideration to working-class organisations and movements. J. F. C. Harrison, in his pioneering work on adult education, Owenism and Leeds Chartism quarried much local material, and developed our understanding of the broad context in which local leaders and movements operated.[10] Edward Royle again drew on his familiarity with the regional evidence to extend our knowledge of the radical 'infidels' and provide a valuable overview of the Chartist movement. Finally, Dorothy Thompson's extensive writings on different aspects of Chartism owed much to her strong West Riding connections.[11]

However, all have their chronological limits and particular concerns. E. P. Thompson's working class was 'made' by 1832 and understandably, after tracing fifty years' nourishment of the Liberty Tree, he leaves the study of the fruit it bore in the 'Owenite and Chartist years' to others. J. T. Ward's main focus is the factory movement, and his insistence on a distinctive Tory-radical presence in the West Riding colours his interpretation of contemporary movements and leads to an underestimation of the 'active' part played by the working class and their local leaders. Derek Fraser, like Alfred Peacock with his important study of Bradford Chartism 1838-40, focuses mainly on one locality.[12] J. F. C. Harrison, though also contributing a valuable local Chartist study, is most notable for the wide sweep of his brush in painting in the broad cultural background against which the movements and leadership of the period should be set. Edward Royle's prime focus is on Owenism and the secularist tradition; whilst the very breadth of Dorothy Thompson's writings

---

9   A notable exception is the wave of Chartist-inflected strikes of summer 1842.

10 Thompson, *Making*; J. T. Ward, *The Factory Movement, 1830-1855* (London: Macmillan, 1962), J. T. Ward, *Chartism* (London: Batsford, 1973) and also numerous local studies; Derek Fraser, 'Politics in Leeds' in Derek Fraser (ed.) *A History of Modern Leeds* (Manchester: Manchester University Press, 1980), pp. 270-300, Derek Fraser, 'The Fruits of Reform; Leeds Politics in the 1830s', in *Northern History*, 7 (1972), pp. 89-111, and numerous articles on elements of local governance; J. F. C. Harrison, *Living and Learning*, J. F. C. Harrison, *Robert Owen and the Owenites in Britain and America: The Quest for the New Moral World* (London: Routledge and Kegan Paul, 1969), and 'Chartism in Leeds' in Asa Briggs (ed.), *Chartist Studies* (London: Macmillan, 1959), pp. 65-98.

11 Edward Royle, *Chartism* (London: Longman, 1980 edn.), Edward Royle, *Victorian Infidels* (Manchester: Manchester University Press, 1974), and Edward Royle, 'Chartists and Owenites – many parts but one body', *Labour History Review*, 65, 1 (2000), pp. 2-21; Dorothy Thompson (ed.), *The Early Chartists*, Dorothy Thompson, *The Chartists: Popular Politics in the Industrial Revolution* (London: Breviary Stuff, 2013 edn.), Stephen Roberts (ed.), *The Dignity of Chartism: Essays by Dorothy Thompson* (London: Verso, 2015).

12 A. J. Peacock, *Bradford Chartism, 1838-40* (York: St Anthony's Press, 1969).

means that local material acts a valuable quarry rather than the central building block of her interpretation of Chartism.

A host of other important early studies of the factory reform and anti-poor law agitations also include substantive engagement with events in, and material from, the textile district.[13] More recent scholarship, notably by Malcolm Chase and Katrina Navickas, has similarly drawn extensively on West Riding evidence in studies of early trade unionism, Chartism and the politics of space and place.[14] The region has also continued to be well-served by a host of local studies of radical, co-operative and trade union activities and the related operational infrastructure.[15] The textile district is equally well-represented in collections of essays and new scholarship examining aspects of radical ideology, culture and organisation.[16]

This study draws on these, and countless other local or more general works, to supplement information from newspapers, Home Office correspondence and a variety of other primary sources. It seeks to piece together a regional picture of diverse working-class movements in one of the most politically challenging and economically decisive decades of the nineteenth century. It deliberately spans the watershed year of 1832 at which so many histories begin or end and argues that what happened after 1840, and the eventual accommodations of the mid-Victorian epoch, cannot be fully understood without appreciating the energy and anger, the hopes and disappointments of the preceding years. It therefore aims to contribute to 'the yet-unwritten story of popular movements in the West Riding in the mid-decades of the Nineteenth

---

13 Cecil Driver, *Tory Radical, The Life of Richard Oastler* (New York: Oxford University Press, 1946); N. C. Edsall, *The Anti-Poor Law Movement, 1834-44* (Manchester: Manchester University Press, 1971); John Knott, *Popular Opposition to the 1834 Poor Law* (Beckenham: Croom Helm, 1986); Robert Gray, *The Factory Question and Industrial England, 1830-1860* (Cambridge: Cambridge University Press, 1996).

14 Malcolm Chase, *Early Trade Unionism*; Idem, *Chartism: A New History* (Manchester: Manchester University Press, 2007); Katrina Navickas, *Protest and the Politics of Space and Place, 1789-1848* (Manchester: Manchester University Press, 2016).

15 For example, essays by Alan J. Brooke, John A. Hargreaves and Robin Thornes in E. A. Hilary Haigh (ed.), *A Most Handsome Town: Aspects of the history and culture of a West Yorkshire Town* (Huddersfield: Kirklees Cultural Services, 1992); all the essays in John A. Hargreaves (ed.), *The Charter Our Right! Huddersfield Chartism Re-considered* (Huddersfield: Huddersfield Local History Society, 2018); John A. Hargreaves '"Hats Off": Methodism and Popular Protest in the West Riding of Yorkshire in the Chartist Era: A Case Study of Benjamin Rushton (1785-1853) of Halifax', *Proceedings of the Wesley Historical Association* 57, 2010, pp. 161-177; John Halstead, 'The Huddersfield Short Time Committee and its radical associations, c.1820-1876', in John A. Hargreaves and E. A. Hilary Haigh (eds) *Slavery in Yorkshire*, pp. 91-144; Dorothy and E. P. Thompson, 'Halifax as a Chartist centre', in Roberts (ed.), *The Dignity of Chartism*, pp. 73-124.

16 John Halstead, 'The Voice of the West Riding: promoters and supporters of a provincial unstamped newspaper', in C. Wrigley (ed.), *On the Move: Essays in Labour and Transport History Presented to Philip Bagwell* (London: Hambleton Press, 2003), pp. 22-57; Janette Martin, 'Popular political oratory and itinerant lecturing in Yorkshire and the North East in the age of Chartism, 1837-60', Unpub. PhD thesis, University of York, 2010; Malcolm Chase, 'Building identity, building circulation: engraved portraiture and the Northern Star', in Joan Allen and Owen Ashton (eds.), *Papers for the People: A Study of the Chartist Press* (London: Merlin Press, 2005), pp. 3-24.

Century', and thereby to unravel some of that 'tangled skein of purposes, influences, and individuals which passes under the name of the working-class movement'.[17]

Not all participants or movements are equally well covered. The emergence of female radical leaders and the hidden activism of working-class women as collectors of subscriptions and signatures, as 'political shoppers' supporting co-operative ventures or sympathetic traders, as worriers of strike-breaking 'black sheep', and as producers and consumers of many of the artefacts that adorned the various movements, has been highlighted in a number of general accounts, particularly of Chartism.[18] However, the full story of the role of West Riding women in the agitations of the era has yet to be written.

Women were also heavily involved in the communal, convivial and cultural activities that many of the movements fostered and supported. These ranged from consumer boycotts and prayer meetings to tea-parties and lectures, and are noted in relevant sections. Unsurprisingly in an area steeped in nonconformity, during an era soaked in religiosity, these undertakings sometimes had a religious dimension. It was also, though, an epoch riddled with doubt and scepticism. As Edward Royle has shown, secularists, freethinkers and 'infidels' were as much a part of the radical spectrum as lay preachers from Primitive or New Connexion Methodist backgrounds. These diverse belief systems were central to the lives of many leaders. However, rather than forming a separate section, they are generally highlighted when they impact on wider endeavours or relationships. Equally, not all instances when socio-political aspirations and confessional convictions collided are systematically explored. So, while the early co-operative movement is the subject of one of the detailed studies, the story of Owenite socialism in the second half of the decade is not tackled in a direct way. Although Simon Cross's investigation of Owenite socialism and anti-socialism in Halifax has made a start, the forensic local studies that Gregory Claeys solicits largely remain to be written.[19]

In contrast, the role of middle-class elites and how they exercised political, socio-cultural and economic power in the emerging industrial towns has attracted significant historiographical attention.[20] This literature has been drawn upon where appropriate.

---

17 Harrison, *Living and Learning*, p. 95.

18 For example, D. Thompson, *The Chartists*; Jutta Schwarzkopf, *Women in the Chartist Movement* (London: Macmillan, 1991); Chase, *Chartism*.

19 Simon J. Cross, 'The Experience of Owenite Socialism and Anti-Socialism in Halifax, 1829-1845', *Transactions of the Halifax Antiquarian Society*, 15 (2007), pp. 91-111; Gregory Claeys, *Citizens and Saints: Politics and Anti-Politics in Early British Socialism* (Cambridge: Cambridge University Press, 1989), p. 208. The standard texts remain, Harrison, *Robert Owen and the Owenites*; Eileen Yeo, 'Robert Owen and Radical Culture', in Sidney Pollard and John Salt (eds.), *Robert Owen: Prophet of the Poor* (London: Macmillan, 1971), pp. 84-114; Edward Royle, 'Owenism and the secularist tradition', in Malcolm Chase and Ian Dyck (eds.), *Living and Learning: Essays in Honour of J. F. C. Harrison* (Aldershot, Scolar Press, 1996); Edward Royle, 'Chartists and Owenites'.

20 Theodore Koditschek, *Class Formation and Urban Industrial Society: Bradford, 1750-1850* (Cambridge: Cambridge University Press, 1990); R. J. Morris, *Class, Sect and Party: The Making of the British Middle Class, Leeds 1820-1850* (Manchester: Manchester University Press, 1990); David Griffiths (2015), 'Huddersfield in Turbulent Times, 1815-1850: Who Ruled and How?', *Northern History*, 52 (2015), pp. 101-124. For Lancashire comparisons see,

However, the main focus remains on working-class agency and the independent agitations, organisations and cultures that local leaders created. These often operated most potently in communities (on the fringes of the main towns) that lay outside the reach and power of the urban elites. New scholarship has also begun to fill another potential gap in the West Riding political landscape: the persistence of working-class loyalism and the growth of operative conservative associations. The latter bodies briefly gained traction in a couple of the main towns and their environs and have been made the subject of detailed study.[21]

Trade unionism, though not the focus of a discrete whole chapter, nevertheless forms a thread which runs through all the major sections of the book. Indeed, one of the study's aims is to restore the centrality of the experience of local trade unionism and its associational culture to the story of how and why Chartism emerged in the form it did. This echoes the approach of Emma Griffin who additionally highlights the role of other associational entities, such as mutual-improvement groups, temperance societies and Mechanics Institutes, in helping to 'nurture the development of a working-class voice'.[22] These connections are noted in passing. Another 'crucially important workers' institution', the friendly society, has, as E. J. Hobsbawm observed as far back as 1957, generally been 'surprisingly and quite unnecessarily neglected by professional historians'.[23] This study does not rectify that oversight, but instead highlights occasions when, local societies, for all their strict 'no politics' rules and convivial, ritualistic elements, firmly aligned themselves with the struggles of their constituent communities.

Whilst not comprehensive, the coverage of this book is, nevertheless, broad. The first two introductory chapters lay the foundations for the later, more detailed studies. Chapter One takes up one of the book's recurring themes: the importance of effective local leadership and organisation to early working-class movements. Chapter Two sketches the industrial context in which these local leaders operated, identifies the common ground of shared perceptions and experiences which existed amongst different groups and strata of workers, and highlights the growth of trades' unionism

---

John Foster, *Class Struggle and the Industrial Revolution: Early Industrial Capitalism in Three English Towns* (London: Weidenfeld and Nicholson, 1974); and Brian Lewis, *The Middlemost and the Milltowns: Bourgeois Culture and Politics in Early Industrial England* (Stanford, CA: Stanford University Press, 2001).

21 Jörg Neuheiser, *Crown, Church and Constitution: Popular Conservatism in England, 1815-1867* (New York and Oxford: Berghahn, 2016). See also, David Walsh, *Making Angels in Marble, The Conservatives, the Early Industrial Working Class and Attempts at Political Incorporation* (London: Breviary Stuff, 2012).

22 Emma Griffin, 'The Making of the Chartists: Popular Politics and Working-class Autobiography in Early Victorian Britain', *EHR*, 129, 538 (2014), p. 591.

23 Iorwerth Prothero, *Artisans and Politics in Early Nineteenth-Century London. John Gast and His Times* (London: Methuen, 1981) p. 349, fn.11; E. J. Hobsbawm, 'Friendly Societies' in *Amateur Historian*, 3 (1957) p. 95. Hobsbawm's call has been answered by P. H. J. H. Gosden, *Self-Help: Voluntary Associations in Nineteenth-Century Britain* (London: Batsford, 1973) p. 27 ff; and Simon Cordery, *British Friendly Societies, 1750-1914* (Basingstoke and New York: Palgrave Macmillan, 2003).

in the early 1830s as an example of the search for 'wider' solutions by an increasingly pressurized and precarious workforce.

The middle chapters look in detail at three spheres of working-class endeavour and activity in the late 1820s and early 1830s. Chapter Three focuses on the popular radical end of the Reform agitation and traces the piecemeal evolution of an independent working-class presence; and, via the Whig 'betrayal' of 1832, the creation of a powerful story and spur for future action. Chapter Four looks at the early co-operative societies and relates this sober, respectable, and often neglected, area of independent working-class activity to the wider political and industrial aspirations of the communities in which it temporarily flourished. The fifth chapter examines a very different sort of movement: the very public and not exclusively working-class campaign for factory reform (to reduce the hours of child labour) in the early 1830s. Here again, though, the contribution of working-class leaders and organisational structures are emphasised, and links with popular radicalism and trade unionism highlighted.

The final two chapters move on from the individual campaigns and organisations of the reform era to focus on the pre and early Chartist years. Chapter Six tackles the abundant yet diverse agitations of the 1833-7 period and traces the development of the formal and informal sides of radical exertions and the progressive peeling off of working-class radicals from their former middle-class and lower middle-class allies. It leads naturally into the final chapter, on the early Chartist years, which witnessed the convergence of a number of streams of popular radical activity and their concentration into a powerful, purposeful force.

This multi-layered, interlocking approach, with its stress on common local leadership and organisation, seeks to minimise the dangers of 'compartmentalisation'.[24] Continuities and linkages, in terms of personalities, ideas and organisations, are highlighted not to create a false impression of a single, unified, homogenous working-class movement; but to recognise the extent of commonality and overlap - possibly more than our imperfect sources reveal. Agitations are not designated as 'political', or 'economic', with popular support swinging between the two according to the force imparted to it by the trade cycle. The two spheres were increasingly seen as being inseparable and interlinked. The working population and their leaders were not passive riders on a pendulum. Their perceptions of what was possible and appropriate in a given context shaped the nature and timing of their activities. Tactical acumen and collective appraisal lay at the heart of their endeavours. Although their aims might retrospectively be categorized as primarily political or economic, backward-looking or progressive, reactive or proactive, working-class leaders' emergence as independent actors and mobilizers of a broad base of support was a social phenomenon of significant proportions.

For all the powerful insights provided by historians stressing the importance of language and culture in sustaining these movements, the emergence of a range of agitations, led by a cadre of politically engaged mainly working-class leaders, at this

---

24 On this, see R. J. Morris, *Class and Class Consciousness in the Industrial Revolution 1780-1850* (London: Palgrave, 1979), pp. 44-5.

particular time and in this form, still requires explanation.[25] As Emma Griffin asserts, we 'now understand the symbolic meaning of green hats, silk bonnets and fustian suits'; but 'risk losing sight of some of the important questions' posed by earlier generations of historians. Chartism, for example, 'was not simply language and symbols: it was also political action on a very large scale'.[26] This action and its antecedents are at the core of this study.

Indeed, the complex interconnected nature of the agitations and movements of the late 1820s and the 1830s forms one of the book's recurring themes. As Edward Royle has noted: 'Members of political unions, vendors of the unstamped press, trades unionists, members of Short Time Committees (for an eight- or ten-hour day), and opponents of the poor law were not different people ... the same people were involved in all these activities and were thinking of them as parts of a whole.'[27] That is not to say that all movements were identical; but they were frequently underpinned by shared ideas, leadership and support and a common quest for 'amelioration'.[28] The campaigns undertaken were not the product of a totally unified and homogenous proletariat. However, amongst large sections of the labour force there existed a commonality of experience and response, which, taken with the radicalising effects of their perceived betrayal by the middle class in 1832, the attacks on trades' unions in 1833-4, and the clearer identification of common enemies and the articulation of shared grievances in the mid-1830s, helped to refine a rough and ready, but nevertheless very real, sense of class.

Class remains a contentious and slippery concept which has been through the historiographical wringer and back again many times in recent decades.[29] In its guise

---

25 On the 'linguistic turn' and the cultural follow up, see, Gareth Stedman Jones, 'The Language of Chartism', in James Epstein and Dorothy Thompson (eds), *The Chartist Experience: Studies in Working-class Radicalism and Culture, 1830-60* (London: Macmillan, 1982), pp. 3-58, and his essay 'Rethinking Chartism', in his *Languages of Class: Studies in English Working-Class History, 1832-1982* (Cambridge: Cambridge University Press, 1983), pp.90-178; Paul Pickering, 'Class Without Words: Symbolic Communication in the Chartist Movement', *Past and Present*, 112 (1986), pp. 144-62; James Epstein, 'Understanding the Cap of Liberty: Symbolic Practice and Social Conflict in Early Nineteenth-Century England', *Past and Present*, 122 (1989), pp. 75-118; James Epstein, *Radical Expression: Political Language, Ritual and Symbol in England, 1790-1850* (London: Breviary Stuff, 2014 edn.); John Belchem, 'Radical Language and Ideology in Early Nineteenth-Century England: The Challenge of the Platform', *Albion*, 20, 2 (1988), pp. 247-59. See p. 381, below, for further discussion of the 'linguistic turn' and its impact.

26 Griffin, 'The Making of the Chartists', pp. 580-1.

27 Edward Royle, 'Owenism and the secularist tradition', p. 16 quoted in Matthew Roberts, *Political Movements in Urban Britain, 1832-1914* (Basingstoke: Palgrave Macmillan, 2009), p. 55.

28 See Samuel Bower jnr., a Bradford radical and Owenite socialist, writing on the reform and trades' union agitations of the early 1830s, *LT* 16 Sept. 1837.

29 For example, see discussions in Neville Kirk, 'In defence of class: a critique of recent revisionist writing upon the nineteenth-century English working class', *IRSH*, 32, 1 (1987), pp. 2-47; Koditschek, *Class Formation*, pp. 1-26; Katrina Navickas, 'What happened to class? New histories of labour and collective action in Britain', *Social History*, 36, 2 (2011), pp.192-204; Griffin, 'The Making of the Chartists', pp. 578-80.

as a cultural process and a tool for understanding people's shared experiences and actions in response to these, rather than as the inevitable outcome of the workings of remote structural forces, it retains much utility and power. In a form which allows for contingency and fallibility, agency and possibility, and which acknowledges that people are not rendered powerless by the social and economic circumstances and the political structures in which they find themselves, it becomes a useful construct rather than a theoretical straitjacket. In contrast to critics such as Craig Calhoun who argue for the potency of 'reactive' community-based popular resistance to capitalist incursions as opposed to class-based organisations and agitations, this account argues that the West Riding evidence suggests that these modes of mobilization coexisted and were complementary.[30]

Admittedly, not all local leaders were especially articulate practitioners of political theory (though some certainly were), and the resultant expressions of class consciousness had limits and areas of ambiguity. The middle class were opposed primarily on the grounds of being corrupt politically rather than for being employers, though this was changing. The particularities of locality and occupation sometimes intruded, but these were often overridden by a sense of commonality and by shared ideas which, though drawing on historic radical claims to political citizenship, were also informed by a desire to restructure economic relations. Particularly through the articulation of the ideal of fair reward for employment, expressed in a number of agitational contexts, traditional notions of moral economy fused with an emerging alternative political economy.

However, there are dangers in focussing too heavily on theoretical discourses and linguistic niceties. At the grassroots level, in the middle of passionately fought campaigns for ten hours or against the provisions of the new poor law, in struggles for the very existence of trades' unions, and for the suffrage and all that went with it in terms of dignity and power, such fine distinctions counted for little. As in the movements themselves, political and economic, old and new, specific and generic elements were interlinked and inseparable. Although often stated in traditional or unsophisticated terms a sense of class emerges clearly from the words and actions of countless local leaders and supporters. Thus, in the aftermath of the trades' union defeat of 1834, a Huddersfield 'Co-operator' penned a bitter and wide-ranging attack on the 'moneyocracy', which denied common interests between masters and men: 'the grand secret is, that the rich live and want to continue to live without adequate labour; and the working man wants to prevent this...' The landed and money systems, and the creation of machinery all aimed 'to barter down the wages of the operative ... which they imagine will not fail to destroy that spirit of insubordination and independence which has troubled them so much lately'. The only effective means of

---

30 Craig Calhoun, *The Roots of Radicalism: Tradition, The Public Sphere and Early Nineteenth-Century Social Movements* (Chicago: Chicago University Press, 2012). However, he notes, that the 1820s and 1830s were 'years of ambivalence' when 'Some unity was forged among factory workers, privileged artisans, and degraded craftworkers; it was this unity which gave birth to Chartism' (p. 212).

opposition to this formidable body of political and economic opponents was 'the justice and humanity of the radical cause'.[31]

The chapters which follow are particularly concerned with the creation and development of this oppositional spirit, nurtured particularly in numerous small industrial communities poised between proto-industrialisation and full-blown capitalism, embodied in their local leaders, and mobilized by them in a multiplicity of organisations and agitations. The 1829-39 period saw the emergence and flowering of a new generation of self-confident, assertive working-class leaders and the development of self-sufficient, more permanent organisations. Operating in a context of long-established community-based radicalism, these two strands held together the fragile structure of early working-class movements, and created the framework on which early Chartism was constructed.

---

31 *Leeds Times* 31 Jan. 1835. The "moneyocracy" included landed, commercial and clerical wealth.

1

Local Leadership and Organisation

This was the celebrated Abram Hanson of Elland – shoemaker, politician, dramatist and medical practitioner. Abram will not be forgotten by the people of Elland, Halifax, and the surrounding villages… A brother of Charles Dickens came down to Elland to take evidence, and make enquiries as to the sanitary conditions of the town. As a matter of course, a public meeting was called, and there was Abram. It was impossible for our friend to be present at a meeting of that kind and keep his mouth closed: accordingly he ventured some remarks. Mr Dickens lifted his head from his book in which he was taking notes, and was astonished at the apparition of a tall, thin and ever-clean person, in leather apron, just as he had left his seat of work. 'Are you a medical man', says he, to which our friend answered with the most imperturbable gravity, 'I am'! 'Where did you study', 'In the College of Nature, Sir', was the reply. Like most of intelligent shoemakers, our friend was an ultra-democrat. He was the right-hand man of Feargus O'Connor for the district…[1]

Q. What do you term their 'managing Committees'?

A. There is not a manufacturing town in Lancashire or Yorkshire in which there is not one Committee or more of working men. They have been formed for various purposes – Sometimes for a 10 Hours Factory Bill – Sometimes for Trades Unions, Anti-Poor Law, and occasionally for other purposes – such as the Dorchester Labourers, and the Glasgow Cotton Spinners. With these Committees I have been for years on terms of the most unreserved communication, and by such means, as much as by personal investigation, I have not only become acquainted with all their circumstances and feelings, but I have

---

1   'Notable Shoemakers' in *BS*, 8 Feb 1879. On Abram Hanson (1796?-1878) and his wife Elizabeth (1797?-1886), see Malcolm Chase, *Chartism: A New History* (Manchester: Manchester University Press, 2007), pp. 22-9.

also obtained their confidence. Generally speaking, they differ with me in what are called Politics; but these differences have never caused any interruptions in our communications. We are agreed upon one principle, – that there must be something wrong in the arrangement of government, when an industrious, sober, skilful, and intelligent workman, cannot by hard labour, earn sufficient money to make himself, his wife and his children comfortable. That 'something' we are all united in endeavouring to find out, and to remove.[2]

Local leaders, such as Abram Hanson, enjoyed a special position within their respective communities;[3] Each wove an individual pattern of involvement within the framework provided by a range of organisations that Richard Oastler, the champion of factory reform, characterized as their 'managing Committees'. In doing so they helped to create and sustain a variety of interlinked movements. This increasingly coherent and effective body of leadership was a distinctive feature of the dense and robust agitational networks that emerged from the late 1820s onwards. At the very same time that railways were revolutionising the transportation of people and goods, local leaders with their campaigning energy were transforming the transmission of ideas. The study of this cohort provides a means of joining national and local scales of action, thereby helping to explain the mystery of the creation of the world's first mass working-class movement: Chartism.

This opening chapter seeks to analyse some of the different dimensions and key features of local leadership and the organisational frameworks within which local leaders operated. The first section, for example, explores relations with national leaders and suggests that effective local leadership was a vital element in any successful agitation or organisation. Section 2 looks at some practical problems which occur when we seek to identify local leaders. The third and fourth sections examine different levels of leadership and the various functions that local leaders played. Section 5 explores the processes by which talented individuals became key figureheads in their localities. Section 6 builds on this discussion to examine the attractions of leadership; whilst Section 7 discusses some of the pitfalls and drawbacks of leadership. The penultimate section examines the local leadership cohort in relation to some key characteristics. The chapter concludes with an overview of some of the organisational structures which local leaders created and serviced. The chapter introduces some of the main personalities, key events and principal organisations whose stories emerge in later chapters.

---

2   TNA: HO 40/40, f. 376, Examination of Mr. Richard Oastler, 7 Feb. 1839.

3   The information on local leaders which appears in this and later chapters is drawn from extensive and consolidated listings of participants in a wide range of working-class movements. Where possible, leaders' birth and terminal years are provided in a footnote. In some cases these dates are provisional, pending further detailed local or family history research. A question mark indicates the most likely date of birth or death, and a plus sign indicates the date of the last mention of the subject in the public record. In addition, occupational or personal information is included where relevant.

1: Local Leadership – An Introduction

The question of leadership is of vital importance to historians of early working-class agitations since it is largely through leaders' words and actions that we study the movements. At times of particular excitement their ideas and endeavours shaped the contours of activity and decided the direction of travel. During more apathetic lulls, they often were the movement. As Edward Royle notes in relation to Chartism, 'its leaders determined the tone, policies and direction of the movement'.[4]

Early histories often explained the successes, and more often the failures, of agitations through analysis of the words and endeavours of key national figureheads. Their lives and characters became a conduit through which to explore the dynamics and shifts in fortune of different campaigns. This focus on national leaders is understandable. Their activities, diligently recorded in the metropolitan press and in their journals and correspondence, are readily accessible; and such figures undeniably played a key role in early working-class movements. In the absence of formal political organisation or rapid means of communication, their command over the public platform and inside track to the radical press, gave the semblance of ideological clarity and the veneer of coherence to a loose network of local societies and supporters.

Subsequent local studies similarly focused on the words and actions of a cohort of town leaders who shaped the tone and direction of local activities, mapped them onto wider concerns and liaised with national figureheads. Their contribution to moulding and nurturing the nascent agitations and organisations of the period was immense. A study of popular politics and trade unionism in South-East Lancashire, for example, identified local leadership as probably the most important single element in the structure of the radical movement.[5] Far from being a collection of uncritical followers or reactive acolytes these local leadership groups were complex and dynamic. They included people who framed key ideas, managed oppositional energy and organised agitational ventures. Most importantly they had identity, experiences and agency of their own.

Beginning with James Epstein and Dorothy Thompson's 1982 exploration of the 'Chartist experience', various collections of essays have extended the range and depth of insights into Chartist politics and culture. Additionally, new studies have explored the cultural dimensions of popular radical endeavours in the 1830s and 1840s and the contested physical and ideological spaces in which they operated.[6] Malcolm Chase's

---

4   Edward Royle, *Chartism* (London: Longman, 1980 edn.), p. 56.

5   For emphasis on the importance of local leadership in the Chartist movement, see James A. Epstein, 'Feargus O'Connor and the English Working-class Movement, 1832-41: A study in national Chartist leadership', Unpub. PhD Thesis, University of Birmingham, 1977; James A. Epstein, *The Lion of Freedom: Feargus O'Connor and the Chartist Movement, 1832-42* (London: Breviary Stuff, 2015 edn.). See also Dorothy Thompson, *The Chartists: Popular Politics in the Industrial Revolution* (London: Breviary Stuff, 2013 edn), pp. 63-72; and David Jones, *Chartism and the Chartists* (London: Allen Lane, 1975). On S. E. Lancashire, see Robert Sykes, 'Popular, Politics and Trade Unionism in SE Lancashire, 1829-42' Unpub. PhD Thesis, University of Manchester, 1982.

6   James Epstein and Dorothy Thompson (eds.), *The Chartist Experience: Studies in Working-class Radicalism and Culture, 1830-60* (London: Macmillan, 1982), Subsequent collections

'New History' drew on some of this new material and dovetailed an appreciation of the complexity and uniqueness of Chartism with a firm sense of its rhythms and chronology. It also included a series of 'pen pictures' sketching the outlines of the lives of a range of Chartist leaders and activists. This focus on the human stories that are central to the Chartist narrative reminds us that people are present at the making of their own history and marks a shift in the direction of what he would later dub labour history's 'biographical turn'.[7]

These studies and the continuing flow of local histories, alongside the re-assessment of the movement's national leaders, have partly addressed Dorothy Thompson's original call for 'much more knowledge about the leadership (of the Chartist movement) at all levels'.[8] However, precursor agitations remain relatively under-researched, despite the diligent work of scholars who have examined the leadership role of key regional and local figures in a range of campaigns and movements.[9] The sterling efforts of a host of contributors have added to the range of local leaders included in the *Oxford Dictionary of National Biography*; but the *Dictionary of Labour Biography* still contains relatively few entries for the key local leaders of the multiplicity of early working-class movements. Our knowledge of trade union leadership, for example, is tantalisingly incomplete. Groundbreaking studies of two notable early leaders (both with extensive involvement in other spheres of working-class endeavour) began to redress the imbalance more than a generation ago, but have not been replicated.[10] There is still some way to go before local leaders are firmly

---

include: Owen Ashton, Robert Fyson and Stephen Roberts (eds.), *The Duty of Discontent: Essays for Dorothy Thompson* (London: Cassell, 1995); Owen Ashton, Robert Fyson and Stephen Roberts (eds.), *The Chartist Legacy* (Woodbridge, Merlin Press, 1999); Stephen Roberts (ed.), *The People's Charter: Democratic Agitation in Early Victorian Britain* (London, Merlin Press, 2003); Malcolm Chase, *The Chartists: Perspectives and Legacies* (London: Merlin Press, 2015). Examples of new approaches include: Robert G. Hall, *Voice of the People: Democracy and Chartist Political Identity, 1830-1870* (Monmouth, Merlin Press, 2007); Katrina Navickas, *Protest and the Politics of Space and Place, 1789-1848* (Manchester: Manchester University Press, 2016).

7   Malcolm Chase, *Chartism*; Malcolm Chase, 'Labour History's Biographical Turn', *History Workshop Journal*, Autumn 2021, pp. 194-207.

8   Dorothy Thompson, 'Notes on Aspects of Chartist Leadership', in *Bulletin of the Society for the Study of Labour History*, 15 (1967), pp. 28-33.

9   For example, John A. Hargreaves (ed.), *The Charter Our Right! Huddersfield Chartism Reconsidered* (Huddersfield: Huddersfield Local History Society, 2018); John A. Hargreaves '"Hats Off": Methodism and Popular Protest in the West Riding of Yorkshire in the Chartist Era: A Case Study of Benjamin Rushton (1785-1853) of Halifax', *Proceedings of the Wesley Historical Association* 57, (2010), pp. 161-177; Robert G. Hall, 'A United People? Leaders and Followers in a Chartist Locality, 1838-1848', *Journal of Social History*, 38, 1 (2004), pp. 179-203; Dorothy and E. P. Thompson, 'Halifax as a Chartist centre', in Stephen Roberts (ed.), *The Dignity of Chartism: Essays by Dorothy Thompson* (London: Verso, 2015); John Halstead, 'The Huddersfield Short Time Committee and its radical associations, c.1820-1876', in John A. Hargreaves and E. A. Hilary Haigh (eds.) *Slavery in Yorkshire: Richard Oastler and the Campaign against Child Labour in the Industrial Revolution* (Huddersfield: University of Huddersfield, 2012), pp. 91-144.

10 R. G. Kirby and A. E. Musson, *The Voice of the People: John Doherty 1798-1854 Trade Unionist, Radical and Factory Reformer* (Manchester: Manchester University Press, 1975).

established in their rightful, pivotal, position as central characters in the drama generated by the upsurge of working-class agitations and organisations in the late 1820s and the 1830s.

Without recommending a return to the uneven methods and diverse interests of late nineteenth century local historians and antiquarians who did so much to establish and embellish the creation myth of West Riding radicalism, there is merit in trying to replicate their eye for human detail and local colour. It is notable that the people they interviewed who were active in the movements of the reform and Chartist years vividly remembered the main leaders in their own district, and also appreciated a fundamental distinction between local and national figures. In an 1895 interview John Bates, a 'veteran reformer' from Queenshead, recalls how, on being

> led to join the local Radical Association, he became acquainted with all the prominent local Radicals of those days. Names of men who were then more popular than some of our present-day local leaders are, or are ever likely to be, are remembered by him with remarkable accuracy. Names such as Ben Rushton, Robert Wilkinson, Thomas Cliffe, Christopher Shackleton, John Crossland, John Snowden and others he speaks of with feelings of emotion, for each and every one of them were well known to him. Of course, they were only characters from the district, but John's acquaintance was by no means limited to local men. He can in detail describe the personality of men such as Feargus O'Connor, John Cleave, Thomas Cooper, John Frost, John West, Samuel Kidd, Ernest Jones, J Raynor Stephens, R Oastler and many others, each and every one of them in his opinion, abler men than the Tilletts, Mann's, Hardies and Cunningham Grahams of the present day.'[11]

The distinction between frontline local and national leaders that Bates draws was clear, but never a divide. Indeed, the interplay between these different leadership levels underpinned the vitality of the diverse campaigns and the robustness of the organisational structures of the period. Both parties understood the benefits of this interdependence. The reach of local campaigns was enhanced by the presence of charismatic national personalities and formal organisations were often created or revitalised in the wake of their tours. Equally, local leaders gained reflected kudos and legitimacy through their familiarity with, and proximity to, leading national figures.

Reciprocally, national leaders benefited from working with respected community figures who served as valuable 'political and cultural go-betweens' and interlocutors in their dialogue with local audiences.[12] Additionally, these local activists arranged the logistics and drummed up support for their speaking tours, served as agents or correspondents for their papers, and provided a generic access point to the local community. Together they discussed tactical options, expanded formal structures and promoted a sense of unity and national purpose. The radical press in general, and later

---

Iorwerth Prothero, *Artisans and Politics in Early Nineteenth-Century London: John Gast and His Times* (Folkstone: Dawson, 1979).

11 'John Bates, The Queensbury Veteran Reformer' in *HC* 7 Mar. 1895. Bates chaired a local Chartist meeting in late 1839, *NS* 21 Dec. 1839. On Bates (1815-1903), see D. Thompson, *The Chartists*, p. 173. Queenshead (later re-named Queensbury) was located halfway between Bradford and Halifax.

12 Hall, 'A United People?', p. 182.

the *Northern Star* in particular, formed a key mechanism in the two-way communication between national leaders and the localities. The *Star* facilitated the 'nationalisation' of radicalism by disseminating the ideas and activities of national figures; but it also broadened the influence and importance of key regional and local leaders. As O'Connor later reflected, before its establishment,

> Grievances were a matter of mere oral tradition; and local grievances were resisted by the brave in their respective neighbourhoods, at great risk. STEPHENS was not known beyond the narrow limits of a portion of Lancashire, and even there, not truly known; ... OASTLER reigned in the hearts of those within his narrow circle; but how much has the 'Star' increased its circumference? BUSSEY was but known to Bradford. PITKETHLY ... could see at one glance the limits of his influence... The talents of HILL ... would have smouldered in the pulpit, and the immediate precincts of his own locality; and many others would have died unknown...[13]

Capable local leadership, however, remained a 'rare and precious commodity' throughout the 1820s and 1830s.[14] The presence of effective local leaders could make the difference between the success or failure of a movement, or the existence of an agitation at all. When two Lancashire delegates came to Halifax in October 1830 to promote the National Association for the Protection of Labour (NAPL), an early general union, they faced immediate difficulties (recorded in a hostile newspaper report) when they found themselves unable to tap this scarce resource:

> THOMAS FOSTER (Manchester delegate) – Will any gentleman name a proper person to fill this chair? (pointing to an unoccupied seat near him).
>
> No answer being vouchsafed, he continued –
>
> GENTLEMEN – We are strangers here, and do not know any suitable chairman – will any gentleman favour us with a name?
> Still a dead silence.
>
> FOSTER (waxing wroth) – If you will not name a person, I will find a Yorkshire chairman myself, by placing two chairs one upon the other!
>
> This appeal was as unsuccessful as the former ones, and the Company looked at the speaker in mute astonishment.

---

13 *NS* 27 Apr. 1839. On Peter Bussey (1805-1869), see A. J. Peacock, *Bradford Chartism, 1838-40*, (York: St Anthony's Press, 1969). On Lawrence Pitkethly (1789-1858), see Felix Driver, 'Tory Radicalism? Ideology, Strategy and Locality in Popular Politics during the Eighteen-Thirties', *Northern History*, 27 (1991), pp. 123-7; and John Halstead, 'Huddersfield STC', p. 93 ff. Pitkethly's name is spelled variously in the sources. This is the form he himself used. On William Hill (1806?-1867), see D. Thompson, *The Chartists*, p. 34.

14 R. J. Morris, 'The Rise of James Kitson: Trades Union and Mechanics Institution, Leeds 1826-51', *Publications of the Thoresby Society*, 53 (1973), pp. 199-200. Emma Griffin, 'The Making of the Chartists: Popular Politics and Working-class Autobiography in Early Victorian Britain', *EHR*, 129, 538 (2014), p. 594 similarly notes the 'dearth of working men versed in the arts of politics' before the 1830s.

> FOSTER, (raising his voice) – Are you sunk so low in everything that is base and slavish that you are afraid to occupy that chair? … Is there no Radical Reformer amongst you?

> A person then called out 'I propose Samuel Hill'; which being seconded, a stout man, with a tremendous walking-stick in his hand, approached the chair and sat down. He opened the business in the following laconic speech: 'Come' – SILENCE!!! at the same time striking the end of his club violently on the floor.[15]

After such an inauspicious start the meeting soon disbanded and the NAPL largely passed Halifax by. Similarly, in Leeds a year earlier, a group of unemployed textile workers who wished to publicise their numbers and condition, graphically saw the difference in the impact of their meetings after enrolling the expertise of James Mann, long-standing leader of the local 'Radical Reformers'.[16]

This reliance on a few outstanding and hard-working stalwarts to provide the main leadership of early working-class movements had many drawbacks. Limited resources sometimes had to be spread thinly and there were limits to the amount of any individual's involvement. The unstamped *Voice of the West-Riding* noted in 1833 that, 'Few of the champions of the 10 Hours Bill have had any lead in the Trades' Union, and few of the leaders in the Trades' Union have been prominent in this measure, not … because they were against it, but because few can lend themselves to so many objects'.[17] Some tried, and occasionally local leaders overstretched themselves. For example, in October 1837 we find John Hanson and Robert Buchanan of Huddersfield excusing their delay in calling a meeting to settle their differences with the radicals of Bradford, on account of 'having a great deal of local business on hand, in town's affairs, besides getting in money to pay off debts contracted by the great West Riding meeting and raising funds to assist the incarcerated Glasgow Cotton Spinners'.[18]

The loss of key figures could severely debilitate an organisation or agitation. Opponents, whether local magistrates or employers or the national authorities, recognised this vulnerability and often sought to demoralise movements by removing or discrediting the local leaders. However, equally damaging losses could occur through natural causes. James Mann's sudden death in the 1832 cholera epidemic was a tremendous setback to ultra-radicals in Leeds, since for fifteen years or more he had been at the very heart of popular radicalism in the town. The defection or desertion of key leaders could also seriously disrupt and weaken a movement. So, when John Tester, revered leader of the Bradford Combers and Weavers in 1825, disappeared in 1832 with £26 destined for strikers at Dolphinholme near Lancaster, it signalled a double loss for Bradford trades' unionism.[19]

---

15 *HCC* 6 Nov. 1830.
16 *LM* 5, 12 Dec.; *LP* 5 Dec. 1829.
17 *VWR* 20 July 1833. The *Voice* was one of a number of illegal newspapers that appeared in the so-called 'War of the Unstamped', part of a long-running radical campaign against 'taxes on knowledge': the imposition of Stamp Duty on newspapers. See below, pp. 325–38.
18 *LT* 28 Oct. 1837.
19 *LM, LP* 4 Aug. 1832 (Mann's obituary). On James Mann (1784-1832), a former cropper turned radical bookseller, see E. P Thompson, *The Making of the English Working Class*

The vulnerability to decapitation was a crucial factor in early Chartist history. It informed both the Government's attempts to repress the Chartist threat in 1839-40 and the movement's own response – the establishment of a more rigorous, formal and permanent party structure – in the early 1840s.[20] The West Riding evidence indicates that, whilst capable leaders remained indispensable, leadership qualities were becoming less rare; perhaps as a result of the working class's own educational efforts and recent political exertions.[21] In spite of arrests, defections and drop-outs, local movements were increasingly able to augment and replenish the circle of leadership. This process of development and organic renewal forms the backcloth to the discussion that follows.

2: Identifying Local Leaders

If the importance of local leaders is not in doubt, a number of practical problems remain before we can accurately identify them and analyse their role. In the first place there is the difficulty of separating true leaders from activists, sympathisers or fringe figures. Not every person who seconded a factory reform resolution or sat on a local radical committee was necessarily a leader.[22] Some local figures such as John Wilson of Leeds, who went round local shopkeepers with George White (a definite leader) collecting subscriptions for Chartist funds in 1839, or Joseph Threappleton who performed the same function for the Huddersfield Trades' Union earlier in the decade were committed activists rather than leaders. Threappleton, for example, spoke only once on the local platform and relied on others to compose and write his letters.[23] The delineating factor here and in similar instances is that such figures carried out local strategy but did not determine it.

It is normally possible to isolate the main active leadership of local movements by introducing a level of participation or involvement: a minimum number of 'mentions' (as a speaker, writer, committee man or organiser, in local newspaper columns, Home Office reports, local histories or other sources) within the span of a particular campaign

---

(Harmondsworth: Penguin, 1968 edn.) p. 645. n. 3. See *LM* 19 July 1834 for James Morgan's allegations against Tester.

20 Neil Pye, *The Home Office and the Chartists 1838-48: Protest and Repression in the West Riding of Yorkshire* (Pontypool: Merlin Press, 2013).

21 This supports Emma Griffin's argument that the 1830s saw an upsurge in the opportunities available for working men to educate themselves and develop organisational and leadership skills, 'The Making of the Chartists', pp. 583-93.

22 The campaigns for factory reform were also referred to as the 'short time' or 'ten hour' agitations (reflecting their aim to limit child factory labour to ten hours a day), and these terms are used interchangeably throughout this book.

23 For Wilson and White's prosecution, see *NS* 27 July, 3, 10 Aug., 21 Sept. 1839. On George White (1812-1868), an Irish-born woolcomber, and his extended career in Chartism, see Stephen Roberts, *Radical Politicians and Poets in Early Victorian Britain. The Voices of Six Chartist Leaders* (Lampeter: Edwin Mellen, 1993); and D. Thompson, *The Chartists*, pp. 161-2. On Threappleton, see TNA: HO 52/25, Depositions of Threappleton and George Beaumont 2 Jan., 14 Feb. 1834 and *LM* 29 Mar., 24 May 1834. For his only public speaking appearance, see *LI* 29 Dec. 1831.

or movement.[24] The frequency of 'mentions' also helps to distinguish the pre-eminent front-line leaders (such as the 'prominent local radicals' identified by John Bates) from the 'second-line' of leadership – the occasional speakers and committee members who together with, and barely distinguishable from, the activists formed a reserve from whom the leadership stock was periodically replenished.[25] The apparent barriers between leaders and activists were in reality fairly permeable. In some accounts activists are synonymous with leaders. In this discussion, however, they are envisaged as a bridging group whose exertions underpinned the everyday activities of key agitations, whether collecting signatures and subscriptions or encouraging the presence of their neighbours at public demonstrations or the local co-operative shop.

Leadership also had more intangible qualitative aspects, related to personality, charisma, presence or other attributes that helped leaders such as Abram Hanson or Ben Rushton of Ovenden to stand out from their peers. These special qualities included an ability to think on their feet, strategize, or organise on a large-scale; or to inspire sufficient trust to act as a representative or serve as collecting points for subscriptions. Evidence for these attributes is often to be found in casual asides in newspaper reports or in the reminiscences of their contemporaries and can be logged alongside more formal public appearances. Yet even after extensive listings and cross-referencing it is still likely that the resulting distillation of local leadership will contain some foreign bodies or exclude perfect specimens. This, in part, is a result of a second problem area: the variability and inadequacy of our sources.

Local newspapers, the chief source of information about local leaders, are not comprehensive or always totally reliable. They tend to reveal most about platform agitations, especially those which attracted respectable middle-class support. Even here coverage is far from uniform, since not all districts are equally well covered.[26] Equally, the political interests of a local paper's proprietor or editor could affect the amount and type of coverage of particular movements. The Tory *Leeds Intelligencer*, for example, gave ample coverage of the factory reform movement, but is less useful for early trade unionism. The *Halifax Guardian*, another Tory paper, sympathised with aspects of the early Chartist movement; in contrast the radical *Leeds Times* reflected the growing divergence of middle-class and working-class radicalism in its changes of editor and its coverage of local movements during the late 1830s.

In part, it was the inadequacy of the reporting of his northern tours in this and other radical papers which prompted O'Connor to float his own newspaper. The

---

24 For the way these difficulties are tackled in other studies, see, Fiona A. Montgomery 'Glasgow Radicalism, 1830-48' Unpub. PhD Thesis, University of Glasgow, 1974, pp. 5-6. John Foster, *Class Struggle and the Industrial Revolution* (London: Weidenfeld and Nicholson, 1974), pp. 131, 151- 2, 154-9 and 317. Dr Foster on p.151 defines his 'main' working-class leaders as those whose activity is recorded three or more times in different years or who were arrested for sedition. Sykes, 'Popular politics', p. 565 defines his Chartist leaders as those who either appeared as speakers at any meeting in 1838-9 or who were known to be on a Chartist committee.

25 Hall, 'A United People?' p. 181 identifies 'about sixty-five [Chartist] activists and leaders' in Ashton-under-Lyne (Lancashire) in the 1838-42 period.

26 For example, Keighley, Huddersfield, Dewsbury, and for a time Bradford, were without their own local papers (printed and edited in the town) during the 1820s and 1830s.

resulting journal, the *Northern Star*, is embarrassingly rich in terms of details on local activities and leaders. Yet even here coverage varied between movements and according to the state of agitation. Equally, much depended upon the particular interests and efficiency of local agents-cum-correspondents. The diligence and dreads of local magistrates and postmasters also determines how amply local movements are covered in another chief source, Home Office papers. Lastly, snippets of information gleaned from the various collections of documents housed in public libraries and museums, and the local histories (often based partly on oral traditions), which supplement our main sources, frequently reveal the incompleteness of our information about leadership.[27]

Third, there is the problem that names by themselves take a researcher only so far. A public profile cannot be taken as incontrovertible proof of leadership: a point which can be illustrated by looking briefly at the role of radical veterans and spokesmen. Most communities had highly respected elders: radicals of vast experience and longevity whose prominence predated the Reform Bill era. These veterans included some notable first-rank leaders such as Benjamin Rushton of Ovenden, handloom weaver and Independent Methodist preacher, born in 1785 and active in radical politics since the time of Peterloo; or Thomas Vevers of Almondbury, 'a veteran in the cause of democracy' who had been 'a Jacobin in the days of Church and King mobs, a Reformer in the days of Horne Tooke and Hardy, a Radical in the days of Hunt and Cobbett and a Chartist in the present day…'. It also takes in less well-known figures such as Thomas Leadbeater of Kirkburton near Huddersfield, 'a labouring man' and 'vulnerable old patriot' in his seventies who was a prominent figure in the Reform Bill era; or Francis Popplewell of Elland, 'a shoemaker and a Radical for 35 years standing', who spoke at local Radical Association meetings in 1837-8.[28]

Not all speakers, chairmen or participants were necessarily leaders. Well-known local personalities – radical veterans, popular speakers or respectable sympathisers – might sometimes be prevailed upon to chair or speak at a meeting in order to add legitimacy, respectability or attraction. Although a number were, or became, genuinely important and active local leaders; others were chosen more as symbolic figureheads to emphasise continuity with earlier agitations. Thus, we find the Leeds

---

27 For example, for 'unseen' Heckmondwike and Liversedge Chartists, see below, p. 430. Our prime sources record only a fragment of an individual's life and involvement in working-class movements, and tend to stress the formal, public and 'overground' sides rather than the informal, private and 'underground' aspects of local activity.

28 On Rushton (1785-1853), see Hargreaves, '"Hats Off"' and E. P. Thompson, *Making*, pp. 437-40. On Vevers (1778?-1843), see obituary in *NS* 27 May 1843 and John Halstead, 'The Voice of the West Riding: Promoters and Supporters of a Provincial Unstamped Newspaper, 1833-34', in Chris Wrigley and John Shepherd (eds.), *On The Move: Essays in Labour and Transport History Presented to Philip Bagwell* (London: Hambleton Press, 1991), pp. 40-2. Formerly a woolstapler and an innkeeper, he was an old Jacobin who had been implicated in post-war insurrectionary planning. He remained a staunch radical, served as a Chartist delegate and addressed a local meeting on distress shortly before his death, see Malcolm Chase, 'Chartism in Huddersfield, the cultural dimension', in Hargreaves (ed.), *The Charter our Right!*, p. 75; *NS* 25 Feb. 1843. For Leadbeater (1760?-1836?), see, *LP* 4 June 1831, *HCC* 27 Nov. 1830. For Popplewell, see *NS* 10 Feb. 1838.

meeting to inaugurate the Great Northern Union in June 1838 being chaired by Mr Hutton 'an old and hard working Radical' and addressed by another old Radical who admitted that he had not attended a public meeting for some time. Six years earlier the Leeds Trades' Union had used Ralph Taylor, a popular ten hours advocate, as their official spokesman at a hostile meeting; whilst around the same time, Huddersfield radicals had delegated Thomas Hirst, the 'noted orator of the operatives' to question parliamentary candidates. As the numbers and confidence of capable working-class speakers increased in the 1830s, so this reliance on the speaking talents of popular sympathisers and allies diminished.[29] Nevertheless, it is still dangerous to take the public appearances of 'platform performers' as the sole measure of their eminence in an agitation. The nature, content and context of their involvement also needs to be taken into account.

Fourth, there are the special challenges associated with identifying trade union leaders. Trade societies, like benefit or friendly societies with which they shared organisational forms and membership, were rarely public-facing, and their quotidian existence often goes unnoticed. They only attracted the attention of local newspapers or magistrates during times of particular excitement, notably strikes, especially those involving attacks on blacklegs, or when wider links within and between unions appeared to be spreading. Especially during the early 1830s, when Yorkshire trades' unionism had a reputation for opacity and secrecy, leaders were coy about revealing their identity and adopted a range of pseudonyms: John Powlett (Secretary, Clothiers), Edward Edwards (President, Clothiers); John Bolland, (President, Worsted operatives); John Polti, (Secretary, Dyers); and John Potter, (Secretary, Carpet weavers). Even a famous figure such as John Tester, the leader of the 'Great Bradford Turn-out of 1825' does not appear in the public record when he re-emerged as trade union official in 1832. There were sound reasons for this anonymity: not least the reality that the threat of victimisation was a fact of life for any trade union leader.

Finally, it needs to be stressed again that names by themselves tell us very little. Who, for example, was 'Mr Smith' who seconded a resolution at a Leeds Great Northern Union (GNU) meeting? Reports from areas with a number of very common family names can be equally hazardous. The Huddersfield area is literally full of Armitages, Brooks, Hirsts, Sykes and Woods.[30] Initials can help, in say, distinguishing between John Hanson of Huddersfield or Abram Hanson of Elland – both prominent radicals; though at other times, forenames are needed. The Huddersfield area for example was blessed with two 'S. Dickenson's both of whom became leading Chartists.[31] Yet even with first names or initials, identification problems are not over.

---

29 See *NS* 9 June 1838; *LM* 6 Oct.; 30 June 1832; R. G. Gammage, *History of the Chartist Movement, 1837-53* (London: Merlin Press, 1969 edn.), pp. 210-2 discusses the emergence after 1839 of 'a new group of Chartist orators'. On Ralph Taylor (1804?-1844), cloth drawer, see obituaries in *LT* and *LM* 8 June 1844, and Morris, 'Rise of James Kitson', pp. 184-5. On Thomas Hirst, originally a cloth-dresser, see John Halstead, 'Notable Co-operator: Thomas Hirst 1792-1833', *Huddersfield Local History Society Journal*, 30 (2020), pp. 61-7; and see below, pp. 217-23.

30 *NS* 9 June 1838; see G. Edmonds, *Surnames around Huddersfield* (Huddersfield, nd). See, Halstead, 'Huddersfield STC', pp. 111-4 for the challenges of trying to identify James Brook.

31 Samuel of Almondbury and Stephen of Huddersfield. Both are spelled as 'Dickenson' or

At a time when radicalism was often a family affair, it is sometimes impossible to know whether a reporter had misheard or guessed at initial or forenames, or whether we are dealing with an unrelated newcomer or a relative of the person we expect.[32] Of the three different 'Busseys' recorded in Bradford radical circles in the 1830s only one was the renowned Peter, though another may have been his brother Thomas.[33] Some duplications can only be detected by familiarity with local sources. The best-known case, concerns the two Joshua Hobsons; both important local radical booksellers – printers and victims of the unstamped. Fortunately, they lived on opposite sides of the Pennines and the Ashton-under-Lyne Hobson died in 1838.[34] More disconcertingly, two radicals both bearing the seemingly rare name of Squire Farrar, one Bradford-based the other operating in Leeds, were active in the 1830s and 1840s.[35] Such cases emphasise the necessity of constant vigilance and the need to examine not only where and when people spoke or acted, but also the content and context of what they said or did.

By triangulating the quantitative measures (of frequency and type of mentions) and the qualitative indicators outlined earlier it is normally possible to identify a recognisable cohort of leaders in most localities. Some leaders spanned a number of different agitations, fulfilled a range of functions and operated at different levels; others focused their attention on particular campaigns or types of involvement. Most centres and their environs had an inner circle of between half a dozen and a dozen key figures, plus a more shadowy penumbra of relative newcomers, occasional delegates or lesser officials whose names crop up just once or twice, and whose true role will only be revealed through more intensive local research. The activities of these leadership cadres and their replenishment forms one of the themes of this introduction. To understand more about the dynamics of such groups it is important to examine the interplay of different levels of leadership and the various roles that leaders performed in their localities.

3: Levels of Leadership

Local leadership operated at three distinct levels: regional, district, township/village; however, in reality there was much fluidity within and between these different layers. The top tier comprised important regional leaders who emerged in the mix of roughly aligned campaigns and agitations of the early 1830s. As noted by O'Connor above, the extension of press and platform later in the decade gave them greater visibility and

---

'Dickinson' at different times. For additional clarity, 'Dickenson' is used when referring to Samuel and 'Dickinson' when referring to Stephen.

32 Reporters who took down names phonetically and hurriedly did not always bother to check them out afterwards. Thus Slater/Slataire; Corless/Corlass/Cawless; Ready/Reedy; Kell/Kelly. If in doubt the first name John or Joseph seems to have been added to a speaker's surname.

33 *Gauntlet* 7 July 1833; *BO* 2 Nov. 1837.

34 See *PMG* 22 Aug. 1835 for a letter from the Ashton 'Hobson'.

35 Squire Farrar of Bradford (1786-1873) was a solicitor's clerk and 'a man of strong and vigorous intellect' (*BO* 15 May 1873). His Leeds namesake was a fruiterer and National Charter Association delegate in 1843.

renown.[36] In early Chartism they became recognisable as prominent platform personalities, as Chartist missionaries or as key West Riding officials and organisers. As such they became popular politicians in their own right and functioned as a vital bridge figures, linking national leaders to the localities. Peter Bussey of Bradford, for example, was accorded the honour of being included in the set of portraits of Chartist Convention delegates published by the *The Charter* in 1839. Lawrence Pitkethly in Huddersfield acted as, in Nicholas Edsall's words, 'an anchor man of popular radicalism'.[37] William Rider of Leeds figured in all the key agitations of the 1830s. Yet not all regional figures were as active in their host communities. Joshua Hobson, publisher and printer of the *Northern Star*, was a leading West Riding Chartist, but appeared rarely on the local platform. Similarly, an appeal by West Riding delegates in June 1839 for the *Star*'s editor William Hill to 'render to the Radicals of Leeds all the assistance he possibly can at their public meetings' apparently went unheeded. Other preoccupations and the pressures of producing the weekly Chartist juggernaut clearly left these two key network figures without the time or energy to engage in much grassroots activity.[38]

The main towns of the textile district all boasted a number of important second tier local leaders, like those remembered by John Bates in Halifax. Not all were necessarily prominent in the same campaigns or at the same time, but their names recur with regularity and together they comprised a committed cohort of active leaders. In reform era Huddersfield a coherent grouping of radicals, co-operators and ten hours advocates was sarcastically labelled the 'the ruling conclave of the Swan Yard'.[39] In the early Chartist period when main town associations often exported speakers and organisational know-how to neighbouring out-townships, such leaders formed the core of the 'Friends from Halifax' who initiated or attended many village Radical Association (RA) meetings; or of the deputation of Dewsbury radicals who advised the infant Ossett RA about conduct and procedures.[40]

The variability of our sources, particularly the rigour with which local activities were reported, means that our knowledge about the size and make-up of this group is sometimes incomplete. Also, at different times, some towns were more 'in advance' of others in relation to trade union or co-operative organisation, or factory or political reform agitations. The vitality, coherence and competing enthusiasms of this leadership cadre also influenced the ebbs and flows of activity during the early Chartist period. Further local research is required to definitively identify them all.

Much also remains to be learnt about the third tier of leadership operating in the small industrial townships and outlying villages that made up such an important part of

---

36 See above, p. 18.

37 *The Charter* 5 May 1839; Malcolm Chase, 'Building identity, building circulation: engraved portraiture and the Northern Star', in Joan Allen and Owen Ashton (eds.), *Papers for the People: A study of the Chartist press* (London: Merlin Press, 2005), pp. 3–24; N. C. Edsall, *The Anti-Poor Law Movement 1834-44* (Manchester: Manchester University Press, 1971), pp. 62-3.

38 *NS* 15 June 1839; 11 June 1842.

39 Swan Yard was the location of the Huddersfield Political Union's meeting room and the place where the printing press constructed by local radicals was initially based.

40 *HHE* 24 Apr. 1834; *LT* 3, 17 June, 12 Aug, 2 Sept., 28 Oct. 1837; *NS* 22 Sept. 1838.

economic profile of the region. Villages to the south and east of Huddersfield and in the Halifax-Bradford hinterland were hotbeds of radicalism and provided a disproportionate number of local leaders and amount of hard-core support for early movements.[41] It was in the bosom of these communities that one of the region's distinctive groups, its parish-pump leaders, flourished. Notwithstanding the missionary efforts of the main town centres, the traffic in radical enthusiasm and leadership was far from being one-way. Many key district leaders as well as much of the vociferous local support traditionally came from these peripheral communities.

Katrina Navickas' work and that of numerous local historians has revealed much about the dynamics of agitational activities and the leadership nurtured in these smaller manufacturing communities. Occasionally village-based radicals such as Ben Rushton, William Thornton or Abram Hanson, based in textile villages or out-townships, became important figures within their district or the region as a whole.[42] Other examples of community leaders who spanned more than one level of leadership include John Smith jnr. of Lepton, Joseph Brook of Little Horton and Abraham Whitehead of Holmfirth.[43]

However, many others remained largely unrecognised outside the confines of their own immediate locality. Their names are only known because they served as local trade union officials or acted as *Star* agents; or because they attended main town gatherings or chaired village meetings. Their activities provided the heartbeat of local agitational endeavour; and as Malcom Chase has noted, in relation to Chartism, they personified 'the real soul of the movement'.

As noted above, these different levels of leadership overlapped and interacted at many points. Few sources illustrate the extent and importance of the interpersonal ties that common endeavours fostered. However, insights are provided by reminiscences such as those of Lloyd Jones', an Owenite socialist,[44] who recalled that on arriving in Huddersfield, 'the first place I used to make for was Pitkethly's and there in his first floor room over the shop, he was sure to be met with … surrounded by a small group of the most thorough radicals, and when business permitted, John Leech, his manager was one of the company'.[45] More generally, it is evident that major West Riding gatherings, smaller local dinners and assemblies, delegate meetings and congresses, as well as private meetings and informal face-to-face contact, all provided opportunities for leaders at all levels to meet together, seal or renew friendships, exchange

---

41 Navickas, *Protest*, p. 106.

42 William Thornton was a woolcomber and Primitive Methodist preacher in Northowram, Halifax. A leading Chartist, he had re-located to Bradford by 1839 and emigrated to escape prosecution in 1840.

43 For John Smith jnr., see below, pp. 360-1. For Joseph Brook, see below, pp. 39-40. On Abraham Whitehead (1801-1868?), a clothier/woollen weaver living at Scholes, a hamlet near Holmfirth, see below, p. 226.

44 Owenite socialists were followers of Robert Owen, famous for his factory workers' welfare and educational innovations at New Lanark and his communitarian experiments. His pre-Marxian socialist ideas influenced a number of co-operative, trade union and radical leaders in the West Riding, including Pitkethly.

45 *NWC* 16 Aug. 1879.

experiences and engage in unseen bridge-building, planning and co-ordination. Local leaders were the mortar that held the whole agitational edifice together.

4: Types of Leader

Local leaders performed a number of different functions. By grouping some of these together it is possible to isolate two pairs of leadership types: speakers and scribes; organisers and officials. The first and most easily identifiable of these four, broad, not mutually exclusive, categories was the public speaker: the prominent agitator and orator who extemporised on familiar themes at major public meetings, who stiffened the resolve of striking workers or who addressed the concerns of non-electors at election hustings.

John Hanson began a speech to a Halifax ten hours meeting in 1832 as follows: 'Gentlemen – Were I standing before you as an orator, I might indeed covet the eloquence of Cicero – "The strength of action and the force of words;" but I must forego the pathetic appeal and pomp of fiction, for, alas! I am no tongue-warrior'.[46] Despite such protestations many, like Hanson, were extremely accomplished public speakers. The reputation of 'the celebrated John Tester, the Bradford spouter' went before him and the *Halifax Express* sarcastically compared 'that redoubted radical, George Beaumont' to Henry Hunt, alleging that his 'efforts, as a demagogue, (so far as his humble sphere and contracted means extend), have not been eclipsed even by the self-dubbed "man of the people" himself'. Beaumont, one of the leading 'Almondbury Orators', was indeed 'acquainted with some of the greatest reformers of the age'.[47]

Thanks to the work of numerous Chartist scholars it is possible to appreciate what working-class orators actually looked and sounded like on the public platform or pulpit.[48] Benjamin Rushton, the Halifax weaver-preacher, addressed village gatherings in worn clothing and clogs, NAPL delegate, McGowan, spoke to a Halifax meeting in 1830 in 'a strong Northern brogue' and Thomas Hirst 'created' an extraordinary sensation amongst local audiences with his 'peculiar yet animating oratory'.[49] However, such glimpses are rare. Sanitized and homogenized press reports often struggle to capture the rhythm, flavour or humour of the speeches. Nor are they necessarily totally accurate. As Chartist veteran R. G. Gammage noted of the *Northern*

46　Oastler Coll., Vol, 2, Item 9, Public Meeting in Halifax on the Ten Hours Bill, 6 Mar. 1832.

47　*Leicester Herald* 27 Feb. 1828; *HHE* 1 Oct. 1831; *HCC* 17 July 1830; *LT* 14 June 1851. On Tester (1800?-1870+) and Beaumont (1792?-1851), see John Sanders, 'Turncoats and traitors, rogues and renegades: reviewing labour's lost leaders in reform era Yorkshire', *Social History*, 48, 4 (2023).

48　Owen Ashton, 'Orators and Oratory in the Chartist Movement, 1840-1848, in Ashton, Fyson and Roberts (eds.), *The Chartist Legacy*, pp. 48-79; Janette Martin, 'Popular political oratory and itinerant lecturing in Yorkshire and the North East in the age of Chartism, 1837-60', Unpub. PhD thesis, University of York, 2010; James Epstein, *Radical Expression: Political Language, Ritual and Symbol in England, 1790-1850*, (London: Breviary Stuff, 2014 edn.); Paul A. Pickering, 'Class Without Words: Symbolic Communication in the Chartist Movement', *Past and Present*, 112 (1986), pp. 144-62.

49　Thompson, *Making*, p. 440; *HCC* 6 Nov. 1830 ('Northern' here means Scottish); *LYC* Mar. 1830.

Star, 'even if they had never mounted the platform before' local leaders' speeches 'were described and reported as eloquent, argumentative and the like; and were dressed up with as much care as though they were parliamentary harangues fashioned in the columns of the daily press'.[50]

Occasionally, though, glimpses of authentic local originality and humour shine through. Take, for example, John Buckley (a radical grocer) addressing the inaugural meeting of the Almondbury Working Men's Association in September 1837:

> Gentlemen, I call you to unite, and with heart and voice, peacefully and respectably, tell the legislators that you are tired of the distinction of elector and non-elector – that you are weary of the few making laws to oppress the many (cheers). I know very well that some of the ten-pounders [electors] are no more fit to vote for representatives than my Billy (his pony) – cheers and laughter.[51]

Even from imperfect newspaper sources, it is possible to detect differences in style, tone and delivery. William Thornton of Bradford, eloquent and humorous, spoke so fast as to defy reporters' short-hand; Benjamin Rushton had a 'fiery eloquence', Abram Hanson a 'ready wit and dry humour'; John Hanson of Huddersfield addressed meetings 'in his usual mild, eloquent and effective manner'. By contrast William Rider had a 'rough tongue' and a humorously sarcastic tone, and Peter Bussey a 'blunt', forceful approach.[52] All initially had to run the gauntlet of a judgemental press. John Tester had previously noted 'the sneering manner ... of certain portions of the public press' and the fact that 'whenever a grammatical mistake occurs in the extempore speech of a mechanic, it is printed in italics, that it may be laughed at by the reader'.[53]

Plain speaking, however, went down well with working-class audiences and helped to reinforce the close relationship that existed between speaker and listener. George White, a West Riding Irishman, revelled in a brusque, humorous style. According to Chartism's first historian, R. G. Gammage, 'George's chief talent as a speaker lay in his ready wit and poignant sarcasms, which were launched forth in language anything but classical...' Frank Peel's history of the Spen Valley recalls another plain-speaker, Benjamin Rhodes, who on the rare occasions on which he mounted the public platform, always treated his audience to something 'racy and original – the quaint humour of deliverance often being heightened by its being couched to some extent in the native vernacular'.[54]

The speakers who got the biggest response at the hustings were frequently those who played upon local or regional loyalties, who appealed to the 'working lads of Yorkshire' and spoke with a West Riding accent or in a rough, humorous vein. Robert Sutcliffe of Halifax though 'no orator' 'spoke plain home-spun stuff'.[55] That is not to

---

50 Gammage, *Chartist Movement,* p. 17.

51 *LT* 9 Sept. 1837. John Buckley (1802–?).

52 *NS* 19 Jan. 1839; Thompson, *Making,* p. 439, *BS* 8 Feb. 1879; *LT* 9 Sept. 1837; *LT* 14 June 1834; *NWC* 16 Aug. 1879 and *The Charter* 5 May 1839.

53 *TN* 11 Sept. 1825.

54 Gammage, *Chartist Movement,* p. 154; F. Peel, *Spen Valley: Past and Present* (Heckmondwike: Senior and Co., 1893), p. 351.

55 For example, Abraham Whitehead of Holmfirth at a Leeds Trades' Union meeting, *LT* 7 June 1834, or Feargus O'Connor at Birstall, *NS* 31 Mar. 1838. For Robert Sutcliffe, see *HG*

say that outside speakers were always at a disadvantage. Newcomers added freshness and colour to the local scene. John Vallance of Barnsley remembers his first impressions of Feargus O'Connor, 'The Language of O'Connor, to ears accustomed to little else than the Barnsley dialect, as spoken by pale faced weavers and swart cobblers, sounded like rich music'. The most successful popular orators were often those, like O'Connor, who combined skilled oratory with a personal, colloquial touch. Joshua Bower of Leeds, a self-made 'Liberal' glass manufacturer, apparently secured much popular support for his parliamentary candidature in 1834 because 'his Radical Views, racy Saxon Language and natural Yorkshire character endeared him to the working-class reformers'. One of these declared at the hustings that, 'It had been said Mr B spoke two languages, not English and French, but English and Yorkshire Was it a fault to be able to speak Yorkshire? (*no, no*)'.[56]

It is probable that local radical leaders were bi-lingual in another sense. Although Lloyd Jones refers to Peter Bussey, rather disparagingly, as 'a moderately good speaker of what is called the blunt, outspoken school' and a contemporary biography acknowledged that 'his manners are somewhat rough', it is clear from his speeches and writings that Bussey, like many other local leaders, was a knowledgeable and coherent advocate of an alternative political economy; and, moreover, he could make himself understood outside his own particular region.[57] As a national movement, Chartism in particular relied heavily upon a universal language of the platform to put across its message. Like the similarly unifying biblical rhetoric of the lower churches, which overlapped with it at many points, this common platform language helped the movement to overcome the potentially divisive effects of accent and dialect. Local leaders undoubtedly had regional accents, but spoke one language for everyday face-to-face contact on purely local occasions, and another, more formal language for the public platform. Command over this ritualised language, with its professions of humility, its specialised vocabulary, its biblical, literary and historical allusions, its set rhetorical devices and its attacks on expected 'Aunt Sallies', was essential for effective radical oratory. Although foreign to its audience (for this reason they liked it to be spiced with humour and local flavour), this platform language was nevertheless expected and demanded by them. Like other attainments and skills, it could set local leaders apart, whilst at the same time making them indispensable to the local movement.[58]

The two-way relationship between speakers and audience is critical to understanding the appeal and standing of popular orators. It was at mass public meetings that they accounted for their actions to their constituents and were confirmed in their leadership role. The leading public speakers had more than a touch

---

23 Jan. 1838.

56   J. Vallance, quoted in Epstein, 'O'Connor' p. 48; Derek Fraser 'The Fruits of Reform: Leeds Politics in the 1830s', in *Northern History*, 7 (1972), pp. 93-4; *LT* 4 Jan. 1834.

57   *NWC* 16 Aug. 1879; *The Charter* 5 May 1839. See also Gammage, *Chartist Movement*, p. 66 and the Huddersfield radicals' insinuations about Bussey's lack of education during the Huddersfield-Bradford controversy, *LT* Sept-Nov 1837.

58   This area of discussion was opened up by Dorothy Thompson in her short paper on 'Chartism as a Historical Subject', *Society for the Study of Labour History Bulletin*, 20 (1970), p. 112. It is also explored in Hall, 'A United People?'.

of the showman in their make-up. Witness the *Leeds Times*' description of Peter Bussey in 1834, riding a white horse and wielding a crimson flag, leading the Bradford contingent to the West Riding Dorchester protest meeting. The huge public gatherings of the 1830s expected such leaders to do a turn – to entertain as well as inform or inspire. As Janette Martin notes: 'A good orator was like a conductor, able to work the emotions of the crowd'.[59] It helped to have powerful lungs and strong vocal cords, but the role also required the quick-wittedness of a comedian, in their ability to deal with hecklers, alongside the theatrical timing and poise of an actor. It is perhaps not coincidental that Abram Hanson, 'the political cobbler of Elland', also performed in local amateur dramatics; so when an acquaintance decided to put on Cobbett's rarely-performed anti-Malthus play, *Surplus Population,* Hanson not only played Cobbett's mouthpiece, Last, the village shoemaker, but also negotiated some realistic props for the ale-house scene. To everyone's amusement, 'when the curtain rose', the audience 'discerned a table with jugs of ale (real) and glasses, and the villagers sat round, each with a churchwarden pipe, smoking like so many steam engines'.[60]

Obviously not all local orators had the thespian flair of Hanson or the popularity of talented national speakers such as O'Connor, Joseph Rayner Stephens, or Richard Oastler. Local agitations, like the ten hours campaign in Halifax, sometimes suffered from a lack of 'native talent' or had to be content with merely functional public speakers. Even well-established town leaders did not always relish their public speaking duties. Lawrence Pitkethly, for example, had a high-pitched voice, and was 'a speaker whose earnestness rather than his oratory, made him popular'.[61]

The second leadership type, the scribe, encompassed a number of roles linked to the written word that often complemented leaders' oral skills. John Tester's friend, Squire Farrar, for example, talked of how 'the harangues and addresses' of this 'young working woolcomber', 'completely threw the provincial aristocracy into the shade. His pen and his tongue acted in concert and it will be difficult to say whether [which] exhibited the most ability'.[62] However, some leaders were particularly noted for their writing skills. John Hanson, 'a very intelligent operative from Yorkshire' penned a number of important ten hours texts including the *Humanity Against Tyranny* pamphlet which served as a reference point for local factory reformers, and drew praise for his 'irresistible' 'reasonings on the factory question' from the editor of *London Mercury.*[63] As Felix Driver notes, 'During the thirties he [also] published an extraordinary account of the political 'menagerie' surrounding Sir John Ramsden, as well as several pamphlets in defence of Owenite socialism.'[64]

---

59 Janette Martin, '"Oastler is welcome": Richard Oastler's triumphant return to Huddersfield, 1844', in Hargreaves and Hilary Haigh (eds.), *Slavery in Yorkshire*, p. 196.

60 *BS* 8 Feb. 1879.

61 *NWC* 16 Aug. 1879; Gammage, *Chartist Movement*, p. 64.

62 PP, Add. Mss., 27,803, f. 332 Baines to Place, 15 June 1825 and f. 556 Farrar to Place, 13 Mar. 1826.

63 *NS* 10 Nov. 1849; *London Mercury* 16 Oct. 1836. On John Hanson (1789?–1877), see Halstead, 'Huddersfield STC' p. 93 ff.

64 F. Driver, 'Tory Radicalism', p. 126.

Hanson's close friend Joshua Hobson not only helped to build a wooden printing-press for the Huddersfield radicals, he also used it to kickstart a career as 'a bold and faithful journalist'.[65] Other notable scribes associated with Hobson's publishing ventures included William Rider, frequent correspondent to the *Voice of the West-Riding* and co-editor of the short-lived *Argus and Demagogue*; William Hill first editor of the *Northern Star*; and pioneer of early socialist thought John Francis Bray.[66] All three may have played a role in keeping the *Voice* afloat after Hobson's imprisonment for publishing it.

Hanson, Hobson and Rider were also inveterate pamphleteers and polemicists. Hobson's press also produced a range of scurrilous pamphlets and political squibs, as well being one of the sources of the extensive campaigning literature produced by the West Riding short time committees. Although Rev. G. S. Bull is sometimes credited with authoring pamphlets that came out anonymously or allegedly from the pen of a worker, the factory movement's proselytizing production line included the output of talented operative writers, such as Hanson, Eli Crabtree and Cavie Richardson.[67]

Other leaders served as local correspondents, filing reports of political activities and accounts of colourful local events for the expanding range of newspaper outlets. Some of the apparent contrast between early Chartist energies in Bradford and Huddersfield can be explained by the efficiency of Peter Bussey in Bradford and the dilatoriness of Samuel Binns in Huddersfield in sending in reports. Even after his outing as an informer in 1834, George Beaumont remained the *Leeds Times*' Almondbury correspondent until his death in 1851.

Prolific writers like Beaumont were also regular fixtures in the correspondence columns of the local press, as the instigators of, or respondents to, countless sectional spats and petty disputes. The local leadership included a number of serial controversialists, such as Thomas Cliffe and Peter Bussey, who regularly displayed their scribal stamina and disputatious propensities.[68] Others, for example Samuel Bower jnr. and John Francis Bray, took to the correspondence columns to propose

---

65 Peel, *Spen Valley*, p. 350. On Hobson (1810-1876), see Simon Cordery, 'Joshua Hobson 1810-1876', in Joyce Bellamy and John Saville (eds.) *Dictionary of Labour Biography*, 8 (London: Macmillan, 1987), pp. 113-19, and John Halstead, "The Charter and Something More!' The Politics of Joshua Hobson, 1810-1876)', in Hargreaves (ed.), *The Charter our Right!*, pp. 83–112.

66 William Rider (?-1897) was a Leeds stuff-weaver, ultra-radical and later leading Chartist, who was eventually employed on the *Northern Star*. William Hill was another former weaver turned schoolmaster, Swedenborgian minister and newspaper editor. On John Francis Bray (1807-1897), see J. F. C. Harrison, 'Chartism in Leeds', in Asa Briggs (ed.) *Chartist Studies* (London: Macmillan, 1959), pp. 68-70.

67 Elijah Crabtree (1797?-?) was a stuff-weaver turned schoolmaster and Methodist New Connexion preacher. Cavie Richardson, originally a hosier, later became a bookseller and teacher.

68 Thomas Cliffe (1797?-1851+) remains a somewhat elusive figure. A prominent Halifax 'ultra radical operative' (*LI* 8 Mar. 1832) from the reform era onwards, he may originally have been a shoemaker, but became 'the keeper of new beershop' in 1832 and later an itinerant bookseller and advocate of the Bradford beersellers. He appeared on radical and Chartist platforms in Halifax and Bradford in the later 1830s, but appears to have withdrawn from politics in the mid 1840s. It is also possible that two 'T. Cliff(e)'s were active at this time.

new ideas or reflect on past failures or current struggles.[69] In all these capacities they were able to showcase their writing skills, their broad intellectual range and the fruits of their prodigious feats of self-education.

Finally, a few local leaders also sought to reveal their poetic talents. The flowering of Chartist poetry that Timothy Randall and Mike Sanders have traced had its antecedents in preceding era in the songs and poetical works emerging from the short time and radical agitations of the early 1830s.[70] Local leader, Abraham Wildman, for example, was a renown vernacular poet in Keighley.[71] However, not all iambic efforts were necessarily so successful, as is evident in Thomas Cliffe's doggerel tribute to Thomas Hirst in the *Voice of the West-Riding* and the regular rejection of his poems by the *Halifax Express*.[72]

The two final leadership functions – organising and office-holding – were again closely linked and formed an underestimated element of local leadership.

Much of the established writing on popular radical leadership focuses on the very visible 'front of house' figures who spoke at public meetings and whose letters filled the columns of the popular press. This section argues for the importance of behind the scenes 'organisers', who contributed immensely to the vitality and cohesion of local movements. Their networking and interpersonal skills, their foresight and resilience and their operational competence and political nous, underpinned the success of many agitations and organisations. In the reform era they were the 'honest and upright workmen' who organised and carried out door-to-door surveys of poverty in the outlying villages around Huddersfield, who organised tea parties and soirées to celebrate co-operative societies' anniversaries, or who arranged the logistics of the 1832 York Pilgrimage, with its detailed marshalling, its feeding stations and its meal tickets.[73] In the Chartist era they were the hidden figures who oversaw the collection of National Rent or National Petition signatures; or the 'few good men and true'

---

69 Samuel Bower jnr. (1807-1850), a bookseller, became a leading Owenite socialist theorist and activist in Bradford (see Theodore Koditschek, *Class Formation and Urban-Industrial Society: Bradford, 1750-1850* (Cambridge: Cambridge University Press, 1990), pp. 506-10). He was also a vegetarian pioneer, living 'chiefly on grey peas'. After a stint at Robert Owen's Queenwood community in Hampshire, he travelled to the United States in 1843 and lived briefly at the Fruitlands community in Harvard, Massachusetts established by Amos Bronson Alcott (father of Louisa May Alcott). He died in New Albany, Indiana in 1850.

70 Timothy Randall, 'Chartist poetry and song', in Ashton, Fyson and Roberts (eds.), *The Chartist Legacy*, pp. 171-195; Mike Sanders, *The Poetry of Chartism: Aesthetics, Politics, History* (Cambridge and New York: Cambridge University Press, 2009).

71 On Abraham Wildman (1803-1870), see *BO* 24 Mar. 1870 (obituary) and J. T. Ward 'Some Industrial Reformers', *Bradford Textile Society Journal* (1963), pp. 131-2. He published his *Miscellaneous Poems* in 1829 and achieved plaudits for his poem 'The Factory Child's Complaint' (*LP* 13 Oct. 1832). The poems of James Bradshaw Walker, secretary of the Leeds Radical Reform Union in the early 1830s, were published in all the main local papers in the late 1830s.

72 *VWR* 11 Jan. 1834; *HHE* 5 Sept. 1833. See below, p. 223.

73 BPP, House of Commons Papers, William Stocks' testimony to the Select Committee on Manufactures, Commerce and Shipping, 1833, VI, p. 599, and *LM* 21 Nov. 1829; *LYC* Mar. 1832; *NS* 5 Jan. 1838; F. Driver, 'Tory Radical?', p. 126.

whose 'continued and unceasing exertions' had contributed to the long-awaited signs of a Chartist 'take-off' in Leeds in December 1838; or the individuals who organised the mechanics of exclusive dealing or, just occasionally, the buying of arms.[74] Collectively they were important nodes in an emerging radical network: individually they served as key brokers supplying energy, expertise and ideological coherence to local agitations.

The background nature of their role sometimes makes it possible to identify only the most prominent local organisers: for example, Luke Firth of Heckmondwike who helped Pitkethly arrange the 1838 Peep Green Chartist meeting; or Samuel Bower jnr., associated with many reform movements in Bradford, who masterminded earlier West Riding rallies in 1834 and 1837.[75] However, just occasionally our sources reveal something of the fine detail of these background endeavours. According to early local historian D. F. E. Sykes, Huddersfield STC member William Armitage 'was not a platform orator. He mainly confined himself to going and begging for the cause, to distributing literature, and to quiet unobtrusive but caustic advocacy'.[76] Another insight into the mechanics of local organisation is provided by the trial in Leeds of two trade unionists (woolcomber John Sutton and woolsorter James Morgan, of the 'Worsted Operative Committee') for allegedly libelling the one of the owners of a prominent and controversial worsted spinning firm, Hindes and Derham. Testimonies revealed them proof-reading, dictating late additions and overseeing the printing of 300 copies of the placard that landed them in trouble.[77]

Most towns had key network figures, such as John Garnett of Keighley who served as the local *Star agent* and correspondent, but who only spoke once at a local Chartist meeting. William Stocks' strengths were similarly 'perhaps more organizational than inspirational'; and his close Huddersfield colleague Lawrence Pitkethly of Huddersfield was perhaps the archetypal network figure.[78] The very day after the sitting Huddersfield MP's sudden death in December 1833 we find Pitkethly dashing to interview a prospective radical candidate, and unwittingly setting in motion a particularly bitter local controversy. His business interests allowed him to travel widely and develop important national links. He served as local correspondent,

---

74 *NS* 22 Dec. 1838; Chase, *Chartism*, p. 42; John Baxter, 'Armed Resistance and Insurrection: The Early Chartist Experience', *Our History*, 76 (1984), pp. 18-20.

75 On Luke Firth (1811-1896?), a woolstapler, see Peel, *Spen Valley*, pp. 351-2. On Bower's role, see J. F. C. Harrison, *Robert Owen and the Owenites in Britain and America: The Quest for the New Moral World* (London: Routledge and Kegan Paul,1969). p. 227 (footnote), Edsall, *The Anti-Poor Law Movement*, p, 73, and *VWR* 26 Apr. 1834 (Dorchester meeting). He later wrote to the *Bradford Observer* with suggestions regarding the 'mode of conducting public meetings' (*BO* 10 Mar. 1842).

76 D. F. E. Sykes, *Huddersfield and its Vicinity* (Huddersfield, 1898), pp. 302-3, quoted in Halstead, 'Huddersfield STC', p. 130. On William Armitage of South Crosland (1815-1893) and his 'good work', see *HDE* 26 Nov. 1885 and below, pp. 434-5.

77 *LM* 13 July 1833. The offending statement was that one of the firm's partners was the son of a 'large dealer in negro slaves until the noblest act ever passed by a British parliament'.

78 On William Stocks jnr. (1782-1851), see F. Driver, 'Tory Radicalism?, pp. 122 and 126; and Halstead , 'Huddersfield STC', p. 118. For Pitkethly as a network figure, see D. Thompson, *The Chartists*, pp. 115.

host and sounding board to a range of prominent figures such as Owen, O'Connor and Oastler. The chance seizure of a number letters to Joseph Broyen of Sutton-in-Ashfield, near Mansfield also reveal the consolidation of informal inter-regional links during the 1838-9 period.[79] Nor was Pitkethly's shop the only co-ordinating hub in Huddersfield. Christopher Tinker's bookshop was another important staging post in an informal and wide-ranging radical network.[80]

The fourth main leadership type, the 'officer', overlaps substantially with the previous three categories. Indeed, many leaders spoke, wrote or took a leading organisational role on account of the office that they held. A few, however, such as John Leech of Huddersfield, 'one of the honestest and best patriots in our town' who managed Pitkethly's shop for a while, or John Ambler of Halifax, 'an old STC man', were perennial officials.[81]

The pivotal role of secretary required literacy and administrative skills, but also resilience, stamina and a sense of public relations. Trade union, co-operative, ten hour and radical organisations all benefited from the abilities and commitment of their secretaries: John Leech and James Brook at Huddersfield; William Rider, Simeon Pollard and John Ayrey at Leeds; Thomas Wilson and John Ambler at Halifax; and John Tester and Peter Bussey at Bradford.[82] They became leading lights and the public face of their respective organisations. Often the role was voluntary and honorary, but occasionally it could be lucrative. John Tester acknowledged that he was 'very well paid' during the Bradford strike and 'still well fed, clothed etc.' afterwards; and his Keighley colleague Thomas Eveleigh received a fee from each member as part of his role as secretary of a Combers' Benefit Club.[83]

---

79 Edsall, *The Anti-Poor Law Movement*, pp. 63-4, discusses the role of organisers such as Samuel Bower and William Stocks. For Luke Firth, a woolstapler, see F. Peel, *Spen Valley*, pp. 351-2. On Samuel Bower see, J F C Harrison, *Quest for the New Moral World: Robert Owen and the Owenites* (New York: Charles Scribner's Sons, 1969), p. 227 (footnote), and Edsall, p. 73. His role in organising the West Riding Dorchester protest meeting is evident in *VWR* 26 Apr. 1834. For Pitkethly as an organiser, see *NWC* 6 Aug. 1879, and TNA: HO 40/47, letters from Pitkethly to Broyen (1837-9).

80 On Tinker (1797-1844), a printer turned bookseller, see Halstead, 'Huddersfield STC', p. 108; and also Halstead, 'The Voice of the West Riding', pp. 37-40.

81 *NS* 17 Mar. 1838, *NWC* 16 Aug. 1879; *NS* 12 May 1838. On John Leech (1803-1871), see Halstead, 'Huddersfield STC' p. 95ff. 'John Ambler' was a common local name and biographical details are hard to trace. The 'old' probably refers to the STC rather than the person. Ambler was also active in the earlier 1835 handloom weavers' campaign (*LT* 14 Mar. 1835). Richard Oastler in 1844 referred to him as a 'good Samaritan' and indicates that he had emigrated or been re-settled away from Halifax (*Morning Post* 15 Apr. 1844).

82 On James Brook, (1798-1870), a joiner and furniture dealer, see Halstead 'Huddersfield STC', p. 94 ff;. On Simeon Pollard (1810-1834), secretary of the Leeds Trades' Union, see John Sanders, 'John Douthwaite and "John Powlett": trades' unionism and conflict in early 1830s Yorkshire', *Labour History Review*, 87, 1 (2022), p.10 ff. John Ayrey (1802?-1871), prominent Leeds radical in the early 1830s, later became a publican and grocer and remained active in radical and Liberal local politics. On Thomas Wilson, see below, pp. 197-201.

83 *LM* 4 Feb. 1826; *LI* 10 Nov. 1825. Given the close connections with the East Midlands, it is not inconceivable that this was the same Thomas Eveleigh (1785?-1855?) who became a prominent co-operative shopkeeper and Chartist in Loughborough in the 1830s.

Money and rewards remained a tricky issue for all working-class associations. In the absence of legal protections, the post of treasurer was particular sensitive, For this reason the role was often entrusted to gentleman-radicals, such as William Cook Esq., treasurer of the Huddersfield NU, or to local tradesmen, publicans or shopkeepers, who had experience of collecting and banking money.[84]

Chairs of branch or public meetings, trade union or radical presidents frequently came from among the same groups. Often chosen because they had the stature and experience to control large gatherings or act as public representatives, they sometimes operated as figureheads or mentors, giving legitimacy or respectability to their adopted organisation, rather than day-to-day working leaders. Delegates, as representatives of their organisations and often carriers of their money, needed to be well endowed with trust and time. They tended to be selected from people with some leisure, financial independence or control over their work process – often shopkeepers, artisans and craftsmen or lower professional people, such as John Ambler, the Halifax clerk who often served as local STC delegate because he had 'more time to spare' and was able to pay some expenses out of his own pocket. An analysis of delegates to the West Riding Chartist delegate meetings of 1838-9 indicates a high representation of such figures.[85]

The balance, however, was gradually changing. Although independent delegates, treasurers or chairs still had many attractions for working-class movements, this period witnessed a growing confidence in, and reliance on, 'their own' – often active and experienced operatives or full-time, professional radicals – rather than prestigious supporters or sympathisers. 'A Friend to the Labouring Class', writing in 1833 at the end of the bitter Holmfirth strike, urged 'Members of the Trades Union', 'Be united, and attend your Lodges, and take your affairs into your own hands, and vote such men into office as will discharge their duty honestly'.[86] Many early Chartist localities positively boasted 'working men' as chairmen. Procedures such as the payment of West Riding delegates to the National Convention, the provision of 4d a mile travelling expenses for Bradford missionary speakers, the regular re-election of local branch officials at Leeds and the sharing of duties amongst the 'impressive array' of early Chartist officials at Bradford, indicated the further democratisation of the movement.[87] It was becoming more possible for working men to take part and to earn all or part of their living through their involvement as active local officials.

---

84 William Cook(e) (1796-1848?) was a merchant and radical. Other examples of 'respectable' treasurers include Thomas Walker, tradesman, (Honley PU 1830), William Stocks jnr., cotton yarn dealer (Huddersfield District Treasurer of the J. R. Stephens Fund, 1839), and James Illingworth, publican (Leeds NU, 1839).

85 For Ambler, see Oastler Coll., 5, 12, Public Meeting in Halifax on the Ten Hours Bill, Sat. 13 July 1833. A rough breakdown of 30 West Riding delegates whose occupation is known reveals: small-scale manufacturers/merchants (3); shopkeepers/retailers/agents (10); tailors/ shoemakers (5); handloom weavers/woolcombers (8); others (4).

86 Anon, *An Address to the Members of the Trades Union* (Huddersfield, 1833), p. 4.

87 A number of 'working men' chaired radical meetings in early 1838. For example, David Sharpe 'an intelligent working man' chaired a Dewsbury meeting on the Glasgow spinners, *NS* 3 Feb. 1838. On the payment of delegates and the local organisational infrastructure, see *NS* 19 Jan, 13 Apr, 8 June 1839, also Peacock, *Bradford Chartism*, p. 18.

As should have become obvious in the preceding discussion, this categorisation of different types of leadership function is intended only as a rough way of dissecting the general body of local leadership. The areas of overlap and omission are enormous. Many of the most prominent and successful local leaders combined a number of different roles. John Tester was the Bradford men's chief speaker, writer, strategist and official in 1825. 'Radical Bob' Wilkinson of Halifax was chairman of the local RA, a prominent local speaker and agent for the *Northern Star*. Most town leaders stand out by virtue of a particular type of involvement. Whilst Lawrence Pitkethly, 'might always be counted on to do his share in laying the staff heavily on the shoulders of both Whigs and Tories', he was most effective as a tireless, behind-the scenes organiser and administrator.[88] Similarly, though he too laid great stress on trade union and radical organisation and was a frequent official, Peter Bussey was perhaps most convincing as a forceful orator and pungent polemicist.

5: The Making of Local Leaders

The absence of detailed biographical information means that little is known about how key local figures actually became leaders. Occasionally, a vital preliminary, the dawn of political and social awareness, is well documented. John Bates for example, remembered the 'turning point in his life' with some precision:

> Owing to my inability to secure new clothes, I ceased attending Sunday School, and mixed with a group of rough lads. But an incident one Saturday night caused me to break from them. It was late, and we were bent upon staying out till morning. During our walk, one of the lads leaped into a garden, and commenced doing wilful damage to the plants. The rest of us protested; and when, presently, he repeated the trick in another garden, I declared I would have no more of the folly, and went home ashamed. This led me to begin associating with some of the young politicians of the day.

Bates later became part of a newspaper reading circle, studied Cobbett, joined the local Radical Association and then became a prominent local Chartist, teetotaller and co-operator. More usually, however, initial involvement in working-class radicalism came as a matter of course to individuals whose minds had been prepared by total immersion in a communal culture with deep-rooted oppositional traditions.[89]

This radical knowledge and enthusiasm might be transmitted by respected elders within the family or wider community. William Stocks snr. was called 'the patriarch of Radicalism in that town [Huddersfield]'; and a report on a local meeting 'on behalf of [the]Glasgow working men' in 1837 noted that, 'It was cheering to every democrat to see both the father and the son (William Stocks, jun.) both engaged in the holy cause of protecting the rights of labour against the tyranny of capitalists'.[90] John Bates speaks of catching the enthusiasm of his 'political father ... a Mr Goldthorpe', whilst Mr Moore, a veteran of post-war radicalism, was one of William Rider's 'political

---

88 *NS* 17 Mar. 1838, *NWC* 16 Aug. 1879.
89 A. C. Carter, *John Bates, of Queensbury, the Veteran Reformer* (Queensbury, 1895), p. 2.
90 *LT* 7 Oct. 1837; *London Dispatch* 15 Oct. 1837. The meeting related to the prosecution of 'the Committee of Operative Spinners of Glasgow'. See below, pp. 354-7.

schoolmasters' in Leeds. For some, the decisive influence came earlier and more intimately. According to his obituary, Joseph Crabtree, a leading Barnsley radical and early Chartist, 'imbibed political excitement at his mother's breast, as he was born during the heat and turmoil of a General Election (Dewsbury 1807), which accounts for his political bias and forwardness in turnouts and radical movements'.[91]

A quick glance at the birth dates and careers of West Riding early Chartist leaders reveals just how many, born between 1800 and 1810, cut their first leadership teeth during the 'hurling time of the Reform Crisis of 1829-34', after being weaned on the disturbances of the Napoleonic era and nurtured on post-war radicalism. Leaders were very aware of this heritage. Radical candidate John Buckley's address to voters at the Almondbury mock election in 1837 began with reference to 'the history of the Irish rebellion. He [then] commented on the Manchester massacre (of which he was a witness). Nor did he forget the Cato-street conspiracy'. Six years earlier, another Almondbury radical, George Beaumont, had toasted the memory of the Peterloo victims at a dinner to celebrate Henry Hunt's election as MP for Preston. He later warned local magistrates that: 'These are not the days of Luddism nor is it as it was in 1819, at those periods the people were like a rope of sand, but now through the Trades Union they are in reality organized'.[92]

Local leaders were immersed in a culture which was itself steeped in indelible radical traditions, like those in the villages outside Huddersfield described by Henry Vincent in a letter to a friend in London:

> You have no idea of the intensity of radicreeal opinions here. You have an index from the numerous public house signs – full length portraits of Hunt – holding in his hand scrawls [sic] containing the words Universal Suffrage, Annual Parliaments and The Ballot. Paine and Cobbett also figure occasionally.[93]

Benjamin Wilson's memories of his early life in Skircoat Green, a Halifax settlement 'long ... noted for its Radicalism', record a natural progression from awareness and interest in politics to involvement in activism and lower-level leadership.[94]

The major step, from radical sympathies and activism to actual leadership, was only accomplished by a handful of local figures. In a few cases special factors such as family background eased the transition. The offspring of 'radical stalwarts' often inherited something of their parents' stature and kudos and moved effortlessly to the forefront of local movements. Alfred Mann, son of Alice and the recently deceased James Mann, for a while took on the mantle of his late father, and served on the committee of the Leeds Working Men's Association in January 1838. Henry, son of John Tiffany, former tailor, 'one of the oldest and best tried radicals ever known in this place' and 'Headmaster of the Radical Association', succeeded his late father as landlord of the

---

91 Carter, *John Bates*, p. 2; *NS* 10 Nov. 1838; Joseph Wilkinson 'Barnsley Obituaries' p. 151, Barnsley Public Library, quoted in C. Godfrey, 'The Chartist Prisoners, 1839-41', *IRSH*, 24 (1979), p. 203.

92 *LT* 19 Aug. 1837; *LP* 21 Jan. 1831; TNA: HO, 52/25, Beaumont and Threappleton to Walker, 13 Apr. 1834.

93 Vincent to Minikin, 26 Aug. 1838, quoted in F. Driver, 'Tory Radicalism?', p. 123.

94 Benjamin Wilson, *The Struggles of an Old Chartist* (Halifax: John Nicholson, 1887), pp. 1-3.

'Labour and Health', Southgate, the chief radical and early Chartist meeting place in Halifax.[95]

Victimisation and persecution could also short-circuit the process. The timely prosecution of Joshua Hobson of Huddersfield, newly-established as a radical printer and bookseller, in August 1833, not only 'rescued' his unstamped *Voice of the West-Riding* 'from oblivion' but also ensured him a special martyr's place in the regional movement.[96] In general, however, people came to be recognised as leaders because of the talents they possessed or the respect they earned over time. Their reputation and capabilities were, of course, linked and at times mutually reinforcing, though for the purposes of analysis it is simpler to discuss them separately.

As well as drawing on their excellent basic skills of literacy, numeracy and verbal ability, the emerging working-class agitations and organisations of the time also benefited from local leaders' particular mix of public speaking flair, intellectual gifts, organisational abilities and tactical nous. Joseph Firth, a Keighley woolcomber, born in 1796 first enters the public record in his mid-twenties as a founding member of the town's inaugural Oddfellow's friendly society lodge. He later served as its Corresponding Secretary and, as 'a 10 Hours Man, a speaker and a thinker and a champion of working men', and led a range of local radical and industrial campaigns in the 1830s and beyond. His fellow comber, John Tester, 'a very intelligent man, and the best speaker amongst them', also demonstrated sophisticated writing skills and strategic acumen.[97]

Secondly, a small group of individuals were recognised as trusted leaders through the reputation they earned or the standing they acquired within their local community. The possession of priceless skills above might initially have created, or burnished, this reputation; but essentially their pre-eminence was founded upon a range of personal qualities – resilience, probity and impartiality – which they had regularly demonstrated in public, occupational or religious settings. Experiences in friendly societies, trade unions or co-operative ventures, or the educational or missionary arms of church, chapel or secularist society, gave them a firm grounding and a solid base of goodwill. Many automatically became community champions to whom people naturally turned at times of political crisis or economic turmoil. They possessed the skills to draw up petitions or write letters to the press and had the eminence to call public meetings to address grievances or expose corruption.

Richard Oastler's friend William Stocks jnr., 'a man of much influence' in Huddersfield, enjoyed something of the status of a local gentleman-leader and had an impressive pedigree even before his overt radical and ten hours involvement in the

---

95 On Alice Mann, see Malcolm Chase, 'Alice Mann [née Burnett] 1791-1865', *Oxford Dictionary of National Biography*, https://doi.org/10.1093/odnb/9780198614128.001.0001 (accessed 4 May 2021). Alfred was a named agent for the *VWR*. He was visited by a spy assessing the state of the various 'Unions' in March 1834, TNA: HO 40/32, f. 49, Bouverie to Phillips, 19 Mar. 1834. On Tiffany, see *NS* 6 Jan. 1838.

96 *VWR* 3, 10, 17 Aug. 1833, 22 Feb., 12 Apr., 4 May 1834.

97 On Joseph Firth (1796-1872), see *Goodfellowship in Keighley: Eboracum Lodge, Independent Order of Oddfellows, 1823-1923.* (Keighley, 1923), pp. 17, 53-4. This reveals that as late as 1871 Firth, presided over a local mechanics' strike. On Tester, see PP, Add MS 27, 803 f332, Baines to Place, 15 June 1825.

early 1830s. In the post-war period he conducted a personal survey (as secretary of the local Sunday School) into the condition of a hundred poor families; in 1826 he liaised with the starving and belligerent local workforce; in 1827 he was involved in agitation against the truck system; in 1829 he chaired the joint manufacturer/workmen's committee of enquiry into the state of the local poor.[98] Another esteemed local figure, Thomas Hirst, leading early co-operator, and Methodist New Connexion preacher, enjoyed similar respect. Co-operative historian C. J. Holyoake recalls the story of the stormy scenes at the end of the 1832 election in Huddersfield, when it took Hirst and Stocks just half an hour to clear the disgruntled crowd. Even when fighting was most furious, the assailants cried out, 'Don't hit Tom Hirst'.[99]

A timeline of the known public involvement of Joseph Brook, a handloom weaver and 'humble operative' of Little Horton near Bradford, illustrates something of the wealth of leadership experience upon which the early Chartist movement was able to draw: 1825, committee member in the great Bradford strike; 1830, speaker at a public meeting of 'friends of co-operation'; 1832-3, Grand Secretary of the Bradford Order, a worsted-based trade union stretching to the East Midlands and possibly beyond. March 1833, (likely) participant in an 'Operatives' political meeting; December 1833, secretary of Bradford committee to erect an operatives' hall; April 1834, leading figure at the Dorchester protest meeting in Bradford; 1834 and 1838, on the platform at local factory reform meetings; 1837-8, active in the anti-poor law campaigns; 1838, witness giving evidence to the Handloom Weaving Commission; 1838-9, prominent Chartist missionary in the Bradford district. Indeed, Joseph was no doubt the Chartist brother and 'frequent speaker' mentioned by William Brook – one of the local Chartists arrested after the January 1840 Bradford Rising.[100] Like other community leaders Brook gave a moral as well as a political lead and enjoyed a close rapport with his 'constituents'. In late January 1837, for example, we find him alleging that the 'immoral and unjust' bastardy clauses of the new Poor Law '… may suit 'gentlemen' very well. (*Aye, in the mills*) Yes in the mills, as you say. I rode on a coach but the other day to Sheffield with a poor girl that had been seduced by her employer in this very

---

98 William Stocks jnr. (1782-1851), a small-scale cotton yarn dealer, fulfilled a key coordinating role in Huddersfield radical politics in the 1830s. Robert Owen's assessment of his influence is in *Crisis* 20 Apr. 1834. On his pedigree, see BPP, Select Committee on Manufacturers, Commerce and Shipping, 1833, VI, pp. 597-600, 637-46; *LM* 3 Feb. 1827, 19 Sept., 12 Dec. 1829. Also F. Driver, 'Tory Radicalism?', p. 126.

99 For the story about Hirst, see C. J. Holyoake, 'Unpub. Letters of Lady Noel Byron, VI', *CN*, 6 Feb. 1892.

100 Further details of Brook's life are sketchy. He may have been the Horton 'worsted hand weaver' (b. 1801) recorded in the 1841 (but not the 1851) census. A reference to thee years' military training as a young man suggests a slightly earlier birth date (*BO* 13 Sept., *LT* 15 Sept. 1838). Brook's name is a very common one and was spelt variously so it is possible that not all the references refer to the same person. However, there is plenty of internal evidence in his speeches to confirm his stature and long-standing importance. The references to his landmarks are as follows: *LM* 11 June 1825, also Union poster at Moorside Mills Museum Bradford; *HCC* 13 Feb. 1830; TNA: HO, 40/32 f. 17, Bouverie to Phillips, 12 Jan. 1834, and *LT* 2 Nov. 1833; *LT* 14 Mar. 1833; *LT* 28 Dec. 1833; *LT* 12 Apr. 1834; *BO* 30 Apr. 1835; *BO* 27 Sept. 1838; HO 20/10 and *NS* 8 Jan., 28 May, 16 July 1842.

town (*great indignation*)'[101] Figures such as Brook served not just as the moral conscience of their constituents, but also as authentic articulators of the oppositional culture and the political hopes of their communities.

6: The Attractions of Leadership

The communal respect enjoyed by local leaders such as Brook was one of the main attractions of their position. Leadership brought them into contact with like-minded people to share ideas and enthusiasms, and to enjoy good fellowship. The touring delegates of the London Working Men's Association, John Cleave and Henry Vincent, were impressed by the mock election that they witnessed in Almondbury in August 1837. The 'village recreation', organised by local radicals, incorporated the full electoral paraphernalia – hustings, bands, flags and speeches – and was attended by 'the townspeople, cottagers, farmers with their wives and daughters'.[102] James Epstein has written about the importance of radical rituals of dinners and toasting in reinforcing solidarity and kinship.[103] Early working-class movements – with their tea-parties and soirées, prayer meetings and schools, newsrooms and shops, as well as their radical dinners and trade union club rooms – had a strong convivial side. Bonds of friendship forged by years of discussion, shared experience and struggle, flourished in this diverse, democratic culture. Although they often come across as dour and serious, it is easy to underestimate local leaders' warmth, humour and pure enjoyment of their role.[104]

The declarations of humility, steadfastness and personal sacrifice which preface the speeches of so many working-class orators were more than a traditional rhetorical device, an expected part of the customary interplay between leader and audience. They also express a genuine passion to effect lasting political and societal change. Countless local leaders were fired by a genuine, lifelong desire to improve the lot of that class to which so many were 'proud to belong'. Joshua Hobson, for example, believed that he had been imprisoned,'for the heinous offence of endeavouring to do good to my fellow men … and labouring to dispel popular ignorance, break up the empire of mystery and introduce a better state of things'. John Bates' politics likewise 'sprang from a desire that was early kindled in me to do something to right the wrongs of the working classes'.[105]

If we accept local leadership as a means of expressing genuine feelings of grievance and class awareness, at another, less conscious level, it also acted as an easily accessible outlet for frustrated talent and aspiration – a means of escape or expression for talented

---

101 *BO* 2 Feb. 1837. The new poor law's bastardy clauses effectively made illegitimate children the sole responsibility of their mothers, whilst simultaneously making it harder to secure paternal financial responsibility for their maintenance. If unable to support themselves and their offspring, mothers would have to enter the workhouse.

102 *LT* 19 Aug. 1837; Vincent to Minikin 4 Sept. 1837, quoted in Alan. J. Brooke, 'The Roots of Chartism in the Huddersfield Area c1826 to c1838', in Hargreaves (ed.), *The Charter Our Right*, p. 30; John Sanders, 'The Voice of the "Shoeless, Shirtless and Shameless": Community radicalism in the West Riding, 1829 to 1839', *Northern History*, 58, 2 (2021), pp. 265-6.

103 Epstein, *Radical Expression*.

104 See Chase, *Chartism*, pp. 142-3, on the convivial side of Chartist associational culture.

105 *VWR* 12 Apr. 1834, 10 Aug. 1833; Carter, *John Bates*, p. 2.

working people. Their exclusion from many of the conventional ways of demonstrating these gifts meant that leadership took on a special importance as a means of displaying their abilities and gaining the respect and recognition of their peers thereby adding to the cultural wealth of their neighbourhoods. Early working-class movements included a number of accomplished writers, speakers and tacticians. Leadership potentially liberated them from the social, geographical or intellectual constraints of their background and widened their horizons enabling them to learn, travel and make their mark in life, whilst still retaining a firm grounding in their host communities.

It was within the bosom of such cohesive communities that local leaders felt most at home and enjoyed the highest respect. Often the appreciation and affection which they inspired was only truly revealed at their death. Stalwarts such as Christopher Shackleton of Queenshead, 'a consistent and zealous advocate of the principle of democracy', or Thomas Roberts, president of the Trades' Union, for whom Thomas Hirst who preached a sermon in 1832, were mourned within their respective communities and beyond.[106] When Hirst died the following year his funeral was attended by thousands, 'including the Trades' Unions, and several other societies' and his family was provided for by numerous subscription books. Local co-operators lauded him as our 'best and ablest advocate' and the *Halifax Guardian* rightly concluded, 'the sight of so many men attending to his last home this popular orator, proves the esteem entertained by his own class for him'.[107] Even the living could be revered and enjoy the gratification of being looked up to and recognised as leading-lights amongst their peers. John Tester, for example, recalled that at Leicester he was 'almost adored by my fellow-workmen, who looked upon me as a sort of demi-god in the cause of Union'.[108]

7: The Drawbacks of Leadership

The downside of such adulation was that local leaders were first in the firing line when things went wrong. At such times they also had to deal with the jibes of detractors and opponents that the real attractions of leadership were fame or fortune. Whilst it is true that some local leaders, such as Tester or Bussey enjoyed the limelight and enjoyed the vicarious thrill of working alongside famous national figures; or that others were flattered to see their name constantly in print, the extent of this phenomenon should not be exaggerated. As Joshua Hobson emphasised in a letter from his cell in Wakefield Prison, he certainly did not become a martyr of the unstamped press out of 'foolishness' or 'a desire 'to be talked about".[109]

The most damaging suspicions about the motives of local leaders were those implying financial self-interest. During an industrial dispute in Leeds in 1830, Patrick Reardon, one of the leaders of the Irish stuff-weavers, 'wished it to be understood that

---

106 *Last Days of Christopher Shackleton, Advocate of Free Thought*, (Halifax: John Spencer, 1855),
   p. 2; *LP* 11 Aug. 1832.
107 *Crisis* 22 June 1833; *HG* 18 May 1833.
108 *LM* 27 June 1834.
109 *VWR* 14 Sept. 1833.

none of the committee had received any allowance from the fund, because it had sometimes been said the committees were careless how long a strike lasted provided they got well fed'.[110] Indeed, such accusations formed perhaps the most common occupational hazard for local leaders, particularly shopkeepers or tradesmen such as Lawrence Pitkethly of Huddersfield who was greatly aggrieved by Robert Owen's jibe (allegedly made to Richard Oastler) that 'my patriotism went only so far as my shop'. Accordingly, he made provisional arrangements 'to leave this shop and to enter upon a branch of trade which could not depend upon the popular cause'.[111]

These cynical interpretations of leaders' motivations do less than justice to the men and women of the West Riding who worked and suffered for the Charter and contributed so much to earlier movements. Leadership required both mental stamina and physical strength. Before Frost's trial in 1839 O'Connor recalled 'the almost super-human exertion of one man, (MR PITKETHLY) who walked twelve hours a day for six days on behalf of the Glasgow men'.[112] Radical and co-operative missionaries' schedules were often crippling. As Hirst recalled, 'He and other members of that society [Huddersfield] went nine or ten miles to lecture in the evenings, and walked back again afterwards, sometimes not reaching home till the morning.'[113] In all he 'travelled thousands of miles and delivered scores of lectures' and eventually paid the ultimate price. He 'died a martyr for the good of his fellow men', his illness (in Robert Owen's words), 'probably caused chiefly, if not entirely, by his over-strenuous exertions in the cause'.[114]

Leaders also faced character assassination and public ridicule in the columns of a predominantly hostile press. Christopher Shackleton of Queenshead on his death-bed in 1855 had reasons to ask a friend to 'do justice to my character that the poisoned tongue of calumny may be deprived of its sting'.[115] The Halifax Commercial Chronicle in September 1830 took particular delight in mocking Thomas Cliffe, 'who sets himself up as the great political bell-weather – the state-cobbler for the Parish of Halifax'. The previous year John Spivey, an Almondbury radical and trade union leader, had been forced to defend his 'character as an operative' by denying allegations that he had used stories of his distressing domestic circumstances to beg for drinking money.[116]

The bitter and often unfounded personal attacks to which local leaders were subjected made them, perhaps understandably, a thin-skinned species: quick to take offence and turn to the columns of the press to right real or imagined slights. The

110 *LI* 10 June 1830. Reardon, who regularly clashed with Leeds ultra-radicals, emigrated to Tasmania a couple of years later (*LM* 15 Sept. 1832).

111 OC No. 677, Pitkethly to Owen, 26 Feb. 1834. On Pitkethly, see *HCH* 5 June 1858, *NWC* 27 Sept. 1879.

112 *NS* 16 Nov. 1839.

113 Proceedings of the Second (Birmingham) Co-operative Congress, Oct. 1831, pp. 5–10.

114 *Crisis* 22 June, 20 Apr. 1833. For an example of Hirst's travels, see *LYC* June 1832.

115 Christopher Shackleton (1808–1853), a handloom weaver and Methodist preacher, became a leading Chartist and was rated by Ben Wilson as 'the finest speaker in the district'.

116 *Last Days of Christopher Shackleton*, p. 5; *HCC* 25 Sept. 1830. See also *HCC* 16, 30 Oct. 1830; *HCC* 20 Dec. 1829.

ranks of local leadership contain some notably cantankerous and implacable disputants such as George Beaumont, Thomas Cliffe, William Rider and Peter Bussey.

To some extent, the single-mindedness and self-righteousness which they display can be seen as a defence mechanism – a necessary part of their armour. It helped to combat, as well as to cause, much of the personal acrimony generated by the often bitter and enervating disputes periodically indulged in by the intense and talented local leaders of early working-class movements. Conflicts within local leadership circles, when political differences were sometimes overlain with personal animosity, could be extremely damaging and debilitating. Huddersfield radicalism never properly recovered its strength after the splits occasioned by the 1834 Huddersfield by-election. Similarly in the early Chartist period, the Leeds movement was weakened by William Rider's breakaway following clashes with other leaders. Inter-district quarrels, like the prolonged controversy between Bussey and the Huddersfield radicals in 1837, strained the nascent movement's fragile unity.

Although vilification by opponents or former colleagues could be extremely distressing, castigation by rank and file supporters was more damaging. Turn-coats were particularly reviled. George Beaumont, and Joseph Threappleton, who provided local magistrates with incriminating evidence about local trades' unionism in 1834, found themselves ostracized by fellow workers. Even extremely well-established leaders such as Lawrence Pitkethly could quite suddenly feel the full force of popular opprobrium. In 1835, for example, he wrote to Robert Own of his pain at finding 'the working bees so much divided, so much spleen, so much dissipation and torrents of abuse heaped upon those who were fighting their battles to an enormous sacrifice'.[117] Pitkethly's abject despair and simmering indignation at this time throws light on another aspect of the relationship between leaders and followers, and a final drawback of leadership – its isolation.[118]

Many local leaders were clearly enduringly popular figures who were extremely well-integrated within the culture and customs of their local community. Others lived in close physical proximity to fellow radicals and occasional inter-marriage between radical families provided sources of cohesion which militated against isolation. John Hanson of Huddersfield, for example, lived next door to Pitkethly, a fellow Owenite socialist and radical, in the late 1830s.[119] Elsewhere it is clear that particular neighbourhoods such as Wilson's Piece in Barnsley or the Nelson Court area of Bradford, or certain villages, such as Queenshead between Halifax and Bradford, or Almondbury outside Huddersfield, provided a disproportionate number of local leaders and amount of communal support for early movements.[120]

---

117 TNA: HO 52/25, Beaumont to Lord Melbourne, 21 Apr. 1834; *BO* 31 Dec. 1835, 21 Jan. 1836; OC No. 730, Pitkethly to Robert Owen, 2 May 1835.

118 The feeling of loneliness is a striking feature of many of the autobiographies of the (often self-educated) working men who led political or trade union movements during the nineteenth century.

119 Both lived on Upperhead Row, Huddersfield in 1839. OC Nos 1139 and 1167, letters from Lunn to Owen.

120 On Wilson's Piece, see F. J. Kaijage, 'Labouring Barnsley, 1816-1856: A Social and Economic History', Unpub. PhD thesis, University of Warwick, 1975, p. 34, (Peter Hoey and William Ashton both lived there). On the Nelson Court area, see Peacock, *Bradford*

Peter Bussey of Bradford, whose letters from the Chartist Convention were read out by his wife to the assembled customers at his beershop, serves as a good example of a local leader who stayed very much in harmony with his constituents. Others however clearly drifted away from their audience in terms of outlook and aspiration. Often the very skills and intellectual pursuits, which made them the automatic champion and mouthpiece of their class, and gave them standing or a living within the local community, distanced them from their fellow workers and neighbours.

They had won their own battle for 'knowledge' – often at great personal sacrifice and effort. Christopher Shackleton of Queenshead had been 'untiring' in his 'struggle for knowledge' despite being 'born in indigent circumstances' and having his 'early education neglected'. George Beaumont of Almondbury never 'had a single shilling laid out in his education', meanwhile John Tester proudly claimed that he had 'attained all I know by my own industry… I have known what it is to work hard for eight hours and study hard for ten more'.[121]

Given this background it is hardly surprising that zeal for education and its moral, regenerative powers occasionally spilled over into smugness or conceit which alienated local leaders from their neighbours. Pride in their hard work and feats of learning could readily morph into disdain for those who had not made similar sacrifices or who remained wilfully ignorant or politically apathetic. Their auto-didactive achievements, like their command over the language of the platform, their cultural range and their wider general horizons, set them up as natural leaders and representatives of their communities, but it could also set them apart from the very people they led.

At times of defeat or despondency such leaders often directed the thrust of their attack inwards against their own supporters – 'Ale-house' radicals in William Rider's telling phrase – rather than outwards towards their traditional enemies. In the aftermath of the 1825 Bradford strike, James Walworth, leader of the Keighley combers and weavers is to be found writing to metropolitan radical Francis Place in the hope of attaining 'useful intelligence' and escaping 'that ignorance which is at present too prevalent amongst the working-classes in general'. Nine years later in the midst of another bout of industrial conflict and collective self-doubt we find Peter Bussey urging the *Leeds Times* to print the Rev. G. S. Bull's stinging 'rope of sand' letter in which the factory reform leader criticised local workers' lack of unity. Bussey comments (on behalf of the Regeneration committee): 'We publish it, although we must confess it contains truth not very creditable to the Operatives – yet we confess it is true, and we only wish it were not so'.[122]

As well as internal doubts, contradictions and pressures, prominent leaders also faced significant external threats. In addition to hard work and sacrifice their activities involved severe risks. Many lived under the constant fear of arrest and incarceration,

---

Chartism, pp. 40, 43 and 48; and C. Richardson, 'Irish Settlement in mid-Nineteenth Century Bradford', *Yorkshire Bulletin of Economic and Social Research*, 120 (1968), pp. 44–5; (George Flinn, a key figure in the Bradford Rising lived there). On Queenshead, see Carter, *John Bates*. On Almondbury as a radical hub, see Navickas, *Protest*, p. 106.

121 *Last Days of Christopher Shackleton*, p. 4; *HCC* 11 July 1829; TNA: HO 20/10; PP, Add. MS. 28,803, f. 335-8, Tester to Place 6 July 1825.

122 *VWR* 10 Nov. 1833; PP, Add Mss. 27,803, f. 554-5 Walworth to Place 28 Jan. 1825 [mistake for 1826]; *LT* 22 Mar. 1834.

and a number served time in tough and degrading penal institutions. George White was imprisoned numerous times for his Chartist activities, whilst Joshua Hobson was convicted three times in four years for selling unstamped newspapers. Confinement broke the health and spirit of more than one local leader in this period.

Often building on widespread low-key harassment of activists, victimisation was also a very real threat. Publicans feared losing their licences and others their livelihoods because of their political sympathies or their involvement in short time or trade union activity.[123] Peter Bussey requested local reporters not to insert the names of 'their committee' into reports of a National Regeneration Society meeting in March 1834 because 'the consequences might be severe to the individuals concerned'.[124]

Whilst radicals, Chartists, socialists, co-operators and ten hours leaders were all threatened with loss of work or actually persecuted during the 1820s and 1830s, trade union officials were in a particularly vulnerable position.[125] John Swift, chief 'writer' and frequent negotiator for the Huddersfield Fancy Weavers' Union in 1824-5, was sacked by his first employer for his part in the Union; and the Union's President, Amos Cowgill, suffered the same fate at the hands of his long-time employer.[126] None of the main speakers at a delegate meeting of the West Riding trades held at Huddersfield in autumn 1834 are named. As one delegate explained, 'being one of the wreck of the old unions, he could not wish to have his name exposed, and thereby subject himself to further persecution'.[127] This was nothing new. Many of the committee of the Bradford Combers and Weavers Association, and their families, were unable to get work in the aftermath of the unsuccessful Bradford strike of 1825.[128] With the exception of John Tester (who re-appeared in Bradford in 1832, though not directly in the historical record of the time), few returned to take a leading part in union affairs or other public roles.[129] The widespread adoption of pseudonyms in Yorkshire trades' unionism of the early 1830s had a pragmatic as well as a ritualistic rationale.

---

123 *NS* 6 July 1839. See also *NS* 17 Aug. 1839 (Dewsbury) and *LT* 7 Mar. 1835 for the fear of persecution being sufficient to prevent the free expression of ten hours opinions.

124 *BO* 20, 27 Mar. 1834.

125 See, for example, *LT* 16, 30 July 1836 for the victimisation of J. Stafford, a Dewsbury ten hours advocate.

126 BPP, Report from the Select Committee on the Combination Laws, 1825, IV, p. 135. John Swift of Newsome subsequently had a varied occupational career as shawl maker, seller of fancy goods, and quack doctor (*LM* 26 Apr. 1834). On Swift and Cowgill, and local fancy weavers' support for the 1825 Bradford Combers' and Weavers' strike, see Alan J. Brooke, 'Labour Disputes and Trade Unions in the Industrial Revolution', in Hilary Haigh (ed.) *Huddersfield*, pp. 224-5.

127 *LT* 25 Oct. 1834.

128 *LT* 2 Nov. 1833; 25 Oct. 1834; J. Tester, *History of the Commencement, Progress, and Termination of the Bradford Contest... etc.* (Bradford, 1826) MS in Bradford Public Library, Box 3, Case 39.

129 *LT* 21 June 1834; On Tester's travels after the defeat, his hopes for journalistic work, his involvement in strikes at Leicester and his return to Bradford, see his letters to *LM* 7, 14, 27 June, 5, 12 July 1834. Also PP, Add. MS 27,803, f. 335, 339, 343, 347, 348, 410, letters from Tester to Place. Joseph Holmes and James Walworth (of Keighley) do not re-appear; T (Thomas?) Eveleigh was the name of a Loughborough co-operative delegate in 1832.

8: Analysis of Leadership

The discussion in sections 3 and 4 allows most local leaders to be positioned within a basic grid, with the horizontal axis relating to different levels and the vertical axis pertaining to distinct types of leadership. A number of leaders, fulfilling more than one function and operating at more than one level, can be located in multiple cells. Keighley grocer and temperance advocate David Weatherhead, for example, was prominent on the local and regional ten hours platform, organised vigorous local opposition to the new poor law and was a consistent radical presence. Later in the decade 'his ardent wishes for the good of the labouring class' led him to spend nearly £300 of his own money 'on behalf of the Radical Association' to buy an old Primitive Methodist Chapel, to act as a 'Working Men's Hall'.[130] Stephen Dickinson, a Huddersfield tradesman and reluctant 'speechifier', nevertheless addressed many local meetings, acted as *Northern Star* local agent, served as district treasurer for the Stephens Defence Fund and also provided local Chartism with one of its regular meeting places.[131]

Leaders in the poorer out-townships and villages such as Benjamin Rushton of Ovenden, John Smith jnr. of Lepton or Joseph Brook of Little Horton (all handloom weavers) contributed in less ostentatious ways but similarly carried out a number of related roles and operated at more than one level.[132] Such multi-tasking reflected the reality that capable local leadership was a precious resource that could sometimes be stretched thinly. However, the evolution and increasing prominence of these parish-pump leaders was one of the distinctive achievements of the period. To understand their contribution more fully it is necessary to drill down into the communal dimension of leadership and to examine a number of other key characteristics relating to gender, age, origins, ethnicity, religion, and occupation, and to note, in passing, that leaders also had other lives.

a) Gender

There is no escaping the fact that the majority of named local figureheads are male. Women leaders are not totally absent; however, the nature of the sources and the lens through which we view leadership means that they are more difficult to see. Much of the female activism comprised leadership from below. Malcolm Chase notes that 'female participation in Huddersfield Chartism was significant', and it is likely that women played a pivotal role in collecting signatures for Chartist petitions and in

---

130 *NS* 27 Apr. 1839. On David W. Weatherhead (1803-1875), radical, short time, and anti-poor law campaigner and leading Chartist, see Ward 'Some Industrial Reformers', p. 131.

131 *NS* 27 Jan. 1838; 26 Jan., 30 Mar.; 22 Feb. 1839. The defence fund was set up in 1839 to support Joseph Rayner Stephens, Lancashire factory reformer, new poor law opponent and briefly Chartist firebrand, following his arrest and prosecution for unlawful assembly and inciting violence. Stephen Dickinson (1794?-1862?), originally a carpenter and cabinet maker/upholsterer, may have turned his hand to shopkeeping. He is listed as a 'woollen draper' in the 1841 census. He moved to Manchester some time in the 1840s.

132 On John Smith jnr. of Botany Bay, Lepton, leader of the local fancy weavers, see below, pp. 360-1.

organising and enforcing exclusive dealing.[133] Equally, it is doubtful whether another form of 'political shopping', in the people's own [co-operative] store', could not have succeeded without the literal buy-in of countless women. In his biography of Elizabeth Hanson, Chase similarly recounts the tale of a female-led ambush of poor law commissioners and two hundred women preventing the delivery of yarn to undercutting 'black leg' weavers.[134] Such activism was not out of the ordinary. A Horsforth magistrate complained in 1832 of women joining a political union and forming 'immense processions'; and it is unlikely that any of the ferocious industrial disputes of the period could have been prosecuted without substantial active female engagement.[135]

Nor was participation confined to outdoor direct action. A few female leaders also took to the public platform and correspondence columns of the local press. As a leading member of the Elland Female Radical Association, Mary Grassby railed against the Poor Law Amendment Act, spoke in favour of the six points of the Charter and welcomed the return of the Dorchester labourers. In addition, she defended her views and her right to express them in letters to the press. When she travelled to Hull in July 1839, she addressed both the Hull Working Men's Association and the (Chartist) Female Patriotic Society.[136] Female radical sympathisers collected subscriptions for unstamped victims and the Dorchester labourers' families, designed and produced of banners and flags and canvassed their neighbourhoods for signatures and support. Family traditions of radicalism or socialism were enduringly strong and activism often involved whole families and communities, with the women-folk at least 'equal to the men in their love of liberty'.[137] The early Chartist period, for example, saw the flowering of many female political associations, such as the Doghouse Female Radical Association which raised 25s for the Stephens Fund in March 1839, the independent-minded women of Bradford, or the Elland Female RA in which the names of a number of previously hidden female leaders, including Elizabeth Hanson and Mary Grassby, emerge.[138]

However, as Jutta Schwarzkopf argues, the roles women undertook in these agitations were primarily auxiliary.[139] Thomas Hirst, recounting a local 'co-operative party' he had recently attended, welcomed the lack of formality: 'Why should any one

---

133 Chase, *Chartism*, p. 42; Chase, 'Huddersfield', p. 66.

134 *VWR* 24 May 1834; Malcolm Chase, 'Elizabeth Hanson' (*née* Fell), 1797/8–1886', *Oxford Dictionary of National Biography*, https://doi.org/10.1093/odnb/9780198614128.013.369109 (accessed 4 May 2021).

135 TNA: HO 52/20, letter from J. A. Rhodes, nd, 1832 (it is more likely that they were joining the Trades' Union rather than a Political Union); *Leicester Chronicle* 19 Oct. 1833.

136 *HHE* 24 Feb. *NS* 17 Feb., 17 Mar., 14, 28 Apr., 13 July 1839. Mary Grassby (1800-1870), born in Northamptonshire, was married to basket maker and leading Elland Chartist, Richard (originally from Hull). She relocated to Hull some time in the winter of 1839-40. Her third child, 'Feargus Roger O'Connor Grassby', was born there in November 1840 (*NS* 16 Jan. 1841).

137 Wilson, *Struggles*, p. 1.

138 Ibid.; *NS* 30 Mar. 1839. On the Bradford women, see *NS* 30 Mar., 6 Apr. 1839. On the Elland Female RA, see *NS* 17 Feb.,17, 24 Mar., 11 Apr. 1838.

139 Jutta Schwarzkopf, *Women in the Chartist Movement* (London: Macmillan, 1991).

be called "Mr" or be above his brothers and sisters? Did we not naked alike come into the world? Shall we not shortly return the same?'[140] Despite the professions of such mildly egalitarian sentiments, female participation in early co-operation generally did not extend beyond the societies' convivial or consumer functions. Equally, though they mobilised female support and witnesses for parliamentary inquiries, short time committees were resolutely male in composition and in their rhetorical conception of the female domestic role.[141] With notable exceptions, such as Elizabeth Hanson's 'powerful and impressive' anti-poor law speeches, female voices are seldom heard on the factory reform or other public platforms of the 1830s. As Katrina Navickas notes, it was rare to see women speaking in public and the era's massive showpiece demonstrations were often 'hierarchically structured ... [and] stratified by political leadership, geography and gender'.[142]

Although largely absent from the public sphere, women nevertheless formed an important component of the infrastructure that underpinned the dense agitational networks of the West Riding. If we wish to understand more about the hidden activism of female leaders it is to the outlying villages and townships that we must turn; for as Malcolm Chase has noted, 'female direction of Chartist activities took place almost entirely at the level of the family and local community.'[143]

b) Age

The patchy nature of biographical information relating to many local leaders makes it difficult to make any definitive comments about the age-range and generational composition of local leadership groups. The presence and role of revered veterans in local agitations has already been touched upon; but what is most striking in many instances is the relative youth of some of the leaders of the key working-class agitations of the period. John Tester was just twenty-five when he led the great Bradford strike; Simeon Pollard was three years younger when he emerged as a leading figure of the Leeds Trades' Union. Ralph Taylor took on the mantle of spokesperson for the Leeds STC in his mid-twenties. Joshua Hobson's youthful appearance was one of features noted by reporters on his first public appearance at a meeting of the Huddersfield Political Union.[144] Even allowing for precocious talent, it is hard to avoid the conclusion that agitation was a young person's game. John Halstead's detailed study of the Huddersfield STC provides some support for this thesis. Over half of the verifiable committee members were born after 1800.[145] The

---

140 *LYC* Mar. 1832.

141 Katrina Honeyman, *Women, Gender, and Industrialisation in England, 1700-1870* (Basingstoke: Macmillan, 2000), p. 128, argues that 'women played a low-key role in the factory campaigns of the early 1830s'.

142 *LT* 17 Feb. 1838; Malcolm Chase, 'Elizabeth Hanson'; Navickas, *Protest*, p. 244. See also, Emmanuelle Morne, '"Glorious Auxiliaries"? Gender, Participation, and Subordination in the Chartist Movement', *Labour History Review*, 85, 1 (2020), pp. 7-32.

143 Chase 'Biographical Turn', p. 198.

144 PP Add. Mss., 28, 803, Tester to Place 6 July 1825; *LT* 3 Jan. 1835; Morris, 'James Kitson', pp. 184-5; *HCC* 30 Nov. 1830

145 Halstead, 'Huddersfield STC', pp. 93-5.

dominant generation in the West Riding early Chartist leadership comprised a cadre of radicals born between 1800 and 1810 who emerged as major leaders during the agitations and organisations of the reform era. Many were brought up in strongly radical communities and were no doubt influenced in their teens by the atmosphere and ideas prevailing during the radical upsurge of the post-war years. Having established their ascendancy in the age of reform, they consolidated their position during the 1830s and along with a few continuing veterans and some slightly older colleagues became the key local leaders of the early Chartist movement.

This outline is only provisional, but it provides a possible mechanism explanation of the frenetic energy and immediacy of the campaigns of the period. These were new generation of young leaders seeking to make sense of a rapidly changing world and on an urgent mission for 'amelioration'.

c) Origins

As well as youth what is striking about a number of key local leaders for whom we have biographical information is how many were originally 'strangers' to the districts they agitated. Lawrence Pitkethly, for example, came to Huddersfield from Edinburgh in the early 1820s; and Samuel Dickenson, a leading Almondbury radical, came to the district in 1822.[146] Neither John Tester, nor Peter Bussey, the two most prominent popular leaders in Bradford in the 1820s and 1830s, were natives of the textile district; and John Halstead has estimated that 87% of the original Huddersfield STC members were 'in-comers in one sense or another'.[147] At one level this merely reflected the mobility and level of immigration that the industrial towns of the West Riding were experiencing at this time. It may also indicate the impact and persistence of artisanal networks fostered by tramping traditions. Links between the West Riding and both the East Midlands and West Country were particularly strong.

By the time that the agitational atmosphere had become more conducive in the early 1830s, a number of these in-comers were already well-established. Peter Bussey had moved to Bradford from North Yorkshire in early 1820s, around the same time that Pitkethly arrived from Scotland and an influx of linen-weavers joined the leadership cadre in Barnsley. These leaders were later supplemented by more recent newcomers, for example J. N. Reid and Robert Buchanan, both Owenite tailors and missionaries, who settled in Huddersfield in the mid-1830s; and George White who came to Bradford from Leicester earlier in the decade.[148] White later re-located to

---

146 Halstead, 'Huddersfield STC', p. 108; *HCC* 15 May 1830. Samuel Dickenson (1795?-1865?) a fancy-weaver, was born in Ashton-under-Lyne in Lancashire.

147 Halstead, 'Huddersfield STC', p. 96.

148 John N. Reid/Reed was a slightly mysterious figure who came to Huddersfield in 1834 and engaged briefly in radical politics. A leading socialist, he wrote letters to Robert Owen as the 'District Master' of the 'Central district committee of the first Huddersfield district' of the successors to the Grand National Consolidated Trades' Union (OC No. 716 John N. Reed? To Owen, 3 Dec. 1834). In 1837 the *Leeds Mercury* printed an allegation that that he had left a wife and children behind in America (*LM* 6 May 1837). Scottish-born Robert Buchanan (1813-1866), a socialist lecturer, was active in a range of radical campaigns in the mid-1830s. According to Lloyd Jones he was 'an ardent student and a remarkably well-read man, [and]

Leeds and forms one of a number of local leaders who moved their base in the region. Joshua Hobson (Huddersfield to Leeds); William Hill (Barnsley to Huddersfield, to Bradford, to Hull, and then to Leeds) and William Thornton (Halifax to Bradford) are other examples of this internal mobility.

In general, local attitudes to outsiders were equivocal. Communities brought up in the tradition of 'Oliver, Castles and Co' often viewed outsiders, particularly complete strangers, with much suspicion.[149] Visiting speakers or recent newcomers frequently had to protect themselves from damning charges of being itinerant opportunists. John Spivey a guest speaker at an Elland meeting on 'Distress' in 1830 was keen to reassure his audience that 'there are a few individuals here from Almondbury; not, however, as itinerant orators, but in accordance with an invitation'.[150] He was right to be cautious. Four years later an anonymous working-class Elland correspondent commented on J. N. Reid's oratory, 'if he and all such like had to earn their bread by the sweat of their brow they would learn more common sense than they can by their present occupation of going about and attempting to gull less educated people than themselves, who luckily for their best interests, have seen so much of, and suffered enough from such demagogues'.[151] Lawrence Pitkethly also clearly resented Reid's intrusion into the local scene in late 1834.

At other times, though, it helped to be a newcomer adding a touch of freshness and colour to the local campaigns. Tom Scriven has sketched out the novelty value and agitational appeal of itinerant speakers.[152] A leading Huddersfield socialist confided to Robert Owen in 1839 that 'we have some good native talent but they have not the command over the prejudiced that a stranger would have'.[153] Outsiders, without a previous track record or reputation and without obvious ties to a particular clique or faction, might be spared some of the jealousy or scorn reserved for local upstarts who were felt to be rising above their station.

In general, particularly in the small industrial villages and out-townships, local roots or acquired standing could be an advantage; and the majority of leaders who operated at this level were long-established residents. Their leadership was built on and contingent upon their close links to their neighbours and the way that they were able to draw on shared community capital in these localities.[154]

---

possessed considerable ability as a writer and speaker' (*NWC* 14 June 1879). He relocated to Sheffield in 1838 and then onto Stoke and eventually London; see Alan J. Brooke, 'Huddersfield Hall of Science', available at https://undergroundhistories.wordpress.com/huddersfield-hall-of-science/ (accessed 1 Mar. 2023).

149 Beaumont himself later warned of 'strangers, who will hold out impracticabilities, and use language violent enough to excite [the] feelings' of workers who attend public meetings', *LT* 24 Apr. 1841.

150 *HCC* 5 June 1830.

151 *LT* 15 Nov, 1834.

152 Tom Scriven, *Popular Virtue: Continuity and Change in Radical Moral Politics, 1820-70* (Manchester: Manchester University Press, 2017), pp. 59-61.

153 OC No. 1184, Read Holliday to Owen, 24 Nov. 1839.

154 For the notion of shared community capital, see Tara J. Yosso, 'Whose culture has capital? A critical race theory discussion of Community Cultural Wealth', in *Race Ethnicity and Education*, 8 (2005), pp. 69-91.

d) Ethnicity

Ethnic tensions were occasionally in evidence in this period, for example between the English and Irish stuff weavers of east Leeds. Also, local leaders' emphasis on a fair wage and an 'Englishmen's' pride in not claiming poor relief sometimes involved distancing themselves from other groups like the 'poor Irish'.[155] Leeds ultra-radicals' endorsement of the candidature of the Tory Thomas Sadler at the 1832 election owed much to the fact that he advocated an Irish Poor Law, whereby the poor Irish would not be 'compelled to resort to the market of labour in England, and thereby reduce the value of the Englishmen's labour'.[156] However, in general, anti-Irish sentiments were rarely expressed from the radical platform. Indeed, Ireland and the 'fate of the oppressed Irish' often figured positively in the political discourse. George Beaumont speaking at an Almondbury meeting on distress in 1829 urged his audience to 'remember the great Catholic Union, and from what a small party it originally sprang, and what was its ultimate tremendous power'. Subsequent efforts to address Irish distress and the thorny issue of Church tithes, drew a supportive response; and opposition to the Irish Coercion Act of Jan 1833 became the first major issue to unify radicals after the passage of the Reform Bill.[157]

Unsurprisingly given the size of the population of Ireland and the well-established patterns of migration before the 'Great Famine', the leadership cadres of political and trade union groups in the West Riding incorporated a number of activists of Irish birth or heritage. These included James Duffy and Charles Connor (in Leeds); George White and George Flinn (in Bradford); and Joseph Mooney and William Cunningham (in Huddersfield).[158] The sizeable Irish element in the local leadership of neighbouring Barnsley included a number of refugees from the unsuccessful Drogheda strike of 1823. Irish weavers and combers were heavily involved in the Bradford strike of 1825, and the radical enclave of Nelson's Court included a number of Irish combers who had arrived following the collapse of the south-west Ireland woolcombing industry.[159] In general, ethnic conflict was confined to particular times (especially harvest season) and places. It rarely intruded into leadership cadres.

---

155 Morris, 'James Kitson', pp. 189-90; *LM* and *LI* June 1830; *Crisis* 27 Oct. 1832.

156 *LP* 4 Aug. 1832.

157 *HCC* 11 July 1829; *LM* and *LP* June-July 1831; Dorothy Thompson, 'Ireland and the Irish in English Radicalism', in Epstein and D. Thompson (eds.), *The Chartist Experience*, pp. 126-8.

158 James Duffy/Duffey (1794?-1843), active in Leeds radical politics in the early 1830s, later moved to Sheffield. Charles Connor, chair of the Leeds Northern [Chartist] Union in 1839, a self-styled 'leveller' and 'revolutionist' became a noted 'Chartist orator' and moved to the Manchester area. George Flinn/Flynn, a woolcomber and physical-force Chartist relocated to Bradford from Kidderminster (See below, p. 379). Joseph Mooney (1791-1843?), a 'woollen printer', was active in a variety of radical campaigns and hustings during the mid-1830s (*LT* 1 Feb. 1834, 28 Mar. 1835; 26 Mar. 1836; *LM* 6 May 1837). William Cunningham (1815?-?) was a radical woollen weaver, living in Holmfirth.

159 Kaijage, 'Labouring Barnsley', pp. 338-40; J. H. Treble, 'The Place of the Irish Catholics in the Social Life of the North of England', Unpub. PhD thesis, University of Leeds, 1968, p. 7.

e) Religion

John Hargreaves' research into popular religion and protest has added weight to the long-established view that the leadership of West Riding radicalism was steeped in Methodism and nonconformity. In this interpretation a range of Methodist sects supplied priceless oratorical training and organisational skills and vital leadership experience.[160] The New Connexion's Thomas Hirst, for example, proselytized the co-operative cause with nonconformist zeal, arguing that 'we could drive the world before us', if the number of co-operative factories matched that of Methodist chapels.[161] Hargreaves' account of the life of Benjamin Rushton of Halifax, another leader with New Connexion origins, emphasises 'the pervasiveness of the influence of popular religion on the culture of the Chartist Movement'.[162]

While this confessional connection may have been true in relation to elements of early co-operation and local trade unionism, and to radicalism in the dispersed villages around Huddersfield, Halifax and Bradford, it was far from being universal. In the main towns the socio-religious pattern of leadership was more diverse. Leeds politics included a vociferous and disruptive group of Carlileite freethinkers and Halstead notes the presence of significant support for 'Republican and Materialist' infidels in Huddersfield in the 1820s.[163] Both low-church evangelicals and high Church Tories became leaders of the factory reform movement and the operative short time committees included a broad range of denominations as well as a number of non-believers. The affiliations of the Huddersfield committee's members, for example, spanned Anglicanism, Primitive Methodism, freethinking and Owenite secularism.[164] Both Bradford and Huddersfield later became thriving Owenite socialist hubs.

It is correspondingly important not to underestimate the scale of religious scepticism or indifference. Woolcombers were famously irreligious in an area where, as Keighley trade union leader, James Walworth, ruefully observed in 1826, 'any one who is known to question the existence of a Divine Providence is shunned like a pestilence'. His colleague, Bradford's John Tester, a woolcomber, had earlier written to Francis Place that, 'I insult no man's religious opinions, no man's irreligious opinions', believing 'that Christianity is destitute of divine origin'.[165] A generation later and despite Bradford's reputation as 'a citadel of dissent', religious observance was, in Tony Jowitt's words, 'very much a minority pursuit'. Prior to the Religious Census of 1851 a local clergyman acknowledged that 'a large proportion of our inhabitants … are either

---

160 Hargreaves '"Hats Off"; R. F. Wearmouth, *Some Working-Class Movements of the Nineteenth Century* (London: Epworth Press, 1948).

161 *LYC* Mar. 1832. The New Connexion broke away from Wesleyan Methodism in 1797. Adherents believed that the laity should share power with ministers.

162 Hargreaves '"Hats Off", p. 164.

163 Halstead, 'Huddersfield STC', pp. 107-11. Richard Carlile's individualistic brand of republicanism and anti-clericalism enjoyed substantial support in the West Riding.

164 Halstead, 'Huddersfield STC', pp. 116. William Stocks jnr., for example, was a devoted Anglican.

165 PP, Add Mss. 27,803, f. 554-5 Walworth to Place 28 Jan. 1825 [mistake for 1826]; PP, Add Mss 27,803, f. 343-6, Tester to Place, 10 July 1825.

opposed or indifferent to the religion of Christ, and in too many cases grossly ignorant and immoral'.[166]

In general, whilst religious affiliation may have given some local leaders a headstart in terms of appeal and influence, leadership was normally contingent on their action and words rather than their belief system.

f) Occupation

Making definitive statements about the occupational make-up of the local leadership of the textile district's agitations and organisations is problematic. In the first place, ease of recognition and the bias of our main sources tends to exaggerate the importance of middle-class leaders or allies. Second, the paucity of detailed biographical information about working-class leaders means that we are relying on imaginative interpretation of snippets of information to piece together a convincing résumé of their working life. Additionally, there are the dangers in inferring too much from fairly crude occupational labels. Newspapers or magistrates often used generic terms such as 'operative', 'labouring man', 'mechanic', or 'working man' when they were unsure about precise occupation. Usually, in the West Riding, it signified work in the predominant local textile trade. Similarly, the designation 'weaver' or 'shoemaker' might be applied fairly indiscriminately. The *Northern Star* describes the speakers at a Halifax radical and anti-poor law meeting in January 1838 as being 'all working men, such as weavers, shoemakers etc'.[167] Such labels tell us little about the type or extent of the work performed or whether the person was an employer, self-employed or a wage-earning journeyman.

Nor can continuous or unchanged employment be assumed. Joseph Firth of Keighley worked initially as a woolcomber, then became a 'respectable farmer and churchwarden' and ended up as an itinerant tea and coffee dealer. John Swift, leader of the West Riding fancy weavers in the mid-1820s, was successively clogger, jumper (Ranter-Methodist), trade union leader, itinerant preacher, quack doctor hawking medicines, lecturer in Chester, and shawl manufacturer in Huddersfield. Peter Bussey, the son of a draper, worked two years as an apprentice cabinet-maker, then went into the worsted trade (probably as a comber) before setting himself up as beershop keeper.[168] Like many other radical beersellers and newspaper agents in the 1830s, Bussey prospered. Not all local leaders were so fortunate. Abraham Wildman, a Keighley radical, poet and Sunday School teacher, was reduced from employing seventeen combers in 1835 to virtual bankruptcy in the ensuing depression; whilst 'old

---

166 J. A. Jowitt, 'The Pattern of Religion in Victorian Bradford', in D. G. Wright, and J. A. Jowitt (eds.), *Victorian Bradford: Essays in Honour of Jack Reynolds* (Bradford: City of Bradford MDC, 1982), p. 37.

167 *NS* 27 Jan. 1838.

168 *Good Fellowship in Keighley*, pp. 17, 53-4 and Ward, 'Some Industrial Reformers', p. 132; *LM* 26 Apr. 1834; Peacock, *Bradford Chartism*, pp. 8-9. By the time of Chartism Bussey 'was running a [worsted] merchant's business as well as his alehouse', D. Thompson, *The Chartists*, p. 113.

Billy Stocks' (William Stock's jnr.), a cotton yarn dealer in Huddersfield, died a poor man in 1851.[169] Very different realities could lie behind identical occupational labels.

Even when the designation is accurate, precise classification is not always easy. The distinction between a skilled artisan and a small shopkeeper, trader or manufacturer could be narrow and hazy. Handloom weavers often considered themselves to be small, independent master-producers. Cloth-dressers (or croppers) worked in a variety of settings but similarly had traditions of independence. Equally, it did not require a great deal of capital or a change of lifestyle for an operative to set themselves up as a beershop keeper, a newspaper agent, a schoolmaster, or a village greengrocer. Often, indeed, the new venture might be backed by part-time work at their former trade. The change was sometimes a matter of necessity rather than choice. Unemployment, victimisation or infirmity drove a number of local leaders into becoming middlemen or schoolmasters. Joseph Hatfield of Heckmondwike was first a carpet weaver, then a regular Methodist New Connexion preacher, before ill-health forced him back to the loom and eventually to the classroom. John Tester bought a few goods and a hawking licence and took to the road in 1826 in the aftermath of the defeat of the Bradford Combers and Weavers. Thirty-eight years later he returned to Bradford to become a teacher of mathematics and natural science.[170] Such figures used teaching, hawking, or small-scale trading as a last resort or safety-net, lower both in status and rewards than their former trades.

With all these caveats, an overview of the West Riding evidence suggests that local leadership was drawn from three main occupational blocks. The first and largest grouping was made up of 'working men', predominantly domestic or workshop-based textile outworkers such as handloom weavers (in the various branches of the woollen industry) and woolcombers; plus artisans from trades such as tailoring and shoemaking. In addition, other traditionally well-paid textile workers, such as cloth-dressers and woolsorters, played key roles in trade unions, the early ten hours movement and, occasionally, radical organisations. The second group comprised a large minority of shopkeepers and retailers – grocers, drapers, booksellers, hairdressers, beershop keepers and publicans – with close links to the working community. A number, such as Lawrence Pitkethly, who toiled initially as a 'wright' (a metal-working craftsman), were originally workers themselves; and many took their identity from their customers rather than their fellow retailers.[171] The final and smallest grouping included small manufacturers, wholesalers and lower professional people such as solicitors, medical practitioners and religious ministers. This diverse group included T. S. Brooke in Dewsbury, Henry Dixon in Halifax and William Stocks jnr., and Read Holliday, 'a manufacturing chemist' in Huddersfield.[172] Holliday, one of the

169 Ward, 'Some Industrial Reformers', pp. 131-2 and 123. Wildman later became a publican in Bingley and then a warehouseman and woolsorter in Bradford. Stocks' moniker is in *HDE* 26 Dec. 1885.

170 On Hatfield (1796?-1869?), see Peel, *Spen Valley*, pp. 349-51. On Tester, see *LM* 28 June 1834; *BO* 9 Feb. 1870; W. Scruton, 'The Great Strike of 1825', *Bradford Antiquary*, 1 (1888), p. 69.

171 Halstead, 'Huddersfield STC', p. 109 on Pitkethly.

172 Henry Dixon was categorized as a 'manufacturer' (*LT* 9 Jan. 1836). On Read Holliday/Halliday (1809-?), see Halstead, 'Voice of the West Riding', pp. 32-3.

original 'managing committee' of the *Voice of the West-Riding*, had strong radical and Owenite credentials. Sympathetic figures of independent means brought with them financial solidity and some echoes of the tradition of the gentleman-leader; though as John Halstead has shown, Holliday, even though an employer, never achieved 'respectability'.[173] In an age of rapid change and greater social mobility the boundaries between these categories could be porous. A case in point is Titus Senior Brooke, a radical Dewsbury 'Chemist, Druggist, Bookseller and Stationer' and perennial Chartist delegate and office-holder. By the time he died in a road accident in 1859 he owned 'a large colliery' and was enumerated amongst the local 'gentry and clergy'.[174] Equally, as countless biographies show, the distinction between a skilled self-employed artisan and small shopkeeper or manufacturer was often narrow.

In the main towns the occupational mix was generally more varied, reflecting the diverse make-up of the local economy. In Leeds radical leaders were drawn from a wide range of backgrounds and included weavers and cloth-dressers and artisans from the 'lower' trades, as well as shopkeepers and full-time radicals. Leaders of short time and trade union organisations had stronger links to factory-based occupations and the upper textile trades and included slubbers, woolsorters and overlookers.[175] In Huddersfield, the peculiar social structure of the town meant that the radical leadership was supplied by a mix of current and former textile workers, shopkeepers, and skilled artisans, albeit reinforced on public occasions by weavers from the outlying townships. A similar occupational composition is identified in John Halstead's analysis of the Huddersfield STC, which reveals that two thirds of members were directly engaged in textile trades, with the remainder 'involved in retail dealing of one kind or another'.[176] In Keighley a report of a Political Union meeting in 1830, which unusually records the speakers' occupations, lists four combers, three weavers and two shopkeepers.[177] At the end of the decade the Chartist local leadership included three combers, a shoemaker and two other 'working men', along with shopkeepers, such as D. W. Weatherhead, a prosperous Chartist grocer.

In the outlying villages communities relied on home-grown leadership resources. Artisans or traders, such as shoemaker Abram Hanson in Elland or shopkeeper John Buckley in Almondbury, occasionally filled pivotal leadership roles. More usually, however, the key community leaders were handloom weavers. These included Benjamin Rushton of Ovenden, Joseph Brook of Horton, Christopher Shackleton of Queenshead, John Smith jnr. of Lepton, and Abraham Donkersley of Almondbury, who all operated in the villages surrounding Huddersfield or in the Bradford-Halifax hinterland.[178] Weavers' prominence reflected not just their numerical superiority in the

---

173 Halstead, 'The Voice of the West Riding', pp. 31-3.

174 *York Herald* 1 Mar. 1834, 24 Sept. 1859. T. S. Brooke (1795?-1859) was later a trustee of the Chartist Land Scheme.

175 Slubbing, the preparatory first stage of woollen spinning, was a skilled male occupation carried out on a 'slubbing-billy' in scribbling mills and the large integrated factories. Male overlookers supervised the work of female and juvenile factory hands in flax and worsted spinning mills. See below, pp. 72 and 87.

176 Halstead, Huddersfield STC', p. 97.

177 *LM* 30 Oct. 1830.

178 Abraham Donkersley (1802?-1872?) was a woollen weaver.

West Riding villages, or the strength of their support for advanced politics, but also the rich traditions of education, organisation and leadership in religious, trade, and community matters which they inherited and perpetuated. Their leadership contribution was immense.

g) Other Lives

Leadership could be a full-time job, both literally and metaphorically. By way of a coda, it is worth noting that the preceding discussion focuses mainly on the visible, proactive elements of local leaders' public careers. Just occasionally the sources allow glimpses into the interior lives of our protagonists. Interpretation of this evidence requires both imagination and recognition that recollections can be misremembered or malleable.

Even with these provisos, the limited evidence suggests that many of our subjects lived well-rounded lives and were firmly embedded in the culture of their host communities. Malcolm Chase has emphasised 'the familial nature of Chartism' and it is clear that family traditions of radicalism or socialism were enduringly strong.[179] As well as husband and wife pairs, the West Riding provides plenty of examples of radical parents, siblings and offspring; for example, Feargus O'Connor Holmes, born to a Keighley Chartist in 1840 or Henry Hunt Rushton, Mary and Ben's sixth child. Radical and socialist babies like the member's child whom Lawrence Pitkethly's son requested Robert Owen to baptise in 1838, were quickly immersed in the established family culture.[180]

Leaders were also well integrated into the social and communal lives of their neighbourhoods. Late nineteenth-century reminiscences, for example, celebrate Abram Hanson's medical pretensions and thespian proclivities. Mid-century newspaper sources reveal George Beaumont's bell-ringing interests; and how, following a likely stroke in 1843, John Hanson focused on developing his musical talents. He contributed to the Huddersfield choral tradition by composing oratorios based on the four seasons, which were performed in the mid-1850s.[181]

Less positively, newspapers also illuminate the ever-present threat of poverty exposed in John Spivey's struggles to support eight children, including a disabled daughter; or Joseph Brook's admission of the financial impact of his wife's 'long sickness'. Isaac Haley, a local operative, similarly reminded a Halifax meeting on the fate of the Dorchester labourers that he needed to work fourteen hours a day 'in order to maintain a sickly wife and a family of small children'.[182] In addition, parish burial registers and newspaper notices chronicle just how frequently local leaders had to cope with the loss of partners or children. For example, the *York Herald* in 1833 recorded the demise of Ellen, the 29 year-old wife of William Thornton, woolcomber, of

---

179 Chase, 'Biographical Turn', p. 198.

180 *Goodfellowship in Keighley*, pp. 80-1; Hargreaves, '"Hat's Off"', p. 169; OC No. 992, Pitkethly jnr. to Owen, 16 Feb. 1838, writing as secretary of the Huddersfield Socialist branch.

181 *BS* 8 Feb. 1879; *LT* 14 June 1851; *HCH* 16 Nov. 1850, 12 Nov. 1853, 23 Aug., 6, 13 Dec. 1856.

182 *LP* 19 Dec. 1829; *BO* 27 Sept. 1838, *LT* 12 Apr. 1834.

Halifax; whilst the *Northern Star* in 1840 sadly noted the death of Ann, 'the beloved and only daughter of Mr. James Penny, grocer, Mill Bridge, Liversedge, aged three years and two months'.[183]

Some leaders also faced personal battles with drink, illustrated in George Beaumont's inebriated confrontation with Joshua Hobson in 1834; and in Charles Connor, a leading Leeds Chartist, being charged with obstruction in July 1839, after continuing the Chartist branch meeting's debate out on the local streets at 7 o'clock on Sunday morning. Ralph Taylor, star pupil of the Leeds Mechanics' Institute and leading short time and trade union spokesman in the early 1830s, ended his days as an alcoholic in the Leeds workhouse a decade later. Though never a 'sot', Abram Hanson's convivial inclinations 'led to his frequenting the public-house too much'.[184]

Given these challenges and competing interests, and the sheer stamina required for sustained campaigning, it is little wonder that there was some inevitable churn in the leadership cadres of early working-class movements. However, the attrition rate should not be exaggerated. Continuity and longevity are more in evidence than change and volatility. In part this is attributable to the firm grounding of local leaders in their respective communities.

9: Local Organisations

> Now I know that the labouring classes are nearly tired of forming first one kind
> of organisation and then another (hear), because we have had a political union
> before, and since that, we have had the Trades Union, and both have failed to
> answer the purpose for which they were intended.

The speaker is Joseph Lodge, an Almondbury leader, trying to persuade the local community, mainly fancy weavers, to set up a Working Men's Association in September 1837. He and other speakers managed to convince sufficient people that this time it would be different, and the Almondbury WMA was established.[185] The years from 1825 to 1839 are full of such attempts to create formal organisations dedicated, as Oastler's testimony at the head of the chapter indicates, to a variety of purposes. Many of these 'managing Committees' displayed similar characteristics and there was considerable crossover in terms of broad aims and personnel. Nevertheless, a number displayed distinctive features.[186]

The first short time committees were the product of delegates meeting from local factories, but soon morphed into looser alliances of interested and committed parties. Subsequent attempts were made to tighten up the organisational structure in the West Riding, with the formation of a Central Committee of local delegates. However, the importance of the interpersonal dynamics of such structures is suggested in Richard

---

183 *York Herald* 16 Nov. 1833; *NS* 1 Aug. 1840. Penny was a key Chartist network figure in the Dewsbury district.

184 *VWR* 5 Apr. 1834; *NS* 13 July 1839; *LM* 8 June 1844; *BS* 8 Feb. 1879.

185 *LT* 9 Sept. 1837. The organisation was still in existence in late 1839.

186 More detailed accounts of particular organisations (with full references) will be given in later chapters.

Oastler's hazy recollections of the personnel assembled at the inaugural meeting in March 1832:

> I think Mr. Nicholson (Halifax,) Printer, was in the chair; who were in the room at that moment I really cannot remember. There were at the meeting two Crabtrees, MYSELF, Hall, Weatherhead, Wildman, I think John Hall, and Etherington and another from Keckmondwike [sic], whom I forget. There were many of the Halifax committee, whose names I never knew. The Secretary is Mr. John Shaw, Grove St., Halifax. Abraham Whitehead and John Hanson were at the meeting. I don't just now remember any more. I think two were there from Bradford. R. [Ralph] Taylor I think was not there...[187]

Throughout the early agitation local committees retained a great deal of independence and continued to raise and distribute their own funds. They operated more as a loose caucus, occasionally quiescent but easily re-activated to meet the exigencies of a fresh crisis or to address new concerns such as the implementation of the new poor law.

Early trade unions drew on long established traditions of 'box-clubs' and friendly societies; and as Malcolm Chase notes, 'benefit functions lay at the heart of most early trade societies'.[188] Unions adopted a variety of organisational forms ranging from individual self-governing local trade societies with loose federated ties, to tiered local, district and occasionally nation-wide structures. The stress however remained on local independence and self-management. Even in the quite elaborate organisational structure developed by the West Riding Fancy Weavers' Union in 1824-5 to overcome some of the difficulties inherent in organising a dispersed and diverse trade, the basic unit remained the separate local society or 'box' of usually fifty to a hundred men and women.[189] Ten years later, the demise of the powerful Yorkshire trades' unions was signalled in reports of lodges selling the box and associated paraphernalia and the closing of their accounts, often with a 'hearty supper'.[190]

The worsted-based 'Bradford Order' of the early 1830s, typical of the 'Trades' Unions' developed in this period, also had an elaborate structure, with separate local lodges feeding into districts (each with a governing committee) which in turn sent delegates to the 'grand lodge' meeting held twice a year at which a 'grand committee' or 'council of direction' was chosen to be the governing power of the union. In practice, though, the 'grand committee' usually turned out (for practical reasons) to be the district committee of the pre-eminent area in the union. Even so, as in the earlier Fancy Weavers' Union, the powers of the central (grand lodge) leadership, which normally comprised at least three full-time officials, were strictly limited, and they often struggled to retain internal discipline and unity of action.[191]

---

187 *PMG* 7 Sept. 1833.

188 Malcolm Chase, *Early Trade Unionism: Fraternity, Skill and the Politics of Labour* (London: Breviary Stuff, 2012 edn.), p. 87.

189 The Union included dyers and scourers as well as weavers and covered an area 30 miles in circumference. BPP, *Minutes of evidence taken before Select Committee on Combination Laws*, 1825, IV, the testimonies of Swift and Cowgill.

190 For example, *LM* 31 May, *HHE* 14 Aug., 16 Oct. 1834.

191 See, for example, the local strike committees mentioned by Swift, BPP, 1825, IV, pp. 138 and 145. In practice both the Bradford and Leeds Trades' Unions of 1831-4 were democratic and

Independence and self-management were also key features of the early co-operative societies. While they occasionally came together in district-wide meetings or co-operative trading endeavours and collectively agreed to send a single delegate to the half-yearly co-operative congresses, they retained their own committees and a proudly autonomous, self-sufficient outlook. This was epitomised in the wish of one Bradford co-operator to see and hear of 'every Society being like a little independent nation of itself'.[192]

Working-class radical political societies of the 1830s adopted a variety of titles, but their basic structure was often similar: a committee of variable size, with a president or chairman and a secretary and treasurer elected annually or quarterly; weekly, fortnightly or monthly meetings (depending on the state of popular interest or a particular agitation); and sometimes regular weekly ½d or 1d subscriptions to cover the costs of agitation and correspondence. Local Political Unions, and Radical Associations frequently linked informally with neighbouring societies, and occasionally developed more formal ties.[193] However, like most working-class organisations of the period they placed great store by their independence and their attempts to put the democratic vision into practice within their own body.

Local leaders developed and serviced a range of different organisations during the agitations of the late 1820s and the 1830s. These varied in terms of their formal structures and links, the degree of formality/informality, the extent of paid officialdom, and the payment of initial subscriptions and regular dues. However, certain organisational features, and some of their associated problems, recurred. In the first place, a number of organisations sought to develop a tiered local/district/regional (and occasionally national) structure, with delegates from each level providing the means of communication and accountability. It was a model of organisation already familiar from Methodism and from the extensive networks of friendly societies or 'secret orders' which were expanding rapidly in the 1820s and 1830s. It was imitated by ten hours leaders in the Factory Reformation Society, the trades' unions of the early 1830s and the anti-poor law campaigners later in the decade. At least one locality (Bradford) successfully adopted this model in the early Chartist period.

The class system which might operate as an extension of, or a substitute for, this form of delegate organisation also owed much to Methodist inspiration. It involved creating or breaking down an organisation into small 'classes' which met regularly for discussion under an elected class leader who collected the nominal (usually 1d) subscriptions and kept a class roll. Class leaders then met regularly to become the driving force of the local organisation. The reorganisation of the Bradford Radical Association (RA) which Peter Bussey proposed in August 1837 was a variant of this. He envisaged sections of twenty-five, each with a leader who would collect subscriptions, distribute political tracts, deal with correspondence and communicate

---

decentralised bodies with much of the power and money being held locally.

192 *WFP* 11 Apr. 1829.

193 For example, the PUs of the Huddersfield area joined together in the reform crisis period to issue addresses and call meetings. The early Chartist period saw more formal ties with district delegate meetings in the Bradford and Huddersfield areas and 'agitation councils' in a number of centres.

information. Leaders would then meet once a week, with a general meeting being held once a month open to all members.[194] The plan was not adopted but interestingly was revived in the late summer of early 1839 when, in the wake of the failures of the Chartist Convention and with the local movement under increasing magisterial scrutiny, it proved a successful means of maintaining enthusiasm and secrecy.[195] According to Cecil Driver, the class system also formed the model for the wide-ranging, deeply penetrating network of committees and groups which Oastler and the early factory reformers sought to achieve in 1831-2.[196]

Ten hours advocates, co-operators, radicals, Chartists and trade unionists all made extensive use of delegates and missionaries to spread organisation and their message, or to raise money or awareness. Thus, when the Fancy Weavers' Union found masters sending work to non-union areas in 1825, they 'posted up a hand-bill on every church door around the neighbourhood [Slaithwaite]' and delegates called a meeting which rejected the lower, undercutting wages. In doing so they recruited thirty new members. In another case (Horton, near Bradford) a deputation went round the weaving shops and received assurances that no more 'lower-rate' work would be taken out.[197] During the major strikes of 1825 and 1834 West Riding delegates took advantage of pre-existing trade union networks to scour the length and breadth of the country to secure urgently needed funds. Within the purely local context the phenomenon of 'main town' radical, short time, co-operative or Chartist societies exporting their enthusiasm and organisational know-how recurred throughout the decade.[198]

The resulting organisations, which were formed in the outlying villages and townships, mirrored the structure of the parent body and normally comprised a committee presided over by a triumvirate of chair, secretary and treasurer.[199] Such local committees with their regular meetings in pub, chapel or school-room, their convivial elements, and their coordinating and money collecting functions, provided the basic organisational unit around which local working-class agitational endeavour developed. In the ten hour and anti-poor law movements these committees planned and held local public meetings, and organised campaigns of resistance. In early co-operation the local committees vetted new members and oversaw any plans for expansion or consolidation; whilst in early Chartism they organised the distribution of petitions and collecting boxes and the provision of lectures. Occasionally the size of the committee might need to be enlarged. During industrial disputes, for example, there might be strength in numbers. Soon after the start of the 1825 strike the original committee, drawn from the various lodges of the Bradford Combers and Weavers Association, was augmented by applying

---

194 *LT* 12 Aug. 1837.

195 Peacock, *Bradford Chartism*, pp. 23 and 29.

196 Cecil Driver, *Tory Radical. The Life of Richard Oastler* (New York: Oxford University Press, 1946), p. 101.

197 PP, 1825 IV, pp. 133 and 146-7.

198 The traffic was not always one way. Navickas, *Protest*, p. 122, cites an example of the periphery (Almondbury) leading the centre (Huddersfield).

199 See, for example, the formation of the Slaithwaite NU branch *NS* 1 Dec. 1838.

to the different tramping societies, which were six in number, to send one man from each, as the representatives of such societies. Afterwards the Irish were assembled together and requested to send one man as their representative. They sent two. Thus was formed the committee which first began to act on behalf of their fellow workmen, and which was a kind of focus, or central point to which the other combers and weavers constantly resorted, to give and receive advice.[200]

This committee like so many others of the period resulted from what was essentially a delegate meeting. Such local or regional meetings of representatives remained a recurring organisational feature of the societies of the early 1830s. In many trade unions the delegating process was formalised and incorporated into the structure of the body with annual, half-yearly or quarterly conferences and regular local district delegate meetings. West Riding delegate meetings became a semi-permanent feature of the ten hours and anti-poor law agitations. Initially, as with the West Riding Chartist delegate meetings, the stimulus might be the organisation of major public demonstration; but the central committees also often took on wider organisational functions and sometimes paid their own full-time or part-time officials.

The payment of officials, and of delegates and missionaries more generally, raised thorny questions of accountability and dependency and laid them open to accusations of self-interest. Consequently, the independent, self-financing representative remained an attractive proposition to early working-class organisations and their supporters. The balance, however, was changing. A Holmfirth 'Friend to the Labouring Class', writing in 1833, urged 'Lodges' to 'send such men to the Delegate-Meetings as you know to be pure advocates for your welfare', rather than 'those sort of men that are more afraid to break down the Master Manufacturer than they are of you having too low wages'. The payment of the Bradford early Chartist 'speakers' shows there was an increasing willingness to compensate working-class delegates for their involvement.[201]

Although highly organised delegate structures evolved in trade unions and early Chartism, it was more usual for meetings to be one-off, small-scale affairs in which questions of payment and accountability scarcely had time to be raised. The worsted handloom-weavers' campaign of 1835, for example, began with a single large-scale meeting of delegates from all the weaving townships in Bradford, Halifax, Leeds and their vicinities. The requests by visiting delegates to support the striking Ashton and Stalybridge cotton-spinners in 1830-1 was met by specially convened meetings of the trades in Leeds and Huddersfield. Operatives responded to worries that Hobhouse's [factory reform] Bill might be lost in spring 1831 by calling a special delegate meeting of one delegate from each of the principal textile factories in Leeds. Similar methods had been used to organise a milk and butter boycott in 1829. The organisation of the West Riding public meeting to protest about the conviction of the Dorchester labourers in 1834 was effected by a meeting of radical and trades' union delegates in Bradford. In most of these instances the delegate body ceased to exist once the specific task had been performed, or the objective achieved.

Indeed, though this was proverbially the age of 'unions', permanent organisations with long-term objectives, formal structures and written constitutions and with

---

200 Tester, *History of … the Bradford Contest.*
201 Peacock, *Bradford Chartism*, p. 18.

extensive regional and national links, were far from being the norm. More usually people came together in a locality in a loose *ad hoc* body to pursue a limited objective over a finite period of time – to fight a wage reduction or win an increase; to publicise distress; to expose a local grievance such as the truck system; to petition parliament on a particular issue; to organise non-electors; to raise subscriptions for unstamped, radical or trade union victims; or to provide information for a parliamentary inquiry. In a number of cases these limited, *ad hoc* bodies evolved into more permanent, formally structured and wide-ranging organisations. The Leeds and Huddersfield operatives' delegate meetings to aid Hobhouse's Bill became the basis of the later short time committees; the Bradford non-electors' committee for the election of 1835 gave rise to a working-class political and educational association; the Almondbury meetings on 'Distress' in 1829 paved the way for the foundation of the Almondbury Political Union; the success of the Leeds woollen workers in winning the big strike at Gott's in 1831 formed the launching-pad from which the Leeds Trades' Union took off.

Accordingly, care should be taken not to read back later organisational features and aspirations into these initial bodies. In many instances a union evolved out of the strike (and the strike out of the wage reduction); and a generalised 'political' organisation arose out of a specific grievance or the need to mobilise wider support for a platform campaign. It is not coincidental that many local short time and Chartist organisations were founded immediately before or after major West Riding meetings. As well as being genuinely idealistic and propagandist, the motives for the formation of such bodies also had a more pragmatic side – to raise funds and to mobilise support for the meetings. The resulting organisations were sometimes short-lived.

In a sense, formal organisations were only necessary where money was changing hands and there was a need to take names and keep a check on subscriptions paid. The vigour and variety of a branch's cultural life was not merely the result of a desire for a cheap, accessible and independent form of conviviality, and the expression of deep-seated political, educational and religious aspirations. It also served the practical need to maintain interest and make sure that people turned up to pay their subscriptions.

In general, whilst formal organisations with, often literally, grand titles and long-term objectives, and with paid officials and a structure for collecting regular contributions, were becoming more common, such trends were not widespread nor were they universally welcomed. As well as a general ingrained mistrust of centralisation, whether local or national, many people also resented, or simply were not able to support, a permanent organisation with paid officials. Only the better-paid occupations or a minority of those in the less well-remunerated trades were able to keep up regular contributions to their trade society. Subscriptions for political or co-operative societies often tailed off quickly after the initial excitement of the 'launch' had died away. Political societies without any obvious immediate short-term 'benefits' were particularly vulnerable. They also suffered from ingrained suspicions about 'nocturnal meetings and penny unions'.[202]

If this ideological opposition to formal organisation gradually diminished during the 1830s, after the apparent success of the political unions of the reform era; fears of

---

202 *LP* 19, 26 Sept. 1829. James Mann's 1829 plan was stymied by concerted opposition, led by Carlileite republicans, to paying the proposed subscription.

embezzlement and misappropriation, fuelled by occasional stories of disappearing treasurers and secretaries, remained strong. A Halifax 'Co-operator' wrote to the *Voice of the West-Riding* in October 1833 about the lack of trust and confidence within the working class and the fact that people were most worried about whether officers would act honestly. His solution was 'proper laws and a careful selection of officers'.[203] However assiduous the choice, a major trade union defeat or a setback for a particular organisation or campaign almost invariably brought in its wake allegations of misuse of funds, extravagance or dissipation. So, in the aftermath of the Leeds Trades' Union's bitter defeat in summer 1834 the Union's President, Thomas Buckley, in an emotional speech, was forced to deny slanders that the committee had all absconded or 'had secured not less than a thousand pounds'.[204]

The final component of the reservations which many people had about formal organisations was the experience, especially where money and strong-minded local leaders were involved, that they led to rivalry and internal strife. For this reason, Joseph Lodge, at the inaugural Almondbury WMA meeting, urged people to 'lay aside all the jealousies and animosities which may have been created in those former unions'.[205] The recurring themes of dishonesty and schism, together with practical difficulties for the majority of the population in keeping up regular subscriptions, constantly bedevilled attempts to set up more permanent working-class organisational structures.

The recognition of these problems makes it imperative to examine the wider, often informal, manifestations of working-class endeavour and not judge the importance of, or the support enjoyed by, a movement solely through the longevity of its bureaucratic structures, the size of its paid-up membership or its impressive moniker. Titles can be misleading and behind elaborate nomenclature we sometimes find just a handful of committed leaders and activists. As a disgruntled Lancashire early Chartist leader complained after 1840 that the agitation was carried on by 'miserable knots of a dozen or two in each town, meeting generally in some beer-shop, and calling themselves branches of the National Charter Association'.[206]

However, popular approval and support was expressed in a number of ways apart from formally enrolling in a trade, political or campaigning organisation. Of the Bradford Chartist prisoners arrested for their part in the 1840 Rising one was 'a Chartist in opinion but has attended only one Meeting'; another 'did not understand it but by what he heard other men say he thought it would better him'; a third was 'a reader of the Northern Star and a Chartist in opinion'; whilst a fourth attended a local meeting in order to hear what they had to say'.[207] At the start of the Bradford strike of 1825 relatively few combers and weavers were paid-up members of the union (many joined after the strike had started), but the vast majority were committed to it. As John

---

203 *VWR* 19 Oct. 1833.
204 *LT* 21 June 1834.
205 *LT* 9 Sept. 1837. Joseph Lodge (1808-1880) was a handloom fancy weaver.
206 Matthew Fletcher, Letters to the Inhabitants of Bury, letter IV, quoted in Dorothy Thompson (ed.), *The Early Chartists* (London: Macmillan, 1971), pp. 27-8.
207 TNA: HO 20/10 (Interviews with Chartist prisoners). Prisoners may have felt that it was in their interests to play-down their involvement somewhat.

Tester recalls, when a strike looked imminent, the union employed twenty people 'to call upon the combers and weavers individually at their respective workshops, to ascertain who would contribute to the support of the strike, should such a thing take place'. More than 14,000 people 'signed their names or caused them to be signed, as a kind of pledge that they would keep their word, and support a strike or strike themselves if necessary'.[208]

In general, formal bureaucratic organisation was not a strongpoint of popular politics. Organisations tended to fade into one another or to die and then revive under a new title following a fresh stimulus. The vitality and strength of popular radicalism often needs to be sought in more informal networks rooted in a culture of meeting rooms, pubs, bookshops and newsrooms and held together by the radical press, continuity of leadership and shared ideas and perspectives. Even so, the study of organisational structures with their dynamic and fluid forms remains an important aspect of the period under discussion.[209] It was one of the achievements of Chartism, building on the experience of the movements which preceded it, that it outgrew the looser old a*d hoc* modes of organisation and eventually established a permanent national organisation, with regular funds, paid lecturers and a democratic structure.

One of those important antecedents was trade unionism, which built on long established traditions and organisational models. The distinctive trades' unionism of the textile district, with its complex structures and cloak of secrecy, both harked back to older structures and modes of operation and looked forward to modern configurations and mutualist aspirations. It is important, then, to examine this pivotal strand of working-class leadership and organisation, and its roots in the industrial structure and economy of the textile district.

---

208 Tester, *History of … the Bradford Contest.*

209 There is renewed interest in this subject. For example, the new political organisations that evolved during the nineteenth century in Europe and North America were the focus of an important 2017 collection of essays, including Maartje Janse's study of the new types of national, mass-based organisations that emerged in the 1830s. Maartje Janse '"Association is a Mighty Engine": Mass Organization and the Machine Metaphor, 1825–1840', in Henk te Velde and Maartje Janse (eds.), *Organizing Democracy: Reflections on the Rise of Political Organizations in the Nineteenth Century* (Basingstoke: Palgrave Macmillan, 2017), pp. 19-42.

2

The West Riding Textile District:
Industry, Trades and Trades' Unionism

This second introductory chapter sketches some of the general background for subsequent explorations of political radicalism, early co-operation, the factory movement, the agitations of the mid-1830s and early Chartism. It firstly defines the geographical area of study – the West Riding textile district – and outlines a few of the distinguishing features of the industrial make-up of each of the six main textile towns and their vicinities. The second section, after briefly highlighting some of the characteristics of the West Riding's slow industrial revolution, looks in more detail at the textile district's labour force. It examines the experiences and organisations of three broad but overlapping categories of workers: the 'upper', more secure, skilled trades, the more insecure, threatened or declining, 'lower' skilled trades, and the depressed (mainly textile) outworkers. It argues that whilst there undoubtedly were gradations of skill and status within the workforce and not all workers were subject to the same pressures and conditions of life and work, the bulk of the labouring population shared many common experiences, values and aspirations, and responded by engaging in wider than 'trade' activities and organisations. The final section looks at one of the distinctive manifestations of this wider response: the growth of trades' unions in the early 1830s. It outlines some of the key features of this movement and provides an introduction to, and reference point for, subsequent discussions of links between radical, co-operative or factory reform endeavours and trade unionism.

1: The West Riding Textile District

This study focuses on one particular part of the West Riding of Yorkshire; namely, the geographical and industrial heartland of the Riding – the textile district.[1] Definitions of this zone vary. A stuff makers' petition of 1772 spoke of

> the district bounded on the North by Settle, on the South by Saddleworth, distant from each other forty miles; bounded on the East by Leeds, and on the West by Haslingden, in Lancashire distant from each other by 35 miles. The space of ground occupied by manufactures, equal to a square of 30 miles, about one half of which are moors and waste ground.[2]

A 1951 historical geography of the 'wool textiles belt' delimited a somewhat smaller 'core area' extending

> from Silsden, down the Aire valley almost as far as Leeds, thence across the Aire-Calder watershed through Morley to Wakefield. From Wakefield the boundary runs up the Calder valley to Dewsbury, and then southward along the Calder-Dearne watershed to the outlying district of Denby Dale. The southern extent of the area approximates the high water-shed between the Calder and upper Don river system. The western boundary crosses over the Pennines to include the remote district of Saddleworth, but cuts across the Calder valley near Sowerby Bridge. From Sowerby Bridge it continues northwards, in an irregular fashion to Silsden.[3]

This central core area, together with adjacent fringes of substantial though not predominant textile employment, was equally recognisable over a hundred years earlier, in the third and fourth decades of the nineteenth century, when boundaries were perhaps less clear-cut and the industry more dispersed. According to M. T. Wild, any variations have tended to be 'more of local than regional significance. The general outlines have altered remarkably little over a very lengthy time span'.[4]

---

1 The term 'textile district' is used here and in the subtitle of this book, rather than the more usual 'woollen' or 'wool' textile region, to signify the multiplicity of fabrics and yarns which were produced in the area during the period. The generic term 'woollen' can be misleading for the West Riding was a major centre of flax-spinning, and produced worsted yarn and stuffs, fancy and mixed fabrics (incorporating silk, cotton and worsted yarns) as well as a wide range of woollen cloths. There was also a significant cotton spinning and weaving sector in the west of the region. Technically speaking the term 'woollen' applies only to cloths made from short wool and spun into woollen yarn to produce a cloth which is then fulled. This specific usage is generally adopted in this study. However, contemporaries occasionally used the word to cover all types of cloths made from wool, including worsteds.

2 James Bonwick, *The Romance of the Wool Trade* (London: Griffin, Farran and Co, 1887), p. 409, quoted in R. M. Hartwell, 'The Yorkshire Woollen and Worsted Industry, 1800-50', Unpub. DPhil thesis, University of Oxford 1955, p. 168. The term 'stuffs' is an alternative for worsted.

3 M. T. Wild, 'The Yorkshire wool textile industry', in J. G. Jenkins (ed.), *The Wool Textile Industry in Great Britain* (London: Routledge and Kegan Paul, 1972), pp. 186-7. See also, Arthur Raistrick, *The West Riding of Yorkshire* (London: Hodder and Stoughton, 1970), p. 21.

4 Wild, 'The Yorkshire wool textile industry', p. 186.

The main concentration of this study is on the central core of the textile region, comprising the six main district or market centres – Leeds, Bradford, Huddersfield, Halifax, Keighley and Dewsbury – together with the innumerable smaller manufacturing towns and villages which made up their environs. A handbill detailing arrangements for the May 1833 Wibsey Moor factory reform meeting indicates how contemporary local organisers divided up their region:

1 Leeds Division – comprising all the Townships of the Parish of Leeds, and also Pudsey, Stanningley, Farsley, and Calverley.

2 Huddersfield Division – comprising Huddersfield, Holmfirth, Honley, and all the adjacent Townships and also Deighton and Brighouse.

3 Bradford Division – comprising all the Townships in Bradford Parish, and also Baildon, Guiseley, Yeadon, Idle, Eccleshill, and Otley.

4 Keighley Division – comprising all the adjacent Townships, and also Bingley.

5 Dewsbury Division – comprising Birstall, Batley, Gomersal, Birkenshaw, Heckmondwike, adjacent Villages, and Mirfield.

6 Halifax Division – comprising all the Townships in Halifax.[5]

These six 'divisions', 'market centres' or 'spheres of influence' remain a useful way of sub-dividing and analysing the central core.

Beyond this primary area, the textile district also included a number of secondary, more peripheral localities – outposts of woollen manufacture, or districts where woollen gave way to other textile, agricultural, extractive or metal-working sources of employment. These fringes, extending towards Skipton in the north west, to Otley in the north, along the Calder valley beyond Hebden Bridge to Todmorden in the west, across the Pennines to Saddleworth in the south west, to Denby Dale and Barnsley in the south east, and to Wakefield and beyond Leeds in the east, have, of necessity, been studied less intensively. For example, although the Saddleworth district was a woollen manufacturing area looking across Stannedge towards the market at Huddersfield, its geographical location on the 'wrong' (Lancashire) side of the Pennines, and the fairly specialised nature of its staple product (high quality woollen cloths) means that it operated as an independent outpost, rather than an integral part, of the West Riding textile region. Equally Todmorden and some of the Calder valley villages were primarily orientated towards the Lancashire cotton industry and have been studied only where they impinge on the story of the main core area.

The non-inclusion of Wakefield – later the West Riding's county town – in this core area raises some issues. Wakefield had been an important woollen manufacturing and merchanting town in the seventeenth and eighteenth centuries. However, its population and woollen manufacturing base grew far less than the main West Riding towns.[6] While it remained an important market for agricultural produce – a

---

5   TNA: HO 40/31 f. 34, (handbill) instructions for 'West Riding Meeting on Wibsey Low Moor'.

6   Herbert Heaton, *The Yorkshire Woollen and Worsted Industry from the Earliest Times up to the Industrial Revolution* (Oxford: Clarendon Press, 1965, 2nd edn.) describes Wakefield as

distinguished visitor in 1835 called it 'the emporium for grain for the manufacturing districts' – its cloth marketing functions declined. In the words of F. J. Glover, 'Wakefield ceased to be a 'generative' urban centre and acquired 'parasitic characteristics' in the early Nineteenth Century'.[7]

Finally, mention should be made of Barnsley, which although in the West Riding and a 'textile' town, possessed a distinct and separate identity. Located on the borderline between the West Riding woollen district and the mining and metal-working zone of South Yorkshire, the town's staple industry in the 1820s and 1830s was linen-weaving, though the local coal-mining industry was also developing fast. The town possessed strong trading links with Leeds and to a lesser extent Huddersfield; and local working-class leaders often aligned themselves with movements of the main textile zone.[8] However, the distinctiveness of the town's products, its geographical location on the outer fringes of the textile area, and the fact that its working-class movements have been the subject of existing detailed studies, mean that Barnsley leaders are included only where they intersect with the story of the central core of the textile district.[9]

It is to the textile heartlands and the six main spheres of influence that we first turn, in order to examine the chief characteristics of the industrial make-up of the region.

a) Leeds

By the end of the fourth decade of the nineteenth century, Leeds was a large and rapidly expanding industrial town.[10] The population of the town itself numbered 88,000 in 1841, with the wider parish and borough containing over 150,000 people.[11]

---

possessing a large number of merchants, wool-staplers, factors and dyers. Although the town had a number of worsted mills (10 in 1835) its textile manufacturing base was not large. See, J. W. Walker, *Wakefield and its History and People, Vol 2* (Wakefield: West Yorkshire Print Co., 1934), p. 529.

7 Sir George Head, *A Home Tour through the Manufacturing Districts of England in the Summer of 1835* (London: Cass, 1968, 2nd edn.) p. 142; F. J. Glover, 'The Rise of the Heavy Woollen Trade of the West Riding of Yorkshire in the Nineteenth Century', *Business History*, 4 (1962), p. 3.

8 Barnsley for example, had ties with the Almondbury operatives' agitation of 1829-30, was linked with Leeds linen workers in the Trades' Union of 1833-4, and supplied speakers and delegates for West Riding meetings of the early Chartist period.

9 For Barnsley and its working-class movements, see F. J. Kaijage, 'Labouring Barnsley, 1816-1856: A Social and Economic History', Unpub. PhD thesis, University of Warwick, 1975.

10 This short study of Leeds draws on a number of secondary sources: E. J. Connell and M. Ward, 'Industrial Development, 1780-1914', in Derek Fraser (ed.), *A History of Modern Leeds* (Manchester: Manchester University Press, 1980); E. M. Sigsworth 'The Industrial Revolution', in M. W. Beresford and G. R. Jones (eds.), *Leeds and its Region* (Leeds: British Association For The Advancement of Science, 1967), pp. 146-55; W. G. Rimmer, 'Leeds Leather Industry in the nineteenth century', *Publications of the Thoresby Society*, 46 (1960), pp. 119-64; W. G. Rimmer, 'The Industrial Profile of Leeds, 1740-1840', *Publications of the Thoresby Society*, 50 (1967), pp. 130-57; also a series of short articles by Rimmer and others in the *Leeds Journal* (Sept. 1953 - Jan. 1959) under the general title, 'Leeds and its Industrial Growth'. Other sources or specific quotes are footnoted separately.

11 Comparative figures in1821 were 48,603 and 83,799. For local demography, see Frank

The wealth of the town originally came from its Cloth Halls and its role as a finishing and merchanting centre for woollen cloth. Although the new factories built around the turn of the century increased the amount of cloth-making in the town itself, the expansions of the mid 1820s and afterwards confirmed the pre-existing trend for actual cloth manufacturing to be located on the outskirts of the town or in outlying villages. Leeds in-township remained primarily a centre of marketing, finishing and dyeing.

Visitors to the town and its environs stressed the novel aspects of industrialisation: the factories, machinery and power, the large labour forces, the slums and the smoke.[12] One foreign tourist spoke of how

> a hundred red fires shot upwards into the sky, and as many towering chimneys poured forth columns of black smoke. The huge manufactories, five stories high, in which every window was illuminated, had a grand and striking effect. Here the toiling artisan labours far into the night.[13]

Certainly, in contemporary terms, there were some spectacularly large establishments. John Marshall, the flax-spinner, employed 1,229 hands (mainly women and children) in the spinning side of his Water Lane 'manufactory' in 1833 and four years earlier the next three largest firms in the industry had been affording 'regular labour' to 698, 560 and 420 workpeople respectively.[14] However, the novelty of these features, and the smoke, obscures the fact that much of the 'industrial' development of the town took in non-mechanised, non-textile sectors and that the town had a very diverse economy.[15]

As well as flourishing textile concerns (woollen, worsted, flax and, on a minor scale, cotton and silk) the town had important chemical, pottery, brick-making, glass-making, engineering and printing industries. These were often initially small-scale enterprises and indeed the bulk of the expansion of the early decades of the nineteenth century took place in services (particularly food and drink), artisan crafts (tailoring, leather and wood-working, building) and in small workshop-based industries. W. G. Rimmer estimated that four out of every five additional workers in the labour force between 1801 and 1841 found employment not in mills and factories but in household and other small-scale production units.[16]

That is not to say that the textile sector in general and the power-driven factories in particular did not exert a major, perhaps disproportionate, influence on the local economy and labour force. A static, single-shot, picture of factory employment does

---

Beckwith 'The Population of Leeds during the Industrial Revolution', *Publications of the Thoresby Society*, 41 (1954), pp. 118-196, and C. J. Morgan, 'Demographic Change, 1771-1911', in Fraser (ed.) *A History of Modern Leeds*, pp. 46-71.

12 Head, *Home Tour*, p. 172.

13 Hermann Fürst von Pückler-Muskau, *Tour in England, Ireland and France, in the years 1826, 1827, 1828, and 1829* (London, 1832), pp. 207-8, quoted in Rimmer, 'Industrial Profile', p. 130, fn. 1.

14 BPP, 1833, VI, p. 155; *LM* 28 Nov. 1829.

15 See, for example, Rimmer, 'Industrial Profile', p. 139, for estimates of the divisions within the town's labour force in 1841: woollen manufacture (13,338); other textile industries (9,473); non-textile industries (37,090).

16 Rimmer, 'Industrial Profile', p. 147. The town therefore contained a large number of servants, craft workers, tradesmen and shopkeepers.

not accurately reflect its pervasiveness. Many 'artisans' worked as craftsmen in factories, or had toiled in their youth as mill-hands, or sent their own children to work in the mills. Equally, traditional industries often serviced the growing textile and mechanised sector. For example, one source of demand for the burgeoning Leeds leather industry, linking the town with the rich farmlands to the north and east, was from machine-makers and factory owners requiring leather for belting and carding rollers.[17] Also new industries like machine-making, drawing on both traditional and newly developed skills, evolved from the demands generated by the textile industry. Textiles, whether directly or indirectly, 'lay at the heart of the town's industrial economy'.[18] The same was even more true of the out-townships and outlying areas which made up the wider district.

As J. F. C. Harrison has noted in his study of Leeds Chartism, the town itself possessed very few depressed handworkers in the textile trades. In the outlying townships and villages of the district the position was different. The 'Borough' of Leeds (including Leeds town and the 'inner' townships) contained over 4,000 handlooms in 1838 and the outer townships and villages nearly another 6,000.[19] By 1830 the nearer out-townships like Holbeck and Hunslet, themselves large and growing settlements, were linked to Leeds township by continuous industrial and residential development along Water Lane and Hunslet Lane. Edward Parsons, an early local historian, wrote of Hunslet in 1834 that,

> no place in the whole district has experienced such a total change in external appearance ... Hunslet Lane still contains a number of good houses connected generally with extensive mercantile establishments, but the whole village, or rather suburb of Leeds, is irregularly and frequently meanly built, consisting of narrow and dirty lanes, branching out from the great thoroughfare to Wakefield, and from the principal street passing by the chapel. The general aspect of the place is strangely uncouth, and perhaps a more dismal scene cannot be presented than the tract of mud and mush called Hunslet Moor, on a rainy day.

Once resplendent Holbeck was now 'one of the most crowded, one of the most filthy one of the most unpleasant, and one of the most unhealthy villages in the county of York.'[20] Both settlements had still some domestic cloth-weaving but were primarily dependent on factory-based textile work and other related industrial developments.

---

17 Rimmer, 'Leeds Leather', p. 129. For the complexity of inter-industry links, see Connell and Ward, 'Industrial Development', p. 154.

18 Connell and Ward, 'Industrial Development, 1780-1914', pp. 151-2. On Leeds engineering firms, see also R. J. Morris, 'The Rise of James Kitson: Trades Union and Mechanics Institution, Leeds 1826-51', *Publications of the Thoresby Society*, 53 (1973), pp. 179-80.

19 J. F. C. Harrison, 'Chartism in Leeds', in Asa Briggs (ed.) *Chartist Studies* (London: Macmillan, 1959), p. 71; BPP, Reports of the Assistant Commissioners for Handloom weavers, 1840, XXIII p. 529.

20 Edward Parsons, *The Civil, Ecclesiastical, Literary, Commercial, and Miscellaneous History of Leeds, Halifax, Huddersfield ... etc.* (Leeds, 1834) Vol 1, pp. 175 and 178. Hunslet Moor was one of the two chief venues for outdoor working-class meetings. On housing in Holbeck and Hunslet, see M. W. Beresford, 'The face of Leeds, 1780-1914', in Fraser (ed.), *A History of Modern Leeds*, pp. 86 and 96-9.

The outlying villages to the south and west of the town – Wortley, Armley, Bramley, Farnley, Beeston – were primarily woollen cloth weaving communities which looked to Leeds as a market centre, but retained links with agriculture and some of the appearance of semi-rural villages. Similarly, the villages in the Leeds-Bradford hinterland – Rawdon, Horsforth, Yeadon, Guiseley, Eccleshill, Idle, Calverley, Farsley, Pudsey and Stanningley – were centres of the domestic manufacture of woollen cloth. Leeds was their natural focal point and the quality of work given out, and wages, tended to diminish the further the village was away from the market centre. Opinions about the merits of villages also varied. For the *Leeds Mercury* 'Pudsey in 1838 now held a distinguished position among manufacturers, rivalling the superior villages of Farnley, Armley and Wortley, in the production of cloth'. However, H. S. Chapman, the Handloom Weavers' Commissioner, found wages lower than neighbouring villages and the people more 'coarse in their manners' and less intelligent. In places like Eccleshill and Idle, where the Leeds woollen district merged with the outskirts of Bradford and touched the mainly worsted weaving townships, wages tended to be lower; and, as at Shipley, the western most extremity of the 'Leeds clothing district', contained a number of worsted looms.[21]

Finally, in the villages on the Leeds-Dewsbury axis – Morley, Batley, Birstal, Gildersome – which specialised in traditional broadcloths and low quality woollens the pull of Leeds gradually diminished in the first half of the century and the area developed into a more independent, self-contained pocket which looked as much to Dewsbury as to Leeds as its natural focus. In general, though, ties with Leeds remained strong throughout the wider area. The town's expertise in dyeing and finishing, signified in numerous small and large (specialist and vertically-integrated) dyehouses and dressing-shops, and in merchanting generally, allied to the town's reputation for making and marketing fine-quality broad-cloths and its overall commercial pull, meant that the town exercised a strong influence throughout the wider textile district.[22]

b) Bradford

Bradford had a long history as a textile town, but in the first half of the nineteenth century it grew from being 'only a small rural town … a really pleasant and picturesque spot' to a major industrial town – 'the Capital of the Worsted Trade'.[23] In

---

21 This was also an area of publicly owned scribbling and fulling mills. On Pudsey, see *LM* 27 Jan. 1838 and BPP, 1840, XXIII p. 551. Pudsey was known as 'the strong hold of Reform in the West Riding', *LM* 27 Jan. 1838.

22 Connell and Ward, 'Industrial Development', pp. 150-1.

23 Edward Collinson, *The History of the Worsted Trade and Historic Sketch of Bradford* (Bradford, 1854), pp. 129 and 97. This section on Bradford is based on: Gary Firth, 'The Bradford Trade in the Nineteenth Century', in D. G. Wright and J. A. Jowitt (eds.), *Victorian Bradford. Essays in Honour of Jack Reynolds* (Bradford: City of Bradford Metropolitan Council, 1981), pp. 7-36; E. M. Sigsworth, *Black Dyke Mills: A History* (Liverpool: Liverpool University Press, 1958) pp. 1-24; Theodore Koditschek, *Class Formation and Urban-Industrial Society: Bradford, 1750-1850* (Cambridge: Cambridge University Press, 1990); M. T. Wild, 'An Historical Geography of the West Yorkshire Textile Industries to *c.*1850' Unpub. PhD thesis,

Theodore Koditschek's striking assessment: 'By 1850, a regional, protoindustrial market town had been transformed into an international capitalist city, the eighth largest in Britain, serving as the global center of worsted production and exchange. No other city in the world at that time experienced so rapid an ascent'.[24] The growth of the borough's population from 13,264 in 1801 to 26,309 in 1821 and 66,715 in 1841 testifies to the speed of the change, much faster than neighbouring Halifax; and contemporary descriptions of the tall chimneys, the 'cloud by day and fire by night' give some feel of its effect.[25] Before the middle of the century the town had become a by-word for urban squalor.

Bradford with its heavy dependence on worsteds had some of the characteristics of a single-industry town.[26] Worsted fabrics, one of the two main branches of the Yorkshire wool textile industry, generally comprised lighter fabrics with the warp and weft lines clearly visible and did not require fulling or finishing.[27] Woollen cloth manufacture had almost disappeared from the district by 1841 and many of the town's smaller industries – comb-making, gear and slay making, and machine-making – supplied the worsted trade. However, in a number of the outlying villages additional industries thrived. Stone-quarrying was carried on extensively in the area, and in the villages and hamlets to the south and south west of the town there existed a complex of coal and iron mines. Iron-working was also carried out here with major foundries at Wibsey Low Moor and Bowling.[28]

The worsted industry however was the mainstay of the local economy. With the consolidation of the Bradford-Halifax-Keighley worsted triangle in the early nineteenth century, Bradford took on a central role in all aspects of the trade. The town housed a major wool market and by 1831 there were forty-three wool-staplers in Bradford, employing numerous woolsorters.[29] Worsted spinning, the first of the worsted manufacturing processes to be mechanised, was carried out in large predominantly steam-powered spinning mills employing mainly female and child labour. By 1820 'the hand spinning of worsted yarn was virtually extinct' in the West Riding; and by 1838 'Bradford contained 36 per cent of the worsted factory horsepower in Yorkshire and 29 percent of the national total'.[30]

The early development of factory spinning and the improvements in the quality of yarn produced, initially gave a boost to the numbers of domestically-based outworkers

---

University of Birmingham, 1972; D. G. Wright, 'Politics and Opinion in Nineteenth Century Bradford, 1832-1880, with special reference to Parliamentary elections' Unpub. PhD thesis, University of Leeds, 1966; and various local histories listed in the bibliography.

24 Koditschek, *Class Formation and Urban-Industrial Society*, p. 79.

25 William Scruton, *Pen and Pencil Pictures of Old Bradford* (Bradford: Thomas Brear, 1889), p. 71.

26 David Ashworth, 'The Treatment of Poverty', in Wright and Jowitt (eds.), *Victorian Bradford*, p. 81.

27 Pat Hudson, *The Genesis of Industrial Capital: a study of the West Riding wool textile industry, c. 1750-1850* (Cambridge: Cambridge University Press, 1986), p. 26.

28 For a description of expansion at Wibsey in 1835, see Head, *Home Tour*, pp. 130-3.

29 Hartwell, 'Woollen and Worsted', p. 249.

30 Sigsworth, *Black Dyke Mills*, p. 4; Koditschek, *Class Formation and Urban-Industrial Society*, p. 79.

in the preparatory and weaving processes. Migrants from North Yorkshire, northern England, the South West and Ireland swelled the numbers of woolcombers, often working in combing shops or their own homes in or near the centre of Bradford.[31] Although constantly threatened by the growing use of, and experimentation with, combing machinery, they were not directly superseded in the 1820s and 1830s and they retained their strong radical and trade union traditions.

The mechanisation of spinning also initially gave a boost to the domestic handloom weavers of the 'inner' out-townships such as Great and Little Horton, Manningham and Bowling, and of the surrounding area. The threat of the power-loom, though voiced frequently during the 1825 Bradford Strike, and opposed violently in spring 1826 when twenty-five looms were destroyed, was not realised until after 1830.[32] As late as 1836 there were only 2,768 power-looms in the West Riding; but the decade which followed witnessed the take-off of worsted power-loom weaving in the large sheds built by merchants and some spinners.[33] In 1838 there were still estimated to be 10,000 handloom-weavers in Bradford parish, though only twenty in Bradford township itself. Twenty years later the first historian of the worsted trade reported that, 'comparatively few pieces are now woven by hand'.[34]

From the strong manufacturing base which had been established, Bradford became an increasingly important merchanting centre. The Wool Exchange, opened in 1828, had various functions including the buying and selling of combings and worsted yarns. A number of foreign merchants established bases in Bradford and the town supplied yarns for the Leicester hosiery and the Huddersfield fancy trades, as well as for export. Worsted stuffs were increasingly dyed in Bradford rather than being sent to Leeds and by 1850 the vertical integration of the industry, which had initially been notable for its horizontal specialisation, was almost complete. By this time Bradford was the centre of the most concentrated wool manufacturing area of the West Riding – providing a central market, a depot for raw materials and cloth, a worsted spinning and stuff finishing centre and a source of finance for the industry.[35]

Much of the area around Bradford formed part of the 'worstedopolis'. Villages like Clayton, Allerton, Thornton, Cottingley, Harden and Cullingworth were primarily the centres of hand-combing and weaving. Although large employers, spinning mills and, later in the decade, power-loom weaving sheds were not uncommon, the majority of the local population were employed by small masters or Bradford manufacturers, and produced a variety of worsted goods for the Bradford market.[36]

---

31 Woolcombing was an important part of the preparatory process for long wools (the basis of worsted yarn). It involved washing and then straightening the wool fibres. This was done by passing a pre-heated metal comb through the wool, which was attached to a wooden post by means of another comb. It was a physically demanding and notoriously unhealthy trade.

32 George Ingle, 'The Bradford Hand-Loom Weavers' Riots of 1826', *Bradford Antiquary*, 3, 17 (1994), pp. 3-16.

33 Firth, 'The Bradford Trade', p. 13. By 1850 there were 30, 000 power-looms in Bradford.

34 Details of the extent of handloom weaving in 1838 are given in BPP, 1840, XXIII, p. 558; John James, *History of the Worsted Manufacture in England … etc* (Bradford, 1857), p. 603. Worsted 'stuffs' were produced primarily for the home market, *LM* 14 Apr. 1827.

35 Hartwell, 'Woollen and Worsted', p. 244.

36 The principal goods in 1838 were shalloons, merinos, wildbores and moreens. The village of

However, the dominance of Bradford and worsted was not total. The villages to the east of the town produced either 'mixed' or woollen cloth, and at Shipley the Leeds clothing district ran 'like a tongue into the worsted district'. To the west of the town villages such as Queenshead (later re-named Queensbury), whose 'inhabitants were colliers, quarrymen and hand loom weavers', looked to Halifax as much as to Bradford as a market centre and focus.[37]

c) Halifax

Halifax ranked next to Leeds and Bradford as a textile centre in the early nineteenth century.[38] Originally a woollen town and stronghold of the domestic small clothier, it developed a more varied manufacturing profile. According to a 1829 witness: 'A great proportion of its population, is not, like that of Leeds, employed in the warp and woollens, nor in stuffs, as at Bradford, or fancy goods, as at Huddersfield, or cottons, as at Manchester, but its trade is a mixture of all these combined...' By the end of the following decade the town's chief articles of manufacture were worsted stuffs, blaizes, broad and narrow cloths, bombazines, crepes and mixed fabrics of wool, worsted and silk.[39]

The Hebble and other brooks served as chief sources of power and their banks became the focal point of industrial activity in the mid-1820s. Local coal was also plentiful and manufacturers, such as James Greenwood, whose extensive and underinsured 'woollen and cotton manufactory' at Wheatley mills (a mile and a half from Halifax) was destroyed by fire in 1830, used both steam and water power.[40] The size of Greenwood's business, though, was not typical. Whilst sizeable, mostly worsted, mills continued to be built in the 1830s in the main valley-bottom, culminating in the Crossley Brothers' first large carpet mill at Dean Clough in 1841, the majority of enterprises remained small-scale, dependent on the 'room and power'

Thornton (4 miles west of Bradford) had 2,000 handlooms in 1838. The finest quality stuffs were made in the immediate neighbourhood of Bradford; lower quality goods came from further afield, BPP, 1840, XXIII, pp. 557-9.

37 BPP, XXIII, p. 551; A. C. Carter, *John Bates, of Queensbury, the Veteran Reformer* (Queensbury, 1895), p. 1.

38 This sketch of Halifax draws on: Wild, 'Historical Geography'; Hartwell, 'Woollen and Worsted'; A. Dingsdale, 'A Yorkshire Mill Town: A Study of the Spatial patterns and processes, processes of urban-industrial growth and the evolution of the spatial structure of Halifax, 1801-1901' Unpub. PhD thesis, University of Leeds, 1974; Sigsworth, *Black Dyke Mills*; Dorothy and E. P. Thompson, '"The Dignity of Chartism": Halifax as a Chartist Centre', in Stephen Roberts (ed.), *The Dignity of Chartism: : Essays by Dorothy Thompson* (London: Verso, 2015), pp. 73-124, and various local histories.

39 *Halifax Courier and Guardian Almanac*, 1894, p. 93, quoted in Dorothy and E. P. Thompson, 'Halifax as a Chartist Centre', p. 74; *Penny Encyclopaedia* (London, 1836) Vol 12, 1838, p. 13 quoted in Hartwell, 'Woollen and Worsted', p. 259. *HCC* 5 Dec. 1829, speaks of a combination of woollens, stuffs, fancy, cotton and bombazines comprising the town's textile manufacture.

40 *HCC* 9 Jan. 1830. The mill employed 650 weavers (all handloom), 50 cutters, 14 spinners (each employing 2 children), 17 twisters, 20 dyers, 60 children, croppers plus others.

system, and relying on an intricate network of horizontal links with other firms.[41] The town was a major market hub and a centre for fulling and finishing. It also contained the full range of artisan town trades as well as a growing number of iron-founding, engineering and wire-drawing concerns. Wire-drawing mills, like the one described by Sir George Head, stood cheek by jowl with textile factories and dyeworks along the Hebble Brook.[42]

Halifax was also the centre of the largest parish in England stretching from Brighouse in the east to Todmorden in the west, and containing twenty-three townships. In the remoter valleys of the outlying district the abundance of good water supplies delayed the inroads of steam power. Here also the worst examples of factory abuses were to be found, epitomised by the notorious Cragg Dale masters.[43] These same outlying districts and upland hamlets contained some of the most extreme examples of the destitution of the handloom weavers. Based in their own homes, paying all their own overheads, they worked, often with the help of their families, on yarn put out by manufacturers, master spinners or middle men and suffered a prolonged and degrading decline which has been amply described elsewhere.[44] The town and wider parish also contained numerous out-working woolcombers who took part in the great Bradford strike of 1825, and who worked in deplorable conditions.[45]

Like the market centre itself the parish economy was diverse. It contained outposts of the Lancashire cotton industry (including significant cotton cloth producing centres such as Todmorden and Hebden Bridge) and silk manufacturing in some of the Halifax out-townships such as Ovenden.[46] However, whilst the textile industries predominated, more than half of the adult working population were engaged in a wide range of other occupations. Some of this employment was in ancillary trades. The wire mills of Halifax, for example, supplied numerous small and a few large master card-makers who employed women and children in the outlying southern and eastern townships to make 'cards' needed for the woollen industry.[47] Small mines and quarries also dotted the area and part or full-time agricultural employment was not insignificant.

---

41 Dingsdale, 'A Yorkshire Mill Town', p. 297. By this system the proprietor of a mill building provided space and power for the entrepreneur.

42 Head, *Home Tour*, pp. 129-30.

43 See George Crabtree, *A Brief Description of a Tour Through Calder Dale … etc.* (Huddersfield, 1833).

44 Thompson, *Making*, p. 313ff. The handloom weavers produced a variety of cloths. Worsted stuffs predominated, but also fine and coarse woollens (the latter woven in the outlying townships especially to the south), cotton and silk; see *LM* 28 Nov. 1829.

45 See J. Whittaker's description in *Crisis* 22 Sept. 1832.

46 A return of mills for the parish in 1831 shows 57 cotton, 35 woollen, 45 worsted and 4 silk; seven years later the figures were 71, 63, 71 and 7 respectively, quoted in Dorothy and E. P. Thompson, 'Halifax as a Chartist Centre', p. 74.

47 Carding was a preliminary 'woollen' process before spinning to open and mix the wool. It was done by a pair of hand cards (wooden paddles covered with leather into which were inserted numerous short metal wires) working against the other. The centres of the card-making trade were Elland, Raistrick, Brighouse, Scholes and Liversedge. It contained a few large firms; for example, John Whiteley and Sons had an average of 800 hands in 1834, see *HHE* 19 June 1834. See also Thompson, *Making*, pp. 273-4.

It was possibly the diversity of the local economy and the absence of a dominant occupational group in the town and its immediate environs which made Halifax a difficult place to rouse and organise in the early 1830s. Later in the decade, though, with the town artisans and the distressed handloom weavers of the outlying villages providing leadership, the wider area became a major Chartist stronghold.

d) Huddersfield

Situated on the River Colne seven miles south-east of Halifax and on the main Leeds to Manchester road, Huddersfield was the market centre for a clothing district which stretched from the junction of the Colne and Calder rivers, up the Colne and Holme valleys and onto the moors of the south.[48] The town itself was very much the product of the industrial revolution. In 1800 it had a population of about 7,000 people and was described as 'a miserable village; the houses are poor and scattered, the streets narrow, crooked and dirty'.[49] Forty years later, with the main streets wider and straighter, the population had risen to 25,000 and the town had become the axis of a major industrial district.

Apart from some canal-side development of iron foundries and lime kilns, the town itself was not a significant manufacturing centre. The peculiar pattern of land ownership in the town meant that industrial development took place on the outskirts and beyond.[50] William Stocks jnr., testifying to a Parliamentary Select Committee in 1833, detailed the effects of the Ramsden family's proprietorial land monopoly, explaining that land 'is let out at a high rate of ground-rent, too valuable to build cottages upon, consequently the poor people are thrown into the different townships round about us. There are comparatively very few workmen in the town of Huddersfield'. Those operatives that lived there tended to be 'the best class of workmen in the woollen manufacture' (presumably woolsorters and cloth-dressers); Stocks adding, 'we have very few resident weavers in the town of Huddersfield'.[51]

The land ownership pattern also meant that the occupational profile of the town was dominated by the small-scale artisans, craftsmen, tradesmen and shopkeepers who served and serviced a growing market centre and industrial focal point. Some dyeing and finishing was done in the town and surrounding area, but Huddersfield, though an important woollen market, never became a major merchanting centre and

---

48 This sketch of Huddersfield draws on the essays in in E. A. Hilary Haigh (ed.), *Huddersfield, A Most Handsome Town: Aspects of the History and Culture of a West Riding Town* (Huddersfield: Kirklees Cultural Services, 1992); D. F. E. Sykes, *Huddersfield and its Vicinity* (Huddersfield, 1898); W. B. Crump and G. Ghorbal, *History of the Huddersfield Woollen Industry* (Huddersfield: County Borough of Huddersfield, 1935); Hartwell 'Woollen and Worsted'; Wild, 'Historical Geography'; J. C. R. Camm, 'Industrial Settlement in the Colne and Holme Valleys, 1750-1960', Unpub. MSc thesis, University of Hull, 1963; R. Brook, *The Story of Huddersfield* (London: Macgibbon and Key, 1968); also directories of the 1820s and 1830s and other local histories.

49 Sykes, *Huddersfield and its Vicinity*, p. 251.

50 Huddersfield town comprised three or four hamlets in the corner of the wider Huddersfield parish. The town 'with the exception of two or three houses is entirely the property of the Ramsden family and yields to them princely fortune', *Pigot's Directory of 1822-3*, p. 616.

51 BPP, 1833, VI, pp. 598-9.

possessed few native merchants or woolstaplers. Equally, whilst the developing textile industry gradually created a demand for machinery, chemicals and dyes, these industries only really became significant in the middle of the century.[52]

The wider Huddersfield district also contained a number of other supplementary industries. The grits, sandstones and flags quarried in numerous small pits provided excellent building stones and an important source of employment; and there was also some small-scale mining of local coal. However, the textile trades remained the area's primary orientation. Although, it included a number of cotton and silk factories such as Meltham Mills, which employed 650 people (mainly women and young girls) in 1835, the bulk of the local economy was geared towards two main branches: the manufacture of 'woollen' and 'fancy' textiles.[53]

From producing a range of traditional good quality 'woollens' – broad and narrow cloths, serges, honleys and kerseymeres – the 1820s saw the area gain a reputation for producing lighter and more fashion-orientated cloths – including shawls, waistcoatings and fancy fabrics made of a variety of yarns, including cotton, wool, silk, alpaca, and mohair. The change of emphasis was noted by contemporaries. William Stocks jnr. in 1833 observed that local employment was split equally between the fancy trade and woollen manufacture. And two years later J. C. Milner confirmed that the fancy trade predominated in the immediate vicinity of Huddersfield.[54] However, as Alan Brooke has stressed, 'there was no rigid distinction between the two trades, weavers lived in the same communities and might change from one branch to another'.[55]

An invaluable picture of these two main textile branches at the height of the distress of 1829 emerges from the letters of a well-informed local correspondent to the *Leeds Mercury*. The 'Fancy Trade ... so called from the variety of patterns which are produced in it', was chiefly carried on in the villages to the north, east and south-east of Huddersfield. At this time it comprised three main branches. The most important and best-paid branch was the manufacture of waistcoatings; next came woollen cord manufacture, a laborious form of weaving requiring some strength; and finally, the most recent and lowest paid branch, that of cassinets.[56] The fancy trade, like the

---

52 This paragraph is based on an analysis of local directories of the 1820s and 1830s.

53 Although the two branches are differentiated here, as they were by contemporaries, a rigid separation should not be assumed. Generically the fancy trade is normally counted as being a sub-branch of the woollen trade. 'Fancy' woollen cloths were those with a fancy weave and/or colour effect. They also used a variety of yarns (woollen, worsted, cotton and silk) to achieve these effects. Although the domestic market was not inconsequential, the trade was predominantly geared to the export market.

54 BPP, 1833, VI, pp. 597-8, 647. Stocks reckoned there to be *c*.12,000 people engaged in the fancy trade with 40,000 depending on it; BPP, Report from the Select Committee on Handloom Weavers' Petitions, 1835, XIII, p. 57. For a comprehensive account of this trade, see Alan J. Brooke, *The Handloom Fancy Weavers c.1820-1914* (Honley: Workers' History Publications, 1993).

55 Ibid., p. 2.

56 *LM* 29 Nov. 1829. The named fancy centres that he names were Huddersfield, Almondbury, Kirkheaton, Dalton, Kirkburton, Shelley, Shepley, Lepton, Skelmanthorpe, Clayton, Denby Dale, Cumberworth, Honley, Lindley, Raistrick and Deighton. Fancy waistcoatings (initially for aristocrats but later for navvies), though producing a good price, were very vulnerable to

patterns it produced, was complex. Controlled by the master-manufacturers who put out the yarn, it became dependent on a fluctuating workforce susceptible to the vagaries of fashion and season. Unemployment and underemployment were common; and though rarely threatened directly by the power-loom, the knock-on effects of mechanisation in other textile sectors increasingly impacted on the fancy trade.[57]

The same 1829 correspondent went onto describe the manufacture of woollen cloth 'which is of by far the greater magnitude and importance, as it employs the greatest part of the dense population of this extensive district'. Confining himself to the major centres of woollen manufacture to the south and west of Huddersfield, along and between the Colne and Holme valleys, he painted a picture of decline, particularly of the old system of small independent clothiers (employing their own family and perhaps some operative piece-makers) selling their pieces 'unfinished' at the Huddersfield Cloth Hall. Even employees of the new vertically integrated factories which he alleged were cornering the trade were apparently suffering in the depth of the winter depression. He estimated that about seventeen mills, 'many of them of considerable extent' had been erected in the last twenty years.[58]

The new factories were primarily located on the outskirts of Huddersfield or in the expanding valley towns such as Slaithwaite. With suitable rivers and streams abundant, water power, occasionally, supplemented directly or indirectly by steam engines, remained the major source of motive power for these and for the older public scribbling and fulling mills. Many of the thirty-nine woollen mills within a two-mile radius of Holmfirth for example were water-powered and were of the old style of country mills which served the 'domestic system'. In spite of the pessimistic picture painted by the 1829 correspondent, two decades later the Huddersfield district remained the centre of a large and important domestic industry.[59]

Major firms like Starkey Brothers of Longroyd Bridge and the Brooke family of Armitage Bridge introduced mechanically-powered spinning into their large-scale and integrated factories from the late 1820s. However, most factories and mills remained small-scale specialist concerns which meshed in with rather than directly challenging the domestic system. Equally, though a few locations saw the introduction of power-looms from the mid-1830s, manufacturers continued to be cautious and the district remained a stronghold of the handloom. All the weaving in the large factories

---

changes of fashion. Cassinets were hard-wearing fabrics made from cotton warp and a woollen weft. They were mainly made for export to Europe.

57 Brooke, *The Handloom Fancy Weavers*, p. 15. On the fortunes and failure of one of the lending fancy firms, Norton Bros. of Clayton West, which at one time employed 1,000 workers, see J. Addy (ed.), *A History of the Denby Dale Urban District* (Huddersfield: Denby Dale Urban District Council, 1974) pp. 75-6.

58 *LM* 12 Dec. 1829. The predominance of the woollen trade refers to the 'greater' Huddersfield area. As centres of woollen manufacture he cites Huddersfield, Lockwood, Thurstonland, Farnley, Foolstone, New Mill, Hepworth, Holmfirth, Thong, Honley, Crosland, Meltham, Linthwaite, Golcar, Slaithwaite, Marsden, Saddleworth, Longwood and Lindley, 'together with a number of small villages scattered in the surrounding district'.

59 Hartwell, 'Woollen and Worsted', pp. 239 and 264-5. In some areas, though, the fancy trade had taken over from the woollen; see, for example, the replacement of the plain broad cloth manufacture by the fancy trade in Holmfirth, *LM* 2 Mar. 1839.

cited in the 1829 *Leeds Mercury* letter was done by hand; and William Stocks jnr. in 1833 confirmed that the numbers employed in the factories were very small in proportion to those employed in weaving out of doors.[60] The process of industrial change was extremely gradual in the Huddersfield area.[61]

e) Keighley

Keighley, a small industrial town on the north-western extremity of the West Riding textile district, is the least well documented of the major textile centres.[62] It existed, in the words of Asa Briggs, 'almost on the frontier of industrialisation'.[63] The town never developed marketing and finishing functions and looked first to Halifax, then increasingly to Bradford, as an outlet for its yarn, tops and pieces. In this sense it was the least self-sufficient of the six chief textile centres.

Initially a woollen town, Keighley's early industrial development was based around cotton mills and the motive power provided by the River Worth and North Beck. By 1805 the town boasted ten cotton factories. Gradually, however, in the second and third decades of the century the emphasis changed and many of the early mills were converted from cotton to worsted. The recovery of fine stuff manufacturing in the 1830s put the seal on this conversion and by 1835 the town boasted twenty-two worsted mills (employing 1,061 people) and just four cotton mills (with 196 employees).[64]

A nineteenth-century authority estimates that as many as eighty per cent of the adult male workforce in this period were either woolcombers or weavers (mainly handloom weavers).[65] They worked for an assortment of established or emerging manufacturers who had risen from the ranks of yeoman farmers and small tradesmen. A few, such as William Sugden the town's largest employer in the 1820s, combed, spun and wove the wool. Others, for example Robert Clough, were primarily worsted spinners who increasingly began to put out work to combers and weavers; or were stuff piece manufacturers who used commission spinners to produce the yarn which they then 'put out'. This general trend saw enterprises to grow in size and become

---

60 BPP, 1833, VI, p. 599.

61 Colum Giles, 'The Huddersfield Woollen Industry and its Architecture', in Hilary Haigh (ed.), *Huddersfield*, p. 280.

62 The following section draws on Asa Briggs, 'Industry and Politics in early 19th Century Keighley', *Bradford Antiquary*, ns 35 (1950), pp. 305-17; Ian Dewhirst, *A History of Keighley* (Keighley: Keighley Corporation, 1974); Hartwell, 'Woollen and Worsted'; Wild, 'Historical Geography'; G. A. Feather, 'A Pennine Worsted Community in the Mid-Nineteenth Century', *Textile History*, 3, 1 (1972), pp. 64-91; John Hodgson, *Textile Manufacture and Other Industries of Keighley* (Keighley: A. Hey, 1879); Robert Holmes, *Keighley, Past and Present: … etc.* (Keighley, 1858); and other local histories.

63 Briggs, 'Industry and Politics', p. 305. The town had a relatively small population (11,176 in 1831), was geographically fairly isolated and did not have its own newspaper until 1862.

64 This and the following paragraph are based on Hartwell, 'Woollen and Worsted', pp. 279-80 and Hodgson, *Textile Manufacture*.

65 It is possible that, as at Bradford, the combers were concentrated in the town itself. Of 33 members in a local Oddfellows' lodge in 1827, 14 were combers, 2 were shoemakers and the rest were assorted town occupations.

more integrated with workers increasingly employed at their employers' premises. However, change was very gradual and the great majority of operatives continued to work in their own homes.

Two dates stand out in the town's industrial history: 1826, when a few months after the defeat of the Combers' and Weavers' strike, the commercial 'Panic' ruined an estimated half of the parish's manufacturers, including many smaller concerns; and 1834-5, when (perhaps significantly after the defeat of another strong worsted union) a number of firms introduced power-looms.[66] The effect on handloom weaving was not immediately catastrophic: merely another twist in the spiral of decline. Major firms like J. and J. Craven who brought in power-looms in 1835 continued to put out work to handloom weavers in Silsden, Sutton, Ikcornshaw and Cowling – a reminder that the network of outworkers stretched out far beyond the town itself and in some cases into Lancashire.

A number of small townships, villages and hamlets came within the orbit of Keighley. A detailed study of one such hamlet, Near and Far Oxenhope, at the head of the Worth valley four miles away from Keighley, has shown the preponderance of hand weaving and combing (either home or workshop-based) in the local economy. Factory employment was confined chiefly to children and teenagers, with a few men being employed as mechanics, joiners and metal-workers in, or servicing, the mills. Agricultural employment was fairly limited and local mines and quarries provided the only other steady source of jobs. Significantly the major economic pull for the hamlet came from Halifax seven miles distant and Bradford ten miles away.[67] This was also the case with other 'satellites' like Bingley, a centre of unfinished low-quality worsteds, which although often considered to be in the Keighley district, in reality came within the orbit of Bradford.[68]

Keighley was never a sufficiently large or diverse commercial centre to counteract this pull. Its major growth point apart from the worsted trade, was in machine-making. A number of firms developed from small beginnings as whitesmiths or makers of agricultural machinery to become manufacturers of spindles, throstles, rollers and flyers for cotton, flax and particularly worsted spinning machinery. The concerns were never large in this period but they developed quickly, particularly after the introduction of power-looms, when a number of established and new firms took up loom-making. By the middle of the century it was an important ancillary trade.[69]

---

66 The Keighley men, and women, were involved in the great Bradford Strike of 1825. Caution about the introduction of, and fear of popular hostility to power-looms is revealed in the case of one power-loom pioneer who stored two looms in the garret of his mill for two years before bringing them out; and another who set them up in the middle of his spinning room lest they should be seen from the outside, Hodgson, *Textile Manufacture*, pp. 59 and 168.

67 Feather, 'A Pennine Worsted Community'.

68 On Bingley, see Harry Speight, *Chronicles and Stories of Old Bingley* (London: Elliot Stock, 1898).

69 Hodgson, *Textile Manufacture*, pp. 240-76

f) Dewsbury

Dewsbury lay at the centre of a compact and increasingly distinct sub-region of the West Riding textile district, specialising in the production of coarse and heavy woollen cloths.[70] Like other 'specialist areas' the dominance of the heavy trade was never total and other branches of textile manufacture and ancillary or related trades were also carried on; for example, cotton and worsted spinning, card-making, metal-working, machine-making and coal-mining. However, by 1840 the area within a six-mile radius of Dewsbury – roughly bounded by Birstall, Cleckheaton, Gomersal, Liversedge, Heckmondwike, Mirfield, Ossett and Batley – had developed its own varied but distinctive pattern of manufacture.

By 1834 Dewsbury had 'rapidly expanded from a village to a considerable town'.[71] Essentially, though, it remained the focal point for a number of small manufacturing hamlets or villages – Dewsbury Mills, Dewsbury Moor, Batley Carr, Hanging Heaton, Dewsbury Bank, Earlsheaton, Chickenley and Gawthorpe – which had yet to be joined into one conurbation. A witness in 1836 could still describe the area as being 'inadequately populated'.[72] Increasingly, however, Dewsbury became the market centre for the producers of the surrounding villages and the focus for the powered section of the industry (mainly the preparatory and finishing processes). A local gazetteer in 1839 reported that 'it contains many extensive establishments for the manufacture of blankets, woollen cloths, and carpets, its market is well frequented, its wealth is very considerable'.[73]

Blanket-making, the chief staple of the area, centring mainly on Dewsbury and Heckmondwike had a long history in the Spen and mid-Calder valleys.[74] After periods of buoyant demand during the late eighteenth century and the Napoleonic Wars, the trade continued a steady expansion during the 1820s and 1830s. Although one pre-eminent firm Hague, Cook and Wormald's was twice the size of its nearest competitor, the industry remained primarily the province of medium and small-scale manufacturers. Indeed, Frederick Glover suggested that 'there were no real economics of scale in the production of heavy woollens before the introduction of the power-loom [from the 1850s onwards]' and that the very size and high overheads of the large

---

70 These included blankets, kerseys, 'duffils', coverlets and 'army cloths'. This study of
    Dewsbury draws on the following sources: Hartwell, 'Woollen and Worsted'; Wild,
    'Historical Geography': D. A. Dean, 'The Economic and Social Development of Dewsbury
    in the 19th Century' Unpub. MA thesis, University of Sheffield, 1963; Frederick. J. Glover
    'Blankets', *Leeds Journal* 7 (1956), pp. 227-31; Frederick. J. Glover, 'The Rise of the Heavy
    Woollen Trade of the West Riding of Yorkshire in the Nineteenth Century', *Business
    History*, 4 (1962), pp. 1-21; Frederick J. Glover, 'A Yorkshire Blanketmaker's Diary', *Bradford
    Textile Society Journal*, (1962-3), pp. 84-109; F. Peel, *Spen Valley: Past and Present*
    (Heckmondwike: Senior and Co.,1893).

71 Parsons, *History of Leeds, Halifax, Huddersfield ... etc*, p. 319.

72 BPP, 1836, XLV p. 221 quoted in Hartwell, 'Woollen and Worsted', p. 276.

73 Parsons, *History of Leeds, Halifax, Huddersfield ... etc*, p. 319.

74 Blanket-making required only a simple weave and was similar to other branches of woollen
    cloth-making except that it required a wider loom. Details of different types and qualities of
    blankets are in Glover, 'Blankets', p. 230.

firms handicapped them during times of depression.[75] Partly because of the markets it supplied – the United States abroad and large government contracts at home – the industry was subject to considerable fluctuation and was sometimes out of step with the trade rhythms of the other woollen sub-districts.[76]

Any major developments in the local textile industry during this period tended to be organisational rather than technical. Dr Glover's study of the industry's leading firm reveals the same inter-connection and interdependence between the 'factory' and 'domestic' sectors found in other textile branches during this period. Although the firm oversaw the preparatory and finishing processes, the manufactured blankets were drawn from three sources. Firstly, from wool put out to their own domestic weavers working mostly on looms owned by the partnership. Secondly from handloom weavers actually employed on the firm's premises. And finally, from the numerous small independent blanket-makers of the area who either worked to order or sold the blankets, both finished and unfinished, at the Leeds, Heckmondwike and Huddersfield markets.[77]

The 1820s and 1830s also saw the rise of the 'shoddy' trade, whereby cloth was woven from yarn mainly comprising reconstituted fibres produced by grinding up old textile rags. The trade developed initially in Batley but later spread more broadly, with the concentration on inexpensive cloths becoming a distinctive feature of the wider Dewsbury area.[78] The development of shoddy fitted in well with existing lines of manufacture: for as well as blankets the townships and villages of the Dewsbury district produced a variety of cheap, coarse woollens. 'Woollen' rather than 'blanket' manufacturers predominated in Ossett, Mirfield, Birstal and Gomersal. Places such as Liversedge and Heckmondwike combined a number of lines; while Dewsbury and Heckmondwike both took advantage of the area's easy access to cotton, worsted and woollen yarns to develop a carpet-manufacturing sector.[79] Finally, in the Cleckheaton and Liversedge localities card-making was an adjunct to local coarse woollen manufacturing.

In general, the area remained under-developed and saw little concentrated capital investment until later in the century. Most local 'mills' were traditional scribbling and fulling mills; and factories also tended to be small-scale and specialised. Although Dewsbury became the major centre of the district its pull was never as strong as the 'big four' textile centres; and the whole district remained decentralised with notable contrasts in specialisms between contiguous settlements.

---

75 Glover, 'Heavy Woollen Trade', p. 14.

76 Large contracts from government sources and from metropolitan wholesale houses could bring the industry quickly out of depression; but their completion could equally plunge it down again. See, for example, a report in the *LI* 11 Mar. 1830. Contractors increasingly looked to Witney and the large Leeds merchants for their blankets in the 1830s, a fact which aided the development of the shoddy trade and a concentration on inexpensive lines.

77 Glover, 'Blanketmaker's Diary', and 'Heavy Woollen Trade', p. 20.

78 See Head, *Home Tour*, pp. 147-51 for descriptions of rag-mills and the shoddy trade in Batley Carr and Dewsbury.

79 For a visitor's description of Heckmondwike 'snow': white blankets left out on the hills to 'dew' (the blankets were sold by weight!), see *LI* 17 June 1828.

g) Industrial villages and out-townships

The Dewsbury area was not alone in boasting a number of diverse industrial settlements and out-townships. The hinterlands of all the main centres contained plentiful examples of overgrown industrial villages, which formed such a distinctive feature of the region. As Edward Royle has emphasised, these outlying settlements contained demographically significant clusters of population. So, for example, whilst the township of Halifax had a population of just over 15,000 in 1831, 'the connected places of Halifax parish', in the words of the 1831 census, contained nearly 110,000 people. Similarly, the population of the connected places of Bradford parish was three times greater than that of Bradford township.[80] Here, in these semi-urbanised communities, town and country intersected, as did the domestic and factory-based systems of production. Although the local population mainly engaged in textile manufacture, work in agriculture or the extractive industries was also common. The recollections of Benjamin Wilson, a future Chartist who lived at Skircoat Green, a township on the fringes of Halifax, indicate something of the diverse profile of local employment:

> when very young I ... was pulled out of bed between 4 and 5 o'clock ... to go with a donkey 1½ miles away, and then take part in milking a number of cows ... I went to a card shop afterwards, and there had set 1500 card teeth for a 1/2d ... I have been a woollen weaver, a comber, a navvy on the railway, and a barer in the delph...[81]

Such out-townships and industrial villages in the hinterland of the main urban centres were often at the heart of radical agitations. Settlements were small enough to be cohesive but large enough to pose a threat collectively to established structures of law and order. In the words of one paranoic but perceptive observer in December 1832, Huddersfield's newly elected MP Lewis Fenton, the industrial villages were overwhelmingly and menacingly working-class:

> Huddersfield is surrounded on all sides by a dense population, composed principally of the operative classes, with a very small number of the leading classes of society in proportion. A vast number of the working-classes have joined these dangerous societies which under the designation of trades', political and other Unions ... are constantly aiming at the subversion of all social order.[82]

Local leaders played on the belligerent reputation of these outlying communities as suppliers of 'bludgeon men' and used it strategically to further their chosen cause. For example, at the height of the anti-poor law protests in 1838, Almondbury radicals issued a satirical placard that referenced the possible mobilisation of a group of hated London police in their area. They proclaimed that 'the swift spindle points and the shuttle tips of the Almondbury hand loom fancy weavers are as sharp as their appetites

---

80 Edward Royle, 'Radicalism in the West Riding, 1790-1890', Huddersfield Local History Society, Annual Luddite Memorial Lecture 2021, available at https://www.huddersfieldhistory.org.uk/events/luddite-lecture/ (accessed 19 May 2022).

81 Wilson, *Struggles*, p. 13.

82 TNA: HO 40/31 f. 3, Fenton to Bouverie, 29 Dec. 1832.

and as the poor weavers wish to appear respectable on so important an occasion they have lots of new clogs which will be freely used if called into action'.[83]

Almondbury is a good example of what Katrina Navickas calls a 'radical locale'. Such places, situated on the outskirts of a main centre, often lay 'outside the policing or jurisdiction of borough authorities' and 'formed distinctive places of political activity'. The West Riding contains plenty of other examples of places that 'fostered continuity in political and religious dissent and a strong sense of trade and community independence' and which connected readily with contiguous communities and similar locales in other districts.[84]

Even more remote and less well-connected settlements such as the mainly handloom weaving hamlet of Mixenden Stones, in the Halifax district, (where the houses were so dispersed 'one would suppose [they] had fallen from Heaven in a thunder-storm'), could be drawn into agitational webs.[85] Indeed, the sense of separation and distance in such communities should not be exaggerated. Haworth, the mythically remote parish of the ten hours supporting Rev. Patrick Brontë, was a mere four miles from its nearest urban centre, Keighley. The people of these locationally peripheral but agitationally central villages may have considered themselves outsiders, in both a geographical and a political sense. Indeed, as Edward Royle has pointed out, their male inhabitants were not fully enfranchised until 1884.[86] However, with their semi-rural, semi-urban make-up, these communities formed a key bedrock of radical and oppositional activities in the 1830s and beyond.

2: Industry, Trades and Workers

As the study of its component elements makes clear, the West Riding textile district was not a monolithic entity. Its economy was extremely diverse and even in the leading wool textile sector there was a significant variety of branches and specialisms. Before looking at how this complex commercial configuration was reflected in the make-up and activities of the region's labour force, it is initially worth emphasising a few key features of the regional and national context.

The first is the gradualness of the economic changes that were taking place. John Foster talks of 'England's very long road to fully fledged industrial capitalism'; whilst from a different ideological standpoint, James Vernon speaks of 'a long and uneven whimper' rather than a 'big bang'. Britain's was a fairly primitive industrial revolution based as much on traditional materials and skills as on new ones. The bulk of industrial technology remained 'rough and ready', the time lag between invention and widespread application was often long and large sectors of the economy were scarcely mechanised at all. The particular phase of the industrial revolution which this study covers saw the highly profitable co-existence and interdependence of craft producers

---

83 *LT* 4 Aug.1838, quoted in Alan. J. Brooke, 'The Roots of Chartism in the Huddersfield Area *c.*1826 to *c.*1838', in John A. Hargreaves (ed.), *The Charter Our Right! Huddersfield Chartism Re-considered* (Huddersfield: Huddersfield Local History Society, 2018), p. 30.

84 Katrina Navickas, *Protest and the Politics of Space and Place, 1789-1848* (Manchester: Manchester University Press, 2016), p. 106.

85 *LT* 9 Sept. 1837

86 Royle, 'Radicalism in the West Riding, 1790-1890'.

with industrial capital. Indeed, as much research has emphasised, the industrial revolution, and the process of urbanisation which went with it, saw a vast expansion in the demand for hand labour. New and traditional industries flourished in tandem and there were many linkages between them.[87]

This national picture was reflected in the West Riding textile district during the 1820s and 1830s. Here, particularly in the woollen sector, the factory and domestic systems existed side by side, occasionally rivals, but more often partners and co-dependents.[88] New vertically integrated factories became a feature of woollen manufacture; and specialist spinning mills became increasingly common in worsted. However, the oft-heralded demise of the domestic system never happened in the period under consideration.[89] Handloom weaving remained central to the woollen and fancy branches until well into the second half of the century and hand-finishing of woollen cloth was also not unknown in this period.

Nevertheless, the 1820s and 1830s saw important changes and an acceleration of some pre-existing trends. In the woollen textile sector, for example, whilst the domestic system survived, the industry as a whole became more concentrated geographically and in terms of ownership. Merchants and the larger clothiers took on the manufacturing role incorporating a wider variety of processes and functions. The Cloth Halls, the key markets for the small domestic clothiers, were gradually by-passed as the larger manufacturing 'houses' increasingly produced for large contracts and bespoke orders. Wealth and control became more concentrated in the hands of large master clothiers and merchant-manufacturers, with small independent clothiers and 'operative piece-makers' becoming scarcely indistinguishable.[90] In the worsted industry, where the domestic system had never existed in quite the same way, the stuff-weavers were increasingly dependent on the large stuff-manufacturers and faced the daunting prospect of pauperisation. The introduction of the power-loom, together with an excess in the supply of labour, and the ease with which the trade could be

---

87 John Foster, *Class Struggle and the Industrial Revolution* (London: Weidenfeld and Nicholson, 1974), p. 13; James Vernon, 'Who's Afraid of the "Linguistic Turn"? The Politics of Social History and Its Discontents', *Social History*, 19, 1 (1994), p. 85; E. J. Hobsbawm, *Industry and Empire. An Economic History of Britain Since 1750* (London: Weidenfeld and Nicolson, 1968), pp. 53-4. Raphael Samuel, 'Workshop of the World: Steam Power and Hand Technology in mid-Victorian Britain', *History Workshop* 3 (1977), pp. 6-72.

88 This point is made in numerous sources; for example, D. T. Jenkins, *The West Riding Wool Textile Industry, 1770-1835: A Study of Fixed Capital Formation* (Edington, Wiltshire: Pasold Research Fund Limited, 1975); D. T. Jenkins and K. G. Pontine (eds.), *The British Wool Textile Industry, 1770-1914* (London: Pearson Education, 1982); Pat Hudson, 'Proto-industrialisation: the case of the West Riding Wool Textile Industry in the 18th and early 19th centuries', *History Workshop*, 12 (1981), pp. 34-61. This section, and the discussion of particular textile branches later in the chapter, draw on these studies and a number of previously cited sources (for example, R. M. Hartwell and M. T. Wild) as well as D. Seward, 'The Wool Textile Industry, 1750-1960', in J. G. Jenkins (ed.), *The Wool Textile Industry*, pp. 34-47.

89 See, for example, *LM* 6 Sept. 1828; 12 Dec. 1829.

90 For the by-passing of the Cloth Halls, see *LM* 2 Mar. 1839. On the 'proletarianization' of the small producers and journeymen, see *LM* 12 Dec. 1829 and Hartwell, 'Woollen and Worsted', p. 331.

learnt or performed by women and children, all added to a declining spiral of stuff-weaving wages in the 1830s.

For large numbers of workers, not just stuff-weavers, the period was one of great uncertainty and psychological dislocation. This is vividly illustrated in the sad case of Luke Earnshaw (1791-1844), Armitage Bridge handloom weaver and delegate to the West Riding Chartist regional meeting in September 1838. Six years later 'his loom was the last standing in the locality' and he took his own life having 'frequently of late declared that he would never work at a power loom, and his work at home having at length been destroyed by the all-engrossing power looms, it is supposed to have preyed on his mind, as for the last week or ten days he had been almost constantly drinking, which has led to this fatal result'.[91]

The cultural transformation wrought by 'the factory' was immense, leading a wide variety of workers to articulate anxiety about the material and emotional impact on themselves and their families.[92] The threat of replacement by machinery and by female and juvenile labour (though not always materialising) remained ever-present. As well as coping with the expected seasonal rhythms of their various trades and the individual family life-cycles of relative abundance and shortage, workers in many trades faced extended periods of unemployment and poverty.[93] The third and fourth decades of the century saw increasingly exaggerated movements of the boom and slump trade cycle. Some of the depressions of the 1825-40 period were exceedingly severe; and throughout the period manufacturers and masters were under pressure to reduce costs. In most cases this meant wages.[94]

People could not readily predict the outcome of the economic and social changes which were happening around them. As Malcolm Chase notes, 'industrialization was not achieved precipitately, nor was it a process of undeviating linear progression'.[95] Given the uncertain economic backcloth and the politically turbulent nature of the times, it is easy to see why a plethora of oppositional activities took root in the communities of the textile district. As noted above, an impressive range of local leaders emerged from the region's small manufacturing towns and villages where ties of community, occupation and class reinforced each other. But even in the main centres, with their more diverse occupational make-up, a common response was often possible because of the shared experiences and perceptions of the bulk of the local labouring population.

A full investigation of the immense variety of processes and occupations in which the working population of the West Riding textile district engaged is beyond the

---

91 *NS* 29 Sept. 1839; *LI* 19 Oct. 1844.
92 Robert Gray, *The Factory Question and Industrial England, 1830-1860* (Cambridge: Cambridge University Press, 1996), pp. 24-5; Colin Creighton, 'Collective Action and Domestic Practices: England in the 1830s and 1840s', in Yvette Taylor and Emma Casey (eds.), *Intimacies, Critical Consumption and Diverse Economies* (London: Palgrave Macmillan, 2015), p. 14.
93 In the woollen trade the spring and fall trades were busiest and winter notoriously slack. Peak earnings were normally in early adulthood.
94 Koditschek, *Class Formation and Urban-Industrial Society*, pp. 91 and 97-9.
95 Malcolm Chase, *Early Trade Unionism: Fraternity, Skill and the Politics of Labour* (London: Breviary Stuff, 2012 edn.), p. 114.

remit of this study. Nor is it possible to systematically examine the economic position, social status, the values, organisational affiliations and political attitudes of all workers. However, it is hoped, by taking some of the key trades and drawing on a wide range of examples, to illustrate something of the common interests, outlook and experiences which workers in a variety of places and trades shared. First, though, the question of factory work and workers needs to be tackled.

Factories were not the typical setting for work and employed a significant number of adult workers in only a few centres.[96] Also links with other settings of work were commonplace and complex. Cloth-dressers sometimes worked in the dressing departments of integrated Leeds factories or in large specialist firms; but elsewhere in the textile district this vital finishing process might still be performed at home or in small independent workshops. The larger factories also increasingly did their own dyeing but the distinctive workplace remained the small dye-shops located along the Timble Beck in east and north east Leeds.[97] Flax was spun mechanically at Leeds but it was dressed, and woven into sacking and canvass, by home-based workers. Finally, skilled 'mechanics' might be employed in the textile factories, in foundries and medium-sized machine-making concerns or in small craft workshops.[98]

The type of work performed in factories varied enormously and was unlikely to be machine-paced. Many factory-based jobs were non-mechanised or semi-mechanised and required much manual dexterity, strength and skill, or involved supervision of others and judgement. The majority of adult male factory jobs in the textile sector – spinning overlookers in flax and worsted and the more numerous slubbers, spinners and dressers in woollen – fall into this category.[99] The factories, especially the large all-purpose 'woollen manufactories', also included numbers of skilled craftsmen within their labour force. At the height of the Leeds (clothiers' and dressers') strike of 1834 one of the union's leaders read a list of people who had 'turned in' at Gott's, the town's largest woollen factory:

> Two joiners; two plumbers and glaziers, two engine men, two engineers, two smiths, four cart drivers, one gas man, one logwood grinder, one boiler feeder, one carpenter, one bricklayer, one stover, a man not right in his head it is considered (*laughter,*) four cloth cutters, three slubbers, two woadmen, thirteen slap dyers, thirty-seven weavers, three mule spinners, fourteen overlookers, twenty-two apprentices, two warpers, six tenterers, twenty-two giggers, two handle setters, two handler weavers, six press setters, eight shearmen, and nine others in different departments.[100]

---

96 A sixth of the working population of Leeds worked in power-driven mills in 1839, Harrison, 'Chartism in Leeds', p. 71.

97 *LI* 29 Dec. 1831 indicates the size (average, 50 men) of some of the big dressing departments; BPP 1833, VI p. 639, for domestic dressing; Morris, 'James Kitson', p. 182.

98 'Mechanics' is used here and elsewhere in its specific sense of a maker or worker with machines, rather than its generic sense of a skilled workman, see *LM* 28 Sept. 1828.

99 The majority of the workforces of flax and worsted mills were juvenile and female. In the smaller woollen mills 75 per cent of the workers were men, two-thirds of them over twenty-one years of age, Hudson, 'Proto-industrialisation', pp. 50-1.

100 *LT* 14 June 1834.

The adult male workers who laboured in factories were therefore not a class or breed apart from the majority of the working population. Wages might often be higher and work more regular, but factory workers were recruited from, lived amongst and often did similar types of work to their non-factory neighbours, a large number of whom in any case had worked as children themselves or sent their own offspring to the factories and mills.[101]

The mid-nineteenth century social structure was 'not a pyramid but egg-shaped', with the bulk of the population located in the 'lumpy' but large middling (skilled and semi-skilled) working-class.[102] If we take into account finer gradations of skill, status and dependency it is likely that in some of the outlying (predominantly outworking) districts of the West Riding a pear-shaped model may be more appropriate. But whatever the precise item of grocery the important point is that the groups at the upper and lower ends of the working class were not dominant in terms of numbers or influence.

Unskilled labourers did not form a vast bottom layer of a social pyramid. While the building and transport industries employed a significant number of labourers in all the major towns, the size of this 'trade-less' sector (and the effect of its generally un-organised and non-political presence) should not be exaggerated.[103] At the other end of the social scale the most skilled and highly paid sections of the working class, (who in Leeds in 1839 were groups like the millwrights, gunsmiths, iron moulders, cloth-drawers, mechanics, brass-founders, turners and printers), were relatively few in number and confined mostly to the main urban centres. The bulk of the working population, though differentiated by varying levels of skill, status and dependency, increasingly shared similar values, aspirations and experiences. It was this common background and lived experience which formed the basis of wide-ranging support enjoyed by many working-class agitations and which underpinned a 'rough and ready' but nevertheless very real sense of class that was a feature of the period. These points can be further explored by briefly examining a few of the key occupational groups within three status and wage categories.

a) 'Upper' Skilled Craftworkers

The 'upper', most highly-skilled and paid sections of the workforce undoubtedly included a number of groups who were consistently aloof from more generalised working-class political and industrial movements.[104] Contemporaries recognised this. Peter Bussey commenting on the 'supineness and apathetic feeling' of the people in

---

101 See Hudson, 'Proto-industrialisation', pp. 48–50; for further discussion of these points, see below, pp. 276–8.

102 See summary in R. J. Morris, *Class and class consciousness in the Industrial Revolution, 1750–1850* (London: Macmillan, 1979), pp. 35–6.

103 Also, in terms of wages, if not status, some labourers were very close to the level of the more depressed outworkers and 'lower' artisan trades.

104 For the distinction between the 'upper' better-paid, higher status and more secure skilled trades and the 'lower' declining or more threatened trades, see Iorwerth Prothero, 'London Chartism and the Trades', *Economic History Review* 2nd ser, 24 (1971), pp. 209–12. This distinction applies as much in the West Riding as in London.

August 1836 singled out for condemnation 'the Aristocratic part of the operatives' who saw themselves as a superior caste and took on the religious and political opinions of their masters. A decade earlier John Tester, leader of the striking Bradford combers and weavers, had attacked even more strongly unspecified groups who, 'on account of having obtained better wages than yourselves have been in the habit of looking upon you as an inferior race of creatures, and who would gladly see you reduced to the worst and most miserable condition.' It is not certain precisely which trades Tester and Bussey had in mind but woolsorters, spinning overlookers and 'mechanics' readily suggest themselves.[105]

Woolsorters, for example, were amongst the best paid and most aristocratic of the wool-based trades. Woolsorting required 'great skill' and a good sorter could earn 'from 25s. to 30s. per week, and very skilful hands even more' in the late 1830s. Apprenticeship was strictly limited and in the Huddersfield area, where 'Gentleman Wool sorter' was apparently a common expression, the sorters apparently wore tall hats as a cherished badge of respectability. The trade was a healthy one, the hours reasonably short and wages were generally sufficient to permit high and regular subscriptions to long-established trade clubs and friendly societies.[106]

The engineering and metal-working trades also had strong trade unions, many, like the branches of the trade itself, of fairly recent creation.[107] All, however, looked back to the traditions and status enjoyed by old-established metal-working groups like the millwrights and smiths, and had adopted many of the customs, preoccupations and appearances of longer-established artisan bodies. Wages in the trade were high. Figures for average earnings in Leeds in 1839 reveal metal-working trades occupying the first four places in the 'weekly wage' list and six of the first seven slots in the 'annual earnings' list. They also enjoyed a high status, partly because of their ten-hour working day, and were expanding fast in the 1820s and 1830s. By 1841, 6.3% of the total population of Leeds and 8.3% of adult male workers were employed in 'Engineering'.[108] However, the relatively large size of the trade hides the numerous

---

105 *LT* 27 Aug. 1836; *LM* 16 July 1825. There is an early reference to clubs of 'mechanics' refusing aid early in the strike and some woolsorters were alleged to have blacklegged.

106 BPP, 1840, XXIII. p.528; Webb. Coll., A, XXXVIII f. 392-416; also, Section C, Vols 99 and 103. For descriptions of the various processes in the woollen and worsted industries, see BPP 1840, XXIII, pp. 528-9; Hartwell, 'Woollen and Worsted', pp. 539-617; J. G. Jenkins, *The Wool Textile Industry*, Ch. 4-12. There were four main groups of processes: preparation, spinning, weaving and finishing. The latter was particularly time-consuming and important in woollen manufacture.

107 This brief discussion of the engineering and metal-working trades draws on: Angela Tuckett, *The Blacksmiths' History: What Smithy Workers Gave Trade Unionism* (London: Lawrence and Wishart, 1974); W. McLaine, 'The Engineers' Union' Unpub. thesis, University of London, 1939; G. W. Daniels, 'A "Turn Out" of Bolton Machine-makers in 1831', *Economic History*, 1 (1926-9) pp. 591-602; G. W. Daniels, 'The Organisation of a "Turn Out" of Bolton Machine-makers in 1831', *Economic History*, 2 (1930-3), pp. 111-6; L. Brentano, 'The Growth of a Trades Union', *The North British Review*, 53 (1871), pp. 59-114; Working Class Movement Library, Salford, Trade Union Rules 1805-1825; Webb Coll. A, XV and IX; and J. B. Jeffreys, *The Story of the Engineers, 1800-1945* (London: Lawrence and Wishart, 1945).

108 Statistical Committee Report on Leeds, 1839 used as the basis for Table IV, 'Wages in Leeds,

fine gradations of status, wage-levels and working conditions within it. The tendency toward specialism and sectionalism in the trade is reflected in the proliferation of trade societies which existed in the period.[109]

The insularity of many of these bodies, alongside their high wages and regularity of employment, set them apart from the majority of working men, including other skilled artisans. However, it would be wrong to read back too many 'aristocratic' tendencies from the mid-Victorian period into the 1830s.[110] The metal and engineering workers did not pursue their trade interests any differently than other groups of skilled artisans. Industrial disputes were no less bitter, violent or acrimonious than in other trades. Equally, they were not totally immune from trade depressions and wage cuts. The formation of a co-operative society by Leeds mechanics in 1829 came at a time when they had allegedly suffered wage cuts of between 15 and 30 per cent.[111] Such instances were rare; but the future prosperity of new trades like machine and steam-engine making, like the wider developing industrial economy as a whole, could not be taken for granted in the 1830s. Towards the end of the decade, when the engineering sector suffered from the general downswing there is evidence of attempts to secure stronger links within the trade and also some indications of Chartist involvement.[112] In spite of their high wages and short hours the 'mechanics' did not have the security or self-confidence to be true 'aristocrats'. In outlook and attitudes, if not in status, they shared much in common with other less well-paid sections of the workforce.

Neither were woolsorters totally immune from trade slumps or the wider political aspirations of the working class. A hundred sorters were said to be unemployed in Bradford in May 1838 and there is some evidence of dilution of the trade and a narrowing of differentials with other groups. Woolsorters participated in the leadership of the worsted trades' union in the early 1830s and also contributed to Chartist funds. In 1848 older members of the trade set up a Chartist farm in the Huddersfield area.[113]

Other highly-paid 'upper' skilled trades can be dealt with briefly. Groups like the printers, bookbinders, and gunmakers generally stayed above the hurly-burly of working-class political and inter-trade activity. Spinning overlookers in flax and worsted mills involved themselves in questions like factory hours, which directly

---

1839' in J. H. Lenton, 'Wages in the Leeds Area, 1770-1850', Unpub. MPhil thesis, University of Leeds, 1969; *LM* 3 Dec. 1831, 15 Oct. 1825, on high status; Rimmer, 'Industrial Profile', p. 158 ff.

109 The best paid were the millwrights (26s and above), the least well-paid, the blacksmiths. Millwrights, iron moulders, smiths, machine and steam-engine makers all had separate 'clubs' and usually more than one network of wider affiliations.

110 On this, see Robert Sykes, 'Early Chartism and Trade Unionism in South-East Lancashire', in Epstein and D. Thompson (eds.), *The Chartist Experience*, p. 154.

111 For a violent dispute involving Leeds machine-makers, see *LM* April-June and 14 Oct. 1837; *LM* 21 Nov. 1829.

112 There was an amalgamation of Manchester and Yorkshire-based societies in the steam-engine and machine-making sector in 1838. On mechanics' subscriptions, see below, p. 447.

113 *BO* 3, 24 May 1838 (see also *LM* 2 May, *LI* 8 Oct. 1829); Webb Coll., A, XXXVIII, f. 401-11; Lenton, 'Wages in the Leeds Area'; Webb Coll., A, XXXVIII, f. 392.

affected them, sometimes in conflict with other groups of workers; but were rarely pre-eminent in any of the wider radical or industrial movements of the time.[114]

Their more numerous equivalents in the woollen sector, slubbers and spinners, also had a rather ambiguous relationship with the wider working community.[115] For example, they were frequently condemned by factory reformers for the over-vigorous exercise of their supervisory role over child pieceners.[116] On the other hand they were not totally aloof or secure and both slubbers and spinners participated in the woollen-based Huddersfield and Leeds Trades' Unions of the early 1830s. Technological improvement in mules and billies and the doubling up of machines increasingly threatened the slubbers' and spinners' control over the work process and their bargaining position. In status and experience there were points of similarity with more traditional artisan trades.

b) 'Lower' Skilled Artisans

Iorwerth Prothero's study of radical politics and culture in London defined an artisan as a member of 'the old specialist, unrevolutionized handworking trades, which required a certain amount of skill, but within wide limits, and had a definite status connotation.'[117] As in the metropolis, the two most numerous sectors at the 'lower' end of the artisan spectrum, building and clothing, both supplied leadership and support for working-class movements in the West Riding.

Building workers comprised a number of separate but closely linked trades: bricklayers, painters, plasterers, glaziers, plumbers, carpenters, joiners and stonemasons.[118] They made up a numerically significant sector of the local workforce and enjoyed wages in the range of 18s- to 24s a week, and sometimes higher. Work was seasonal, but included a well-recognised skill factor. Their average working day was shorter than most groups and this, together with the large degree of control which they exercised over their work process, gave them a relatively high status.[119] They

---

114 See, for example, their stance (and also the slubbers') in favour of eleven hours, *LM* 2 Dec. 1837.

115 Much actual spinning remained in the domestic sector. Factory spinning only really took off after 1840. Slubbing, the preparatory first stage of spinning, however, was performed in the scribbling mills and the large integrated factories on a 'slubbing-billy'. Wages were high (in the range of 21s to 24s) and the trade remained a skilled, male preserve and essentially a hand operation until well into the 1840s.

116 See, for example, *NS* 20 Apr. 1839.

117 Prothero, *Artisans and Politics*, p. 5. On artisans' role in early working-class movements generally, see pp. 3-6.

118 The discussion of the builders which follows draws on the following sources: R. W. Postgate, *The Builders' History* (London: The Labour Publishing Company, 1923); W. H. Oliver, 'Organisations and Ideas behind the Efforts to Achieve a General Union of the Working Classes in England in the early 1830s', Unpub. PhD thesis, University of Oxford, 1954; Webb Coll., A, X-XIII and local newspapers of the period.

119 Rimmer, 'Industrial Profile', p. 158 ff. reveals approximately the same number of adult males employed in 'building' as in 'dress' and 'engineering', in the 1841 Census (all were not skilled, though). On wages and the large number of building firms in the 1830s, see Lenton, 'Wages in the Leeds Area', and W. R. Rimmer, 'Working Men's Cottages in Leeds, 1770-1840',

organised themselves into associational bodies which displayed many of the familiar hallmarks of a typical artisan trade society.[120]

The prime concerns of these societies were the maintenance, and occasionally the improvement, of wage levels, working hours and customs. Apprenticeship regulations were not strictly enforced, and in this sphere in particular the building trades can be differentiated from the higher (new and traditional) skilled trades. However, without any major threats from mechanisation or the possibility of being undercut by child or female labour, building workers remained in a relatively strong bargaining position throughout the 1820s and 1830s. The trades won significant advances during the building booms in the middle of each decade, but suffered wage reductions with the onset of general depression at the beginning and at the end of the 1830s. Working hours and customs were also strong 'trade' considerations. For example, the Huddersfield masons struck unsuccessfully in May 1832 to achieve a shorter working Saturday and the following year protested strongly about the 'degrading contracting system' which they alleged led to the competitive undercutting of wages for individual trades.[121]

In the late 1820s and early 1830s long-established intra-trade links were formalised through the establishment of national and regional federations of individual trades.[122] Local co-operation between the different building trades was also commonplace, including joint, often staggered, industrial action.[123] The next step, the linking of these national and regional trade bodies into a national confederation of building trades, occurred in the conducive atmosphere for trades' and general unionism of the early 1830s, with the formation of the Operative Builders' Union (OBU). One of the chief constituents of the OBU, the stonemasons (numerically most important of the building trades in the West Riding) had a strong base in the region and it appears that loose local 'operative builders' federations existed in a number of West Riding towns.[124] The defeat of the OBU in the Lancashire strikes of 1833, however, provoked much earnest discussion in local trade branches about the relative merits of 'exclusive government' and 'general union'.[125] Eventually the exclusives won the day and sometime in 1834 the wider confederation ceased to exist. However, in a number of

---

Publications of the Thoresby Society, 46 (1961), pp. 165-199. Also, local directories. On working hours and status, see, for example, *LM* 3 Dec. 1831.

120 These included a tramping system, a high degree of decentralisation, convivial and ceremonial aspects.

121 *LP* 25 May 1832; *HHE* 4 May 1833. General contracting involved the practice of one master getting the contract and then sub-contracting (at the lowest price).

122 For example, the 'Manchester Order' of Bricklayers in 1829, and the General Union of Carpenters and Joiners established in July 1827, see *TN* 16 Aug. 1828.

123 See, for example, *LM* June-Aug 1824 and April-May 1825; one year the bricklayers led the assault, the next the joiners.

124 The Huddersfield Operative Stonemasons (OSM) lodge, formed or re-constituted in November 1832, was the 'parent lodge' and first 'Grand Lodge' of the national OSM. On local builders' confederations, see *HHE* 2 Feb. 1833 (Bradford); *Crisis* 28 Dec. 1833 (Leeds) and statement of Liverpool building workers in Webb Coll., A, X, f. 80.

125 *Pioneer* 1 Mar. 1834 (letter of James Pontey).

trades, notably the masons, the framework for a national union survived and prospered.

After losing the major battles over union recognition and control in 1833-4 the builders generally returned to lower-key trade activity during the remainder of the decade. For a time, though, they operated at the very forefront of schemes for co-operative production and wider trades' union organisation. The 'Journeymen Masons' of Huddersfield, for example, sought 'contracts on their own account' in October 1833 and after a short strike in December the Bradford masons followed suit. Around the same time the Huddersfield 'Operative Joiners' raised subscriptions for the Derby silk-weavers and formed a committee to visit all the trades in the neighbourhood. Ten months later their headquarters served as the location for a West Riding trades' meeting to discuss the projected successor of the now virtually defunct Grand National Consolidated Trades' Union (GNCTU), Robert Owen's British and Foreign Consolidated Association (BFCA).[126]

Involvement in broader political and social movements is more difficult to discern. The leading trades, the masons and the carpenters and joiners, supplied a few local radical leaders. Building trades' banners were present at the 1833 ten hours meeting on Wibsey Moor, and builders (particularly joiners) occasionally figure amongst those arrested at Chartist, anti-poor law and (non-building) trade disturbances.[127] In general, though, their main preoccupation was to preserve the wages and customs of trades which, though often prosperous, felt vulnerable. They can perhaps be best described as a middling group of skilled artisans who shared things in common with both the better-paid 'higher' skilled trades, for example machine-makers, and with the 'lower' skilled groups such as the tailors and shoemakers.

The shoemaking and tailoring trades formed the two most numerous artisan trades in the second quarter of the nineteenth century.[128] Although generally designated as coming within the 'skilled' sector neither trade required a high degree of skill or strength, nor were the workers required to buy expensive tools and equipment. Production was generally concentrated in small craft shops or in small domestic units; and the borderline between journeyman and small master was often very hazy.

Neither trade was highly paid. Leeds shoemakers earned only slightly more than local handloom weavers in 1839 and their wages compared unfavourably with other leather-related trades. The decline of wages since the early 1820s was not due to the

---

126 *VWR* 5 Oct.; *LT* 7, 28 Dec. 1833; *Pioneer* 4 Jan.; *LT* 25 Oct. 1834. In 1835 Dorchester subscriptions were collected at the OSM headquarters.

127 *LI* 6 July 1833; see, for example, *LT* 14 June 1834 prosecution of a master joiner for assault on a 'black sheep' during the Leeds clothiers' and dressers' strike.

128 For figures in London in 1831 and 1841, see Prothero, *Artisans and Politics*, pp. 341-3. Rimmer, 'Leeds Leather', p. 134, estimated that there were 7,000 adult males making shoes in the West Riding as a whole in 1831, approximately a sixth of these were in Leeds. On shoemakers and shoemaking, see also R. A. Church, 'Labour Supply and Innovation, 1800-60: The Boot and Shoe Industry', *Business History*, 12, 1 (1970), pp. 25-45; E. J. Hobsbawn and J. W. Scott, 'Political Shoemakers', *Past and Present*, 89 (1980), pp. 86-114. On tailors and shoemakers in the pre-1832 period, see Thompson, *Making*, Chapter 8 (Artisans and Others). On the London tailors see, Prothero, *Artisans and Politics*, pp. 250-2, 268-70, 300-5, and 333-8.

inroads of machinery, but to the sheer expansion of the trade and the numbers employed in it.[129] Female and juvenile labour was not yet a problem, nor did competition from France or the highly capitalised outworking Northampton trade yet pose a serious threat. It is more likely that in the West Riding displaced weavers, who found shoemaking with its independent traditions and relative ease of acquisition an acceptable substitute for the loom, contributed to the dilution of the trade.[130]

Tailors, though less numerous and slightly better paid than the 'Sons of Crispin',[131] nevertheless formed a substantial and increasingly threatened body of artisans. The pressures creating a large dishonourable 'sweated' sector in London also existed in the West Riding, though less acutely. Again, technical innovation posed no real threat, but the growing domestic market for ready-made and inferior bespoke goods encouraged the proliferation of small masters, thereby often undercutting established 'honourable' masters.

Both shoemakers and tailors had a strong occupational consciousness with long traditions of mutuality and trade organisation. Respectable shoemaking 'club men' or 'flints' strove (sometimes successfully, occasionally violently) to uphold wage rates and the honour and integrity of the trade by striking against masters who employed non-union 'scabs'.[132] However, the respectable part of the trade was coming under increasing pressure. At the end of a long and bitter dispute in 1834, for example, three of the leading Leeds manufacturers succeeded in reducing wages to the level of a number of the smaller (presumably less unionised) shops.[133] It is likely that this increasing vulnerability led the already radically inclined shoemakers to view wider political movements like Chartism as a more fruitful channel for their proverbial energies and intelligence.

Fair and equal (usually higher) wages and the maintenance of traditional customs formed the main pre-occupations of the West Riding tailors' societies, but they also aspired to a shorter working day.[134] At times their wage demands succeeded, as in the favourable economic climates of 1824 and 1835, but there is some evidence of increasing antagonism and industrial conflict later in the decade. In 1836, for example, union recognition became a key issue in Leeds when a minor dispute escalated into a trial of strength between the united masters and workmen. The outcome is not known but a union defeat is indicated by the men's announcement later in the year of the opening of a 'large and commodious Work Shop for Our Men'.[135]

---

129 Lenton, 'Wages in the Leeds Area', Table 4: Wages in Leeds, 1839; Church, 'Labour Supply and Innovation'; Rimmer, 'Leeds Leather'.

130 Rimmer, 'Leeds Leather'; for possible links between shoemakers and Yorkshire textile trade unionism, see *LT* 28 Sept., *HHE* 3 Oct. 1833 (Rochdale shoemakers) and the cordwainers' initiation ceremony detailed by George Beaumont in TNA: HO 52/25, Walker, Batty to Melbourne, 15 Feb. 1834.

131 This collective nickname originated from St Crispin, the patron saint of shoemakers.

132 *LM* 10 Apr. 1824, 19 Feb.; *LI* 23 June, 7 July 1825. See also, *HG* 19 Oct. 1833.

133 *LT* Dec. 1834 - Feb. 1835.

134 *LT* 17 May 1834; *LI* 11 Jan. 1827; *LP* 22 May, *HCC* 29 May 1830; *LI* 23 Aug. 1834; but see *LT* 30 July 1836 for long hours.

135 *LM* 12 June 1824; *HG* 6 June, *LT* 22 Aug., 5 Sept. 1835; *LM* 17 Sept., *LT* 26 Nov. 1836. See also *HG* 29 Nov. 1835 (Bradford).

The relative openness and vulnerability of both trades encouraged them to establish strong internal trade links and also to participate in moves towards general unionism. The precise pattern of the shoemakers' national unionism is not clear. However, for a time in the early 1830s the strong links within the trade were formalised into a major national organisation.[136]

The participation of the tailors nationally in the flowering of general unionism in 1833-4 is well attested.[137] West Riding tailors were closely involved in these developments. The Leeds tailors, for example, considered themselves part of the GNCTU in May 1834 and sent £10 'towards supporting in their brethren in London'. The 'Consolidated' principle met some opposition after its first introduction in Bradford in April 1834, but 'operations were resumed' in October, and the local 'Consolidated' union branch remained in existence until at least the disputes of mid-1835.[138]

The contributions of both trades to early working-class movements, however, went far beyond involvement in national intra- and inter-trade organisations. The participation of shoemakers in radical politics was extraordinary and long-standing. There is hardly a locality, radical agitation or organisation in the West Riding in which it is not possible to identify a shoemaker-leader. The trade was also involved in early co-operative ventures. Tailors likewise supplied a number of prominent local leaders; and Huddersfield in particular seems to have been notable for its radical tailors and co-operators.[139] This widespread involvement in trades' unionism, radicalism and co-operation owed something to long-established traditions within the two leading clothing trades but it also indicates the increasing vulnerability to, and attempts to counteract, wage cuts and loss of status. This sense of marginality, resented all the more because of strong traditions of independence and strong-mindedness, was echoed in the experience of the third and most important trade 'bloc': the textile outworkers.

c) Textile Outworkers

The textile outworkers, the largest category of workers in the West Riding labour force, shared much in common with the declining 'lower' skilled artisan trades. They worked outside, but often as an adjunct to, the factory system on materials owned and put out by the master-manufacturers. They had strong trade traditions and a fierce independence but had lost, or were in the process of losing, any semblance of artisan status. Their story has been amply and poignantly told by E. P. Thompson and will re-surface at many junctures in the chapters which follow.[140] The purpose of this section

---

136 *Pioneer* 11 Jan. 1834; *Destructive* 25 Jan. 1834.

137 Terry Parssinen and Iorwerth Prothero, 'The Tailors' Strike of 1834 and the Collapse of the GNCTU: A Police Spy's Report', *IRSH*, 22 (1977), pp. 65-107. See also *VP* 21 May 1831 for contact with Leeds tailors.

138 *LT* 17 May 1834 (see also *Pioneer* 21 June 1834 for a similar sum from the 'North Union of Tailors, Halifax'); *LT* 22 Aug., 5 Sept. 1835.

139 Hobsbawm and Scott, 'Political Shoemakers'; for Huddersfield see *LT* 28 Oct. 1834.

140 Thompson, *Making*, Chapter 9 (esp. pp. 310-46). This section is based on this; also, BPP, 1840, XXIII, pp. 527-90, regional studies and local newspapers.

is not to replicate or to challenge Thompson's principal conclusions, but to briefly re-state their importance and to emphasise the enduring influence of their traditions and experiences on the wider working community. The two largest and 'classic' groups of outworkers during this period – handloom weavers and woolcombers – will serve as our prime examples.

Handloom weaving included a number of different branches. Most of these were not in direct competition with the power-loom in the 1820s and 1830s, but all experienced a decline in wages, attacks on established customs and increasing overheads.[141] Wages varied considerably within and between branches, being higher nearer the larger urban centres where the higher quality work tended to concentrate, and in the woollen and fancy trades.[142]

The weavers were inveterate organisers and had strong traditions of trade solidarity and mutual assistance. The fancy weavers of the Huddersfield area, for example, established an extensive trade union in 1824-5; organised again in 1827 to recover wage levels and to protest against truck payments; were prominent in the activities of the Almondbury Political Union in 1829-32; formed the Fancy Trades' Union in 1832-4; were involved in further unions and local Chartist branches in 1837-9; and set up a 'Central Committee' in 1842 which pressed for local Boards of Trade and wage equalisation.[143] Both demands remained key themes of weavers' associative bodies throughout the period.

Handloom weavers were not uniformly radical. The woollen-weaving villages of the Leeds clothing district included some acknowledged bastions of Whiggery. However, by the end of the 1830s, when the effects of wage-cutting, over-working and under-employment were increasingly being felt, even places like Pudsey, 'peculiarly a village of clothiers', had its Chartist branch.[144] Elsewhere in the textile region advanced political radicalism flourished consistently amongst the woollen and fancy weavers of Huddersfield, the blanket weavers of Dewsbury and the worsted weavers of the Halifax and Bradford areas. All these groups provided radical and Chartist leaders and their painful decline served as a point of reference for all workers.

Like the handloom weavers, the woolcombers of the worsted trade worked predominantly in a domestic setting for declining wages with tools and on materials owned by their employers. Although not particularly skilled, the work to straighten fibres with heated metals combs required great strength and was notoriously unhealthy. According to one contemporary observer handcombers' homes had become 'consuming dens instead of life-sustaining shelters where the functions of health are desecrated and rendered morbid'.[145] Overheads were few and the distinction

---

141 In Bradford, and in larger enterprises in the Huddersfield and Leeds districts, weavers sometimes worked in large 'loomshops' or weaving sheds added to mill buildings.

142 BPP 1840, XXIII, p. 551. H. S. Chapman, the Handloom Weavers Commissioner, worked on the basis of a 2:3:5 ratio for wages in cotton: worsted: wool.

143 Webb Coll., A, XXXVIII, f. 151-6.

144 Thompson, *Making*, p. 318; BPP, 1840, XXIII, p. 536. See also, Morris, 'James Kitson', pp. 189-190 on the small enclave of English and Irish stuff-weavers in the east end of Leeds, a particularly volatile, unpredictable handloom weaving branch.

145 The Rev. Scoresby (the new incumbent at Bradford) in 1840, quoted in Firth, 'The Bradford Trade', p. 16. See also *Crisis* 22 Sept. 1832 for a description of combers' 'dungeons' in the

between a journeyman woolcomber and a small master was very slight. The trade increasingly became the preserve of a mass of dependent outworking combers, employed by large master combers and spinners.[146]

Wages had declined substantially since the high point of 1825. However, though the strike defeat of that year was a major blow to a long-established and traditionally strong union, it's an exaggeration to say that the post-defeat woolcomber was 'translated almost overnight from a privileged artisan to a defenceless outworker.'[147] It is likely that it was technical difficulties rather than the cheapness of combers' labour which kept the threat of machinery at bay. Indeed, the combers' union revived in 1827 and by August of that year wages were approaching the 1825 level. Reductions later that year and in 1829, 1832 and 1833, ensured that the general trend was downward; but the combers were often able to make good at least some of the damage.

This semblance of the maintenance of wages rates in an increasingly over-stocked trade, which was moreover relatively easy to learn, can partly be explained in terms of the combers' trade union heritage and belligerent reputation.[148] Trade organisations stretched back well into the eighteenth century and, despite setbacks and defeats, remained strong right until the combers' sudden extinction by combing machinery in the late 1840s. The combers were also 'almost without exception rabid politicians'; and in the Chartist era 'the combing shops rang with wild denunciations of wrongdoers, or of fervid admiration of the champion of democracy [Feargus O'Connor]'.[149] The attraction of Chartism, like the appeal of trades' and general unionism to the combers earlier in the decade, may have owed something to strong traditions, but it was clearly also related to the combers' loss of status and earnings.[150] Although the decline may not have been as precipitate as E. P. Thompson contends, it is clear that independence, honour and health were all gradually sacrificed in the fight to eke out a living wage.

Finally, outside these classic branches of outworking, in less well-known corners of textile or related outworking, outlines of similar stories of increasing intensification of work, threats of mechanisation, pressure on wages, breakdown of established ways of working, involvement in trade and trades' unions and, increasingly, the growing appeal of radical politics and newspapers can be discerned. These can be seen in the examples of the home based flax-dressers of Leeds who formed part of the Linen Trades' Union in 1833-4; the silk-dressers of Ovenden who were prosecuted for

---

Halifax district.

146 This discussion of the woolcombers draws on Thompson, *Making*, pp. 311-13; Sigsworth, *Black Dyke Mills*, pp. 7-9; Webb Coll., A, XXXIII, f. 139-41; Jonathan Smith, 'The Strike of 1825', in Wright and Jowitt (eds.), *Victorian Bradford*, pp. 66-7.

147 Thompson, *Making*, p. 312.

148 On wages in the late 1820s and 1830s, see Lenton, 'Wages in the Leeds Area'; on the influx into the trade, see William Scruton, *Bradford Fifty Years Ago: A Jubillee Memorial of the Bradford Corporation* (Bradford: G. F. Sewell, 1897) pp. 95-6; on the ease of learning the trade, see *LM* 1 Dec. 1832. The work was however becoming more difficult and time-consuming due to the increased combing of short stapled wools. This was a wage-reducing pressure.

149 Peel, *Spen Valley*, quoted in Thompson, *Making*, p. 313; W. Cudworth, *Rambles around Horton* (Bradford, 1886), quoted in Peacock, *Bradford Chartism*, p. 3.

150 The combers were a leading component of the Bradford Trades' Union of 1832-4 which in turn was connected with the GNCTU.

neglect of work in 1836 (they had taken time off to read unstamped papers); and the female card-setters of the Halifax area who turned out 'on the orders of the Trades' Union' in 1834.[151] Not all of these rich and nuanced narratives can be investigated here; but it is proposed to briefly look at one special feature of the creative response of the textile district's working population to their predicament in the early 1830s: the establishment of trades' unions.

3: Trades' Unionism, 1831-4

The dominant theme in trade unionism in the late 1820s and early 1830s has long been identified as the trend 'towards "national" unions and towards general unions: the former bringing local clubs of one particular trade into a loose union, the latter linking societies of different trades in one union'.[152] Malcolm Chase's comprehensive study of *Early Trade Unionism* argues that: 'The notion of general union between different trades presaged a new kind of way of seeing work itself, the solidarities and commonality of a single craft being extended beyond the frontier of the skill concerned'.[153] Yet many of the details of this 'revolutionary' development remain obscure and he concurs with J. F. C. Harrison's view that, 'The complex story of the development of British trade unionism in the years 1831-34 has never been satisfactorily unravelled'.[154]

Most conventional accounts of this period focus on the GNCTU and the influence of Robert Owen. However, as Malcolm Chase notes, the GNCTU 'was very far from being an isolated phenomenon' and the impact of Owen and Owenism may have been exaggerated.[155] Earlier iterations of general unionism such as the impressively broad and long-lasting Manchester-based NAPL, whose delegates failed to rouse Halifax in November 1830, have struggled to command an appropriate amount of historical attention'.[156]

The same applies to another of 'the great Unions of the North', the woollen-based Clothiers' Union, and its worsted equivalent, the Bradford Order.[157] Despite valuable sorties by various historians into the area that he mapped out, G. D. H. Cole's concise account remains the standard text on Yorkshire trade unionism in the 1820s and

---

151 TNA: HO 40/31 f. 165, *Pioneer* 12 Apr., *True Sun* 5 June 1834; *LT* 26 July 1834 (on Linen Trades' Union); *HG* 5 Mar. 1836 (silk-dressers); *HHE* 19 June 1834 (card-setters).

152 W. H. Fraser, 'Trade Unionism', in J. T. Ward (ed.), *Popular Movements c. 1830-1850* (London: Macmillan, 1970), p. 100.

153 Chase, *Early Trade Unionism*, p. 113.

154 J. F. C. Harrison, *Robert Owen and the Owenites in Britain and America: The Quest for the New Moral World* (London: Routledge and Kegan Paul, 1969), p. 208.

155 Chase, *Early Trade Unionism*, p. 111.

156 This is despite a detailed account in R. G. Kirby and A. E. Musson, *The Voice of the People: John Doherty, 1798-1854. Trade Unionist, Radical and Factory Reformer* (Manchester: Manchester University Press, 1975). See Robert Sykes, 'Trade unionism and class consciousness: the "revolutionary" period of general unionism, 1829-1834', in John Rule (ed.), *British Trade Unionism, 1750-1850: The Formative Years* (London: Longman, 1988), p. 180, for a comparative assessment of its importance. For Halifax, see *HCC* 6 Nov. 1830 and pp. 18-9 above.

157 *Crisis* 19 Apr. 1834.

1830s.[158] As noted in a study of these two West Riding unions in the 1831-34 period, more than two generations on, a comprehensive history of early trade unionism in Yorkshire 'is perhaps overdue'.[159] It is not proposed to provide this here. Instead, this section explores a number of the distinguishing features of Yorkshire trades' unionism and the important legacy of its eventual defeat. Other aspects of the history of local trades' unions are dealt with in later chapters, including connections with the factory movement, with early co-operation (through 'commercial orders' and ideas of national union), and with political radicalism (during parliamentary elections and the Dorchester campaigns).

'Trades' unionism' as it developed in the West Riding textile district manifested both of the two strands of development outlined earlier: vertical links within a trade and horizontal ties between trades, with the latter becoming increasingly important. The strengthening of intra-trade links through the enhancement or revival of national structures can be seen in a number of artisan trades from the mid-1820s onwards. Examples include the sawyers and hatters; the stonemasons, whose Huddersfield lodge became the 'parent lodge' of the national Operative Stonemasons; and groups like the tailors and shoemakers with their strong traditions of mutuality and extensive tramping networks.[160]

Alongside this consolidation of vertical ties, a range of horizontal links developed within and between unions in different industrial sectors. The Potters' Union and the Builders' Union, for example, included all the various branches in their particular trade. Contemporaries recognised the novelty of this new form of 'union'. William Lovett, a leading metropolitan radical, wrote in summer 1834 of how

> the first of these new arrangements were formed about eighteenth months since, and took the name of Trades' Unions, instead of Societies. The first in the field … was the builders, who formed a union of all the branches in the building line, under the title of the 'Operative Builders'.[161]

The leading West Riding unions were of this ilk, a fact which alarmed employers and magistrates alike. The Coroner at the inquest of James Benson, a blackleg woollen-weaver allegedly murdered by trade unionists at Farsley near Leeds in 1832, voiced the fears of local 'respectables' in his assessment of the state of the district:

---

158 G. D. H. Cole, *Attempts at General Union, 1818-1834* (London: Macmillan, 1953). Other additions to the literature include, Morris, 'James Kitson', pp. 188-92; Derek Gregory, *Regional Transformation and Industrial Revolution: A Geography of the Yorkshire Woollen Industry* (London: Palgrave Macmillan, 1982), pp. 225-35; Chase, *Early Trade Unionism*, p. 119.

159 John Sanders, 'John Douthwaite and "John Powlett": Trades' Unionism and Conflict in Early 1830s Yorkshire', *Labour History Review*, 86, 1 (2022), p. 3.

160 TNA: HO 40/18 f. 524 (Sawyers' Union in the north, 1825); TNA: HO 52/25, Warwickshire (districts of the Hatters' Union in 1833); John Sanders, 'Working-class movements in the West Riding textile district 1829 to 1839, with emphasis on local leadership and organisation', Unpub. PhD thesis, University of Manchester, 1984, p. 92 (stonemasons); Parssinen and Prothero, 'The Tailors' Strike of 1834' (tailors); Chase, *Early Trade Unionism*, pp. 122-3 (shoemakers).

161 *True Sun* 18 Aug. 1834.

so extensive and alarming is the Combination called the Trades Union. It extends through every manufacturing town and village in the West Riding… This Union is composed of branches of the different trades. The Clothiers, Stone Masons, Potters etc. I have reason to believe have each their separate Societys and all centre in the Trades Union.[162]

The apostrophe which is sometimes inserted at the end of trades' is significant, because the West Riding trades' unions were unions of 'trades', often within an identifiable industrial sector.[163] The Clothiers' Union, for example, covered the four main branches of woollen cloth manufacture: slubbing, spinning, weaving and dressing. The card-makers' trades' union in the Halifax-Dewsbury area comprised, 'operative thick and small wire-drawers, cardmakers, curriers etc. etc.'[164] The Leeds Dyers' Union, (the 'Society of Operatives, Dyers, Singers, Dressers and Makers-Up in the Stuff Department'), struck in July 1833, ostensibly to boost the wages of lower paid workers such as 'helping hands, stockers etc.'[165]

The trades' unions that were created were often of more than local import and quickly stretched beyond their original heartlands. What Robert Owen termed 'the Great Union of the Woollen Trade', (the Clothiers' Union), spanned the West Riding woollen district and extended across the Pennines to Lancashire.[166] The Linen Trades' Union covered Leeds, Barnsley, York and Knaresborough and had links to the West Country and Ulster.[167] The Bradford-based worsted trades' union (the Bradford Order) boasted forty districts in 1833 including Leicester, Nottingham, Derby, Kendal and Banbury.[168]

The culmination of this movement was the Grand National Consolidated Trades' Union which, as its name suggests, was, or aspired to be, a consolidation or confederation of existing trades' unions.[169] It was the linkages for mutual support and the potential for coordinated actions implicit in general unionism that particularly alarmed local employers and the authorities. However, before examining their

---

162 TNA: HO 52/20, Lewison to Melbourne, 24 Dec 1832. 'Mercator' in *LM* 10 Nov. 1832 also suspected that the Trades' Union extended to all operatives in every trade in Leeds.

163 Contemporaries often equated a 'trade' with a 'calling or occupation', *Pioneer* 29 June 1834.

164 TNA: HO 40/32 f. 233, Ramsden and Harrison to Melbourne, 17 Mar. 1834. The union aimed at wage equalisation but was broken in summer 1834, *HHE* 19 June 1834.

165 *LT* 4, 20 July 1833.

166 *Crisis* 12 Apr. 1834.

167 On the Linen Trades' Union, see the Address 'To the Flax and Hemp Trade of Great Britain' dated Leeds 30 Nov. 1832 in TNA: HO 40/31 f.165 This was picked up by an employer in Yeovil and sent to Lord Melbourne. George Loveless, the Tolpuddle martyr, had the same flyer on him when he was arrested, and at his trial he attributed the 'cause of their being here' to it, see Oliver, 'Organisations and Ideas', p. 240. See also, *LM* 28 Sept. 1833; OC No. 615, James Ray to Owen, 14 Nov. 1833; *Crisis* 12 Apr. 1834; *VWR* 8 Mar. 1834; *Pioneer* 29 Mar. 1834, and *True Sun* 5 June 1834, for Isaac Clark, Leeds flax-dresser, reporting on his visit to branches in Northern Ireland and Lancashire gathering pledges of support for the Leeds Clothiers' Union.

168 TNA: HO 40/32 f. 19, Bouverie to Phillips 12 Jan. 1834; *True Sun* 27 May 1834. This body was also known as the 'Bradford Trades' Union' or the 'Worsted Operative Committee', *LM* 13 July 1833.

169 See *Crisis* 19 Apr. 1834 (John Browne, secretary of the GNCTU Executive).

response and the ensuing conflicts in the West Riding, it is worth setting this development in a wider context.

First, whatever its novel features in terms of the wider links which were forged and the new trades and groups of workers which were 'unionised', all these new structures were founded on the solid bedrock of small-scale, local trade society activity which stretched back over decades and which carried on largely unnoticed even in this 'revolutionary period'.[170] The concerns of these small local trade societies mirrored very closely those identified by Iorwerth Prothero in his extensive study of London artisans: the maintenance of customary working practices, the prevention of the dilution of the workforce by unskilled or non-club interlopers; defences against the ravages of sickness, accident and unemployment and, finally, fair wages.[171] Strikes were rare and usually comprised small-scale, short-lived conflicts, barely meriting a mention in the local press. Occasionally these long-established undercurrents and the new surface movements for inter-trade links collided; as, for example, in the summer of 1831 when a NAPL missionary visited the Brushmakers' Society in Liverpool. The local secretary highly approved of the general union but stressed that they were so well organised and had no fear of major reductions that they did not need the wider association.[172]

Second, one of the common names given to the Yorkshire-based worsted union, the 'Bradford Order' indicates the close links between contemporary developments in trade unions and those happening in friendly societies. Just as early trade societies were barely distinguishable from benefit and friendly societies, so the upsurge of trades' unionism in the 1830s needs to be set in the context of the simultaneous growth of 'secret orders' like the Ancient Foresters, the Oddfellows, and the Druids.[173] A Bradford correspondent writing in the aftermath of the industrial defeats of 1834 blamed the growth of trade unionism on central government, which altered the law 'with respect to Benefit Societies, which, from a dislike they had to be under the control of a government at that time unpopular, has driven most of the sick clubs of the good old plan into Secret Orders or Unions, so that in Bradford there are only two or three remaining.' A Leeds correspondent two years earlier had confirmed the trend for 'benefit societies' to merge 'into institutions which, in my estimation, are of an objectionable character.'[174]

Friendly societies, for all their non-partisan strictures were not above showing their true colours. So, for example, at the height of trades' union moral panic in June 1833, we find the Court of the Royal Foresters at Kirkburton near Huddersfield

---

170 Sidney and Beatrice Webb, *The History of Trade Unionism* (London: Longmans, Green and Co., 1894), p. 113.

171 Prothero, *Artisans and Politics*, pp. 28-38.

172 *VP* 2 July 1831. On the brushmakers, see William Kiddier, *The Old Trade Unions, From Unprinted Records of the Brushmakers* (London: George Allen and Unwin, 1930). The trade and its society were small-scale, localised and insular. But see *NS* 21 July 1838 for the contribution of some Leeds brushmakers to Chartist funds.

173 On the 'secret' or 'affiliated orders', see P. H. J. H. Gosden, *Self-Help: Voluntary Associations in Nineteenth-Century Britain* (London: Batsford, 1973) p. 27 ff; and Simon Cordery, *British Friendly Societies, 1750-1914* (Basingstoke and New York: Palgrave Macmillan, 2003).

174 *LM* 27 June 1834; 2 June 1832.

resolving that 'the name of a Black Sheep never be mentioned any more in this court'. The passwords, oaths, ceremonies, designations and organisational structures of Yorkshire trades' unions also owed much to the practices of the 'affiliated orders'. Indeed, John Tester later acknowledged that the forms and ritual of the Oddfellows (practised by the Rochdale flannel-weavers) became the basis of the clothiers' procedures.[175]

Third, the proponents of the new general unionism of the 1830s had learnt from the experiences of the combinations and conflicts of the previous decade, particularly the Bradford strike of 1825. John Corless, a leading local trade unionist, speaking to a meeting of NAPL members at Bradford in early 1832, reassured his listeners (probably combers) that 'They did not wish them … to rush into the fire, as was done in the union of 1825'.[176] The defeat of that year had undoubtedly had a sobering effect, but it had in no way diminished the instincts for trade and wider union organisation. Indeed, in some ways, it acted as a testing ground for inter-trade co-operation.

The story of the 'Great Strike' of 1825, 'a pitched battle between labour and capital' has been amply told elsewhere.[177] Its massive scale (over £14,000 spent on strike pay and thousands of combers, weavers and mill-workers thrown out of work), its duration (twenty-three weeks) and the regional and national links and advanced ideas it engendered, places it amongst the key industrial struggles of the early nineteenth century. The contest was not about 'the men's hostility to new machinery', but about wages and conditions.[178] However, it quickly developed into a dispute about the recognition of the innovative alliance between the combers and weavers organised within the Bradford 'Union Association of Wool-Combers and Stuff-Weavers'. As one hard-line employer frankly admitted in October: 'the advance required, when the struggle was once begun, … [was] secondary to the great object of breaking up this mischievous Combination'.[179] The masters' went to great lengths to secure this end. They won the war, when, with the onset of winter, their widening of the dispute and the start of extreme depression in the trade, the strikers were forced to turn in on any terms they could get. However, the trade unionists at least won the union recognition battle; a point which dismayed the same hard-line employers who believed that 'dispensing with a disclaimer' requiring workers to abjure the union, 'conceded nearly

---

175 'A Kirkburton Friendly Society', Documents of the Royal Foresters in Kirkburton, 1833 onwards, in the Tolson Memorial Museum, Huddersfield.; Gosden, *Self-Help*, p. 31; *LM* 5 July 1834.

176 *LM* 4 Mar. 1832.

177 TN 4 Sept. 1825; Smith, 'The Strike of 1825'; William Scruton, 'The Great Strike of 1825', *Bradford Antiquary*, (1880-8) pp. 67-73, and J. T. Ward, 'A Great Bradford Dispute', *Bradford Textile Society's Journal*, (1961-2), pp. 117-31. This and the following paragraphs draw on these accounts, but also a number of primary sources notably, John Tester, *History of the Commencement, Progress, and Termination of the Bradford Contest… etc.* (Bradford, 1826) MS in Bradford Public Library, Box 3, Case 39; local newspapers (mainly the *Bradford and Wakefield Chronicle* and the *Bradford Courier*); and the collection of documents in the BPL on the 'Bradford Combers and Weavers' Strike, 1825'.

178 Ward, 'A Great Bradford Dispute', p. 118.

179 Hindes and Patchett to Moulden (solicitor acting on behalf of the Associated Masters), 28 Oct. 1825 in BPL, Bradford Combers and Weavers' Strike, 1825, Box 3, Case No 38.

all that was worth contending for'.[180] The Minute Book of the Associated Masters' meetings also reveals that the strikers on occasions came perilously close to winning the dispute. Their eventual defeat was not an ignominious one. The strike, as even hostile newspapers admitted, had been an efficiently organised, extremely well-disciplined affair. John Tester, the combers' and weavers' leader, proudly claimed that 'He had heard of no disturbance during the strike except a base fellow of the name of Ryan having been sledged by an old woman or two'.[181]

In addition, the disputants and the wider working community in the textile district, and the country at large, showed remarkable resilience and solidarity. The conflict generated local 'unions of trades' and advanced ideas of 'a general Union among all workmen' and 'a Union of Unions', which re-appeared in the early 1830s during the key dispute of that era, the Derby strike of 1833-4.[182] As well as showing the need for greater secrecy, and the need to avoid a 'general strike' in a particular branch, the Bradford dispute illustrated the possibilities of intra- and inter-trade co-operation and tested the logistics of cross-regional mutual support.[183] Some of the lessons learnt were put into practice during the general unionism upsurge of the early 1830s.

The story of Yorkshire trades' unionism in this period is complex and often 'shadowy'.[184] The leading unions built on strong associative traditions stretching back into the eighteenth century. The clothiers, combers, and croppers (cloth-dressers) all had collective muscle memory of associative endeavour and of vigorously pursuing industrial aims.[185] Their emphasis on secrecy, ceremony and oaths also harked back to earlier days and mimicked the rituals of friendly societies. Yet in the mutual support networks that they established, the organisational frameworks they developed and the tactics they adopted, they were at the forefront of new conceptions of 'union'. General unionism was a vital stage in the process by which, in Malcolm Chase's words, 'Workers' associations, from being essentially reactive responses to economic circumstances, were becoming increasingly pro-active in pursuit of a creative role in the shaping of those circumstances'.[186] This duality, grounded in past traditions but

---

180 On the union's appreciation of their limited 'victory', see Walworth's speech in *LM* 12 Nov. 1825. On hardline employers' disappointment, see Hindes and Patchett to Moulden 28 Oct. 1825.

181 See *BWC* 15 Oct. 1825; *LM* 12 Nov. 1825, for the lack of any 'outrages'. For a 'union of trades' (Norwich), see *LM* 20 Aug. 1825; *LI* 10 Nov. 1825.

182 *BC* 22 Sept.; *BWC* 8 Oct. 1825.

183 John Tester's public admission that once the strike was won the union would seek to equalise other areas was a crucial factor in persuading reluctant masters in other worsted areas to turn-out their men and cut off 'supplies' of funds to Bradford.

184 Thompson, *Making*, p. 558.

185 For the long traditions of organisation, see Adrian Randall, *Before the Luddites: Custom, Community and Machinery in the English Woollen Industry, 1776-1809* (Cambridge, Cambridge University Press, 1991); Alan J. Brooke, 'Labour disputes and Trade Unions in the Industrial Revolution', in Hilary Haigh (ed.), *Huddersfield*, pp. 221-3; Thompson, *Making*, pp. 569-79.

186 Chase, *Early Trade Unionism*, pp. 112-3 and 114.

aspiring to a more equitable future world, lay at the heart of Yorkshire trades' unionism.

Its pre-eminent organisation, the 'Clothiers Union' was known by a variety of names: the 'Leeds Trades' Union', the 'Yorkshire Trades' Union', the 'Woollen Trades' Union of Leeds' or simply 'John Powlett', after the fictitious name of its secretary. The precise origins of this iteration of 'woollen' trade unionism and its exact links to the NAPL remain obscure.[187] G. D. H. Cole is probably right in asserting that, while some of the expansion of Yorkshire trades' unionism took place under the auspices of the NAPL, formal connections were weak. However, the inspiration of the NAPL model and the indirect connection through the Rochdale flannel-weavers (a woollen branch), who were themselves early members of the association, should not be ignored.[188] One of the avowed intentions of the new trades' union was the 'protection of labour', and this phrase and the 'National Association' title recur in references to trades' unionism in Yorkshire.[189] Certainly, following the Clothiers' successful prosecution of their long strike at Gott's iconic factory in October 1831, evidence of links with Lancashire become more plentiful. NAPL delegates were in the area in early 1832 and the association's Manchester committee kept a close eye on developments in West Riding. John Doherty, writing in the *Poor Man's Advocate*, following his resignation as secretary of the NAPL, talks of 'the management' of the association being 'passed into the hands of the spirited and intelligent operatives of Yorkshire'.[190]

The torch, if passed, was handled adroitly in the ensuing period. The victory at Gott's, the largest woollen mill in Leeds, led to the imposition of the union list of 'fair' prices across the town and its vicinity and paved the way for the expansion of the union into all areas of woollen cloth production. Important district committees operated in places such as Halifax, Huddersfield and Dewsbury, with local committees at Batley, Holmfirth, Morley and Slaithwaite.[191] These are merely the branches whose existence or activities are revealed in the local press. The scale, power and mode of operation of the union is illustrated in the evidence that emerged following the inquest on the murdered Farsley blackleg, James Benson, in December 1832. This revealed the provisory identity of 'John Powlett', the precautions the union took to ensure secrecy, and its elaborate processes for negotiating local 'statements of prices'. In answering one of 'Mercator's' probing questions during the subsequent battle of words

---

187 Sanders, 'John Douthwaite and "John Powlett"', p. 9; *Crisis* 12 Apr. 1834 (Owen). Simeon Pollard, the Leeds Trades' Union's secretary claimed to 'having been connected to the above Union for nearly five years', *LM* 22 Dec. 1832.

188 See *LM* 12 June 1830 and 14 June 1834 for connections with Rochdale flannel-weavers.

189 See, for example, *LM* 6 Oct. 1832, 28 July 1833.

190 *UPCI* 24 Mar, 7, 21, May 1832 (for the Manchester perspective on developments in Yorkshire); Cole, *Attempts at General Union*, p. 42, and Kirby and Musson, *The Voice of the People*, p. 233 support this conclusion. See also, *PMA* 21 Jan. 1832. Less flattering evidence of a Lancashire connection emerged in John Tester's later salacious allegation that a NAPL leader 'had been spending his days in the bowling alleys of Leeds and his nights in the brothels' in 1832, *LM* 7 June 1834.

191 *HHE* 26 Jan. 1833 (Halifax); *LM* 29 Mar. 1834 (Huddersfield); *LT* 7 Sept. 1833 (Dewsbury); *LM* 22 Sept.

about the purposes and tactics of trades' unions, the Clothiers' president also affirmed the underpinning strand of mutuality:

> ... Is it not a fundamental principle of the Union, that the work men engaged in particular branches of the woollen trade are to be supported by the workmen in all other branches of that trade, so that if a dispute should arise betwixt a master and any individual portion of his workmen, all the rest will support the demand of that portion, even to the extent of a general strike against such an employer?
>
> Answer: yes.[192]

The union had some notable successes. In the Huddersfield area local manufacturers agreed to pay at the Leeds benchmark and weavers and croppers restored their wages to former levels.[193] The union also won a protracted and exceptionally bitter, but 'most glorious victory over the Holmfirth Gentlemen', through the judicious use of co-operative self-employment.[194] The bullish assessment of a metropolitan delegate to the April 1833 Co-operative Congress in Huddersfield that 'the Trades' Unions of Huddersfield and the neighbourhood were 40,000 strong, and they had expended [£]27,000 in strikes within a very short time', may have exaggerated local strength; but six months later Robert Owen similarly pronounced that it was 'in many respects the centre of the operations of the working men in this country'.[195] Owen's assessment may also have been typically hyperbolic, but it accurately reflected the strength and importance of what Richard Oastler dubbed 'the workman's army'.[196]

The Clothiers' Union was widely recognised as a major organisation. The *Poor Man's Guardian* proclaimed it 'the Great Union ... in the North'; and its officials wielded significant power and influence regionally and nationally.[197] 'John Woodhouse, alias John Powlett', one of the 'Triumvirate of Secretaries and Treasurers (who sit daily at the White Hart Inn [Huddersfield])' was in all likelihood the 'J. Woodhouse' who attended the 'Special Meeting of Trades' Union Delegates' in London in February 1834 that formally established the GNCTU.[198] Simeon Pollard, the main incarnation of 'John Powlett', secretary of the Leeds Trades' Union, featured prominently in the regional press throughout the 1832-4 period and even the London-based *Poor Man's Guardian* celebrated how 'JOHN POWLETT, the *nom de guerre* of their Secretary, has struck terror into the heart of many a mill-tyrant and

---

192 *LM* 8 Dec 1832 - 2 Feb. 1833.

193 Alan J. Brooke, 'Labour disputes', p. 226.

194 For the strike see, *LM* Aug. - Oct. 1832; *Crisis* 4 May 1834; *Wakefield and Dewsbury Journal* 25 Oct. 1833; Brooke, 'Labour disputes', p. 226; *An Address to the Members of the Trades Union* (Huddersfield, 1833), p. 4.

195 *Crisis* 27 Apr. 1833, (J. R. Turner, the London United Trades' Association's delegate); *Crisis* 23 Nov. 1833.

196 Richard Oastler, *Facts and Plain Words on Everyday Subjects* (Leeds, 1832), p. 45.

197 *PMG* 2 Nov. 1833. On John Powlett, see Sanders, 'John Douthwaite and "John Powlett"', pp. 14-16.

198 *LM* 24 May 1834 (Letter of Joseph Threappleton, a paid informer); W. H. Oliver, 'The Consolidated Trades' Union of 1834', *Economic History Review* 17 (1964-5), pp. 79-80; Oliver, 'Organisations and Ideas', pp. 477-90; *LT* 7 June 1834; and *LT* 20 Feb. 1836 for a report on the death of John Woodhouse, aged thirty-three.

bull-headed manufacturer'.[199] Pollard later appeared on the public platform in Derby in early January 1834 to pledge support for the locked-out silk workers. Significantly, the meeting resolved that 'Delegates here present from Yorkshire, Birmingham and Nottingham, do take immediate steps to consolidate the different branches into a division of the Grand National Union'; though tantalisingly the Clothiers' Union always appeared to be on the verge of formal affiliation to the incipient national union.[200]

A second and more incontrovertible constituent of the GNCTU was the so-called Bradford Order, or the '"National Friendly Society" of operative Worsted Manufacturers, and other industrious operatives', to give the union its full title.[201] This was not, as earlier researchers have supposed, a 'minor Yorkshire union', but one of the major supra-regional unions of the 1832-4 period.[202] Contemporaries placed it alongside the Builders' Union and the 'Consolidated Union'. Factory Commissioner and bitter opponent of trades' unions, Edward Carleton Tufnell, judged it 'one of the most extensive in England', since it had spread beyond the confines of the West Riding worsted area to take in other areas of worsted or related manufacture.[203]

Like the woollen-based Clothiers' Union, its origins were closely tied to the NAPL. Bradford combers joined the National Association in March 1831 and, though there is little evidence that initial enthusiasm was converted into many paid-up members, important seeds had been sown.[204] In January 1832 a local correspondent reported that the NAPL was 'prospering there', and Peter Bussey confirmed that Bradford delegates would be attending a national association meeting in Manchester.[205] This vigorous engagement is corroborated by John Tester who returned to Bradford in April 1832 when Bussey, the Bradford District Secretary, was 'at the head of it ... receiving eighteen shillings a week ... for acting the part of an "agitator"'.[206] Shortly after Tester's reappearance he replaced Bussey as 'head' and, at the instigation of another local leader, the Bradford men changed tack and aligned themselves to the clothiers' model of organisation, with its structure of local lodges, district committees and grand lodges (and its 'Grand Council of Direction' and three

199 *PMG* 2 Nov. 1833.

200 *Pioneer* 25 Jan. 1834; *Crisis* 25 Jan. 1834.

201 E. C. Tufnell, *Character, Object and Effects of Trades' Unions; with some remarks on the law concerning them* (London: James Ridgway and Sons, 1834), p. 126.

202 Oliver, 'Organisations and Ideas', Chapter 7.

203 *Pioneer* 28 June 1834; Tufnell, *Character, Object and Effects*, pp. 60-1; *LT* 12 Apr. 1834.

204 *VP* 5 Mar., 16 Apr., 31 Aug. 1831 (see also Kirby and Musson, *Voice of the People*, p. 250). Significantly, a meeting of Leicester woolcombers in late December 1830, on the question of joining the NAPL, had been chaired by John Douthwaite, later the Bradford 'Grand Master' and GNCTU Executive Committee member, *VP* 8 Jan. 1831.

205 *PMA* 28 Jan. 1832; *LM* 4 Feb. 1832.

206 *LM* 5 July 1834. See also *UPCI* 31 Mar. 1832, *LP* 5 May 1832 for Bussey as a union agitator.

Grand officers).[207] It also adopted the rules and ceremonies of the Leeds clothiers; but essentially formed a distinct worsted-based trades' union.[208]

The worsted union's prosecution of a major dispute centring on the question of union recognition with their old adversaries Messrs. Hindes and Derham based at Dolphinholme near Lancaster, put an early strain on the nascent union's funds.[209] The practicalities of supporting the locked-out worsted operatives, mainly combers, at a distance of over fifty miles, proved challenging for the re-born union; and their position was not helped when John Tester disappeared with twenty-six pounds intended for the Dolphinholme workers. The long contest was eventually lost when the masters successfully trained up a cohort of imported blackleg labour. The dispute cost the union over £2,000, the majority coming from No 1 Bradford district.[210]

Hereafter, though spreading in the East Midlands, the union's resources were stretched thinly in the West Riding worsted area during 1833, a position not helped by the added encumbrance of the Derby strike.[211] The Yorkshire connection to Derby has rarely been touched upon in histories of the dispute, but it appears certain that 'initially at least the Bradford "Grand Council" thought of the Derby strike as their own.'[212] It may have been this link and the union's obvious weakness in early 1834 which prompted the leadership, possibly after the Keighley delegate conference of early February 1834, to seek a tie-in with wider general union schemes which were currently being canvassed, and to send John Douthwaite, the Union's Grand Master, to London to attend the trades' conference which inaugurated the GNCTU.[213]

The strong connections between Yorkshire trades' unionism (through Bradford, Leeds and Huddersfield) and the Consolidated Trades' Union have hitherto been

---

207 *LM* 5 July 1834. Tufnell, *Character, Object and Effects*, pp. 59-65; also, TNA: HO 40/32 f. 17, Bouverie to Philips, 12 Jan. 1834, Nottingham informant's report referring to the visit of 'Joshua Brookes, the Grand Master from Bradford' to the Nottinghamshire lodges.

208 *LM* 5 July 1834; Tufnell, *Character, Object and Effects*, p. 59.

209 The firm, Hindes and Derhams of Dolphinholme, Leeds and Bradford, was the successor concern to that which had advocated a hardline in 1825. On the strike, see *LM* Nov. 1832 - Jan. 1833 and 13 July 1833; and Tufnell, *Character, Object and Effects*, pp. 59-65.

210 For the allegations against Tester, see *LM* 27 June, 19 July 1834. Tufnell, *Character, Object and Effects*, p. 61. Tufnell asserts that the true figure cost was nearer £4,000.

211 On East Midlands connections, see A. Temple Patterson, *Radical Leicester: A History of Leicester 1780-1850* (Leicester: Leicester University College, 1954), p. 285; M. I. Thomis, *Politics and Society in Nottingham, 1783-1835* (Oxford: Blackwell, 1969), p. 70; TNA: HO 52/22, Cook to Lamb, 8 Oct 1833; TNA: HO 40/32 f. 7 Rolleston (?) to Bouverie; f. 17, Bouverie to Phillips, 12 Jan. 1834; f. 19, for a transcription of a circular to the Districts from Joseph Brookes [Brook?], Grand Secretary of the Bradford Grand Council, dated 3 Nov. 1833 (indicating that the union cannot afford any more disputes).

212 Oliver, 'Organisation and Ideas', quoting HO 40/32 f. 17 makes the connection. See also *Pioneer* 28 Dec. 1833 for the Derby union structure which corresponds to that cited (for the worsted union) by Tufnell, *Character, Object and Effects*, p. 126 ff; Sanders, 'John Douthwaite and "John Powlett"', p. 13.

213 See *HG* 8 Feb. 1834. The Keighley meeting is referred to obliquely in TNA; HO 52/24, Adnutt(?) to Melbourne, 15 Mar. 1834 and HO 40/32 f. 19, transcription of Joseph Brookes' circular. On John Douthwaite and his significant role in Yorkshire trades' unionism, see Sanders, 'John Douthwaite and "John Powlett"', pp. 3-4.

largely ignored; but, with Douthwaite forming one of the five Executive Council members, it is clear that with the worsted-based union was a key constituent of the GNCTU.[214] This eminence is confirmed in the choice of Douthwaite to chair of a Birmingham 'Grand Meeting of the Trades' Unions' on the Dorchester sentence in late March 1834.[215] The Bradford leader remained an important player in the troubled, complex history of the GNCTU before returning to the West Riding in 1835.[216]

The failure of the GNCTU marked the end of the first phase of what Sidney and Beatrice Webb called the 'revolutionary period' of trade unionism. Malcolm Chase has highlighted the exceptional scale of industrial conflict nationally during this time.[217] The textile district was at the heart of this unrest, particularly in the period from spring 1831 to summer 1834. Beyond the two flagship unions covering the woollen and worsted manufacture, other branches and trades were also part of the heady general union mix. George Beaumont, self-proclaimed 'founder of the fancy union' alleged that he had helped to set up thirty-six lodges of a revived Fancy Weavers' Union in the villages to the south and east of Huddersfield. By the summer of 1833 the union had secured significant wage increases.[218] The Linen Trades' Union, initially established by the flax-dressers of Leeds but also incorporating linen-weavers, similarly took its inspiration and structures from the Clothiers.[219] The recently unionised but traditionally active Leeds stuff dyers, with their own fictitious secretary, 'John Polti' became the centre of a bitterly contested dispute.[220]

A brief summary of another vicious conflict in Leeds, involving carpet weavers, provides an insight into the confrontational atmosphere and the communal solidarity of the general union era. The origins of the dispute with John Howard dated back to 1828, but came to a head in May 1833 when weavers successfully won an advance from local carpet manufacturers.[221] Howard, a major employer, however, resisted. He responded by prosecuting ten workers for leaving their work unfinished, securing them a month's hard labour in Wakefield's House of Correction. In Peter Bussey's words, one old man, who had worked for Howard and his father for thirty years, 'enriching the coffers of this manufacturer, enabling him to bring up his family in idleness and extravagance, to prey upon the vitals of the working classes' now had 'consolation' of spending 'the last few days of his life in a loathsome dungeon'.[222]

---

214 On this connection, see *BO* 5 June; *LT* 7 June 1834 (Bussey's letter); TNA: HO 64/15, Ball (a London spy) to Roe, 5 Apr. 1834; Oliver, 'Organisation and Ideas', Appendix I, pp. 477-90 (report on the inaugural meeting of the GNCTU); OC No. 684, William Pare to Owen, 16 Apr. 1834.

215 *Crisis* 5 Apr. 1834; *LM* 12 Apr. 1834.

216 Sanders, 'John Douthwaite and "John Powlett"', pp. 29 and 33-4.

217 S. and B. Webb, *The History of Trade Unionism*, p. 113; Chase, *Early Trade Unionism*, pp. 129-30.

218 Brooke, 'Labour disputes', pp. 226-7; TNA: HO 52/25, Deposition of George Beaumont, 2 Jan. 1834.

219 *VP* 7 Apr. 1832; Chase, *Early Trade Unionism*, pp. 119-21.

220 For the dyers' turn-out, see *LT* and *LM* 4 July – 21 Sept, 1833 and Morris, 'Kitson', p. 190.

221 *Gauntlet* 7 July 1833 (Peter Bussey's letter); *LM* 4, 11 May 1833.

222 *HHE* 18 May 1833; *Gauntlet* 7 July 1833: *LT* 6 June 1833.

On their release the imprisoned workers 'were escorted into this town and through its principal streets, in an open coach adorned with laurels, evergreens etc. and attended with a band of music and a great number of their friends and well-wishers', including 'the tailors' trades' union'. Howard, undaunted, persisted with his 'endeavours to break up all unions' and took out further warrants, resulting in four more workers being sentenced to two months' hard labour. While Peter Bussey sought wider support, some of the weavers took matters into their own hands. In late June Joseph Ellis was imprisoned for assaulting three 'black sheep' working for Howard; and the following week, in a 'DIABOLICAL OUTRAGE' a mare belonging to Howard being stabbed and bruised. The weavers nevertheless enjoyed widespread sympathy and the liberation of the imprisoned four was marked with another 'numerous procession' this time involving striking dyers, whose dispute now took centre stage.[223] The end of the seventeen-week contest with Howard was signalled in late summer with the manufacturer's triumphal paid letter outlining his successful recruitment of new workers and a defiant response from the carpet-weavers' pseudonymous secretary, 'John Potter'.[224]

Beyond the constant struggles of the unions' leadership to maintain internal discipline, what is most notable about the trades' union upsurge of 1831-4 is not just its strength in the textile branches, but also the breadth of its appeal. The range of trades which associated for 'the protection' of their 'labour' is remarkable. In addition to the various textile unions, it included all the building trades and main urban artisan groups, also coal-miners, machine makers, 'journeymen smiths', steam-engineers, iron foundry workers, quarrymen, brick-makers; and rural workers such as the Idle (the place, not the predilection) 'United Delvers' and the '1st Lodge of Operative Agriculturalists' of Farnley Tyas, who subscribed to the Derby Fund and poignantly displayed a banner at a Dorchester protest meeting.[225]

As the *Voice of the West-Riding* noted in November 1833, 'The "Trades' Unions" form a new element in society'.[226] The variety of trades involved, their penchant for secrecy and ceremony, and the undercurrent of coercive behaviour collectively spooked local magistrates and employers. They responded with placards, propaganda, prosecutions and their own weapon – the imposition of 'the document', requiring workers to disown their unions or face losing their jobs.

The story of the trades' union moral panic in 1832-3, the deployment of the employers' own '2,000 horsepower Union' the following year and the subsequent decimation of Yorkshire trades' unionism has been told elsewhere.[227] However, a few aspects of the narrative are worth exploring further.

The first is the strength of the forces that the trades' unions were up against: a largely hostile press; vigilant authorities willing to employ spies and informants to

---

223 *LT* 13, 27 June; 4 July 1833; *Gauntlet* 7 July 1833.
224 *LM* 31 Aug., 7 Sept. 1833. It is not clear under whose jurisdiction the strike took place. Bussey's involvement suggests that the carpet weavers were aligned with the worsted Bradford Order.
225 *Pioneer* 29 Mar. 1834; *BO* 24 Apr. 1834.
226 *VWR* 9 Nov. 1833.
227 Sanders, 'John Douthwaite and "John Powlett"', pp. 18-33.

undermine the unions; and a manufacturing class prepared to establish its own union to break those of the operatives. As Richard Oastler noted in relation to the final conflict in summer 1834, 'the "Leeds strike" is a strike of the Masters, not of the men'.[228] The groundwork for this pivotal assault had been laid the previous summer when master dyers responded to the demands of their workers by presenting 'the document', and instituting a mutual bond of £500 to be forfeit if any master employed a trade unionist.[229] They were quickly followed by a number of woollen manufacturers who stopped their mills and in the words of a *Pioneer* editorial 'threatened [their operatives] with worse than the guillotine – "loss of bread" – unless they denounce the holy compact of defensive alliance'.[230]

The tactic was not an immediate success and both parties entered phoney war period for the remainder of the year. With trade poor and resources stretched by disputes in Leicester and support for Derby, the unions approached the new year in a precarious position. They had cause for concern. Internal frictions exposed in the Huddersfield by-election may have exacerbated fraying allegiances. A local magistrate, commenting on the state of the trades' union in the Dewsbury area in March 1834, believed it to be in decline with many willing to renounce it 'if they had a favourable opportunity', adding 'the committeemen who make a good livelihood by agitation are of course active in keeping it up'.[231]

A second key event – the prosecution of the Dorchester labourers – exposed that vulnerability. The effect was immediate and electrifying; in part because Yorkshire unions were directly implicated in the spread of general unionism to Dorset, but mainly because secrecy and oath-taking formed integral parts of local trades' unionism. Joseph Brook, the Bradford Order's Grand Secretary, told a Dorchester protest meeting that he had committed the offence for which the Tolpuddle men were arraigned hundreds of times.[232]

The Northern military commander, General Bouverie, who had deployed spies to ascertain the state of the unions, reported 'a considerable schism amongst the Unions' on the question of oaths – many wanting their abandonment, but the leaders allegedly needing their force.'[233] This ambivalence is evident in the views of James Morgan, a woolsorter and trade union activist, who admitted that he was 'not one of those who are for much pageantry, or idle show', whilst arguing for the essentially harmless nature of the union's 'forms and ceremonies'.[234]

There is plenty of evidence to suggest that G. D. H. Cole was wrong to suppose that the Leeds Union never administered oaths. His downplaying of the secretive and ceremonial aspects of local trades' unionism misses the point that they were integral

---

228 Oastler Coll., 3, 29, pamphlet dated 10 June 1834.

229 For the Dyers' turn-out, see *LT* and *LM* 4 July - 21 Sept. 1833; Morris, 'Kitson', 190. The union was called the 'Society of Operatives, Dyers, Singers, Dressers and Makers-Up in the Stuff Department', *LT* 4 July 1833.

230 *LT* 24 Aug 1833; *Pioneer* 12 Oct. 1833.

231 West Yorkshire Archives Service (WYAS), Leeds, Harewood Papers (HP), Box 2, Armitage to Harewood, 17 Mar. 1834.

232 *VWR* 12 Apr. 1834.

233 TNA: HO 40/32 f. 58, Bouverie to Phillips 14 Apr. 1834.

234 *LT* 19 July 1834. James Morgan (1805-1851+).

features, and part of the attraction, of the associational culture of the period.[235] They also had practical benefits. James Morgan contended that they were 'in some measure the causes of why our lodges are governed in silence without drunken squabs, or pothouse differences'.[236] More strategically, these practices were 'a means of reinforcing loyalty and solidarity in contexts of collective financial vulnerability and individual economic precarity'. Ritualism, in Malcolm Chase's words, acted as 'a form of cultural mortar that bound memberships together in [a] shared sense of purpose, responsibility and obligation'.[237]

The exceedingly well-timed Dorchester blow was quickly followed by a concerted West Riding masters' offensive, in the second week of May, involving the widespread presentation of 'the document'. The decisive conflict in Leeds, a lock-out of unionised workers, 'was waged with extreme ferocity in an atmosphere of class antagonism and bitterness'.[238] Within a few months the Unions generally were said to be 'in a state bordering on decomposition.'; and the local stamped press jubilantly reported the convivial decommissioning of union 'boxes' and the death of 'John Powlett'.[239]

Defeat brought the usual recriminations, with the Trades' Union President having to deny allegations that committee members 'had run away to America; ... [or] had got a fine public house at Huddersfield or Manchester'.[240] The reality was more prosaic. Following in the wake of the 'commercial orders' which had been optimistically floated a few months earlier, self-manufacturing 'Co-operative Lodges' were now envisaged as a defensive tactic to employ victimized or unemployed union members.[241] One such venture, 'The Leeds Joint Stock Trading Company' ('Woollen Manufacturers') which included Major Schofield, 'an officer in the union', amongst its shareholders, appears to have survived until summer 1836, but this in all probability was an outlier.[242] By the end of summer 1834 the West Riding trades' unions had effectively been smashed. The defeat was both daunting and debilitating and left a lasting legacy. The implications of its decimation were quickly appreciated. A Huddersfield 'Co-operator' writing in February 1835 noted, 'The Union is dead; the masters know it and will now take advantage of their mechanical strength and the

---

235 Cole, *Attempts at General Union*, pp. 73-5. For evidence about oaths and the ritualistic side of trades' unionism, see, for example, *LM* 14 June 1834 (Tester) and TNA: HO 44/26, James Hartley's testimony in, Harewood to Melbourne, 9 Mar 1833. On this see also, Sanders, 'John Douthwaite and "John Powlett"', pp. 16-18; Chase, *Early Trade Unionism*, p. 137; Thompson, *Making*, pp. 558-9.

236 *LT* 19 July 1834.

237 Chase, *Early Trade Unionism*, p. 137.

238 Sanders, 'John Douthwaite and "John Powlett"', p. 30.

239 *LM* 5 July 1834, *HHE* 15 May, 14 Aug. 1834.

240 *LT* 21 June 1834.

241 *LT* 14, 21, 28 June 1834. On commercial orders, see below, pp. 227-9.

242 Schofield/Scholefield was a regular speaker at the Leeds unionists' outdoor meetings in late May and June 1834. An official notice of the 'Court for the relief of insolvent debtors' lists Schofield, formerly a publican and weaver, as the salesman of the company. Other shareholders included two journeymen cloth-dressers and two journeymen cloth makers (one also a publican), see *LI* 11 June 1836.

workman's weakness. Thus you see the moneyocratic car moves on, crushing the millions beneath its iron wheels'.[243]

The Yorkshire unions' obsession with secrecy makes it difficult to ascertain exactly how far the strands of intra- and inter-trade connections extended at the height of the general union upsurge. Contemporaries certainly thought that they were extensive. 'Mercator', writing in the *Leeds Mercury* in 1832, believed that the Leeds Trades' Union's 'machinery is constructed with admirable skill, and worked with consummate tact', and that it covered operatives in 'all trades' not just woollen workers. A sympathetic manufacturer was similarly convinced that 'the Trades' Union extends itself to all trades'.[244] G. D. H. Cole suggests that the Leeds Union originated with an attempt to form a 'General Union of Trades' and hints that it included non-textile sectors. There is some contemporary evidence to support this view of the Leeds Trades' Union being a wider local general union.[245] Similarly, the *Pioneer* (originally the builders' paper) talks of the Bradford Order including 'a great variety of different trades', and the catch-all inclusion of, 'and other industrious operatives' in its title supports this reading of the potential breadth of the union. Certainly, Peter Bussey was particularly amused in April 1834 by the fact that the 'general union' had spread to the Low Moor ironworks outside Bradford owned by the father of the local Whig MP, John Hardy.[246]

The extent of trade union expansion is not in doubt, but the precise nature and extent of the linkages remain unclear. In June 1833 the *Halifax Guardian* bemoaned the fact that 'the system of combination in every branch of trade and mechanics appears to be quite the fashion' in Huddersfield.[247] There are also tantalising indications of the existence of formal structures such as the monthly committee of delegates from 'all the trades' in Leeds, whose 'practice' was to lay aside 'all frivolous distinctions as respects the particular division to which they belong'.[248] Similar inter-trade collaboration is suggested in regional meetings, like the October 1833 meeting of 'the various District and Provincial Committees connected with the Trades' Union'; or the half-yearly meeting of trades' union delegates from across the country held in Keighley in February 1834 that two missionaries from John Fielden's National Regeneration Society (NRS) addressed.[249] The main players such as the clothiers, worsted workers and building trades were certainly in close touch with each other.

---

243 *LT* 14 Feb. 1835.

244 *LM* 10 Nov; 1 Dec. 1832.

245 Cole, *Attempts at General Union*, p. 59; see, for example, *LM* 10 Nov. 1832 and the list of 'turned in' workers at Gott's (see p. 87, above).

246 *Pioneer* 28 June 1834; *LT* 12 Apr. 1834, the ironworks were owned by the father of the local Whig MP, John Hardy. Bussey was now once again Secretary of the Bradford Union.

247 *Crisis* 27 Apr. 1833. Turner's estimates are exaggerated, but his broad impression of local trade union strength is accurate. *HG* 15 June 1833.

248 *Pioneer* 30 Nov. 1833.

249 *HHE* 17 Oct. 1833; Kirby and Musson, *The Voice of the People*, p. 286; *HG* 8 Feb. 1834. The visit of the delegates promoting the NRS' 'Eight Hour Plan' probably coincided with the bi-annual Grand Lodge meeting of the Bradford Order. John Fielden of Todmorden, MP for Oldham (1832-47) was a cotton factory owner sympathetic to many radical causes including ten hours, press freedom, repeal of the new Poor Law and universal suffrage.

However, apart from the *Pioneer*'s reference to a delegate committee from 'all the trades' meeting monthly in both Leeds and Sheffield, there is little definitive evidence that trades' unions linked formally with other similar bodies locally, in a formal proto-Trades' Council type of organisation. Malcolm Chase is probably correct in characterising the Leeds Trades' Union as 'a loosely connecting affiliation'.[250] It is clear that extensive structures existed for funds to be shared and distributed, underpinned by the notion, in Peter Bussey's words, of 'one trade assisting another'. Adherence to this fundamental principle may have lain behind Bussey's attempts, as one of 'the few remaining veterans who still adhere to the Trades' Union', to liquidate the debts contracted by the union in early autumn 1834.[251] However, it still remains uncertain how far such linkages went beyond solidarity and mutuality.

In many ways, though, a fixation on the precise extent of formal inter-union structures and cross-regional linkages is a red herring. The sharing of the similar titles and the same system of organisation, of itself, symbolised the strengthening pre-existing ties and traditions of mutual aid and co-operation; but as Malcolm Chase emphasises, 'The general unionism of 1829-34 was about more than just mutual support'.[252] Excessive attention to official bodies and paid-up membership misses much of the excitement and importance of the trades' union upsurge of the early 1830s. Trades' unionism was a system or style of trade union organisation which spread rapidly amongst a wide cross-section of different trades in the early 1830s. It was also an idea and a movement with which large numbers of people, whether or not they were subscribing members, felt an affiliation. The trades' union, in the phrase of Leeds radical stalwart, William Rider, was 'the apple of the operatives eye'.[253] Groups of workers in related occupations built on often pre-existing, separate societies to form their own trades' union which may or may not have linked formally with similar configurations. It was this extended and highly secretive network of aligned unions which frightened middle-class observers. Many trades' union leaders and adherents clearly felt themselves to be part of a wider endeavour. Although most were never formally part of a single national body, they nevertheless adopted common practices and linked together 'in an informal movement whose seemingly Government-endorsed decimation left a residue of bitterness'.[254]

The legacy of this epoch was not, then, organisational. Samuel Bower jnr., writing three years later, reflected on emasculated unions and a pivotal loss: 'It is ... true, that a great portion of the working classes still maintain in their respective trades, the old protective and strike system, but even that is sufficiently exploded to render it impossible that it should ever again become the focus of a national movement'.[255] Rather it was in ideas, people and politics that the impact was felt. As the *Poor Man's Guardian* wrote defiantly a year after the defeat:

---

250 *Pioneer* 30 Nov. 1833; Chase, *Early Trade Unionism*, p. 119. A 'Sheffield Trades' General Union' existed as early as March 1830.

251 *LT* 12 Apr. 1834; 20 Sept. 1834.

252 Chase, *Early Trade Unionism*, p. 114.

253 Oastler Coll., Vol.3, 12, Rider's 'Observations... etc.' (1833).

254 Sanders, 'John Douthwaite and "John Powlett"', p. 37.

255 *LT* 16 Sept. 1837.

Although the visible existence of these once general and powerful bodies is no more, the elements of which they were formed... and the object at which they aimed, are still in existence... Although the forms, the name, the organisation of the thing is gone, the soul, the elements, the men, the intelligence remain.[256]

The 'soul' was articulated through a range of interlocking ideas. These included a general demand for equalisation and protection of labour, based on traditional notions of equity and fairness. These increasingly coalesced with more sharply defined radical tenets to become part of the system of ideas which heightened a sense of class awareness. Behind these ideas, expressed in trade unionists' speeches and letters, lay an alternative moral and economic interpretation of contemporary trends, underpinned by an assertion of labour as the source of all wealth. This viewed the unprotected operatives as being dragged into 'wretchedness, poverty, misery and degradation' by wage reductions enforced by 'our cruel, ambitious and slave-driving task masters.'[257] Low wages, long hours and child labour caused by overproduction, excess competition and the spread of machinery were the product of 'the inordinate love of gain' by some masters who thereby harmed the operative and 'the upright and kindhearted manufacturer'. The latter were becoming rarer, resulting in the creation of 'two distinct classes': 'the very rich and the very, very poor.'[258] The only solution was working-class union. In the words of a Huddersfield woollen weaver, 'Let us no longer be guided by the degrading principle, "*Take care of number one;*" but let us be "EACH FOR ALL AND ALL FOR EACH," and then our Union will be formed on a firm foundation.' This would secure a 'fair remuneration for labour'; and the higher, fairer wages, by boosting domestic consumption, would benefit all.[259] These ideas found practical expression in co-operative endeavours, equitable labour exchange schemes and the adoption of co-operative production practice by trades' unions in proto-syndicalist 'commercial orders'.[260] All flourished briefly at this time.

A few of 'the men' to whom the *Poor Man's Guardian* alluded had been lost prematurely or had deserted the union cause.[261] However, many, including important figures like Joshua Hobson, John Douthwaite, Peter Bussey, William Hill, George White, Joseph Firth, William Rider and Joseph Brook survived and went on to play a leading role in subsequent campaigns and early Chartism. The lessons they learnt and which they doggedly repeated in succeeding agitations was that working population had been duped by the Whig-liberals and that the only effective remedy was 'the justice and humanity of the radical cause'.[262]

---

256 *PMG* 1 Aug. 1835.
257 *PMG* 11 Aug. 1832.
258 *LM* 29 Dec. 1832 (letter of Edward Edwards, President of the Trades' Union).
259 *PMG* 11 Aug. 1832; *UPCI* 24 Mar. 1832 (Peter Bussey's letter). See also the newspaper controversy about 'Trades' Unions', *LM* Oct.-Dec. 1832.
260 On 'commercial orders', see Chase, *Early Trade Unionism*, pp. 126-8; and above, pp. 227-9.
261 Thomas Roberts, President of the Leeds Trades' Union was a victim of the 1832 cholera epidemic. Simeon Pollard, secretary of the Leeds Trades' Union, and John Woodhouse, secretary of the Huddersfield Trades' Union, died in 1834 and 1835, aged 24 and 33, respectively. Key deserters included George Beaumont and John Tester.
262 *LT* 14 Feb. 1835.

As Malcolm Chase has noted, 'the public declaration of affinity and shared purpose that general unionism entailed was in itself a profoundly political statement'.[263] The annihilation of Yorkshire trades' unionism amplified this legacy. It permeated all subsequent agitational endeavours. The organisational lessons drawn from the mobilisation of the trades' unions, the kudos that local leaders gained though their defence of the unions and their experience of confronting perceived government repression all fed into the tactical and ideological mindset that informed early Chartism. The struggles of the early 1830s convinced them that the most effective way of opposing their formidable political and economic opponents was by embracing 'real radical principles'.[264]

Samuel Bower jnr., a Bradford radical and Owenite socialist, reflecting in 1837 on 'five years of excitement and exertion', cited the formation of the Trades' Union' as one of the 'two great sources upon which ... [the working classes] ... had successively confidently relied' for 'amelioration'. The other was political reform.[265] It is to the leaders, organisations and ideas generated in this second major sphere of working-class endeavour – political radicalism – that we must turn for our first major study.

---

263 Chase, *Early Trade Unionism*, p. 107.
264 *LT* 31 May; 24 May; 14 June 1834.
265 *LT* 16 Sept. 1837.

3

Popular Radicalism and Reform, 1829-32

> There was an old saying, that there is a lightening in shifting, even if it is for the worse (*laughter*); but as to the difference betwixt the Whigs and the Tories, he remembered the conduct of the former at the time when the Reform Bill was passing. He then lived at Holmfirth. The Whigs then said, "Come lads, we have a great stone to mount, and except the labouring Radicals will assist us, we cannot get at the top. (*Laughter.*) Help us, and we will assist you." As soon as they got at the top of it, instead of letting the Radicals get up too, they chopped off their fingers as they were making the attempt. (*Cheers.*)

Luke Bradley's vivid imagery at a Huddersfield meeting in aid of the 'Dorchester Victims' in July 1835 illustrates just how quickly and how firmly the memory and myth of the great Whig betrayal became fixed in popular radical consciousness.[1] A rich store of what Tara Yosso calls 'linguistic capital' was accumulated in the close communities of the region and was readily passed down the generations.[2]

There were plenty of stories to draw on. The West Riding had long and proud radical traditions, including both 'constitutional' and 'conspiratorial' elements. Indeed, the textile district had been one of the chief centres of agitation and direct action in the post-war period;[3] so when popular radicalism re-emerged from its long, but

---

1 *PMG* 11 July 1835. Luke Bradley (1803?-1870?), a cloth-dresser and preacher based in Lockwood, Huddersfield, delivered Chartist sermons in the 1840s (e.g. *NS* 21 Jan. 1843) and was later active in the temperance movement (*HCH* 12 July 1851).

2 Tara J. Yosso, 'Whose culture has capital? A critical race theory discussion of Community Cultural Wealth', *Race Ethnicity and Education*, 8 (2005), p. 79.

3 John A. Hargreaves, '"A Metropolis of Discontent": Popular Protest in Huddersfield c.1780-c.1850', in E. A. Hilary Haigh (ed.), *Huddersfield, A Most Handsome Town: Aspects of the History and Culture of a West Riding Town* (Huddersfield: Kirklees Cultural Services, 1992), pp. 191-208; Malcolm Chase, *1820: Disorder and Stability in the United Kingdom* (Manchester: Manchester University Press, 2013), pp. 115-7, 122-6.

fruitful hibernation towards the end of the 'silent' 1820s, old leaders and rivalries, old enthusiasms and banners re-emerged.[4] Equally, the time-honoured critique of 'old corruption' was voiced in yet more strident terms. However, the extent of direct continuity should not be exaggerated. The radical language of 1829-32 was richer and more nuanced after the gains of 'the decade of the silent insurrection'; and, though a few honoured veterans once more took up the radical reins the profile of local leadership was now more extensive and more broadly based.[5] The reform period saw the emergence of a new generation of radical leaders who were to remain key local figures throughout the ensuing decade and beyond.

The historiography of the reform era is something of an enigma. On the one hand, in Philip Lockley's phrase, it is 'a moment in modern British history fraught with familiarity'; on the other, significant questions remain unanswered.[6] One of these is the precise role of local working-class leaders and political organisations in the unfolding drama.

The key episodes of the main storyline are well known. Political historians from J. R. M. Butler and Norman Gash to Michael Brock and Derek Fraser have sketched the general background to the Reform Bill and its passage; noting the role of the aspiring middle class, the splits in the aristocratic elite and the dilemmas faced by radical reformers over whether to support the measure.[7] Interpretations of these key events were refracted through a variety of Whiggish, 'tory' and Marxists lenses. More recent work generated by proponents of 'new political history' has challenged many of the assumptions of previous generations and has initiated debates about the extent to which the 1832 Reform Act fuelled significant democratic advances, merely accelerated existing processes or even hindered change.[8] Whatever their precise

---

4   Some of the main West Riding radical leaders of the post-war years, such as James Mann and Thomas Mason of Leeds, re-appeared in the agitations of the reform era; but only Mann appears to have retained his former eminence. A few of the era's key splits had also been pre-figured in the post-war agitation: for example, between Mann/Baines in 1819, and Mann/Brayshaw, (a supporter of Carlile) in 1821-2. Other veterans, like Thomas Vevers of Huddersfield, William Smith of Bradford or Thomas Leadbetter of Kirkheaton, also featured on the popular platform. For the bringing out of dusty old banners at a Leeds RRA meeting see *LI* 3 June 1830.

5   John Belchem, *'Orator' Hunt: Henry Hunt and English Working Class Radicalism* (London: Breviary Stuff, 2012), p. 127, talks of how the 'new ideology' based on the labour theory of value 'did not displace the old attitudes, concepts and aims: it reinforced them'. See also, Peter Gurney. 'The Democratic Idiom: Languages of Democracy in the Chartist Movement', *The Journal of Modern History*, 86, 3 (2014), p. 570, on popular radicals' use of 'the relatively new, future-oriented language of democracy'.

6   Philip Lockley, *Visionary Religion and Radicalism in Early Industrial England: From Southcott to Socialism* (Oxford: Oxford University Press, 2012), chapter 9.

7   J. R. M. Butler, *The Passing of the Great Reform Bill* (London: Longmans, Green and Co, 1914); Norman Gash, *Politics in the Age of Peel* (London: Longmans, 1953); Michael Brock, *The Great Reform Act* (London: Hutchinson, 1973); Derek Fraser, 'The Agitation for Parliamentary Reform', in J. T. Ward (ed.), *Popular Movements c.1830-1850* (London: Macmillan, 1970), pp. 54-77.

8   James Vernon, *Politics and the People: A Study in English Political Culture 1815-1867* (Cambridge: Cambridge University Press, 1993); Frank O'Gorman, 'Campaign Rituals and

historiographical lineage or ideological persuasion, however, most histories of the
Reform Bill era tend to concentrate on politics 'from above' and on the mobilisation of
public opinion and mass support by middle-class reformers, the eventual beneficiaries
of the measure. In general, little attention has been paid to the primarily working-class
radical agitations and organisations of the period.[9]

This gap has long been recognised. More than two generations ago Asa Briggs
spoke of the need to pay attention to these 'crucial years ... to clarify the matrix of
radical movements out of which Chartism emerged'. Subsequently, Dorothy
Thompson argued that the 'whole question of the popular end of the Reform Bill
agitation of 1831-2' needed to be examined before an adequate history of Chartism
could be written.[10] That plea remains largely unanswered. Nancy Lopatin-Lummis's
work on political unions has thrown fresh and long overdue light on a neglected key
feature of the period; but her necessarily broad-brush approach inevitably misses
something of the nuances and complexities of the local context and the extent to
which reforming leadership and organisational structures were contested.[11] Katrina
Navickas' assessment that, 'The historiography of popular politics and the 1832
Reform Act remains thin', still remains valid.[12] This is no more so true than in relation
to one of the fascinating sub-plots of the drama: the role of working-class radical
leaders and their supporters in the maelstrom of political intrigue and activity. This is
an aspect that the ensuing exploration hopes to illuminate.

The chapter falls neatly into two halves, with the parliamentary recess of
Christmas/New Year 1830-1 forming a convenient dividing line. The first part, after
briefly tracing the political and economic background, looks at the limited re-
awakening of popular radicalism in 1829-30. In particular it examines the
development of an overtly political response to distress in two areas, Huddersfield and
Leeds, and traces the emergence of political unions here and elsewhere in the textile
district. It then follows the rising tide of political interest and activity stimulated by
national developments, the election of 1830 and the news of revolution in France.

Ceremonies: The Social Meaning of Elections in England, 1780-1860', *Past and Present*, 135
(1992), pp. 79-115; Philip Salmon, *Electoral Reform at Work: Local Politics and National Parties,
1832-1841* (Woodbridge: Boydell Press, 2002).

9   Exceptions include Fraser, 'The Agitation for Parliamentary Reform', who brings out the
    important working-class strands and lessons drawn; Asa Briggs 'The Parliamentary Reform
    Movement in Three English Cities', *Cambridge Historical Journal*, 10 (1952), pp. 292-317,
    who emphasises the popular radical contribution; and Iorwerth Prothero, *Artisans and Politics
    in Early Nineteenth-Century London, John Gast and His Times* (Folkstone: Dawson, 1979), pp.
    268-99, who traces the radical agitations in London.
10 Asa Briggs 'The Parliamentary Reform Movement', quoted in Dorothy Thompson,
    'Chartism as a Historical Subject' in *Society for the Study of Labour History Bulletin*, 20 (1970),
    pp. 11-12.
11 Nancy Lopatin-Lummis, *Political Unions, Popular Politics and the Great Reform Act of 1832*
    (Basingstoke: Palgrave Macmillan, 1999).
12 Katrina Navickas, *Protest and the Politics of Space and Place, 1789-1848* (Manchester:
    Manchester University Press, 2016), p. 121, fn. 1.

The second half, on the reform crisis of 1831-2, is necessarily briefer since this period has been covered extensively elsewhere. It focuses in particular on working-class responses and radical leadership at four key pinch points of political excitement: firstly, the publication of the Reform Bill and its reception by working-class radicals in Spring 1831; secondly, the period in October and November 1831 when the House of Lords rejected the Bill and ultra-radicals temporarily seized the initiative; thirdly, 'The SIX DAYS of May 1832' when the Bill was again in jeopardy; and finally, the build up to, and holding of, the first reformed elections.

The chapter focuses on the 'popular end' of reform era agitations and seeks to provide a detailed account of radical groups and their leaders. It follows conventional wisdom in emphasizing the importance of the agitations of these years in conditioning later activities and establishing future leadership, organisational patterns and tactics. But it also acknowledges the very real ideological and tactical dilemmas which radicals of all persuasions faced at the time. Equally, it highlights the wider concerns and interests of local leaders and their constituents. Although the focus is necessarily on 'political' organisations and campaigns, these are broadly defined and recognized as being just one of a number of manifestations of working-class endeavour. As the previous and subsequent chapters seek to show, co-operative, trade union and short time organisations and campaigns drew on a common reservoir of support and some of the same leaders. Although energies and enthusiasms might flow from one cause to another, the different movements were rarely competing rivals. As a Birmingham co-operator wrote in April 1831:

> The cause of co-operation ... has been much cramped by the agitated state of politics. Reform is now so loudly called by the people, they have no breath to speak a word for Co-operation. Not that I wish to bring the two in opposition, I believe they are streams flowing from the same fountain – a desire for Improvement.[13]

A 'desire for Improvement' underpinned the varied working-class radical campaigns of 1829-32. These, the chapter argues, were crucial to the development of the multi-faceted movements which came together in Chartism. They gave a number of community-based leaders the experience of organising and directing an independent working-class agitation. For them and their supporters the pre-reform campaigns, the provisions of the Bill itself and the local conflicts and controversies which marked its progress all served to confirm a hatred of the aristocracy and to heighten a sense of separateness from the middle class. Leaders who had consistently advocated the full radical programme retained and later proudly displayed their scars from their conflicts with the dominant Whig-liberals and their supporters. Leaders who had gone along with the middle-class reformers in the hope and expectation that it would be 'the first step to an emancipating series' were left with feelings of betrayal and shame and a sense of having been used as a 'reserve army'. Both sets of leaders absorbed what they saw as the key tactical lesson of the reform agitation – the potency of an open

---

13 *Carpenter's Political Letters and Pamphlets*, No. 30, *A Political Observer*, 16 Apr. 1831. The Birmingham man, John Powell, occasionally corresponded with John Heaton, a leading Huddersfield co-operator, *A Political Reformer*, 19 Mar. 1831.

constitutional platform backed up by the potential mobilization of mass popular support. Together these experiences and these insights set in motion the vital process – which started earlier in some places than others and was not a single irreversible trend – of the peeling-off of working-class radicals from their former middle-class radical and Whig-liberal allies. The origins of this process can be traced back to the summer of 1829 and it is here that we begin our investigation of the popular radical end of the reform era.

1: Political and Economic Background

Apart from occasional protests about the Corn Laws, popular radical activity had been fairly circumscribed in the two years before 1828. The defeat of the Bradford combers and weavers in 1825 and the economic crash of 1826 had both taken their toll on local enthusiasms and agitational inclinations. The subsequent revival of radicalism and reform in the late 1820s can partly be explained by changes in the atmosphere of national and local politics. The political tempo had begun to quicken in 1828, with the 'restitution of full civil rights', first to Nonconformists and then, more controversially, to Roman Catholics.[14] Their emancipation evoked a strong response in the West Riding and remained a key political issue in 1828 and early 1829.[15] Relations between rival Whig and Tory elites became increasingly embittered and the rising political temperature helped to forge an open alliance between Whigs and radicals.[16]

The eventual granting of Catholic emancipation can be seen as the first step towards the Reform Act. It gave a severe jolt to the finely balanced mechanism of parliamentary politics, and provided valuable lessons for both extremes of the political spectrum. The ultra-Tories deduced from both the fact and manner of passing the Catholic Relief Act, that parliament was not representative and therefore should be changed; whilst the ultra-radicals saw clearly that a well-organised mass movement had foisted change upon an unwilling government by force of popular pressure. Moreover, the form and tactics of the Catholic Association – its unified structure and mass allegiance; and its processions, simultaneous meetings and veiled threats of physical-force – provided a successful agitational model for radical reformers to imitate.[17] Most importantly reform was now seen to be possible.

At the same time as the Catholic emancipation issue was inducing uncertainty at the centre of national politics and bitter rivalries in the localities, contests for the offices of local government, an underestimated locus of political ambition, were also

---

14 Malcolm Chase, *Early Trade Unionism: Fraternity, Skill and the Politics of Labour* (London: Breviary Stuff, 2012 edn.), p. 110.

15 On the Catholic Emancipation issue generally see Norman Gash, *Mr Secretary Peel: the Life of Sir Robert Peel to 1830* (London: Longman, 1961), p. 545 ff. For responses and events in Leeds, see A. S. Turberville and F. Beckwith, 'Leeds and Parliamentary Reform, 1820-1832' *Publications of the Thoresby Society*, 41 (1954), pp. 18-19 and 22-4. For local events, particularly in Leeds, see *LM* and *LI*, May 1828-Mar. 1829.

16 For the big 'Liberal' meeting in early December, see *LM* 6, 13 Dec. 1828. For opposition to Catholic emancipation in Halifax, a Methodist stronghold, see *LI* 25 Dec. 1828.

17 Fraser, 'The Agitation for Parliamentary Reform', pp. 34-7.

becoming more animated and similarly divisive.[18] The trend was particularly noticeable in Leeds where the town's closed corporation was increasingly challenged by a new group of merchants and manufacturers, mostly but not exclusively Whig or 'Liberal' in politics and nonconformist in religion, seeking political power to match their economic strength. With the parliamentary reform movement dormant in the 1820s, they made town and parochial administration their political battlefield and the vestry (the only area where popular participation was possible) their means of attacking the unreformed corporation.[19]

The chief focus of this challenge was the key office of churchwarden and the controversial question of church rates.[20] The relatively democratic and open nature of the vestry meant that the popular radicals were valuable allies for the Whig-liberal 'economists'. In 1828 this posed few problems since, as well as sharing much common ground with the 'Liberals' on the emancipation issue, the radicals were, if anything, even more fiercely opposed to church rate expenditure. James Mann later recalled:

> When a meeting was about to take place in the parish church vestry, respecting the inhabitants of Leeds being taxed for the support of the new churches, and the erection of the walls around them, Mr Baines went to him (Mr Mann) and asked him if he would endeavour to prevail upon the friends of reform to support him on that occasion...[21]

Mann obliged, joined the 'Liberal' alliance and supported Baines and his fellow Whig-liberals at the December vestry meeting.[22] However, as the Tory menace subsided with the passing of the Emancipation Bill in 1829, this 'Liberal' coalition fell apart when it became apparent that the respectable Whig-liberals would not go as far as the radicals in disallowing church rates.

A split ensued and, though the 'Bainesocracy' continued to control the vestry during the five years after 1828, they were never again able to do so from such a strong base. Popular mistrust of Baines increased and apathy towards local government politics returned.[23] The radicals, in response to both national and local stimuli, increasingly pursued their own independent course during 1829, and Leeds politics gradually took on its distinctive fragmented pattern.

---

18 On this important but 'unglamourous' branch of local history see Malcolm Chase, 'The 'local state' in Regency Britain', *Local Historian*, 43 (2013), pp. 266-78.

19 See Derek Fraser, 'The Leeds Churchwardens, 1828-50', *Publications of the Thoresby Society*, 53, 1971, pp. 1-2; Derek Fraser, 'Politics in Leeds, 1830-52' Unpub. Ph.D Thesis, University of Leeds, 1969, pp. 23-4; Derek Fraser, 'Politics and Society in the Nineteenth Century', in Derek Fraser (ed.), *A History of Modern Leeds* (Manchester: Manchester University Press, 1980), pp. 273-4; Turberville and Beckwith, 'Leeds', p. 19. Dr Fraser uses the term 'Liberal' to denote Whigs, Reformers and Radicals, 'Churchwardens', p. 5, fn. 7.

20 Fraser, 'Churchwardens', pp. 2-4; W. R. Ward, *Religion and Society in England, 1790-1850* (London: Batsford, 1972), pp. 110-11. The questions of church expenditure and new 'Parliamentary' churches were also major local issues at Dewsbury where, in 1828, William Rhodes of Earlsheaton, a radical, successfully led vestry opposition, *LM* 21 June 1828.

21 *LP* 5 Dec. 1829.

22 *LM* 20 Dec. 1828.

23 *LP* 5 Dec. 1828; see also the *Patriot's* vitriolic comments on the small attendances at vestry meetings, *LP* 5 May 1829.

The chief focus of local political interest and ambition in Huddersfield lay in the vestry election of the Constable, 'the principle [*sic*] officer of the town', who also had the power, in theory, to select a paid deputy. The town provides a good example of a vestry highly sensitive to popular influence and radicals frequently used it as a battleground in skirmishes with local Tory and Whig elites. As at Leeds, parochial and town administration provided radical, dissenting and excluded groups with their only accessible avenue to local political status and power. Friends of 'popular rights' in Huddersfield won some victories in 1826, but radicals suffered a defeat over the question of the Deputy Constable's expenses in December 1828.[24] The late 1820s saw an escalation of conflict which both nourished and fed off the 'religio-political' animosities aroused by the Catholic emancipation and witnessed the beginning of the gradual ascendency of local radicals.[25]

The 'Reform Question' had remained in the background of national politics in the 1820s: ever-present but often overshadowed by more immediate controversies concerning Catholics, corn and currency. At times the cause seemed hopeless.[26] In 1829, however, with the centre of politics invigorated by the debates and divisions on Catholic emancipation and Peel's currency measures, interest in reform revived. In May, the *Leeds Mercury* reported rumours of impending reform legislation;[27] and two weeks later the ultra-Tory Marquis of Blandford moved his famous resolution in favour of reform. With Cobbett and Hunt once again taking on the mantle of national leadership and reports of extreme depression and suffering filtering in from Lancashire and Spitalfields, radical reformers who, for example at Leeds, had earlier in the year merely been going through the motions of an annual dinner to Paine, now began to rouse themselves once more.[28]

A further stimulus was provided from another 'politico-religious' source: Richard Carlile and Rev. Robert Taylor's 'Infidel Mission' in the summer of 1829 to follow up the latter's release from prison for blasphemy.[29] The 'Missionaries' struggled to find an audience in Leeds, but animated freethinking radicals in a number of other centres.[30] In Huddersfield, for example, a correspondent informed Carlile in September that his

24 *LI* 4 Dec. 1828; on the 1820s background and the victories of friends of 'popular rights' see *LM* 30 Sept. 1826.

25 For a religio-political dispute in a neighbouring area see J. A. Jowitt, 'Parliamentary Politics in Halifax, 1832-47', *Northern History*, 12 (1976), pp. 176-7 (the Halifax vicarial tithes dispute). This ascendency eventually saw the election of William Stocks jnr., William Leadbeater and William Cooke to the office of Chief Constable in the early 1830s, see David Griffiths, *Pioneers or Partisans? Governing Huddersfield 1820-1848* (Huddersfield: Huddersfield Local History Society, 2008), pp. 22-3.

26 Lord John Russell stopped proposing his annual reform motion in 1827. On moderate reform proposals affecting Leeds in the 1820s, see Turberville and Beckwith, 'Leeds', pp. 5-10 and 19, and Gash, *Mr Secretary Peel*, pp. 469-73. On the currency question, see Briggs, 'The Parliamentary Reform Movement', p. 294.

27 *LM* 23 May 1829.

28 *LP* 17 Jan., 7 Feb. 1829. ff. On Cobbett and Hunt's 'last major exercise in political co-operation', see Belchem, *'Orator' Hunt*, p. 148.

29 On Carlile, see Joel. H. Wiener, *Radicalism and Freethought in Nineteenth Century Britain: the Life of Richard Carlile* (Westport Connecticut: Greenwood Press, 1983).

30 For Leeds, see *LI* 18, 25 June; *LP* 27 June, 4, 11 July 1829.

'visit has taken effect with vengeance here ... infidelity engrosses the whole conversation' and plans were initiated to erect an Infidel Chapel.[31] It is likely that, as John Halstead speculates, local leaders with Owenite socialist sympathies would have engaged in the resulting controversies.[32] Equally, it is possible that the ensuing theological debates may have distracted them from developments on their doorstep.

The first stirrings of popular radicalism in the West Riding in the summer of 1829 were more than just a reaction to outside stimuli, particularly the change in the atmosphere of national politics. They owed much to local conditions and experiences during the 'silent 20s'; and formed just part of a wider long-term working-class response which soon involved trade unionism, co-operation, and the factory agitation. Moreover, the re-awakening had a proactive aspect. The predominantly working-class meetings which took place in the second half of 1829 also contributed to the development of a movement for reform, both locally and nationally. In a few key pockets of the textile area at least, the 'tide of popular interest' had turned 'back to political agitation' well before E. P. Thompson's 'summer of 1830' watershed.[33]

The other key factor causing this tide to turn was distress. The working population of the West Riding suffered greatly during the long, harsh winter of 1828-9. In Leeds the January poor relief figures showed an 8.3% increase on the previous year, and were 21.3% up on the 1827 amount. Even the normally sanguine *Mercury* was forced to accept the existence of 'great distress'. By the middle of April, the full extent of the 'lamentable depression' became apparent. In the Dewsbury-Heckmondwike area only a quarter of the blanket weavers were employed, and many were reportedly starving. Around Huddersfield the curse of underemployment meant long hours at a pittance for those lucky enough to find work. Only Bradford's staple worsted trade provided some semblance of regular employment for its workers.[34] This geographical pattern of distress persisted throughout May, with reports speaking of the wretched condition of the woollen operatives within the Huddersfield/Halifax/Dewsbury triangle, and of the unprecedented stagnation of the fancy trade outside Huddersfield. Even in the absence of any signs of disturbance, the authorities took no chances and reinforced the military presence in the distressed areas.[35]

The temporary improvement of the Fall trade proved a false dawn and, by the start of October the *Mercury* was again bemoaning the dullness of trade in Dewsbury, Heckmondwike, Huddersfield and Halifax.[36] Many weaving villages and hamlets in these areas faced the prospect of the on-coming winter without having experienced even a semblance of prosperity during the past twelve months. It is against this background that the development of a working-class agitation in 1829 must be set.

---

31 *The Lion*, 2 Oct. 1829, quoted in John Halstead, 'The Huddersfield Short Time Committee and its radical associations, c.1820-1876', in John A. Hargreaves and E. A. Hilary Haigh (eds.) *Slavery in Yorkshire: Richard Oastler and the Campaign against Child Labour in the Industrial Revolution* (Huddersfield: University of Huddersfield, 2012), p. 110.
32 Halstead, 'Huddersfield STC', p. 111.
33 E. P. Thompson, *The Making of the English Working Class* (Harmondsworth: Penguin, 1968 edn.), pp. 891-2.
34 *LM* 31 Jan; 14 Feb; 11 Apr; 2 May 1829.
35 *LM* 2, 16 May; *LI* 7, 21 May 1829.
36 *LM* 20, 27 June, 11, 25 July; *LI* 23 July 1829; *LM* 8, 22 Aug; 3 Oct. 1829.

However, distress does not provide a catch-all explanation of the gradual radical revival. The textile district had known even worse times in 1826 when local banks failed and workers in the Bradford area attacked the installation of power-looms. There had been little radical campaigning during that depression and the years since had rarely been prosperous. Also citing 'distress' begs the question of why people should put forward an essentially 'political' programme of reforms in response to the everyday experience of 'economic' hardship. This can only be unpicked by looking at how the workers' agitations developed in a couple of key areas and by examining the ideas they expressed and the actions they proposed.

2: The First Stirrings, 1829

a) Almondbury Operatives

The first group to respond to their predicament were the woollen and fancy weavers in the villages to the south and east of Huddersfield. Towards the end of May they called a public meeting at Almondbury to discuss the best method of relief and the Corn Laws.[37] Possibly because it emanated from the denizens of an unassuming collection of working-class settlements, the significance and power of the resulting agitational outburst has perhaps been underestimated. Only Katrina Navickas and local historians such as Alan Brooke have recognized the importance of this key 'radical locale', citing it as an example of the periphery leading the centre.[38] On Monday 1st June between 1,500 and 2,000 poor, dishevelled workers gathered slowly in a secluded quarry (Almondbury Bank). The occasion was sparse and sombre, but laced with black humour. No banners were unfurled; just the simple effigy of an ill-clad weaver bearing the caustic epithet 'Wellington's Prosperity', accompanied by a band playing the 'Dead March'.[39]

The eventual meeting though not explicitly radical, used its terms of reference widely. The Cobbettite favourites – currency and the Corn Laws – formed the local speakers' main subjects and the aristocracy their main targets. The only direct reference to parliamentary reform however came from an outsider, James Mann of Leeds, who cited parliamentary indifference to distress as evidence of the need for reform, and quoted the Catholic Association as the means of achieving it. He urged the meeting to 'form bonds of Union and demand reform if they meant to effect anything'. The meeting's convenors, however, were clearly unwilling to press so far so soon.[40]

---

37 *LM* 30 May 1829.

38 Navickas, *Protest*, pp. 106, 122. Alan J. Brooke, 'Economic Distress and the Revival of Radicalism in the Huddersfield Area 1826-1830', in 'We are Weary of Slavery', available at https://undergroundhistories.wordpress.com/we-are-weary-of-slavery/ (accessed 14 May 2022). A short account of this agitation is given in John Sanders, 'The Voice of the "Shoeless, Shirtless and Shameless": Community radicalism in the West Riding, 1829 to 1839', *Northern History*, 58, 2 (2021), pp. 9-12.

39 *LM* 6 June; *LP* 6 June 1829. On the significance of Almondbury Bank as a radical venue see Navickas, *Protest*, p. 242.

40 *LM* and *LP* 6 June 1829.

A second meeting on Monday 15 June, which delegates from Bradford, Halifax, Heckmondwike and 'other places' were also rumoured to be attending, attracted another sizeable audience, and passed resolutions condemning a familiar catalogue of abuses – the national debt, the currency, the Corn Laws and machinery. The apparent unanimity however hid some underlying tensions which had shown themselves at the end of the first meeting on the question of seeking the manufacturers' help.[41] These were now brought clearly into the open by the presence of another outsider, William Ashton, a radical Barnsley linen-weaver.[42] Ashton's speech, vetoed by the *Mercury* as 'a very intemperate and inflammatory harangue', was well received by the audience of hungry, unemployed weavers, and provided a focus for those who were dissatisfied with the conciliatory tone and direction of the meetings. He commented firstly upon what 'appeared to be a laxity, a tameness in some of the persons, who had the management of the meeting'; and decried as 'a waste of time' their strategy of not petitioning or forming a Union with other districts, until they could see what concessions the local manufacturers might give. In the past employers might have helped the struggling mechanic, but now 'the manufacturer found himself floating down the same stream with the same millstone round his neck, and it would be in vain for him to extend that hand to another which could not rescue him'. Equally local remedies were of no avail: distress now registered on a national scale which 'required a general co-operation to alleviate it'. He ended with an emotional exhortation to adopt 'vigorous measures'[43] which had been successful at Barnsley in resisting wage reductions:

> nature never intended them to be slaves: Labour was required from many, but those who were subjected to it were entitled to a compensation, and when they could not get that, the hand of oppression was upon them, and resistance became a part of their duty ... (cheers). They were then bound to co-operate, and by their exertions hurl down the tyrants who oppressed them.[44]

It is clear from the warm reception afforded to Ashton's speech that many suffering handloom weavers were equally willing to identify their employers as amongst their oppressors.

Ashton's remarks did not endear himself to all of the local leadership, but his plea for a coordinated response to distress was quickly answered with the establishment of an operatives' committee to communicate with other towns and villages. George

---

41 The advocates of 'co-operation' had originally won the day and during the following week a deputation of workmen waited upon the principal tradesmen and manufacturers of the area, *LM* 13 June 1829. The response, however, was poor, *LP* 6 June 1829.

42 On Ashton see Bellamy and Saville (eds.), *Dictionary of Labour Biography*, 3 (London: Palgrave Macmillan, 1976), pp. 5-7; and Dorothy Thompson, 'William Ashton, c.1806-1877', *Oxford Dictionary of National Biography*, https://doi.org/10.1093/ref:odnb/48212 (accessed 4 May 2021).

43 In Barnsley these had included coercive threats against 'notorious' manufacturers and blacklegs in order to counter proposed wage reductions. See F. J. Kaijage, 'Labouring Barnsley, 1816-1856: A Social and Economic History', Unpub. PhD thesis, University of Warwick, 1975, p. 325 ff.

44 *LP*, *LM* 20 June 1829.

Beaumont, fancy weaver and emerging leader, was appointed secretary; and another fellow weaver and future Chartist, Samuel Dickenson, now confidently attributed distress to political causes. Yet amongst others of the organisers the hope persisted that the manufacturers might join them, and on this premise, the meeting once more adjourned.[45]

By the beginning of July, however, William Ashton's prediction of employer indifference seemed to be coming true. The *Mercury* of 4 July regretted that the Almondbury meetings had elicited little response from the masters, and made a final plea for them to join their workmen in reporting the exact size of the problem of distress to parliament. In the meantime, the operatives' committee organised a third Almondbury Bank meeting, which eventually took place on Monday 6 July, the date from which the later Almondbury Political Union took its foundation. The speeches largely repeated the themes and arguments of earlier meetings. Church and crown wealth in particular were attacked, and the advent of machinery and wage reductions equated with increases in pauperism and crime. Although the locally-inspired fusion of 'political' and 'economic' themes provided by Ashton at the earlier meeting had given way to a more general radical analysis in terms of rich versus poor, and poverty amidst plenty, the occasional foreboding utterances gave the meeting a more desperate tone.[46]

With collaborative overtures to masters rejected and parliament seemingly indifferent, indeed hostile, to the plight of 'the working-classes', 'self-protection' became the speakers' watchword. Samuel Dickenson, at the end of a humorous, rousing speech, advised his audience to 'knit themselves together in one firm body' and to 'remember the great Catholic Union, and from what a small party it originally sprang'. John Eckersley followed up Reuben Earnshaw's recommendation 'to form a Union' with a proposal to form committees in 'their different villages', on the Almondbury model, to investigate the extent of distress.[47] Edward Dixon, for his part, encouraged his famished audience to forget their pride as Englishmen and 'claim on the parishes'. They should feel 'no shame' since they had 'been overtaken by poverty by the mismanagement and misgovernment of the country'. He pledged that, 'if they were refused relief, and would let their cases be known to the committee at Almondbury, the public should be made acquainted with it. He hoped by such an exposure that they should hear no more cases of starvation through neglect'.[48]

Yet despite the emphasis on independent action and self-help, the Almondbury operatives' committee continued to actively seek their masters' participation. This eventually bore fruit towards the end of July; though it may have been fears of

---

45 *LP, LM* 20 June 1829.

46 *LM* 4, 11 July; *LP, HCC* 11 July 1829.

47 John Eckersley (1800-1885?), like Samuel Dickenson, was a Lancashire-born fancy weaver. Reuben Earnshaw (1790?-1839), radical and a factory reform stalwart, also had a background in the fancy trade. He promoted a patented 'composition' to reduce the amount of oil used in the manufacturing woollen goods and was a partner in 'Reuben Earnshaw and Co.','fancy cloth manufacturer' when he died (*LT* 6 May 1835; *LM* 11 Jan. 1840).

48 *HCC* 11 July 1829. These were not mere idle words, as Beaumont and Dickenson showed in early 1830 when they successfully exposed a case of unjust poor relief refusal, *LI* 4 Mar. 1830. The 1841 census includes a 60-year old Edward Dixon, cloth-dresser, living in the household of a shoemaker in Almondbury.

workers' direct action, evidenced by recent events in Barnsley, that jolted a number of influential masters meeting in Huddersfield to form their own committee, with William Stocks jnr. as secretary. They joined the operatives in a 'cordial union', 'with a view of giving the Government and the gentry around us a true state of our country'.[49]

The strategy drew on recent precedents and involved pairs of 'trustworthy workmen', some drawn from the Operatives' Committee, visiting 'the labourers in their homes' in twelve predominantly 'fancy' townships during August and early September, and enumerating their family and financial circumstances. The rigour, scale and speed of the resulting survey was impressive and marked it out 'as an epic of early social investigation and self-help'.[50] The primary object, 'to obtain one great result', was underpinned by extensive aggregate figures and tables.[51]

These statistics revealed the cruel reality of over a third of the total population of approximately 33,000 in the twelve townships existing on not more than 2½d (1p) each per day. This finding, along with the numbers living at slightly higher levels, formed part of a printed circular distributed, as promised, to leading members of the government and local gentry. The publication of this document in September was the apogee of the Almondbury operatives' mid-summer agitation.[52]

Their sense of achievement, however, was short-lived; for despite securing the collaboration of local manufacturers, revealing the prevalence of extreme distress, and bringing it to the attention of the government, no response was forthcoming. As William Stocks jnr. later recalled, the joint committee had not expected to receive immediate financial amelioration, but they had at least hoped for a parliamentary inquiry which might suggest some mode of relief. Although the damning figures caused a stir in radical circles in London, the governmental response was indifference.[53] This appeared to confirm Samuel Dickenson's earlier assessment that, 'The Legislature of this country seemed to have a peculiar grudge against the working-classes'. It thereby revealed both its unrepresentative nature and its want of humanity. By the time the next public meeting on distress was called in December, 'privations' were more extreme, the operatives' tone angrier, and their leaders' analysis more explicitly radical.[54]

The upsurge of popular activity in the area to the south-east of Huddersfield during the summer of 1829 requires close and careful examination. Taking the question of timing first, the most salient factor was the failure of the spring trade. The West Riding weaving communities expected and, to a certain extent, could allow for harsh winters; but the total absence of a revival in the spring, following upon two years of declining wages and insufficient work, opened up the vista of a hopeless

---

49   *LM* 25 July 1829; William Stocks' testimony to the Select Committee on Manufactures, Commerce and Shipping, BPP 1833, VI, p. 643.

50   John Sanders, 'The Voice of the "Shoeless, Shirtless and Shameless": Community radicalism in the West Riding, 1829 to 1839', *Northern History*, 58, 2 (2021), p. 9. See *LM* 1 Aug; 21 Nov. (letter from 'K'), 12 Dec. 1829 for the mechanics of the survey.

51   BPP 1833, VI, p. 643.

52   Ibid.; *LI* 19 Nov. 1829 (where the tables were reprinted); *LM* 19 Sept. 1829.

53   BPP 1833, VI, p. 643; Belchem, *'Orator' Hunt*, p. 151.

54   *HCC* 11 July 1829; *LM* 12 Dec. 1829.

future. By the time of the second meeting on 15 June, half the audience (estimated at between 1,500 and 2,000) were totally without work and only eighteen in full employment. In addition, the poor harvest of 1828 had by this time worked its way through into higher food prices, a fact which helps to explain the stress placed on the Corn Laws as a grievance at the initial meetings.[55]

Less easy to define, but equally important, was the change in overall political atmosphere in 1829. Rumours of reform, the re-emergence of Cobbett and Hunt as popular leaders, and the extent of political uncertainty at the centre, all helped to convince local workers that something could be achieved by agitation. This, together with the feedback from other discontented groups, in Leeds, Barnsley, Spitalfields and Lancashire, reinforced the Almondbury operatives' resolve to continue with their meetings. For the first time in years there seemed a point in printing handbills, borrowing a hustings cart, and nominating a committee.[56]

In explaining why Almondbury in particular became the focus of a popular agitation in the summer of 1829, two factors seem especially pertinent. Firstly, it lay at the heart of an area, and more especially a trade, which had suffered more than most since the halcyon days of 1825. After the slump of 1826, the fancy trade remained in a state of uncertainty, characterised by low production and meagre wages. In addition, the depression of 1829 hit the Almondbury area disproportionately hard.[57] The skilled, independent-minded and previously well-paid fancy weavers felt their degradation particularly severely.

Yet distress was not confined to this district. Contiguous areas around Dewsbury, Elland and Mirfield suffered equally. A second more intangible factor – a recent history of trade and community organisation and activism – appears to have been also important. As Katrina Navickas has noted, places such as Almondbury lay largely outside the control and surveillance of urban elites. Radical traditions ran deep in the villages lying to the south and east of Huddersfield.[58] Although not totally dominated by the fancy trade, they nevertheless formed a cohesive occupational community in which the values of 'moral economy' were joined with the expertise and experience derived from a tradition of independent action and self-help.[59] For example, during the prosperity of 1824-5 the fancy weavers had constructed a complex, highly disciplined trade union which fought for higher wages and the maintenance of customary measurements. In 1825 their leaders had participated in the establishment of a democratic local Mechanics' Institute. At the height of the 1826 depression they organised a meeting of the unemployed on Almondbury Bank, collected detailed information about local conditions, and delegated a deputation to acquaint Lord Harewood of their findings. When trade revived in May 1827 they again organised

---

55 *LM*, *LP* 20 June; *LM* 11 Apr. 1829.

56 The Almondbury radicals, like George Beaumont, were well connected to other radical centres, see *LT* 14 June 1851.

57 BPP 1833, VI, p. 646; *LM* 13 Jan. 1827; 21 Nov. 1829 (letter from 'K'). Whilst the Bradford stuff and Leeds broadcloth markets recovered somewhat during the summer months, the picture in the fancy and 'low woollen' trades was one of unmitigated gloom.

58 Navickas, *Protest*, p. 106.

59 On moral economy, see E. P. Thompson, 'The Moral Economy of the English Crowd in the Eighteenth Century', *Past and Present*, 50 (1971), pp. 76-136.

themselves to retrieve former wage levels and protest against the cancerous growth of the truck system.[60] Set against this backdrop their position at the forefront of a popular agitation in 1829 becomes more comprehensible.

One vital aspect of this ability and willingness to respond in 1829 lay in the existence of a cadre of capable and experienced local leaders who formed themselves into the 'Almondbury Operatives' Committee'. The most prominent were the public speakers – Jonathan Brook, Edward Dixon, John Eckersley, Samuel Dickenson and George Beaumont; but other members (perhaps the organisers) included Reuben Earnshaw, Joseph Sykes, Solomon Thwaite and possibly John Spivey.[61] Information on these leaders is far from complete. However, it appears that all were respected figures within the local working community; and at least four can positively be identified as having previously taken part in local agitations. Five can definitely be assigned as fancy weavers, and the rest were certainly 'workmen'. Some became leading radicals and later Chartists.[62]

Two main strands may be identified in the analysis of distress expounded by these leaders at the 1829 meetings.[63] The first saw distress as a consequence of the exploitative nature of 'Old Corruption'. In this view, the aristocracy, 'the drones', 'the useless ones' or most crudely, 'the rich', used their power to exploit the poor, 'the labouring or useful classes' through paper currency, heavy taxation, the Corn Laws, the Church, and ultimately by placing 'garrisons in our cities and towns and police at our doors'. The remedy lay in currency reform, reduction of taxation, repeal of the Corn Law, and the sale of Church and Crown lands to pay off a national debt contracted by an excessive army waging unjust war against France. The corollary to this analysis, that fundamental political change was necessary to change things permanently, although ever-present, often remained unspoken, except by radicals such as James Mann and Samuel Dickenson.

The second line of thinking incorporated elements of an alternative 'moral economy' into an attack on capital, competition and machinery. It traced a simple line

---

60   On the Fancy Weavers' Union, see *LM* Sept. 1824-Aug. 1825; BPP, 1825, (417) p. 121 ff; on the local Mechanics Institute, see *Rules and Regulations of the Kirkburton and Dogley-Lane Mechanics Institute, for the Disseminating of Useful Knowledge* (Huddersfield, 1825) in the Tolson Memorial Museum, Huddersfield; on 1826 see, Stocks, BPP 1833, VI, p. 644, *LM* 15, 22 July 1826; on 1827, see *LM* 13 Jan., 2, 16, 23 June, 7, 21 July 1827. Also, *BC* May - June 1827.

61   John Eckersley, *HCC* 11 July 1829, had recommended a committee of eight to ten people in other villages. Solomon Thwaite (1797-1877), of Kaye Lane, Almondbury, was a fancy weaver (as were Dickenson, Beaumont, Eckersley and Earnshaw) and it is likely that most of the others (described like Jonathan Brook as 'operatives') were similarly employed in the fancy trade.

62   Earnshaw, Beaumont, Brook and Dickenson were described as 'honest and upright workmen' by Stocks, BPP 1833, VI, p. 599, and *LM* 21 Nov. 1829; Thwaite and Spivey had been prominent members of the Fancy Weavers' Union in 1825, Beaumont had taken part in anti-truck activities in 1827, Earnshaw had sat on the committee of the Kirkburton and Dogley-Lane Mechanics Institute ; Dickenson, Thwaite, Beaumont, Sykes and Spivey all had future radical and Chartist connections.

63   This, and the two following paragraphs are based on the reports of the meetings in *LM, LI, LP, HCC* June-July 1829.

of causation from capital to machinery leading to excess competition, over-trading and wage reductions resulting in distress, degradation and crime. George Beaumont, who had personal experience of the factory system, for example, argued that machinery 'introduced for the aggrandisement of the few to the injury of the many', 'had been the principal cause of the increase in pauperism and crime', and maintained that 'competition and hand labour could not flourish together'. Edward Dixon, whilst recognising its benevolent potential, still cited machinery as the 'primary cause' of recent wage reductions, and suggested a shift in the burden of taxation from the poor to the new machines.

It would be misleading to distinguish too rigidly between these two strands, for in the minds and speeches of the Almondbury operatives they were very much intertwined. Edward Dixon, for example, attributed the increased use of machinery to a home market crippled by the government's fiscal policies, and argued that it was 'paper money [which] gave such facilities to bankers as enabled them to make liberal advances, and which served to augment the power of the steam-engine, and by suddenly creating large capitals, led to a system of over-trading, and to that detestable spirit of competition, which has produced so much mischief and distress in the country'.

As regards tactics, the Almondbury leaders had no intention of 'going it alone' in their initial response to distress. They consistently and actively sought the co-operation of local employers; and in the conduct and tone of their meetings, if not always in the content, they took care not to alienate local middle-class opinion. This strategy had ample precedents in the Fancy Weavers' Union's agitation against illegal measurements in 1824-5, and in joint attempts to eradicate the obnoxious truck system in 1827.[64] Seen in this context the conciliatory attitude of the local leaders is more comprehensible. Their response to distress was essentially conditioned by local economic conditions and the recent experience of the dominant occupational community. The vigour of this response is thrown into starker relief by briefly looking at responses to distress elsewhere in the textile region.

In the Halifax area both local economic circumstances and social realities mitigated against imitation of the Almondbury example. A meeting of workers at Sowerby Green, which discussed remedies for the depressed state of trade in early July, may have taken its lead from Almondbury; but its recommendation – a petition to landowners to reduce rents – was essentially a pragmatic, short-term solution which reflected the preoccupations of a dispersed, semi-rural population engaged in a diversified local economy. In Halifax itself a similar public meeting later in the month chaired by a local radical, Thomas Cliffe, failed to attract more than thirty or forty people.[65]

---

64 Also in 1826 unemployed weavers had sought their employers' aid in organising a public meeting and spoke warmly of their attempt to prolong employment, *LM* 8, 15 July, *BC* 13 July 1826.

65 *HCC* 11 July; *LP* 25 July, 1 Aug. 1829. Lack of suitable leaders and a recent history of activism may have hindered agitations here; also, the more diverse local economy may have partly cushioned some of the worst excesses of distress.

Barnsley, a domestic linen-weaving centre fifteen miles south-east of Huddersfield and contiguous to some fancy-weaving hamlets, serves as a more useful comparison. It too possessed a single, solid (if not stable) occupational community (in this case reinforced by ethnic bonds) which suffered greatly from low wages and scarcity of employment in the depression of 1829.[66] After vigorously resisting proposed wage reductions in May, the Barnsley men watched developments amongst the fancy weavers closely. They delegated first Ashton and then Frank Mirfield to the Almondbury meetings; and they followed the fancy weavers' formula by holding a series of meetings on distress which culminated, towards the end of June, in a deputation of 500 linen weavers presenting a memorial to Earl Fitzwilliam. Six weeks later the weavers' committee again paralleled Almondbury developments (in their attempts to win over public sympathy) by publishing comprehensive statistics on the number of unemployed looms. Yet as well as these 'constitutional' responses to distress, the Barnsley operatives also kept open their coercive extra-legal options, and when the masters proposed further 25% reductions in the third week of August, they resumed full-scale hostilities. In a year of ferocious industrial conflict in the north, the five-month Barnsley strike was one of the most bitterly and fiercely fought contests.[67]

The question of leadership is important in explaining differences between the fancy and linen weavers' responses. Whilst the Almondbury men saw their best hope of salvation in uniting with local manufacturers to fight an idle, corrupt aristocracy; the Barnsley leaders identified the 'tyrants who oppressed them' nearer home: the unscrupulous undercutting masters, who were pushing the weaving community into the vortex of low wages, long hours and infrequent work. This difference in outlook can be explained by two factors. Firstly, the type of leadership differed. The early Almondbury agitation was dominated by moderate, 'respectable' members of the local weaving community; whereas the Barnsley leadership included a greater proportion of young 'radicals' and importantly, a leaven of vociferous Irish trade unionists, including a number of refugees who had come to England following the failure of the great Drogheda turn-out of 1823.[68] Secondly, although the trade depression was no worse in Barnsley than in Almondbury, the economic and social context, within which local leaders were operating, also differed. In Almondbury the employers, by their former record and present actions in not reducing wages further and eventually co-operating

---

66 *LM* 16, *LI* 21 May 1829. The following paragraphs are based on Kaijage, 'Labouring Barnsley', pp. 325-40 and *LM*, *LP* June-Oct. 1829.

67 The strike had a potent mix of elements – daily meetings at times of particular excitement, arson, shooting, threatening letters, looms smashed, houses stoned, yarn captured, blacklegs assaulted. Eventually, after most of their committee had been arrested or fled in fear of arrest, the weavers' resistance began to disintegrate in early winter. A sequel to the dispute was the conviction and transportation of Ashton and Mirfield for their alleged part in the Dodsworth Riot. An interesting connection with Ashton's Almondbury appearance is contained in the *Patriot's* allegation that Baines (whose paper Ashton had denounced there) was involved in a conspiracy against them, see *LP* 10 Apr. 1830; also see Ashton's letter, *LP* 28 Aug. 1830. Both returned ten years later to become Chartist leaders.

68 Kaijage, 'Labouring Barnsley', pp. 338-40; J. H. Treble, 'The Place of the Irish Catholics in the Social Life of the North of England, 1829-51', Unpub. Ph.D thesis, University of Leeds, 1968, p. 9.

with their men, ensured that the weavers channelled their energies into a broadly based quasi-political agitation. By contrast, in Barnsley the mutually antagonistic positions of capital and labour, reinforced by the residential separation and proximity, were merely confirmed by provocative wage-cuts and the ensuing local class war.[69]

As well as vigorous 'industrial' and 'political' activities to preserve a meagre standard of living, working people in the West Riding also took practical measures to ease their predicament. The prominence of the Corn Laws as a grievance in the early Almondbury public meetings reflected concern about one component of working-class distress: the price of bread. Throughout the summer operatives in various parts of the region attempted to regulate the price of another vital commodity, dairy produce, by means of a 'consumer boycott'. The idea had a long pedigree in the eighteenth century and originated at this time in Lancashire.[70] It was first put into practice in Barnsley in late June with the posting of notices urging the inhabitants to refrain from buying milk above 1½d a quart and butter 6d a lb. Two weeks later a meeting of Leeds workers proposed similar mass abstinence. In August Huddersfield followed suit; whilst five miles away at Kirkburton (a woollen and fancy weaving centre) the poor inhabitants committed to abstaining from milk, old milk and butter until the prices were fixed all year round at 1½d, ¾d and 9d respectively. The chances of success were undoubtedly higher in the smaller, tightly knit weaving communities like Kirkburton, where according to the *Mercury* the resolution 'is strictly acted upon, and any person who does not conform to it is prosecuted with the utmost vigour by his neighbours, and all friendly intercourse with him is suspended'.[71] The proposed 'boycott' in Leeds, with its greater population and more varied occupational structure, is therefore of special interest; and it is to developments in this area that we must next turn.

b) Leeds Radical Reformers

Although Leeds, with its diverse industrial base, escaped the worst ravages of the 1829 slump, high food prices and the proximity of distress provided sufficient stimulus for the operatives to follow Barnsley in calling a public meeting to fix maximum prices for the necessities of life. The meeting was 'convened in consequence of messages, communicated to the work people in each mill by certain individuals claiming to act as a committee' attracted over 1,000 people, 'chiefly weavers and other operatives' to Woodhouse Moor. There they listened to attacks on the Corn Laws and machinery before passing resolutions fixing both dairy prices and arrangements for a permanent

---

69　Many of the fancy merchants lived in Huddersfield itself. On the 'ghetto situation' of the linen-weaving community see Kaijage, 'Labouring Barnsley', pp. 43, 304-5.

70　The notion of enforcing a 'fair' price for dairy produce owed much to the well-established tradition of food riots. It also links in with other traditional tactics available to local communities. It was a short step from consumer boycott, to exclusive dealing, to co-operative trading. In Lancashire the 'boycott' movement of June-July 1829 was highly organised and had radical political overtones, Robert Sykes, 'Popular Politics and Trade Unionism in SE Lancashire, 1829-42', Unpub. PhD Thesis, University of Manchester, 1982, pp. 355-6.

71　*LP* 27 June; *LM* 11 July; *LI* 13 Aug; *LM* 15 Aug. 1829.

committee.[72] In both its venue and method of calling, as well as in the choice of the Union Inn as a regular meeting place for the delegate committee, the meeting foreshadowed later trade union and factory reform developments amongst the operative community.[73]

The weavers' concentration literally on 'bread and butter' issues clearly disappointed local radicals. The *Patriot* which gave the meeting only a short paragraph disapproved of the dairy boycott, preferring abstinence from excisable articles, or better still, an agitation for real radical reform. James Mann, (the radical bookseller), who the organisers permitted to speak after the main resolutions had been passed, urged the latter course.[74] However, as when he spoke at Almondbury in June, it is clear that high food prices and unemployment in themselves did not as yet provide a sufficiently rich ground-soil in which the seeds of ultra-radicalism might flourish. At least, though, some of the preliminary spadework was being done.

Mann was keen to maintain the momentum of the gathering and suggested further meetings on the subject of distress. However, the only assembly of note in the following weeks was a demonstration by 200 unemployed (factory) weavers against the *Mercury*'s reports of 'tolerable' employment. Yet, the atmosphere remained cordial, the men apparently attributing distress to the Corn Laws, machinery and the national debt.[75] In spite of improving trade, the *Patriot* persisted in its attempt to link distress and reform – arguing, for example, that a reformed parliament was the only guarantee against decreasing employment and remuneration.[76] More importantly, along with the *Trades' Free Press*, it reported fully on radical meetings in the capital, especially those of the London Radical Reform Association.[77] This latter body probably provided the inspiration for a group of Leeds radicals to circulate handbills in early September calling a public meeting of the friends of Radical Reform to form a 'Radical Union'.[78]

This meeting may well have been connected with the earlier Woodhouse Moor gatherings, organised by the 'operatives' committee'. But whatever its precise origins, the meeting, chaired by Mann and held on a Monday evening to allow working men to attend, was a great success. An enthusiastic audience packed Mr Heaps' room opposite the Free Market Tavern, capable of holding 400, and hundreds remained outside unable to gain admission.[79] Reading from a copy of the *Trades Free Press*, William Taylor, in his first public speech, went through a series of resolutions passed at a recent London meeting, before proposing that reformers should start a weekly

---

72 *LM* 11 July 1829. For Turberville and Beckwith's curt dismissal of the speakers and their views, see 'Leeds', p. 21. The gathering was probably the work of hand woollen-cloth weavers, dressers and ancillary workers who worked in the large, but as yet only partly mechanised woollen 'manufactories' of Leeds.

73 Similar delegated bodies met in late 1830 to aid Ashton-under-Lyne strikers, and later Gott's 'turn-outs' in Leeds. The Leeds Operatives Committee (STC) of March 1831 was called by similar mechanisms.

74 *LP* 11 July 1829.

75 *LM* 25 July 1829.

76 *LM* 22 Aug., 5 Sept. (trade); *LP* 5 Sept. 1829.

77 On this body see Prothero, *Artisans and Politics*, pp. 275-81.

78 *LM* 12 Sept. 1829.

79 Probably John Heaps, a radical acquaintance of Cobbett, and later auditor of the Leeds RRA.

penny subscription. Thereafter the speeches of three more experienced campaigners – James Mann, John Foster of the *Patriot* and Edward Baines of the *Mercury* – dominated the proceedings. Mann, for example, voiced his belief that the labouring population would lead the reforming vanguard, and advocated support for a 'Union' with the object of Radical Reform. Foster again emphasised the connection between Reform and distress. Even Baines appears to have been affected by the radical enthusiasm of the meeting. In a long speech he spoke critically of the present 'inefficient representation', and whilst arguing the annual parliaments were too frequent, and the ballot unmanly, he nevertheless still pronounced 'that universal suffrage is not a wrong but a right'.[80]

However, the meeting was far from being unanimous and with the audience split between the radical reformers and those, like Baines, who urged a broad front for 'full, fair and free representation', the meeting adjourned for a week. A leading article in the *Mercury* on the following Saturday continued in a more pungent vein. It condemned as inappropriate the calling of a 'nocturnal meeting', and attacked the way the idea of a penny subscription had been presented. Furthermore, it pronounced haughtily that since 1819, 'the Radical Reformers have very much fallen off in Leeds both in numbers and in talent, … and … though they may, and would no doubt, act efficiently with others (if they would lay aside their peculiar dogma) they are, as they exist in this place at present, wholly unfit to take the lead in the promotion of any great national measure'. The article ended by strongly urging the upper and middle classes to join together to counterbalance the influence of the 'Radical Reformers'.[81]

The split between the latter and the 'liberal' faction dominated by Baines had other than purely ideological grounds. Indeed, at this time a strong personal animosity between Foster (and to a lesser extent Mann) and Baines was overlain by an intense commercial rivalry (between the *Mercury* and *Patriot*) which gave rise to allegations of sharp practice and chicanery.[82] Things came to a head the following Monday at the resumed meeting from which Baines was a notable absentee. Reported in the *Halifax Commercial Chronicle* as 'Leeds Radical Reform Dis-Union', the disruption of the meeting began at the door over the refusal of a group of Carlileite republicans, led by John Smithson, to pay the 1*d* entrance money. James Mann, sarcastically dubbed the 'well *tried* Radical pamphlet vendor', eventually began the meeting by reviewing the progress of unions elsewhere in the country. He was followed by Zachariah Orrell, a young radical, who praised local Tory philanthropist and recently elected MP for Newark, M. T. Sadler's recent pronouncements on distress. His speech urging the necessity of sweeping political change, interspersed with attacks on Baines and his comments about the previous meeting, was subject to frequent interruptions.[83] The

---

80 *LP, LM* 19 Sept. 1829. 'William Taylor' does not reappear in the sources. It is possible that this was in fact Ralph Taylor's inaugural speech.

81 *LP, LM* 19 Sept. 1829. The 'peculiar dogma' was universal suffrage, annual parliaments and the ballot.

82 See, for example, *LM* 19 Sept. 1829 ('The Conspiracy'). Also, *LM* 5 Dec. 1829, for the allegation that Mann went round local pubs on Saturday evening trying to gain converts from the *Mercury*.

83 *HCC* 26 Sept. 1829. John Smithson 'head of the Carlile gang', was a furniture broker. Zachariah Orrell (1806?-?), a woolsorter, was allegedly sacked in 1829 for his radical views (*LP* 31 July 1830). He later became an ally of Smithson and a member of the 'moderate'

final break, however, came when James Duffy, an Irish radical, proposed the formation of a society with subscriptions of $1d$ per week. Uproar ensued with Smithson and Cunliffe, both Carlileite veterans of the post-war agitation, opposing 'penny unions and nocturnal meetings' on the grounds that they would put off many respectable advocates of reform. Eventually the meeting was only placated by the election of a large committee to consult Baines on the question of requisitioning a public meeting on reform.[84]

When the committee first met the next evening radical reformers, heavily outnumbered by Bainesite Whigs and Carlileites, refused to co-operate with the latter. At the following Monday's meeting, Mann, after first reading the accounts of the aborted society, quickly tried to dissolve the assembly. However, after Smithson and Cunliffe insisted on speaking, the meeting ended amidst scenes of 'indescribable confusion'. The *Mercury*, the following Saturday, could scarcely conceal its satisfaction that the Leeds radicals had, 'wisely determined to discontinue their weekly meetings' and had 'called upon those in the more wealthy classes, who are favourable to reform, to petition for this important measure'. The radical *Patriot*'s version was slightly different. It correctly attributed the radical defeat to Baines' alliance with the Carlileites, but denied that the reformers had totally dissolved their meetings. Rather they had decided to discontinue them for a while to see if the influential classes kept their promise to help the reform cause.[85]

The short-lived autumnal agitation of the Leeds radical reformers had important implications for the future pattern of politics in Leeds. It isolated the Mannite radicals and demonstrated their inability to control public meetings in Leeds. It taught them that conditions were not yet right for the emergence of an independent ultra-radical agitation fired by the frustrations of working-class distress. Equally, they now knew that without the establishment of a strong popular base, they could easily be outnumbered and outmanoeuvred in public by an alliance of Carlileite republicans and Bainesite Whigs.

One way of securing such a base was grafting reform issues onto the body of more general grievances, in times of economic depression.[86] As autumn turned into winter and stagnation set in, local conditions became more promising for the popular radicals. The *Intelligencer* and *Mercury* made the deteriorating state of trade the subject of a two-month war of words, which was both a symptom and a component of an increasing local polarisation.[87]

A number of unemployed Leeds operatives responded to the onset of this sharp depression by gathering on Hunslet Moor in late November, 'to ascertain the number of men out of work, and to publish the truth to the country'. Organisation was

---

Holbeck PU in 1831.

84 *HCC* 26 Sept. 1829. Joseph Cunliffe ,'formerly a preacher at a small Antinomian Chapel' was a worsted spinner, see *LI* 24 Sept., *LM*, *LP*, 26 Sept. 1829. The names of the Committee are in the *Mercury*.

85 *LI* 24 Sept; *LP*, *LM* 3, 10 Oct. 1829. The Reform Union possibly continued a shadowy sort of existence.

86 The radicals' initiative had been unfortunate in coinciding with the best autumn trade in years.

87 *LM*, *LI* Nov-Dec. 1829.

rudimentary, and the meeting, which eventually attracted about 300, people lasted just twenty minutes – sufficient time only to elect a chairman, read some resolutions and hear a short speech from James Mann, supporting their grievances and suggesting a week's adjournment to ensure better publicity. The five resolutions concentrated solely on distress and Baines' damagingly false account of its incidence. Yet although non-partisan and even occasionally deferential in tone, they exhibited a firm appreciation of the value of labour. The fifth resolution for example, declared that,

> the operatives by no means wish to assume a situation that does not belong to us yet as we are well aware, that labour is the source of all wealth, and that we are the support of the middle and higher classes of society and therefore unless we obtain labour and a fair remuneration for it, the middle class must soon sink to our level, and the whole community become dis-organised.[88]

Such a possibility clearly worried the Leeds bourgeoisie, twenty members of whom kept their eyes on the proceedings from a short distance, mindful perhaps of recent trouble in Barnsley and reports of trade union disturbances in Lancashire. Baines, for his part, devoted considerable space to ridiculing the poor 'Saint Monday' attendance and insinuating radical connivance in formulating the resolutions. However, although both Mann and Foster (the radical *Leeds Patriot*'s proprietor and editor) were present, the obvious inexperience of the organisers, as well as the limited scope of the resolutions, all tend to confirm that the meeting was a grassroots gathering to express genuine and deep-felt grievances. The organisers had apparently consulted Mann before calling the meeting but appear to have followed his advice that, 'it should be entirely their own doing – an expression of their own feelings and opinions'.[89]

The replayed meeting the following Monday was better organised and attended. Nominally the same group who had convened the first meeting remained in charge; and although radical speakers monopolised the platform, the tone and content, both of their speeches and the additional resolutions, remained close to the sentiments of the original meeting. This at least gave Mann and Foster the opportunity to indulge in personal attacks on Baines, though it was John Ayrey who most clearly voiced the popular belief that, 'Mr Baines, though once a journeyman, was now in better circumstances, and … did not feel for the labouring classes because he had got his cake buttered on both sides'; consequently, 'the poor had turned their backs upon him, and would for ever hate him in Leeds – (Cries of 'They will, lad')', a prediction which proved largely correct.[90]

The speakers also expressed hatred of what Baines stood for. James Mann, for example, attacked the 'advocates of free trade' and, 'the great capitalists' who were 'triumphing in their distresses'. Likewise, popular fears that 'machinery is throwing large numbers out of employment' found a champion in John Ayrey, who, after noting the *Mercury*'s coverage of new machinery and railroads rather than on distress, declared that, 'they had sufficient machinery at present'. Indeed, he challenged the

---

88 *LM, HCC* 28 Nov. 1829.
89 *LM, HCC* 28 Nov. 1829; *LP* 26 Dec. 1829.
90 *LP, LM* 5 Dec. 1829. Although he later took over the Saddle Inn in Leeds, Ayrey may originally have been a cloth-dresser, the trade recorded for his eldest son in the 1851 census.

Mercury's prediction that the general spread of railroads would save enough corn to make repeal of the Corn Laws unnecessary. He continued in a topical vein:

> Was not the corn bill one of the greatest evils to commerce which we have? And would not the substitution of locomotive power for horses do away with the labour of two men for every horse that was supplanted? He thought they neither wanted rail-roads nor locomotive carriages, they had already sufficient conveyance by water and by land.[91]

Ironically, when the meeting ended, between 300 and 400 people returned to Leeds by the Middleton Railway in order to demonstrate outside the *Mercury's* office!

Predictably the *Mercury* reacted with renewed hostility to the day's events, particularly the manhandling of its reporter. It printed an account of proceedings from a sceptical correspondent who connected the meetings with September's ill-fated 'Reform Union'.[92] There is no reason to disbelieve Foster's and Mann's vigorous denials of any collusion in the actual preparation of the original meeting. However, once the agitation was underway, they literally jumped on the hustings wagon; and seeing both the commercial and political potential of a reservoir of discontent, naturally sought to tap it.[93] It is clear that this outburst of grassroots feelings, allied to news of the progress of the London Radical Reform Association, gave the radical reformers fresh heart. By the middle of December handbills were being distributed, publicising a meeting of 'the association of the friends of Radical Reform on the principles of universal suffrage, annual parliaments and vote by ballot'.[94]

This meeting at the Union Inn yard of 'the members of the Association recently formed in Leeds' marks the public re-emergence of the radical 'union' (which had maintained a shadowy, small-scale existence since the defeats of September) under a new title, the 'Radical Reform Association'. Connections with the recent Hunslet Moor meetings were stressed by Mann, who praised those gatherings for drawing public attention to distress. However, the explicitly ultra-radical resolutions reflected the composition and preoccupations of the platform. So much so, in fact, that a non-member complained about the absence of any discussion of distress. The radical speakers were far from preaching to the converted. Indeed, the meeting once again demonstrated their inability to control a large public gathering and after Mann had been repeatedly heckled by 'infidel' republicans and supporters of Baines, the meeting was adjourned for a week, amidst much confusion and disorder. On reflection, the radicals cancelled this further meeting, allegedly on account of Cobbett's imminent arrival in the area – a move which brought a sharp rebuke for their timidity from Henry Hunt.[95] This equivocation confirmed the weak base on which the Leeds RRA was founded.

---

91 *LP* 5 Dec. 1829.

92 *LM* 5 Dec. 1829.

93 *LP* 5 Dec. 1829. The *Patriot's* circulation was anything but healthy at this time, and there had been difficulties with printing, *LP* 12 Dec. 1829. Interestingly, at one time the Union Inn room was used as a printing room.

94 *LP* 19 Dec. 1829. On the chequered history of the RRA in London, see Belchem, 'Orator Hunt', pp. 148-51.

95 *LP, LM* 26 Dec. 1829; *LM* 9 Jan. 1830.

3: Radical Reformers and Political Unions in Early 1830

a) Radicals and 'renegades' in Leeds, January-September 1830

By the winter of 1829-30 both Cobbett and Hunt were vying to be recognised as the natural spokesman of the popular radicals, and their activities in the London RRA were reported widely in the provincial press. Cobbett, particularly focusing on the currency question, had once more taken on the mantle of a national leader; and in early 1830 he undertook an extensive speaking tour of the North of England. Except at Huddersfield, where organisational mistakes limited numbers, his lectures in the West Riding attracted sizeable and even 'respectable' audiences.[96]

For the ultra-radicals, however, the tour was less illuminating. Cobbett extemporised on currency and taxation rather than reform, and the prohibitive price of admission only gave credence to the *Mercury*'s and *Intelligencer*'s insinuations that his motives were pecuniary. Even so, his mere presence in the area added a few degrees to the local political temperature, and at a meeting of the Leeds RRA in early February, James Mann (who had spoken to Cobbett in Leeds) publicly thanked him for his lectures. This meeting, as well as demonstrating that the reformers were not moribund, also showed them to be closely in touch with parliamentary and other national developments, such as the formation of the Birmingham Political Union in January and the subsequent establishment of the Metropolitan Political Union in London. However, it also indicated that their fortunes were to some extent dependent on external stimuli.[97]

The split between the 'Radicals' and the 'Moderates' remained wide, despite an attempt by Thomas Mason, a popular local figure, to bridge the gap at a further public meeting of the Leeds RRA in mid-March. The meeting voted its approval of the Metropolitan Union's proceedings; and after Foster's opening lines had literally almost brought the house down, he continued outside to ridicule Mason's approval of a petition for 'full, free and equal representation'. Predictably another rumpus with Smithson's Carlileite faction ended the evening's proceedings, and provided useful sparring for the main fight three days later.[98]

Here at a 'respectable' public meeting on 'Retrenchment and Reform', the radical reformers got their comeuppance. What the *Mercury* termed a 'foolish and factious attempt' by Mann, Foster and Ayrey to include a commitment to universal suffrage, the ballot and triennial parliaments in the proposed petition shattered any semblance of

---

96 *LM, LP* 9, 16, 23, 30 Jan. 1830. Cobbett spoke at Halifax, Huddersfield, Dewsbury and Leeds. His Leeds audience included several magistrates and bankers as well as most of the town's merchants and manufacturers. See *HCC* 30 Jan. 1830 for the widespread acceptance of Cobbett's ideas in 'respectable' circles.

97 *LP* 13 Feb. 1830. For example, one speaker condemned Russell's Bill to enfranchise Manchester, Birmingham and Leeds, and another approved the 'Birmingham Union'. James Mann was also in touch with grassroots developments in Leeds and spoke at a stuff-weavers' meeting to protest against the spread of power-looms, *LP* 20 Feb. 1830.

98 *LP, LM* 20 Mar. 1830. Thomas Mason had been a major figure on the local popular radical platform, along with Mann and Brayshaw, in the post-war period. (See, for example, *LM* 24 July, 7 Aug., 4 Sept., 13, 27 Nov., 11 Dec. 1819).

unity amongst the reformers. It merely invited the united opposition of Whigs, 'Liberals', republicans and 'renegade radicals', like Mason who cited the continual splits as his reason for not joining the radical reformers. This powerful alliance easily carried the day, and when the unamended petition was forwarded to London it allegedly contained over 13,000 signatures.[99]

Although easily outnumbered, the radicals, and Foster in particular, were 'neither disappointed nor dismayed at the very small minority we are in'.[100] By April the RRA had moved further away from its earlier, conciliatory, approval of the Birmingham Political Union; and familiar speakers now praised Hunt and the more radical platform of the Metropolitan Political Union.[101] But whilst members may have found consolation in James Duffy's maxim, 'if we are few and united, we are better than a thousand divided', their persistent weakness and inability to dominate their own meetings may have prompted them to reconsider their position and adopt a more conciliatory approach, in line with that shown by operatives in neighbouring areas.[102]

Exactly a week after the last, embittered, meeting of the RRA, a public meeting requisitioned by 138 householders, opened on Hunslet Moor with the vaguely worded intention of 'forming an Union of all Classes of the people to promote an Effectual and Radical Reform in the Commons' House of Parliament'. The speakers, who included most of the leading lights of the RRA, as well as the Rev. George Beaumont, (a radical Wesleyan Methodist preacher from Norwich), reiterated familiar arguments that 'real radical reform' formed the only lasting solution to distress and its many causes, and the meeting approved the establishment of a 'Leeds Union' based on the Metropolitan principles, as well as a list of people to act as Political Council until July 1831.[103]

The absence of any mention of this body in the following two months, however, suggests that the putative 'Leeds Union' got off to a slow start. Initially, the parliamentary recess, a good June in the woollen trade and a bitter strike in the stuff sector all focused attention elsewhere. Soon, however, the nascent Political Union's fortunes were overtaken by outside events – notably the King's death and the candidature of Henry Brougham, an avowed reformer, in the Yorkshire county election.

---

99 *LM* 20 Mar., *LI* 25 Mar. 1830; Turberville and Beckwith, 'Leeds', p. 29.

100 *LP*, *LM* 20 Mar. 1830. Foster's consistently cantankerous character may not have helped the radical cause. His career in Leeds is interspersed with personal-financial vendettas, for example, with Fothergill (1829), Baines (1829–30), Oastler (1833). According to Dr. Rob Sykes the same pattern was repeated when he moved to Bolton.

101 *LP* 10 Apr. 1830. The leading speakers were Mann, Foster, James, Duffy, John Watts, John Ayrey, and Joseph Oates.

102 This weakness was shown, for example, in a meeting on proposed (disenfranchising) poor rates legislation, chaired by a future Chartist, Joshua Barnard, *LP* 29 May 1830. This issue was easily taken over by the 'moderate' alliance *LP* 5, 12 June 1830.

103 *HCC*, *LM*, *LP* 5 June 1830. Unfortunately, only the names of the three auditors survive and we can only speculate that the Leeds PU was more broadly based than its predecessor.

The intricacies of this election campaign have been covered in detail elsewhere.[104] Brougham and Viscount Morpeth, the two Whig candidates, attracted huge gatherings throughout the region, and their overwhelming endorsement at the polls was a great triumph for Baines, the Leeds reformers, and 'the stray sheep of the Radical interest'.[105]

The attitudes and activities of the main flock of local radicals at this time tend to be lost amidst all the electioneering excitement. Their thunder was stolen by Brougham's candidature; and attempts by Mann and Foster to expose the limits of his commitment to reform at the huge Leeds meeting of July 27 failed miserably. Outgunned in the local contest, the Leeds popular radicals set their sights further afield – to Hunt's candidature at Preston and events in France – for solace and inspiration.[106]

Whatever its immediate psephological impact, the news from France undoubtedly heightened political interest and expectation. Ultra-radicals, in particular, eagerly seized upon its inspirational potential. In Leeds, for example, James Mann first used the French experience as a propaganda tool on 2 Aug, a couple of weeks earlier than Professor Gash had previously allowed.[107]

The coincidence of a keen local election and events in France gave radicals in different parts of the textile area a boost. However, before examining how they sought to cash in on the resurgence of political interest occasioned by the coincidence of a keen local election and the July Revolution in France, it is first necessary to retrace our steps and see how working-class radicals in Huddersfield and other places both contributed and responded to the quickening of the pulse of popular radicalism.

b) The Birth of the Almondbury Political Union

In the Huddersfield area, a good autumn trade in 1829 provided but a brief respite from the suffocating hardship which the distress survey had exposed; and as the customary November lull rapidly deepened into full depression it is possible to sense the growing impatience of the local operatives and their committee. In the fancy trade those lucky enough to find employment were faced with a 25 per cent reduction in wages; whilst in the more extensive woollen trade the 'truly deplorable' condition of the operative piecemakers was matched only by the abject poverty of any surviving small clothiers. The deteriorating local situation came to a head at a respectable public meeting called in mid-December, 'to take into consideration the present DEPLORABLE STATE OF THE OPERATIVES AND LABOURING CLASSES'.[108]

---

104 Norman Gash, 'Brougham and the Yorkshire Election of 1830', *Proceedings of the Leeds Literary and Philosophical Society*, 8 (1956), pp. 19-35; see also Turberville and Beckwith, 'Leeds', pp. 30-2; *LM* 17, 24, 31 July 1830.

105 *LI* 29 July 1830.

106 These two events formed the subject matter of another Hunslet Moor meeting, *LP* 7 Aug. 1830.

107 *LP* 7 Aug. 1830. Norman Gash, 'English Reform and French Revolution in the General Election of 1830', in R. Pares and A. J. P. Taylor (eds.), *Essays Presented to Sir Lewis Namier* (London: Macmillan, 1956), p. 263 ff. cites its first use as 18 August.

108 *LM* 14; 21 Nov. and 12 Dec. (letters of 'K'); *LI* 19 Dec. 1829.

On the operatives' side the tone was set by George Beaumont, who after reminding his audience of the increasing distress, urged them to 'form themselves into bodies and societies, and join the societies of Reformers in other towns, and let us tell the Government, we will be oppressed no longer'. The solutions to their dire situation were political rather than charitable. Speaking with his distinctive mix of humour and grit, and holding a letter from the Huddersfield Relief Committee, he mocked the news that it had re-opened its 1*d* a quart soup kitchen for the winter:

> Here is the envy and admiration of the world – a Soup Shop! – (*Tremendous laughing, and cheering which continued for some time.*) I do not want to give offence. Was it reasonable that they should bear to be relieved by soup? They did not want soup – they wanted an opportunity of earning their own living by working – (*cries of order, order from the chair*). Let those who want to thrust soup down their throats, thrust it down their own. (Order, from the Chair). Gentlemen, as I am not allowed to proceed, I must withdraw. [*Tremendous cheering, mixed with hissing, followed the concluding remarks of this speech, which threw the whole meeting into confusion.*][109]

This theatrical outburst which shocked many of the 'respectable' members of the platform, pleased the operatives in equal measure. The next speaker, the Rev. Drawbridge, was roundly hissed when he claimed that distress was attributable to God rather than government. Other operative speakers, 'men of acute minds, ready speech and, lively feelings' and some 'errors of opinion' in the *Mercury*'s patronising assessment, followed Beaumont's lead. John Spivey, 'whose appearance evinced great distress' in the words of the *Chronicle*, spoke movingly of his eighteen-year-old disabled daughter and neatly summarised the values of the local weaving community in asserting that, 'they did not want charity, they wanted work and wages'.[110]

William Stocks jnr., in a long sympathetic speech, endorsed this plea, arguing that wage rises were indispensable to everyone's prosperity and advocating a wage-fixing system by local 'boards of appeal'. The response of the local manufacturers, however, was characteristically cautious and non-committal. John Woods of Dalton, a major fancy manufacturer, feared foreign competition whilst Joseph Batley of Armitage blamed distress solely on the Government's currency policy. This latter point was later embodied in the meeting's resolutions which, after reiterating familiar sentiments about the ubiquity of distress, modestly recommended the formation of committees in each locality to help parish officers raise money and dole out relief. To carry these resolutions into effect, the meeting appointed its own committee whose composition (like the resolutions themselves) merely reflected the pervading influence of the 'respectable' predominantly Whig-liberal gentlemen and manufacturers who had convened the meeting.[111]

---

109 *LM* 12, *LP* 19 Dec. 1829. These comments gave rise to a post-meeting controversy and prompted Beaumont and Spivey to deny that they were opposed to charity in itself; and to argue that the money for relief should come from landowners, pensioners and the clergy, through essentially 'political' reforms, (*LM* 16 Jan. 1830). (Square brackets in original.)

110 *LM* 12, 19 Dec; *HCC* 12 Dec. 1829.

111 *LM* 12, 19 Dec; *HCC* 12 Dec. 1829. The committee contained the names of many leading Whig-Liberals; William Stocks jnr., Dickenson and Dixon were the only 'radical'

Clearly, the operatives' committee as a whole had not turned its face on co-operation with this powerful group. Edward Dixon, for one, recalled the anti-truck association of 1827 and pressed for renewed action about this continuing abuse. For all the strong words, radical reform was not yet seen as a viable option; so that when, at the end of the meeting, a workman proposed radical reform and universal suffrage to protect them once relieved, as the *Patriot* disappointedly noted, 'he met with no support from the crowd'. And significantly it was Beaumont and Spivey who proposed the meeting's final motion of thanks to the 'kind-hearted Manufacturers and Gentlemen who had assisted this far'.[112]

However, as distress persisted throughout the early months of 1830 and radicalism gathered momentum in Birmingham and London, the active members of the operatives' committee adopted a more explicitly radical stance. In the absence of any large public meetings, the committee continued to function as both a relieving and an agitating body, with leading figures like Beaumont, Spivey and Dickenson endeavouring to keep the reality of distress, and the grievances of the operatives in the public eye. They had little trouble in achieving this since wage reductions, the introduction of machinery and the general state of trade continued to figure prominently in the local press.[113]

The operatives' growing dilemma – whether to continue on the road of collaboration with the local 'respectables' or to pursue their own independent course – came to a head in early March 1830 with a further all-party meeting on distress in the Huddersfield Court House. Like the similar meeting three months earlier, the platform contained representatives of all sections of the local community. However, unlike the earlier meeting where the crowd had rejected the endorsement of universal suffrage, the mention of radical reform now met with a more favourable response. After William Stocks jnr. had first raised the subject, the ever-controversial George Beaumont proceeded to emphasise the futility of petitioning under the present representative system. The Irish Catholics had won their rights by union, and he therefore urged his audience to imitate the 'noble example' of Birmingham. For their part the 'moderate' Tory and 'liberal' Whig speakers offered only sympathy and the usual solutions: currency reform, retrenchment and reduced taxation.[114]

That some at least were not happy with this, was shown towards the end of the meeting when John Spivey, after being called to order for advocating parliamentary reform, announced their intention of shortly holding a meeting on the subject. Three weeks later placards signed by 21 householders, announcing a 'REFORM' meeting appeared in Almondbury; and on Easter Monday a large working-class audience convened on Almondbury Bank to consider 'the propriety of forming a Political Union, to correspond with the one lately formed at Birmingham'.[115] The meeting

representatives. The town's leading Tory, John Whitacre, withdrew (*LI* 17 Dec. 1829).

112 *LM*, *HCC* 12 Dec. 1829; *LP* 19 Dec. 1829.

113 For developments in London, see Prothero, *Artisans and Politics*, pp. 275-6. *LP* 4 Feb; *HCC* 20 Feb; *LI* 4 Mar; *LP* 3 Apr; *LM* 13, 20 Apr. 1830.

114 *LP* 19 Dec. 1829; *LM*, *LP* 13 Mar. 1830. The other radical working-class speakers were John Spivey, William Leadbeater and Samuel Dickenson, all fancy weavers.

115 *LP* 3; 17 Apr; *LM* 17 Apr. 1830. The Leeds RRA (on the London model) had been formed four days earlier.

marks a reversion to the independent line of action pursued in the previous summer's series of meetings, and must be seen as the first significant break with the Huddersfield manufacturing and mercantile establishment.

The meeting also signalled a split within the operatives' leadership cohort. It is impossible to date this precisely, but if Samuel Dickenson's account in May is to be believed, it seems that the original operatives' committee had dissolved itself or fallen into disuse some time before the April meeting. Old stalwarts like Dixon, Eckersley and Earnshaw did not participate at the Huddersfield meeting in March; and by this time the initiative had clearly passed from the 'Old Committee' to a 'radical caucus' – Beaumont, Dickenson and Spivey – all of whom remained in the public eye throughout the early months of the year.[116]

It was this group which dominated the Easter Monday meeting with their coherent and articulate radical analysis of the operatives' situation. Conciliation and compromise remained the keynote of the speeches. Samuel Dickenson for example, exhorted, 'all classes in society, both high and low, rich and poor ... [to] come forward and join in one strong bond of union', which would demand 'an extension of our suffrages and political privileges, that cannot be gained by petitioning ... privileges that must be gained by the united efforts of the middle and labouring classes'. So, although John Spivey was 'decidedly of the opinion that the London Union is preferable' – a view which the majority of the audience clearly shared – he nevertheless recommended the adoption of the Birmingham model in terms which foreshadow later 'first step' reactions to the Reform Bill:

> ... if we can get the elective franchise extended as to the house-holder or rate-payer, I say it would not only better our conditions, but in many respects be equivalent to universal suffrage (*No, no, 'let us have the other and all: it is all one expense whether we have all or part'*). Again I say these little differences ought to be conceded... We are all agreed that Reform is indispensably necessary (*'It is'*) and I say that of Birmingham is likely in my opinion to bring in the greatest multitude from the wealthy class of society to unite with us.'[117]

Spivey's conciliatory pragmatism was supported by Thomas Baxter (who five years earlier had been prominent in the Fancy Weavers' Union) and by a leading fancy manufacturer, John Woods, who urged general resolutions and warned that 'if they thought nothing less than annual parliaments and universal suffrage would do, they must be content to go by themselves, as the majority of the community would not go as far as that'. The meeting took Woods' advice and did not adopt either the Birmingham or London model; a hesitation noted by radical reformers in the capital.[118]

However, the genuine hopes which the meeting raised of a unified assault on the corrupt system soon faded when it became evident that the middle-class inhabitants of Huddersfield were unwilling to join Almondbury in a broad-based reform union. The attempt at compromise and co-operation had not only failed but left a residue of

---

116 *LM* 1, 8, 15 May 1830, *LP*, *HCC* 15 May 1830.
117 *HCC* 15 May 1830.
118 *LP* 8 May 1830 (London Radical Reform Association).

bitterness and resentment. Beaumont for one 'was extremely sorry that they had lost so much time and made so much labour in visiting, and otherwise inviting the middle class of the neighbourhood to co-operate with them', only to find that 'they seemed to be inclined to stand aloof from them as long as they could'. His declared solution was working-class self-help, 'Let the lower orders depend only on their own exertions for bettering their own circumstances', and, 'unite in one strong bond on union, and loudly and firmly call for a real and radical reform in the Common's House of Parliament'. He 'thought the middle class would, ere long, unite with them, but at all events they should go steadily on' and form 'a general political union between the middling and labouring classes of Almondbury and its neighbourhood'. The Birmingham compromise was not revived, and the meeting elected a political council of nine to manage a local union modelled on the Metropolitan example.[119]

The establishment of a Political Union at Almondbury formalised a process of radicalisation which had been set in train the previous summer. It forms an interesting contrast with the ultra-radical agitation in Leeds. The emerging radical leadership in both areas shared a broadly similar analysis of distress, and had broken, temporarily at least, with local Whig-liberals. The radical press and James Mann in particular provided another common link.[120] Yet the distinctive trajectories followed and the different outcomes that their agitations achieved reflect the very different starting-points. Whereas, the Leeds men regularly struggled to cope with the factional nature of local popular politics and to mobilise consistent grassroots support from a diverse working population, Almondbury radicalism was firmly rooted in the values, traditions and recent economic experiences of the dominant occupational community.[121]

4: New Political Unions in Later 1830

a) Political Unions and the Yorkshire Election, March-August 1830

Almondbury and Leeds were beacons of hope as the cause of radical reform struggled to maintain momentum in the spring of 1830.[122] But they were not the only centres of local activity. In Keighley, where workers were actively organising to secure wage

---

119 *LM* 1 May (Beaumont's letter urging middle class reformers to take up the issue); *LM*, *LP*, *HCC* 15 May 1830. The President was Samuel Midgley (1785?-1859?), an Almondbury shopkeeper and major local figure right into the Chartist period. Six of the nine council members were active in radical politics in 1838-42.

120 For example, Mann had sent the Almondbury radicals twelve copies of the rules of the London Metropolitan Union, *LM* 17 Apr. 1830. The Almondbury radicals' tactical dilemma reflected contemporary discussion in the press, such as the *Leeds Mercury's* (1 May 1830) criticism of the *Weekly Free Press'* advocacy of separate unions for every class and party. For a reference to wider contacts and correspondence, see Beaumont's speech at Elland, *HCC* 5 June 1830.

121 Possibly because of its 'out of town' location, Lopatin-Lummis, *Political Unions*, significantly underestimates the importance of the Almondbury PU. There is abundant evidence that the organization lasted well beyond the putative end-date of autumn 1830 (p. 45).

122 See Belchem, *'Orator' Hunt*, pp. 155-7, on internal tensions and Hunt's unsuccessful attempts to launch a national campaign.

rises, John Bradley (a radical painter) chaired the inaugural meeting of a Political Union in early April. The 'respectable' founders enrolled about a hundred members in an association based initially on the Birmingham (household suffrage) principles. By early May, however, the London RRA was claiming that the Keighley reformers were 'embracing the whole measure of political regeneration' offered by the Metropolitan model. Another Political Union was also formed at nearby Haworth, but no information survives about its allegiance or longevity.[123]

The picture is similarly incomplete about the formation of a union in the 'populous clothing village' of Morley (four miles south west of Leeds) on Easter Tuesday. Around a hundred members were enrolled and the thousand strong meeting adopted the London (Metropolitan) resolutions. Radical sentiment was still evident in late May, when the presence of 'the Morley Reformers' and 'the Gentleman amateurs of the Morley Band' at the Leeds radicals' Hunslet Moor meeting were highlighted in the local press.[124] The precise backcloth to this radical upsurge in the village remains obscure, though once again the local industrial atmosphere may have contributed. It is perhaps significant that the petition passed by the Easter meeting referred to the injury caused to the handloom weaver by the unrestricted use of power-looms. Whilst these machines were not yet a direct threat in Morley itself, nor had the village suffered disproportionately during the previous winter's distress, it is possible that the failure of a violent clothiers' strike the previous November had left a residue of bitterness which heightened political awareness.[125]

In Bradford, by contrast, the operatives remained quiet. They had suffered less than their neighbours in the winter of 1829-30, and although wages stayed low, employment was fairly full. The 'liberal' part of the manufacturing class, for their part, seemed content to let Leeds take the lead, whilst they supervised the contentious installation of power-looms in some of their shops.[126]

Generally, however, the fertile nature of the local industrial ground was a factor in the growth of these radical seedlings. Economic and political grievances were seen as inseparable and intertwined, but with a fundamental root-cause. Abram Hanson, making his first recorded public speech, at the Easter Monday Almondbury meeting, for example, argued that,

> The evils of Machinery and the unjust monopolies with all their various ramifications, are but so many effects emanating from the grand source of all evils – mis-government. (*Hear, hear.*) … So that it is in vain for us to look for permanent relief until that den of corruption, the House of Commons, be changed by a Radical Reform. (*Applause.*) Now the question is, – How is Reform to be obtained? I answer, by establishing political unions in every town and village throughout the empire, to investigate into the theory and practice of Government, and to unite all under one great bond of union, so that we may be

---

123 *HCC* 27 Mar. 1830, *LP* 22 May 1830; *LM, LP, HCC* 10 Apr. 1830.
124 *LM* 17 Apr.; *HCC* 5 June. The 'Morley people' were involved in an altercation on Holbeck Moor 'on their return home', *LP* 12 June 1830.
125 *LM* 17 Apr; *LP* 1 May 1830; *LM* 14 and *LI* 12 Nov. 1829.
126 *LI* 18, *HCC* 20 Feb. 1830.

enabled to bring all the moral power of the people into one grand focus, and to demand with one voice our just and natural rights. (*Hear, hear.*)[127]

In Halifax, which like Bradford saw a spring revival in trade, the situation was again slightly different. Although Cobbett's visit in January had not nurtured the formation of any permanent political organisation, the town remained a Cobbettite stronghold. Yet independent working-class activity remained absent, apart from the lone involvement of Thomas Cliffe in the Almondbury agitation.[128]

Shoemaker Abram Hanson, another 'outsider' who attended the early public meetings at Almondbury was more successful than Cliffe in transposing some of the fancy-weavers' radical enthusiasm to his native area: Elland-cum-Greetland. Like the townships to the south and east, Elland, a populous area between Halifax and Huddersfield, producing mainly coarse woollens and a few fancy fabrics, suffered greatly in the depression of 1829-30. By April 1830 the *Chronicle* was expecting the speedy formation of a reform union in the area. That such a meeting did not happen immediately may well have been due to the wish of local reformers to watch, and perhaps learn from proceedings at Almondbury. Contact between the two centres was certainly close and when a public meeting was finally held at Nabs End, Elland in early June, the principal speakers apart from Hanson and Cliffe, were all Almondbury men.[129]

Yet developments in the two places, although seemingly synchronised, were not identical. The most striking features of the Elland public meeting, apart from its impressive size and festive air, were its respectability, caution and constitutionalism. The focus of attack was upon the 'corrupt aristocracy' and their 'placemen, pensioners and tax-eaters' who had distorted the balance of the constitution. According to Hanson this was to be achieved by 'co-operation between the middle and lower classes of society' since it is 'the middle class, united with the honest industrious labourer that constitutes a nation'. This sentiment, together with Thomas Cliffe's observation that 'the labourers were not dissatisfied with their employers', forms the keynote of the meeting. It goes a long way towards explaining why Hanson, to the obvious surprise of the Almondbury delegates, was content merely to propose a vague motion which postponed the formation of a loosely-defined Political Union until a second meeting in early July.[130]

The projected meeting never took place, Hanson ruefully observing that, 'the great mass of the people remained in a state of apathy with regard to their political privileges'.[131] Lethargy, however, was less discernible in Almondbury, now firmly

---

127 *LM* 17 Apr. 1830.

128 See, for example, *HCC* 12 June 1830 for a meeting of 'friends of Cobbett' to start subscriptions to get him elected to parliament. Cliffe chaired the Almondbury meeting on 10 May.

129 *LM* 11 July 1829; *HCC* 17 Apr; 5 June 1830.

130 *HCC, LP, LM* 5 June 1830. The meeting attracted 3,500-4,000 people (half allegedly women and children). The requisitioning committee included tradesmen and five 'very respectable inhabitants'. At the end of the meeting the band struck up 'God save the King' and 'several national and patriotic airs'.

131 *LM, LP* 10 July 1830. Another factor in the Elland postponement was the death of the King

committed to Hunt and the Metropolitan model, which hosted another outdoor Political Union meeting on Almondbury Bank on 5 July. A range of speakers, including Hanson, addressed familiar themes in front of a healthy crowd. The meeting was celebrated as the first anniversary of the Almondbury Political Union, cementing the symbolic link with the sombre gatherings to complain about 'Distress' the previous summer. Equally, the presence on the platform of George Bolland of Huddersfield foreshadowed the imminent emergence of a radical reform response in Huddersfield itself.

The landownership pattern in the town meant that the bulk of the working population lived outside Huddersfield township.[132] And hitherto the agitation to link the issues of distress and parliamentary reform had flourished amongst the fancy and woollen weavers in the villages outside Huddersfield, rather than amongst the shopkeepers, artisans and tradesmen of the town. Attempts by the Almondbury leadership to gain the co-operation of the respectable middle class had failed to achieve more than a few token displays of concern and sympathy. The strong opinions voiced by the operatives at the town meetings of December 1829 and March 1830 perhaps made local notables wary of broaching the reform question. In the words of one disgruntled 'Looker-on' in July 1830 'why there never is a public meeting in Huddersfield, but the respectable part of the Inhabitants suffer the insulted with the impertinence of an ex-Linen Draper's [William Stocks jnr.] well-trained band of Almondbury Orators'.[133]

This was not the case, however, ten days later when about 150 'respectable' freeholders met in the Court House to consider the state of the representation. The stimulus here was not distress, but the imminent county election. The speakers, comprising the full range of 'Liberal' opinion from solid Whigs (George Senior) to 'liberal' Whigs (John Wood) to town-radicals (William Stocks jnr. and George Darwent), all urged support for Brougham – a candidate pledged to retrenchment and a 'more perfect representation of the people'. When the election campaign finally got underway, popular support in Huddersfield swung firmly behind the local 'Liberals'' advocacy of Brougham and Morpeth. So strongly, in fact, that when their candidate Duncombe visited the town local Tories had to ask George Darwent to silence the continual booing and hissing.[134]

The July meeting and subsequent events in Huddersfield are perhaps symptomatic of the ambiguous effect of the Yorkshire election upon what had hitherto been a predominantly grassroots working-class agitation for reform. Whilst the election campaign eventually aroused political interest and gave a wider currency to notions of political change, it also largely stole the thunder of the small pockets of radical reformers in places like Almondbury and Elland. Throughout the region Brougham and Morpeth were met by massive, well-orchestrated crowds keen to support a liberal 'first-step' towards change.[135] However, amidst all the noise and ballyhoo of

---

and the start of the resulting election campaign.
132 Stocks in BPP 1833, VI, p. 637.
133 *HCC* 17 July 1830. The 'ex-Linen Draper' was William Stocks jnr.
134 *LP, LM* 24, 31 July 1830.
135 *LM, LP* 17, 24, 31 July 1830.

electioneering the voice of an unrepresented labouring population was largely drowned out.

b) Aftermath of the July Revolution, August–December 1830

Yet, if local radical reformers were dismayed by their lack of impact at the election hustings, the news of the 'Revolution in France' (which reached the columns of the local press on 21 July) gave them fresh heart and added another twist to the spiral of growing political anticipation.[136] In Keighley the PU passed a resolution urging all the religious denominations to preach sermons and take a collection for the orphans and widows in France. In Elland, where the reformers had finally re-convened their meeting in mid-August, many of the numerous (1,500) audience wore tricolour emblems, and the hustings were bedecked with a huge tricolour flag. George Beaumont declared early on that, 'it would be a consolation to every friend of freedom, to know that the heroic people of France had bravely struggled, and had been successful in emancipating themselves from the iron hand of tyranny and oppression'. Yet despite the invocation of 'revolutionary' slogans, the establishment of a moderate reform union on the Birmingham model reflected the respectable roots of the meeting and repeated the restrained tone of the previous gathering in June.[137]

Two weeks later the leading Elland reformer, Abram Hanson, attended a more radical repast attended by nearly two hundred reformers at Huddersfield to 'celebrate the triumph of the French people over despotism', and spoke alongside James Mann of Leeds, Thomas Cliffe of Halifax, and (in the *Intelligencer*'s words) 'that little busy-body George Beaumont, Dickenson, Vevers and other noted "reformers" resident in Almondbury and its neighbourhood'. The contingent which marched in from the south east was certainly a strong one. Indeed, the paper's sarcastic comment that Almondbury formed 'the grand focus of West Riding radicalism' contained more than a grain of truth. Although the paper dismissed the dinner as a failure (indeed, there was no immediate follow-up) it was undoubtedly important in bringing the experienced operative campaigners from the fancy-weaving townships into closer contact with radical sympathisers amongst the shopkeepers and tradesmen of Huddersfield.[138]

In Leeds, which as usual was slightly slower off the mark than other places, the news from France was well received by a wide cross-section of 'liberal' opinion. On general emotive issues like this, past, often very bitter, differences were forgotten;[139] and John Smithson, scourge of the radicals' earlier efforts to form radical reform unions, joined with leading popular radicals at a lively and well-supported dinner to celebrate the 'French Revolution'. The event just about managed to steer clear of

---

136 See, for example, *LM, LP* 7, 14 Aug. 1830.

137 *LP* 28 Aug.; *HCC, LP* 21 Aug. 1830.

138 *LI* 9, *LM* 11 Sept. 1830. The dinner marks the first recorded public appearance of Lawrence Pitkethly. The other town-based radicals included Hopkinson and (possibly James) Brook. Important out of town speakers included familiar Almondbury names, plus Vevers (presumably Thomas – a radical stalwart) and Benjamin Lockwood, the Kirkheaton surgeon who became treasurer of the Almondbury PU.

139 See, for example, the platform at a public meeting, *LM* 25 Sept. 1830, which included Baineseite Whigs, more radically inclined Whigs, Carlileite republicans and popular radicals.

contentious issues and confined itself to general resolutions and safe toasts to Hunt, Cobbett, O'Connell and, interestingly, Oastler. In the words of Foster's *Patriot* the meeting was 'orderly' and 'respectable' and 'included some of the most intelligent operatives and little tradesmen this town possesses'.[140]

This coming together may have reflected a certain loss of impetus amongst the radical reformers in the early autumn; with the revival of trade, the anti-climax following the West Riding election and the last throes of Wellington's ministry all contributing a sense of suspended animation. Radical leaders continued to be active. James Mann, for example, spoke at meetings at Keighley and Huddersfield, as well as at the public dinner in Leeds where he criticised the exclusion of the 'productive classes' in Lord John Russell's proposed Bill, and put forward his own ideas for equal electoral districts.[141] But reform was just one issue competing with a number of others. A flourishing Fall trade and wage rises in both the woollen and worsted areas also helped to divert interest away from 'Distress and Reform' – except in the fancy-weaving districts where, at the height of the autumn trade, 3,000 operatives were still totally without work.[142]

The Almondbury Political Union, now unequivocally in the Huntite orbit, went from strength to strength. Samuel Midgley, the union's President, read a letter from Hunt to a well-attended meeting in late September and resolutions spoke of him as 'the most proper person' to act as 'our leader and adviser'.[143] Leaders from the Almondbury 'grand focus', in close contact with Preston radicals, threw their weight behind Hunt's plan for a mass petitioning campaign and engaged in local missionary work. In the middle of October, for example, Beaumont and Dickenson addressed a meeting of over 400 in Honley, a contiguous fancy and woollen township, resulting in the formation of a Political Union on the Metropolitan principles.[144] The following Saturday 'Reformers from the different hamlets surrounding Almondbury entered the town with tri-coloured flags and various inscriptions upon them, attended by a band of music' in support of a large Almondbury Political Union meeting to petition the new King about 'Distress and Reform'. Robert Lodge of Honley chaired the outdoor gathering and spoke at length alongside Thomas Ledger, the new Secretary of the Honley Political Union, emphasising close local ties and their commitment to Hunt's strategy.[145]

The birth of the Huddersfield Political Union in November 1830 also owed much to outside stimuli.[146] Processions from Almondbury, Kirkheaton and other outlying

---

140 *LP, LM* 23, *LI* 21 Oct. 1830. The *Mercury* had printed Oastler's 'Yorkshire Slavery' letter that very day.

141 *LM* 30 Oct; 11 Sept; *LP* 23 Oct. 1830.

142 *LM* 2 Oct. 1830. For the atmosphere and concerns of autumn/early winter 1830 see *LM, LP, HCC, LI* Aug-Dec. 1830.

143 *LP* 2 Oct. 1830. On Hunt's attempts to revive the Great Northern Union and his struggle to make a 'breakthrough to mass support', see Belchem, *'Orator' Hunt*, pp. 159-62.

144 *LM* 23 Oct. 1830.

145 *LP* 30 Oct. 1830. Robert Lodge (1791?-1846?) was a tailor. Thomas Ledger (1796-1833) was a woolsorter and 'a true, honest and virtuous character', whose loss in 1833 was mourned by his wife and four children, and by his community.

146 It also had faced some local middle-class hostility, with local printers refusing to print

townships swelled an exclusively working-class crowd. The platform included a range of 'outside' radical speakers such as Samuel Dickenson (who chaired the meeting), Thomas Cliffe of Halifax, Beaumont and Spivey of Almondbury, Thomas Walker of Honley, the itinerant Joseph Mitchell (of Preston) at this point still Hunt's 'most trusted lieutenant', and, interestingly, Benjamin Rushton of Halifax.[147] All added vital experience and expertise to procedures.

In addition, the meeting also brought into prominence important local radicals like Joshua Hobson, John Hooper and Joseph Hopkinson. It was these town-radicals (hitherto anonymous or concealed from our 'public' gaze) who comprised the officers and Council of the new Political Union formed 'upon the Metropolitan principle'. It is possible to allocate occupations to just a handful of the seventeen names who made up the 'Political Council'. The treasurer, George Darwent, was a joiner, as was Joshua Hobson at this time. Another member can positively be identified as a tailor, and two others as master manufacturers. Beyond this it is only possible to surmise that the new union's council drew its membership and support from a wide range of town artisans, shopkeepers and small manufacturers.[148] Interestingly the meeting prefigured future alignments, and illustrated common concerns, by denouncing Baines' attack on Oastler and condemning the former's misrepresentation of 'the state of the working-classes' in general.[149]

By this time the political temperature, both national and local, had risen appreciably. Newspapers carried reports of vociferous attacks on Wellington and his ministry. Widespread fears that he would go to war to help the Dutch against the new regimes in Belgium and France sent waves of indignation and resistance out from the capital.[150] In the local context the passions and interest aroused by agricultural disturbances in Kent, industrial conflict in Lancashire and particularly by Oastler's letter on factory conditions all added to the volatile political atmosphere and a sense of expectancy.[151]

---

publicity for the meeting, *LI* 28 Oct., *HCC* 30 Oct. 1830. This remained a problem in Huddersfield and eventually prompted the establishment of an independent working-class press, see below, pp. 326–7.

147 Thomas Walker was 'a respectable tradesman' who served as treasurer of the Honley PU (*LM* 23 Oct. 1830).

148 Lopatin-Lummis, *Political Unions*, p. 60 correctly highlights the PU's uncompromisingly radical objectives, but perhaps underplays its working-class credentials. For example, George Beaumont and Samuel Dickenson were fancy weavers, John Hanson was an operative; and Thomas Vever's pub and John Heaton's co-operative shop were radical hubs.

149 *LI* 4 Nov, *HCC* 6 Nov. 1830. William Lucas of Swan Yard (a publican) was secretary – thus establishing the PU's long connection with Swan Yard. This meeting marks Benjamin Rushton's first recorded public appearance in the early 1830s. The absence of Lawrence Pitkethly from this meeting is puzzling but may have been because he was preoccupied with an allegation of embezzlement, see *LM* 8 Jan. 1831. On Mitchell and his later defection from Hunt see Belchem, 'Orator Hunt', pp. 158–61, 181–2.

150 On the 'first crisis of the Reform period' in London see Prothero, *Artisans and Politics*, pp. 277–80.

151 See *LM, LP, HCC, LI* Oct–Dec. 1830. Brougham's elevation to Grey's Cabinet also meant a Yorkshire by-election.

Feelings ran high on the 'Yorkshire Slavery' question and on 17 November 300 people (mainly working men) successfully disrupted a 'respectable' anti-slavery meeting at Kirkheaton, a fancy township which had sent a strong contingent to the inaugural Huddersfield Political Union meeting. They heavily defeated a proposed abolitionist petition and loudly hissed a local gentleman who claimed that the condition of the West Indian slaves was ten times worse than that of the English poor. The operatives' spokesman, Thomas Leadbeater (a radical veteran of thirty years' standing) in a speech which again demonstrates the fusion of issues, declared instead, that the first object of all impartial men should be a fair representation, by which slavery at home and abroad would be abolished. In spite of John Wood's (a local manufacturer) offer of a separate meeting on reform, if they would allow the petition to pass, the operatives remained adamant and, undeterred, arranged for their own meeting.[152]

This took place on the first Saturday of December when about a thousand people, with bands and tricolours, gathered in a field to hear speakers from Almondbury, Honley and their own locality propose familiar resolutions, and the drawing up by a Political Council of a petition similar to those discussed earlier at Almondbury and Huddersfield. Although radicalism was not new to Kirkheaton, the formal establishment of a Political Union there marks another stage in the spread of radical organisation in the Huddersfield area.[153]

Outside the Huddersfield-Leeds axis, information is less abundant. In Keighley, where a Political Union had been in existence since spring, local radical reformers, like their counterparts around Huddersfield, appear to have resumed their activities in late October, with a joint meeting on France and reform. For once it is possible to speak with some certainty about the occupational composition of both platform and audience. The latter, numbering perhaps a thousand, were mainly woolcombers and handloom (stuff) weavers. The main speakers, who comprised two shopkeepers, three weavers and four combers, similarly reflected the predominance of the worsted trade in the local economy.[154] All were figures of some standing in the local working community who could turn readily from what with hindsight we term 'industrial' to 'political' concerns.[155] The Keighley Political Union provides the most clear-cut West Riding example of an alliance between operatives and local radical tradesmen. This fusion of interests explains why in terms of outlook, the Keighley 'Union' stood by the class collaborationist principles (of Birmingham) on which it was founded. However, even the *Mercury* was forced to admit that, though the October meeting displayed 'moderation and good sense', the resolutions were 'ultra'.[156]

---

152 *HCC* 27 Oct. 1830.

153 *LP, HCC* 11 Dec. 1830. Lopatin-Lummis, *Political Unions*, p. 47, says that the Kirkheaton PU was formed by Thomas Leadbetter between the summer and autumn of 1830, but I have found no reference to confirm this.

154 *LM, HCC, LP* 30 Oct. 1830. Beaumont and Mann also spoke.

155 For example, radical spokesmen like Gillet Sharp, Joseph Firth and Joseph Wood formed part of a delegation which tackled local manufacturers on the question of a proposed reduction for combing and weaving a month later, *LP* 25 Nov. 1830.

156 *LM* 30 Oct. 1830. The resolutions urged annual parliaments, universal suffrage and the ballot as the solution to increasing distress.

Elsewhere in the textile area the existence of political organisations amongst the operatives, whether independent or allied to elements of the lower middle-class, is difficult to substantiate. In Bradford, for example, which was without its own local paper at this time, the stream of local political life runs very murky and is lost at certain points.[157] In October the *Patriot* reported a meeting in Bradford on France, convened by Members of the 'Philosophical, Mechanical and Chemical Society'. The audience which was chiefly 'composed of operatives' passed an address signed by over 100 names and raised £2 14s in subscriptions to the 'brave Parisians'. A dinner was was held the following week, but no reports of this survive.[158]

In Halifax, which like Bradford enjoyed a relatively prosperous year, the symptoms of any independent political activity are similarly difficult to find. The most prominent local radical, Thomas Cliffe, who spoke at many 'away' public meetings throughout the summer and autumn of 1830, cuts an isolated, almost comic figure at 'home'.[159] The dispersed settlement and varied economy of the Halifax area made it a particularly difficult place to organise and it was only towards the end of the year that local radicals were finally stirred into action. Thomas Cliffe now advertised the proposed delivery of 'An Address to the people of Halifax' at the Union Cross Inn, and possibly as a result of this local reformers agreed to petition for complete reform and appointed a committee to meet at the same venue to arrange preliminaries for a public meeting.[160]

The Dewsbury area remains even more of an enigma at this time. After a poor start to the year, the blanket and carpet trades enjoyed something of a minor recovery in the summer and autumn months. There was no distressed group of workers to provide the necessary leadership and support for any incipient working-class radical reform movement. The major Whig-liberal factory owners remained firmly in control, and it was they who led the vociferous campaign for the reinstatement of Michael Stocks jnr. (a radical Whig) to the local magistracy, an issue which monopolised local political interest during October and November.[161] When, with trade deteriorating, a reform meeting was finally held in December it was a relatively tame, 'respectable' affair. The predominantly working-class audience (of about 800) heard speeches from local Whigs and from town-radicals sympathetic to reform and working-class aspirations, but the meeting endorsed vague resolutions which urged, for example, only a 'more extensive franchise'.[162]

---

157 D. G. Wright, 'Politics and Opinion in Nineteenth Century Bradford, 1832-1880, with special reference to Parliamentary elections', Unpub. PhD thesis, University of Leeds, 1966, has little concrete evidence about alignments at this time.

158 *LP* 16 Oct. 1830; *HCC* 30 Oct 1830.

159 *HCC* 25 Sept, 16 Oct, 6 Nov. 1830.

160 *HCC* 18 Dec. 1830; *LP* 15 Jan. 1831.

161 *HCC* 13 Nov, *LI* 11 Nov. See also WYAS: HP, Box 1 for the extensive local correspondence on the Stocks controversy.

162 *HCC*, *LM* 18 Dec. 1830. The town-radicals, many of whom remained important local figures throughout the decade, included Thomas Todd (1788?-1864), an oil, wine and spirit merchant; Titus Senior Brooke (1795?-1860), druggist; Morritt Mathews (1771?-1850?), a Quaker currier; and Newsome, possibly Samuel Newsome (1806-1845) a boot and shoemaker, who spoke on the local factory reform platform in 1836.

The fact that, by the end of the year, previously quiet areas like Dewsbury were becoming involved in a swelling reform movement is a good indicator of the rising political temperature. In early November, the Duke of Wellington made his famous declaration on the pristine condition of the British constitution. It was a statement badly out of touch with reality in the country at large, and even the mildly Tory *Halifax Chronicle* rejected its sentiments.[163] Soon his ministry fell. Brougham joined Grey's new cabinet – thus necessitating a further Yorkshire election. However, unlike the previous contest, this election aroused little interest, and Sir John Johnstone (a 'milk and water' Whig, according to the *Intelligencer*) was chosen without the Tories even bothering to field a candidate.[164] The year ended with both national and local politics in a state of suspended animation, with everyone waiting to see what a new government, under a supposedly sympathetic king, would do.

5: Reactions to the Reform Bill, March–June 1831

The prospect of reform held out in the King's Speech in January 1831 did not excite an immediate response amongst the workers of the West Riding: other matters took priority. Woollen weavers in the villages around Leeds and woolcombers in Keighley, for example, took advantage of an unseasonal boom to recover wage levels.[165] Meanwhile delegates from the striking Ashton-under-Lyne and Stalybridge cotton-spinners addressed a 'meeting of the trades' in Huddersfield and also a similar gathering at the Brewers Arms, Leeds.[166] The radical connections with the Leeds meeting – John Watts was chair, James Duffy spoke, and subscriptions were invited at Mann's and Smithson's – indicate the futility of compartmentalising working-class agitations. Local radicals, including Mann, Watts and Duffy, had also been involved at another Brewers Arms meeting three weeks earlier to form a committee and open a fund for O'Connell. This, together with a dinner in Huddersfield to salute another radical hero, Henry Hunt, whose election at Preston had fired the local imagination, indicates that it was the working-class radicals who were most active in the early months of 1831.[167]

However, the local middle-class reformers gradually stirred themselves and held a number of 'respectable' meetings (normally indoors, during the day) in various centres. Possibly because of a deal struck beforehand with the radicals, the respectable Leeds meeting of 10 February displayed considerable unanimity and force.[168] The first issue of the pro-Whig *Halifax and Huddersfield Express* reports a similar gathering at Halifax, which resulted in the formation of a Political Union on the Birmingham model. All the local indicators, including Thomas Cliffe's apparent statement that he would 'be

---

163 *HCC* 13 Nov. 1830.
164 *LI* 9 Dec. 1830; Turberville and Beckwith, 'Leeds', p. 33.
165 *LM* 15, 22, 29 Jan. 1831.
166 *LP* 15 Jan; *LM* 5 Feb. 1831. For this strike see R. G. Kirby and A. E. Musson, *The Voice of the People: John Doherty, 1798-1854 Trade Unionist, Radical and Factory Reformer* (Manchester: Manchester University Press, 1975), p. 119 ff.
167 *LP* 15, 22 Jan. 1831. John Watts was an Irish born 'operative'. A beer-retailer of that name is recorded in *LT* 9 June 1838.
168 *LM* 12 Feb. 1831; Turberville and Beckwith, 'Leeds', pp. 34-5. The platform was predominantly middle-class Whig and Whig-Radical.

content with a moderate reform', point to a local atmosphere of collaboration if not total unity.[169] At neighbouring Elland, where the Birmingham model had been adopted the previous year, a predominantly respectable meeting passed moderate pro-Reform resolutions and a petition.[170]

Elsewhere in the area the position was not so clear-cut. The middle-class reformers of Huddersfield did not risk a public meeting on the subject – particularly as feelings were running high about county MP Sir J. Johnstone's ill-timed, sanguine remarks on the state of local employment. The only major public statement on the subject of reform was a joint address by the Huddersfield, Honley, Kirkheaton and Lepton Political Unions.[171] No political activity is recorded in the Dewsbury area where industrial strife was the chief local issue.[172] Meanwhile in Bradford, Home Office reports spoke of a Political Union being formed in January, with future Chartist leader Peter Bussey among the participants.[173] The Keighley Political Union's meeting and petition in February were uncompromisingly radical, whilst reformers in Manningham and Heaton, near Bradford, held meetings to petition for a 'full and fair representation'. Speakers at Manningham included James Mann, James Stockdale (who spoke at a later NAPL meeting), Henry Rawnsley (an operative who was involved in Bradford radicalism later in the decade), William Smith (a radical veteran originally from Kendal) and William Fox (a future Chartist leader). These meetings may have been called as a rejoinder to a middle-class moderate pro-Reform meeting in Bradford.[174] Whatever their precise origins and complexion, they mark the end of what might be termed a prelapsarian phase of popular radicalism, before the Whigs unveiled their proposals for parliamentary reform.

These were made public in the first week of March and the following week the Reform Bill received its first reading in the Commons. The terms of the Bill were, in the context of the times, far-reaching and it was generally agreed that the Bill was more radical than expected.[175] In looking at the reactions of local working-class leaders

---

169 *HHE* 12, 19, 26; *LM* 19 Feb. 1831. This may have been the meeting that Lopatin-Lummis refers to in *Political Unions*, p. 70, though it pre-dates the publication of the Reform Bill. The platform at the first meeting included a wide spectrum of pro-Reform opinion from the Whig Rawdon Briggs to the radical veteran John Rowbottom. The only dissension was about the ballot. The 'moderate and liberal' Tory paper, the *Halifax Commercial Chronicle*, had ceased publication in late December because of the ill-health of the proprietor, *LM* 24 Dec. 1830.

170 *HHE*, *LM* 26 Feb. 1830. Abram Hanson was a notable absentee.

171 It is possible that the Almondbury PU had been subsumed within the Huddersfield PU by this point.

172 *LP* 5 Mar; *HHE* 12 Feb; *LP* 26 Mar. 1831. There was also a meeting at Kirkheaton, *HHE* 12 Feb. 1831, but no indications of who spoke survive.

173 Lopatin-Lummis, *Political Unions*, pp. 62-3.

174 *LM* 26 Feb; *LP* 5 Mar. 1831. Stockdale (1794?-1851?) may have been a Manningham-based woolcomber. It is not clear whether Rawnsley was also a woolcomber (1785?-1871+), or a 'weaver' who spoke at anti-poor law and radical meetings in Bradford in 1837 (*LT* 11 Feb., 1 Apr. 1837; *BO* 6 July 1837). On Smith (?-1835), see Peter Bussey's tribute, *PMG* 11 July 1835. William Fox (1805-1861+) was a handloom worsted weaver based in Great Horton.

175 *LM* 5, 12 Mar. 1831; Turberville and Beckwith, 'Leeds', p. 35.

to the proposals it is necessary to differentiate between their immediate responses and what they said a few months or years later.

At the time the vast majority of radical leaders followed Cobbett's lead in supporting the Bill whilst distrusting the Whig's motives, and hoping for a more democratic measure.[176] At a Leeds reform meeting on 10 March James Mann expressed his pleasure 'in coming forward in support of a measure, which, though it did not come up to what he thought the people had a right to, yet he approved of it as a bold measure, one calculated to destroy the influence of that oppressive oligarchy which has so long ruled the people of England'.[177] At Huddersfield operatives and respectable supporters of reform for once came together to discuss the proposals. William Stocks jnr. expressed a commonly-held view when he stated that although 'we could have wished that the measure had gone further', he believed that it went beyond what many had expected. And Samuel Dickenson mapped out the logic of what became known as 'first step' support for the Bill: 'He knew that it would not satisfy the generality of the people, because they would be excluded; but if they broke down the boroughmongers' domination, they might get more'.

The tone of the meeting and the immediate effect of the proposal, however, was best captured by George Beaumont who, 'thought it was high time that there was a better and kinder feeling between the middle and labouring classes – they ought to form themselves into a strong phalanx, to arm themselves with reason, and face in battle array, the aristocratical borough-mongers.'[178] This same pattern of working-class radicals joining with respectable reformers was repeated in Keighley, where Abraham Wildman, a radical leader, alleged that the ultra-Tories were now the Jacobins and believed that whilst the reform proposal was admittedly 'a revolutionary one, but it was a revolution not of blood, but of light from darkness – of freedom from tyranny – of knowledge from ignorance'.[179]

This honeymoon period did not last long in some places. The Huddersfield radicals later claimed that 'as early as March 1831, a Petition was sent up to parliament, signed by 6,000 persons, exposing the partiality and defects of the Bill, asking for Universal or Household Suffrage ... short Parliaments ... Vote by Ballot ... and ... no Property Qualifications...'[180] However, there is plenty of evidence from the turn-out

---

176 W. H. Maehl, *The Reform Bill of 1832: Why Not Revolution?* (New York: Holt, Rinehart and Winston, 1967), pp. 24 and 59-60. On the general welcome for the Bill in London see Prothero, *Artisans and Politics*, p. 282. At the Leeds meeting Smithson, a later supporter, voiced great distrust and scepticism about aristocratic motives, Turberville and Beckwith, 'Leeds', pp. 35-6.

177 *LM* 12 Mar. 1831. Mann criticised the exclusion of the working class but his cautious initial reaction differed from that given in his obituary: 'he never for one moment could be prevailed upon to support a Reform Bill, which did not secure even ONE of the great features of ... real Reform...', *PMG* 11 Aug. 1832.

178 *LM* 12 Mar. 1831.

179 *LP* 12 Mar. 1831.There were many such meetings throughout the Riding, see *LM* 12 Mar. 1831.

180 According to *The Woodites' "forget me not!": being a sketch of a new political farce called the Whig Tomfoolery Election, ... etc.* (Huddersfield, 1833), p. 5, a meeting 'to petition against Lord John Russell's Bill as partial and insufficient' was held on the same night as the 'Committee of

at public meetings, and the sentiments expressed, to indicate genuine popular support for the measure.[181] At the end of a predominantly working-class meeting in Bradford to discuss joining John Doherty's NAPL, three hearty cheers were proposed and given for the Reform Bill.[182]

When Lord Grey decided upon a dissolution after the second reading of the Bill had passed by just one vote, this popular support was expressed in the widespread backing of Whig candidates at the May 1831 election. In Leeds a fund to defray the expenses of voters travelling to York included sizeable contributions from workmen at a cloth dressing factory and at a machine-making firm. In Halifax the PU convened a numerous meeting which determined to support four 'liberal' candidates who would vote for 'the Bill'.[183] Only in Huddersfield did the radicals pursue a more independent line when they drew up a cart, bedecked with two tricolour flags bearing the inscriptions 'Universal Suffrage', 'Vote by Ballot' and 'We are weary of Slavery', opposite the main hustings for the election meeting and addressed the candidates on a wide range of subjects, including distress and the recently published factory bills of Sir John Hobhouse.[184] The incident indicates that the working class and their leaders were concerned with other matters than purely reform, and that from its very inception the operatives' short time campaign was inextricably bound up with reform politics.[185]

The Huddersfield incident, however, was not typical of the general response to the election and the Reform Bill. The majority of radical leaders welcomed it as an important first step and favoured the return of a strong pro-reform ministry.[186] They also recognised that it would be political suicide to oppose the provisions of a Bill which, whatever its shortcomings, generally travelled a fair way along the newly resurfaced road of radical reform. Nevertheless, a few radicals had already had second thoughts, and these, together with a few consistent opponents of the measure, formed the main pockets of resistance to 'first step' acceptance. Leadership of these clusters of ultra-radicals was assumed by Henry Hunt who had been one of the few dissentient voices when the Reform Bill had been published. He argued not only that it did not go far enough, but that because of its disenfranchising clauses it was, as far as the working-class was concerned, positively retrogressive.[187]

Operatives' met to support Hobhouse. No report of this meeting survives, but it was probably held on 12 March.

181 *LM* March - early April 1831; but note the poor turn out for the county meeting on Reform. The contrast with the 'York Pilgrimage' the following month is striking.

182 *VP* 16 Apr. 1831.

183 *LM* 30 Apr. 1831. The cloth dressing firm, (James Brown's), was the largest in Leeds. Taylor and Wordsworth's, machine-makers, also employed traditionally well-paid and articulate working men. But see Thompson, *Making*, p. 900 for Baines' estimate in 1831 that only one of the 'mechanics' there would actually get the vote. Speakers at Halifax included three prominent radicals, Joseph Nicholson, Thomas Wilson and John Rowbottom.

184 *LM* 30 Apr. 1831.

185 For further discussion of this see below, p. 256. In Leeds, the strike at Gott's was also a major focus of interest.

186 The Yorkshire election aided this end by electing four 'liberals' and was a major triumph for Baines and his Leeds Association. See Turberville and Beckwith, 'Leeds', pp. 37-8, and Fraser, 'Politics in Leeds', pp. 37-45.

187 For Hunt's evolving reaction to the Bill, see Belchem, *'Orator' Hunt*, pp. 170-6.

Hunt's views and their adoption or reiteration in Huddersfield and Leeds in particular, coming at a time when the progress of the Bill was in the balance, incited heated and bitter controversy. In Leeds, for example, James Mann, a long-standing acquaintance and supporter of Hunt, sought to call a meeting to defend him from attacks in the press. But with feelings running high on the evening preceding the election, the meeting was easily taken over by Carlileite republicans and other 'first-step' supporters, mainly operatives, who passed resolutions in favour of a united front to pass the present Bill. The radicals took both their defeat, and the manner it was reported in the *Mercury*,[188] badly and the meeting effectively ended any hopes of a *rapprochement* between the various factions on the radical wing of Leeds politics.

The ultra-radicals held no more public meetings and the loose organisational framework inherited from the RRA finally collapsed. James Mann, writing from Harrogate in late May, now declared the Bill to be 'founded on no just or equitable principle' rather being intended 'to unite the middle-class and the aristocracy, to prevent the labouring classes from obtaining that just reform to which they are entitled'. Mann's analysis with its emphasis on the iniquity of the Bill's stress on property as the basis of representation, however, was not shared widely in Leeds and the summer of 1831 saw the ultra-radicals there weak and in disarray.[189]

The picture in Huddersfield and neighbouring radical strongholds was somewhat different. They put up a vigorous and more broadly endorsed defence of Hunt. In May the 'Councils of the Political Unions of Huddersfield and neighbourhood' called a joint meeting to congratulate the Preston electors on returning Hunt once more, and to thank him for his work on behalf of the labouring class.[190] Held in the large Political Union room in Swan Yard, this district meeting was a milestone in the development of an independent working-class political agitation in Huddersfield. In contrast to the initial cautious acceptance of the Reform Bill the meeting was unequivocal in its condemnation of the proposal and its praise of Hunt. George Beaumont vigorously defended him and was particularly vociferous about middle-class insinuations regarding the working-class's moral and educational failings:

> if his fellow workmen could all live in large towns, and pay £10 a year rent, this would instantly expel the darkness of their ignorance, and they at once became intelligent and intellectual beings. (Laughter.) ... They, (the middle-classes) had their roast and boiled, and fared sumptuously every day, while the labouring classes dined off their scanty meal of potatoes and gruel. Many of this class drank more every day, than most of them earned, but it had never been discovered that this unfitted them from the exercise of their political privileges. (Hear, hear.)

Traditional contrasts between rich and poor, and between the corrupt, dissolute aristocratic 'do nothings' and the productive classes were also emphasised, but special

---

188 *LM* 7 May, *LP* 14, 21 May 1831.

189 *VP* 11 June 1831. Leeds radical reformers found it 'inconvenient' to send a delegate to a Manchester meeting. The ascendency of the Carlileites was indicated by (unfulfilled) plans to start a rival to the *Patriot*, *LP* 2 July, 13 Aug. 1831.

190 *LP* 21 May 1831. The four joint secretaries were Beaumont, Thomas Vevers, a veteran radical from Almondbury, Joseph North, an Almondbury schoolmaster, and Thomas Ledger of Honley.

bitterness was reserved for the perceived desertion of the working-class reformers by their natural allies in the middle-class. This sense of betrayal had undoubtedly been exacerbated by the attitude of many of this same group (led by predominantly Whig-liberal merchants and manufacturers) to Hobhouse's Factory Bill. Thus it was not incongruous for John Spivey, an Almondbury radical, to devote almost all of his speech to detailing the harmful effects of the factory system. Equally, the meeting was particularly harsh on the press, notably the *Leeds Mercury*, which as well as being one of Hunt's bitterest critics had also been prominent in attacking the factory reform proposals.[191]

Indeed the local radicals' desire to exercise more control over their reading matter and raise the standards of political education resulted in the proposal to establish 'a working man's news-room' at Swan Yard. This would not only furnish subscribers (at 1*d* or 2*d* a week) with 'cheap and early news', but also be a centre for reading 'sterling works on politics and the science of Government' and for lectures on 'moral and political subjects'. The venture, which got off the ground the following Monday, provided a place for both formal and informal discussions, a hub for the dissemination of radical ideas and newspapers, and a base for future expansion.[192] It was an important step in the development of an independent, predominantly working-class, radical culture in the town and an expression of the strong educational, self-improving, perspectives of radical leaders.

Abram Hanson's presence at the Huddersfield meeting and a public dinner to Hunt held in Elland the following day, attended by 'a few friends from Huddersfield', indicates the continuing and close links between the radicals of Huddersfield and those of the neighbouring villages. In Hanson the Elland ultra-radicals had a leader of undoubted ability and perception. 'His plan of radical reform' announced at Huddersfield the previous day included not only universal suffrage but also foreshadowed his later Chartist involvement in advocating equal electoral districts and the payment of MPs.[193] Yet in contrast to the Huddersfield leaders it is hard to say how much popular support he carried with him.

Elsewhere there is some patchy evidence of second thoughts on the Reform Bill, possibly inspired by the Huddersfield and Elland meetings. A hastily-convened meeting gathered on Bradford Moor in mid-May, for example, to consider the best way of securing a more extensive franchise. Although small, the meeting was almost exclusively working-class. Speakers included Peter Bussey, John Watts (of Leeds), John Corless (a leading radical and trade unionist), Henry Rawnsley (radical operative), William Fox, James Stockdale, and George Hopkins (woolcomber and future *Northern Star* agent).[194] Their speeches included strong attacks on the middle-

---

191 *LP* 4 June 1831. The meeting marked the coming together of the PUs of Huddersfield, Almondbury, Horbury, Kirkheaton, Lascelles Hall, Lepton and Dalton.

192 *LP* 4 June 1831. 'Joseph' (probably Joshua) Hobson proposed the resolution to set up the news-room; and it was here in 1833 that he printed and edited the unstamped *Voice of the West-Riding*. For a later reference to 'the ruling conclave of the Swan Yard', see *HHE* 24 Apr. 1834.

193 *LP* 4 June 1831.

194 Corless/Corlass/Cawless' name suggests Irish heritage. A 'John Corless' of Bradford died in an accident aged 62 in 1862 (*LM* 16 Oct.1862).

class' desertion and some fierce assertions of working-class rights and independence. According to Corless, 'such men as constituted the middle class could have no idea of the wants and wishes of those who lived by labour'. The 'working class' could not expect fair representation of their interests by those who benefited from their subjugation; indeed, the middle class just wanted to use 'the working man' as

> a stepping stone to their own further elevation (*Applause*). The middle-class had all along shown a jealousy of the lower-class, and now they had got representation for themselves, they would either oppose the rights of the labouring classes, or refuse any support in obtaining them.[195]

Although other speeches were more restrained or traditional in their targets, an impressive line-up of local working-class leaders were united in their condemnation of a Bill which, in Peter Bussey's words, 'united the middle and higher classes together to the exclusion of the lower-class', which would not benefit 'the working man' and which, if it passed, would make further reform more difficult.[196] The meeting endorsed a series of ultra-radical resolutions unanimously. Although only a pin-prick in the side of the overwhelming body of pro-Reform opinion, it damaged the illusion of total unity in Bradford, and for this reason soon aroused the *Mercury*'s wrath and ridicule.[197]

The *Mercury*'s remarks about the Bradford radical reformers invoked the censure of the Huddersfield working-class radicals when they met a couple of weeks later to express their opinion on the reform measure which Russell had re-introduced. The indoor Saturday evening meeting attracted over a thousand people to hear a strong radical platform condemn 'the present Whig Measure of Reform as a deep laid policy, to render the Legislature more inaccessible than ever to the community at large', and reiterate demands for the full radical programme. The resolutions also indicate how the radical leaders' vision of the need for fundamental political change took in the whole range of working-class endeavours. For example, Abraham Donkersley and Benjamin Whiteley recommended 'the people to avoid these ineffectual struggles, called 'Turn-outs' – 'Strikes' etc. and to insulate themselves as much as possible from the influence of corruption, by Temperance Societies, Co-operative Societies, Trades' Unions, etc. The Hydra must be attacked at all points'.[198]

The increasing identification of the middle-class with 'the Hydra' and the repeated advocacy of working-class 'union' was an important step in the evolution of a distinctive radical working-class identity. But, as yet, such an analysis was confined chiefly to 'advanced' strongly radical areas like Huddersfield and to radical caucuses in a few other West Riding towns and villages. It was not yet widely accepted; the majority of the people continued to view the reform proposals as better than nothing.

---

195 *LP* 11 June 1831.

196 Ibid.

197 *LM* 11 June; *LP* 25 June 1831.

198 *LP* 25 June 1831. The meeting was chaired by Samuel Dickenson and included contributions from Thomas Leadbeater, Oates (the *Voice of the People* reporter), Hobson, John Hanson, George Beaumont, William Sykes, Abraham Donkersley and Benjamin Whiteley of Holmfirth. The meeting particularly stressed the need for no property qualifications. Benjamin Whiteley (1791?-1841+), a cloth-dresser, was involved in the factory reform agitation and local politics.

However, the amount of popular interest and excitement aroused after Lord Russell had re-introduced his reform measure in late June should not be exaggerated. Apart from some activity in the Halifax area where a radical meeting on Ovenden Moor in mid-July, chaired by local weaver and future Chartist Benjamin Rushton, established a pro-universal suffrage political union on the London model, the summer and early autumn period saw little radical or reform campaigning.[199] The chief focus of public concern moved to local industrial conflict and to the question of Irish distress.[200] Here too, though, the ultra-radicals found an issue on which their analysis of political and economic relationships diverged appreciably from that of the respectable, largely pro-reform, middle-class; and future alignments were prefigured in the support which M. T. Sadler won in radical circles for his humanitarian approach to Ireland.[201]

In Huddersfield the events of spring and summer 1831 were also crucial for drawing the lines for later conflicts. Joshua Hobson, writing from Wakefield Prison in December 1833, recalled that in Huddersfield the 'Radicals' were not 'a distinct party from the 'Liberals' ... until sometime after the introduction of the afore-mentioned 'bill' ... it was the '<u>Bill</u>' that caused the first rupture between them; the one ... lauding it up to the skies, and the other regarding it with distrust and suspicion, if not hatred'. The radicals came to oppose it 'as being neither intended nor calculated to benefit the Working Classes' and viewed it as 'a change to prevent further changes' and not as 'the first step to an emancipating series which would lead to Universal Suffrage, but intended as a barrier'.[202]

Such sentiments were not universal. The Bill enjoyed widespread popular support; and a number of key radical (and later Chartist) leaders, despite reservations about the Bill's 'partial and incomplete' nature, supported its passage in a pro-Reform alliance with middle-class 'Liberals'. Their loyalty they believed would soon be matched by reciprocal support for a further extension of the suffrage. Eventually, however, the hopes of the 'first step' supporters dissolved. The belief that the Reform Bill has been a 'fraud', a 'cheat' designed 'to unite the middle with the higher classes to oppress the working-class', 'to crush them for ever – to be final',[203] passed rapidly into the radical liturgy. The local working-class radicals who had earlier courted unpopularity and vilification were seemingly justified in their scepticism; indeed, their untarnished image at this time often formed the basis of the support which they carried through

199 *LP* 23 July 1831. George Beaumont, Abram Hanson and Thomas Cliffe also spoke. Ovenden, a stuff-weaving village 1¼ miles north west of Halifax, was a strong radical and later Chartist centre.

200 *LM*, *LP* June-Sept. 1831 for meetings and letters on Irish distress and the disputes at Leeds and Dewsbury.

201 *LP* 25 June; *LM* 18 June 1831. The radicals stressed the 'deeper' causes of Irish poverty, especially taxation and exploitation by the Church and an absentee aristocracy. See also a letter from an Almondbury 'Radical' linking the issue with the development of the mechanised Leeds flax-spinning industry, *LP* 23 July 1831. The *Mercury* strongly attacked Mann for supporting Sadler (now the officially adopted Tory candidate for Leeds) in preference to Macauley (a putative Whig candidate), *LP* 14 Sept. 1831. The other Whig candidate was John Marshall jnr., son of the leading Leeds flax-spinner.

202 *VWR* 28 Dec. 1833; *Woodites*, p. 4.

203 *VWR* 5 Oct. 1833; 3 May 1834.

into the Chartist era. Stephen Dickinson of Huddersfield pertinently reminded a local audience in January 1838 that, 'he had been always against the Reform Bill, so called, and had thought that with that great man, Mr Hunt, that it was but a mere hoax upon the people, and as such would never do any good'.[204] By contrast those leaders who had supported the Bill looked back on the role with shame and regret. Indeed, their bitterness and disillusionment were often all the more extreme for having been the dupes of the Whigs. Thomas Cliffe rhetorically asked a Halifax meeting in January 1838, 'what were the thanks they received from those in working [for] whose benefit they had been instrumental?' and proceeded to instance the hatred Baines' hypocritical attitude to the mass platform. The treachery of the Bainesite middle-class, and their scheming manipulation of working-class support to secure their own political ends, remained constant and potent themes in the speeches of local radical leaders from the Bill's passage right through into early Chartism.[205]

6: The Crisis of October 1831

In late summer 1831, with parliament in recess, the main topic of local political discussion was the choice of possible election candidates for the new constituencies.[206] Working-class radicals do not appear to have taken any major part in these deliberations – though they will have noted with interest the *Leeds Intelligencer's* change of attitude to the Reform Bill. The editor now criticised the measure as insufficiently democratic, as a disenfranchiser of the poor, and strongly favoured the candidacy of M. T. Sadler, the locally connected sitting MP for Newark.[207] Sadler's sympathetic approach to Irish distress had returned him to prominence in the summer of 1831 causing James Mann to endorse him in preference to Macauley, one of the local Whigs' proposed candidates, much to the *Mercury's* annoyance. Sadler's reputation as a philanthropist gave him a high standing amongst the Leeds operatives, and when towards the end of September the West Riding factory reformers identified support for ten hours as a key test for any potential candidates, the outlines of future alignments were clearly discernible.[208]

With local and national radical interest focussed mainly on the 'Liberty of the Press', the reform issue remained fairly dormant.[209] It only took on new life when the Bill reached the House of Lords. With the future of reform seemingly in the balance, popular radical leaders again faced difficult decisions about confronting or collaborating with middle-class reformers. At Leeds, for example, Mann and Foster appeared on a predominantly 'Liberal' platform to launch a pro-reform petition.

---

204 *NS* 27 Jan. 1838.

205 *NS* 27 Jan. 1838. Cliffe at one time had been accused of being a 'partisan' of the *Mercury*, *LP* 29 Jan. 1831 (To correspondents).

206 Turberville and Beckwith, 'Leeds', pp. 40–5; *LP* 3 Sept. 1831, for rumours of John Wood of Dalton standing at Huddersfield; Jowitt, 'Parliamentary Politics', pp. 177–8 for machinations at Halifax.

207 Turberville and Beckwith, 'Leeds', p. 44.

208 *LM* 17; *LP* 24 Sept. 1831.

209 *PMG* 17 Sept. 1831 for a Huddersfield meeting; Prothero, *Artisans and Politics*, p. 285 for developments in London.

In Huddersfield 'a numerous body of men' including 'several leaders of the Political Unionists' sought to gatecrash a respectable public meeting called to petition the Lords in favour of the Reform Bill. It was a rowdy affair with the radicals routinely hissed and shouted down. Even the pugnacious Beaumont was stung by the shabby way he had been treated by 'the "great men"' who led the proceedings. By contrast in Bradford where respectable, middle-class Whig-liberals similarly took the lead, no working-class radicals spoke.[210]

When the House of Lords rejected the Bill on 8 October, as Beaumont had teasingly dared them to do ten days earlier, the *Mercury* reported a 'strong sensation' in Leeds, though 'it was rather "deep" than "loud".[211] The popular ferment and collective violence experienced in other parts of the country at the Bill's rejection was not repeated in the West Riding. This lack of activity may reflect the broad consensus which existed on the question in the textile district and the absence of readily identifiable targets to attack. However, it also possibly indicated a certain world-weariness on the part of the populace, as well as the existence of competing issues and concerns.[212]

The Lords' rejection gave local ultra-radicals the chance to seize the initiative and press for their 'full rights'. It not only confirmed their traditional views about the tyrannical aristocracy, it also gave other radicals who had flirted with the local liberals the opportunity to break out from the tactical straitjacket in which they were in danger of becoming confined. Not all, however, took the opportunity.

In general, the popular radical leadership's response reflected the state of local relationships with middle-class Whigs and Whig-liberals. In Halifax for example the local PU issued a loyal address to the King and publicly thanked the Whig ministers and supporters of the Bill for their efforts.[213] However, in places where attitudes to the Bill and to local Whigs were more equivocal, moves were immediately set in motion to put forward a truly radical programme. A 'Radical Reformer' writing from Bradford Moor on 11 October condemned the House of Lords' actions, but argued for a West Riding meeting to press for a wider Bill; and from Leeds there were reports that the radicals were at last stirring themselves to form 'a real Radical Union'.[214] Huddersfield, however, led the way. At a hastily-convened meeting in the Political Union room on 20 October John Hanson condemned the useless cry of 'the whole bill and nothing but the bill', and resolutions were passed to organise a wider district meeting to press for full political rights.[215]

The Leeds radicals also took to organising independently. The 'real Radical Union' mentioned by the *Patriot* in late October took a step closer to becoming a reality a week later when about a hundred working-class radicals met to consider forming a

---

210 *LM, LP* 1 Oct; *HE* 1 Oct. 1831 and *LP* 29 Oct. 1831 (for the Huddersfield meeting and Beaumont's displeasure); *LM* 8 Oct. 1831 (for Bradford).

211 Turberville and Beckwith, 'Leeds', p. 39; *LM* 15 Oct. 1831.

212 Gott's strike was coming to an end and the fate of Hobhouse's Bill was also in the balance.

213 *LM* 22 Oct. 1831.

214 *LP* 15, 29 Oct. 1831.

215 *LP* 29 Oct. 1831. Speakers included many of the leading radicals including Beaumont who sought to explain his appearance on the Whig platform in late September.

political union to press for universal suffrage, the ballot and annual parliaments.[216] They projected a spectacular launch for the new union and delegated Mann to travel to Manchester to invite Henry Hunt.[217]

The ploy was not a spectacular success. Whilst Hunt was still popular enough to attract crowds along his route through Keighley, Bradford and Bingley, poor health and radical organisation, plus determined opposition from Baines and his allies, reduced the impact of his visit to 'the focus of Whigism [sic] and delusion in Yorkshire'. The planned outdoor meeting on Woodhouse Moor was abandoned and instead Hunt addressed a large crowd from the window of a hotel. Although Hunt delivered what John Belchem judges to be 'his best speech during the entire Reform Bill agitation', the encounter was mainly notable for his vitriolic clash with Baines and his endorsement of Sadler in preference to Macauley.[218] However, the visit did give the final push in the formation of a separate working-class political union and the Leeds Radical Political Union (RPU) was duly established at a meeting on 17 November.[219]

The importance which Baines and the middle-class Whig leadership placed on securing working-class support (and by implication legitimacy) for their cause is demonstrated by their counter-moves to establish a rival political union. The Leeds or 'Holbeck' Political Union arose out of the deliberations of a group of 'respectable mechanics' but it was tied very closely to Baines and was launched on the same day as the 'Huntite' RPU. For a couple of months the bitter rivalry between the two unions epitomised a growing chasm between two very different 'Schools of Reform'.[220]

In organisation the two bodies were very similar. Both were broadly based on the rules of the London Metropolitan Political Union with regular membership subscriptions, elected officers and a committee.[221] The key differentiating features were their class perspectives and political ideas. The RPU supported the traditional radical programme and pledged itself 'never to be satisfied with any mode of representation which excludes that class from the right of voting whose industry alone produce wealth'. It deprecated Lord John Russell's new Bill, arguing that it deprived the 'labouring classes' of their rights, and rejected the notion of a broad pro-reform alliance. In William Rider's words, 'The Whigs in building the superstructure of reform' had constructed 'a castle in the air, and they would never succeed till they began at the foundation – the working-classes, the people, the rabble'. The chief leaders included the veteran James Mann, John Ayrey, the young Robert Howard,

---

216 *LM* 5 Nov. 1831. The meeting took place in the lodge room of a local friendly society.

217 *LM* 5 Nov. 1831; *LP* 12 Nov. 1831. Mann was a long-standing acquaintance and supporter of Hunt, see Belchem, 'Orator' Hunt, pp. 76, 178, 188.

218 Belchem, 'Orator' Hunt, pp. 188-9; *LP* 12 Nov. 1831; Turberville and Beckwith, 'Leeds', p. 46. Convinced of radical support the Leeds Tories formally invited Sadler to be their candidate on 12 November.

219 *LM, LP* 19 Nov. 1831.

220 *LM, LP* 19 Nov. 1831. All sources agree that Baines was the force behind the rival venture. For reasons of clarity the 'Huntite' union will be referred to as the RPU and the rival union as the Holbeck Political Union.

221 Doubts about the legality of such unions delayed their actual formation, *LP, LM* 26 Nov., 3, 10 Dec. 1831.

William Rider, John Watts and J. B. Walker; and all put across an unequivocal brand of radicalism which emphasised the independence and rights of the working class.[222]

By contrast the Holbeck Political Union espoused a more limited reform programme which saw the Reform Bill as a necessary first step on the road to full reform and advocated the virtues of class collaboration.[223] This aspect was institutionalised in the Union's Political Council, which comprised equal numbers of 'Operative' and 'Middle-Class' members. The occupational composition of these constituents indicates the groups from which the union drew its chief support. On the operative side it is likely that the union reflected the views of some of the well-paid workers in the 'upper' skilled trades, employed in the factories, workshops and warehouses of Holbeck and Hunslet. The middle-class Council members comprised a varied selection of lower middle-class craftsmen, traders and lower professional people in the area together with a couple of merchants and two major manufacturers. The driving force appears to have come from these latter two – the chair Joshua Bower, a self-made wealthy glass manufacturer and the treasurer John Whitehead, a machine manufacturer – and from two experienced Carlileite republicans, Joseph Lees and John Smithson.[224]

The relative strength of the two organisations is difficult to judge. Both drew large audiences for their early indoor meetings, though it is interesting that the RPU was sufficiently strong to disrupt at least one Holbeck PU meeting in December.[225] It is likely that with the factory reform issue also engaging much public attention and provoking hostility to Baines, the RPU, temporarily at least, enjoyed the ascendency in terms of popular support.[226] The RPU ceaselessly attacked the 'Holbeck Union' and its connections with Baines and the 'Leeds Association', the main Whig-liberal

---

222 *LI* 24 Nov; *LP* 10, 17 Dec. 1831. Robert Howard is an elusive and enigmatic figure who served as treasurer of the Leeds Radical Reform Union. He was active on the radical platform in the early 1830s and was sufficiently eminent to have shared a coach with James Mann and Henry Hunt (*LI* 10 Nov. 1831). His 'oratorical notoriety' (*LM* 1 Dec. 1832) may have been the result of a speech impediment which was mercilessly mocked by his opponents (*LI* 12 Jan. 1832). Not surprisingly perhaps he had a quick temper and was twice charged with assault. He appears to have left Leeds in 1834 following his acquittal for passing on a forged bill of exchange (*LT* 5 Apr. 1834). James Bradshaw Walker (1806?-1844+), secretary of the Leeds Radical Reform Union in the early 1830s, was a former cloth drawer who became a 'schoolmaster' and aspiring poet. He struggled to make a living through either endeavour (*NS* 23 Nov. 1844).

223 The respective political programmes were very close, but the means to achieve them very different, see *LI* 29 Dec. 1831 for Joshua Bower's views.

224 *LM* 17, 24, 31 Dec. 1831; 7 Jan. 1832. Council members for whom an occupation is known comprised two machine-makers, two flax-dressers, a flax spinning overlooker and two woolsorters. The vice-chairman William Nichols was foreman at Messrs Taylor and Wadsworth's (Machine Makers) who supplied machines to Marshalls, the pre-eminent flax-spinning firm. John Marshall jnr. was also one of the two Whig candidates for Leeds. See also *LI* 29 Dec. 1831, for complaints about the unwillingness of the respectable middle-class to join.

225 *LM* 17 Dec. 1831.

226 *LP, LM, LI* 3-31 Dec. 1831. Major ten hours meetings were held on 10 and 12 December. *LP* 21 Jan. 1832.

electoral organisation. For 'Quiz', writing to the *Patriot*, the Holbeck Political Union was a Whig tool a 'mere Mercury-council-chamber'. The RPU blamed the similarity of names on its rival and coined the 'Holbeck' title as a deliberately denigrating alternative.[227] The Huntite radicals of the RPU not only promulgated an uncompromising reform programme but also discussed and adopted issues – notably factory reform and Ireland – which highlighted their distance from the Whig-liberal mainstream and also their proximity to Sadler.[228] This represented not a diversion from, but merely an extension of, their political radicalism. The separate paths, which had been evident since 1829 with the formation of the RRA, and whose roots stretched back to the early 1820s, had by New Year 1832 become institutionalised and seemingly irreversible. The Huntite radicals stood apart and clearly differentiated from the local Whig-liberal establishment and their Carlileite and Cobbettite radical allies.[229]

The intertwining of radical and factory reform issues and the bitter separation of predominantly working-class radicals from middle-class Whig-liberals also became more pronounced in the Huddersfield area. Two events in particular caused the local political temperature to rise – the visit by Henry Hunt, and the local radicals' public call for a National Convention.

The Huddersfield radicals' support for Hunt and his criticisms of the Reform Bill have already been noted; and when Hunt visited the West Riding at the Leeds radicals' request, in early November, he naturally took in Huddersfield. Accompanied by Foster and Mann he arrived in the town on 10 November and attracted a large audience to a public meeting which voted against the Reform Bill and the Whig ministers.[230] The visit and its outcome incensed local Whig-liberals, one of whom, Thomas Barlow of Netherton, attacked the local radical leaders in less than restrained terms as,

> Huntite-rabble – traitor-radicals – hair-brained zealots – a gang too idle to earn an honest living – notorious Deists – fire-brands – drunkards – greedy alike for riot and plunder – bad husbands – bad neighbours – bad parents – pests – rearing up children in the disbelief of God, and the contempt of everything good, and along with Hunt, the revolutionizing cat's paws of the Tories!![231]

The detailed content of the ensuing controversy which raged for a few weeks in the local press is not important, but the whole episode reveals an unbridgeable chasm between radicals and Whig-liberals in Huddersfield.[232] The basis of this divide went beyond mere 'political' questions. As the radicals later surmised:

---

227 *LP* 10 Dec. 1831; 7, 21 Jan. 1832; *LM* 31 Dec. 1831 (James Morgan); *LI* 12 Apr. 1832. On the 'Leeds Association', see Derek Fraser, 'The Fruits of Reform; Leeds Politics in the 1830s', *Northern History*, 7 (1972), pp. 92–3.

228 See, for example, Robert Howard's speech at an early meeting, *LP* 10 Dec. 1831.

229 Fraser, 'Fruits of Reform', p. 94, says that the 'Radical Union gradually deserted its political Radicalism in favour of a commitment to the social improvement of the working class'. A Leeds dinner to honour Cobbett was chaired by Joshua Bower and included speeches from prominent 'Holbeck' PU members, *LP* 10 Mar. 1832.

230 *LM* 12 Nov. 1831 gave the figure as 5,000.

231 *Woodites*, p. 5.

232 *LM* 19, 26 Nov; *LP* 26 Nov., 10 Dec. 1831.

...the origin of all this whiggish abuse arose, first, from the opposition of the radicals to the Reform Bill ... secondly, from their coincident advocacy of the Ten-hour-Bill, which the green-eyed jealousy of Party has childishly argued, was got up for the purpose of strangling this tender whiggish-pet, Lord J. Russell's Bill[233]

The factory and political reform issues also became caught up in the second major source of controversy in late 1831 – the Huddersfield radicals' adoption of the 'National Convention' idea.[234] On 1 November John Hanson, Joshua Hobson and John Leech, 'as joint secretaries of the General Committee of the Political Union and Operatives of Huddersfield and its vicinity' issued a circular to fellow 'Radical Reformers' requesting their co-operation in sending delegates to a proposed meeting in Manchester, which would 'arrange a plan and frame Resolutions for a grand Meeting all over Britain and Ireland on the same day and hour, so that the people may come in all respects well-prepared to meet the tyrants on one great and general principle'. The document urged united action by 'one grand and simultaneous movement', 'one phalanx', displaying 'an irresistible front': effectively a general strike. For all its rhetorical flourishes the circular's tone, reflecting the radical, even revolutionary frisson attached to 'national holiday' idea, is one of bitterness, class awareness and imminent confrontation.[235]

The immediate stimulus for the circular came from the Huddersfield Political Union meeting on 20 October which formed a committee to call a 'district general meeting'. This committee formed the basis of the 'General Committee' which apparently comprised representatives of the Political Union acting with 'persons deputed from the surrounding hamlets, villages, and factories, for the express purpose of organising the whole labouring population of the district'. The wider context for the circular can be found in the ideas for a 'holiday' and 'a grand and solemn National Conference' which William Benbow was advocating at National Union of the Working Classes (NUWC) meetings in London and which, through the medium of the *Poor Man's Guardian*, Manchester Huntite leaders were also taking up.[236]

A major Political Union meeting in late November confirmed Huddersfield's position as the leading radical centre in the Riding. It endorsed an uncompromising reform programme and revealed growing tensions and a sense of imminent decisive conflict. An address to Lord Wharncliffe, an influential local peer and political intermediary, emphasised the political unionists' determination that 'no other class shall be entrusted (or ought to be relied upon) to redress their wrongs or obtain their

---

233 *Woodites*, p. 5.

234 On the currency of this and related ideas see Prothero, *Artisans and Politics*, p. 288 ff. For a more detailed discussion see Iorwerth Prothero, 'William Benbow and the Concept of the General Strike', *Past and Present*, 63, 1 (1974), pp. 132-71, and Terry Parssinen, 'Association, Convention and Anti-Parliament in British Radical Politics, 1771-1848', *EHR*, 87 (1973), pp. 517-21.

235 *PMG* 5 Nov. 1831. see Chase, *Early Trade Unionism*, p. 128. It is clear that 'the people' are equated with the 'labouring population'.

236 *LP* 29 Oct. 1831; Prothero, *Artisans and Politics*, p. 288; *PMG* 10 Sept; 1, 22 Oct., 5 Nov. 1831.

rights'.[237] Local radicals spoke of 'incurring the displeasure of their employers' and asserted that 'their aim has always been to employ moral and not physical force, now it would seem that they are to be put down'; it was therefore up to the 'property-men' to decide 'whether robberies – murder – and incendiarism are to be the order of the day'. Most striking of all is the total rejection of the 'Whig administration', it being 'equally as deaf as the Tories to the cries of a degraded, enslaved, insulted and starving population; and much more disgusting, vile and irritating because they make so many more pretensions to an assimilation of feeling with us than the Tories...' The meeting ended with a resolution which called for 'great and simultaneous meetings' and 'a grand National Holiday' on 26 December when 'every wheel and every wheel's connection shall rest from their labour, and that the whole population shall shout with an irresistible voice, and that the whole country shall reverberate the glorious sound – liberty'.[238]

The meeting made no direct mention of a National Convention, whether through radicals' fears of arrest or a reluctance to supply Edward Baines with further ammunition for his campaign against them. In an article headed 'Proposed Illegal Convention' the *Mercury* of 26 November had used allegations of Huddersfield's involvement in the proposed meeting in Manchester the following Monday to smear both the 'Huntites' and 'the Committee of Operatives' (STC). James Brook, the secretary of the STC, and John Hanson, another prominent member, replied vigorously, stressing the separateness of the two committees and, at first, denying knowledge of the Manchester meeting. However, in face of a continued *Mercury* onslaught against the 'absurd and illegal national convention', Brook was forced to argue for the legality of delegate meetings and question the status of Baines' Leeds Association.[239]

The vigour of the *Mercury*'s attack owed much to its seizure of a golden opportunity to simultaneously both attack factory reformers and ultra-radical opponents of the Bill (who in Huddersfield were in many cases one and the same); and to disrupt the increasingly close relationship between working-class radicals and Tory factory reformers like Sadler. It had been particularly incensed (and perhaps worried) by the address of gratitude which a deputation from the Huddersfield STC, led by Brook, had presented to Sadler in early November; and the 'National Convention'

---

237 Lopatin-Lummis, *Political Unions*, p. 119.

238 *PMG* 10 Dec. 1831. The date of the meeting is not certain. The *Patriot* did not report it and only the resolutions are given in the *PMG*. The Manchester Political Union of the Working Classes had convened a delegate meeting, but on the day chosen for simultaneous meetings, 28 November, only two gatherings were held. The Huddersfield PU meeting may have been held on this day. I am grateful to Dr. Sykes for this information.

239 For this controversy see *LP*, *LM* 3, 10, 17 Dec. 1831. The inclusion of the word 'Operatives' in the title of the 'General Committee' which called for the National Convention, and the fact that the circular was signed by three prominent ten hours' men, in the *Mercury*'s view, appeared to commit the STC to the Convention. Brook and Hanson replied that the STC was not involved in party politics and that the word 'Operatives' had been added to signify the wider committee which had been created at the 20 October meeting. Their replies are not totally consistent or convincing.

controversy only added heat to Whig-liberal/radical rivalries in Leeds and Huddersfield.[240]

The 'National Convention' issue with its whiff of illegality, its hints of prosecutions and its potential damage to the factory cause put the Huddersfield radicals on the defensive. They abandoned the National Convention idea and were spared participation in what turned out to be a fiasco.[241] However, the simultaneous meetings idea remained on the agenda; and although there is no evidence that any other areas took up the call, the Huddersfield district proceeded with its 26 December 'holiday' meeting. The rally held on Almondbury Bank was a large-scale affair and attracted an impressive platform of speakers from the wider Huddersfield district who unequivocally insisted on full reform and rejected Whig leadership.[242]

The Boxing Day meeting marks the culmination of the Huddersfield radicals' response to the rejection of the Reform Bill. The tone of the speeches and the preceding agitation illustrate the completeness of the split from the Whig-liberals and the vitality of independent working-class radical activity in one of the key West Riding districts. This energy was not confined to the town of Huddersfield. Indeed, much of the real strength and popular support on which the Huddersfield PU drew came from the predominantly handloom-weaving villages and out-townships.[243] The mutual hostility felt between the radicals and local Whig-liberals is evident in rumours of the formation of a rival Whig-sponsored, predominantly middle-class political organisation in Huddersfield.[244] It also shows itself in the speeches and letters of the radical leadership.

This antagonism, although generally expressed in 'political' terms and having perceived injustices and lack of representation as its most explicitly stated causes, had deeper roots. These enabled local leaders and their supporters to embrace simultaneously both ultra-radical political solutions and the factory reform movement. Both cross-fertilising agitations drew on and developed broad anti-capitalist sentiments which stressed the interconnection of employers' (particularly factory employers') 'political' and 'economic' roles. The same Whig 'factory lords' who supported a limited Bill also opposed factory regulation and the operatives' hopes of thereby curbing the 'malevolent system of competition, machinery, tyranny and oppression'.[245] This distrust and hostility lay at the heart of the Huddersfield radicals' rejection of a partial Bill. They discerned 'from the character and interests of the enfranchised middle men', that it would prevent further reform,

---

240 *LM* 26 Nov; 3 Dec. 1831; Cecil Driver, *Tory Radical. The Life of Richard Oastler* (New York: Oxford University Press, 1946), pp. 114-5. The *Mercury* alleged that Oastler not Sadler wrote the address.

241 *LM* 7 Jan. 1832; *PMG* 17, 31 Dec. 1831, 4, 25 Feb. 1832. Only three real delegates turned up (information from Dr. Sykes).

242 *LI* 29 Dec. 1831; *LP* 7 Jan. 1832. Lawrence Pitkethly chaired the meeting and was one of eleven future Chartists who spoke. Robert Howard and Thomas Harrison of the Leeds RPU also attended.

243 The out-townships also contained factories and the 'General Committee' aimed to include representation from these, *LP* 29 Oct. 1831.

244 *LP* 24 Dec. 1831. There were also rumours of a local Whig newspaper being started.

245 *LP* 3 Dec. 1831, letter from an 'Oppressed Operative'.

for their interests are not identical with the Working Classes, except in the broad feature – that is as far as national prosperity goes, but in the particular, viz., in the tug between wages and profits, &c. they are opposed – this distinction is mostly overlooked, and it was on this Error that the hopes of the *step* advocates were founded – and as for the character of these middle-men, they were anti-reformers till the panic times. – Nay, we find them in the earlier stages of Reform resisting it in the shape of Gentlemen-Cavalry – Constitutional Associations – Watch and Wards – supporters of the Six Acts:- hence we find the shopocracy, the millocracy, and every other ocracy always arrays itself against the rights and interests of the working man.'[246]

Not everywhere was as 'advanced' as Huddersfield. Although Thomas Wilson chaired a working-class meeting in Halifax in late December to support Sadler's Factory Bill, he also appears to have taken a leading role in the 'collaborationist' Halifax PU and a broad-based Whig-liberal-radical alliance which, despite the occasional rumpus, held together until the second half of the decade.[247] Thus when some Halifax PU members attended a Huddersfield meeting in February 1832 on the propriety of supporting the Reform Bill, one of their number, Thomas Cliffe, argued that the radical reformers took an erroneous view and opposed their own true interests by withholding support. A noisy and heated discussion ensued and his resolution was defeated; but it is unlikely that the Halifax radicals' perceptions and tactics changed in any way.[248]

The wider concerns and ultra-radical ideas of the Huddersfield leadership ensured that the continuing suffering of distressed workers and the growing threat of cholera became potent political as well as economic or medical issues.[249] A meeting on 'Distress' convened largely at the instigation of the Huddersfield PU in April 1832 arose from Thomas Vevers' attempts to raise broadly 'political' questions at a meeting to solicit subscriptions for the prevention of cholera. In echoes of 1829, the radical meeting also received report-backs from PU members who had been appointed (at the November meeting) to enquire into local hardship, and pledged itself to set up a

---

246 *Woodites*, p. 4.
247 This assumes that Thomas Wilson (1786-1853), later a stationer and bookseller, was the same person as the pre-eminent local co-operator. Wilson was an extremely common local surname.
248 *LP* 24 Dec. 1831; 25 Feb. 1832; Jowitt, 'Parliamentary Politics', pp. 177-8. Wilson was the town's leading co-operator and a key working-class leader. Lack of information makes it impossible to speculate about the line adopted by popular radical leaders in Bradford, Dewsbury and Keighley.
249 Turberville and Beckwith, 'Leeds', pp. 34 and 49 for the arrival and spread of cholera. Local newspapers were full of remedies, but also some pungent social and political analysis. See, for example, the very bitter, 'A Specific for the Cholera. To the Medical Gentlemen, Merchants and Factory Lords of Huddersfield and its Vicinity' from 'an Oppressed Labourer', *LP* 3 Dec. 1831. On the Cholera outbreak generally see R. J. Morris, *Cholera, 1832: The Social Response to an Epidemic* (London: Croom Helm, 1976).

'Central Committee' in Huddersfield and 'District Committees' in villages to collect evidence.[250]

In addition to the impressive array of speakers, the meeting is most notable for the breadth of its concerns. As well as discussion of cholera and distress, we find George Beaumont extolling the virtues of Trades' Unions, exclusive dealing, and a 'national holiday' to pass the Ten Hour Bill; Thomas Hirst recommending 'union and co-operation', John Heaton urging the idea of co-operative manufacturing during strikes, and Thomas Vevers attacking the Reform Bill and advocating unity with the oppressed Irish. The vocabulary of the speakers was largely traditional – the veteran Thomas Leadbeater attacked 'corrupt government' and the clergy; Pitkethly the extravagant Whigs and Tories; Peter Thornton excessive taxation; though particular emphasis was placed on targets nearer home – 'the pseudo-aristocracy, the creatures of monopolised machinery' and the 'factorymongers' who were depressing the people.[251] The meeting, which ended with the news that Leeds operatives had resolved to strike for two days to attend the 'York Pilgrimage', provides a vivid illustration of the fusion of leaders, ideas and concerns which was taking place in the rarefied atmosphere of the reform crisis period. It also serves as a useful reminder of the impossibility of isolating distinct, separate movements and leaders from the agitational melting pot of these hyperactive years.

7: The 'May Days', 1832

The relatively small crowd at the Huddersfield meeting on 'Distress' in early April indicates that even in this radical stronghold, the Huntites were unable to retain a large following in the politically dormant period of late winter to early spring 1832. However, with the Reform Bill increasingly under threat, there was a resurgence of interest in reform from the middle of April onwards.[252] This coincided with renewed ten hours activity and, particularly in Leeds, resulted in the inflaming of local political passions and the further polarisation of opinion.[253]

When Lord Grey's administration resigned in early May over the King's refusal to create sufficient peers to carry the Reform Bill, ultra-radical opponents of the Bill were in a tactical cleft stick; and they remained at a disadvantage throughout the 'May Days'. They had no intention of re-joining a broad pro-Reform alliance yet their willingness to let the Reform Bill perish was not calculated to endear them to the

---

250 *LP* 14 Apr. 1832; *PMG* 10 Dec 1831. Unlike in 1829 this investigation was to be an explicitly radical, working-class affair. Pitkethly refers to it obliquely in his letter to Francis Place, 2 May 1832, PP, Add Mss, 35,149, f. 168.

251 *LP* 14 Apr. 1832. As well as familiar figures like Beaumont and Pitkethly, the meeting also included veterans like Vevers and Leadbetter, co-operators like Hirst and Heaton, Christopher Tinker, future unstamped victim and Chartist, and Daniel Frazer, ten hours leader. David Green, radical and future leading Owenite socialist, also spoke. The meeting ended with a vote of thanks to Oastler and Sadler.

252 Turberville and Beckwith, 'Leeds', pp. 50-1; *LP* 28 Apr. 1832 for Huddersfield radicals' invitation to Capt. Wood.

253 April saw the 'York Pilgrimage' and also the start of Sadler's parliamentary inquiry. For the controversy aroused by an anti-Baines demonstration see *LI* 3, 10; *LM* 5, 12 May 1832.

majority of the local population. For whilst it is unlikely that vast numbers of people had genuine hopes of the Reform Bill being of great benefit to them, they had grown accustomed to the idea of an, albeit unsatisfactory, measure of reform being granted. The possibility of total defeat and a return to Tory rule evoked genuine popular emotions which local groups of ultra-radicals were unable to combat.

The extent of popular outrage which the 'May Days' provoked should not be exaggerated. The news of the resignation was received in Leeds with murmurs of discontent 'not loud but deep'. And as radicals and Chartists later reminded their Whig opponents, it helped that many manufacturers closed their mills to allow their workpeople to attend the massive pro-reform demonstrations.[254] Although led by the Whig-liberal Bainesocracy and orchestrated by their lower-middle class and working-class allies in bodies like the Holbeck Political Union, these rallies drew on a broad base of support. The size of the meetings held throughout the textile district, leaves no room for doubt about this being a genuinely popular outburst of disappointment and frustration.[255]

The ultra-radicals remained in a decided minority. Attempts to draw away support from the big Leeds meeting of 14 May by counter placards failed. The RPU, which only two days earlier had denied that it was 'an expiring Union', made no impact and the editor of the *Patriot*, John Foster, received only bruises from a largely hostile crowd for his attempts to address the meeting.[256] The great West Riding meeting at Wakefield nine days later was held in a carnival atmosphere in the knowledge that the Bill was safe. But here the Huddersfield radicals, in their own words, also 'displayed the same uncompromising opposition, being convinced that a real Reform would sooner be obtained by rejecting this shadow (of a Bill), than by accepting it'. Pitkethly succeeded in briefly addressing the meeting to advocate universal suffrage but was shouted down.[257]

Outside these two active and well reported centres, little is known precisely about the attitudes and allegiances of working-class radicals. At Halifax it is likely, given Cliffe's declaration three months earlier for moderate reform, that the radicals supported public meetings and petitions in support of the House of Commons and the Reform Bill. However, as disagreements between Whigs and radicals over the choice of candidates soon revealed, relationships may have been very delicately poised.[258]

Bradford remains an enigma largely because of the paucity of local evidence. The middle-class pro-reform lobby embraced all groups except the extreme 'Church and King' Tories, but the attitude of the local working-class leaders remains unclear.[259] Dr. Wright asserts that the Bradford Political Union, headed by Peter Bussey, held

---

254 *LM* 12 May 1832; Turberville and Beckwith, 'Leeds', pp. 52-3. The day of the Wakefield West Riding meeting was made a general holiday in Leeds.

255 Turberville and Beckwith, 'Leeds', pp. 52-3; *LM, LP* 12, 19 May 1832.

256 Turberville and Beckwith, 'Leeds', pp. 51-2. The RPU admitted that it had got rid of some 'milk and water radicals', *LP* 19 May 1832.

257 Turberville and Beckwith, 'Leeds', pp. 52-4; *Woodites*, p. 5; *LM* 26 May 1832.

258 Jowitt, 'Parliamentary Politics', p. 178. See also Benjamin Wilson, *The Struggles of an Old Chartist* (Halifax: John Nicholson, 1887), p. 1, for 'great rejoicing in radical Skircoat Green after the passing of the Bill'.

259 Wright, 'Politics and Opinion', p. 97.

frequent out-door meetings 'to press for universal or household suffrage and stoutly to oppose the limited political programmes and social and economic assumptions of the capitalist leaders'. But local papers provide no evidence for the existence of this body beyond possibly the June 1831 meeting to urge a fuller measure of reform.[260] In late Spring 1832 the chief working-class leaders appear to have been preoccupied with developing links with the NAPL and trades' union developments. The excitement of the 'May Days' may have largely seemed an irrelevance or diversion.[261]

In Dewsbury, which, like the other remaining centre Keighley, was not a projected parliamentary borough, the evidence is more plentiful and suggests that the broad pro-reform alliance, taking in the leading Whig-liberal manufacturers and town radicals, and embodied in the Dewsbury Political Union, held firm. The 'May Days' meeting of 18 May attracted a large audience and is particularly interesting in revealing the radicals' attempts to press for a 'more effective measure of reform' in place of the 'partial and incomplete' Bill.[262]

The varying reactions in the different West Riding centres and the mixing of tricolours and yellow 'Liberal' banners at early May public meetings indicate that the ultra-radicals were still very much in a minority when reform itself was in the balance. However, the lasting importance of the 'May Days' to popular radicalism was not so much in what local radicals actually said and did as in the creation of a potent radical and later Chartist trope, which reflected and embodied a collective sense of bitterness, disillusionment, and in some cases shame, about the whole Reform Bill episode. As John Belchem notes, 'Chartism derived its vigour and assertive working-class independence from a powerful myth: the pervasive belief that the people had been deliberately deluded by the Whigs and manipulated by the middle-class reformers during the Reform Bill agitation'.[263]

Central to this trope was the image of Edward Baines jnr. calling for three groans for the Queen at the massive Leeds meeting of 14 May. Oastler in particular was offended and constantly referred back to it, but it became part of a more general working-class attack on the Whigs. At the time of the Dorchester meetings in 1834 the *Voice of the West-Riding* reprinted an extract from 'The History of an Old Rusty Blunder-buss', a satirical pro-trade union tract allegedly picked up by 'John Powlett' in London, which talked of the Dorchester protesters making a rope 'long and strong with which they vowed, either to pull back all the six victims from Botany Bay, or else

---

260 D. G. Wright, 'A Radical Borough: Parliamentary Politics in Bradford, 1832-41', *Northern History*, 4, 1 (1969), p. 137; *LP* 11 June 1831. Dr. Wright, in 'Politics and Opinion', p. 96, states that the Bradford PU was not referred to by name until the 1832 election.

261 *LP* 5 May 1832. Unlike the trade union meeting of the previous year, no 'political' sentiments were reported. Future disagreements with Huddersfield radicals and later electoral alignments suggest that popular radicals still shared some common political ground with lower middle-class 'radical-liberals', determined mainly by common hostility to the Tories. This is confirmed by Peter Bussey at a dinner in his honour, *NS* 19 Jan. 1839.

262 *LP* 17 May 1832. Two town-radicals urged the stopping of money and the boycotting of excisable articles until parliament granted a 'more extensive franchise', shorter parliaments and the ballot. The Dewsbury PU dated back to July 1831, *LM* 28 July 1832 (anniversary). I have been unable to uncover information about 'May Days' events in Keighley.

263 Belchem, *'Orator' Hunt*, p. 169.

to HANG ALL THE TAX-REFUSING, KING-KILLING, QUEEN-INSULTING, KING-DETHRONING, QUEEN-GROANING, INDUSTRY OPPRESSING, INNOCENCE-TRANSPORTING, LYING, GREEDY, WILY WHIGS'.[264]

A second more general element was the recollection of leading Bainesite Whigs adopting the rhetoric of violence and advocating a series of ulterior measures to enforce their claim to the franchise. Six years later when local Chartists were constantly being assailed by the *Mercury* for their allegedly violent language and tactics in pressing for what they saw as 'their Reform Bill', the *Northern Star* regularly reminded their Whig opponents of their former antics. The paper even went so far as provide a free engraving of 'Whig Loyalty and Moral Force' depicting the two Baines' (father and son), Joshua Bower and other Leeds liberals on the May 1832 platform.[265] The Whig victory of 1832 was projected as a triumph for 'physical force' threats with an effective popular mobilisation giving numerical heft to a constitutional, 'moral-force' stance. This was the model that the Chartists alleged they were simply reproducing in 1838-9.

The final strand of this image was the memory of the factory owners' manipulation of their operatives to carry a measure which benefited only themselves. As George Hodgson told a meeting of locked-out Leeds woollen workers in June 1834:

> It was but the other day that the operatives were led in great numbers to the West Riding meeting at Wakefield, for the purpose of carrying the Reform Bill. At that time, the very individuals who were now attempting to put down trades' unions, were arraying them to carry by force of numbers, a political reform which he was sure would not otherwise have been obtained from the aristocracy of the country. That reform which had thus been obtained appeared to him to have been the ultimate means of strengthening the hands of corruption and oppression.[266]

Peter Bussey reminded a Queenshead Chartist audience of the same events in 1838.[267] Together these fragments of collective myth and memory made up a recurring theme which consistently informed future working-class perceptions, tactics and enmities in the West Riding.

8: The First Reformed Elections, June–December 1832

The Reform Act of June 1832 created four Parliamentary boroughs in the West Riding textile district – Leeds (two members) containing the township of Leeds, ten

---

264 *VWR* 3 May 1834. The author may well have been Rev. G. S. Bull, see *BO* 2 Feb. 1837.
265 *NS* 6 Apr. 1839 (O'Connor at Leeds). *NS* 29 Dec. 1838; 5 Jan. 1839. The engraving is reproduced in Turberville and Beckwith, 'Leeds', illustration facing p. 49.
266 *LT* 24 May 1834, quoted in Thompson, *Making*, p. 908. George Hodgson (1790-1867) of Wortley, a woollen weaver/clothier, was a prominent trade union leader during the 1834 Leeds lock-out and remained an influential local figure. He testified to the 1838 Handloom Weavers' Commission and acted as a 'second' for Lloyd Jones in a debate with a local Wesleyan minister on the merits of Owenite socialism (*LT* 4 Aug.; 10 Nov. 1838). He supported the class collaborationist Complete Suffrage Union in 1842 and served on the General Council of the National Charter Association a couple of years later.
267 *NS* 10 Nov. 1838.

'out-townships' and four additional villages; Bradford (two members) containing the townships of Bradford, Bowling, Horton and Manningham; Halifax (two members) containing the township only and Huddersfield (single member) again including only the 'town' of Huddersfield itself and none of the outlying townships and villages in the wider parishes of Huddersfield and Almondbury. The size of the electorate in all cases was fairly small.

Leeds not surprisingly had the largest number of voters (4,171) followed by Bradford (1,137), Huddersfield (603) and Halifax (531).[268] The electorate comprised just a small proportion of the local population, and contained very few working-class voters. Dr. Wright estimates just 6% for Bradford and the figures for other towns were similar.[269] The reality of what the £10 franchise meant in practice can be seen in Leeds where Baines' estimates revealed that in Holbeck, a mainly working-class area, there were but a hundred and fifty voters; and that only two of Marshall's adult male workers would be entitled to vote, none at Messrs O. Williams and Sons woollen factory, and that only one voter was anticipated from amongst Taylor and Wadsworth's highly-paid machine-makers.[270] Dewsbury and Keighley were not made into parliamentary boroughs and here the residents' only direct interest at election times was in the massive West Riding constituency, in which some residents and electors in the enfranchised boroughs were also allowed to vote.[271]

The first reformed elections in the three of the four parliamentary boroughs have already been the subject of much intensive scrutiny and it is not proposed to repeat this.[272] Rather, after outlining the main features of the contests in each of the constituencies, a number of more general aspects will be examined.[273]

---

268 Turberville and Beckwith, 'Leeds', p. 70; Wright, 'Politics and Opinion ', p. 106; *LM* 13 May 1837; Jowitt, 'Parliamentary Politics', p. 173.

269 Wright, 'Radical Borough', p. 159. Jowitt estimates the 'working class' voters (even generously categorised) comprised less than 5% of the electorate. And the electorate in Halifax was only 1.7% of the total population. (Comparable figures in the other towns are Leeds (3.5%), Huddersfield (4.5%) and Bradford (4.8%)).

270 E. Baines, *The Life of Edward Baines* (London, 1859), pp. 157-9, quoted in Thompson, *Making*, p. 900.

271 See F. M. L. Thompson, 'Whigs and Liberals in the West Riding', *EHR*, 74 (1959), pp. 214-8. The West Riding constituency (two members) was the largest in the country with 29,000 electors in 1836. Many were freeholders living in the industrial areas. However, it is not proposed to discuss the West Riding elections in any detail except where they impinge upon the local story, since the constituency, and the factors effecting its behaviour, stretched well beyond the woollen textile district. The West Riding candidates normally addressed meetings in all of the main textile towns; but these contests were not normally the main focus of popular political interest and involvement.

272 For Leeds, see Turberville and Beckwith, 'Leeds', pp. 40-88; Fraser, 'Politics in Leeds', pp. 62-91; 'Fruits of Reform', pp. 90-96. For Bradford, see Wright, 'Politics and Opinion', p. 106 ff; 'Radical Borough', pp. 138-9; for Halifax, see Jowitt 'Parliamentary Politics', pp. 173-80; B. Wilson, *Struggles*, pp. 1-2. Driver, *Tory Radical*, p. 178 ff covers the 'Reform Bill Excitement' in the West Riding.

273 Most space will be devoted to Huddersfield, which has been less well covered in existing studies.

The wider significance of the contest at Leeds where the Whig-liberal pairing of Marshall and Macauley defeated the Tory factory reformer Sadler, has long been recognized.[274] It created an important, but not permanent alliance between Tories and radicals which focused particularly on the factory question. Ten hours became the biggest single issue in the campaign and amidst growing bitterness and vituperation factory reformers and ultra-radicals moved even closer together. Yet, whilst the alliance held firm and the contest became increasingly polarised with Whig-liberal political reform pitted against Tory-radical factory reform; as Dr. Fraser has stressed, 'the actual campaign was profoundly affected by the choice of candidates'.[275]

It is worth emphasising that not all Tories voted for Sadler, especially the factory owners.[276] Equally, the ultra-radicals did not mothball their organisation or recant their views when they endorsed Sadler. Their stance was pragmatic and, given their position on the Reform Bill, their long-standing commitment to factory reform, their record of antipathy to Baines and their rivalry with the 'moderate' radicals of the Holbeck PU, was not unexpected.

The Bradford contest, in which the Whig-liberal candidates E. C. Lister and John Hardy defeated the 'liberal' Tory George Banks, was a low-key affair which in contrast to, and perhaps because of, Leeds aroused little passion. Hardy, son of the Low Moor iron-master, enjoyed support from mild Tories, whilst Banks was pro-Reform Bill and spoke in favour of factory reform. Lister had been prominent in the parliamentary reform campaign and came from a family of leading worsted-spinners. Although Bussey and other combers' leaders questioned the candidates closely on the radical programme, the election passed off quietly, with the show of hands unusually being fairly evenly divided.

The Halifax contest threw up four candidates – Michael Stocks, a prominent local liberal with radical sympathies, Charles Wood, the son-in-law of the Whig leader Lord Grey, Rawdon Briggs jnr., a prominent local Whig banker, and James Stuart Wortley, part of a major Yorkshire Tory landowning family. Stocks and Briggs were the popular favourites, but it was Briggs and Wood who secured a Whig-liberal rather than a liberal-radical victory. As at Bradford there was no support for the pro-factory reform Tory from the working-class radical leadership, who strongly supported Stocks and, despite strained relations with the Whig-liberal leaders, joined the lower-middle class shopkeepers and tradesmen in endorsing Briggs. Wood was not a popular candidate but, drawing votes from 'moderate' Tories and respectable Whigs, easily defeated the maverick Stocks.[277]

Huddersfield saw a straight radical versus Whig contest, with local Tories failing to field a candidate. The popular favourite was Joseph Wood, a retired army captain with a small estate at Sandal near Wakefield. Wood was an honorary member of the Huddersfield PU and 'had also familiarized himself with the condition of the Working Classes … by entering the weavers' cottages, accompanied by Mr W. Stocks jnr., a long tried friend of the poor'. Wood also secured the support of Oastler and the ten

---

274 See, for example, Thompson, *Making*, p. 908, and Ward, *Leeds*, p. 96.
275 Fraser, 'Politics in Leeds', p. 64.
276 Fraser, 'Politics and Society', p. 277.
277 On Stocks, a local mine-owner, see Jowitt, 'Parliamentary Politics', pp. 177-8.

hours movement when he unhesitatingly pledged himself in favour of factory reform.[278] The Huddersfield contest is often set alongside the Leeds election as an example of a Tory-radical alliance in operation, and certainly, as at Leeds, factory reform was a major issue. But in reality, the contests had different emphases and characteristics. In Huddersfield the alliance was very much radical-led and involved the coming together of radicals and 'Oastlerites'.[279] Many Tories abstained or voted on the Whig side. The special nature of the constituency, in particular 'the peculiar and almost feudal connexion subsisting betwixt this Town and the Ramsden family', also conditioned political perspectives and alliances.[280] The Ramsdens, with their strong Whig connections, owned virtually the whole of the town and the strength of the 'Ramsden interest' gave credence to the radical jibe that Huddersfield would in effect be a pocket borough.

The decision of local Whigs to run J. C. Ramsden, son of Sir John, as their candidate appeared to confirm radical prejudices. However, he was given an extremely hostile reception at a public meeting in late June and soon dropped out.[281] His replacement, Captain Fenton, was scarcely more popular. A leader of a Volunteer Association in the post-war period, to the local radicals he was scarcely distinguishable in politics from the hardline repressive Tories of that era. According to the radicals, 'many of the Whigs themselves looked upon him with suspicion.[282]

The long campaign became increasingly bitter and vitriolic as the Whig and radical positions became increasingly polarised: the Whigs opposing factory reform and further extension of the suffrage; the Radicals supporting Oastler on ten hours, pressing for 'real' reform and condemning 'Ramsdenian tyranny', both political and commercial.[283] On nomination day, Fenton, who had scarcely dared speak in public during the campaign was regularly shouted down and Captain Wood overwhelmingly won the show of hands.[284] The two-day poll however gave Fenton a comfortable majority: many Tories as the *Mercury* had predicted, abstaining or voting for Fenton for fear of Wood's election.[285] Popular disappointment and resentment at this 'Oligarchical illustration of the Reform Bill' vented itself in attempts to seize the Poll Book and in the breaking of windows of 'notorious Fentonians'. Special constables were called out and the military sent for and, with an armed guard round his house, Fenton spent his victory night in a pane-free house after an attack by 'several hundred of the wretches' (his description).[286] Eventually after the 'Specials' and

---

278 *Woodites*, pp. 5-6.

279 Driver, *Tory Radical*, p. 187 uses this term.

280 *Woodites*, p. 1.

281 Ibid., p. 8; *LM* 30 June 1832.

282 *Woodites*, p. 9; see also WYAS: HP, Box 1, Lewis Fenton to Harewood, 18 Dec. 1820 (writing about a Volunteer Association being formed).

283 A particular source of grievance were the canal dues on Ramsden's canal, *Woodites*, p. 10.

284 *Woodites*, pp. 11-12. According to W. Moore (the local Whig postmaster) to F. Frieling, 15 December 1832 (in TNA: HO 52/20), the labouring population 'literally hate and despise Fenton!'

285 *LM* 8 Dec. 1832; only 413 out of 603 potential electors actually voted, *Woodites*, p. 13, and much 'promised' radical support evaporated.

286 TNA: HO 40/31, f3, Fenton to Bouverie, 29 Dec. 1832. For contrasting descriptions of the

the 'antiquated sons of carnage' (the troops)[287] agreed to keep a low profile, two respected radicals William Stocks jnr. and Thomas Hirst managed to persuade the crowd to disperse.

The West Riding election of 1832 tended to be overshadowed by the local contests. However, it remained the chief focus for Keighley and Dewsbury radicals. At Dewsbury a broad alliance of Whig-liberals and town-radicals remained the dominant force, preaching class collaboration and wide public consultation by electors in the use of their votes.[288] In Keighley the Whig candidates were shouted down and two leading radicals and short time men, David Weatherhead and Abraham Wildman, requested Oastler to stand. The 'Factory King' did not take up the suggestion but provocatively attended the poll, where the two Whig candidates, Morpeth and Strickland, were returned unopposed.[289]

Throughout the textile district as a whole it is impossible to discern a single pattern of working-class involvement or response. Local conditions, the state of relations with lower middle-class radical-liberals and middle-class Whigs, personalities and the 'track-record' of particular candidates clearly counted for much. However, a number of general themes and questions are worth exploring.

In the first place, how much impact did the working-class radicals make? At first sight this would seem to be minimal. 'Radical' candidates were fielded only at Huddersfield and Halifax and neither stood on the full radical programme. Captain Wood was 'a reformer of the Cartwright school' who advocated 'cheap government, cheap law, cheap religion, cheap bread' and favoured the extension of the suffrage (though he did not commit himself to how far), the ballot and shorter Parliaments. His popularity was also based on his advocacy of 'a good day's wages, for a good day's work' and his support for factory reform.[290] Michael Stocks in Halifax favoured triennial parliaments, abolition of sinecures and pensions, abolition of the Corn Laws, and the prohibition of children under twelve working in factories. However, he opposed the Ten Hours Bill and did not favour household suffrage until education was more widely diffused.[291] Both candidates received the backing of popular radical leaders, but their radicalism was also sufficiently moderate to attract the support of middle-class and lower-middle class, more liberally inclined, radicals – the shopkeepers, town tradesmen and small masters who existed very much on the class borderline. It was these who served with working-class leaders on the election

---

extent and cause of the 'Riot' see *Woodites*, pp. 13-15 and the letters of the unpopular and jumpy Whig postmaster, William Moore to F. Frieling (G.P.O.) in TNA: HO 52/20, 13 and 15 Dec. 1832. Moore gives a vivid account of the disturbances, which he blamed on 'the influence of about a dozen demagogues' and Oastler. The radical line was to deprecate window smashing but to blame the Whigs and their 'Specials' for over-reacting and provoking a disturbance.

287 *Woodites*, p. 14. For further discussion on radical rhetoric see below, p. 460.

288 See November public meeting, *LM* 1 Dec. 1832, at which George Crabtree (local ten hours leader), Vevers and Pitkethly (urging universal suffrage) also spoke.

289 *LM* 8 Dec. 1832; Driver, *Oastler*, p. 203.

290 *Woodites*, p. 5.

291 Jowitt, 'Parliamentary Politics', p. 178

committees and at Halifax worked with them in the Political Union. But, despite their willingness to play practical politics, in neither case were working-class radicals successful.

The popular radicals equally did not make a large impact in Bradford, and at Leeds they were junior partners in an alliance which left them vulnerable to the constant jibes and invective of the *Leeds Mercury*. However, it should be remembered that the full marshalling of radical forces behind Sadler only occurred after attempts to get a radical candidate had failed.[292] As early as mid-July Frank Phillips, the radical chair of a 'committee of operatives' meeting held at the Union Inn (the STC and Trades' Union headquarters) had urged the operatives of Leeds to follow the Huddersfield men and solicit a man of 'disinterested and independent principles'. The person he had in mind was George Wailes, a lawyer on the radical side of the Whig-liberal bloc who had been prominent on the Reform Bill platform at Leeds. Eventually further meetings of 'influential persons among the operatives' resulted in a formal coming together of the Union Inn pro-Wailes committee (including people such as Phillips, J. Bottomley and David Black) and the 'Radical Union' (including Mann, Ayrey and Rider).[293] These 'political' meetings formed just part of a series of gatherings held in late July to early August which demonstrate the convergence of some key facets of working-class endeavour and aspiration into one coherent force which, after Wailes declined an invitation to stand alongside Sadler, was put behind Sadler's candidature.

The context of this coming together is worth noting. Cholera was rampant in Leeds and by the end of the first week of August had carried off James Mann, the pre-eminent ultra-radical, Thomas Roberts, the president of the Trades' Union, and Thomas Inchbold, the leading ten hours printer in Leeds.[294] Unemployment was also rife, swelled partly by local manufacturers' attempts to send cloth to be worked in the outlying areas of Leeds in order to by-pass the control of the Trades' Union.[295] In addition, the *Mercury*'s attempts to play down the extent of local distress had, as in 1829-30, infuriated the operatives and demonstrated Baines' 'unreserved hypocrisy' towards them.[296] A series of meetings of the unemployed on Woodhouse Moor were convened by the same committee who were pressing for Wailes' candidature.[297] These attacked Baines not only for his journalistic inexactitudes but also for his political role and his stance on the factory reform question. In particular the operatives resented and rejected the candidates foisted upon them by Baines. David Brook, short time and

---

292 Turberville and Beckwith, 'Leeds', pp. 57-8. There was no intention of withdrawing support from Sadler – rather to run the two in tandem.

293 *LP* 14, 21, 28 July 1832. Wailes was a particular advocate of the ballot. Francis (Frank) Phillips (1791?-1841+), an 'operative', may originally have been a cloth-dresser (see *LI* 26 July 1832). However, he is listed as a hairdresser in the 1841 census and when he sold tickets for a Chartist Grand Soiree (*NS* 16 Jan 1841). J. may be a mistake for T. (Thomas) Bottomley (1796?-1841+), a cloth-dresser and future Chartist. David Black, an 'operative' was very active as a Chartist in 1839, but disappears thereafter.

294 *LM* 4 Aug. 1832. Inchbold was a Tory.

295 *LP* 4 Aug. 1832 (F. Phillips' and Wm. Ross' speeches).

296 *LP* 28 July 1832.

297 *LP* 14, 28 July; 4 Aug; *LM* 28 July 1832. The meetings comprised 'unemployed weavers etc', presumably factory-based weavers, and possibly dressers.

probably Trades' Union leader, asked how Marshall could be expected to represent the working-classes when he was 'a capitalist … who possessed a mechanical power, whereby he could crush not only the infant population, but the adult population to the very earth'. Baines for his part has shown himself 'a most dangerous character' by 'his intrigues with members of Government, his connections with manufacturers, and his ardent love for machinery, coupled with his propensities for enslaving little children'. Equally Baines had not endeared himself to the operatives by his allegations that the STC was unrepresentative and was misusing its funds.[298]

A number of common themes pervade the pro-Wailes and unemployed meetings. First, a stress on labour as the source of all wealth and on the dignity and independence which was due to every working man. Second, a deep hostility to capitalists and employers – 'property-men' and 'profit men' – in both their political and economic roles. Christopher Ellwand alleged that the working men were now 'slaves of the capitalists and it was through them that they had acquired their mansions and their carriages', whilst James Mann (in his last public speech before he died) asked 'were these men who employed large quantities of machinery the most proper men to send to be law-makers for the working-classes?'[299] The attack on the misuse of machinery formed the third common strand. David Brook admitted that 'he was one of those who, fifteen or sixteen years ago, when men were sent to prison, and hanged for breaking a few machines, did not think that machinery was a blessing; but he now believed that it might be of advantage if made subservient to manual labour'; and John Drake likewise argued for restraints 'within proper limites' to allow the labouring class to reap the benefits of machinery.[300] Fourthly, other strands of an alternative political economy are also very much in evidence, notably the stress on the need for higher wages and shorter hours as the means of 'regulating supply and demand for labour', increasing employment and creating an enlarged domestic market for manufactured and agricultural goods. Finally, there is the floating of alternative strategies to achieve these broad economic and political objectives, including co-operative production through 'an institution of the working-classes for the purpose of establishing a manufactory by their own united efforts'; and exclusive dealing with shopkeepers to ensure that their interests are looked after.[301]

The meetings favoured a broad working-class front in favour of Sadler, because he supported ten hours (a crucial touchstone), favoured agricultural reform and advocated an Irish Poor Law (whereby the poor Irish would not be 'compelled to resort to the market of labour in England, and thereby reduce the value of the Englishman's

---

298 LP 28 July 1832. David Brook (1796?-1871?), a cloth-dresser, was a prominent in the ten hours campaign and meetings of out of work operatives. He testified to Sadler's Committee in 1832.

299 LP 4 Aug. 1832. Christopher Ellwand (1801-1857?) was a woollen weaver active in ten hours, trade union and radical circles in the early 1830s.

300 LP 28 July 1832. Brook, a cloth-dresser or 'cropper' (as Mann had been), was old enough to have been involved in the Luddite disturbances.

301 LP 4 Aug. 1832. A committee was established to set up this institution – possibly the precursor of the later 'commercial orders'. It was clear that something more than a temporary expedient to deal with unemployment is envisaged.

labour'); and Wailes, because he had consistently advocated an extended suffrage, the ballot and short parliaments.[302]

It is likely that this fusion of the operatives' broad political demands and economic grievances would have commanded widespread popular support.[303] However, Wailes' disinclination to stand, coupled with Mann's untimely death, killed off any chance of achieving such a broad alliance. Although many of the operatives who had supported the Union Inn initiative and the unemployed meetings no doubt fell in behind Sadler, it is likely that the more moderate elements in the Trades' Union leadership inclined more naturally to the 'Liberal' than the Tory side.[304] This predilection, together with the demands of a major dispute at Holmfirth, their efforts to spread the union to the outlying 'woollen' villages, and the need to defend the union from increasingly ferocious public attacks, may help to explain their reluctance to become overtly involved in the latter stages of the Leeds election campaign.[305]

A second major question raised by the 1832 elections concerns another aspect of Trades' Union engagement: their involvement in mass demonstrations and exclusive dealing.[306] Although formal organisation was not always a radical strongpoint there can be no doubt that leaders such as Pitkethly, Stocks and Beaumont in Huddersfield were extremely effective in linking with unions to mobilise popular support and orchestrating outdoor demonstrations. Captain Fenton, the victorious candidate at Huddersfield, spoke with some fear and perhaps even awe of radical boasts that 'in three hours they can at any time assemble a force of 20,000 robust members of these unions without the town...', whilst William Moore, the local Whig postmaster, believed 'their system is a well organised system, worthy of a better cause'.[307]

The harnessing of this support to persuade shopkeepers and others to favour the popular candidate proved more difficult. The potential for exclusive dealing implicit in the Reform Bill had been early recognised and the tactic had been advocated from the very start of the campaign.[308] 'Wood for ever' stickers quickly appeared in shop windows in Huddersfield and the Leeds Trades' Union quickly had to dissociate itself

---

302 *LP* 28 July, 4 Aug. 1832.

303 Although popular support did not win elections, it did help to give legitimacy and moral justification; and the *Mercury* showed some unease about the potency of this combination, *LM* 28 July 1832.

304 See *LM* 25 Aug. 1832 for the allegation that twelve leading members of the Trades' Union had been given tickets for one of Baines' election dinners; *LM* 8 Dec. 1832 for Thomas Roberts, late President of the Union, being a supporter of reform, and of Marshall and Macauley. Roberts worked for Benjamin Gott, a Tory, with whom the union had its first major dispute. Roberts' death, *LP* 7 July 1832, may have strengthened the hand of the radicals who called the pro-Wailes and unemployed meetings.

305 *LM* 4 Aug., 6 Oct; 20 Oct. 1832 ff. for letters between 'Mercator' and 'John Powlett'. For early questioning of the candidates, by Ralph Taylor, about trades' unions, see Turberville and Beckwith, 'Leeds', pp. 63 and 67.

306 John Foster, *Class Struggle and the Industrial Revolution* (London: Weidenfeld and Nicholson, 1974), p. 53 ff. emphasises the importance and success of exclusive dealing in Oldham.

307 TNA: HO 40/31 f. 3, Fenton to Bouverie, 29 Dec. 1832, Fenton had in mind 'trades', political and other unions'; Moore to Frieling, 15 Dec. 1832, TNA: HO 52/20.

308 See *LM* 12 Mar. 1831 (Samuel Dickenson); *LP* 14 Apr. 1832 (George Beaumont).

from canvassers (presumably for Sadler) who had used the Union's name.[309] However, after the initial excitement had died away, there is little evidence of systematic exclusive dealing for political ends in either Leeds or Huddersfield. The complaint of the Leeds shopkeepers in early October 1832 was that the Trades' Union was threatening exclusive dealing in order to bolster its funds, and this was also a grievance at Huddersfield.[310] Here the Trades' Unions publicly demonstrated their support for Wood and the collection of money for union funds may have been scarcely distinguishable from extracting promises.[311] However, the lack of widespread complaints or evidence of its adoption suggests that the tactic was but little used or, if adopted, was not successful. This may have been due to the practical difficulties of a large body of radical supporters in the out-townships and villages pressurizing town-based shopkeepers, and also to the realisation that exclusive dealing could be a double-edged weapon.[312] Although mass mobilisation had managed to drive away one Whig candidate, it was not a sufficiently powerful weapon to prevent the easy election of his successor. The victory of William Cobbett at Oldham encouraged a re-appraisal of the possibilities of exclusive dealing and a more systematic approach at the following year's by-election. But then, as in 1832, it was insufficient by itself to alter the local balance of power.

The impact of the working-class radicals in the West Riding at the 1832 elections was not as great as that enjoyed by their peers across the Pennines. In the post-Reform Bill honeymoon period, their analysis of the defects and implications of the measure was not totally accepted. Nevertheless, the election campaign, and the preceding agitations, had a profound effect on future lines of development. From its gradual inception in Almondbury in 1829 the operatives' agitation for 'real radical reform' gave a number of local activists invaluable experience of independent organisation and aided their emergence as significant figures who became, and were to remain, the leaders and voice of the unenfranchised right through the decade. This was not a universal phenomenon. In some places radical leadership remained in the hands of more 'moderate' liberally-inclined, predominantly lower middle or middle-class leaders, only a handful of whom stayed the course right through into Chartism. However, in a number of places the backbone of early Chartist leadership is already discernible.

In these communities the working-class radicals (with some lower middle-class leaders and allies) became clearly and irreversibly differentiated from the 'Liberals' and henceforth pursued a largely separate line of development. In a few places they engaged in alliances with individual talismanic Tories; but here, as in cases where working-class radicals attached themselves to the cause of a Whig-liberal or a 'radical-liberal' candidate, the arrangement was essentially pragmatic, limited and consistent with wider political or economic aspirations.

---

309 *LM* 30 June 1832.

310 *LM* 29 Sept., 6 Oct. 1832. There were also complaints from Bradford, *LM* 10 Nov. 1832.

311 *Woodites*, p. 6.

312 Excessive pressure could be counter-productive and powerful local Whigs had ways of pressurising radicals, see *Woodites*, pp. 15-16. See also James Mann's remarks on exclusive dealing, *LP* 23 Oct. 1830.

Collectively, the popular radical agitations of the 1829-32 period, the passing of the Reform Act and the reformed elections were critically important in forging working-class identity and a sense of separation. The Reform Bill drew, and the reformed elections scored more deeply, a precise line across the nation. This new demarcation was easily grafted onto pre-existing delineations. Increasingly the people, the non-electors and the working-class became synonymous. Leeds ultra-radical William Rider was able to talk of the chasm existing 'betwixt themselves and the ten-pounders'. As 'Geo. Dickinson' (in all probability Samuel Dickenson) bluntly told a hostile respectable pro-Reform meeting in Huddersfield in late September 1831: 'you (*turning to the gentlemen on the magistrates' bench*) consider yourselves of a different order – you despise the poor man. (*Tremendous disapprobation.*) There is one thing I wish to tell the gentlemen in this room. There is no way for the labouring man but one, and that is to unite and protect their own interests. (*Cheers from the Radicals*)'.[313]

This sense of class was both a product and a cause of the coming together of organisations, ideas and grievances witnessed, for example, at the Huddersfield distress meeting of April 1832 or the Leeds unemployed and political meetings of early August. The various strands of working-class endeavour were never in reality that separate or discrete. All were born out of common concerns about standards of living, unemployment, political inequality, injustice. And they were informed by shared, and widely-held ideas about competition, over-production, over-working, machinery, labour being the source of wealth, pauperism, inequality, and the politically-determined nature of oppression. The heat of the reform crisis and its aftermath served to make links, and shared ideas and aspirations, more explicit and obvious; and to identify, in the 'shopocrats', 'millocrats' and 'capitalists', common enemies who opposed working-class hopes and interests, whether manifested in trades' unions, political unions, short time committees or co-operative societies. This analysis was not universally or immediately accepted, but during the middle years of the decade, through slow trickles and occasional boosts, it infused and charged up the consciousness of large sections of the working population – artisans, out-workers and factory workers. The energy and frustration stored up in these post-Reform years helps to explain the early and powerful genesis of Chartism in the West Riding textile district. However, before exploring further the charging of working-class batteries in the fitful, but important agitations of the mid-1830s, it is necessary to look at other aspects of the working-class response to their economic, social and political predicament, beginning first with early co-operation.

---

313 *LP* 21 July 1832; *HHE* 1 Oct. 1831.

4

Early Co-operation, 1829-34 and Beyond

Early co-operative societies formed an important stratum in the multi-layered working-class response to the severe socio-economic dislocation of the period. They also provided a setting in which traditional and advanced ideas intersected and practical nostrums to engender fundamental social and economic change were played out. Their significance and persistence, and their links to other working-class enterprises, have generally been underestimated. The condescension and marginalisation that Peter Gurney notes in relation to the history of later co-operative endeavours, also applies to the preceding period.[1] Early co-operation, with its earnest overtones and prosaic day-to-day concerns, has not garnered the same historiographical attention as more emotionally-charged popular agitations such as the fight for the vote or the campaign to reduce the working hours of factory children.

Few historians have followed the lead of E. P. Thompson in emphasizing the significance of the early co-operative pioneers; or built on J. F. C. Harrison's foundational studies of Owen and the Owenites and the fusion of the co-operative and radical movements.[2] There are, however, some noteworthy exceptions. Robin Thornes has revealed the richness and variety of co-operative practices in West Yorkshire and beyond; and demonstrated important elements of continuity that challenged the foundation myth constructed around the Rochdale Pioneers. M. Purvis's contemporaneous work endorsed this conclusion and highlighted the volume

---

1 Peter Gurney, *Co-operative Culture and the Politics of Consumption in England 1870-1930* (Manchester: Manchester University Press, 1996), pp. 2-3.
2 E. P. Thompson, *The Making of the English Working Class* (Harmondsworth: Penguin, 1968 edn.), pp. 872-5, 884-6; J. F. C. Harrison, *Robert Owen and the Owenites in Britain and America: The Quest for the New Moral World* (London: Routledge and Kegan Paul, 1969).

and diversity of co-operative activity during the supposedly moribund 1835-50 period. More recently, John Halstead and historians of the Huddersfield area have celebrated the life of one of the key advocates of early co-operation in the north: Thomas Hirst of Huddersfield.[3]

Figures like Hirst generally do not appear in Gregory Claeys's landmark study of the intellectual origins of early British socialism. This includes a re-examination of Owen and his influence on co-operative and trade union endeavours. Claeys concludes that, though his flirtation with both was brief, it had a lasting impact through his pivotal role in the emergence of 'social radicalism', which brought together different strands of radical social and political thought and profoundly influenced the later complex interactions between Owenism and Chartism.[4] How far these connections were anticipated in the pre-Chartist era provides one of the running themes of this chapter. It also seeks to contribute to the local and regional studies that he argues are necessary for a fuller picture to emerge.

Subsequent research has similarly tended to focus on Owen and the ideas of Owenite theorists, and on metropolitan debates and developments.[5] This concentration means that early co-operative endeavours are generally viewed (if noted at all) in terms of what they prefigured rather than what they actually did. The quotidian practice of early co-operation in its heartland, the industrial north, remains under-reported and underestimated; despite the fact that, as Peter Gurney has stressed in relation to the later Chartist period, for many local leaders 'consumption ... was regarded as an intensely political sphere'.[6]

Historians of consumerism like Gurney have examined co-operation through a different lens: arguing that consumer co-operation needs to be considered on its own terms as a challenge to the dominant, capitalist-based, mode of consumption.[7] Few of

---

3   Robin Thornes, 'Change and continuity in the Development of Co-operation, 1827-1844', in Stephen Yeo (ed.), *New Views of Co-operation* (London: Routledge, 1988), pp. 27-51; Robin Thornes, 'The origins of the co-operative movement in Huddersfield: the Life and times of the 1st Huddersfield Co-operative Trading Association', in E. A. Hilary Haigh (ed.), *Huddersfield, A Most Handsome Town: Aspects of the History and Culture of a West Riding Town* (Huddersfield: Kirklees Cultural Services, 1992), pp. 171-88; M. Purvis, 'Co-operative Retailing in England, 1835–1850: Developments Beyond Rochdale', *Northern History*, 22 (1986), pp. 198-215; John Halstead, 'Notable Co-operator – Thomas Hirst 1792-1833', *Huddersfield Local History Society Journal*, 30 (2020), pp. 61-7. On the foundation myth of the Rochdale Pioneers, see John K. Walton, 'Revisiting the Rochdale Pioneers', *Northern History*, 80 (2015), pp. 215-45

4   Gregory Claeys, *Citizens and Saints: Politics and Anti-politics in Early British Socialism* (Cambridge: Cambridge University Press, 1989).

5   For example, Ben Maw, 'Robert Owen's Unintended Legacy: Class Conflict', in Chris Williams and Noel Thompson (eds.), *Robert Owen and his Legacy* (Cardiff: University of Wales Press, 2011), pp. 155-73.

6   Gurney, *Co-operative Culture and the Politics of Consumption*, p. 15.

7   Ibid.; Ellen Furlough and Carl Strikwerda (eds.), *Consumers against Capitalism? Consumer Co-operation in Europe, North America and Japan, 1840-1990* (Lanham: Rowman & Littlefield, 1999); Lawrence Black and Nicole Robertson (eds.), *Consumerism and the Cooperative Movement in Modern British History: Taking Stock* (Manchester: Manchester University Press, 2009).

these studies, however, have reached back into early history of co-operation. For example, the pioneering societies of the reform era fall outside the scope of Peter Gurney's account of 'the contested and uneven development of the working-class consumer in England between the First and Second Reform Acts'.[8] Like the benefit and friendly societies with which they shared organisational structures and aspirational vitality, early co-operative ventures remain under-researched and their significance under-appreciated.

Part of the reason for this may be the relative dearth of sources, itself an indicator of the societies' humble origins and the extent to which they quickly became absorbed into the everyday fabric of their communities. Detailed information is lacking for all but a few of the many co-operative bodies that flourished in the West Riding textile district during the 1829-34 period and beyond. Even in those instances where adequate records exist, the nature of the evidence is unbalanced. Accounts rely heavily on the writings and doings of a handful of the keenest apostles, sometimes, as in the case of Huddersfield, refracted through the world-view of later co-operative advocates.[9] The attempt to reconstruct the story of early co-operation is nevertheless worthwhile, not least because it focuses on an underestimated source of labour's potency: the collective use of purchasing power for both practical and idealistic ends. Early co-operators, as much as their Chartist and Anti-Corn Law League successors, 'harnessed seemingly mundane, quotidian acts of buying and selling in order not merely to tinker at the margins but to change the world'.[10] As E. P. Thompson noted, 'This juxtaposition of the little store and the millenarial plan is of the essence of the co-operative mood between 1829 and 1834'.[11]

1: Introduction

Although there are areas of significant overlap, the history of West Riding early co-operation is not the same as the story of Owenites and Owenism.[12] A few recognisable Owenites played a part in the early co-operative societies and Owen's ideas influenced the thinking of a number of leaders. However, their importance should not be exaggerated. The nostrums which were most influential – labour as the source of all wealth, the unnatural effects of competition and industrialisation, the relation of distress to intemperance, crime and ignorance – were those which were already most familiar to skilled artisans and outworkers.[13] Many of Owen's key tenets, such as on

8   Peter Gurney, *Wanting and Having: Popular Politics and Liberal Consumerism in England, 1830-70* (Manchester: Manchester University Press, 2015), p. 4.

9   For example, G. J. Holyoake, *The History of Co-operation in England* (London, 1875) and his series of articles in *CN*, 2 Jan - 6 Feb. 1892. On Holyoake, see Peter Gurney, 'George Jacob Holyoake: Socialism, Association and Co-operation in Nineteenth-Century England', in S. Yeo (ed.), *New Views of Co-operation*, pp. 52-72.

10   Gurney, *Wanting and Having*, pp. 17-18.

11   Thompson, *Making*, p. 872.

12   For this see Harrison, *Robert Owen and the Owenites*; Sidney Pollard and John Salt (eds.), *Robert Owen: Prophet of the Poor* (London: Macmillan, 1971).

13   For this point in a London context see Iorwerth Prothero, *Artisans and Politics in Early Nineteenth-Century London, John Gast and His Times* (Folkstone: Dawson, 1979), pp. 246,

family and marriage, and his general paternalistic perspective, were widely rejected. Indeed, his views on religion were an anathema to many leading West Riding co-operators.[14] His vision of 'Community' was not generally shared – even amongst the advocates of something more than co-operative retailing and manufacturing. They preferred more 'practical' limited schemes based on 'home colonisation' ideas.[15] There are grounds for treating with some caution J. F. C. Harrison's assertion that, 'for five years the British working-class movement was saturated with Owenism'.[16]

Robin Thornes's detailed study of West Yorkshire and M. Purvis's overview of post-1834 activities have outlined the extent of continuities in the 'history of co-operative formations from the 1820s to the 1840s and beyond'.[17] This chapter similarly stresses the degree of commonality with earlier modes of activity and organisation, and links with other contemporary working-class 'unions'. The ideas and organisational know-how on which the early co-operators drew were of ancient usage. During the second half of the eighteenth century there had been co-operative corn mills and small co-operative stores in Yorkshire.[18] In the frequently harsh economic climate of the 1820s, co-operative retailing provided a practical response to austerity and scarcity in the more isolated villages around Huddersfield. The oldest society, Meltham Mills, can be traced back to 1827.[19] Convenience, notions of fair price, and worries about food adulteration all played their part in the co-operative explosion of the late 1820s. For this reason, the formation of early societies should be set in the context of contemporary campaigns, such as the 'milk and butter' boycotts of 1829 and the attempts to challenge the truck system.[20] Some of the early co-operative societies which set up a shopkeeper as storekeeper can similarly be viewed as engaging in an extension of exclusive dealing – a traditional artisan tactic.[21]

Nor was co-operative production unfamiliar by the early nineteenth century. Trade societies occasionally used their funds to buy raw materials and set their members to work for the society, in order to meet the exigencies of a crisis like a major strike. Such enterprises usually ceased when normality returned.[22] Co-operative production had been actively canvassed at the end of major contests like Bradford (1825) and Kidderminster (1828).[23] Some early co-operative leaders and societies in the West Riding saw self-employment as more than a temporary expedient. For example, 'D. Wilson' of Halifax asserted in March 1831: 'We … are steadily persevering

---

255-6.

14 See below, pp. 221-2.

15 For a discussion of this see Prothero, *Artisans and Politics*, pp. 247, 252-3; and Malcolm Chase, *The People's Farm: English Radical Agrarianism 1775-1840* (London: Breviary Stuff, 2010 edn.).

16 Harrison, *Robert Owen and the Owenites*, p. 196.

17 Stephen Yeo, preface to Thornes, 'Change and Continuity', p. 28.

18 Harrison, *Robert Owen and the Owenites*, p. 197.

19 Owen Balmforth, *Handbook of the 27th Co-operative Congress, Huddersfield 1895* (Huddersfield, 1895), pp. 103-11; Thornes, 'Origins', p. 182.

20 See above, pp. 130 and 133.

21 Prothero, *Artisans and Politics*, p. 248.

22 Ibid., p. 250; Thompson, *Making*, p. 869.

23 See above, pp. 102-3.

towards the principle [sic] groundwork of Co-operation – Independence from the control of competitive employers'.[24] But for many societies it was clearly just a form of unemployment benefit.

The idea of working people clubbing together, with small weekly subscriptions, for mutual benefit and insurance also had a rich heritage, especially in the northern weaving communities with their long traditions of mutuality. The early years of the nineteenth century saw a tremendous growth in the number of friendly or benefit societies which were often connected very closely with a trade society or community. These locally organised bodies, with their rituals and oaths, used members' weekly contributions to cover the effects of the potential ever-present levellers of working people's social condition: ill-health, injury, unemployment and death.[25] It therefore required little or no advance in working-class culture to convince people of the advantages to be gained through clubbing together to buy in bulk and sell cheap, or to produce for themselves. Indeed, many of the early, 'practical' school of co-operators promoted their societies as a more beneficial alternative to benefit and savings societies.

Early co-operative societies, like benefit societies, appealed to the sense of respectability and independence of skilled artisans like the 'decent and respectable working men' who made up the audience for a Bradford co-operative meeting in 1830. Indeed, the local society's stated desire was to hear of 'every Society being like a little independent nation of itself'.[26] As William Carson stressed, the early societies aimed 'to obtain the comfort, respectability and humble, yet true independence of the working classes'.[27]

The societies were a conscious response to the severe economic straits in which many artisans and outworkers found themselves in the late 1820s. Indeed, the Halifax co-operators considered them 'the only effective remedy for Distress'.[28] Their development and progress must be firmly set in the context of public meetings to address local suffering, of complaints about truck payments and power-looms, of wage disputes and consumer boycotts, and of the growth of political and trade union organisations.

Links with popular radicalism and trade unionism will be explored throughout this chapter, but particularly in the later sections which look at relations with Owen and the schemes for 'national union' which developed in the 1833-4 period. However, the initial focus is on the early expansion of co-operative societies in the late 1820s and early 1830s; and it is with some intensive local studies that we start.

2: Leeds, Bradford and the Villages

The story of early co-operation in the Leeds region begins in late 1828, with a meeting of a local benefit society and an address by William Carson of Birmingham

---

24 *Carpenter's Political Letters and Pamphlets*, No. 27, 'Political Pilot', 26 Mar. 1831.

25 On friendly societies, see Simon Cordery, *British Friendly Societies, 1750-1914* (Basingstoke and New York: Palgrave Macmillan, 2003).

26 *HCC* 13 Feb. 1830; *WFP* 11 Apr. 1829.

27 *WFP* 19 Dec. 1829.

28 *Carpenter's Political Letters and Pamphlets*, No. 27, 'Political Pilot', 26 Mar. 1831.

on the propriety of forming a 'Co-operative Trading Fund Association'.[29] The inspiration came directly from London via the medium of the *Weekly Free Press*. But there was also an indirect connection with Brighton from where Dr. William King's practical approach and advice, expounded in the *Co-operator*, won many converts.[30]

The link with benefit societies existed at a number of levels. In a general sense, co-operative societies were seen as being a superior sort of friendly society – a benefit club with profits. Indeed, a number of the societies which grew up in the Leeds area relieved their members in sickness.[31] At the first Leeds meeting Carson had argued that his plan would remove the precarious balance upon which benefit societies generally existed. Moreover, the hefty subscriptions would ensure that membership of the new institution was select and respectable. He proposed an organisation of sixty members of different occupations each paying a shilling a week in order to raise capital to buy commodities at discount prices. In addition, members could manufacture for each other and sell any excess, the proceeds being added to capital.[32] In essence the scheme was practically based and firmly rooted in traditional artisan concerns relating to independence, security and respectability. Of the four stages of co-operation which Dr. King had outlined – fund-raising, retail store, employment of members, acquisition of land – only the first three were aspired to. No mention was made of Owen or communities.

The roots of this meeting, and of the beginnings of co-operation in Leeds can be traced back to the 1828 'Benefit Societies' Campaign' against Courtenay's Bill that sought to regulate their activities.[33] In Leeds, as in London, this was perceived as an attack on the societies' (and the working-class's) independent management of their own affairs and was vigorously opposed.[34] An impressive, well-coordinated national campaign, led by the London societies in which Carson also took part successfully scotched Courtenay's Bill and then proceeded to set about producing its own Bill to clarify benefit society legislation.[35] In order to do this the London coordinating committee urged full co-operation with the Society for the Diffusion of Useful Knowledge (SDUK) which was circulating a questionnaire in an effort to draw up

---

29 *WFP* 27 Dec. 1828.

30 *WFP* 29 Nov. 1828, for the advertisement of G. C. Penn. For the connection between Penn and the London co-operators and Brighton model, see Prothero, *Artisans and Politics*, pp. 241-2. On King see, Andy Durr, 'William King of Brighton: Co-operation's prophet?', in S. Yeo (ed.), *New Views of Co-operation*, pp. 10-26.

31 *LM* 18 July 1829. Thomas Wilson of Halifax also spoke of the benefits likely to accrue to members in sickness or unemployment, *HCC* 13 Feb. 1830.

32 *WFP* 27 Dec. 1828.

33 T. F. Courtenay, a well-connected Tory MP, had a long-standing interest in their activities. The story of the little known, but important working-class campaign against the Bill in the late 1820s is outlined in Prothero, *Artisans and Politics*, pp. 232-8.

34 *LM* 26 Apr., 3 May 1828. A 'Union of Benefit Societies' was created. Meetings were also held at Halifax and Bradford, *LI* 1 May 1828.

35 This Bill, the work of artisans, resulted in landmark friendly society legislation the following year, see Prothero, *Artisans and Politics*, pp. 235-6. For meetings in Leeds on this new Bill, see *LM* 23 Aug., 18, 25 Oct., 1 Nov. 1828; 10, 24 Jan., 18 Apr. 1829 and *LI* 30 Oct., 20 Nov. 1828.

guidelines for mortality tables and benefit society rules.[36] At this point, Carson, a delegate of the Birmingham friendly societies, first appeared in Leeds seeking to persuade local societies to fill in the SDUK schedule. It was not an easy task: any form of centralism or 'improving' paternalism was regarded with great suspicion; but he eventually succeeded in carrying the day.[37] It was in this context that the Birmingham delegate, who had been in contact with leading London co-operators during 1828, forged the links which led onto the December meeting and the first co-operative venture in Leeds.

Although the December meeting voted unanimously in favour of the 'Trading Union' scheme, the new society took a few months to get off the ground. As late as April 1829 it was still categorised in the *Weekly Free Press* as one of the societies which was 'forming' (presumably acquiring capital) rather than 'Formed and Trading'.[38] In July, however, the *Leeds Mercury* reported that a number of 'Co-operative Societies' existed in the area and by October there is conclusive proof of three societies in the immediate vicinity of Leeds.[39] The origins of two – the West End Co-operative Society and the Brewery-field Co-operative Society, Holbeck – dated back to April; whilst the third, the first Leeds Co-operative Society of the 'North East Co-operatives' who held their general meeting in late October 1829, was possibly the original society which Carson had helped to set on its path.[40] Progress had been slow, for only now was a committee appointed to draw up rules and arrange for the opening of a shop.

The harsh economic winter of 1829-30 made practical co-operation highly topical. In addition to the three societies already in existence 'four or five more' were reported to be forming in early October. By November there were said to be eleven societies in the Leeds area, and a delegate meeting at the Saddle Inn on Christmas Day 1829 included representatives of sixteen societies.[41] William Carson, who delivered the keynote address to this gathering, was the inspiration behind much of this activity.[42] His work included selling the idea to the better paid and well organised artisan trades. In November a meeting of nearly a hundred 'mechanics' voted to form a co-operative society for their 'mutual protection as they alleged that their wages had been reduced from 3 to 6/- in the pound'.[43]

The following week Carson, himself a former secretary of the Carpenters' union and now a self-made architect,[44] was instrumental in encouraging the 'journeyman

---

36 Prothero, *Artisans and Politics*, p. 236.

37 *LM* 25 Oct., 1 Nov. 1828.

38 *WFP* 17 Jan.1829 stated that a Leeds society had been formed, but in following issues the more tentative state was recorded, *WFP* 24 Jan. 1829.

39 *LM* 18 July 1829; *WFP* 3 Oct. 1829.

40 *WFP* 3 Oct, 7 Nov; *LM* 5 Dec; *LP* 31 Oct. 1829. The West End Society had 90 members, the Brewery Field (Holbeck) 56 and the first Leeds about 40.

41 *WFP* 3 Oct., 7 Nov. 1829; 2 Jan. 1830; *LI* 31 Dec. 1829.

42 *LM* 5 Dec. 1829 emphasised his role. Carson himself claimed to have established eighteen societies in Yorkshire, *VP* 9 July 1831.

43 *LP* 21 Nov. 1829. 'Mechanics' here is used in the specific sense of engineering workers. This is indicated by the way of expressing wage-levels and the meeting place, the Bay Horse Inn.

44 Webb Coll. A, XI, f. 170 gives a reference to PP, Add. Mss. 27,799, f. 133, for Carson in 1822. See also *LM* 5 Dec 1829 for Carson's approval of, and role in, the carpenters' club in

carpenters and joiners' to establish a 'Co-operative Trading Society'.[45] It is not clear how many of the sixteen putative societies represented at the Christmas delegate meeting actually materialised. Given the extreme distress of the early months of 1830 and the apparent strictness of the rules regarding credit and 'compulsory purchasing', it is likely that they very quickly ran into difficulties. Carson had hinted at some of these problems at the delegate meeting, in his warnings to societies not to allow credit or allow members to withdraw their 'shares' in the common stock at short notice. Letters from two of the leading societies (West End and Holbeck) in February and March, referring to 'difficulties' and 'attempts of enemies to overturn the society' provide supporting evidence that all was not well.[46] The visits of James Watson, as missionary of the British Association for the Promotion of Co-operative Knowledge (BAPCK) and the wider links these stimulated, may have given Leeds co-operators a temporary boost; but it is likely that problems continued.[47]

The ever-present threat of fraud materialised in August 1830 when the Holbeck Society's agent expropriated £61: a case which revealed opposition to the societies from both a Tory magistrate and the radical *Leeds Patriot*.[48] Other sections of the local community were also hostile. The master carpenters and joiners were highly suspicious of their journeymen's attempts to 'have a fund', and 'Anticipator' writing to the *Mercury* in late 1829 threatened not to give any work to any 'co-operative joiners, glaziers etc.'[49] Shortly afterwards John Heaton in Huddersfield spoke of master manufacturers sacking co-operators amongst their workmen. He also hints at local collusion between local masters and shopkeepers and wrote at the turn of the year that, 'in some towns the grocers begin to see their craft is in danger, and are taking various plans to put down Co-operation'. These included giving co-operative agents unfavourable terms for their 'wholesale' purchases and undercutting the societies' retail prices.[50]

The pioneering Leeds bodies had a number of features common to many of the early co-operative societies. The 'principal object' was to provide their members with everyday provisions 'at a cheap rate'. Non-members, in other words the general public, were allowed to shop at the store 'on as good terms as at other places'. All transactions were for 'ready money', thereby avoiding 'the baneful practice of running

London.

45 *LM* 5, 12 Dec. 1829.

46 *WFP* 2 Jan., 27 Feb., 27 Mar. 1830.

47 *WFP* 27 Feb., 27 Mar. 1830; and 16 Jan. 1830. On Watson (1799-1874), see W. J. Linton, *James Watson, A Memoir… etc.* (Manchester: Abel Heywood and Son, 1880).

48 *LM*, *LP* 28 Aug. 1830. *LP* 3 Apr. 1830 also published a letter from 'A Labourer' which argued that co-operation was alright in principle, but would only impoverish shopkeepers.

49 *LM* 5, 19 Dec. 1829.

50 *WFP* 9, 2 Jan. 1830. On shopkeepers' worries see, 'Anticipator's' letter in *LM* 19 Dec. 1829. John Heaton was a fancy-weaver, who had been an active committee man of the West Riding Fancy Weavers' Union in 1825 and served as their secretary two years later (*LM* 12 Feb. 1825; 7, 21 July 1827). He became agent of the Huddersfield Co-operative Society and represented it at the first two Co-operative Congresses. He 'left home, family and situation' in December 1831 to take on the role of agent for the Liverpool co-operative warehouse (*LYC* 4 Feb. 1832).

on bills at the provision dealers' shops, and paying ten, twenty and thirty per cent for credit'. However, already by December 1829 Carson was warning of the 'evil' of giving credit to members. The Leeds societies also had strict rules (with fines) binding members to shop only at the 'Society's warehouse or shop'.[51]

In contrast to other places, self-employment does not figure prominently in the early history of the Leeds societies.[52] Carson spoke in January 1830 of hopes of starting to manufacture cloth at Leeds; but whilst the co-operative production would not have been a major step for trades like the carpenters and joiners, it was beyond the finite horizons of the early co-operative adherents.[53] 'M', writing to the *Leeds Mercury* about the objects of the societies, spoke of communities as 'wild and visionary plans'; and William Carson himself stressed the providential, moral and educational nature of the societies.[54] The limit of the Leeds co-operators' initial aspirations was a 'general warehouse' to reap the advantages of bulk buying and to provide a co-operative meeting place, and this formed the object of their Christmas delegate meeting.[55]

The lofty beliefs voiced by some of the leading local co-operators, that they were engaged in something beyond mere retailing, no doubt helped to keep a few of the Leeds societies afloat in the difficult months of 1830.[56] But this very high-mindedness, with its concomitant moral strictness and superiority, together with the lack of retail experience, the societies' legal vulnerability, and their inflexible rules, gives grounds for supposing that the co-operative whirlwind was largely played out in Leeds by the second half of 1830.

Exactly how long the Leeds societies survived is not certain. Carson, at the third (London) Co-operative Congress in April 1832, speaks of the first Leeds society gradually increasing 'its trade and capital, till it had been able to open a large co-operative store in Liverpool'.[57] This may only mean that the society subscribed money to the Liverpool wholesale scheme. Certainly, by the time J. Whittaker reached Leeds on his northern tour in September 1832, the local society had ceased to exist and only a few co-operators remained to read the propaganda which he deposited.[58] The families of the skilled 'upper' and 'lower' artisan trades, on whose membership, custom and support the early societies relied, had by this time moved on to other shops and other causes.

---

51 *LM* 18 July 1829; *WFP* 2 Jan. 1830; *LM* 26 Dec. 1829.

52 *LM* 26 Dec. 1829, see the letter from 'W.W.' of Thorne, near Doncaster.

53 *LM* 2 Jan. 1830. Self-employment, clubbing together to build a house in their spare time, was not uncommon amongst journeymen carpenters, see Prothero, *Artisans and Politics*, p. 250.

54 *LM* 2 Jan., 19 Dec. 1830.

55 *WFP* 2 Jan 1830; *LI* 31 Dec. 1829.

56 See, for example, Peter Cummins's letter from the Holbeck Society, *WFP* 27 Feb. 1830, which speaks of 'our cause'.

57 Proceedings of the Third (London) Co-operative Congress, 23-29 April 1832 (London, 1832), hereafter Proc. (London) C.C. April 1832 p. 63 ff. On the Liverpool venture, see below, pp. 208-10.

58 *Crisis* 22 Sept. 1832.

The 1st Bradford Co-operative Society, dating back to 2 February 1829, was the oldest West Riding society represented at the London Congress. As at Leeds the direct stimulus came from G. C. Penn's advertisement in the *Weekly Free Press*. By March 1829 the society had accumulated £20 capital and had already started trading, by taking a house and putting 'one of their members in as agent'.[59] The idea spread quickly and at the end of March four societies, 'formed and trading', were reported in the town. It is not certain whether the three additional societies were located in the town or comprised the Clayton, Horton and Queenshead societies whose existence was noted in October 1829.[60] The 'No. 1 Trading Association' based at Diamond Street was well established by the end of July and by the time James Watson spoke to 'Friends of Co-operation' in Bradford in early February 1830, there was an additional society in Bradford and five flourishing societies in the out-townships and villages of the area.[61]

This initial flowering of Bradford co-operation did not last long, but it throws up some interesting names which indicate close ties with local workers' organisations and their economic and political aspirations. For example, John Atkinson, writing to the *Leeds Patriot* in July 1829 'on behalf of a large number of woolcombers' about wage negotiations with local manufacturers, gave his address as the 'No. 1 Trading Association Depot', Diamond Street. Atkinson was later a co-operative delegate and a speaker at trade union and Dorchester meetings in 1832 and 1834.[62] According to Robin Thornes, a fellow unionist and later Chartist, Peter Bussey, was listed as secretary of the Bradford Moor Co-operative Society in 1831.[63] Two of the chief speakers at the co-operative public meeting in February 1830, Joseph Brook and William Rouse, both handloom-weavers, also served as important local leaders.[64] Brook was involved in just about every working-class agitation in Bradford in the 1830s, and was particularly notable as a leading trade unionist; whilst William Rouse of Bowling, like Brook, gave evidence to the 1838 Handloom Weavers' Commission and was a leading Chartist. Even if Brook and Rouse were not active co-operative leaders, their presence, and the resolutions passed at the meeting (relating distress to unnecessary competition and the individualistic system), indicate that co-operation dovetailed neatly with local workers' analyses and remedies for contemporary ills.

Exactly who these rank and file co-operators comprised is difficult to say. Initially at least it appears that the societies attracted members from the predominant local

---

59 *WFP* 11 Apr. 1829. This was probably John Atkinson.

60 *WFP* 11 Apr., 17 Oct. 1829.

61 *LP* 1 Aug. 1829; *HCC* 13 Feb. 1830. The societies were at Little Horton, Sheerbridge, Fairweather Green, Sticker-Lane and Smidhills.

62 *LP* 1 Aug. 1829; *LYC* July 1832 (delegate to North West District Council meeting); *LT* 2 Nov. 1833, 12 April 1834. Atkinson was probably a relatively young man at this point. In 1838, for example, he testified at the inquest of his father-in-law, Jonas Barker, a stuff weaver, aged 53, who 'hung himself in a fit of temporary insanity brought on by excessive drinking' (*BO* 8 Nov. 1838).

63 Thornes, 'Change and Continuity', p. 35.

64 *HCC* 13 Feb. 1830. On Brook, see above, pp. 39-40. On William Rouse of Bowling (1797-1861), see *BO* 11 Oct 1838; *NS* 6 Apr. 1839. He died tragically in an industrial accident at a dyeworks in 1861 (*BO* 27 July 1861).

textile out-working groups like the combers and weavers. However, these were the very groups who would have found it difficult to maintain regular subscriptions and exist without credit.[65] Some of the better-paid and more determined may have achieved this. But it is likely that membership was also drawn from the higher-paid, ancillary textile and other skilled town trades – groups like woolsorters. tailors, shoemakers, joiners, and mechanics.[66]

The two main sources for the later history of the Bradford society, the statistical tables gathered for the 3rd (London) and 4th (Liverpool) Co-operative Congresses, paint a picture of a small, yet flourishing society with thirty members and £120 in funds by April 1832. This money no doubt came partly from a co-operative store; but, in addition, the society possessed a school, a library of seventy volumes and held regular Sunday lectures and discussions, including some on the principles of labour exchange. More importantly by April 1832 it 'occasionally' employed its own members to make 'heald, yarn and shoes'; and by October it engaged its own shoemaker.[67]

Little is known of the progress of Bradford co-operation after 1832. The society's banner, bearing the motto, 'members without union are powerless; union without knowledge is useless' was spotted amongst the vast crowd at the Wibsey Moor ten hours meeting in July 1833.[68] The following May, the society celebrated its fifth anniversary with a dinner at Mr. Hills School-Room. Between eighty and ninety people of both sexes attended, and the good-humoured proceedings were helped along by renditions from several musicians and glee-singers.[69] How long co-operation in Bradford survived after this date is impossible to say. In November the *Leeds Times* intriguingly reported 'a numerous meeting of the operatives' to consider forming 'themselves into a branch of the Grand National Consolidated Union – the principle of which, we believe, is co-operation'. In the opaque associational atmosphere of the time, and with masters cutting woolcombers' wages, it is likely that local workers opted to take a different direction. There are no indicators of co-operative activities in the town until the Bradford Socialists announced the opening of a co-operative store in May 1840.[70]

Early co-operative societies developed in some of the smaller, remoter villages of the West Riding as well as in the main centres and their environs. The areas around Halifax and Huddersfield in particular saw a proliferation of societies. Co-operative enterprises in Meltham Mills, Kirkheaton and Almondbury all pre-dated the main Huddersfield society (the Huddersfield Co-operative Trading Association) founded in

---

65 Initial subscriptions for the Bradford Society were a hefty 1s a week for a year. Sales were for 'ready money only', *LYC* Mar. 1832, letter of 'D.W.'. The Huddersfield and Halifax societies subscriptions were 3d per week.

66 The Leeds evidence and the type of goods produced suggest this.

67 Proc. (London) C.C., Apr. 1832; Proc. (Liverpool) C.C., Oct. 1832.

68 *LT* 4 July 1833. In 1832 Charles Simons, later chair of the Bradford STC, had become secretary of the society.

69 *VWR* 24 May 1833. William Hill, future editor of the *Northern Star*, was a leading ten hours man and radical. His school became the chief local working-class meeting place.

70 *LT* 22 Nov., 27 Dec. 1834, 3 Jan. 1835; Thornes, 'Change and Continuity', p. 43.

April 1829; and at the end of that year the Milnsbridge Co-operative Society was advertising for orders for its goods, and co-operators of the eighty-strong Longroyd Bridge society sat down to a dinner of 'old English fare'.[71] Early in the new year four additional societies were started.[72]

A period of inactivity or decline followed this initial flourish, as a number of societies experienced difficulties. The storekeeper at Milnsbridge was discharged and the Huddersfield co-operators appointed a deputation 'to attend' to the affairs of Cowons Society in 1830.[73] However, most remained in existence and another burst of activity in early 1832 saw the formation of seven new societies in the area. By this time Huddersfield was acknowledged to lie 'in the heart of Co-operative Societies' and the district was reckoned to contain at least fifteen of the forty West Riding societies which a *Leeds Times* correspondent estimated in July 1833.[74]

Although relations with the main Huddersfield Society were close and its leading light, Thomas Hirst, represented their interests at congresses, many of the local societies pursued a fairly independent existence. Some were probably little more than small associations of villagers intent on securing a cheap, convenient and pure supply of food or handloom weavers' necessities. In practice they may have comprised little more than an informal association of friends or family, or a closed body run for the profit of shareholders.[75] Size of membership varied from place to place, but never reached more than forty members. A sample of twelve societies in the Huddersfield vicinity in 1832 gives an average size of twenty-two and a median size of only seventeen members.[76] It is little wonder, then, that few aspired beyond successful co-operative retailing, and that Hirst found 'a great want of knowledge among the Societies' on his local tours. Of the twelve societies for which we have information in 1832, only one had a school, just one possessed a library of any size, and only three employed any of their own members. Not surprisingly none of the societies had discussed the principles of labour exchange at this stage.[77]

Apart from a few names, we know little about these village societies' leaders or members. The Milnsbridge Society's membership in December 1829 chiefly comprised 'workmen employed in the various branches of manufacturing carried on

---

71 *WFP* 24 Jan 1829 (Almondbury); Balmforth, *Handbook*, p. 109 (Kirkheaton); *WFP* 2 Jan 1830 (Milnsbridge and Longroyd Bridge); *LYC* Oct. 1832, *CN* 2 Jan. 1892.

72 Owen Balmforth, *The Huddersfield Industrial Society Limited: History of Fifty Years' Progress* (Manchester: Co-operative Wholesale Society, 1910), p. 21 (for the new societies). See also *WFP* 23 Oct. 1830 (for Armitage Bridge).

73 Balmforth, *Huddersfield Industrial Society Limited*, p. 21; *CN* 2 Jan. 1892.

74 *LYC* Oct. 1832; Balmforth, *Huddersfield Industrial Society Limited*, p. 21; *LT* 20 July 1833. New societies started in 1833-4 included Farnley Tyas and Lowerhouses (in the Almondbury area). Thornes, 'Origins' p. 172, calculates that 38 societies were established in West Yorkshire between 1827 and 1832.

75 According to Balmforth, *Handbook*, p. 110, the original motive for the Kirkheaton venture was convenience for local weavers, plus any resulting profit. There were few other shops in the village.

76 *LYC* Oct. 1832; Proc. 3rd (London) C.C., Apr. 1832 (tables).

77 Proc. 2nd (Birmingham) C.C., Oct. 1831, p. 5; *LYC* Oct. 1832; Proc. 3rd (London) C.C., Apr. 1832 (tables).

in this neighbourhood'.[78] Here and elsewhere this meant mainly woollen or fancy weaving. The few self-employing societies, for example, all produced 'woollen cloths'. How long these small local societies survived is difficult to say. Some clearly followed the national pattern and folded in the difficult years of 1833-4. However, a number, defying the downward trend, continued to provide evidence that, in Robin Thorne's words, 'the movement was far from dead'.[79]

Virtually nothing is known about early co-operation in Dewsbury or Keighley. The co-operative missionary James Watson visited Dewsbury in early 1830 and the 'First Dewsbury Co-operative Association' was reported to be doing well eight months later. The following year it was apparently manufacturing woollen cloths. Three other societies also existed in the area but have left no trace.[80] The Keighley Society, formed in November 1829 boasted forty members and funds of nearly £250 by April 1832. It had discussed the labour exchange idea, but had not yet engaged in manufacturing.[81] Further information about these main town societies and any ancillary village societies in the Dewsbury and Keighley districts will have to await the discovery of fresh sources or intensive new local research. However, it is instructive to examine two areas for which information on early co-operative activity is more abundant: Halifax and Huddersfield.

3: Halifax

The impetus for co-operation in Halifax came initially from the simple theory expounded in Brighton's *Co-operator* and the practical example set in neighbouring Bradford.[82] One of the Wilson family came across the Bradford society in Spring 1829 and returned home with copies of the *Co-operator* and the *Associate* for his family and friends. Thomas Wilson, speaking at the 4th (Liverpool) Co-operative Congress, takes up the story: 'In May 1829, he and eight other persons laid down a shilling each, and with this nine shillings and five pounds lent by his brother, they commenced business in a small room in a back entry'.[83]

The first Halifax Co-operative Trading Society was, in essence, the product of a proud body of local workers, which evolved in the context of a period of depressed trade.[84] An obsession with respectability pervades Thomas Wilson's account of the motives and attitudes of the early members:

> They said they were fast tending to the condition of the poor Irish, and with the poorhouse and parish relief before them, they endeavoured to better their situation, for they considered that if they applied for parish

---

78 *WFP* 2 Jan. 1830.

79 Thornes, 'Origins', p. 180.

80 Linton, *James Watson*, pp. 21-2; *WFP* 11 Sept. 1830; *LYC* 1 Oct. 1831. Later in the decade local Chartists established a Joint Stock Co-operative Society, *NS* 12 Oct. 1839.

81 Proc. 3rd (London) C.C., Apr. 1832 (tables).

82 *LYC* Mar. 1832.

83 *Crisis* 27 Oct. 1832. At its inception the Society was very much a family affair – five of the nine original members being 'Wilsons'.

84 See, for example, *HCC* 10, 31 Oct., 14 Nov. 1829.

relief, they should be degraded, and could not lift up their heads and walk erect, as every free, honest and hard-working Englishman ought to do...[85]

Theirs was self-help born out of fear of social degradation. Diligence and sobriety were pre-requisites for membership. The committee, therefore, carefully vetted intending co-operators, for they believed 'that the future welfare of the Society would in a great measure depend upon the conduct of its early members', and so 'invited such only to join us as we had reason we believe would prove good and useful members'.[86]

The new-born society made quick progress. Within seven weeks membership had risen to thirty, over three pounds had been raised in subscriptions, and trading profits amounted to 17s 14½d. The society could now afford to draw up and print both a set of rules and two thousand copies of an 'Address to the Labouring Classes' – a tract written by the President, Thomas Wilson, and distributed throughout the textile district. Meanwhile the society's small co-operative store prospered. As 'D.W.' recalled: 'though our place of sale was somewhat obscurely situated, ... it attracted considerable public custom, an account of its being found a cheap shop'. In fact, such was the early success of the store that at the end of November the society was able to remove to a better location.[87]

The co-operative shop was more than just a source of cheap, unadulterated food, it was also a social and cultural centre, however humble, for the Halifax co-operators. The early movement combined astute promotional instincts with a strong convivial sense; as, for example in April 1830, when about two hundred wives of members and female customers in Halifax were treated to a 'Tea feast' to 'both see and taste the blessings of co-operation' and hear lectures on its advantages. It was at the store that the co-operative papers could be bought and discussed; and here also that a member taught 'about 20 infant scholars'. The strong sense of purpose and identity bred in such an atmosphere helps to explain some of the early attractions of the co-operative society.[88]

In the second quarter (ending on 28th December 1829) no less than eighty people applied to admission to the society, sixty-five of whom were admitted at the quarterly meeting, giving a total membership of nearly 130. Yet, inevitably after the initial excitement, membership and rates of capital growth began to slow down in 1830. By the beginning of autumn the society was facing a minor crisis. In the words of 'D.W.', 'The sale at our store had somewhat diminished this quarter, and ... a considerable number of our members had paid little towards their subscription, but on some account had given over both to pay their subscriptions forward, or, to come to the store'.

The situation was rectified by a 'purge of the drones'. Wayward members 'were accordingly visited, and such as either could not or would not engage to attend to their duties as members, had their subscriptions returned to them, upwards of £27 was

---

85 *Crisis* 27 Oct. 1832.
86 *LYC* Mar. 1832.
87 Ibid. 'D.W.' was in all probability David Wilson, secretary of the society.
88 Ibid.

paid in the way during our second year ... But though we thus lost many members, we lost no real strength, as our sale of goods increased in consequence rather than diminished'. 'D.W.'s interpretation is optimistic, in true co-operative style, for the bulk of any slight increase in trading profits was absorbed in payments to leaving members. The society continued to face similar problems in the following two years, when the additional factors of higher food prices and increased competition from the town's grocers acted as a further drag on progress.[89]

Nevertheless, the society managed to take most of these early problems in its stride. 'D.W.' writing in March 1832, had reason to feel satisfied with the stability and size (about sixty to seventy members) of the society: 'We have now, we think, obtained a pretty firm possession of the first step on the co-operative ladder, *viz.* a well stocked shop. We are preparing, in concert with another society, to ascend the second viz to employ ourselves upon our own capital'.[90] The idea of manufacturing and retailing 'their own goods in addition to buying and selling their own provisions' had been present from early on.[91] However, this second step was only fully embraced in 1832, in conjunction with other local societies.

The Halifax Co-operative Society, like its Bradford equivalent, was not an isolated phenomenon. A correspondent writing to the *Halifax Commercial Chronicle* spoke of other smaller societies in the area in November 1829; and three months later Thomas Wilson mentioned the progress of 'the various societies in this town and neighbourhood'. It is likely that Halifax played a major role in the development of these; as in the case of the Northowram Society formed in February 1831 after a formal public meeting addressed by Wilson and Bancroft of the Halifax society.[92] By the time of the 3rd (London) Co-operative Congress there were nine other societies in the Halifax district; six months later this figure had risen to sixteen.[93] The majority of these societies were so small as to have left few traces for the historian, but they were no doubt mainly based in the small clothing villages and out-townships like Northowram which surrounded the market centre. Many, like the Ripponden society, were founded in 1832, when J. Whittaker reported in the *Crisis* that, 'the societies in Halifax, and in the villages adjacent, seem to be in a very flourishing state'.[94] The close relationship with the main Halifax society is indicated by the fact that none ever sent a delegate or letter to Congress, preferring to let Thomas Wilson speak on behalf of the whole district. The interdependence of Halifax and its co-operative hinterland can further be seen in the coming together of founder and junior societies in an attempt to attain the 'second step of the co-operative ladder'.

The origins of the 'Halifax District Co-operative Manufacturing Association' (HDCMA) lay in the growing belief amongst co-operators in late 1831 and early 1832 that 'an attempt ought to be made to form an union of societies, for the purpose of

89 Ibid. For indications of criticisms of the society in early 1830 see T. Wilson's speech, *HCC* 13 Feb. 1830.
90 *LYC* Mar. 1832.
91 *HCC* 13 Feb. 1830.
92 *HCC* 14 Nov. 1829, 13 Feb. 1830; *HHE* 19 Feb. 1831.
93 Proc. (London) C.C., Apr. 1832; Proc. (Liverpool) C.C., Oct. 1832. (tables).
94 *Crisis* 22 Sept. 1832. On Ripponden, see Thornes, 'Change and Continuity', pp. 41-2.

finding employment for some of our members upon our own capital in the way of manufacturing some kind of useful articles'. They proposed nothing too ambitious, rather 'to commence in a small way, at first, after the manner of individual societies'. Accordingly, after meetings and discussions between some of the local societies during the early months of 1832, the HDCMA was eventually established by the societies in Halifax, Holdsworth and Shibden. Capital was raised by £5 shares, with each member society buying according to its means, and each in its turn employing members when wanted. A central committee, meeting monthly and comprising not more than three members from any one society, administered the Association. Any day-to-day business was supervised by two committee-appointed agents: a manufacturing agent to manage the working department, and a wholesale agent to superintend the storage and sale of the goods produced.[95]

The Association had commenced operations by the time of the London Co-operative Congress (April 1832) and the statistical tables record that the Halifax Society had four members employed making 'merinoes, stuffs and lustrings'.[96] By summer the HDCMA had orders for 'pieces' from Liverpool, Manchester, Barnsley and Keighley as well as a stand in the local Cloth Hall. In general profit was small, but the Association survived at least until the Liverpool Congress (October 1832) when five men were listed as being 'partially' employed by the Halifax Society; and perhaps well beyond that date.[97]

Like other manufacturing societies in the West Riding the Halifax co-operators were stymied by the preponderance of the textile trade in their area. They supported the Liverpool wholesale venture strongly,[98] and from an early date were keenly aware of the possibilities in the mutual exchange of co-operatively manufactured goods. 'T.W.' wrote in April 1832:

> If our Birmingham friends will engage to appear in our fabrics, we will engage to cut our beef and pudding (when we can get any) with their knives and forks, and sup our broth and oatmeal porridge with their spoons, and if our London brethren will do so too, we will appear, as soon as possible, with their silk handkerchief round our necks.[99]

Three months later resolutions in favour of labour exchanges were passed at a sub-council meeting at Halifax; yet local leaders realised all along the impossibility of a viable exchange in their locality. Like northern co-operators in general they were 'impelled, at the outset, to look towards a national plan of co-operation'.[100] J. Whittaker recalled that, on explaining the benefits of labour exchanges to Halifax co-operators,

---

95 This discussion of the Manufacturing Association is drawn from *LYC* April, August 1832, articles by Thomas Wilson.

96 Proc. (London) C.C., Apr. 1832. 'Lustrings' is probably a mistake for 'lastings' a hard, tightly-woven fabric.

97 Proc. (Liverpool) C.C., Oct. 1832 (table).

98 *LYC* Aug. 1832. By this time Halifax had contributed nearly £11 to the venture.

99 *LYC* Apr. 1832.

100 Thompson, *Making*, p. 871.

they seemed much pleased with what I said, but thought they could not open one, for the same reason as Manchester, viz, on account of the similarity of their trades, yet if the London Exchanges would take their lastings, merinoes and stuffs (patterns of which, and the prices, I brought up with me) ... in exchange for treacle or tea, it would be the saving of them and their families.[101]

As elsewhere in the textile district ideology was circumscribed by economic realities.

Little information exists about either the leaders or the rank and file members of the Halifax Society. Thomas Wilson, President and frequent congress delegate for the society, is the most conspicuous individual; but his public appearances on political platforms and in the press, as a prolific writer on co-operative issues, give no clues as to his occupation. His brother, David, the society's first secretary, was also a prominent figure; but the remainder of the Wilson family, who played such an important part in the beginnings of the society, are cloaked in obscurity. One key figure who it is possible to name is J. Nicholson, a radical printer, who represented the society at the London and Huddersfield Congresses and chaired the Northowram meeting.[102]

The list of articles manufactured by the 'Manufacturing Association', taken with the occupational make-up of Halifax at this time, suggests that the majority of local co-operators were textile hand-workers. To these may perhaps be added a few skilled artisans, especially those, like shoemakers and tailors, capable of making and selling basic goods to their fellow co-operators. But, given the level of subscriptions (3d), the regular habits and occasional sacrifices needed to become and remain a member, these can only have come from amongst the better paid and most regularly employed men in their trades.

It is difficult to judge exactly how far up the co-operative ladder ordinary co-operators' aspirations went. The rank and file in Halifax certainly gave active support to the *Lancashire and Yorkshire Co-operator* and to the Liverpool warehouse; and they also advocated the national system of co-operative manufacturing.[103] In neighbouring Ripponden the society responded to 'the astonishing changes which the course of a series of years have produced to the labouring classes' by advocating 'the attainment of independence by means of a common capital'. This was to be achieved by 'a weekly subscription to a common fund', by co-operative retailing, 'by employing its members

---

101 *Crisis* 22 Sept. 1832.

102 *HHE* 13 Feb. 1831. It is likely that this is Joseph Nicholson of Halifax, who printed the first set of rules for the Huddersfield Co-operative Society in 1835. Nicholson was prominent in the Halifax PU in the early 1830s and supported the ten hours cause in 1832. He chaired the committee that sought the election of Protheroe (the Liberal-Radical candidate) in the 1835 election. Two years later he led the committee to erect a proposed 'People's Hall' in Halifax in 1837. A 'Whig' nominee in the controversial 1837 Poor Law Guardians elections, he never appeared on the Chartist platform. However, he remained involved in mutual improvement societies and Mechanics' Institutes in the 1840s and 1850s. The waters are muddied somewhat by the naming of Joseph Nicholson, 'a carpet weaver' of Charlestown, Northowram, alongside 'others, Members, and Co-Partners of "the first Halifax Co-operative Trading Society"' in a deed of assignment (for debt) in 1840 (*HHE* 7 Mar. 1840).

103 *LYC* April 1832. 'J.N.' reported he sold 12 copies of the paper every month.

as circumstances admit', and by 'living in community with each other, on the principle of mutual Co-operation, united possessions, equality of exertions, and of the means of enjoyment'.[104] However, as Robin Thornes has noted, the rules of a majority of societies made no mention of community or indeed of co-operative manufacturing. It is likely that, with the exception of a few societies and their leaders, grassroots ambitions rarely stretched as far as land ownership or an actual community.[105]

Evidence about links with other working-class movements is scarce but suggestive. The 'Bancroft' who addressed the Northowram co-operative meeting may have been the 'J. Bancroft' who spoke at a Halifax ten hours rally in July 1833 and a factory workers' meeting on the same issue in March 1836.[106] Political and trade union links were much stronger, despite Thomas Wilson's protestations to an 1830 meeting that 'radicalism and combination formed no part' of the character of co-operative societies. At the very same Halifax gathering the visiting BAPCK missionary, James Watson, entertained the audience with amusing attacks on Wellington, Peel and other members of the government.[107] The repeated declarations of the society's non-political nature may betray concerns about its vulnerability to accusations of radical connections.[108] Certainly, both Wilson and Nicholson appeared on the local radical platform; and at the height of the reform crisis, we find a Halifax 'Christian Co-operator' presuming that the votes of the society's trustees 'will be given to men who act as the popular side'.[109] Given the deep-rooted communal radicalism of the area it probably felt natural for some societies (despite their leaders' misgivings) to be asking potential members in October 1831, 'are you a real Radical Reformer?'; just as it was normal eight years later for the Ripponden Chartists to be meeting in the 'Co-operative Committee Room'.[110]

Nor should the denial of any links with trade unions, repeated by Wilson at the Liverpool Congress, be taken too literally.[111] Six months later, at the Huddersfield Congress, we find him accepting an appointment as '*pro tem*' missionary for an area of thirty miles around Huddersfield, with a mandate to cultivate 'the extensive field which was then opening for missionary exertion among the Trades' Unions'.[112] Co-operative and trade societies were not mutually exclusive institutions and can be seen as different responses to the same stimuli. Although understandably reluctant to admit any connection, both forms of working-class 'union' moved closer together as external

---

104 J. H. Priestley, *The History of the Ripponden Co-operative Society* (Halifax, 1932), pp. 31-2, cited in Thompson, *Making*, p. 873.

105 Thornes, 'Change and Continuity', pp. 41-2; *LYC* Mar. 1832 for Nicholson arguing in favour of community.

106 *HHE* 13 Feb. 1831; Oastler Coll.Vol. 5, Item 12, 'Public Meeting in Halifax on the Ten Hours Bill', Sat. July 13, 1833; *VWR* 20 July 1833; *HG* 2 Apr. 1836.

107 *HCC* 13 Feb. 1830.

108 For example, *LYC* Oct. 1832.

109 Nicholson often chaired and Wilson spoke at early meetings of the Halifax PU; and in 1834 Wilson chaired meetings on Dorchester (*LT* 12 Apr. 1834) and of non-electors (*HHE* 18 Dec. 1834). For 'Christian Co-operator', see *LYC* 17 Sept. 1831.

110 Proc. (Birmingham) C.C., Oct. 1831, p. 5; *NS* 5 Jan. 1839.

111 *Crisis* 27 Oct. 1832.

112 *Crisis* 19 Oct. 1833.

pressures mounted in the second half of 1833; and indeed, with the development of 'Commercial Orders', they had multiple points of intersection.

The co-operators naturally saw their particular type of union as best calculated to improve the lot of the working class; but the value and legitimacy of other approaches was also accepted. A series of letters from a 'Halifax Co-operator' (possibly Wilson) to the *Voice of the West-Riding* in late 1833 illustrates the convergence of concerns and the commonality of ideas on which radicals, trade unionists and co-operators all drew. Speaking of trades' unions, the writer acknowledged their value, especially now that co-operative 'Commercial Orders' were developing: 'they have taught the people a better knowledge of their power, and are now leading them to the system of co-operation, and will eventually be the cause, in a great measure, of their political, social, physical and moral emancipation, ...' However, he stressed the superiority of the co-operative model:

> There is a great difference between a step gained in the primary object of the trades unions (I say primary because I think they have another object now in view) and a step gained on the co-operative principle; in the former if you get your wages up at one time, the masters have got plenty of wealth have the power of having another struggle with you when a favourable opportunity presents itself, which must always be disadvantageous to you; but in the latter, if by subscription you can gain a shop, or factory, or both of your own, it is a point achieved which neither the power of the masters nor anything else ... can ever deprive you of.[113]

Reflecting the chiliastic mood of the time he had previously asked, 'Is not the master manufacturers at this moment doing their best to overthrow you. But by co-operation you become your own masters and compel those proud tyrants who long for your moral annihilation, to become what you are at present – labourers'.[114]

In the embittered post-reform atmosphere of 1833, the potential power of political shopping and the notion of co-operation as an explicit extension of exclusive dealing came to the fore. According to the 'Halifax Co-operator', the 'gospel sound of co-operation' was increasingly heard, and the working people were beginning to identify their real enemies: the 'monopolists' who held political and economic power over them. Notable amongst these were the shopkeepers: 'they are enemies of the Trades Union, they are opposed to the enfranchisement of the people, they are foes to co-operation, and when a contest takes place between the aristocracy and the working classes, we always find the shopocrat in the ranks of the aristocrat'. Instead of 'the evil' of 'buying their groceries and all other kinds of goods at the shops of their enemies', the people needed to join their friends 'by regular trading at the [co-operative] stores and contributing Three-pence per week'. As Robin Thornes notes, this plea for self-

---

113 *VWR* 19 Oct. 1833.
114 *VWR* 12 Oct. 1833.

reliance and political shopping was echoed later in the decade in Chartists' endorsement of co-operation and exclusive dealing.[115]

Little is known about co-operation in the Halifax area after the collapse of so many working-class organisations during the summer of 1834. A Halifax delegate may well have been the fourth speaker who addressed a meeting at Huddersfield of the 'British and Foreign Consolidated Association of Industry, Humanity and Knowledge' (the GNCTU's successor) in October 1834. If so, then local co-operators suffered greatly at this time. The delegate reports that after trading profitably for four years, 'during the late disturbances and suspension of trade many of their brethren became poor and would have been obliged to go to this parish if they had not had a fund in the society, thus many of the shares which amount to nine pounds odd, with the profits which had accumulated, have now gone'.[116]

In spite of blows like this the Halifax society struggled on, and indeed accommodated the seventh and final Co-operative Congress, a small, mainly West Riding affair, comprising representatives from just twelve societies, held on the 20 and 21 April 1835. As G. J. Holyoake recalled, 'co-operation was coming to be regarded as a minor matter'; and this was the last meeting of delegates from stores described as a 'Co-operative Congress'. Not surprisingly the home society was represented by a couple of the Wilson family, who remained loyal to the end.[117] White's Directory of 1834 lists John Wilson as a 'shopkeeper and Dealer in Groceries and Sundries' at 41 Northgate, and four years later the same source locates the Co-operative Society, with agent James Wilson, at 34 Northgate. However, the society would appear to have been struggling. This, at least, would seem to be the import of a resolution passed by the Huddersfield Co-operative Society in 1836 to admit young men from Halifax who wanted to join the society.[118] The end probably came in the pivotal winter of 1839-40 when the last rites of 'the First Halifax Co-operative Trading Society' were announced in the *Halifax Express* in the form of a deed of assignment for debt executed by the creditors of the society.[119]

4: Huddersfield: Early Development and Links with Liverpool

The story of early co-operation in Huddersfield is fairly well documented. As well as the usual information from the co-operative and unstamped press, congress reports and the jubilee histories, the Huddersfield picture has been further enlivened by a series of articles by G. J. Holyoake in the *Cooperative News* at the end of the nineteenth century, based on the actual correspondence and minute books of the Huddersfield

---

115 *VWR* 12 Oct. 1833; Thornes, 'Change and Continuity', pp. 44-5.

116 *LT* 25 Oct. 1834. Fears of recriminations from employers forced delegates to remain anonymous. However, internal evidence suggests that the speaker was a Halifax man.

117 G. J. Holyoake, *The History of Co-operation in England* (London, 1875), Vol I, p. 191. A. Pahlman, 'Rise and Fall of the North-West of England Co-operative Company', *Co-operative Review*, 9, (July 1935), p. 211.

118 *CN* 16 Jan. 1892.

119 *HHE* 7 Mar. 1840.

Society.[120] Historians of the district have drawn on these and other sources to provide excellent accounts of local societies and their leaders.[121]

The 'Huddersfield Co-operative Trading Association' dates from the 20 April 1829.[122] The society's motto was taken from Isiah – 'They helped everyone his neighbour and everyone said to his brother, be of good courage', pointing to the strong religious component evident in Huddersfield and in northern co-operation generally. 'Christian Co-operators' were commonplace in the societies of Huddersfield and Halifax; and like their contemporaries across the Pennines, Yorkshire co-operators appear 'to have combined Owenite Co-operation very easily with Christian principles'.[123]

The nonconformist influence is very evident in the idiom and register of the letters to the *Voice* from a 'Halifax Co-operator' in 1833; one of which concludes, 'you cannot serve two masters – God and Mammon, and such as ye sow, so shall ye reap, therefore sow ye in the ground that will bring fruit, meet unto salvation which is Radical Reform and Co-operation, so shall ye be blessed upon earth and your children shall rejoice in you'.[124] Samuel Glendinning, a prominent Huddersfield co-operator, was a committed Primitive Methodist; whilst Thomas Hirst, a leading regional figure, served as a lay preacher in the Methodist New Connexion. His speeches on co-operation are replete with biblical references and lessons from Methodism.[125] However, as Robin Thornes points out, nonconformity did not have a denominational monopoly; as indicated by the active role that Rev. C. B. Dunn, the liberally-inclined curate of Cumberworth, played in his local society and the wider regional movement.[126]

The society at Huddersfield was run by a committee of thirteen, meeting every Wednesday evening. Here any prospective members were vetted 'in order that the said committee be able to determine from his circumstances, situation and disposition', whether they possessed 'that confidence in the candidate which is necessary to the admittance of a member of this society'. They also had to check their age, because initially the society operated a limit of forty years old, though this was later extended to fifty. The first President of the society was Amos Cowgill, formerly leader of the Fancy Weavers' Union. In addition, Christopher Wood was paid 45*s* per quarter to act as part-time secretary, and the society also employed a full-time salesman and a full-time agent, John Heaton, (another former fancy-weaver and trade unionist) at the rate

---

120 *CN* 2 Jan. to 6 Feb. 1892. Many of the details in the following section have been taken from this source. Holyoake received the letters and records directly from W. R. Croft, a late nineteenth century local historian. It is likely that he thereby avoids many of the inaccuracies and anachronisms which riddle some of his other writings on co-operation.

121 Thornes, 'Origins' and Halstead, 'Hirst'.

122 *CN* 2 Jan. 1892. Proc. 3rd (London) C.C. (table). See also *WFP* 24 Jan., 14, 28 Mar., 11 Apr. 1829.

123 A. E. Musson, 'The Ideology of Early Co-operation in Lancashire and Cheshire', *Transactions of the Lancashire and Cheshire Antiquarian Society*, 68 (1958). p. 135.

124 *VWR* 12 Oct. 1833.

125 Halstead, 'The Huddersfield STC', p. 116; Halstead, 'Notable Co-operator', p. 61; *PMG* 17 Sept. 1831. For an example of Hirst's speeches, see *LYC* Mar. 1832.

126 Thornes, 'Origins', pp. 176-7. Cumberworth is situated on the Huddersfield/Barnsley border.

of 20*s* per week. Wood was one of the society's three trustees (the legal deed-holders) who were elected by the members at a General Meeting.[127]

The officers' duties were not always popular, and the society's rules counselled members 'not to insult the agent, salesman, or any officials of the society in the execution of their duties by impertinent, upbraiding, or abusive language'. A strict moral tone pervades the rule book. Credit, though permissible in cases of 'extreme necessity' was granted up to the amount of a member's subscription 'and no more', only after the formal consent of the committee. In addition, the society required that 'every member shall pledge himself to purchase all he can at the society's stores, and any member not complying with this rule must show cause to the committee how it has so happened'.[128]

The society initially made great progress. At the first annual general meeting in April 1830 the committee had to consider limiting 'the number of members to 250, until after the next general meeting.[129] By the time of the second (Birmingham) Co-operative Congress in October 1831 the society was one of the largest and richest in the country, and had already attained the first two rungs of the co-operative ladder – a successful co-operative store, and the start of co-operative manufacture.[130] John Heaton, speaking to Birmingham co-operators a month before the Congress, was justifiably proud of achievements in his area:

> The labourers in the district from which he came ... had formed themselves into societies on the co-operative principles. They subscribed a small sum each weekly, which they employed in trade, first by buying the necessities of life at wholesale prices, and retailing them out again to themselves and the public at retail prices, the difference being put to a common fund. In this manner it accumulated, until they were able to employ their own shoemakers, tailors etc; and at length, as in their own society at Huddersfield, their profits and subscription united enabled them to set their members at work at their own trades. They had now fourteen of their own members at work for the society on its own capital. They were manufacturing woollen cloths, waist-coatings etc. etc.[131]

As at Halifax, the mainstay of the Huddersfield Society was the co-operative store. Although its precise origins are not known, it is possible that a £50 loan from Charles Wood, recorded in April 1829, marks the start of co-operative trading. The problem experienced by the various small societies in the Huddersfield area in getting a good wholesale price prompted them first to delegate just one man to buy for the whole

---

127 The paragraph is drawn from *CN* 2, 16 Jan. 1892; Proc. 3rd (London) C.C.; and John Heaton's letter in *Carpenter's Political Letters and Pamphlets*, No. 26, 'A Political Reformer', 19 Mar. 1831. The legal name of the shop was 'Christopher Wood and Co.'

128 *CN* 16 Jan 1892. The society's rules were first printed in 1835. The limited permission of credit may help explain why the society survived up to this date, and beyond.

129 *CN* 2 Jan. 1892.

130 Proc. 2nd (Birmingham) C.C., Oct. 1831 (table).

131 *LYC* 1 Oct. 1831.

district, then to unite and open a shop in Huddersfield which supplied all. The shop located in Westgate opened in December 1829, buying in bulk and selling in retail quantities such articles as flour, oatmeal, starch, sugar, currants, raisins, soda, tobacco, malt and hops.[132] With a location on one of the chief retailing thoroughfares in Huddersfield, and its wider district links, it is unsurprising that the co-operative store flourished. In 1830, for example, the store's profit, along with members' subscriptions, raised over £150 for the society and enabled it to increase the salaries of its officials.[133] By the end of this year the first step on the co-operative ladder had been very successfully attained and consolidated.

The Huddersfield society was very much in earnest. Already, by late spring 1830, it was contemplating two additional enterprises: first, a sick society, whose rules Charles Glendinning was instructed to draw up in May 1830; and second, co-operative manufacturing, for which a committee had been formed as early as April 1830.[134] This early adoption of co-operative manufacturing at Huddersfield shows that the vision of the early co-operators quickly went beyond the retail store. The organising committee acted with speed, and by October 1830 the Huddersfield society was advertising 'broad and narrow cloths of every description and quality, Kerseymeres, Waistcoat pieces, stuffs for pantaloons and gowns'.[135]

Business appears to have thrived, for in May of the following year four persons were appointed to act with nine committee men in the dispatch of business in the furnishing, clothing, wool and fancy sections. Yet ambition was still not satisfied, and in October 1831 the society resolved, 'to apply to the sister of Lord Harewood or to Lady Byron, for a loan of £400 to carry on the manufacture of woollen goods for the advantage of members'.[136] It is possible that this money was sought in order to buy the steam-engine and machinery which, according to William Carson in July 1831, the Huddersfield co-operators were about to purchase.[137] All the evidence – and there is no reason to believe that the capital investment was not carried out – points to the local co-operators seeing self-production not as a temporary expedient to combat unemployment but as an end in itself.[138]

Yet having produced their own woollen and fancy cloth, the question remained of how to dispose of it in an already saturated local market. A. Parker, Secretary of the 1st Huddersfield Co-operative Society, outlined the problem as early as October 1830:

---

132 *CN* 2 Jan 1892. *WFP* 2 Jan. 1830.

133 *CN* 2, 16 Jan. 1892.

134 *CN* 2, 16 Jan. 1892, for additional loans contracted and the new ventures. It is not known if 'Charles' was related to Samuel Glendinning. The venture again highlights close parallels with benefit societies.

135 *Chester Co-operative Chronicle*, 1 Oct. 1830, quoted in R. G. Garnett, *Co-operation and the Owenite Social Communities in Britain, 1825-45* (Manchester: Manchester University Press, 1972), p. 131.

136 *CN* 2 Jan. 1892.

137 *VP* 18 July 1831.

138 *CN* 2 Jan. 1892. The society certainly acquired a £500 loan from Lady Byron the following year. *VWR* 12 Oct 1833 refers to, 'all kinds of drapery, and hosiery goods a large assortment of blankets and flannels, woollen cloth of every description, manufactured by the society, and the commercial order...'

We have done a good deal of business with several Co-operative Societies, in exchange and otherwise, but our principal sales are to the regular merchants, who have to supply the country, and of course, Co-operators amongst the rest, consequently the profits are got by the capitalist instead of Co-operators.[139]

The solution was to 'consume each others productions as much as possible', and in order to achieve this end the writer, at the instigation of 'several societies in Yorkshire' and elsewhere, suggested a delegate conference of 'practical Co-operators' to promote the 'cause of Co-operation' and particularly the 'exchange of goods'. Thus the Huddersfield Society, having consolidated links locally, was at the forefront of moves to establish a wider national network of exchange and a co-operative forum.[140] Another, related solution was to use the purchasing agency associated with the first Liverpool Co-operative Society as a medium through which to exchange goods. Huddersfield's early and enduring links with this scheme illustrate its pragmatic but entrepreneurial, outward-looking approach.

The full story of this Liverpool venture has yet to be written, but from its inception it had strong West Riding connections. As a port and major commodity market Liverpool had obvious advantages for buying everyday necessities in bulk; and when it became known that a co-operative society was about to be formed there, it was a 'Yorkshire Co-operator' (John Heaton) who immediately seized on its potential utility. He spoke of a 'wholesale warehouse' being established in connection with the local society to supply the 'Co-operatives' in the West Riding and elsewhere; and even identified 'the rapid progress they are making with the Liverpool and Manchester railway' as being advantageous to his plan.[141] The Liverpool co-operators responded quickly, pledging their help and by June they were advertising their rates of commission for executing wholesale orders. By September the Liverpool society had processed nearly £700 worth of orders on behalf of various societies, including the '2nd Bradford' and the Huddersfield Society.[142] However the scheme never really took off – the first purchasing agent left in disgust, the Liverpool treasurer John Finch spoke of 'the want of encouragement from the different societies in the country' and these latter complained of inferior goods, high prices and the withholding of money balances.[143]

The idea of a co-operative wholesale warehouse in Liverpool revived at the first Co-operative Congress held in Manchester in May 1831.[144] In addition to the

---

139 *WFP* 6 Nov. 1830.

140 Ibid. See also J. Heaton's letter, *Carpenter's Political Letters and Pamphlets*, No. 26, 'A Political Reformer', 19 Mar. 1831.

141 *WFP* 2 Jan. 1830. Heaton suggested that this might facilitate the Liverpool society opening a co-operative warehouse in Manchester.

142 *WFP* 23 Jan, 12 June, 25 Sept. 1830.

143 *VP* 30 July, 13 Aug. 1831.

144 Proceedings of the 1st (Manchester) Co-operative Conference – extracts reprinted in, F. Hall and W. P. Watkins, *Co-operation – A Survey of the History, Principles and Organisation of the Co-operative Movement in Great Britain and Ireland* (Manchester: The Co-Operative Union Ltd, 1934), pp. 365-70.

advantages for bulk-buying such a scheme also provided a means by which the manufacturing societies might exchange their produce for other co-operatively manufactured goods or for food. Equally, it offered an acceptable way of using the quite sizeable capital sums which the societies had now accumulated.[145] After long and acrimonious debates about the best model to adopt, the North West of England United Co-operative Company was formally launched on 12 December 1831, with premises on prestigious London Road, Liverpool, and with John Heaton (the Huddersfield society's own experienced agent) appointed as warehouse agent.[146]

The ambitious venture required individual co-operative societies to join the company (at 4s per head), and use it as a medium through which to purchase essential commodities and promote the 'sale and exchange of all articles of co-operative manufacture' – with the warehouse taking out a 1% commission to cover its costs. It opened too late to catch the Christmas trade and never really got off the ground. The Huddersfield society recorded in 1832 that 'the Liverpool concern has not been of much profit to us as co-operators' and as early as February 1832, Thomas Wilson of Halifax, a trustee of the company, can be found appealing to co-operators everywhere to remedy the shortfall in subscriptions and purchases.[147]

This and similar appeals appear to have had some effect; and by June 1832 the Halifax society, which had paid over £10 in subscriptions, was now expecting it to 'act as a kind of medium for exchange, a general broker for all the societies goods'. Four months later Thomas Wilson reported a small profit and expressed hopes for a future increase in business, provided everyone paid up their contributions.[148] Unfortunately these subscriptions never materialised in the more challenging environment of 1832.[149] Although not revealed in the Congress report, it is probable that the delegates' meeting at Liverpool in October 1832 authorised Thomas Hirst of Huddersfield to write to Lady Byron for a £500 loan to bolster the company's sagging finances. The loan duly arrived courtesy of 'Miss Chaloner ... [who] ... has long been a friend of your cause, though she disapproves entirely of Mr. Owen's principles'.[150]

In spite of this financial boost the Liverpool company continued to struggle in 1833. At one stage, the Huddersfield society recommended all societies to subscribe 5s per member to make up the losses which had been incurred.[151] The Huddersfield Congress in April resolved on stringent cost-cutting measures to 'alter the mode of

---

145 For example, by June 1831 the Halifax society's capital was £200.

146 *VP* May-Aug 1831; Proc. 2nd (Birmingham) C.C., Oct. 1831, pp. 22-4.; Proc. 3rd (London) C.C., Apr 1832, pp. 48-50.

147 Pahlman, 'Rise and Fall', p. 208. Proc. 3rd (London) C.C., Apr. 1832, pp. 48-50; *CN* 2 Jan 1892; *LYC* 4 Feb. 1832.

148 Proc. 3rd (London) C.C., Apr. 1832; *LYC* Apr., Aug., Oct. 1832.

149 A comparison of the statistical tables of the London and Liverpool Congresses reveals the extent of retrenchment.

150 *CN* 16, 23, 30 Jan. 1892. Lady Byron had earlier sent £100 as a stop-gap. Miss Chaloner, with aristocratic connections in Yorkshire and Kent, was involved in a number of charitable initiatives 'intended to promote the welfare and improve the moral condition of the poor', including managing a 'Loan Fund' in Tunbridge Wells (*LI* 28 Jan. 1830; *Kentish Gazette* 8 Oct. 1833). Her loan was for three years at 4% interest.

151 *CN* 16 Jan. 1832.

carrying on the store, change the agent, give up the large premises held in London Road, and take one Frederick Street at a much smaller rent, so that the rent of the warehouse, salary of the agent, interest on the money borrowed, and other contingent expenses would not amount to more than £100 a year'.

This drastic pruning granted the ailing company a temporary reprieve. During the nine months before the Barnsley Congress of March 1834, 'it appeared that even with the difficulties the manager had to meet with, and the disappointment or jealousies which had been created in the minds of the societies, that the small business which had been done had more than covered expenses by seven pounds'. In the end the granting of another year's grace proved futile. The amount of business done during the interim was minimal, with only Huddersfield and Halifax trading with the company, resulting in a £20 loss. The next congress in Halifax in April 1835 finally laid the Liverpool venture to rest.[152] The Huddersfield Society remained invested to the very end. Just four days before the Halifax Congress its annual general meeting ordered that £38 be appropriated to the 'Liverpool Fund'.[153] The society which gave birth to the idea, whose subscriptions and loans had helped to nurture the infant company, now found itself paying the funeral expenses.

It is now necessary to go back in time and see how the Huddersfield Society fared during 1832 – a year of contraction in many of the larger societies. The scant evidence available seems to point to Huddersfield following the general pattern, with membership falling from 150 to 100, and total funds only increasing by £28 in the six-month period between the London and Liverpool Congresses.[154]

This shedding of membership does not appear to have dulled the enthusiasm of the Huddersfield co-operators. The society continued to employ some of its members (ten were recorded in April and twelve in October 1832) in the production of 'woollen cloths, valencias, shawls etc.' Furthermore, it continued to advocate the importance of large-scale co-operative production. Huddersfield delegate Thomas Hirst, ever the showman, addressed the inaugural public meeting of the London Congress, in a typically direct and humorous fashion:

> 'I have on my back ... a Co-operative shirt, and here's a Co-operative coat, and here's a Co-operative waistcoat (loud laughter). All my friends have Co-operative clothes, and for my own part. I would sooner go without clothes at all, than be clothed in any other way, so strong an advocate am I for Co-operation.

---

152 Pahlman, 'Rise and Fall', pp. 210-11, quoting extracts from the Reports of the 6th (Barnsley) Congress and the 7th (Halifax) Congress.

153 *CN* 16 Jan. 1892.

154 Proc. 3rd (London) C.C., Apr. 1832; Proc. 4th (Liverpool) C.C., Oct. 1832 (tables). Another possible indicator of loss of membership or of an attempt to attract new members can be seen in the resolution passed at the 1832 AGM to divide and share out the profits of the society, *CN* 2 Jan. 1892.

Afterwards he exhibited several specimens of handkerchiefs, flannels, gown prints, Britannia metal tea-pots and knives manufactured by various northern co-operative societies.[155] Similarly, the co-operative bazaar organised in conjunction with the Congress in Liverpool was well furnished with 'woollen cloths etc. of all descriptions from Huddersfield.[156]

Perhaps because of the strong Methodist influence, the Huddersfield society always had a strong missionary instinct. From its early days members were employed to go out and visit other societies in the country. Soon after the formation of the Rochdale Co-operative Society in October 1830, for example, 'John Heaton was appointed to visit Rochdale at their desire and at their expense'. Not that the Huddersfield Society was miserly in its outreach work: Thomas Hirst recalled at the second (Birmingham) Co-operative Congress that his society had spent £20 in the previous year in correspondence advising different societies. And in April 1833 it agreed to pay 1 d per month per member towards the missionary cause.[157]

Hirst himself never acquired anything more than ill-health for his frequent and strenuous co-operative tours. Even local proselytizing could be exacting, as Hirst recalled, 'He and other members of that society (Huddersfield) went nine or ten miles to lecture in the evenings, and walked back again afterwards, sometimes not reaching home till the morning.' The Huddersfield society was always at the forefront of any proposal for the formal organisation of missionary work. Indeed, at the Birmingham Congress, Hirst claimed that only five out of 150 members of his society objected to the proposal for establishing co-operative missionaries. So, when the Congress decided to shelve this plan until the next Congress, the Huddersfield co-operators took the initiative themselves by appointing their president Amos Cowgill as a permanent missionary with a weekly wage of 18s.[158]

The Huddersfield Society's instinct for propaganda also manifested itself in their appreciation of the value of newspapers and the press. At the Liverpool Congress, for example, Thomas Hirst voiced the belief that Dr. King's Co-operator 'had converted hundreds if not thousands to the cause'. As early as April 1830, the minute-book of his society records that 'the Huddersfield society agreed to purchase one £10 share of the Weekly Free Press and Co-operative Journal'.[159] In October of the following year, Hirst exuded warm praise for the Voice of the People, the Free Press and Carpenter's Letters, and the Midland Representative at the Birmingham Congress. He further 'suggested to the Conductors of those Newspapers, that they should bring out a plan, such as was adopted at Huddersfield, to amalgamate the Political Unions and Co-operative Societies, so as they might both pull together'. This gives substance to intriguing rumours which were circulating seven months earlier in Huddersfield that the Leeds Patriot was to be sold and given to John Heaton, and suggests that as early as October 1831 co-operators and radicals were considering pooling resources to bring out

---

155 Proc. 3rd (London) C.C., Apr. 1832, p. 38.
156 Proc. 4th (Liverpool) C.C., Oct. 1832, published in LYC No. 10 (Oct. 1832).
157 CN 2 Jan. 1892; Proc. 2nd (Birmingham) C.C., Oct. 1831, p. 5; CN 16 Jan. 1892.
158 Proc. 2nd (Birmingham) C.C., Oct. 1831, p. 5. CN 2 Jan. 1892.
159 LYC Oct. 1832; CN 2 Jan. 1892.

material together.[160] The link was a natural one. Many of the members of the BAPCK in London were involved in radical activity and the nascent unstamped struggle; and Hirst himself chaired a radical 'Liberty of the Press' public meeting at Huddersfield in August 1831.[161]

Hirst's enthusiasm had cooled somewhat by the time of the London Congress in April 1832. He complained bitterly to an unreceptive audience that, 'we [co-operators] were deserted in the hour of need. Mr. Carpenter deserted us (*loud murmurs, and cries of 'no, no-no such thing'*) the TRADES FREE PRESS deserted us, THE VOICE OF THE PEOPLE deserted us – and we were thus left without any advocate to support our cause'. Nevertheless, he was able to declare defiantly that 'we have now got a press of our own (*loud cheers*), a co-operative press, and I trust we shall find it will succeed without the aid of those who have left us'.[162] This suggests that the Huddersfield co-operators may have had a stake in the 'Union Free Press' that was operating in Swan Yard by January 1833 if not before.[163]

The vacuum left by what Thomas Hirst saw as the 'desertion' of many former friends in early 1832 was filled for the rest of the year by an enlarged and more expensive version of the *Lancashire and Yorkshire Co-operator*.[164] Its demise at the end of the year was another blow for the northern co-operators, and to counteract this, Hirst talked of bringing out 'a new co-operative journal to be called *The Cooperative Economist* – an excellent name not yet used'.[165] Although there is no evidence that the idea ever materialised, the concept of starting their own newspaper remained in the minds of the local co-operators, and in 1833 they resolved to publish a monthly paper to be called, significantly, the *Christian Co-operative Advocate* at 2d.[166] Again, no traces of this project survived and it is unlikely that it ever got off the ground. However, the germ of the idea for a local paper did not perish, it merely incubated in the heated atmosphere of the time and emerged to maturity in the *Voice of the West-Riding*, a radical unstamped journal which was launched in Huddersfield in June 1833.[167]

As well as appreciating their uses for publicity and propaganda, the Huddersfield co-operators also recognised the educative value of newspapers. Hirst spoke at the Birmingham Congress of how his society encouraged its members to read the co-operative newspapers themselves, and also to get their fellow workmen, 'to stay at home and read the paper instead of going to the public-house'. A year later Hirst wrote to Mr. Francis Trench, a friend of Lady Byron, of the growing thirst for

---

160 Proc. 2nd (Birmingham) C.C., Oct. 1831, pp. 15-16; *LP* 26 Mar. 1831.

161 Prothero, *Artisans and Politics*, p. 255; *PMG* 17 Sept. 1831.

162 Proc. 3rd (London) C.C., Apr. 1832, pp. 35-6. It is not clear whether Hirst is referring to local moves in Huddersfield to set up a press at the Swan Yard radical headquarters (if so, this would be earlier than hitherto realised), or to the *LYC*.

163 John Halstead, 'The Voice of the West Riding: promoters and supporters of a provincial unstamped newspaper', in C. Wrigley (ed.), *On the Move: Essays in Labour and Transport History Presented to Philip Bagwell* (London: Bloomsbury Academic, 2003), pp. 28-30.

164 *LYC* Mar. 1832. This began a new series of monthly, 16 page, 2d papers.

165 *CN* 30 Jan 1892. Hirst envisaged this replacing the *LYC*.

166 *CN* 16 Jan. 1892.

167 For a full discussion of the origins and history of the *Voice*, see Halstead, 'The Voice of the West Riding:', pp. 22-57; and below pp. 327-34.

knowledge amongst the society's men, evident in the sizeable numbers who were subscribing towards a library and meeting regularly to improve each other's minds.[168] In 1833, the co-operators apparently discussed establishing a co-operative school. Whether this meeting bore fruit is not known, but certainly by early 1834, a Sunday School was being held in the Union Room, Swan Yard.[169]

Education was a vital component in the conception of working-class self-help and independence that co-operators shared with many radicals. Thomas Hirst, speaking at the London Congress, urged his fellow workers not to rely on government intervention: 'The remedy was co-operation; they must work for themselves – they must unite and gain knowledge – and union combined with knowledge was the most powerful engine by which despotism could be over thrown or good effected'.[170] The reverse side of this high-minded zeal, despair at 'the ignorance of the working classes themselves', revealed itself in this same speech, and two months later when Hirst was attacked by ultra-radicals for his 'soft' questioning of J. C. Ramsden, the Whig election candidate. Hirst responded by deprecating the operatives' conduct (in shouting down the local dignitary), and asserting that 'they had furnished the strongest possible proof of the necessity of a better education than they had received'.[171]

Although condemned in the heat of the moment as a turncoat, Hirst's role here and at later meetings as spokesman of the operatives indicates that, as at Halifax, there was considerable overlap in the local leadership of co-operation and radicalism.[172] Whilst some of their radical colleagues might occasionally find the co-operators' moderation and even-handedness frustrating, they nevertheless often shared a common platform and many of the same basic tenets, read the same newspapers and in all probability collaborated on local efforts to create an independent press.[173]

The radicals increasingly viewed the co-operation with admiration. At a radical reform meeting in June 1831, for example, local workers Abraham Donkersley and Benjamin Whiteley proposed a resolution recommending 'Temperance Societies, Co-operative Societies, Trades' Unions etc.' as ways of attacking 'the Hydra' and a means of people insulating 'themselves ... from the influence of corruption'.[174] By late 1833 radicals had additional practical reasons for commending their colleagues' efforts:

> The co-operators of Huddersfield have weathered the storm – they have become respectable in the town, and what is more they have three

---

168 Proc. 2nd (Birmingham) C.C., Oct. 1831, p.16; *CN* 30 Jan. 1892. The reference is probably to the Huddersfield Society for Intellectual Improvement, which started in November 1832 and was recommended to members of the co-operative society in late 1833, see *LT* 23 Nov. 1833, *VWR* 4 Jan. 1834. John Hanson, a prominent radical, and Edwin Lunn, a future leading Owenite socialist, were members in the mid-1830s.

169 *CN* 16 Jan. 1892; *VWR* 1 Feb. 1834.

170 Proc. 3rd (London) C.C., Apr. 1832, p. 67.

171 Ibid. *LM* 30 June 1832. Hirst's supine questioning was condemned by George Beaumont and Lawrence Pitkethly.

172 *LM* 30 June 1832; *LP* 11 Aug. 1832.

173 See, for example, *LP* 14 April 1832, describing Hirst's conciliatory speech as 'very long and desultory'. On commonality, see above, p. 203.

174 *LP* 25 June 1831.

votes for the favourite candidate. If every 200 labouring men in this town had done like this society, they would have been in possession of a capital, and the privilege of voting.[175]

The first post-Reform election of 1832 had earlier revealed a common interest in using consumer preferences for political 'purchase' via exclusive dealing and had cemented formal links between co-operators and radicals in the town. In addition, in June, the society resolved that, 'our trustees do give their vote and interest to Joseph Wood as member for this borough, and that Thomas Hirst and Christopher Wood be appointed to attend Captain Wood's Committee from the body'.[176] This connection caused some embarrassment, notably with Lady Byron, the Huddersfield society's benefactor. When she heard rumours that Hirst was using the £500 loan, which she had arranged, 'for the purpose of forwarding secret unions of a very dangerous political tendency', she asked for clarification. Hirst denied the report and went on to assert that, 'Co-operation has nothing to do with politics. Neither have we to do with secret unions of a political nature... There is not a single member of our society that is connected with any political union, either secret, or public', a statement which was palpably untrue.[177]

The secrecy associated with West Riding trades' unionism makes it difficult to fully assess the precise nature and extent of links with early co-operation in the Huddersfield area. A number of leading figures in the Huddersfield society certainly had strong trade union connections. Thomas Cliffe's poetic tribute to Thomas Hirst in 1834 refers to his role in 'Unions' Trade Society';[178] and Hirst himself delivered the sermon in front of the massed ranks of operatives at the memorial service in Huddersfield for Thomas Roberts, late President of the regional Trades' Union.[179] At the Liverpool Congress Hirst recalled the genesis of the inspiration for co-operation: 'finding that they could not maintain their families, pay their rent and live without being rogues or thieves, they wanted the masters to advance wages'. The employers refused; a turn-out was 'ordered' and during the long 'unnatural contest' which ensued £200,000 was allegedly paid for 'men to walk about with their hands in their pockets, meditating mischief against their employers'. He continued, 'their object in commencing co-operation was to put an end to this war; to a considerable extent they had succeeded; [since] nearly the whole of the masters in Huddersfield had given an advance in wages...'[180]

---

175 *VWR* 4 Jan. 1834.

176 *CN* 2 Jan 1834. The Society donated £3 to the Committee to help defray election expenses. Holyoake is mistaken in assigning the original resolution to June 1831.

177 *CN* 16, 23 Jan. 1892. There was much contemporary discussion about secret (trade) unions in Yorkshire following the Farsley murder, see above, pp. 99-100. Samuel Glendinning was a member of the Huddersfield PU; Hirst, Wood and Heaton all had radical connections. The three trustees (Wood, William Hodgson and Thomas Dickinson) all voted for Capt. Wood in the 1834 election, as did Amos Cowgill, now a draper, *VWR* 11 Jan. 1834.

178 *VWR* 18 Jan. 1834. See below, p. 223.

179 *LP* 11 Aug. 1832 estimated that the crowd of numbered 20,000.

180 *Crisis* 27 Oct. 1832. The last sentence may refer to the recent success of the Huddersfield Trades' Union. The £200,000 figure is clearly wrong. £20,000 was a figure commonly

The dispute he had in mind may have been the Bradford Strike of 1825, though local disputes involving the Fancy Weavers' Union at the same time may also have driven home the same lesson.[181] Certainly there was an important connection with these earlier conflicts through the person of Amos Cowgill, President of the Fancy Weavers' Union in 1824-5 and now President and official missionary of the Co-operative Society.[182] John Heaton, the society's agent had also taken a prominent part in the Fancy Weavers' Union at this time; and at a Huddersfield radical meeting on Distress in April 1832 he repeated the suggestion 'that he had made several years ago, that when strikes for wages took place, instead of keeping the men for doing nothing, the money should be appropriated to the establishment of manufactories, in opposition to those masters whom the strike was made'.[183]

Heaton's other public statements, with their focus on questions of wages, and their attacks on tyrannical employers and the 'old' competitive system, indicate his trade union heritage and concerns.[184] It seems reasonable to assume that, particularly in terms of ideas and organisational experience, a trade union background provided an important resource upon which the co-operators were able to draw. Equally, the employment of Cowgill and Heaton by the Huddersfield society can be seen as a response to the blacklisting that followed their earlier involvement as high-profile trade union leaders. Two local STC members also had co-operative connections: Samuel Glendinning temporarily oversaw the society's 'woollen manufacturing department' and John Hirst was the co-operative store's manager.[185]

No membership records survive for the first Huddersfield Co-operative Society, and so any remarks about the co-operative rank and file must be based on scattered fragments of indirect evidence. The nature of the society's products and the occupational structure of the area suggest, unsurprisingly, that fancy and woollen weavers were well represented. However, in addition, to textile outworkers, and possibly some factory-based workers, other skilled town trades with artisan status or aspirations may also have been represented.[186] John Heaton in his general remarks on

---

quoted for the cost of the Bradford strike.

181 It is just possible that Hirst is referring to more recent strikes, such as Leeds (1831) or Holmfirth (1832).

182 See above, p. 45.

183 For example, he formed part of a weavers' deputation and spoke at a public meeting (*LM* 12 Feb. 1825); *LP* 14 Apr. 1832.

184 See *WFP* 2, 9 Jan. 1830; *Carpenter's Political Letters and Pamphlets*, No. 26, 'A Political Reformer', 19 Mar. 1831.

185 On Glendinning (1802-1883) a woollen merchant (draper), radical, STC member and Primitive Methodist preacher, see J. T. Ward's article in *Halifax Daily Examiner* 2 June 1958; *Huddersfield Weekly News* 14 July 1883; and Halstead 'Huddersfield STC', pp. 93 ff. On John Hirst, see Halstead 'Huddersfield STC', pp. 93 ff. Thomas Hirst had a son, John, but he would only have been fifteen at the time of the committee's creation.

186 See, for example, the list of manufactured products on sale at the store, *VWR* 12 Nov. 1833. Too fine a distinction between factory-based and 'out' workers should not be drawn. The better-paid adult male factory workers could certainly have afforded the subscription. See also John Heaton's assessment in March 1831, 'we are doing pretty well, considering the very low state of wages among us', *Carpenter's Political Letters and Pamphlets*, No. 26., 'A Political Reformer', 19 Mar. 1831.

co-operative progress in the Huddersfield district in October 1831 for example, mentions the employment of tailors and shoemakers.[187] Both of these trades were ideal for the start of self-employment, since they required little capital outlay and produced goods which could easily be sold in the co-operative store. In 1831, for example, a certain William Hodgson was remunerated for labour performed for the society with a suit of clothes, taking in both hat, shoes and shirt.[188]

Three years later J. N. Reid testified that, 'twenty of them [tailors] had worked into the shop in Westgate (Huddersfield) about £100 in goods!'[189] In addition the Huddersfield co-operators employed their own butchers, their own engineer, as well as their own agent and salesman. Therefore, although drawn preponderantly from the textile trades, it is probable that the membership of the Huddersfield Co-operative Society also included representatives from the various skilled, better-paid trades to be found in any sizeable market town of the day.[190] This tentative conclusion is supported by the evidence of Barnsley, a linen-dominated town, twenty miles away, where the growing Barnsley West End Co-operative Society reported to Congress in April 1832 that, 'we have in our society, linen manufacturers, bleachers, weavers, shoemakers, joiners, masons, dyers, mechanics etc...'[191]

In the case of Huddersfield, it would appear from the support given to the missionary cause and the Liverpool warehouse, that rank and file aspirations went beyond a 'mere trading association'. Similarly, co-operative manufacture was undertaken not as a temporary expedient, but as a major stride along the co-operative path. Once having commenced co-operative production ordinary co-operators accepted the economic logic of a national scheme of exchange. Yet the very local economic conditions which proved favourable to contact with, first, the Liverpool concern, and later the Birmingham Exchange, also discouraged rank and file support for a comprehensive system of locally-based exchanges. The principles of labour exchange had been discussed as early as April 1832, but the fact that no concrete progress was made towards the establishment of an exchange in the Huddersfield area indicates the limits which economic realism could place on co-operative aspirations.[192]

The views of a key component of the early co-operative rank and file – its female adherents – remain largely hidden. Their discipline and support was vital to the success of the early societies, but apart from the role of benefactors like Lady Byron and Miss Chaloner, women appear only fleetingly in the historical record. However, female co-operators clearly played an important role in the day-to-day activities and the cultural life of the societies. The location, content and timing of events like tea-parties and 'co-operative festivals', with their informal, convivial atmosphere, teetotal refreshments and educative aims, were designed to have broad appeal. Thomas Hirst, for example, recalled a tea party at a local society where 'the company consisted of

---

187 *LYC* 1 Oct. 1831.

188 *CN* 16 Jan. 1892.

189 *LT* 25 Oct. 1834. Reid, an intriguing figure, arrived in Huddersfield from London in 1834 and for a short period became a leading radical and socialist agitator.

190 *CN* 2, 16 Jan. 1892.

191 *LYC* Apr. 1832.

192 *VWR* 4 Jan. 1834; Proc. 3rd (London) C.C., Apr. 1832 (tables).

men and women, and almost every woman had a bairn [child] on her lap. There was none of the old custom of "Mr President"; but all appeared to be brothers in one family'. Seven years later the *Northern Star*'s correspondent's account of the Huddersfield society's 1838 annual festival notes that the 'large room of the Socialists … was decorated in the most tasteful manner' and that 'the women looked beautiful, the men cheerful, and "all of them happy"'.[193]

Yet, as in trades' unionism and radicalism, female participation in co-operation can hardly have been passive or decorative. The active role that women played in organising and enforcing exclusive dealing that Malcom Chase noted, can equally be applied to co-operation, its logical extension. They were essentially early co-operation's foot-soldiers, maintaining resolve and discipline and often making sacrifices. At the London Congress in April 1832, Thomas Hirst declared proudly that women were not kept in the background in the Huddersfield society and that 'it would take hundreds of London men to make one good co-operative woman (loud laughter)'.[194] How far this rhetorical flourish translated into individual membership or participation in decision-making remains to be investigated. Iorwerth Prothero notes that the strict no-credit rule was unpopular with the wives of London co-operators, and it is likely that the easing of this policy in a number of early West Riding societies came as the result of pressure from this direction.[195] However, there is still much to be discovered about women's involvement in and influence on local societies including: how far shopping was gendered; what roles women played in the internal life of societies; and to what extent their views informed strategy.

5: Hirst, 'Community' and Owenism

John Halstead's exploration of the career of Thomas Hirst, 'a considerable figure in national co-operative circles', outlines what little is known of his early life: his birth in 1792, his economic struggles and the early death of his first wife.[196] Whatever his precise role at the inception of Huddersfield co-operation, Hirst quickly became a key figure in the local society, and (along with Thomas Wilson) the leading co-operative personality in the West Riding. 'Personality' is the correct term, for Hirst appears to have been an unusually charismatic figure. The *Lancashire and Yorkshire Co-operator* in March 1832 testified to the 'extraordinary sensation' created by 'his peculiar yet animating oratory and force of argument'.[197] The context of this praise is an article on missionary activity, in which Hirst was deeply involved. The fact that the work was initially unofficial and unpaid did not deter him, and in the year separating the Birmingham and Liverpool Congresses (October 1831 - October 1832), he inflicted a punishing schedule upon himself.[198]

---

193 *LYC* Mar. 1832; *NS* 5 Jan. 1838.

194 Malcolm Chase, *Chartism: A New History* (Manchester: Manchester University Press, 2007), p. 42; Proc. 3rd (London) C.C., Apr. 1832, p. 36.

195 Prothero, *Artisans and Politics*, p. 248.

196 Halstead, 'Notable Co-operator', pp. 61-2, 64.

197 *LYC* Mar. 1832.

198 See *LYC* for details of his prodigious missionary efforts in this period.

The inspiration and training for this missionary work came from Hirst's strong religious sense and his work as a preacher in the Methodist New Connexion. The Methodist example was always to the front of his mind: 'If we co-operators had as many factories as there are methodist chapels in England, we could drive the world before us'. Yet he was not a religious bigot; he believed strongly that co-operation should be non-denominational: 'I think the Missionary's path is plain before him, he has nothing to do with the theological opinions of any man ... I have been called an infidel, but if co-operation is infidelity, I don't believe there is such a thing as infidelity in the world'.[199]

Perhaps because of his prestigious position within the local religious community, Thomas Hirst epitomised the strong element of respectability evident in the early co-operative societies. He saw co-operation as a means of moral regeneration, writing to Lady Byron shortly before his death in 1833:

> I have endeavoured always in my advice to the working-classes, to show them that if they would endeavour to improve their morals, and conduct themselves legally and peaceably, saving their money instead of spending it in drunkenness – and thus try to raise themselves from the social degradation and misery that the 'higher classes' would help them'.[200]

At the height of the reform crisis, Hirst confronted an ultra-radical who came to Huddersfield with stories of half a million men at Attwood's command, of arming, and taking the magazines, telling him that 'they wanted no more Olivers. That the workmen would not break the peace, or destroy the lives or property of the masters or employers – and the weapons of their warfare were morality, truth and knowledge, which was power'. However, his rejection of topical political scare tactics in favour of more moderate 'moral-force' ideas should not diminish Hirst's stature as a reformer. Like many other Methodist leaders of working-class movements his beliefs fused a strong commitment to fundamental political change with a strong egalitarian streak. Although attacking William Carpenter, editor of the *Weekly Free Press*, at the London Congress, he admitted that he had always admired his writings and principles and had taken his paper from its commencement.[201]

Hirst's ideas combined important elements of a traditional radical analysis, with a developing alternative political economy. Whilst accepting primogeniture, paper money, the funding system, the East India monopoly and the Corn Laws as partial causes of the 'present evil system', he never missed an opportunity to attack the misuses of machinery and the evils of competition and monopoly. 'To monopoly and its

---

199 *LYC* Mar. 1832; Proc. 2nd (Birmingham) C.C., Oct. 1831, p. 5.

200 *CN* 23 Jan. 1892. His stress on legality brought him into conflict with London radicals and co-operators, when he stated his view that 'according to the existing institutions of the country, the Government was bound to prosecute [Carpenter] for selling his unstamped papers', Proc. 3rd (London) C.C., Apr. 1832, p. 40.

201 *Crisis* 27 Oct. 1832. *LYC* March 1832. Proc. 3rd (London) C.C., Apr. 1832, p. 40. On Carpenter, his radical politics and support for co-operation, see Prothero, *Artisans and Politics*, pp. 230-1, 247-8, 279-8.

concomitants, we may therefore point as the great source of our evils. The whole system of trade is now one great system of falsehood and fraud'. Competition for foreign markets, in his view, only instigated a vicious cycle of cut-price selling and wage reductions; and he argued strongly for an increase in wages to enlarge the domestic market.[202]

He expected little of the unproductive classes or political economists. Possibly referring obliquely to his personal experience, he asked,

> How many representations had been made to the Government upon the alarming increase of pauperism and bankruptcy, and when, at length, the evidence became irresistible, and the facts of the case could no longer be denied, what remedy had our sapient legislators suggested for the cure of this enormous evil? The Malthusian philosophers asserted it to be the necessary consequence of avaricious and redundant population.[203]

Equally insensitive were the manufacturers and 'tyrannical capitalists' who decried every attempt of the labouring classes to improve their 'impoverished condition'. 'In his part of the country they had been compelled to labour not only twelve, but sixteen and eighteen hours a day – and if human nature could endure, they would be made to work the whole twenty-four'. The solution was simple. The working-classes must ensure their own salvation by using their intrinsic economic power, in co-operation: 'for 'labour is the only source of wealth' ... Is this not as plain as two and two make four?'[204]

Hirst characterized himself as 'a common, hard-working man' and his world-view may have been informed by his own occupational background as a cloth-dresser, a hitherto highly-skilled and well-remunerated branch of the woollen trade with strong radical and associational traditions. It may also have been shaped by his personal experience of bankruptcy in 1814 and 1820.[205] When he was finally released from debt in 1822 the words 'Dealer' and 'Chapman' (pedlar) were included in his occupational designation, indicating some retail experience prior to his involvement in co-operation.[206]

Whatever his precise career path, Hirst's conception of co-operation was extremely broad. For him the co-operative society was the ultimate working-class 'union'. So, in a speech at the Birmingham Congress, he 'showed the difference between Benefit and Trade Societies and Political Unions, and the Co-operative

---

202 Proc. 3rd (London) C.C., Apr. 1832, pp. 35, 63-79; *Crisis* 27 Oct. 1832.

203 *LYC* Mar. 1832.

204 *CN* 23 Jan. 1892; *Crisis* 27 Oct. 1832; *LYC* March 1832.

205 *Liverpool Mercury* 5 Oct. 1832; Halstead, 'Notable Co-operator', pp. 61-2. It is possible that he ran an independent workshop operating in the hinterland between skilled craft operative and small master status. On cloth-dressers (also known as croppers), their 'privileged' position, role in Yorkshire Luddism in 1812, and subsequent decline see, Thompson, *Making*, pp. 547-9. 570-80, 601-2.

206 *LI* 9 Dec. 1822.

Societies, and that the latter embraced all the objects of the former'.[207] His vision also extended vertically beyond the co-operative store, employment of members and exchange of produce, to community. In March 1832 he is to be found urging co-operators to 'keep your eyes fixed upon the ground-plan of community', and two months later, declaring that the, 'community of property, equality of right and privilege – these are the fundamental principles of our system'.[208]

This interest in community was long-standing. When the subject had been raised at the Birmingham Congress (October 1831), Hirst urged perseverance and patience, stressing the necessity of building any community from the bottom, on the solid foundation of successful co-operative societies. He reiterated this line of argument at the London Congress, and illustrated his caution two months later by rejecting, as unsuitable for a community, a potential 1,200-acre site at Kirkby Mallory (Leicestershire), which Congress had recommended.[209] However, his interest in some sort of communal experiment remained strong, and by the time of the Liverpool Congress his ideas looked set to take on a more concrete form. Chairing the debate on community he declared that,

> Community was the principle [*sic*] object of their pursuit at Huddersfield, and in order to prepare themselves a few of their members would take some land as soon as possible. They were now in treaty with a gentleman for some land in the neighbourhood of Huddersfield, upon a loan for ever, with power to purchase at a stipulated price. They thought it advisable to go cautiously and prudently to work and to have their land situated near the scene of their present occupations, for they could not get out of the present into the new system of society at a bound.[210]

Caution and realism are the hallmarks of this first tentative step towards community; and Hirst concludes by advocating William Thompson's ideas, by which 'their wishes would be accomplished in less time, and with much greater chance of success than by waiting till some such magnificent sum as that proposed by Mr. Owen was subscribed by the wealthy'.[211] Exactly what Hirst had in mind for Huddersfield can be seen from the outline of a letter sent to Mr. Francis Trench a little later in the year. In this Hirst speaks of 'the formation of a home colony on real co-operative principles'; the idea being to rent (and later buy) 150-200 acres of land 'somewhere in the manufacturing districts' and settle on it a number of 'intelligent and industrious

---

207 Proc. 2nd (Birmingham) C.C., Oct.1831, p.15. For a discussion of the concept of 'union', see Chase, *Early Trade Unionism*, pp. 112-3; Harrison, *Robert Owen*, p. 200; and W. H. Oliver, 'The Labour Exchange phase of the Co-operative Movement', *Oxford Economic Papers* ns. 10 (1958), p. 359.

208 *LYC* Mar., June 1832.

209 Proc. 2nd (Birmingham) C.C., Oct. 1831, pp. 11-15; Proc. 3rd (London) C.C., Apr. 1832, pp. 85-95; *LYC* June 1832.

210 *LYC* Oct. 1832. Hirst spoke of a £1,500 loan for the venture having been offered by a gentleman who had been at New Lanark and had visited the Orbiston Community.

211 *LYC* Oct 1832.

agriculturists'. If the experiment succeeded, the latter would be able to exchange their farm produce for goods manufactured by the co-operative societies in that district, 'until such time as a manufactory could be built on the estate, to furnish all the necessary clothes'.

Instead of needing the £250,000 thought essential by Owen, Hirst talked in terms of £10,000 which 'under proper management and due economy, together with the well-directed industry of the people, would give an enlightened public a practical proof of what co-operation properly directed was capable of accomplishing, and furnish those proofs which Mr. Owen's speculations have failed to produce'.[212] There is no evidence that the 'home colony' scheme ever got off the ground in Huddersfield. Its timing was unfortunate, coming as it did in a worsening economic climate, and at the very time when Hirst's health began the deterioration which ended in his death. However, it says something for the sophistication of the Huddersfield co-operators that such a scheme could be so actively, and optimistically, promoted amongst them.

The fact that it may have been Hirst's hobby horse may distort any assessment of rank and file interest in community as a co-operative goal. In May 1832 a general meeting of co-operators had discussed the question of promoting a community, and had been addressed on the subject by Mr. Vandaleur of Palatine. The meeting, however, considered community to be 'impolitic and impractical' at that time, 'particularly in regard to the cultivation of land at Chat Moss [near Manchester]'.[213] The failure of the latter experiment no doubt brought home the practical difficulties involved in making even the first move in the direction of community. For the most committed members the attraction of Hirst's 'home colony' scheme may have been its communitarian goal (however distant); for others it offered the chance of land ownership and cultivation on a small scale; but for the majority of co-operators, it probably remained beyond their experience and aspirations.

Hirst's preference for communities on the Thompson model raises important questions of Hirst's attitude to Owen, and of how far he and other West Riding co-operators can be labelled 'Owenite'. The epithet itself is far from satisfactory and critics, like Iorwerth Prothero, have argued that, through the all-embracing nature and use of the term, 'Every inoffensive member of a co-operative society or the Consolidated Trades' Union stands in grave danger of being labelled "Owenite"'.[214]

Nowhere is this truer than in the West Riding. It is clear that Hirst was not always happy about Owen's primacy in the co-operative movement. Not only did he think Owen's community schemes grandiose and impractical, he also disagreed fundamentally with Owen's views on formation of character and, most importantly, religion. Equally, though, he recognised the dangers to co-operative unity and, at the London Congress, sought to minimise them: 'Although Mr. Owen and I on scriptural

---

212 *CN* 30 Jan. 1892. Trench, a co-operative sympathiser, may have been the gentleman who offered a loan.

213 *CN* 2 Jan. 1892. On Chat Moss, see Musson, 'Early Co-operation', p. 125. Vandaleur had founded a flax-growing 'little colony' on co-operative principles in County Clare (*Liverpool Mercury* 5 Oct. 1832).

214 Iorwerth Prothero, 'William Benbow and the concept of the "General Strike"' in *Past and Present*, 63, 1 (1974), pp. 155-6.

grounds are very widely opposed to each other, yet I give him the right hand of fellowship, in the truest sincerity. All sectarianism should instantly cease' – an olive branch that testifies both to the nub of their differences and Hirst's standing in the national movement.[215]

It is open to question how far the reconciliation worked. Although Owen was a well-respected and generally popular figure in the West Riding, it must be remembered that many of the early co-operative societies were founded while Owen was still in America. In terms of ideology and organisation they owed more to traditional sources and the early co-operative propagandists such as Dr. William King, William Thompson and William Carpenter than to Owen himself. Those aspects of 'Owenite' ideology which were most acceptable to West Riding co-operators (for example, labour as the source of all wealth, the evils of competition and the misuse of machinery), were also the ones with which they were most familiar.[216] In other areas, especially religion, the divergence was fundamental and deep. One co-operator even went as far as to dissociate Yorkshire co-operation completely from Owen, 'the Co-operative Societies of Yorkshire are not based on the principles of Mr. R. Owen, but on Christian principles – justice, temperance, economy, benevolence, peace, union of exertion and enjoyments'.[217] So it is no surprise to find that one of Hirst's last acts was to write to Owen imploring him to desist from his attacks on the Christian faith.[218] For Hirst, and the many West Riding co-operators who followed his lead, the 'Owenite' cap is a very poor fit.

Hirst's death in May 1833 was not unexpected. A year of exhausting missionary effort began to take its toll soon after the Liverpool Congress which he had chaired the previous autumn. His health continued to deteriorate in the early months of 1833, prompting offers of financial and medical assistance from Lady Byron. Robert Owen, in Huddersfield for the Co-operative Congress (April 1833), found Hirst on his deathbed, and realised that 'his illness was probably caused chiefly, if not entirely, by his over-strenuous exertions in the cause'.[219] He died a month later, on 8 May, leaving a widow and four children.[220] His funeral was attended by 'thousands' of mourners 'including the Trades' Union and several other Societies, and headed by radical stalwarts William Stocks jnr. and Capt. Wood of Sandal'. The *Halifax Guardian* rightly concluded, 'the sight of so many men attending to his last home this popular orator,

---

215 *CN* 30, 9 Jan. 1892; Proc 3rd (London) C.C., Apr. 1832, p. 38.

216 For a discussion of Owen's influence and interaction with artisans in London see Prothero, *Artisans and Politics*, pp. 239-64.

217 *LT* 20 July 1833.

218 *CN* 6 Feb. 1892. See also Dr. William King's letter to Hirst, 3 April 1833, *CN* 23 Jan. 1892.

219 *CN* 23, 30 Jan., 6 Feb. 1892. *Crisis* 20 Apr. 1833. The exact illness is not known. Earlier in the year Hirst complained of being 'extremely ill of an inflammation of the lungs', *CN* 23 Jan. 1892.

220 *Crisis* 22 June 1833. Immediately after his death a public subscription was started and a hundred memorandum books circulated in town and country. Lady Byron's pledge to the dying Hirst to look after his family was also fulfilled. Mrs. Hirst received £50, and in 1835 his two sons began three years' education at Mr. Craig's school, Middlesex, at Lady Byron's expense. *CN* 6 Feb. 1892.

proves the esteem entertained by his own class for him'.[221] The local co-operators realised the extent of and reasons for their loss: 'We had lost the best and ablest advocate of our cause in this part of the country; he has travelled thousands of miles and delivered scores of lectures, – has spent his all and died a martyr for the good of his fellow men...'[222] A final tribute came the following year from the pen of aspiring (and often derided) radical poet Thomas Cliffe of Halifax:

> His name shall stand a useful monument,
> Tho' fools may treat it with a 'fools' contempt,
> The British nation will in future see
> The fruits of 'Unions' Trade Society;
> Co-operation seized his mind of late,
> And that he thought would heal the social state.
> His time, his talent, and his purse did aid;
> (For sure he ne'er could have his service paid;)
> But what he knew, or fancied could be found
> A permanent relief he echoed round![223]

6: The Huddersfield Congress, and Commercial Orders, 1833-4

It must have been galling for Thomas Hirst that, after innumerable missionary tours and journeys to congress, illness should prevent him from participating in a co-operative gathering on his own doorstep. The choice of Huddersfield for the spring 1833 congress reflected both a shift in co-operative preoccupations towards exchange and liaison with the trades' unions, and a recognition of the influence of the West Riding co-operative societies.[224] The multi-layered aspirations of the co-operators increasingly focused on co-operative production and exchange, which by its very nature necessitated the search for allies within the working class. The *Poor Man's Guardian*, in approving the choice of Huddersfield for the congress, noted both trends:

> They [the Huddersfield societies] seem convinced from the first acts of the Reformed Parliament that little will be done to benefit the working-class – indeed they feel confident that no plan of reform can permanently benefit them, unless such as shall place them beyond the grinding influence of commercial competition, surplus capital and increasing productive powers... They, therefore, aim at being their own masters and uniting capital and machinery in their favour. Many of these societies have already their own machinery and are employing several of their members, especially in the manufacture of cloth. They are striving to extend the consumption of their manufactures through

---

221 The considerable size of the funeral is attested by at least two independent sources, *HG* 18 May 1833, *Crisis* 22 June 1833.

222 *Crisis* 22 June 1833, letter of A. Turner (Sec) to Owen, 29 May 1833.

223 *VWR* 18 Jan. 1834.

224 Proc. 4th (Liverpool) C.C. Oct 1832, pp. 36-7; *LYC* Oct. 1832. Owen had wanted the congress to be held in London.

the medium of exchange, and feel they would benefit each other in proportion as working men were united on the same principles in every part of the Kingdom. Many Trade and Benefit Societies are making arrangements for employing their members with their funds, instead of paying them to do nothing, or, what is worse, to invest them in Saving Banks and the funds.[225]

The chronological and geographical context of the congress is significant. It was held at a time (April 1833) of working-class disillusionment with the outcomes of last year's political agitation, and concern over the recent ravages of economic depression. Few places had suffered more than the villages of the Huddersfield area.[226] In addition the location of the congress meant that it took place in a highly unionised atmosphere. After returning to the metropolis, J. R. Turner, the delegate of the United Trades Association of London, reported that 'the Trades' Unions of Huddersfield and the neighbourhood were 40,000 strong, and they had expended [£]27,000 in strikes within a very short time'. Six weeks later the *Halifax Guardian* bemoaned the fact that in Huddersfield 'the system of combination in every branch, of trade and mechanics appears to be quite the fashion'. Indeed, while the congress was taking place Owen was able to consult with 'a Trades Committee' which was sitting at the same time.[227]

In such a conducive atmosphere it is hardly surprising that proposals for closer links between trades' unions and co-operative societies were aired. However, this process was greatly helped by a greater receptiveness for such ideas on the part of the unions. At the opening of the Congress 'several speakers stated that the Trades' Union in and about Huddersfield amounted to 20,000 persons, and that they were about adopting measures to employ their unemployed, and felt by means of exchange, it might greatly facilitate their operation'.[228] This growing co-operative and labour exchange awareness among the trades' unions antedated the Congress, and formed the basis of Thomas Hirst's optimism, in October 1832, for the spread of co-operation in the northern textile districts:

> The fact was, the trades' unions were at length beginning to see the utter inutility of striking either against a reduction, or for an advance of wages, so long as the present wretched and degrading system of competition existed. They also began to lament their egregious folly in having subscribed and paid away tens of thousands of pounds to men for walking about the streets with their hands in their pockets. (*Hear*). There was now a turn-out in Yorkshire, and men were being supported in this way, but they had wisely resolved by the advice of the

---

225 *PMG* 30 Mar. 1833.

226 *Crisis* 20 Apr. 1833. The question of distress had always been a prime concern of co-operators and radicals in Huddersfield, e.g. *PMG* 28 Apr. 1832.

227 *Crisis* 27 Apr. 1833. His figures appear somewhat exaggerated, double the figure given in Congress reports, *HG* 15 June 1833. The committee may have been the stonemasons.

228 *Crisis* 19 Oct. 1833. Although extracts of the Congress' proceedings had been published in the *Crisis* in early May, a full account was given, by public demand, in the bumper London Congress edition of the *Crisis*.

Co-operatives, never to do so again. They would establish united trades manufactories, manufacture for themselves, raise their own food, and exchange each others surplus produce...[229]

It is open to debate how far this new receptiveness was due to co-operative propaganda or to the exigencies of the industrial situation, or indeed whether it had existed, untapped, all along. However, it appears to have been matched on the part of the co-operators by an increased awareness of the potential of labour exchange and the role of trades' unions. William Pare, a leading co-operator, remarking on the situation in Birmingham in December 1832, found that, 'The different Trades Unions, which we are meeting every night, are taking the matter [labour exchange] up with spirit, and, being already organised, they are capable of doing us great good'. Tangentially acknowledging the power and influence of trade union leadership, he added, 'I conceive it to be of the utmost importance to cherish these Trade Unions. Only convince these fine hearted men that our plan will really do them good, and you have an army on your side at once'.[230] The trades' unions of the woollen textile district, being equally well-organised, offered no less of an incentive.

The Huddersfield Congress was comparatively short (lasting only three days) and small-scale. It was very much a 'provincial Congress', and received little advance publicity.[231] The themes of distress and labour exchange dominated its proceedings. The issue of distress was a perennial concern of the West Riding co-operators, and the topicality of parliamentary debates on it, ensured that it remained at the forefront of the delegates' minds.[232] However, the much-quoted local evidence collected during the recent ravages of industrial depression served to emphasise the need for co-operators to develop far-reaching solutions to deal with the major problems created by the present system.

The solution proposed, and continually stressed at private and public meetings alike, was for a national system of labour exchanges; in the words of J. R. Turner, 'a general union of the working-classes throughout the kingdom'. Turner, having floated the idea of a 'National Association of the United Trades of Great Britain and Ireland' a few weeks earlier, became, with Owen, one of the principal advocates of the scheme.[233] Yet support for the idea was widespread amongst the delegates, and significantly, it was two Yorkshire members (C. Wood of Huddersfield and Thomas Wilson of Halifax) who proposed the congress's first major resolution:

---

229 *LYC* Oct. 1832. The strike referred to was probably the Holmfirth clothiers' strike.
230 *Crisis* 15 Dec. 1832.
231 Earlier congresses had lasted six days. Initial meetings were held in the co-operative store. A large number of delegates came from northern societies. *Crisis* 20 April, 4 May, 19 Oct. 1833.
232 See, for example, *LP* 25 Feb.1830, 'J.B.' refers to the formation of a co-operative association 'for the purpose of alleviating the poor'. Also, *PMG* 25 Apr; *LP* 11 Apr.1832 and *Crisis* 27 Oct.1832 for Hirst's involvement in this issue. For contemporary activity see *Crisis* 4 May 1833, a report on a public meeting addressed by Thomas Wilson and William Stocks jnr.
233 *Crisis* 4 May; 20 Apr. 1833.

> That this Congress view the establishment of Branches of the National Equitable Labour Exchange as a highly desirable consummation, according to the plan explained, and earnestly recommend the Co-operative and Benefit Societies, and the Trades' Unions in the different parts of the Kingdom to unite themselves into an association, for the purpose of promoting the National Equitable Labour Exchange.[234]

This ambitious, outward-looking, stance is one of the key features of the congress, and marks an important development in the early co-operative movement. It showed itself in practice at the Easter Monday public meeting at the White Hart Inn, where Abraham Whitehead, clothier and leader of the Holmfirth strike, shared the platform with Owen and Turner, and put his weight behind trades' self-employment and 'Exchange Banks'.[235] The following day delegates discussed 'the extensive field which was then opening for missionary exertion amongst the Trades' Unions', and passed a series of resolutions (favourable to labour exchange) including one for the formation of a Missionary District Association taking in a circle of thirty miles around Huddersfield. It further showed itself in the symbolic addition of the subtitle 'The National Co-operative, Trades' Union and Equitable Labour Exchange Gazette' to the banner-head of the *Crisis*; and, more importantly, in the authorisation of a national congress in October of 'delegates from the Co-operative Societies and Trade Unions of Great Britain and Ireland'. The final seal of approval came from a sub-committee of six delegates, looking into the establishment of labour exchanges and liaison with the trades' unions, which declared that,

> the best means of obtaining the co-operation of the Trades' Unions in Labour Exchange, is for the Congress here assembled to urge on the attention of the delegates the necessity of the members of their societies who do not belong to Trades' Unions, to join Trades' Unions and for these who do unitedly to use their utmost exertion in explaining and teaching the principles of exchange.[236]

As with any congress it is virtually impossible to measure the direct impact of the Huddersfield meeting upon the various parties involved. Unfortunately, 1833 is a barren year for information on the Huddersfield society. We can guess that their request to Sheffield for a specimen of a labour exchange note may have been stimulated by the discussions of the congress, but it is likely that the local co-operators were more preoccupied with internal problems – 'the storm' referred to by the *Voice* the following year – caused by the economic situation and the mismanagement of an agent.[237] They made no progress towards establishing an exchange in the immediate

---

234 *Crisis* 4 May 1833.
235 *Crisis* 4 May 1833. He quoted the example of a trade union victory in Holmfirth gained by self-employment.
236 *Crisis* 19 Oct. 1833.
237 *CN* 16 Jan. 1892; *VWR* 4 Jan. 1834; *LT* 1 Nov. 1834 (J. N. Reid's Speech).

locality – though by summer there was talk of one being formed in Barnsley.[238] Nevertheless, it is possible that local co-operators took the advice of congress and made their influence felt in the trades' unions. These latter bodies were, by April 1833, becoming more receptive to the ideas and practices of labour exchange. J. R. Turner found that the 'Trades' Unions of Huddersfield and neighbourhood regretted they had not known before the working of the exchange system'. And the 'Trades Committee' sitting at Huddersfield, to whom Owen explained 'the principles and practice of labour exchange', afterwards passed a resolution 'pledging themselves to use their utmost influence in urging on the attention of their fellow workmen to the important advantages derivable from the Labour Exchange'.

By August 1833 a friend was reporting to Owen that, 'the Trades Unions of Yorkshire and Lancashire [are] looking to Labour Exchange Banks for relief. Many are looking to the London and Birmingham Banks with dense anxiety'.[239] Yet, in addition to this flirtation with the idea of labour exchange, some unions were taking practical steps to employ their members, by the formation of 'Commercial Orders'.

These were a fascinating addition to the range of working-class associative entities spawned in the hyperactive years of 1833 and 1834. 'Order', with its friendly society connotations and mystique was, like 'union', a common buzzword of the era. Commercial orders left behind few traces, but essentially operated as co-operative production wings of the trades' unions. Although legally separated from the parent union body, in practice they used subscriptions from union members to set up facilities to begin their own manufacturing. They were not confined to the West Riding. In November 1833 the Staffordshire Colliers met to form themselves into a 'Political and Commercial Union' and resolved to collect subscriptions to establish 'a Colliers' Fund for the purchasing, renting and working of Pits on their own account'.[240] The idea of self-employment of members was in itself very traditional. In the past trade societies had frequently set up their own workshop as a strike tactic or to aid blacklisted members. However, in this instance, the unions appear to have envisaged a lasting entity, which would give regular employment to some members, and consequently also improve the bargaining position of the remainder.

When Robert Owen met various local working-class representatives in Huddersfield on 1 November 1833, the first resolution of the meeting significantly listed 'Commercial Orders' alongside Trades' Unions, Co-operative Societies and Benefit Societies as 'associations for the improvement of the working classes'.[241] Apart from the influence of co-operators and co-operative ideas (of whose effect there is no direct evidence), the crucial factor in the emergence of commercial orders in 1833 was the autumnal counter-attack of the woollen master manufacturers on the West Riding trades' unions. As the Leeds Builders' union secretary, James Pontey, recalled in March 1834:

---

238 OC No. 632, J. Marshall to Owen 11 Aug. 1833.
239 *Crisis* 27 Apr., 4 May 1833; OC No. 632, J. Marshall to Owen 11 Aug. 1833.
240 TNA: HO 40/31 f. 110, Placard for a meeting of Staffordshire Colliers.
241 OC No. 620, Resolutions of the Huddersfield Meeting, 1 Nov. 1833.

Ever since the 2000 horsepower [master manufacturers'] Union was attempted to be formed [Oct. 1833], the Union saw the necessity of a general union, and of taking their affairs into their own hands, since then they have opened several lodges, under the title of the 'Commercial Orders', the object being to raise a capital, and commence for themselves.[242]

Unlike their temporary forerunners, commercial orders were not restricted to the confines of a particular strike or lock-out. So when the masters' attack on the unionists reached a stalemate and was called off, in mid-October, the commercial orders continued and flourished. An editorial in the *Voice* of 22 February 1834, on Derby and the need for self-employment, mentioned an example from Huddersfield:

In this age of 'Unions' there is one formed for this express purpose; and we have the pleasure of knowing, that the members of one section of it are nearly all clothed with goods of their own manufacture – that many of the members are kept constantly employed – that in less than one week they have cut up and sold upwards of £30 worth of woollen cloth: and we have the additional pleasure of knowing that every day adds to the numbers of these 'Commercial Orders' – that their organisations are proceeding with great rapidity in many of the principal towns in the West-Riding.[243]

This was certainly the case at Leeds where Pontey reported around the same time that the 'Commercial Orders' 'are all in a very flourishing state and expect soon to have some union-cloth to send out to our friends'.[244] Whilst in Huddersfield, the *Voice* reported that Lodge No.1. of the commercial order had appointed two representatives to consult the Masons' Union on the possibility of building a Trades' Guild Hall.[245]

The optimism of these two sources, however, should not induce an exaggerated impression of the overall importance or longevity of commercial orders. The adoption of co-operative practice (albeit itself derived from traditional strike tactics) by the trades' unions was of great symbolic significance. It illustrated the convergence in ideas and praxis of these two forms of working-class 'union' at a time of great uncertainty. Furthermore, it showed that the trade unions were now willing to put a foot, tentatively, outside the existing system, in order to combat the perennial problems of fluctuating wages and employment.

Yet the system of commercial orders can only have been small-scale and incomplete. A sympathetic Huddersfield shopkeeper, writing to the *Leeds Times* in the middle of the regional anti-union lock-out in May 1834, related that 'the men of Huddersfield are forming themselves into a society for the express purpose of manufacturing on their own account', and advised the Leeds strikers (and indeed the

---

242 *Pioneer* 1 Mar. 1834.
243 *VWR* 22 Feb. 1834.
244 *Pioneer* 1 Mar. 1834.
245 *VWR* 1 Mar. 1834.

whole working class) to do likewise.[246] The union leaders at Leeds had similar ideas and called a trades' delegate meeting on 29 May. This decided to invoke traditional trade union practice to meet the exigencies of the crisis: the employment of turn-outs 'by appropriating the surplus funds of unions, and by endeavouring to obtain the application of the idle money of the different societies.'[247]

This may have achieved temporary relief for some of the workers but it is doubtful whether anything of permanence came out of it. Two weeks later we find one of the unionists urging the men to vote for money to be taken out of their sick funds and put into a fund for 'establishing manufactories of their own'.[248] As the contest came to its bitter, humiliating end in the second week of June, self-employment remained the one ray of hope for the future. A West Riding meeting 'of Delegates from the different Manufacturing Districts Connected with the Trades' Unions' (at Mirfield Moor) on 23 June recommended the committee at Leeds 'to open Co-operative Lodges' to raise funds to employ victimised and unemployed union members, and eventually all members. The *Leeds Times* believed that 'available funds were already at the service of the Union, and that two establishments have been obtained to carry the resolution into effect'.[249] It is possible that one survived until 1836.[250] However, it is likely that the hopes invested in commercial orders and other self-employing enterprises largely floundered in the famine of funds following upon the fall of the trades' unionism in the West Riding.

7: Owen and the 'Grand National Moral Union'

The Huddersfield Congress of April 1833 brought Owen and J. R. Turner into direct contact with a powerful trade union body – and they were undoubtedly impressed.[251] G. D. H. Cole believed that the 'germ of the idea of the Grand National Union' was possibly 'engendered' in Owen's mind on this occasion.[252] However, it must be remembered that Owen had already been in contact with trade union delegates; and also that the plan for a 'National Association of the United Trades of Great Britain and Ireland', which envisaged a 'Union of Trade, Benefit and Co-operative Societies, and of Societies of depositors' establishing branches of the National Exchange Bazaar in every town, antedated the congress.[253] It seems more likely that the atmosphere at the Huddersfield Congress (with the discussion of labour exchange and direct contact with union leaders) rubbed off on Owen and helped to mature further some already-present ideas.

Perhaps because of the perceived isolation of the venue, there appears to have been little follow-up in London to the ideas and hopes of the Huddersfield Congress.

---

246 *LT* 24 May 1834.

247 *LT* 31 May 1834.

248 *LT* 14 June 1834.

249 *LT* 21, 28 June 1834.

250 *LI* 11 June 1836.

251 See *Crisis* 27 Apr. 1833, J. R. Turner's report to U.T.A.

252 G. D. H. Cole, *Attempts at General Union, 1818-1834* (London: Macmillan, 1953), p. 94.

253 For example, *Crisis* 6 Apr. 1833, report of a 'most satisfactory conference with the delegates of the Trade Unions'; *Crisis* 20 Apr. 1833, proposals dated 30 Mar. 1833.

Owen, for his part, continued to lecture weekly, tour occasionally, and gradually formulate his plans. By mid-summer these were beginning to take the shape of 'A united body, a moral union, a national moral union of the productive classes'.[254] He further expanded this theme in his weekly Sunday lecture prior to the special Co-operative and Trades' Union Congress, held in London during early October 1833. He outlined the great, bloodless, transformation which would come like, 'a thief in the night'. His plans were a logical extension of the ideas on co-operative production and exchange which had been aired so forcibly and frequently six months previously at the Huddersfield Congress. The old corrupt competitive world was to be transformed into the new moral world by means of 'National Companies', which would, by 'simplification and combination', take over all manufacturing.

> All trades shall first form associations of lodges, to consist of a convenient number for carrying on the business; these lodges shall be called parochial lodges; all individuals of the specific craft shall become members, and these shall include all producers of wealth, or whatever contributes to knowledge or happiness. These parochial lodges, shall meet weekly, they shall also select delegates to form county lodges to meet monthly, and these again shall select delegates to form provincial lodges amounting to perhaps ten in number for Great Britain. They shall superintend the trade of the provinces, and send delegates to the grand national congress, which shall probably, meet in London.[255]

Owen summarised the existing situation, on the third day of 'the General Congress of Delegates': 'A number of trades are already united in lodges, but by far the greater number are divided, and those who are united are only individually so'. Although some trades were linked vertically on a national basis, there were few horizontal inter-trade links. He wanted 'another line of lodges, which shall take charge of the whole general interest of all of the working-classes'. In order to achieve this 'new line' Owen envisaged a very broad amalgamation and rationalisation of existing working-class institutions, especially co-operative societies and trades' unions, into 'national companies or associations' which would take over the manufacturing of the country.

It was a grandiose scheme of singularly Owenian dimensions; a fact which immediately worried some of the Congress's members. The Birmingham delegate, for example, feared that the 'new Unions' would supersede the labour exchange; an objection which Owen quashed in true style, declaring that in comparison with this present scheme labour exchange was 'a mere drop in the bucket'. Thomas Simpson, the representative of the Potters' Union, stated categorically 'that any plan which would have a tendency to destroy the present Unions would be decidedly opposed by the society to which he belonged', though he added that 'they could have no objection to one which would draw them in, by forming a junction with them'.[256] Owen's rational truths were not always so self-evident to working-class leaders and organisers,

---

254 *Crisis* 15 June 1833.
255 *Crisis* 12 Oct. 1833.
256 *Crisis* 19 Oct. 1833.

who often showed a natural parental reluctance to kill off the offspring they had nurtured.

This may also have applied to co-operators and trade unionists in the West Riding. It is doubtful whether the London Congress itself, a small and hastily convened affair, had any immediate impact on the region. The post-Hirst Huddersfield society was only able to send a letter; Thomas Wilson did not attend, nor seemingly did any delegate from Halifax or Yorkshire as a whole.[257] The patchily representative nature of the congress may partly explain why Owen felt the need to follow the unveiling of his plans with an extensive tour of the Midlands, Potteries, Lancashire and Yorkshire – the key industrial areas of the country. He announced the tour on the penultimate day of congress, stating its purpose, in typically patrician terms, to be the formation of a 'provisional council of gentlemen in different parts of the country, for the purpose of effecting the great object of National Union'.[258]

Little is known of Owen's progress in the early part of the tour because his first letters from the provinces apparently never reached the *Crisis* office in London. Fortunately, by the time he reached Yorkshire in late October his epistles were getting through. He arrived in Huddersfield on Sunday 27 October and pronounced it 'in many respects the centre of the operations of the working men in this country'. He remained there six days, 'holding meetings with the Trades' Unions, Co-operative Societies and Commercial Orders, into which divisions and societies the productive operatives are now formed'. He saw his main object as being 'to unite all these into one common interest for their common benefit, that their strength might not be frittered away by these separate interests and sub-divisions'.[259]

It is difficult to assess exactly how far he succeeded. Certainly a special meeting of 'delegates and others from the various societies and trades' unions in the neighbourhood of Huddersfield', which he chaired on 1 November, passed an important resolution recommending 'all Trades' Unions, Co-operative Societies, Commercial Orders, Benefit Societies, and all other associations intended for the improvement of the working-classes, to form themselves into Lodges, make their own laws and regulations to unite under the 'Grand National Moral Union of the Productive and Useful Classes', as proposed by the Congress held in London at the National Equitable Labour Exchange from the 7th to the 14th August 1833'. Yet this 'recommendation' in all probability applied only to local societies. With reference to the wider area of the West Riding, and its powerful union bodies, a further resolution merely recommended 'delegates of the Unions meeting in Leeds to take into consideration the Grand National Moral Union'.[260]

---

257 Ibid. The contents of the Huddersfield letter are not known. Holyoake, in a paragraph originally concerned with 1833, mentions that 'a letter was sent to the 'consolidated meeting' in London, asking whether this Huddersfield Society could be admitted as a lodge'. [*CN* 16 Jan. 1892]. It is possible that this was the letter that was read to Congress. However, it seems more probable that such a letter would have been sent in 1834.

258 *Crisis* 19 Oct. 1833.

259 *Crisis* 23, 30 Nov. 1833.

260 OC No. 620, Resolutions of the Huddersfield Meeting, 1 Nov. 1833, The date of the congress is wrongly given as August, instead of October.

Significantly, it was to Leeds that Owen travelled from Huddersfield. There he 'communicated with the Trades' Union officers' and 'arranged matters for future proceedings'; but apparently little else. He soon moved on to Halifax where he introduced his plans to the 'leading men amongst the working-classes'. According to Owen these made 'a very favourable impression', but no evidence survives to record if anything of substance was achieved. The following day he returned to Huddersfield and held another meeting 'to forward the measure proposed the preceding week, and to enlist in our cause some leading men who had taken part in promoting the Ten Hours Bill'. He later returned to Leeds, but there is no evidence that he won anything more than rhetorical endorsement for his grand scheme when he met Simeon Pollard, secretary of the powerful Leeds Trades' Union, and 400 delegates in mid-November.[261]

Throughout this tour, the stress was on personal contacts, not only amongst the most influential of the local leaders of the working-class but also with the master manufacturers, whom Owen visited in all these places and sought to convert to his plan for national redemption.[262] The latter category included John Fielden of Todmorden, to whose house Owen travelled from Huddersfield. Here the two men began the series of discussions on measures to improve the condition of working-people, which engendered the idea of the National Regeneration Society with ambitious plan for a universal eight-hour working day.[263]

Hereafter the story of Owen's northern tour becomes more convoluted, with the Grand National Moral Union (GNMU) and the Eight Hours scheme vying for his attention. Owen in his usual fashion had little difficulty in reconciling them both. They readily dovetailed into his grand plan to usher in the new moral world.[264] The GNMU would be strengthened by the affiliation and incorporation of a new 'line' of Regeneration Societies, whilst the demand for an eight-hour day would reciprocally gain strength by having the weight of the GNMU behind it. If in the latter part of his tour Owen's new enthusiasm for eight hours tended to overshadow his advocacy of the Moral Union, he nevertheless considered the 'foundation' of the latter scheme 'well laid in Yorkshire and Lancashire'.[265] On returning to London in early December he reported enthusiastically that he had made more progress in the six weeks of his northern tour than in the previous two years: 'I have had a great deal of intercourse with, and have acquired a great deal of experience amongst, the working-men, and know their condition in all parts of the country'.[266]

The GNMU is perhaps the most elusive of all the working-class organisations which emerged in the bountiful period of 1829-34. This may well be because it was primarily a figment of Owen's imagination. Historians are divided about its material

---

261 *Crisis* 7 Dec. 1833.

262 *Crisis* 23 Nov. 1833.

263 Ibid.

264 *Crisis* 7 Dec 1833, for example, an extract from the 'Catechism of the Regenerating Society': 'Q. Suppose a union of all industrious classes be accomplished what should be its first measure? A. They should fix a minimum time [eight hours] and a minimum remuneration for their daily labour'.

265 *Crisis* 30 Nov, 7 Dec. 1833. See also, OC letters, Nos. 600, 603, 607, 610, 664, 668.

266 *Crisis* 7 Dec. 1833.

existence and the extent to which it foreshadowed, melded into, or coexisted with the GNCTU.[267]

In spite of the weight of evidence that Owen's initial plans for a national organisation of the working-classes never attracted more than a series of good intentions, the suspicion still remains that, in the months following the London Congress, they amounted to more than this. For example, a resolution passed at a 'General Meeting of Operatives at Derby' on 2 January 1834 that 'the Delegates here present from Yorkshire, Birmingham and Nottingham, do take immediate steps to consolidate the different branches into a division of the Grand National Union'.[268] If any functioning collective organisation was to have evolved at this time, it is likely to have emerged from the practicalities of receiving and distributing aid to centres, like Derby, which were bearing the brunt of the concerted assault on trades' unions in the latter part of 1833.

Whatever its possible shape or structure, the 'Grand National Moral Union' left few traces. It may have just comprised an agreed centre for communications, a model set of rules and procedures, or an informal network of sympathisers like 'the provisional council of gentlemen in different parts of the country' which Owen envisaged at the end of the London Congress.[269] Certainly during the subsequent six-week tour, Owen built up a loose network of personal contacts among influential trade union, co-operative and short time leaders in the north and midlands.[270] Many of these were undoubtedly sympathetic to ideas of labour exchange and national union, and by winning their adherence to his cause, Owen could in a limited sense be said to have established the skeleton of a national organisation. Yet it was only a loose framework, which did not touch the rank and file. As Owen himself admitted after returning from the north, 'We did not communicate with the Trades Unions as Unions; but we communicated with the leaders, and recommended them to communicate to the members'.[271] So, while the representatives of the trades' unions, commercial orders, co-operative societies and benefit societies who met Owen in Huddersfield in early November 1833, may have afterwards considered their associations as constituents of the GNMU, it is likely that they had some difficulty in convincing their members of this fact.

What is evident, nonetheless, is that operatives in the woollen textile district were strongly supportive of the struggles in the East Midlands and their trades' unions were heavily involved in the general union developments which culminated in the GNCTU.[272] In the maelstrom of early 1834 organisational labels and affiliations were

---

267 Cole, *Attempts*, pp. 90-5; W. H. Oliver, 'Organisations and Ideas behind the efforts to achieve a General Union of the Working Classes in England in the early 1830s', Unpub. Oxford D.Phil Thesis, 1954, p. 149. For more recent discussions, see Chase, *Early Trade Unionism*, pp. 122-7; John Sanders, 'John Douthwaite and "John Powlett": Trades Unionism and Conflict in Early 1830s Yorkshire', *Labour History Review*, 87 (2022), pp. 21-2.

268 *Pioneer* 25 Jan. 1834.

269 *Pioneer* 11 Jan. 1834; *Crisis* 19 Oct. 1833.

270 OC No. 600 contains a letter of introduction (for Owen), from Lawrence Pitkethly to John Clarke in Barnsley. Also, *Crisis* 23, 30 Nov, 7 Dec. 1833.

271 *Crisis* 14 Dec. 1833.

272 Sanders, 'John Douthwaite and "John Powlett"', pp. 13-15, 27-9. See also above, pp. 106-10.

readily interchangeable and, in this context, the GNMU can be said to have existed on an abstract level – as a name to which various working-class unions felt attached.[273] This sense of identity was strongest in the areas of Owen's greatest influence and prestige – London, the co-operative societies, and the areas where he toured in the early winter of 1833. In these places the Grand National Moral Union had most reality. And here also the idea survived longest. A precis of Thomas Wilson's advertisement for the Sixth Co-operative Congress at Barnsley, addressed primarily to 'Co-operative Societies', but also inviting 'Trades' Unions', 'Regeneration Societies' and the 'London and Birmingham Labour Exchanges', appeared in the *Crisis* of 22 March, a week after the original insertion.[274] Significantly (and perhaps on Owen's editorial instructions) the title of the Congress was now given as, 'The Congress of the Grand National Moral Union of the Working Classes'.[275] So, despite the advent of the GNCTU, it is clear that, as late as March 1834, Owen and some of his adherents still believed in the concept of an all-embracing GNMU.

It is likely that most co-operative members in their small local societies allowed these fine distinctions of nomenclature to pass them by; and in the main centres, core business remained a priority. An advert in the *Voice* in February 1834 promoted the variety of goods now available to 'the Poor Man's Family' at the Huddersfield co-operative store: groceries, drapery, hosiery, cutlery, hats, shoes, best Sheffield Tobacco and various sorts of snuff, all 'as good, and at prices equally low, as any other shop in the Town'.[276] An account of the Huddersfield society's Annual General Meeting the previous month paints the picture of a flourishing society which had 'weathered the storm'. Labour exchange remained an active option: the *Voice* reporting that the society had 'opened a communication with the Birmingham Exchange Bazaar, and that they have articles of various descriptions, which they have received in exchange for cloth of their own manufacturing'.[277] As Malcolm Chase suggests, such persistence in the face of obvious difficulties may have been due to the fact that the 'idea was important for what it symbolized, as much as it managed to achieve in practical terms. It held out the prospect that the labour movement might step outside of the capitalized industrial system'.[278]

The transformative appeal of the GNCTU, as well as residual loyalty to Owen, may have influenced the society's decision to send a letter to the 'consolidated meeting' in London, asking whether they could be admitted as a lodge.[279] Unfortunately, Holyoake does not mention the date of this letter, so we can only surmise that the 'consolidated meeting' referred to was either the extraordinary Trades' Union Congress of February 1834, or, possibly, the Executive Council of the GNCTU. Such a request is not surprising considering the process of convergence between co-operative societies and trade unions which gained momentum during

---

273 For example, *Crisis* 9 Nov. 1833 contained letter from James Tucker. Also OC No. 620.
274 The original notice, signed by Thomas Wilson 'on behalf of the Barnsley District' appeared in *Crisis* 15 Mar. 1834.
275 *Crisis* 22 Mar. 1834.
276 *VWR* 8 Feb. 1834.
277 *VWR* 4 Jan. 1834.
278 Chase, *Early Trade Unionism*, p. 127.
279 *CN* 16 Jan. 1892.

1833 and the early part of 1834. It may well have been occasioned by the recommendation of the Barnsley Congress (31 March to early April 1834) urging all co-operators to join the Consolidated Union.[280]

The degree to which West Riding co-operators were caught up in the events of early summer 1834, when 'the all engrossing subject of the day appears to be UNION' is unclear.[281] Well known co-operative leaders and sympathisers mounted the public platform in Huddersfield and elsewhere to attack the harsh sentences passed on the Dorchester labourers.[282] However, when the final assault on local trade unions materialised in late May, a Huddersfield 'observer' drew a lesson from the co-operative experience to bemoan the lack of working-class solidarity. Referring to the 'people's own shop', he complained of wives of trade unionists buying at the shops of their oppressors: 'and these same wives will not go to the co-operative shop, or a friends', it is too 'vulgar, ungenteel and unostentatious', 'it is homely, such as they see every day – too like themselves in manners'. He urged them, 'Get you husbands to enter co-operative societies, or commercial orders, and spend your money at them now'. The profits will enable them to start their own factories and secure an independence from masters and shopkeepers. He concluded, 'Political equality and co-operation are the panaceas', a recipe revisited in the early 1840s after another episode of defeat and despair.[283]

8: Postscript: Huddersfield, 1834 and Beyond

Despite the circumstantial evidence of the Halifax society's struggles beyond the mid-1830s and the possibility that the Bradford Co-operative Society No1's glee-singing at its fifth anniversary celebrations in May 1834 was its swansong, other societies appear to have survived the general associational carnage of the period, possibly by focussing on core business.[284] The 100 member-strong Clayton society, near Bradford, for example, held a tea-party in March 1835 to mark the opening of a new shop, which aimed to 'purchase and retail to the members and neighbourhood nearly all the necessities of life' and thereby benefit 'the industrious poor'.[285] Meanwhile in the Huddersfield area new societies were formed in Skelmanthorpe (1834), Kirkheaton (1835), Hopton and Carr Green (1836) and Clayton West (1838).[286]

The Huddersfield society itself does not appear to have been unduly affected by the defeat of West Riding trades' unions, and the general collapse of working-class

---

280 *Crisis* 12 Apr. 1834.

281 *VWR* 24 May 1834.

282 *VWR* 12 Apr. 1834. Hobson, who regularly urged co-operation and exclusive dealing during 1834 chaired the Huddersfield gathering. Other sympathetic speakers included (David?) Green, J. F. Bray, Thomas Cliffe, and Lawrence Pitkethly. Thomas Wilson chaired the Dorchester meeting at Halifax.

283 *VWR* 24 May 1834; Thornes, 'Origins', p. 184.

284 See above, p. 204; *VWR* 24 May 1834.

285 *LT* 7 Mar. 1835. The paper opined 'that (unconnected with unions for strikes) these institutions when properly managed will prove invaluable'.

286 Thornes, 'Origins', pp. 180-2. It is not clear whether the Kirkheaton society was connected to the earlier venture.

organisations in the summer of 1834.[287] At a general meeting on 12 August 1834, for example, the committee recommended the purchase of two rooms and a jenny, and for the society 'to employ others as soon as opportunity offered'.[288] According to J. N. Reid two months later, 'at the present time they were doing well and had £2,400 worth of stock in the shop'.[289]

The 'Huddersfield Co-operative Trading Association', shared in the general trading prosperity of the following two years. Total (that is, accumulated) profits by 1 October 1835 came to £1,450. By October of the following year, £725 had been added to total profits and the society was in a position to start repaying the loan contracted with Lady Byron over five years earlier. In the same year 'the society attained to the dignity of buying a horse and cart, to vend goods in the country' – possibly the first ever co-operative mobile shop. Its expansion took other directions. One James Wimpenny was employed as permanent manufacturer to the society at 25s per week, plus a suit of cloth of his own choosing every year. In addition, the Society resolved to lodge £500 of its funds in a money club at the White Hart Inn 'for the benefit of its business'. Between October 1836 and October 1837 the society managed to add nearly £250 to total profits, as well as repaying a further £136 to Lady Byron, whilst the following year the annual accretion was £500 and total profits nearly £3,000.[290]

When the Huddersfield society took advantage of changes in friendly society legislation to become 'The Huddersfield Co-operative Trading Friendly Society' in 1838, other local societies followed suit. A few of the neighbouring certified societies like Skelmanthorpe, Hopton and Clayton West, remained committed to Huddersfield's stated ideals of co-operative manufacturing and of renting or purchasing land to establish a co-operative community: 'to arrange the powers of production, distribution, consumption and education in order to produce among members feelings of pure charity, and social affection for each other, and practically plant the standard of peace and good will on earth to all men'.[291] Others, like Paddock and Kirkheaton, pragmatically limited their ambitions to low priced food and clothing. Interestingly, as Thornes has shown, a few of these small pioneering societies in the Huddersfield area paid dividends, anticipating an innovation associated with Rochdale by more than a decade.[292] Huddersfield's success consolidated its position at the forefront of local co-operation. Its 'Co-operative Stores' (No. 10 Westgate) served as the natural meeting place for 'Delegates from the Different Co-operative Societies' in the district (or possibly region) in May 1839.[293]

---

287 The Underbank Co-operative Society at Holmfirth appears to have been equally unaffected. fifty members dined at the Masons Arms, *LT* 12 July 1834

288 *CN* 16 Jan. 1892. 'Rooms' is probably a mistake for 'looms'. Thornes, 'Change and Continuity', p. 39 wrongly attributes this purchase to Halifax.

289 *LT* 1 Nov. 1834.

290 *CN* 16 Jan. 1892.

291 Thornes, 'Origins', pp. 180-2; *Rules of the Huddersfield Co-operative Trading Friendly Society* (Huddersfield, 1838) p. 6, quoted in Thornes, 'Origins' p. 181.

292 Thornes, 'Origins' p. 182.

293 *NS* 11 May 1839.

The notice of this meeting and other coverage in the *Northern Star* indicates that Huddersfield co-operation continued to be a source of inspiration and funds during the early Chartist years. As well as using financial services based at the White Hart Inn, the main local radical and trade union meeting place, the society availed itself of the facilities of the town's Socialists' large room for its annual 'Co-operative Festival' on New Year's Day 1838, featuring tea, music, lemonade, brandy-snap, raisins, singing and speeches. In addition to declarations of the merits of co-operation, participants passed an eclectic range of resolutions toasting the virtues of Robert Owen, Richard Oastler, John Fielden, Feargus O'Connor and J. S. Buckingham, and celebrating the full range of popular aspirations, from press freedom and radicalism to temperance and ten hours.[294] Ten months later the Huddersfield Northern Union branch acknowledged the society's generosity in defraying some of the costs of the giant West Riding Chartist meeting at Peep Green. George Barker, a speaker at the rally and founding member of the NU, was one of a number of leaders who spanned both organisations.[295]

As Barker recollected in 1841, 'when we commenced we had but one store, now we have three, and have been manufacturing woollen cloth for six years'. Such hard-earned success, though, was hard to replicate. It sometimes bred frustration that every other group of two hundred 'working men' had not done the same, or that the working-classes were 'more willing to trade with other people than among themselves'. Another local leader, Joseph Bray, commented in 1841, that had they embraced co-operation fully, 'the Charter would be the law of the land before this'.[296] The following year, according to Thornes' conservative estimate, at least thirty-one West Yorkshire co-operative societies were legally registered as friendly societies; and he further calculates that 'there may have been at least sixty societies in West Yorkshire by 1842, thirty-two of them in the Huddersfield area'.[297]

At this date the Huddersfield society had a large grocery store that, in G. A. Fleming's words, produced 'profits which are periodically divided, also employment in various kinds of manufactured goods is given to the members of the society, which are afterwards sold and the profits added to the common stock'. Fleming, a leading socialist, however, further noted in 1842 that, '[The Owenite Rational Society] seems originally to have been established on the ruins of the Co-operative Societies, which were so rife in this country from 1829-34 ... we believe that there are still a few of them in existence, but with the exception of one at Huddersfield, their condition is anything but satisfactory'.[298] Fleming may have erred on his estimate of the number of local societies, but was probably correct in his assessment of their general health. The 'flood' of Chartist co-ops, as Thornes noted in 1839-40, slowed to a 'trickle' as the decade, progressed. With Chartist efforts and resources focused first on the revival of political campaigning in 1841-2 and then on the 'Land Plan', expansion faltered. John

---

294 *NS* 6 Jan. 1838. James Silk Buckingham, journalist, social reformer and temperance advocate, had served as MP for Sheffield between 1832 and 1836.

295 *NS* 5 Jan. 1839; Thornes, 'Origins', pp. 183-4.

296 *NS* 16 Jan. 1841, quoted in Thornes, 'Origins', p. 184.

297 Thornes, 'Origins', p. 184.

298 Ibid., p. 180.

Butler calculates that only five societies were established in Yorkshire between 1844 and 1849 and it is likely that many of the smaller societies (often comprising no more than a single store) ceased operations.[299]

According to Thornes, the main Huddersfield society was one or three or four societies still operating in the town in 1851, with a further seven in the surrounding area. It survived until at least 1853.[300] This longevity, and the corroborating evidence of M. Purvis's survey of co-operative activity in the 1835-50 period, adds weight to Thornes' argument that 'the decade 1834-44, far from being one of virtual inactivity, was a period in which co-operation became more deeply entrenched as a strategy of the labour movement, and one in which the organizational form of retail co-operative later characterized as the Rochdale model became firmly established.'[301] Whatever the precise chronology of the demise of the original society, it is clear that when the 'modern' Huddersfield Industrial Society was formed in 1860, there lay behind it a wealth of co-operative experience and tradition in the town and surrounding region.

9: Conclusion

The story of early co-operation in the West Riding woollen textile district does not fit easily into the grand narratives of labour history. Nor does it readily slot into accounts of the growth of liberal consumerism. Instead, rather like the perception attributed to trade unionists' wives quoted earlier, its preoccupations may have been judged too 'unostentatious', 'homely' and everyday to merit sustained historiographical attention following the pioneering studies of E. P. Thompson and J. F. C. Harrison. Bulk-buying and dividends, tea-parties and glee-singing may lack the vicarious frisson of machine-breaking or drilling on the moors. Whatever the reason, the importance, ambition, and resilience of the societies that prospered and survived in a number of towns and outlying villages of the region deserve to be more widely acknowledged.

Some were located in fairly isolated communities and limited their aspirations to the provision of cheap, unadulterated food. Others, however, sought to scale all rungs of the co-operative ladder from retailing to community and adopted a range of innovative practices to attain these ends. In contrast to popular radicalism, where the periphery at times led the centre, co-operative societies in the main town centres were generally pre-eminent in size, influence, and ambition. In Thomas Hirst and Thomas Wilson, Huddersfield and Halifax produced leaders of regional and, in Hirst's case, national standing. But the societies also relied on the work of countless other diligent officers and staunch advocates to underwrite their activities.

The societies' leadership cadre did not just identify the debilitating impact of distress on their communities, they proposed practical and radical solutions to the economic dislocation it caused. Their efforts provide a case study in working-class agency. The resulting organisational template did not fit everyone. Relatively high

---

299 Thornes, 'Change and Continuity', p. 48 (on the Chartist land plan, see Chase, *Chartism*, p. 247 ff.); John H. Butler, 'The Origins and Development of Retail Co-operative Movement in Yorkshire during the Nineteenth Century', Unpub. PhD thesis, University of York 1986, p. 169.

300 Thornes, 'Origins', p. 185.

301 Purvis, 'Co-operative Retailing'; Thornes, 'Change and Continuity', p. 49.

subscriptions, stringent vetting procedures and strictures on access to credit excluded some from the orbit of the nascent societies. Equally their focus on sobriety and respectability, sometimes expressed in tones of resigned disappointment, may have put off other potential members. Ultra-radical contemporaries on occasions were certainly frustrated by some co-operators' gradualism, high-mindedness and even-handedness; but they increasingly admired their doggedness and their practical achievements. The co-operative organisations created during this period were strongly embedded in their localities and generally reflected their political affiliations and mutualist proclivities of their host communities, hence their connections with radicalism, trades' unionism and friendly societies.

As Robin Thornes shows, the associational forms these leaders constructed were many and varied. They also spanned two worlds. On the one hand, they built on traditions of artisanal independence and solidarity, and harked back to earlier food boycotts, anti-truck campaigns and concerns about food adulteration. These aimed to create a social economy to replace the existing political one and thereby 'recuperate some of the characteristics of an older, moral economy'.[302] On the other, their co-operative stores posed a direct challenge to the dominant mode of consumption and to the 'shopocracy'. They also opened a second front for exclusive dealing and pioneered mechanisms for the distribution of profits that prefigured developments later in the century. Equally, they effectively channelled contemporary ideas of the value of labour to create structures for co-operative production and exchange that consciously challenged the competitive industrial system and anticipated syndicalism. Together, co-operative retailing and production embodied coherent critiques of capitalism and the role of labour that were to influence later iterations of co-operation.

At the same time, these societies also reflected their nonconformist environs in their studied respectability, their educational aspirations and their proselytising fervour. Yet, for all that, a veneer of hard-headed realism informed their day-to-day activities and some of their pronouncements, they also displayed a strong convivial streak, and often adopted innovative and entrepreneurial approaches to achieve their mission. They were infused with idealism as much as pragmatism. In addition to shops providing 'all kinds of goods necessary for the people, and at reasonable prices', they also had grander, loftier aims. Commenting on the futility of masters' attempts 'to shackle ... the working-classes' through the introduction of 'the document' in autumn 1833, the *Voice* asserted that instead co-operation and political education were about to emancipate 'the producers of wealth' and 'conduct us into the "new age"'.[303]

This belief in social transformation was an important area of commonality that they shared with Robert Owen; and, for a brief period, Owen exerted a strong influence on West Riding co-operation. However, his role should not be exaggerated. He came onto the scene fairly late. Other co-operative theorists and advocates were more important in kick-starting the early growth of societies; and his anti-religious sentiments remained a constant barrier to the full acceptance of his views and his primacy in the movement. Consequently, early co-operation in the West Riding, like

---

302 Stephen Yeo, 'Introductory: Rival Clusters of Potential: Ways of Seeing Co-operation', in S. Yeo (ed.) *New Views of Co-operation*, p. 4.
303 *VWR* 12 Oct.; 28 Sept. 1833.

the wider associational culture, can perhaps be more accurately described as Owen-lite rather than Owenite.[304]

Whatever their precise ideological classification, the early co-operative societies were certainly an important element within the heady brew of ideas, agitations and organisations that bubbled up during the reform era. They deserve to be set alongside other contemporary and sometimes overlapping working-class endeavours; whether the forging of intra- and inter-trade alliances, the challenging of local elites' domination of political spaces, the building of an independent press, or the fight to reduce the long working hours of factory children.

---

304 Chase, *Early Trade Unionism*, pp. 124-6.

5

The Early Factory Movement, 1830-4

At first sight, the West Riding factory reform movement would appear to require little further investigation. Cecil Driver's excellent life of Richard Oastler and J. T. Ward's exhaustive history, both incorporating detailed consideration of the woollen textile district, seem to have had the subject boxed off two generations ago.[1] More recent studies have explored the mainsprings of Oastler's ideology and his radical connections; or have sought to locate his role and the broader campaign against child labour within the context of the anti-slavery movement and the shifting religious and political affiliations of the era.[2]

Another important strand of research has examined the rhetoric, languages and broader cultural dimensions of the factory agitation and their links to the wider political and social landscape. In particular Robert Gray's 1996 study of the 'factory question' brings out the different layers of activity engaged in by the key constituencies and the subtle distinctions between textile towns and between the Lancashire and the West Riding experiences. In particular he investigates the various voices that strained to be heard and the discourses about the nature of industrial transformation that they articulated. What emerges is a complex history, but one which significantly locates factory reform as an important 'episode in the making of

---

1   Cecil Driver, *Tory Radical, The Life of Richard Oastler* (New York: Oxford University Press, 1946); J. T. Ward, *The Factory Movement, 1830-1855* (London: Macmillan, 1962).

2   Matthew Roberts, 'Richard Oastler, Toryism, Radicalism and the limitations of Party, c.1807-1846', *Parliamentary History*, 37 (2018), pp. 250-73; Stewart A. Weaver, 'Richard Oastler', *Oxford Dictionary of National Biography*, (Oxford: Oxford University Press, 2004); Felix Driver, 'Tory Radicalism? Ideology, Strategy and Locality in Popular Politics during the Eighteen-Thirties', *Northern History*, 27 (1991), pp. 120-38; John A. Hargreaves and E. A. Hilary Haigh (eds.), *Slavery in Yorkshire: Richard Oastler and the Campaign against Child Labour in the Industrial Revolution* (Huddersfield: Huddersfield University Press, 2012).

the working class' albeit one displaying a gendered class-consciousness. What Gray calls the 'discourse of patriarchal protection' brought together ideals of fair employment, defence of the family economy and radical claims to citizenship. Gray's emphasis on the workers' defence of the family economy has been taken up by historians of domestic practices and relations of intimacy, notably Colin Creighton's accounts of how the 'Ten Hours Movement' embodied operatives' attempts to confront the material and emotional pressures on the family and prefigured twentieth century discourses on children's rights.[3]

The factory movement also features, though not as a leading theme, in diverse accounts of class relations in Bradford, the emergence of popular conservatism and the growth of child labour.[4] Many of these studies draw extensively on evidence from the West Riding. Indeed, earlier accounts of the movement in Lancashire complained, perhaps justifiably, about the 'Tyke-centricity' of much of the existing literature. In particular, they noted the overemphasis on Yorkshire's Tory-radical leadership and the playing down of pre-1830 activities in Lancashire.[5]

The time has perhaps also arrived for a re-assessment of the West Riding evidence; to both take on board the import of new approaches and to challenge the enduring legacies of the interpretations implicit in J. T. Ward's formidably thorough narrative accounts.[6] Matthew Roberts, for example, notes the persistence of myths relating to

3 S. A. Weaver, 'The Political Ideology of Short-Time', in G. Cross (ed.), *Worktime and Industrialization: An International History* (Philadelphia: Temple University Press, 1988), pp. 77-103; Robert Gray, 'The Languages of Factory Reform in Britain, c. 1830–1860', in P. Joyce (ed.), *The Historical Meanings of Work* (Cambridge: Cambridge University Press, 1987); Robert Gray, *The Factory Question and Industrial England, 1830-1860* (Cambridge: Cambridge University Press, 1996), p. 7; Colin Creighton, 'Collective Action and Domestic Practices: England in the 1830s and 1840s', in Yvette Taylor and Emma Casey (eds.), *Intimacies, Critical Consumption and Diverse Economies* (London: Palgrave Macmillan, 2015), pp. 13-35; Colin Creighton, 'The Ten Hours Movement and the Rights of Childhood', *International Journal of Children's Rights*, 20 (2012), pp. 457-85.

4 Theodore Koditschek, *Class Formation and Urban-Industrial Society: Bradford, 1750-1850* (Cambridge: Cambridge University Press, 1990); Jörg Neuheiser, *Crown, Church and Constitution: Popular Conservatism in England, 1815-1867* ((New York and Oxford: Berghahn, 2016); Peter Kirby, *Child Labour in Britain, 1750-1870* (Basingstoke: Palgrave Macmillan, 2003); Jane Humphries, *Childhood and Child Labour in the British Industrial Revolution* (Cambridge: Cambridge University Press, 2010); Sonya. O. Rose, *Limited Livelihoods: Gender and Class in Nineteenth-Century England* (London: Routledge, 1992), ch. 3

5 R. G. Kirby and A. E. Musson, *The Voice of the People, John Doherty, 1798-1854, Trade Unionist, Radical and Factory Reformer* (Manchester: Manchester University Press, 1975) p. 346 ff. Robert Sykes, 'Popular Politics and Trade Unionism in South East Lancashire, 1829-42', Unpub. PhD thesis, University of Manchester, 1982, p. 425 ff.

6 As well as his standard history of *The Factory Movement* and his summary account, 'The Factory movement', in J. T. Ward (ed.), *Popular Movements, c. 1830-50* (London: Macmillan, 1970), J. T. Ward also published a number of valuable local studies and cameos, notably: 'Bradford and Factory Reform', *Bradford Textile Society Journal*, (1960-1), pp. 41-52; 'Leeds and the Factory Reform Movement', *Publications of the Thoresby Society*, 46 (1961); 'Matthew Balme (1813-1884) Factory Reformer', *Bradford Antiquary*, 40 (1960), pp.217-28; 'Squire Auty', *Bradford Antiquary*, 42 (1964), pp. 104-23; 'Some Industrial Reformers', in *Bradford Textile Society Journal* (1963), pp. 121-36; 'Two Pioneers in Industrial Reform', *Bradford*

the factory movement and Oastler's relationship to his supporters.[7] And just as he seeks to set the record straight in relation to the 'Factory King's' radical credentials, this chapter seeks to recalibrate assessments of the operatives' role in the factory agitation. This not to deny the contributions of humanitarian elites or the existence of cross-class interactions and alliances. Rather this account seeks to reassert the agency of the operatives. It does this through exploring issues of leadership and organisation and the early factory movement's links to wider, working-class endeavours to challenge existing political and economic power structures.

The pre-eminence afforded in the movement's historiography to prominent national and regional figures, such as Oastler, Sadler, Bull, Fielden and Ashley, has not gone without challenge. Gray, for example, has emphasised the importance of working-class radical perspectives in short time campaigns.[8] However, with notable exceptions, like John Halstead's study of the Huddersfield short time committee (STC), even local studies tend to follow J. T. Ward in assigning the role of 'prime movers' to Oastler and his colleagues.[9] 'King Richard's' contribution is justifiably celebrated; and it is understandable that historians, using his papers as a key source, should highlight the special position which Oastler enjoyed within the West Riding factory movement.[10] The Ten Hours Bill became his obsession. A prolific propogandist, he helped to provide the funds, the organisational framework and much of the oratorical fire for the prolonged campaigns. But equally he was the first to acknowledge the pivotal role of the operatives and their 'managing Committees' in the movement's joint endeavours.[11] As E. P. Thompson pointed out many years ago, there are dangers in underestimating 'the part played in the agitation over twenty and more strenuous years, by men such as John Doherty and the workers' own Short-Time Committees'.[12]

It is with such figures and their organisations that this chapter is primarily concerned. Without attempting a detailed narrative of the West Riding experience, it hopes to show that the early ten hours campaigns brought to prominence a number of important local working-class leaders. It provided them with a popular platform, priceless organisational experience and a context within which to develop a broader analysis of political and economic relations. More fundamentally though, the chapter seeks to emphasise that the early West Riding factory movement was a popular

---

Textile Society Journal, (1964).

7   Roberts, 'Richard Oastler', p. 252.

8   For Oastler, see C. Driver, *Tory Radical*; for Sadler, see J. T. Ward, 'M T Sadler', *University of Leeds Review*, 7 (1960); for Bull, see J. C. Gill, *Parson Bull of Byerley* (London: S.P.C.K., 1963); for Fielden, see Stewart A. Weaver, *John Fielden and the Politics of Popular Radicalism, 1832-1847* (Oxford: Clarendon Press, 1987); for Ashley, see G. F. A. Best, *Shaftesbury* (London: New English Library, 1975 edn.).

9   John Halstead 'The Huddersfield Short Time Committee and its radical associations, c.1820-1876', in Hargreaves and Hilary Haigh (eds.), *Slavery in Yorkshire*, pp. 91-144. For example, A. J. Peacock, *Bradford Chartism, 1838-40* (York: St Anthony's Press, 1969); Koditschek, *Class Formation*, ch. 15.

10   *VWR* 22 June 1833, for the monarchical moniker.

11   TNA: HO 40/40, f. 376, Examination of Richard Oastler, 7 Feb. 1839.

12   E. P. Thompson, *The Making of the English Working Class* (Harmondsworth: Penguin, 1968 edn.), p. 384.

working-class cause which had important connections with both local radicalism and trades' unionism. These links will be examined through the local leaders' ideas and activities and through the organisations and communities in which they operated.

After an initial examination of the outlines of the early factory movement in the West Riding, the first section of the chapter looks at the formation, character and key organisational features of the early STCs. The second section examines relationships with popular radicalism, with gentlemen leaders and with Yorkshire toryism. It seeks to explain and put in perspective the Tory and Anglican connections which have traditionally received so much attention. The third section begins by looking at links with Yorkshire trades' unionism and examines some of the common aims, ideas and support which drew both movements together. It emphasises the pervasive influence of factory employment on all sections of the community and argues that support for factory reform was not based only on humanitarian considerations or derived solely from obscurantist opposition to the 'present unnatural, overgrown, overstrained factory system'.[13] As well as being driven by a strong sense of moral outrage, workers inside and outside factories also saw the regulation of children's employment as a legitimate means of seeking to reduce adult hours and ultimately improve the wage-levels and employment prospects of all. The final section examines the more systematic interlocking of what for shorthand purposes might be termed radical, trade union and short time ideas and concerns during the increasingly bitter eighteen months which followed the first reformed elections. It looks in particular at West Riding involvement in the 'Eight Hours Plan' and argues that, though this formed a natural progression and not an aberration for factory reformers, its timing was inappropriate in the West Riding.

1: Introduction

The early West Riding factory movement was never a static or homogenous entity. It therefore requires careful and detailed analysis. Even within the relatively short period of time under consideration there were changes within, and important variations between, different localities. Attempts to attribute these too rigidly to broad 'economic' factors are not very satisfactory. The greater concentration of adult male factory-based workers in the Leeds and Huddersfield woollen industries may help to account for the earlier 'take-off' here rather than in the predominantly child and female-labour based worsted factories of the Bradford and Halifax area. But this does not explain the early prominence of Keighley (a worsted centre) or the initial involvement in Leeds of flax-spinning overlookers.

A positive kaleidoscope of other factors – traditions, and the recent history of working-class leadership and organisation, political and industrial relationships with leading groups of local master-manufacturers, individual concerns and personal loyalties – appear to have been equally or more important. For example, in Halifax the leading predominantly Whig-liberal master-manufacturers led by Jonathan Ackroyd retained a united front against factory reform. They also managed (just) to maintain a working political relationship with local 'radicals'. Independent working-class

---

13 James Brook, speaking at Huddersfield, *LI* 29 Dec. 1831.

leadership was not particularly well developed and the town never became an early stronghold of the ten hours movement. Similar factors may also have been significant in the Dewsbury area where two of the leading employers – Thomas Cook and John Halliley – were politically and personally more popular than their Halifax counterparts.

Similarly, there can be no simple explanation for why the issue emerged with such force and impact in the early 1830s in the West Riding. Unlike in south east Lancashire, the movement was not associated with a particular group of workers.[14] Admittedly, some sections of the West Riding factory workforce, like the cloth-dressers, felt their wages and status increasingly under threat, but they did not occupy the central position enjoyed by Lancashire's cotton mule-spinners. Nor did the movement gather force in the aftermath of trade union defeats. On the contrary, the advent of the West Riding factory agitation coincided with the emergence of an aggressive brand of trade unionism in the form of the 'Leeds Trades' Union'. The timing of the factory reform upsurge appears to owe more to extraneous or more intangible factors, to the interventions of Hobhouse and Oastler, to the general political and economic climate and, most importantly, to the operatives' perception of possibilities. Working-class morale, well-being and organisation were slowly recovering in tandem with the gradual rebound from the depths of the 1826 depression. With political change now seeming possible and factory legislation on the parliamentary agenda, and with trade improving and collective action and organisation spreading amongst local workers, the adoption of the factory hours issue was symptomatic of a more confident and assertive local workforce.

The early factory movement in the West Riding was a diverse, multi-faceted agitation, which continued almost non-stop during the first four years of the 1830s. However, a number of episodes and periods of activity stand out and provide useful marker-posts in any general survey. Oastler's famous 'Slavery in Yorkshire' letter which appeared in the *Leeds Mercury* on 16 October 1830 was a major landmark and starting point. It provocatively compared the conditions of child workers in Bradford's worsted spinning mills with those endured by slaves in the West Indies and immediately sparked debates about the merits of legislation.[15] The West Riding factory reform movement, however, took on a new dimension the following spring when, after the publication of John Cam Hobhouse's Factory Bill, local operatives began to organise themselves in support of the Bill. The coming together of Oastler and the operatives' committees was achieved in June 1831 by the so-called 'Fixby Hall Compact'. After the dilution and effective defeat of Hobhouse's proposals in the autumn of 1831, a major new campaign for factory legislation began in late 1831, culminating in the introduction of a Ten Hours Bill by Sadler in March 1832. The

---

14 Sykes, 'Popular Politics and Trade Unionism', p. 425 ff. stresses the central role of the cotton mule-spinners whose earnings and control over the work process were under increasing pressure at this time.

15 On the background to the letter's publication and its 'sensational' impact, see John A. Hargreaves, 'Introduction: "Victims of slavery even on the threshold of our homes": Richard Oastler and Yorkshire Slavery' and '"Treading on the edge of revolution?" Richard Oastler (1789-1861)', in Hargreaves and Hilary Haigh (eds.), *Slavery in Yorkshire*, pp. 1-11, 213-4.

government responded by setting up a Parliamentary Committee under Sadler's chairmanship and this, together with the prodigious West Riding meeting of Easter 1832 – the 'York Pilgrimage' – became the major *foci* of local committees' activities in the spring and early summer of 1832. For the remainder of the year attention switched to the coming parliamentary elections, particularly those at Leeds and Huddersfield where factory conditions and legislation became the single most important issue.

Sadler's defeat at Leeds at the hands of the two Whig opponents of factory legislation - T. B. Macauley and John Marshall, the famous Leeds flax-spinner – was a crucial set-back for the regional and national movement. A major delegate conference at Bradford in January 1833 sought to tighten up organisation, and plan future strategy. This involved a significant campaign of meetings and petitions to back up the reintroduction of the Ten Hours Bill into the new reformed Parliament in March 1833. The outcome was a Royal Commission to enquire further into factory conditions. Opposition to the activities of what was perceived as the masters' commission became a major focus of local endeavour in late spring and early summer of 1833. Amidst fears that the Commission's findings would result in a hybrid bill – giving more generous protection to the youngest children, but leaving all other workers untouched – West Riding delegates organised another major demonstration which gathered on Wibsey Moor on 1 July in 'a mood of bitter resentment'.[16] Although in some senses the culmination, this massive show of popular support also marks the beginning of the end of the first continuous phase of agitation. Althorp's Act of August 1833 – providing for the restriction of nine to thirteen year-old's labour to eight hours a day and for 'young persons' under eighteen to work no more than a twelve hour day – appeared to outbid the factory reformers in humanity.

Hereafter the local movement was in decline. A West Riding delegate meeting in October 1833 planned to re-organise on the basis of 'Factory Reformation Societies' and a number of STCs transformed themselves into 'Reformation' branches. Early in 1834 a number of these re-configured themselves again, into branches of the 'National Regeneration Society' and began the West Riding's brief flirtation with the 'Eight Hours Plan'. By this time, however, other pre-occupations, notably the defence of trade unions and trade unionists, had taken over as the focal point of local operatives' concerns. The factory reform issue faded and local committees disappeared from view in the summer of 1834 amidst the collapse of Yorkshire trades' unionism.

2: The Early Short Time Committees

As many commentators have noted, Oastler did not invent the term 'White Slavery', nor was he the first to use the 'clumsy' slavery metaphor.[17] For Oastler, an ardent abolitionist, and in the hands of his radical colleagues, 'white slavery' was a powerful rhetorical device to expose the double standards of their opponents, many of whom were leading anti-slavery advocates.[18] However, a number of short time speakers of all

---

16 Ward, 'Leeds' p. 100.
17 Hargreaves, "'Treading on the edge of revolution'", pp. 212-3. Roberts, 'Richard Oastler', p. 268. Recent scholars, like Roberts, have noted the problematic nature of the epithet.
18 Gray notes that images of slavery both resonated with the popular cause of abolition and with

political persuasions were happy to engage in hyperbole equating the conditions of factory children with those experienced by slaves in British colonies, or even to say that they were worse. Whilst few local leaders adopted the overtly racist, negrophobic views frequently voiced by William Cobbett, some had clearly absorbed the negative tropes, underpinning ideas of natural English superiority, that became commonplace in a 'particular strand of radical discourse' during the 1820s.[19]

Other local leaders were aware that this was difficult comparative territory and sought to keep their anti-slavery and ten hour beliefs and activities separate. Like Oastler, they 'did not conceive abolition and factory reform as mutually exclusive'.[20] Indeed, a number of leading local short time advocates remained consistent opponents of colonial slavery. However, they increasingly found it difficult to stop ideas from one sphere bleeding into the other. So, for example, when the ultra-radical and ten hours supporting leader John Ayrey demanded 'the immediate and unconditional emancipation of the slaves' during a heated debate in Leeds about the 1833 Slavery [Compensation] Bill, he was joined by Cavie Richardson, a key West Riding factory reformer, who argued that:

> There were in this country men, women, and children who were no better than slaves; they paid the taxes of the country, and were they to be called on to pay a compensation for the liberation of negro slaves? If they were called on to compensate the slave himself for his suffering they would not object to it, but they did object to a demand for compensation to the oppressor of the slave, and they repudiated such a demand.

These sentiments were poignantly endorsed by a lone, unnamed 'Negro' (an escaped slave) in the gallery who asserted that 'the slave holders should be made to pay the twenty million to the slaves. (cheers.) He stated that the only thing which the slaves required was to be paid for their labour.'[21]

Although they were not organised as early or as rigorously as their Lancashire counterparts, and they did not yet characterise the issue as equivalent to 'slavery', the Yorkshire workers were conscious of the factory reform issue well before Oastler's intervention in October 1830. As in other spheres, the great Bradford strike of 1825 provided a touchstone and inspiration for later developments. The dispute generated debates about child factory labour – the critique on health grounds, the moral and educational arguments, and the relationship to adult hours and labour – which were to re-emerge in the early 1830s.[22]

---

long-standing radical rhetoric in which the slave was the antithesis of the free-born Englishman (*The Factory Question*, p. 39)

19 Ryan Hanley, 'Slavery and the Birth of Working-Class Racism in England, 1814-1833', *Transactions of the Royal Historical Society*, 26 (2016), pp. 103-24.

20 On Oastler's abolitionist background, see Hargreaves, '"Treading on the edge of revolution"', pp. 211-2; Roberts, 'Richard Oastler', p. 27.

21 *LI* 27 July 1833. For a reiteration of this view by John Ambler, 'an old STC man', five years later, see *NS* 12 May 1838.

22 On Lancashire, see Kirby and Musson, *The Voice of the People*, pp. 346-64. The

In the aftermath of the strike, possibly as a way of dissipating some of the bitterness engendered, a few master-manufacturers, led by the Tory worsted-spinner John Wood, reduced children's hours and increased breaks in an unsuccessful effort to 'organise a voluntary ten-hour day in the Yorkshire worsted industry'.[23] In February 1829 a further initiative by master worsted spinners in Bradford recommended a reduction of the hours of work for under-16s to twelve hours a day and the extension of existing (cotton-based) legislation to the worsted industry. The Tory *Leeds Intelligencer*, which claimed to have first raised the issue the previous October, reported the meeting under the heading 'Infant White Slavery'.[24]

The concept of 'White Slavery' also had an established niche in the traditional radical vocabulary.[25] But its meaning tended to be more general, and took in the whole of the working population and their place within a tyrannical political system. The common radical usage, which often contrasted 'respectable' responses to black slavery abroad and white slavery at home, can be seen in the speech of Samuel Dickenson, a leading Almondbury radical, at an Elland public meeting on distress in June 1830:

> A great deal of talent and eloquence had been employed on the condition of the black slaves; but why should such men advocate the abolition of slavery abroad, in preference to slavery at home? (*applause.*) In his opinion, before they flew on wings of benevolence to rescue aliens and strangers from wretchedness, they ought to emancipate not only the labouring population, but England herself from slavery. (*cheers.*) Where did slavery exist to a greater extent than in England? The nation, and especially the poor, are slaves to a debt that neither is, nor can be paid; they were slaves to taxation unjustly imposed; (*cheers.*) slaves to a useless standing army; slaves to a hive of drones who despoil the hive of its honey; (*applause*) in fact, the people were enslaved and shackled by a system of unparalleled extravagance, and this made them slaves to oppression and to hunger. (*applause.*)[26]

The very week before Oastler wrote his letter, John Smithson, the chief Carlileite republican in Leeds, used the white-slavery, black-slavery antithesis in a long speech in support of the 1830 French Revolution. Amidst a more general tirade against the 'lamentable ignorance of the working classes', he specifically referred to 'the factories of Leeds' and argued that the only reason why black slavery had not been introduced

---

Woolcombers' and Weavers' Eighth Address, *LM* 29 Oct. 1825 is particularly interesting. See also Charles Button's speech to a Leeds meeting to honour the Radical MP, Joseph Hume, *LM* 13 Aug. 1825, and John Tester's speech, *LM* 18 June 1825.

23 J. T. Ward, *Chartism* (London: Batsford, 1973), p. 57. Wood was instrumental in Oastler's Damascene conversion to the factory cause, Hargreaves, 'Introduction', pp. 5–7.

24 *LM* 28 Feb. 1829. The participants included some of the town's largest and most prominent firms, but it is doubtful whether the initiative was acted upon; *LI* 8 Mar. 1829.

25 Kirby and Musson, *The Voice of the People*, p. 407, fn. 14.

26 *HCC* 5 June 1830.

in England was because 'white slaves could be hired cheaper, and thrown upon the parishes when they were not wanted'.[27]

Having overcome their initial surprise, local radicals in Leeds and Huddersfield were quick to welcome and use Oastler's 'very able letter, in favour of white slaves, both male and female, young and old, in England'.[28] The letter caused such a stir not because of the novelty of the ideas and information it conveyed, but because of the source from whence it came and the fact that it touched a raw nerve of deep-seated grievances. As Cecil Driver perceptively surmises, 'most of the workers who read it or had it read to them in the public houses, saw in it an indictment of the whole industrial system. They read into it, indeed, many of their own grievances, including things Oastler knew nothing about. They felt that the regulation of child labour might be made the beginning of an improvement of their own lot'.[29]

The operatives did not formally organise themselves until the following spring when fears of the dilution or defeat of Hobhouse's Factory Bill prompted the formation of 'Committees of Operatives', later to be called 'Short Time Committees'.[30] The emergence of the West Riding committees was not quite as 'spontaneous' or without precedent as is generally suggested.[31] In Spring 1830, for example, Leeds workers had received delegates from the Bolton cotton-spinners who were advocating a new Factory Bill.[32] Local operatives' committees were an established way of organising to respond to a variety of issues. In 1829 delegates from all the principal factories in Leeds had met at the Union Inn to form a committee which sought to regulate the price of milk and butter.[33] The method of calling and location of the 1831 (Short Time) 'Committee of Operatives' were identical. Also, in 1829 workers in the Huddersfield area had formed their own 'Committee of Operatives' which investigated, publicised and made a political response to local distress.[34]

The early STCs were predominantly working-class in origin, composition and style. They met informally at first in pubs and taverns and quickly adopted a familiar committee format and later a delegate structure. Although respectable lower middle-class supporters (shopkeepers and tradesman predominantly) also joined, Cecil Driver is correct in suggesting that 'the initiative came entirely from the workers', many of

---

27 Oastler Coll., Vol, 4, Item 3, J. Smithson, *Substance of a Speech Delivered… on Thursday. September 23rd, 1830* (Leeds, 1830), pp. 5-6. For Carlile's virulent racial discourse, see Hanley, 'Slavery', pp. 120-1.

28 *LP* 23 Oct. 1830; *LM* 23 Oct, 6 Nov. 1830. Smithson himself proposed the vote of thanks to Oastler at a Leeds meeting and Oastler's letter was reprinted and distributed widely as a broadsheet, C. Driver, *Tory Radical*, p. 51 and Ward, *Factory Movement*, p. 35.

29 C. Driver, *Tory Radical*, p. 51.

30 The full title was 'The Short Time Bill Committee of Operatives'. The 'Committee of Operatives' designation continued to be used until well into 1832. In line with previous writers however, the generic title 'short time committee' and its abbreviation 'STC' will mainly be used in the text.

31 See, for example, Ward, *Factory Movement*, p. 41.

32 *LM* 17 Apr. 1830. See Kirby and Musson, *The Voice of the People*, pp. 361-2 for the Lancashire background.

33 *LM* 11 July 1829.

34 See above, pp. 125-33.

whom 'knew one another from their political or trade union activity'.[35] Huddersfield and Leeds, two of the leading early centres, both had a strong trade union and radical traditions and a number of short time leaders came from this background. But contacts and experience gained through local friendly societies, co-operative societies, Mechanics Institutes or religious activities may also have been important. The skills and expertise developed in these and other contexts by key individuals such as Joseph Firth of Keighley, George Beaumont of Almondbury or Ralph Taylor of Leeds,[36] complemented the experience and lessons brought to the campaign by non-operative leaders like Oastler, Bull, Williams Stocks jnr., and William Osburn jnr., with their diverse experience in anti-slavery and anti-tithe organisations, temperance associations, the Church Missionary Society, and Sunday School unions.[37]

The latter influence is worth noting because it is often the factory movement's Anglican connections that are stressed. Methodism admittedly supplied some of the most ardent apologists for child labour, but it also provided a training ground for Oastler and a number of other local short time leaders.[38] Driver states that, 'many of the operatives' leaders ... belonged to one or another of the Wesleyan sects'. This may be overstating the case but certainly local leaders, such as Cavie Richardson and Benjamin Bradshaw in Leeds, and Samuel Glendinning and Daniel Fraser in Huddersfield, had strong nonconformist backgrounds. When faced with problems of developing their organisation they naturally turned to the Wesleyan model of class meetings and missionary activity.[39]

The diverse local, independent, predominantly working-class STCs were the key organisations of the early factory movement. Yet they are generally little studied, meaning that common misconceptions, such as the belief that the Huddersfield STC

---

35 C. Driver, *Tory Radical*, p. 82.

36 Joseph Firth had been a combers' delegate and founder of the Keighley Political Union in 1830, and was also a leading figure in a local Oddfellows lodge. George Beaumont was involved in both the anti-truck and distress agitations of 1827 and 1829-30. Ralph Taylor was a promising member of the Leeds Mechanics Institute and possibly an early leader in the Leeds Trades' Union.

37 Oastler had preached in Methodist chapels in his youth, and had been actively involved in the anti-slavery movement before his leading role in the Halifax tithes dispute of 1827. Bull had organisational experience in the Church Missionary Society and the formation of temperance associations. William Stocks jnr. of Huddersfield had been involved in countless local agitations and organisations (e.g. Sunday Schools, anti-truck, distress meetings) before 1830. William Osburn jnr. was a Leeds Sunday School superintendent and evangelical Anglican.

38 Ward's writings, and those of J. C. Gill, on Rev. G. S. Bull, have rightly illustrated the significant contribution of a few important Anglicans. Thompson, *Making*, p. 383, makes the point about the Methodist mill-owners. For Oastler's nonconformist upbringing and his father's links with the New Connexion Methodists, see C. Driver, *Tory Radical*, pp. 14-17 and D. Colin Dews, 'Richard Oastler: the Methodist background, 1789-1820', in Hargreaves and Hilary Haigh (eds.), *Slavery in Yorkshire*, pp. 79-90.

39 C. Driver, *Tory Radical*, p. 101; Cavie Richardson of Leeds was a Methodist local preacher on the East Circuit in late 1827, *LM* 15 Dec. 1827 (see also *LM* 24, 31 Dec. 1831). For Benjamin Bradshaw (1799-1869), a cloth-dresser, from New Wortley near Leeds, and a Primitive Methodist preacher, see, BPP 1831-2, XV, pp. 129-40. On Glendinning, a Primitive Methodist, see Halstead, 'Huddersfield STC', p. 116.

mainly comprised factory workers, have been repeated down the years.[40] Equally, the extent of working-class agency and diversity in these bodies has been consistently underestimated. Until more forensic local studies like that undertaken by John Halstead in relation to Huddersfield are available, the early West Riding STCs and their leaders will remain somewhat opaque. However, their centrality to the factory reform campaign merits closer examination of their composition and pivotal role.

First in the field were Leeds and Huddersfield. The Leeds committee, comprising 'delegates appointed by the operatives of the principal woollen, worsted and flax manufactories in Leeds and its neighbourhood', featured John Hammond as 'Chairman' and Ralph Taylor as 'Secretary'.[41] According to J. T. Ward, John Hammond was a 'woollen worker', and Taylor a 'Radical operative agitator'.[42] However, 'Hammond' and John Hannam, a flax-spinning overlooker, who gave evidence to Sadler's Committee in 1832, may well be the same person.[43] Equally, whilst Ralph Taylor, may have been 'an excitable ultra-Radical' and an 'agitator', there is no direct evidence to connect him with the public meetings of either of the two main radical camps in the early 1830s. Indeed, it was as an advocate of the local trades' union that he gained prominence and eventually notoriety. He was certainly a talented writer and speaker, 'the most promising young man that the Institute has trained' according to a teacher at the Leeds Mechanics Institution.[44] Possibly because of fears of victimisation, the names of other active members of the committee are difficult to discover.[45] David Brook, a cloth-dresser who testified to Sadler's Committee, was certainly a leading member; and Benjamin Bradshaw, another dresser, may have been.[46] But other names, like (Joshua) Drake, who addressed a ten hours meeting in

---

40 For example, Jörg Neuheiser, *Crown, Church and Constitution: Popular Conservatism in England, 1815-1867* (New York: Berghahn, 2016), p. 202.

41 *LM*, 2 Apr. 1831.

42 Ward, *Factory Movement*, p. 41.

43 For Hannam's testimony as 'chairman' of the local STC see, Parliamentary Papers, House of Commons Papers, Select Committee on Bill for Regulation of Factories 1831-2, XV (hereafter BPP 1831-2, XV), p. 290. J. T. Ward indexes 'Hammond' and 'Hannam' as separate individuals. However, the similarity of their names, their position and their views indicate that they were one and the same. 'Hammond' signed a letter as Chairman of the 'Committee of Operatives in Nov. 1831. Ward, 'Leeds', p. 31 gives 'Hannam' as the 'new' chairman of a rally of mill-delegates on 10 Dec. 1831; whilst Driver, *Tory Radical*, p. 119 gives 'Hammond'. Tellingly, consecutive issues of the *Leeds Times* report of the same 1835 meeting of 'overlookers and operatives employed in the flax mills' record it as being chaired first by John Hammond and then by John Hannam (*LT* 21, 28 Feb. 1835). Hammond/Hannam and Taylor are the two leading STC figures at the great Leeds meeting of 9 Jan. 1832, (Oastler Coll., 4, 6, *The Ten-Hour Bill. Report of the … great Leeds Meeting … January 9, 1831* [mistake for 1832] (Leeds, 1832), pp. 28-30).

44 Ward, 'Leeds', p. 91; *LT* 14 June 1834; R. J. Morris, 'The Rise of James Kitson: Trades Union and Mechanics Institution, Leeds 1826-51', *Publications of the Thoresby Society*, 53 (1973), pp. 184-5.

45 The threat of victimisation was taken very seriously. At least three of the Leeds witnesses to Sadler's Committee were dismissed on their return home, see Ward, 'Leeds', pp. 93-4.

46 For Brook's involvement, see Oastler Coll., 4, 6, *The Ten-Hour Bill. Report of the … great Leeds Meeting … January 9, 1831* [mistake for 1832] (Leeds, 1832), pp. 34-5.; BPP 1831-2,

late 1831; James Ross, an operative who retaliated against John Nicholson's pro-factory poem, 'the Factory Child's Mother'; and Robert Howard, treasurer of the Radical Political Union, who spoke at ten hours' meetings in winter 1831-2, are more speculative.[47]

Some of the early committee men were certainly radicals but formal links with radical organisations did not become pronounced until the election campaign of 1832.[48] It is probable that the original STC crossed the very sketchy and provisional party affiliations that were commonplace at the time. The factory delegates who set up the original committee doubtless comprised the senior or most articulate adult male workers in their establishments – spinning overlookers in flax and worsted, cloth-dressers, weavers or perhaps slubbers in woollen. Politically, a number may have been inclined to the 'first step' radicalism embodied in the 'Holbeck' Political Union, which favoured a broad pro-Reform Bill alliance with the main body of Whig-liberals.[49] As the factory reform issue became more polarised along party lines it is probable that their political and factory reform affiliations came increasingly into conflict. This would certainly help to explain the divisions and drop-outs in 1832-3 and the replacement of Leeds by Bradford as the seat of the West Riding Central Committee.[50] Allegations of financial mismanagement were another factor. First Hannam and Taylor, then later Oastler and Sadler, were accused of misappropriation.[51] In addition, it is likely that the heat of the election contest and the formal support for an official Tory candidate exacerbated tensions within the operatives' committee. The Leeds

XV, pp. 59-72; and *LP* 12 Jan., *LT* 14 Mar., 4 July 1833. Brook also testified to the 1834 Select Committee on Handloom Weavers' Petitions, 1834. Bradshaw chaired meetings of out of work trade unionists during the Leeds 1834 lock-out (*LT* 7, 14 June 1834) and addressed a meeting of the Hull and East Riding National Charter Association in 1841 (*NS* 20 Feb. 1841)

47 The 'Drake' who spoke at the operatives' meeting in December 1831 (*LP* 17 Dec. 1831) may have been Joshua Drake, a fifty-six year-old woollen weaver, who gave evidence to Sadler's Committee. (A 'John Drake' spoke at an unemployed workmen's meeting in late July 1832, *LP* 4 Aug 1832). Ross may have been the cloth-dresser who later penned a rhyme 'The Voice of Labour' (*LT* 17 May 1845). For his earlier poetic retaliation, see Ward, 'Leeds', p. 92. Robert Howard spoke at ten hours meetings at Huddersfield, *LI* 29 Dec. 1831 and Leeds on 9 Jan. 1832, (Oastler Coll., 4, 6, *The Ten-Hour Bill. Report of the ... great Leeds Meeting ... January 9, 1831* [mistake for 1832] (Leeds, 1832), pp. 27-8). It is possible that amongst the more senior of the twenty-three Leeds witnesses who testified to Sadler's Committee there were a few committee men. The names of William Swithenbank (cloth-dresser), Daniel and M. Best (flax overlookers) and S. Binns (flax overlooker) suggest themselves as likely candidates.

48 Brook and Ross, for example, spoke at a 'Radical Union' meeting in favour of Wailes' candidature for the Leeds election, *LP* 28 July 1832. They may have been involved in the 'committee of operatives for the support of Mr Wailes' which met at the Union Inn, and which sought the co-operation of the Radical Union, *LP* 28 July 1832; see also, Ward, 'Leeds' p. 95.

49 This was certainly the case amongst the leadership of the Leeds Trades' Union, which had close links with the STC.

50 On this see C. Driver, *Tory Radical*, p. 211 and Ward, 'Leeds', p. 97.

51 For Hannam and Taylor's denial of misuse of funds, see *LP* 28 July 1832. The best account of the accusations against Oastler and Sadler (by John Foster, former short time ally and editor of the *Leeds Patriot*) is in C. Driver, *Tory Radical*, pp. 251-5.

STC was never the same force within the regional movement after Sadler's defeat and when the local committee came into public view again it had a new chair, John Stubbs, and a new secretary, William Rider, a leading ultra-radical.[52] Hereafter the streams of factory reform and political radicalism in Leeds run very closely.

Thanks to the diligent work of John Halstead and earlier researchers much more is known about the origins and membership of the Huddersfield 'Committee of Operatives'.[53] The initiative came originally from factory workers, 'chiefly overlookers', meeting in early March 1831 at the Ship Inn, Huddersfield. They arranged rules and formed a committee to 'render aid and furnish information to Mr Hobhouse'. 'On the very same evening' the local radicals were holding a meeting at 'their Union Room' to 'petition against Lord John's (Reform) Bill as partial and insufficient'.[54] The Ship Inn meeting 'was convened almost unknown to the radicals', and in the main comprised people who 'took little part in politics'. It was not until some weeks later (possible as late as June 1831) that 'some of the leading radicals of Huddersfield joined the party who met at the Ship Inn'.[55]

Analysis of the composite lists of Huddersfield STC members compiled by Halstead and prior researchers reveals some intriguing results. Reflecting the dispersed nature of settlement and industry, only seven, out of seventeen, lived in the town centre and fewer still were natives of Huddersfield. The occupational make-up of the district was also mirrored in the predominance of workers in the textile trades (weavers, cloth-dressers and cotton spinners) but also in the presence of a small but significant group of shopkeepers and dealers. Although a number of members had prior or current links with factories, the strong initial connection with local factories via the overlookers was soon superseded. The eventual composition of the committee reflected the continuing importance of domestic manufacture and the fact that, in Halstead's words, 'Huddersfield ... in 1830 [was] still more of a marketing centre than a manufacturing one'.

The political orientations of the committee members also became more clearcut. By the summer of 1831 the STC had a strong radical presence. This included the

---

52   The relegation of Leeds from its former prominence has never been adequately explained. On this era, see Ward, 'Leeds', pp. 96-9. Hannam and Taylor, after issuing an *Address* warning the operatives against any compromise with eleven hours supporters, (*BLPFCF* 15 Feb.1833), drop out of prominence in 1833. Hannam, together with Benjamin Bradshaw and Charles Greig, formed a deputation of three operatives not in the STC who (with STC permission) waited on the Factory Commissioners in May 1833, (Oastler Coll., 3, 12, W. Rider, *Observations on Power and Drinkwater's 'Replies'...* (Leeds, 1833), p. 7).

53   Halstead, 'Huddersfield STC', pp. 91- 144; John Sanders, 'Working-class movements in the West Riding textile district 1829 to 1839, with emphasis on local leadership and organisation', Unpub. PhD thesis, University of Manchester, 1984, pp. 336-7. This discussion also draws on *LM* 3 Dec 1831 (James Brook's letter); *The Woodites' "forget me not!": being a sketch of a new political farce called the Whig Tomfoolery Election, etc.* (Huddersfield, 1833), an account of the 1832 election in Huddersfield; and *NS* 9 Dec. 1843, Joshua Hobson's recollection of the foundation of the committee.

54   The date of this 'Union Room' meeting is not known. A major meeting of local Whig-liberals in favour of the Reform Bill was held on Monday 7 March – so it was presumably on the Saturday before or after this meeting that the radicals met.

55   *Woodites*, p. 5.

committee's secretary, James Brook, a joiner/furniture dealer; the current chair, John Leech; Lawrence Pitkethly, who employed Leech as the manager of his draper's shop; Samuel Glendinning, a small woollen cloth merchant and future chair; George Beaumont, fancy weaver and a leading light in the Almondbury operatives' political campaign of 1829-30; John Hanson, a woollen-spinner; and Joshua Hobson, joiner and fellow member of the Fixby Hall delegation. Additional, non-STC figures like Daniel Fraser, who went to London in July 1832 as a lobbyist and witness for Sadler's Committee and spoke at local radical and ten hours meetings added further agitational heft to the factory reform campaign.[56] Unsurprisingly, Huddersfield, with this leaven of articulate and committed radical leaders, quickly became and remained one of the most active short time centres.

Bradford and Keighley also responded quickly to the need for organisation, but in contrasting fashions. As at Huddersfield, factory overlookers called the first Bradford meeting, which was chaired by John Hall, overseer at John Wood's worsted spinning factory, in April 1831. The composition of the early STC reflected its philanthropic origins, with Wood as secretary and Joseph Woodhall as chair, and garnered support from a broad base which included Anglicans and Tories, like future regional leader, Mathew Balme, superintendent of John Wood's factory school.[57] In contrast to Huddersfield, though perhaps not surprisingly given the town's recent industrial history, none of the leading working-class radicals and trade unionists – figures such as Peter Bussey, Joseph Brook, William Sharman, John Corless – are to be found on the early factory reform platform.[58] They may well have had other pre-occupations – notably the various Reform Bill crises, and the re-establishment of a strong trade union. Equally, it is likely that, in common with some radicals in some other places, they were suspicious of Tory involvement in the local STC and found it difficult to share the platform with local manufacturers and clergy. Indeed, the only working-class radical who appeared on the local ten hours platform before the second half of 1833 was George Wooller, former secretary of the Bradford weavers, who had been ostracised by other leaders during the 1825 strike. Suspicions of Oastler remained strong amongst sections of the Bradford radicals right through the 1830s. The speakers at a major rally on 27 December 1831 included a Horton curate, the Rev. G. S. Bull, two Tory manufacturers, two doctors, Oastler and Joseph Woodall. The only working-class speakers were James Brook (of Huddersfield) and Ralph Taylor (of Leeds).[59] In Bradford the early factory reform struggle became primarily a contest

---

56 Ward, 'Some Industrial Reformers', pp. 121-6; Halstead, 'Huddersfield STC'; Sanders, 'Working-class movements', p. 337; F. Driver, 'Tory Radicalism?', pp. 125-7.

57 Ward, *Factory Movement*, p. 41. On the early Bradford STC which had Wood as secretary and Joseph Woodhall as chair, see Ward, 'Bradford', p. 41; Ward, 'Balme', pp. 217 ff.; Balme was an 'early member' (though it is not clear how early) of the STC. John A. Hargreaves, 'Mathew Balme (1813-1884), factory reformer', *Oxford Dictionary of National Biography* (Oxford: Oxford University Press, 2004).

58 Sharman and Corless have left few traces. William Sharman, who chaired a meeting of Bradford weavers in 1834 (*LT* 18 Jan. 1834), may been the shopkeeper/grocer of Bolton Road, Bradford (1791-1861+). John Corless was a leading Bradford trade unionist who clashed with John Tester in 1832 (*LT* 19 July 1834).

59 *LM* 31 Dec. 1831.

between rival groups of manufacturers. Viewed from a working-class perspective, it is questionable whether, in the early period at least, D. G. Wright's assertion, that 'Bradford was always the chief centre of the factory movement and supplied more leaders and supporters than any other town', holds water.[60]

The Keighley Committee, had more in common with Huddersfield than Bradford. From the start the leading lights included some notable radical working-class leaders. D. W. Weatherhead, a grocer and leading town-radical, chaired the first major public meeting in January 1832. Other speakers and fellow committee men included a number of radicals, such as Joseph Firth, woolcombers' leader and radical; James Bedford, a radical shoemaker; and Gillet Sharp, a leading woolcomber, radical and local Overseer of the Poor. Abraham Wildman, a small master woolcomber, radical and local poet, was another important network figure who helped to link Keighley with the wider movement.[61] In contrast to Bradford, few local manufacturers sympathised with factory legislation; a factor which gave an added edge to local campaigns. When the Keighley masters met secretly at Bingley in early 1832 the local STC committee responded by plastering the town with posters proclaiming 'BEWARE: A TEN HOURS BILL IS OUR BILL: A TWELVE HOURS BILL IS THEIR BILL'.[62]

The Dewsbury district responded more slowly than elsewhere and never established itself as a major focus of the early factory movement. Many of the small manufacturing centres had their own STCs by early 1832; but apart from Matthew Crabtree of Mirfield, who testified to Sadler's Committee in 1832, his brother Mark, and Charles Etherington of Heckmondwike, who chaired a West Riding delegate meeting in June 1833, few major figures emerged from these and little is known about their composition or vitality.[63] In Dewsbury itself established town-radicals like T. S. Brook found it hard to shake off their deep-rooted suspicions of Tories like Sadler; and it is only in early 1833 that any notable radical presence – in the shape of John Dibb, a

---

60 D. G. Wright, 'Politics and Opinions in 19th Century Bradford', Unpub. PhD thesis, University of Leeds, 1966, pp. 102 and 104. The town's three leading spinners, John Wood, Matthew Thompson and John Rand, who owned over half the machine power in the town, all favoured factory reform.

61 *LM* 4 Feb. 1832; Briggs, 'Keighley', p. 304; Ward, 'Some Industrial Reformers', p. 131 ff.; *LP* 12 May 1832; Ian Dewhirst, *Victorian Keighley Characters* (Nelson: Hendon Publishing Co, 1990), pp. 21-3. Sharp (1781-?) testified to Sadler's Parliamentary Committee. Bedford (1801-1871+) was later a Chartist,

62 Quoted in C. Driver, *Tory Radical*, p. 151.

63 BPP 1831-2, XV, pp. 95-101. Mark Crabtree (1807-?) and Matthew Crabtree (1810-1851+) were both radicals and ten hours advocates who had worked as children in the factory system. Mark became an operative blanket weaver and small manufacturer, but was later bankrupted by a large wholesaler. He was employed by the Chartist Convention in 1839 as a doorkeeper and messenger. He remained active in the factory reform movement in the 1840s. Matthew Crabtree, based in Leeds, contributed to the Oastler Liberty Fund (*NS* 30 Dec. 1843) and later became a railway contractors' agent. Etherington, who with another Heckmondwike delegate, attended one of the first West Riding delegate meetings at Halifax in March 1832, (*PMG* 7 Aug. 1833) and spoke at the big Dewsbury meeting of February 1833 (*LP* 11 Feb. 1833), was a pro-Duncombe Tory and a 'blanket dealer' who went out of business in 1841.

Dewsbury 'Clog and pattern maker', and Jeremiah Marsden, a Earlsheaton 'operative' – is discernible.[64]

Halifax, which, according to Ward, contained 'the most bitter opponents of legislation, the worst conditions, the most cowed operatives', had to wait until December 1831 before a meeting of 'overlookers and other operatives' at the Waterhouse Arms Inn formally established a local STC. The meeting, chaired by the ubiquitous leading local co-operator Thomas Wilson, included a vote of thanks to 'our Friends from Bradford for their kind assistance rendered to us this Evening'.[65] The occupational and political profile and routine activities of the resulting body remain largely unknown. It enjoyed little support from local manufacturers or clergy and in general the Halifax agitation appears less forceful and successful than in other areas.[66] The Halifax committee provided no witnesses for Sadler's Committee and their reliance on outside speakers for public meetings was noted by friends and foes alike.[67] Writing about 'a public meeting of the friends of the ten hours' bill', the *Leeds Times*' local correspondent acknowledged that 'The operatives of Halifax have long been backward in advocating their rights, but on this occasion the short time committee were determined to muster native talent, and on Saturday the ice was broken…'[68]

Membership of the local committee included John Denton (secretary in 1833), John Shaw (an earlier secretary) and John Ambler, a clerk who regularly served as a delegate; but the other members remain fairly anonymous.[69] Established town-radicals tended to be lukewarm. Eli Crabtree was part of the 'native talent' assembled for the ice-breaking June 1833 meeting, whilst Joseph Nicholson, a radical printer, had earlier chaired the West Riding delegate gathering and spoken at a major short time rally in Halifax on 6 March 1832. But another speaker at this earlier meeting, Thomas Cliffe, now keeper of 'a new beer shop', perhaps revealed the real reason for some radicals' ambivalence about the factory agitation in his insinuation that the meeting had been got up for 'political purposes'.[70] In the period before the 1832 elections many 'first step' supporters of the Reform Bill were seemingly unwilling to jeopardise their alliance with local Whig-liberals.

---

64 See, for example, T. S. Brook's attack on Sadler, *LP* 11 Feb. 1832. Brook was later a leading Chartist; *HG* 23 Feb. 1833. Jeremiah Marsden (1789-1857?) was a blanket weaver.

65 Ward, *Factory Movement*, p. 50; Oastler Coll., 5, 12, Public Meeting in Halifax on the Ten Hour Bill, Sat. 13 July 1833, (John Ambler's speech); *HHE* 24 Dec. 1831.

66 J. A. Jowitt, 'Parliamentary Politics in Halifax, 1832-47', *Northern History*, 12 (1976), pp. 176-7

67 *VWR* 20 July 1833; *LM* 10 Mar. 1832.

68 *LT* 20 July 1833.

69 *LM* 4 Feb 1832; Oastler Coll., 5, 12, Public Meeting in Halifax on the Ten Hour Bill, Sat. 13 July 1833; *VWR* 20 July 1833. Oastler writing in 1833 could not recall the names of the local committee men who had attended a West Riding delegate meeting at Halifax in March 1832, *PMG* 7, 14 Aug. 1833. John Denton was possibly an Ovenden based woolcomber (1797-1861+).

70 *VWR* 20 July 1833; *PMG* 7 Sept. 1833; Oastler Coll., 5, 2, Halifax Public meeting on Sadler's Bill. Tues. 6 March 1832. Speakers at this latter meeting included 'William Thornton of Illingworth', possibly the future Chartist leader, and 'Mr Nicholson', a prominent local radical, *LP* 10 Mar. 1832. Nicholson had served as the local collection point for subscriptions to defray the expenses of West Riding witnesses for Sadler's Committee, *HHE* 14 Apr. 1832.

The STCs spread from their initial base in four of the main textile centres by concentrated bursts of campaigning and missionary activity. The first big push in late autumn 1831 resulted in the new committees at Dewsbury and Halifax, and also in smaller townships like Batley, Gomersal, Heckmondwike, Holmfirth and Morley.[71] A further local missionary drive after the January 1833 delegate conference at Bradford resulted in the establishment of twelve new committees, mainly in the woollen cloth manufacturing villages of the Bradford-Leeds hinterland.[72] The process of committee men from the large towns going to outlying towns and villages, 'addressing gatherings wherever they could find a forum in schoolrooms or primitive methodist chapels, in assembly rooms or taverns', was one already familiar to working-class organisers of co-operative societies, trade union branches or political unions, and one which was to be repeated in the early Chartist years.[73]

Other aspects of the later Chartist experience were also prefigured in these early committees. They stressed democratic forms and procedures. Officials were elected for a fixed period or rotated. Public meetings and delegate conferences served as the source of legitimacy and binding decisions.[74] Regional representatives to lobby parliament in 1833, like the Chartist supplementary delegates later in the decade, had to undergo an elaborate selection procedure.[75]

Although the local committees display differences in style and emphasis, the reverse side of this democratic character, the propensity to act like independent, self-governing republics, was possibly less marked than in other working-class bodies. It manifested itself mainly on the question of money. Each local committee had its own fund which it disposed of at its own discretion. Oastler also had his own private fund derived from his personal income and the donations of friends. Possibly because of fears of embezzlement and misuse or just plain suspicions about centralisation, 'there was never any attempt to establish a single fund for the organisation as a whole'.[76] The Bradford conference in January 1833, however, moved toward a more coherent structure when it decided to convert the movement as a whole into a membership organisation whereby 'only those who formally joined the association and paid their regular dues were to share in the determination of policy and tactics'.[77] The reasons may partly have been financial, but can perhaps also be attributed to a desire to tighten up the organisational framework of the campaign in the aftermath of internal divisions and electoral defeat at Leeds.

---

71 C. Driver, *Tory Radical*, pp. 101-2; Ward, *Factory Movement*, p. 50.

72 *BLPFCF*, 28 Dec. 1832; 1, 8 Feb. 1833.

73 C. Driver, *Tory Radical*, p. 216.

74 For the mandatory nature of delegate decisions see the Leeds STC's adherence to the decisions of a short time delegate meeting (*LT* 25 Apr. 1832) in Oastler Coll., 3, 12, W. Rider, *Observations*, p. 6 ff. See also below, p. 284, for Oastler's reluctance to agitate for the eight hours plan without proper authority.

75 See C. Driver, *Tory Radical*, p. 211. For a discussion of the practice of accountability in Chartism, see Peter Gurney, 'The Democratic Idiom: Languages of Democracy in the Chartist Movement', *Journal of Modern History*, 86, 3 (2014), pp. 581-2.

76 C. Driver, *Tory Radical*, pp. 146-7.

77 Ibid., p. 211.

The early structure of committees in Yorkshire was described by Oastler in March 1832: 'We have established "operative committees" in all the towns, and in Leeds there is also a "general committee" ... We have also in Leeds a "central committee" for the West Riding of Yorkshire, composed of members from the different local committees; ...'[78] The precise origins of the regional central committee are not known. The model may have been borrowed from Lancashire. With Ralph Taylor and William Osburn jnr., both of Leeds, as the first secretary and chair, it became an important coordinating body – responsible for organising the 'York Pilgrimage' and the West Riding's evidence to Sadler's Committee in 1832, and coordinating local responses to the Factory Commissioners and the great Wibsey Moor meeting in 1833.[79]

Cavie Richardson was one of two 'missionary' agents appointed and paid by the committee in summer 1832.[80] It held regular meetings during this period, but in practice the main burden of day to day work probably fell on Oastler and the 'host' committee.[81] In Leeds, which also had its own operatives' committee and a 'general committee' of respectable supporters, it is likely that organisational overlap and confusion added to the frustrations of late 1832.[82] After the Bradford conference of January 1833 had re-affirmed the pivotal position of the central committees in Lancashire and Yorkshire, occasional West Riding delegate meetings continued to be held, usually, like their trades' union and later Chartist counterparts, at some convenient inn on the main coaching routes.[83] The main town committees increasingly became the focus for activities and organisation within their wider districts – indeed six such divisions were explicitly delineated in the instructions for the Wibsey Moor meeting. However, a tiered local/district/regional committee structure was not formally achieved until the last West Riding delegate meeting in October 1833 which established the short-lived Factory Reformation Society.[84]

Although initially responding to a particular situation and tending to follow independent lines of action, the early STCs, like other *ad hoc* working-class organisations, quickly became semi-permanent and developed a wide range of functions. They became canvassers of support, collectors of money and information, and the vehicle through which campaigns were mounted and propaganda distributed.

Campaigning was on a monumental scale. Driver, for example, notes the sheer volume and intensity of local leaders' work in early 1833: 'In the 18 days following the conclusion of the Bradford Conference, 15 public meetings were held in the Riding

---

78 *PMA* 24 Mar. 1832. The Leeds 'general committee' was predominantly middle class.
79 C. Driver, *Tory Radical*, p. 144.
80 Oastler Coll., 5, 6, C. Richardson, *A Short Description of the Factory System* (Bawtry, 1832).
81 See C. Driver, *Tory Radical*, p. 144. The first meeting I can trace is the one at Halifax on 6 March 1832 referred to in Foster's controversy with Oastler, *PMG* 31 Aug., 7 Sept. 1833. It is interesting that when Bradford became the 'host' committee Cavie Richardson is referred to as Secretary of the Bradford Committee. It is possible that he became the West Riding Secretary, *BLPFCF* 1 Feb. 1833.
82 On the Leeds General Committee, see C. Driver, *Tory Radical*, p. 145 ff.; Ward, 'Leeds', p. 93.
83 For example, Yew Tree Inn, Robert-town (Birstall) 29 June and 28 Oct. 1833.
84 Oastler Coll., 3, 21, *Address to the Friends of Justice and Humanity ... from the Meeting of Delegates of the Short-Time Committees* (Bradford,1833).

and at least a dozen new short time committees were established'.[85] The breadth of activity is also staggering, including extensive use of press and platform, petitioning and parliamentary lobbying techniques, mass demonstration and harassment, and extensive multi-faceted propaganda.[86] Many of these same campaigning tactics and methods were adopted by the subsequent anti-poor law and Chartist movements.

The gains for local working-class leaders from their involvement in the local and regional committees were immense. In the first place they had the opportunity to develop a wide range of organising and managing skills.[87] The 'York Pilgrimage' of 1832, with its hired resting stations, its food tickets and logistical challenges, and the Wibsey Moor meeting of July 1833, with its detailed instructions devised by a 'Committee of Management' under John Hall the Bradford Secretary, were both impressive triumphs of planning, organisation and discipline.[88]

Careful preparation, combined with imaginative improvisation, also marked the response to the Factory Commission's arrival in the West Riding in May 1833. Selected local short time men shadowed the commissioners' every move, reporting back on who they met, the condition of mills they visited, even what they ate. The commissioners' coming was always known in advance and local committees were able to organise a five-week programme of continuous, if varied, harassment and protest, culminating in a spectacular open-air meeting in Huddersfield at which the commissioners were burnt in effigy.[89]

Alongside, and often in harness with, these varied and highly effective public demonstrations proceeded more mundane organisational work: the collection of signatures for the various petitions which accompanied every phase of the campaign; the lobbying of local and national support, and the collection of all forms of statistical, medical or anecdotal evidence and information. Indeed, nothing better illustrates the organisational skill and calibre of the early short time leaders, both 'operative' and 'respectable', than the speed and efficiency with which the central and local committees marshalled evidence and witnesses for Sadler's Committee in 1832.[90]

The second major spin-off for later working-class movements was in nurturing local speaking and writing talents. The local STCs provided the wider movement with some extremely effective and accomplished advocates. The ten hours platform

---

85 Driver, *Tory Radical*, p. 215.

86 See Creighton, 'Collective Action and Domestic Practices', p. 15.

87 For examples of the speed of distribution of publicity, the drumming up of support and the stage-managing of meetings, see C. Driver, *Tory Radical*, pp. 223 and 236.

88 The best account of the York Pilgrimage is in C. Driver, *Tory Radical*, pp. 154-63. See also, press reports in *LM*, and *LP* 21, 28 Apr., *LI* 26 April 1832. Reports of the 1833 Wibsey Moor are in *VWR* 6, 13 July, *LT* 4 July, *LM* 6 July, *LI* 6 July 1833. A copy of the instructions for the meeting is in TNA: HO 40/31 f. 34.

89 On the response to the Factory Commissioners see, Oastler Coll., 3., 22, C. Richardson, *A Speech Delivered April 19, 1833, Before the Short-Time Committee ...* (Leeds, 1833), p. 7; Oastler Coll., 3, 12, W. Rider, *Observations*, p 7 ff.; *BLPFCF* 12 Apr.; *LI* May - June 1833; *VWR* 1, 15, 22 June 1833; and *LT* 25 Apr., 23, 30 May 1833. See also C. Driver, *Tory Radical*, pp. 228-236 and pp. 553-5 and Ward, *Factory Movement*, pp. 94-8. For the Huddersfield meeting see *PMG* 29 June; *LT* 20 June; *VWR* 22 June 1833.

90 Driver, *Tory Radical*, pp. 168-70; and Appendix B, pp. 550-3.

provided local working-class leaders with an opportunity to develop their oratorical skills, a chance (rare at the time) to reach a wide audience and a means of legitimising their leadership role. The appearance of their speeches and letters in print further enhanced their standing and their skills. Although the West Riding movement's two key middle-class leaders, Oastler and Bull, were prolific writers as well as 'speechifiers', operative leaders such as Cavie Richardson in Leeds and Huddersfield's John Hanson, whose *Humanity Against Tyranny* served almost as the local orator's standard text, also contributed enormously to the propaganda effort of the early movement.

The value to concurrent and later agitations of these propagandising skills and experiences – the third chief area of gain – cannot be overestimated. After the early days when 'the correspondence columns of the various local newspapers had provided almost all the publicity that had seemed necessary', the factory movement produced an astonishing amount and variety of literature.[91] This included cheap broadsheets for the wider public, pamphlets of all sorts, newspaper reprints of meetings and correspondence, and one-off propaganda tracts for public gatherings. All served to back up the platform campaigns. Thousands of these items were printed for, and distributed through, the local committees. Broadsheets were 'posted on walls and fences, hung in reading rooms and shop windows, and put in the taverns where the operatives gathered'.[92] The need for an effective distribution network provided a *raison d'être* and a continuing strand of work for the local committees.

Regional and local leaders were extremely conscious of the importance of the press as an adjunct to their public meetings and petitions. In September 1832 the West Riding movement started its own cheap unstamped paper, *The British Labourer's Protector and Factory Child's Friend* – a miscellany of reprints from other papers, correspondence, comment, medical testimony, poetry and anecdote.[93] Priced at only ½d and printed in an accessible pamphlet-like size, it lasted until April 1833 but never attracted a large readership; possibly because of its sanctimonious tone (typically the last issue ends with two prayers), and its desire, in the words of the prospectus, to 'carefully and universally ... avoid all party politics'.[94]

The *Voice of the West-Riding*, founded by a group of Huddersfield radicals (possibly with local co-operators' support) had no such scruples. Although inaccurately described by Joel Wiener as a 'factory journal', the *Voice*, published and printed by Joshua Hobson, a local STC member, nevertheless gave the ten hours movement full coverage.[95] The first issue, which came out in the middle of the Factory

---

91 Ibid., p. 142.

92 Ibid., pp. 143-4, for a detailed description of ten hours propaganda. The Oastler Collection at the Goldsmith's Library, University of London, contains numerous examples of all types of publicity.

93 For details of *BLPFCF*, see J. H. Wiener, *A Descriptive Finding List of Unstamped British Periodicals, 1830-6* (London: Bibliographical Society, 1970), Ref. 56. The paper was edited by Rev. G. S. Bull.

94 *BLPFCF*, 21 Sept. 1832; 19 Apr. 1833.

95 On Hobson and the *Voice*, see John Halstead, 'The Voice of the West Riding: promoters and supporters of a provincial unstamped newspaper', in C. Wrigley (ed.), *On the Move: Essays in Labour and Transport History Presented to Philip Bagwell* (London: Hambleton Press, 2003); Joel Wiener, *The War of the Unstamped: The Movement to Repeal the British Newspaper Tax,*

Commissioners' investigations, asked the people of Huddersfield in typically unrestrained fashion,

> ... how do you intend to act when the men who are 'commissioned' to do all in their power to perpetuate Infanticide and Murder, shall visit your town in order to prosecute their infamous 'inquiries'. We know of a fact that they have more dread of visiting Huddersfield, than of any other town in Yorkshire. 'Tis a pity they should be disappointed ...[96]

The advent of the *Voice* had other implications. It gave the Huddersfield committee, and the movement as a whole, access to an independent, sympathetic printing press. Hobson, first at Huddersfield then later in Leeds, became the West Riding movement's printer-in-chief.

Finally, the early factory movement in general and the STCs in particular helped to develop and strengthen further, a pre-existing network of contacts amongst local working-class leaders. Not only did they meet together at major events like the Wibsey Moor meeting or at the regional delegate conferences, but they corresponded, spoke at each other's town meetings and transacted business together. The extent and content of such informal contact rarely emerges from our sources; an exception is John Foster's references to meetings with Abraham Wildman, Ralph Taylor and Matthew Crabtree in Leeds in late Spring 1832. Nevertheless, its importance in cementing friendships, sharing affiliations and developing common ideas was inestimable.[97]

3: Ten Hours, Radicals and 'Tory-Radicals'

The early factory movement had important connections with radical and 'Reform' politics. Oastler wrote his letter at a time when radicals of all persuasions were assimilating the lessons of the 1830 French Revolution and when local working men in a number of localities were organising an essentially political response to distress. The operatives formed their STCs shortly after the introduction of the first Reform Bill at a time of growing political uncertainty and excitement. And the campaigns of late 1831 were conducted in a steamy political atmosphere in the knowledge that Sadler, now the factory movement's parliamentary leader (and a leading opponent of the Reform Bill), was the official Tory candidate for Leeds. The great surge of agitation in favour of Sadler's Bill in the early months of 1832 first rode and then was eventually drowned by the wave of popular excitement surrounding the last reform debates in parliament.

Matthew Roberts has argued cogently that, 'Like the popular radicals with whom he was allied, Oastler personified the pervasive anti-party sentiments held by the working-classes in the 1830s and 1840s'; and that his 'involvement in factory reform, and subsequently the anti-poor law movement, did much to foster anti-party

---

1830-36 (Ithaca: Cornell University Press, 1969), p. 190.

96   *VWR* 6 June 1833.

97   *LP* 12, 19 May 1832.

sentiments'.[98] However, try as Oastler and the Huddersfield factory reformers might to stress their non-party purity – 'the terms Whig, Radical or Tory, affect me no more than calling me James, George, or John' said James Brook in 1831 – it was impossible in practice to divorce the early factory movement from the political context in which it arose and in which it was conducted.[99] From early on Oastler had been accused of party motives, of trying to distract attention from the issue of parliamentary reform.[100] Sadler's involvement increased suspicions still further, particularly amongst the many radicals who supported the bill as a 'first step' and were instinctively reluctant to jeopardise progress by flirting with Tories. This appears to have been the case at Halifax, where radical support was slow to materialise, and may also have been a factor amongst the independent working-class radicals of Bradford whose ingrained hostility to toryism was also significant.

Radicals who followed Hunt in rejecting the Reform Bill as a Whig manoeuvre to deceive and divide, however, generally cared less about their bedfellows. In Huddersfield and Keighley, ultra-radicals allied themselves closely to the factory cause and supplied a number of the key leaders of the early STCs. In Leeds, whilst factory and radical reform organisations remained distinct, they moved closer together.[101] Radicals involved themselves directly in the factory campaigns of late 1831 and early 1832, and took cognizance of developments on the ten hours issue at their own meetings. Successive meetings of the Leeds RPU in January 1832 cited 'discussions on the factory question' as evidence of the Whigs' insincerity and read Sadler's Factory Bill with warm approval.[102] At a Huddersfield radical meeting on distress three months later, George Beaumont (a radical, trade unionist and STC member) was urging a topical ultra-radical course of action in the event of defeat for the 'ten hour bill': 'It is doubtful whether the government will pass that bill. If they do not, do not petition or demonstrate; they are not our government; we have not appointed them; but let us say 'we will fix a month, and a certain day of that month, and then we will pass that...''[103]

Suggestions such as this, or the call for a National Convention and simultaneous meetings signed by three leading radicals and the ten hours men in Huddersfield (Hanson, Hobson, and Leech) in November 1831, occasionally embarrassed the wider movement, with its emphasis on constitutional tactics and non-party high-mindedness. But they also serve to emphasise that the radicals who bridged the two agitations were 'real' radicals, not sleeping Tory populists interested in social questions devoid of any radical political content. Oastler, as he later stressed, had no illusions about Joshua Hobson's politics, he was 'a right-down thorough-paced Radical; a Church-leveller, a real Republican, for an elective King, an elective House of Lords,

---

98 Roberts, 'Richard Oastler', p. 270.

99 Oastler Coll., 2, 9, 'Public Meeting at Bradford, 10 Dec. 1831'; see also Brook's letter in *LP* 3 Dec. 1831.

100 See, for example, *Woodites*, p. 5.

101 Derek Fraser, 'Politics in Leeds, 1830-52' Unpub. Ph.D Thesis, University of Leeds, 1969, pp. 56 and 61-4.

102 *LP* 21, 28 Jan. 1832.

103 *LP* 14 Apr. 1832. The idea he was alluding to was the 'Grand National Holiday' originally espoused by William Benbow. Beaumont had moved a resolution in favour of such a scheme in late November 1831, *PMG* 10 Dec. 1831.

for no property qualifications; for annual parliaments, vote by ballot, settlement of the National Debt etc etc.'[104]

Where ties existed already, the passing of the Reform Bill and the ensuing election campaign cemented the bond between radicals and factory reformers. The factory reform question became the biggest single issue in the Leeds and Huddersfield elections and the basis of a workable Tory-radical alliance. However, this was not a universal phenomenon. Where radical involvement in the STCs was weaker, other issues predominated and other patterns of popular support evolved. In Halifax, Michael Stocks, the radically-inclined 'Liberal' pronounced himself 'an enemy to the Ten Hours Bill', whilst the unpopular Tory candidate James Stuart Wortley was only a lukewarm supporter of factory reform. On the election hustings Stocks and the local Whig banker Rawdon Briggs jnr., an opponent of legislation, easily won the show of hands.[105] The Bradford election was a fairly tame affair. Two Whig-liberals, E. C. Lister and Charles Hardy, headed the poll above George Banks, the Tory candidate. Both were strong opponents of the factory reform, and although Banks won some unpopular acclaim by making ten hours 'the most prominent feature in his political programme', he never secured the support of the working-class radicals within the Bradford Political Union.[106]

By contrast, the Leeds RPU had formally pledged its support for Sadler as early as September. Its two most prominent leaders, John Ayrey and William Rider, allied themselves closely with the factory issue and after Sadler's eventual electoral defeat became leading figures in the STC. John Ayrey, mounted on a white charger, 'white being the colour (because no party-colour) adopted by the friends of the Ten-Hour Bill', led the Leeds division to the great Wibsey Moor meeting.[107] In Huddersfield, where links were even stronger, Captain Wood the popular Radical candidate symbolically entered the town in a procession headed by factory children. They bore a white standard proclaiming 'Oastler is our champion' and flags whose slogans illustrate something of the fusion of social and political aspirations which the particular local circumstances of late 1832 engendered: 'Wood and Oastler and the Ten Hours Bill', 'No New Sarums', 'The Ten Hour Bill and a tax on Machinery', and 'A good day's wage for a good day's work'.[108] Wood's triumphal entry into Huddersfield, which recalls the famous occasion when Sadler's carriage was unhitched and dragged through the streets of Leeds by local operatives, is an appropriate point to consider in more detail general questions of gentlemanly leadership, deference and Tory-radicalism in Yorkshire.[109]

The concepts of 'gentleman' leaders and 'democratic' working-class organisations are not antithetical in the context of the early nineteenth century. The English radical tradition of leadership by independent country gentlemen, which can be traced

104 Oastler Coll., 8. 12, R. Oastler, *The Huddersfield Dissenters stark staring mad!...* (Leeds 1835), p. 7.

105 Jowitt, 'Parliamentary Politics', pp. 178–9.

106 Ward, *Factory Movement*, p. 77; Wright, 'Politics and Opinion', p. 114.

107 *LI* 6 July 1833.

108 *LP* 11 Aug. 1832.

109 C. Driver, *Tory Radical*, p. 198.

through Hunt, Cobbett, Cartwright and Burdett as far back as Wilkes, was particularly strong outside London. The provincial radicals often lacked support and leadership from local worthies; consequently, independent disinterested gentlemen-leaders, with their stress on strict constitutionalism and their professed willingness to suffer or even die for the cause, had a great appeal.[110] Such figures were, in Belchem and Epstein's characterisation, 'simultaneously of the people and not one of them'. The gentleman radical was thereby 'a liminal figure: at home on the platform but otherwise moving outside and beyond any given local community'.[111]

The role of such gentlemanly leaders was far from being purely ornamental. They often played a vital role in early working-class movements. By adroit use of the radical press and the popular platform they held together the fragile framework of local societies and sympathisers and provided much needed coordination and ideological direction. They also had the advantage of not being vulnerable to victimisation or to charges of being professional agitators. Their ample resources of time and money gave them an independence which no shopkeeper or working man could match. To movements, one part of whose legacy was betrayal, desertion and unprotected embezzlement, such 'Champions of the People' had obvious and not inconsiderable attractions.

The tradition of the gentleman-leader was particularly strong in the West Riding. Wildly cheering crowds lined the route of William Cobbett's progress through northern market towns and weaving villages in the winter of 1829-30.[112] Henry Hunt, who had built up an immense personal following the post-war years, also evoked an enthusiastic response when he travelled across from Lancashire to Leeds in November 1831.[113] Later in the decade Fergus O'Connor, Hunt's conscious successor, enjoyed his strongest and most consistent support in these same textile towns and villages.

Elements of this tradition also help to explain the support enjoyed by local gentlemen-radicals like Captain Wood or General Johnson, the radicals' candidate in Huddersfield in 1835. Lower down the social scale, in the purely local context, some of the established town-radicals – people like William Stocks jnr., Lawrence Pitkethly and Thomas Vevers in Huddersfield, T. S. Brooke in Dewsbury, Henry Dixon in Halifax – drew sustenance and support from this tradition.[114] It highlighted their high-minded independence, their constancy and their willingness to place the cause of 'the

---

110 This discussion of the tradition of gentlemanly leadership draws on, John Belchem, 'Radicalism as 'Platform' Agitation in the periods of 1816-21 and 1848-51: with special reference to the leadership of Henry Hunt and Feargus O'Connor', Unpub. DPhil thesis, University of Sussex, 1974, pp. 33-5; and James A. Epstein, 'Feargus O'Connor and the English Working-class Movement, 1832-41: A study in national Chartist leadership', Unpub. PhD Thesis, University of Birmingham, 1977, pp. 176-9.

111 John Belchem and James A. Epstein, 'The nineteenth-century gentleman leader revisited', *Social History*, 22, 2 (1997), p. 179.

112 *LM, LP* 9-30 Jan. 1830.

113 *LP* 12 Nov. 1831.

114 On Stocks, see Robert Owen's assessment in *Crisis* 20 Apr.1834; on Pitkethly; 'that gentlemanly radical', see *NS* 19 Jan. 1839, and F. Driver, 'Tory Radicalism?', pp. 124-6; on Vevers, see obituary, *NS* 27 May 1843; On Brook, see *NS* 28 Sept. 1839; on Dixon 'that stirling old Radical', see *LT* 31 Dec.1836, 18 Feb.1837.

People' above self-interest. The Scottish writer and economist, William Thomson, for example, dedicated the second edition of his popular *The Age of Harmony* to 'Laurence Pitkethly, Esq. Huddersfield, the patriotic advocate of the Rights of his Country, and the warm and disinterested friend of the productive classes...'[115]

It is in this wider national and local context that the popularity and support enjoyed by Richard Oastler, and other respectable Tory leaders of the factory movement like Sadler, Ashley and G. S. Bull, must be placed. It is easy to misinterpret their role and to generalise from it into assumptions of deference and 'backwardness' on the part of their working-class co-workers and supporters. Although the worst offenders in peddling a fanciful picture of the malleable 'unskilled Northern worker' with his 'continuing peasant mentality', 'his idealised memory of paternal government and his nostalgia for a pre-industrial past', unquestioningly accepting the leadership of 'the Tory social reformers in the North' have long been challenged, elements of this view have 'stubbornly persisted'.[116] Equally, it needs to be re-emphasised that the leadership of Tories such as Oastler, Sadler and Bull, and lesser local figures like William Osburn jnr. in Leeds, was not achieved automatically or accepted uncritically. The intense personal respect, affection and allegiance which Oastler in particular enjoyed, and which in the early Chartist years Fergus O'Connor also inspired, was hard-won. It should not be mistaken for deference, naivety or vacuity on the part of the operatives.

In the case of Oastler it is also worth noting that this following was initially confined to and remained strongest in areas like Huddersfield and Leeds with which he had close personal ties. The so-called 'Tory-Radical' alliance was the product of a particular mix of local conditions and personalities. It was never endlessly reproducible.[117] In Bradford, where personal connections were weaker and fewer regular points of contact existed, Bussey and the working-class radicals remained suspicious and aloof.[118]

It is often overlooked that the initiative for the 'Fixby Hall Compact', the beginning of what the *Leeds Mercury* termed the 'unnatural coalition', came from the Huddersfield operatives and not from Oastler. They asked him to become a member of the STC. Their decision was based on more than just blind gratitude that he had taken up an issue about which they had long been concerned. It owed much more to a realistic appraisal of the opposition they were up against and to an appreciation, stemming perhaps from Oastler's pronouncements in favour of ten hours, that he was widening his perception of the issue and beginning to think along their, broader, lines. His past record as scourge of the Vicar of Halifax and creator of a popular anti-

---

115 Oastler Coll., 9, 9, William Thomson, *The Art of Harmony; Or, A New System of Social Economy... etc* (2nd edn., Glasgow, 1834). Reprinted in Gregory Claeys, *Owenite Socialism: Pamphlets and Correspondence, Vol. IV, 1832-1837* (Abingdon and New York: Routledge, 2005), p. 305 ff.

116 R. N. Soffner, 'Attitudes and Allegiances in the Unskilled North, 1830-1850', *IRSH*, 10, (1965), p. 429 ff.; repudiation by Dorothy Thompson, 'Notes on Aspects of Chartist Leadership', *Bulletin of the Society for the Study of Labour History*, 15 (1967), pp. 30-1; Roberts, 'Richard Oastler', p. 252.

117 F. Driver, 'Tory Radicalism?', pp. 122 and 138, comes to much the same conclusion.

118 Bussey in fact never spoke at an official ten hours meeting until April 1838, *BO* 3 May 1838.

tithe organisation in 1827 also helped; as did his local reputation.[119] Fixby Hall lay just four miles outside Huddersfield and at least one of the delegation of six short time men who walked to the Hall on Sunday 19 June – Joshua Hobson – had family connections with the Thornhill Estate.[120]

At the start it was essentially a pragmatic relationship, which had attractions and advantages on both sides. Oastler was an asset to the STC. He was a respected figurehead and a popular drawing-card for their public meetings. He had access to money and a network of respectable contacts. His record as a prolific writer and speaker also made him a very valuable ally. Conversely the operatives of the STC had much to offer him. They possessed detailed inside information about the workings of the factory system. They had access to various networks of contacts which were outside his normal social range. Also, they included in their midst a number of experienced organisers and talented writers and orators.

However, the relationship quickly became more than just a trade-off of information, skills and contacts. It worked and survived firstly because, as in all successful partnerships, both sides quickly came to know, respect and like each other. When Oastler first met the Ship Inn delegation he was 'struck with their intelligence and their civility… These men surprised me by the knowledge which they communicated and the sensible manner in which they conveyed that knowledge'.[121] Shared endeavour in agitation quickly cemented bonds of affection and respect. Secondly, although coming from different ideological starting points, they increasingly came to identify common enemies and to articulate a shared hostility to 'over-grown capitalists' and the ravages of unrestrained industrial capitalism.[122] Indeed, Matthew Roberts has identified a number of 'radical currents in Oastler's ideology' and argues that these allow us 'to understand his widespread popularity with northern labourers without resorting to crude explanations such as a deferential affinity for toryism, or an immature obsession with gentleman leaders'.[123]

Finally and most importantly, the limits of the alliance were stated and appreciated from the outset. Accounts of the 'Fixby Hall Compact' from both sides stress the frank exchange of views and the acknowledgement of fundamental political and religious differences. Indeed, both sides repeatedly turned this potential weakness to their advantage. The proof of their humanitarian purity was in their willingness to rise

---

119 On this see C. Driver, *Tory Radical*, pp. 33-5.

120 Joshua Hobson's grandfather (another Joshua) who died in 1833, allegedly at the age of 104, was a small tenant farmer and carpenter on the Thornhill estate, *VWR* 30 Nov. 1833; *NS* 9 Dec. 1843.

121 Oastler's most-often quoted account of the compact in *Home* 6 Mar. 1852 owes something to the embellishments of hindsight or fading memory. For example, it is unlikely that the deputation of outworkers and small tradesman claimed that they could only come on Sunday because 'we are in the mills all the rest of the week from early in the morning till late at night'. An earlier account talks of 'three or four manufacturing operatives' coming to see him, in Oastler Coll., 16, 6, R. Oastler, *A Letter to the Bishop of Exeter* (Manchester, 1838), pp. 4-5. However, Hobson's recollections in *NS* 9 Dec. 1843 largely tallies with the main outlines of Oastler's account.

122 See, for example, John Hanson's testimony BPP 1831-2, XV p. 404.

123 Roberts, 'Richard Oastler', pp. 263 and 252.

above considerations of mere party or sect. If anything they came to glory in their 'unnatural coalition'. Oastler at the West Riding hustings in December 1832 stoutly defended the existence of Political Unions, 'the people's standing army', and Trades' Unions, 'the workman's army'.[124] He came to admire the radicals' perseverance and to respect their openness.[125] He preferred Joshua Hobson with his clear Republican views to hypocritical 'Whigs and Reformers', because Hobson was at least an 'honest radical'.[126] The Huddersfield radicals for their part, as Oastler later stressed, knew their co-worker 'perfectly well; they know that I never blink any question: they know that I am an out-and-out ultra Tory; but I received their thanks and their invitation [to speak at a meeting to welcome Fergus O'Connor] because they also know that I am the Workman's Friend – the Friend of Labour'.[127]

The strength of the radicals' loyalty and friendship meant that they were usually prepared to tolerate Oastler's aberrations or tell him politely when he was out of his depth. Thus in May 1833, when Oastler was peddling the 'pendulum loom' to the Trades' Union Committees of Huddersfield and Leeds in the belief that it was a potential challenger to the power-loom, William Rider, then Secretary of the Leeds STC, wrote 'as an operative weaver', (in what for him was fairly restrained terms), to ask if Oastler was really serious and to give his opinion that he considered the loom injurious to the weaving trade.[128]

In spite of such occasional disagreements, the mutually understood contract which Oastler entered into with key local short time leaders was largely adhered to. But the importance of the Tory-radical alliance in the West Riding should not be over-stressed. It arose out of a particular mix of local political conditions and personalities, and can be explained in these terms.[129] It was never as universal or as rock-solid as some historians have imagined. Indeed, the alliance was only operational in the formal sense in the early years, during the Huddersfield and Leeds elections of 1832. When both places had by-elections in late 1833 and early 1834 the potential weaknesses and limitations of the alliance were exposed. In Huddersfield radicals were split between those like William Stocks jnr., John Hanson and James Brook who supported Sadler's candidature and the main body of radicals who supported Captain Wood.[130] In Leeds, where the Tories chose Sir John Beckett, an old-fashioned 'political' Tory, as their

---

124 Oastler Coll., 2, 11, R. Oastler, *Facts and Plain Words on Everyday Subjects* (Leeds, 1832), p. 45.

125 Ibid., p. 19; Oastler pays tribute to Pitkethly 'an Ultra-Radical' in a speech to a Huddersfield meeting, Tues., 18 June 1833, in Oastler Coll., 3, 2.

126 Oastler Coll., 8. 12, R. Oastler, *The Huddersfield Dissenters stark staring mad!...* (Leeds 1835), p. 7.

127 Oastler Coll., 12, 2, R. Oastler, *Damnation: External Damnation to the Fiend-Begotten 'Coarser Food' New Poor Law* (Leeds, 1837).

128 *LT* 16, 23 May 1833.

129 In Huddersfield, for example, the deep-felt resentment against the 'Ramsden Interest' and the early split off of the working-class radicals from the 'Liberals' were important factors. The existence of a cadre of strong-minded, independent radical leaders and Oastler's local connections also helped to create 'special' conditions.

130 On the 1834 Huddersfield Election, see C. Driver, *Tory Radical*, pp. 255-9; and below, pp. 313-5.

candidate, a number of the leading factory reformers, like John Ayrey and Cavie Richardson supported the radical 'Liberal' candidate, Joshua Bower.[131]

The alliance was never a blind allegiance. Tactical considerations remained as important as personal bonds. Yorkshire did not have a peculiar hybrid breed of working-class leaders or supporters espousing a doctrine called 'Tory-Radicalism'. It was an alliance not an ideology and, as Felix Driver argues, always 'selective and fragile'.[132] The coalition was at all times conditional and only ever between certain, important sections of the radical leadership and some local Tories. The radicals who supported Oastler were 'real radicals'. But plenty of other radicals remained at best lukewarm and at worst deeply suspicious about any close political relationship with a party that was still tainted with the blood of Peterloo. Equally, whilst it is true that figures like Oastler, Bull, Sadler, John Wood of Bradford, and Perring of the *Leeds Intelligencer* do not have equivalents on the other side of the Pennines, and that they formed a more socially-aware and active grouping, Yorkshire toryism was not dominated by such figures. Nor, as Matthew Roberts points out, were their conceptions of toryism always compatible.[133]

The respectable Tories who involved themselves in the 'Factory Question' formed just one wing – a minority one – of the 'Party'. There is a danger of inadvertently transcribing later 'official' Tory endorsement of the issue into accounts of the early years. Factory reformers were often adopted as parliamentary candidates for reasons of political expediency or for lack of other suitable candidates.[134] In places like Halifax the majority of Anglican churchmen remained aloof. The opponents of legislation included many Tory manufacturers. Benjamin and John Gott of Leeds abstained in the 1832 election but voted for Beckett in 1834; and it is likely that after Sadler's defeat in Leeds many leading Tories were glad to see him fail once more at Huddersfield.[135]

Jörg Neuheiser is correct in arguing that 'the political orientations of the activists within the factory movement were decidedly more complex than scholars usually maintain'.[136] However, with notable exceptions, such as Cavie Richardson, who became a founding member of the Leeds Operative Conservative Association in 1835, few of the operatives' leaders in the 1831-4 period can be identified as potential Tories. Even Richardson's political affiliations, like his occupational status, remain a bit cloudy and provisional. In 1831, for example, he 'candidly' stated 'that I am no Whig, and I am very far from being a Radical'; but he supported the *Leeds Patriot* as 'the people's paper' and in 1833 endorsed the 'liberal' Joshua Bower, in preference to traditional

131 Derek Fraser, 'The Fruits of Reform; Leeds Politics in the 1830s', *Northern History*, 7 (1972), pp. 97-8.

132 F. Driver, 'Tory Radicalism?', p. 138.

133 Roberts, 'Richard Oastler', pp. 255-6.

134 Factory reformers, like Sadler at Leeds and Huddersfield, held out the possibility of attracting some radical votes – one of the few ways of eroding the 'natural' Whig-liberal majorities in most West Riding constituencies. On the difficulties of attracting suitable candidates see, Jowitt, 'Halifax', p. 178, One major landowner and three local Tories all declined the 1832 nomination. Also see *LI* 6 May 1831, for the failure to attract high-status Tories for the 1831 West Riding election.

135 Thompson, *Making*, p. 384; Fraser, 'Politics in Leeds', pp. 105-7.

136 Neuheiser, *Crown, Church and Constitution*, p. 205.

Tory, Sir John Beckett.[137] Equally, no amount of reading back of later affiliations by earlier researchers can change the basic arithmetic. The conversion to conservatism (often late in life) of a number of radical ten hours men, such as Hobson, Hanson and Leech in Huddersfield, long after radicalism had declined, cannot be taken as evidence that they 'fully shared their leaders' views', and of latent toryism.[138] The Operative Conservative societies which emerged in the mid-1830s, with their deferential and anti-radical leadership, were very different to the STCs and were not prefigured in the politics of the so-called 'Tory-Radical alliance'.[139]

Although more in evidence in the West Riding than in other areas, the Tory social reformers did not rule the head or heart of the Tory party. Oastler was a radical Tory, or as Matthew Roberts posits, 'both a tory and a radical', who on occasions 'trod the edges of revolution'.[140] It was his radicalism, his willingness to defend the rights of labour, not his Toryism, which evoked a popular response. From the start the Tory-Radical alliance was in reality a Radical-Tory alliance. Indeed, the reversal of proper nouns gives the phenomenon its true weight and emphasis.

4: Ten Hours, Trades' Unions and Factory Workers

The paucity of information about trade union leaders and organisation, and the ambiguity of some of the evidence available, makes it particularly difficult to estimate trade union support for, and involvement in, the factory movement in the West Riding. However, a broad survey of the early period reveals good grounds for believing that, whilst not underestimated as seriously as in Lancashire, the extent of overlap between the early factory movement and trade unionism has also been understated in Yorkshire.[141]

---

137 Oastler Coll., 4, 8, C. Richardson, *Address to the Working Classes of Leeds and the West Riding* (Leeds, 1831), pp. 7 and 4. In this he asserted that he was poor, even if he did not have to earn 'my bread by the sweat of my brow' in 1831. According to Neuheiser, *Crown, Church and Constitution*, pp. 103–4, fn. 35, Richardson was a hosier in 1830 and may have been a bookshop owner and teacher in 1834. This trajectory fits with other working-class leaders, mainly radicals, who were involved in the trade of agitation. He also helped to form the Leeds Protestant Association in 1835 (*LI* 3 June 1837), but left Leeds the following year.

138 J. T. Ward was particularly guilty of creating retrospective Tories; see, for example, J. T. Ward, 'Some Aspects of Working-class Conservatism in the 19th Century', in J. Butt and J. T. Ward (eds.), *Scottish Themes: Essays in Honour of Professor S. G. E. Lythe* (Edinburgh: Scottish Academic Press, 1976), p. 140. For a more nuanced consideration of this phenomenon, see Halstead, 'Huddersfield STC', and 'The Charter and something more! The politics of Joshua Hobson', in John A. Hargreaves (ed.), *The Charter Our Right! Huddersfield Chartism Re-considered* (Huddersfield: Huddersfield Local History Society, 2018), pp. 83–112.

139 See below, p. 351.

140 Thompson, *Making*, p. 380; Roberts, 'Richard Oastler', p. 273.

141 Sykes, 'Popular Politics and Trade Unionism', p. 425, argues that Prof. Ward's account of the factory movement vastly underestimates trade union backing for the short time agitation. See also, Kirby and Musson, *Voice of the People*, Chapter X, for some of the long standing formal and informal links between factory reform and trade union leaders and organisations in south east Lancashire. Ward's *Factory Movement*, has comparatively little to say directly on the subject of Yorkshire trades' unionism and its links to the factory campaign (see pp. 57, 106,

STCs and trades' unions in the West Riding flourished simultaneously in an atmosphere of increasing intra- and inter-trade co-operation and at a time of growing confidence in the possibilities of collective action. As Colin Creighton has noted the discourse of the factory movement 'emphasised the collective and relational above the individual'.[142] The two endeavours shared similar organisational features, a few of the same leaders, and a common concern to offset what they perceived as the detrimental effects of unrestrained competition. For a time they were effectively, if not organisationally, different arms of the same movement.

In Leeds the 'Committee of Operatives' (STC) entered the public arena just a few weeks after the operatives at Gott's factory had begun the strike which acted as a catalyst in the development of the Leeds Trades' Union. The two bodies met at the same venue, Mr and Mrs Blunt's Union Inn, and initially at least had similar delegate structures.[143] Contemporary observers often did not bother to distinguish between them in a precise way. The *Leeds Mercury*, making the most of an incident at the end of the 'York Pilgrimage' when an effigy of its editor Edward Baines jnr. was paraded round the town and burnt outside the paper's office, commented that,

> we understand that the Operatives' Committee, or the Trades' Union, were incensed partly by the refusal of the Mercury to support the 10 Hours Bill, and partly by the insertion of a letter from 'A Merchant' in our columns that day, concerning the alleged dictation of the Trades' Union to the manufacturers...[144]

Interestingly, the effigy was prepared at the Union Inn, and ultra-radicals, like Mann, Ayrey and Rider, as well as some members of the Trades' Union, were allegedly implicated in the incident.[145] The 'York Pilgrimage' itself provided nervous Huddersfield magistrates with further evidence of the influence and power of the Leeds Union in the area. In a letter to the Home Office they enclosed a report of a Huddersfield PU meeting on distress at which it was announced that, 'the operatives of Leeds had resolved to strike work for two days in order to attend the county meeting at York, on Easter Tuesday, in support of the Factory Bill...'[146] Trades' union and friendly society support had been widely canvassed since November 1831; and it is doubtful whether either the York Pilgrimage or the 1833 Wibsey Moor meeting could have been so successful without their active participation.[147]

---

112).

142 Creighton, 'Collective Action and Domestic Practices', p. 27.

143 The STC was initially comprised delegates from all the main textile factories in the town. The Leeds Trades' Union Committee was drawn from each of the main woollen establishments.

144 *LM* 5 May 1832.

145 Ibid., and *LP* 12 May 1832.

146 TNA: HO 52/20, Haigh, Fenton, Kaye and Walker to Melbourne, April (nd) 1832. See also, *LP* 14 Apr. 1832.

147 An 'Address to the Friendly Societies and Unions', written by John Leech on behalf of the Huddersfield STC, was circulated widely in the West Riding in November 1831. See below, p. 272, for evidence of union banners at the Wibsey Moor meeting. An 'Ancient Gardeners'

Workers as well as magistrates could be jumpy about possible links between the ten hours and trade union activities. When the government appointed a Royal Commission to investigate the practicality of Ashley's Factory Bill in April 1833 it was widely rumoured in the West Riding that the ulterior motive was to seek information about the trades' unions.[148] Such fears do not appear quite so fanciful in the light of the Commissioners' attempt to implicate short time leaders in the calling of strikes, and of the publication of a virulent attack on trades' unions early the following year by Edward Carleton Tufnell, a Commissioner in Lancashire. In his tract he states unequivocally that the Leeds Trades' Union Committee advocated 'the ten-hour factory bill' as part of a wider policy 'to diminish the quantity of goods brought to market, and thus, as they foolishly supposed, to raise the rate of wages'.[149] This statement recalls a resolution condemning the 'serious injury' caused by the system of low wages and unrestricted hours of labour, which brought loud applause from the trades' union members who had flooded a meeting of Leeds shopkeepers in October 1832.[150]

Ralph Taylor, the local STC secretary, acted as the union's chief spokesman at this meeting and was an active member and committed supporter of the Leeds Trades' Union in its early days.[151] Although the evidence is patchy, there are other indications of common leadership and involvement at Leeds. John Hannam, the Leeds STC chair, informed Sadler's Committee that his employer, Mr Harris 'is not altogether a friend to the Bill, yet he has kindly given me liberty to join a union'.[152] Another Leeds witness, David Brook was certainly a trade union member and may also have been an active and important leader in the local Trades' Union.[153] Finally Benjamin Bradshaw, like Brook, a cloth-dresser and witness in 1832, reappears in June 1834 chairing two of the Leeds Trades' Union's last public meetings before their eventual defeat.[154]

Other West Riding STCs also had trade union connections. George Beaumont who considered himself 'the founder of the fancy union' was one of the original members of the Huddersfield STC.[155] Other members were sympathetic to the union cause and worked closely with the Trades' Union in the 1832 election.[156] Joseph Firth and Gillet Sharp of Keighley had served as combers' delegates in local industrial

(friendly society) banner was also spotted.

148 Oastler Coll., 3, 12, W. Rider, *Observations*, p. 5.

149 E. C. Tufnell, *Character, Object and Effects of Trades' Unions; with some remarks on the law concerning them* (London: James Ridgway and Sons, 1834), p. 55.

150 *LM* 6 Oct. 1832.

151 *LM* 6 Oct. 1832 and *LM* 7 June 1834. See also Ward, 'Leeds', p. 94. For an allegation that 'he swindled the union' see *LT* 14 June 1834.

152 BPP 1831-2, XV, p. 290.

153 See Brook's testimony, BPP 1831-2, XV, pp. 59–72, esp. p. 64. Also, his evidence to the 'Select Committee on Handloom Weaver's Petitions', BPP 1834, X, p. 35. A 'Brook' spoke at the Leeds Trades' Union meeting, *LT* 7 June 1834.

154 *LT* 7, 14 June 1834.

155 TNA: HO 52/25, Deposition of George Beaumont of Almondbury, 2 Jan. 1834.

156 For example, Pitkethly, Leech, Hobson, Hanson and Brook.

disputes. At Holmfirth Abraham Whitehead, radical factory reformer and co-operator, was a leading figure in the local clothiers' successful 1832 strike.[157]

The evidence on the overlap of leadership is not, however, overwhelming. After the publication of the Royal Commission's Report in July 1833, speakers at a Halifax meeting indignantly repudiated any links with trade unions. One (B. Carter) denied that local leaders were 'the men who in every rash and headlong strike had assumed the command of the discontented members of the operative body'. Another, Mr Ambler (in all likelihood John Ambler), asserted that 'he had never in his life had anything to do with any strike, nor any trades, or political union - The only Union with which he had ever been connected was the Sunday School Union'.[158] The evidence from a relatively 'backward' ten hours and trade union centre like Halifax may not be typical, but it suggests caution. None of the known Bradford trade union leaders were actively involved in the early factory reform agitation and in the Dewsbury area, where evidence is scant, the only obvious connection between the two 'movements' appears in the decision of local factory woollen spinners to support the short time campaign by refusing to work more than eleven hours a day.[159] In Leeds Ralph Taylor parted company with the Leeds Trades' Union ostensibly because he was unhappy about the direction it had taken.[160] William Rider, the new STC Secretary, although a defender of trades' unions, was never an actual leader. The *Voice of the West-Riding* commenting on the 1833 Halifax meeting had a straightforward, common-sense explanation for this lack of obvious overlap in leadership: 'few of the champions of the Ten Hour Bill have had any lead in the Trades Union, a few of the leaders in the Trades Union have been prominent in this measure, not ... because they were against it, but because few can lend themselves to so many objects...'[161]

The Yorkshire unions at this time were large-scale flourishing organisations. The *Voice*'s view deserves to be given due weight. Whatever the precise degree of overlap between the local leadership and formal organisations of STCs and trade unions, there can be no doubt that they drew on a common reservoir of aims, ideas and support. Thus although none of the known Bradford trade union leaders appeared on the local platform, Bradford banners at the 1833 Wibsey Moor meeting included those of 'the United Society of Cordwainers Bradford', the 'Friendly United Mechanics' and the 'Friendly Society of Operative stone masons'.[162] Occupational groups like the masons were particularly attentive to issues relating to working hours.[163]

---

157 *LP* 25 Nov. 1830; *LM* 15 Jan. 1831; *Crisis*, 4 May 1833.

158 Oastler Coll., 5, 12, Report of a ten hours meeting in Halifax, Sat. 13 July 1833.

159 *VWR* 13 July 1833. The spinners met at the Wellington Inn, the usual trade union meeting place.

160 *LM* 7 June 1834.

161 *VWR* 20 July 1833.

162 LT 4 July 1833; Oastler Coll., 6, 7, *Great Meeting of the West Riding in Support of the Ten-Hour Bill* (Leeds, 1833) p. 1. The banner of the 'United Order of Joiners' was also present. John Douthwaite, a key figure in Bradford trade unionism, appeared on the 'factory' platform later in the decade.

163 See above, p. 92. See also Ralph Taylor's reference to their (short) working hours, *LI* 29 Dec 1831.

The early factory movement's interest in the question of adult hours has long been recognized.[164] But it perhaps needs re-emphasising and re-examining. The concern existed from the very start. The Leeds committee's open letter to Hobhouse leaves no room for doubt:

> As the factory system stands at present, one adult and one child, and in some branches one adult and several children, are employed together; which, if the Bill pass would cause the adults to give up work at the same time with the children. Hence the objection of the manufacturer and, so far as we are concerned, our support of the Bill.[165]

Although possibly detrimental to their battle for public opinion, the Leeds operatives were never afraid to admit that economic self-interest played a part in their support for legislation. When an unpopular woollen master manufacturer, Mr Bruce, asked the crowd at a Leeds factory reform meeting in January 1832 to confirm 'that this ten-hour bill is not only to restrict the labour of children, but to restrict the labour of adults'; the collective response was unequivocal: 'That is what we want'.[166] An individual Leeds cloth-dresser, David Brook, gave his personal stance as follows: 'I have supported the Bill ... on this principle, that I really do think it is absolutely necessary, in the first place, that children should be protected from excessive labour; that is the first point in my mind; with a hope, I confess, that it will benefit myself and others as well'. He felt that the Leeds operatives generally, 'will ... be very glad if the Bill should pass for the children alone; at the same time they do contemplate it may in a measure relieve them from the excessive labour they have been subjected to'.[167] Such admissions do not lay the STC and their supporters open to charges of hypocrisy, of cynically using the child-hours issue as a 'front' for wider industrial objectives. They never disguised the mixed nature of their motives.[168]

The depth of operative anger and the strength of genuine humanitarian feeling, however, should not be underestimated. Joshua Brook of Leeds described his children as 'more like dogs dozing on a warm hearthstone than like children'.[169] In the words of another Leeds 'witness', 'the labouring classes are straightforward people; they are not political economists; they are determined to support the Ten Hour's Bill on the score of humanity' – even, as other witnesses stressed, to the point of making material sacrifices.[170] As Colin Creighton notes, ten hours advocates 'consistently emphasised the importance of the quality of interpersonal relationships, and most especially the

---

164 See, for example, C. Driver, *Tory Radical*, p. 83.

165 *LM* 2 Apr. 1831.

166 Oastler Coll., 4, 6, *The Ten-Hour Bill. Report of the ... great Leeds Meeting ... January 9, 1831* [mistake for 1832] (Leeds, 1832), p. 28. The weavers of Bruce's firm, Bruce, Dorrington and Walker, had recently been granted an advance of wages.

167 BPP 1831-2, XV, pp. 70-1.

168 C. Driver, *Tory Radical*, pp. 83-4 and Thompson, *Making*, p. 373, both stress this point. Creighton, 'Collective Action and Domestic Practices', p. 15, also emphasises it.

169 Drake's testimony to Sadler's Committee, quoted in Gray, *The Factory Question*, p. 33.

170 Stephen Binns, BPP 1831-2, XV, p. 187; for example, John Hanson, BPP 1831-2, XV, p. 405.

bonds between parents and children'.[171] The infants they were talking about were not some remote paupers but their own, their friends' and neighbours' children.[172] As more than one witness stressed, parental feeling was not the preserve of the rich alone. The humanitarian arguments remained at the very heart of the factory reformers' case and tied in neatly with a wider moral critique of the factory system – its effects on the family, its reversal of traditional roles, and its pernicious effects on children's health, morals and education.[173]

The humanitarian and moral arguments, though often to the fore, were rarely voiced in isolation. Economic and 'trade union' justifications for legislation remained a constant theme right from the Leeds Operatives' first 'frank declaration in favour of regulating adult labour' in March 1831.[174] They lay behind the cry of 'Ten hours and a time-book' and the opposition to any measure which would allow children to work in relays. Through them were voiced the hopes of the Leeds cloth-dressers (whose normal day was eleven hours) that, 'the ten hours' bill will enable us to work no more than ten hours'.[175]

The magic and meaning of 'ten hours' are easily lost over the passage of time. It was a key objective of many early trade unions and was cited in local disputes involving stonemasons, engineers and shoemakers in the 1820s and 1830s. 'A Labourer', writing on the economic and political situation in April 1830, urged the working classes to 'unite to work only twelve hours a day' including two for refreshment. This would spread work, benefit the 'philanthropic capitalist' and harm only the 'greedy employers' who 'burn the midnight oil'. The significance of ten hours was well appreciated by all working men and women. It corresponded to their conception of 'a fair day's work' and recalled an idealised pre- or early industrial age. As Ralph Taylor stressed to a Bradford audience in December 1831, 'all trades unconnected with machinery keep to the practice of working ten hours a day, which before the introduction of machinery was the general rule of all trades.'[176] The reference to the present is as important as the allusion to the past. 'The old practice of working ten hours a day'[177] was a mark of respectability and independence which separated off the better-paid skilled artisans from the mass of working men and women. As John Hanson told a Halifax meeting in March 1832, 'You have the example around you, in numberless instances, that those trades which are pursued only about ten hours per day are more remunerated than those which are carried on to sixteen or eighteen hours per day'.[178] Little wonder then that the Leeds committee, with its trades' union connections, should consistently advocate ten hours and

---

171 Creighton, 'Collective Action and Domestic Practices', p. 26.
172 See below, p. 279.
173 For debates about such critiques and the meanings attached to them, see Gray, 'Languages', pp. 148-51; Neuheiser, *Crown, Church and Constitution*, pp. 212-14; and Creighton, 'Collective Action and Domestic Practices', pp. 17-19.
174 C. Driver, *Tory Radical*, p. 83; *LM* 2 Apr. 1831.
175 David Brook, BPP 1831-2, XV, p. 68.
176 *LM* 3 Dec. 1831.
177 Ibid.
178 Oastler Coll., 2, 9, pp. 70-2, Report on Halifax ten hours meeting, 6 Mar. 1832.

repeatedly pose the double-edged question of whether, 'the poor Factory child or even adult-operative, should work longer than a full grown mechanic?'[179]

However, short time leaders and supporters also believed that more fundamental, long-term industrial benefits would accrue to all workers from factory legislation. In the first place, restrictions on long hours and over-working would curb the evil effects of excessive competition and over-production, notably the creation of a wage-reducing and longer-working 'vortex'.[180] This in turn would tend to 'equalize and extend labour, and call into employment numerous male adults who are now compelled to be idle, and subsist on eleemosynary [charitable] aid'. Trade 'would actually be increased, by a number of consumers being created', and the demands of the home market being enlarged. The outcome would be greater regularity and better remuneration in employment for all.[181]

This alternative economic analysis, with its themes of over-production, wage equalisation, underemployment and under-consumption, runs through the Leeds Operatives' Committee's first open letter to Hobhouse. It pervades short time leaders' evidence to Sadler's Committee; and it remained the staple fare of the writings and speeches of the chief working-class leaders, like Ralph Taylor and John Hanson. It provided the rationale for the widespread belief that wages would not fall as a result of legislation.

Witnesses to Sadler's Committee, such as Hanson, Mark Crabtree and Daniel Fraser, all stated confidently that the operatives wanted the Ten Hours' Bill 'even if they should be losers by it at first'. However, they thought that it would never come to this: Crabtree believing that any decrease in wages would be offset by greater regularity of employment and Hanson that ten hours would 'ultimately give them all the benefits of their labour'.[182]

The operatives may have had other reasons for their confidence. The views of David Brook, who was also prepared to accept 'short labour and decreased wages to long hours and larger wages', are worth noting. Brook worked in a factory and, possibly in the role of trade unionist, 'had a great deal of communication with a great body of intelligent operatives' in the Leeds area. They wanted factory regulation and less time to be worked, but did not anticipate any reduction. Pressed further on whether the operatives were 'prepared for the alternative' of a wage reduction taking place he replied, 'They are, and will submit to it; and, generally speaking they will submit to it cheerfully, rather than work the long hours they do'. However, he added an important rider 'let me not be misunderstood; they will submit to it, not however without attempting to keep them up'.[183] Although never explicitly stated, it is clear that the operatives' confidence that a reduction would not take place was founded not

---

179 *LM* 3 Dec. 1831.

180 Hanson, BPP 1831-2, XV, p. 401. See also Ralph Taylor's speech in Oastler Coll., 2, 9, pp. 60-9, Report on Bradford ten hours meeting, 10 Dec. 1831.

181 Hanson, Oastler Coll., 2, 9, pp. 70-2, Report on Halifax ten hours meeting, 6 Mar. 1832; *LM* 2 Apr. 1831, (Leeds operative's letter); see, for example, Daniel Fraser, in BPP 1831-2, XV, p. 412.

182 BPP 1831-2, XV, pp. 412, 100 and 405. As Creighton, 'Collective Action and Domestic Practices', p. 27, notes, this remained a consistent feature of factory reformers' arguments.

183 Ibid., p. 64.

just in their belief in the laws of an alternative political economy, but in the knowledge that they were joined together in a powerful and hitherto extremely successful Trades' Union. Particularly in the context of spring and early summer 1832 they were willing to risk restriction of adult as well as children's hours and leave the fighting to any ensuing wage reductions to the Trades' Union. As Brook later tells the Sadler's Committee, the workmen knew they would 'not get as much for ten hours as they got for sixteen; but we may get as much perhaps for ten as we do for eleven, the regular day'.[184]

The question of wages lay behind any equivocation on the operatives' part about the ten hours proposal. Although a popular lobby in favour of the *status quo* or eleven hours never materialised, some manufacturers and their overlookers did mobilise some working-class opposition to the Ten Hour Bill. John Hammond speaking in Leeds in early 1832 regretted that 'a few of my brother workmen who erroneously suppose that their wages will be reduced by this measure, oppose it more strenuously than do the largest manufacturers'.[185] A number of the better-paid adult male workers feared that the masters would not give 'six day's wages for five day's work'.[186] The support of articulate and skilled sections of the workforce like the dressers and slubbers, the combers and the woolsorters was crucial to the early STCs. Consequently, great efforts were made to placate and reassure them.[187] To this end short time leaders used their wider economic arguments and the testimony of sympathetic employers to assert positively that the price and remuneration of labour would rise as a result of restriction; or they asked rhetorically, 'what has been the effort of no bill at all!' – low wages; or they simply back-tracked on the wider 'industrial' aims of legislation.[188] Thus when Messrs Bruce, Dorrington and Walker's operative cloth-dressers initially voted 22-17 in favour of eleven hours (instead of ten) in the belief 'that the factory bill was intended to restrict the hours of adults, and would have a tendency to reduce wages', they were 'informed by the committee at Leeds that the bill will only restrict the hours of children under a certain age'.[189] They immediately changed their minds and fell into line with the unanimity (in favour of ten hours) expressed by cloth-dressers in the other main factories. What is most interesting here, though, is not so much their turnaround as their initial understanding of the purposes of the Bill and the closeness of the original vote.

The early campaign against child labour enjoyed substantial support from both factory and non-factory workers.[190] However, any distinction between the two groups

---

184 Ibid., p. 66.
185 Oastler Coll., 4, 6, *The Ten-Hour Bill. Report of the … great Leeds Meeting … January 9, 1831* [mistake for 1832] (Leeds, 1832), p. 29.
186 William Ellis, a flax-spinner and operative member of the Holbeck PU in late 1832, voiced this fear at the same meeting.
187 For example, Oastler Coll., 5, 3, *A Word, addressed to the Wool-Sorters Combers, and others connected with Mills and Factories on the subject of the Ten Hours Bill* (Halifax, 1832).
188 See Taylor's speech in Oastler Coll., 2, 9, pp. 60-9, Report on Bradford ten hours meeting, 10 Dec. 1831; and Hanson, Oastler Coll., 2, 9, pp. 70-2, Report on Halifax ten hours meeting, 6 Mar. 1832.
189 *LI* 29 Dec. 1831.
190 For example, a 'very large majority' were in favour of ten hours (as opposed to eleven) at

should not be too sharply drawn, especially if it attempts to assign separate motives. The ten hours agitation was not an alliance between factory operatives cynically attempting to gain trade union objectives by subterfuge and backward-looking, domestic hand-workers seeking to curtail the progress of machinery and the factory systems in general. As we have seen, the 'domestic' and 'factory' system interlocked at a number of points and were often mutually reinforcing.[191] Neither structure existed in a pure, fully developed state. As yet factory workers made up only a relatively small proportion of the total labour force, particularly the adult male workforce. Many of those who toiled in factories were skilled craftsmen working in non-mechanised or semi-mechanised settings. Their children might also work in the factories. But the majority of factory children can only have come from, and after adolescence would return to, the ranks of handloom weavers, woolcombers and other home or workshop-based operatives. Many of these same 'domestic' workers had previously been emplyed in factories and, though often reluctant to compromise their pride and independence by sending their own children to the mills, sheer economic expediency often demanded it. They, therefore, could empathise with the humanitarian arguments for regulation.

The textile outworkers in particular also had pressing economic reasons for supporting the curtailment of children's hours. The mills and factories were the central features of the over-working system which made their labour marginal. As the first victims of over-production, they were the underemployed and the under-consumers personified. The handloom weavers even came to evolve their own particular arguments for restriction – attributing the poor quality of the yarn they had to work with to the children's long hours and arguing that, 'If they were not worked so long, their attention to piecing would be more vigorous, and it would be much better for the weaver'.[192]

The impossibility of arbitrarily separating out 'factory' and 'non-factory' leadership and support is nowhere better illustrated than in the careers of leading factory reformers and radicals. Many had first-hand experience of factory conditions. James Brook and Samuel Glendinning, secretary and chair respectively of the Huddersfield STC, had both been factory children, so had George Beaumont, another leading figure in the local committee.[193] Although brought up 'in a domestic manufactory in the woollen business', John Hanson had worked (at Lockwood's mill) as a factory-based woollen spinner. He lived next to the factory and in 1832 his two daughters were currently working in the mills.[194] Other local STC members and radical sympathisers in the Huddersfield PU also had direct personal experience of factory

---

Marshall's flax-spinning factory; see the letter of Humphrey Boyle, an overlooker at the mill and leading Carlileite Radical, *LM* 14 Jan. 1832. Equally, the size and success of major public rallies and demonstrations could not have been achieved without support in the wider working community.

191 See above, pp. 78-9.

192 Oastler Coll.,9, 12, *The Report and Resolutions of A Meeting of Deputies from the Hand Loom Worsted Weavers residing in and near Bradford, Leeds, Halifax etc., Yorkshire* (Bradford, 1835) p. 7.

193 Oastler Coll., 3, 3, Report on Hebden Bridge ten hours meeting, 24 Aug. 1833; *HCC* 11 July 1829.

194 BPP 1831-2, XV, pp. 399 and 403.

work. Daniel Fraser had worked for forty-two years as overseer at a silk-throwing factory; whilst it had been John Spivey's 'lot to pass a period of his life in different factories... He had seen the hired overlooker pacing the room with strap in hand, like the slave driver of the West Indies'.[195]

In Keighley two of the leading figures, Joseph Firth (now a handcomber) and James Bedford (now a shoemaker) had both been factory boys; whilst Abraham Wildman's sisters and Gillet Sharp's children had all worked in the mills.[196] Matthew Crabtree of Mirfield and his brother Mark had both been pieceners at Hague and Cook's factory. In Leeds, where all the initial committee were mill delegates, John Hannam, the local chairman, had long experience of factories. Although his own children no longer worked in the mills, his sister's child was currently employed in a flax-spinning factory. The son of another prominent member, David Brook, lasted only three months in a factory, before his father sent him back to school because of deteriorating health.[197]

Even short time leaders without direct personal or family involvement often had extensive second-hand knowledge and experience. Abraham Whitehead of Holmfirth lived 'near to parents who have been sending their children to mills for a great number of years' and his business as 'a clothier' brought him frequently into contact with the factories.[198] Equally, many of the shopkeeper radicals who served on local committees in Huddersfield and Keighley had daily contact with factory workers of all ages.

The essential passion at the heart of the early factory movement in Yorkshire came not from middle-class philanthropists or working-class idealists and obscurantists, but from hard-headed practical men and women with genuine hopes and grievances and extensive first-hand experience of and daily contact with, the realities of factory life.

5: Fusion, Disillusionment and Regeneration, 1833-4

The early STCs made an immense contribution to the development of working-class leadership and organisation. In many places they aided the emergence of an identifiable group of local leaders who were to remain the key articulators and organisers of working-class protest and aspiration right through into early Chartism. Their involvement in the early factory movement gave them vital organisational and agitational experience. It also helped them to refine an increasingly coherent and sophisticated analysis of political and socio-economic relations. For whilst the committees' formal links with political radicalism and trade unionism should not be over-stressed, it is clear that these connections and points of overlap helped to facilitate the fusion of an older, essentially 'political' critique of society and newer, essentially 'economic' elements into an alternative political economy which challenged the orthodox 'pounds, shillings and pence doctrine' espoused by the ruling Whig-liberal middle-class.[199] This convergence of ideas and perspectives gathered pace in the

195 Ibid., p. 407; *LP* 4 June 1831. Spivey was a leading Almondbury radical and trade unionist.
196 For Firth, see *LM* 4 Feb 1832, and BPP 1831-2, XV, p. 294. For Bedford, see *LT* 4 July 1833.
  For Wildman and Sharp, see BPP 1831-2, XV, pp. 153-6 and 208-14.
197 BPP 1831-2, XV, pp. 95 ff., 283, 288-9, and 63.
198 BPP 1831-2, XV, p. 18.
199 For an attack on the 'cold calculating Scotch philosophy', see John Hanson's speech in

eighteen months that followed the first reformed elections and was matched by more explicit radical involvement in the STCs, by closer formal identification with trade union issues and by the adoption of the 'Regeneration' plan in early 1834. However, all these developments were underpinned by the articulation of common ideas.

The clearest local statements of the economic aspects of this alternative working-class synthesis generally come from the mouth or pen of John Hanson. But elements of this analysis pervade the writings and speeches of many leaders and the testimony of witnesses to Sadler's Select Committee. Two inter-related themes predominate.

Firstly, the critique of competition, and its concomitant evils of over-production and over-working.[200] According to this line of argument, prevention of the excesses of competition would benefit the operative materially, by reducing long working hours, equalising wages and preventing underemployment, and also morally, by giving 'the poor an opportunity to attend to their families – for recreation and mental improvement'. It would also benefit the 'fair honest and humane' employer at the expense of the unscrupulous, undercutting master'.[201]

The second main strand was the attack on the misuse and over-use of machinery. Although some factory reformers opposed machinery *per se* and sought to reduce its influence, many leaders were cautiously favourable.[202] John Hannam, for example, told Sadler's Committee, 'I am quite an advocate for machinery, but not under the present system'. Machinery had not delivered its expected benefits, instead of increasing 'the comforts and conveniences of life' it had aided over-production, and displaced adult labour. John Hanson was merely re-iterating a view common to many radicals, trade unionists and co-operators when he told the Committee,

> I never pretend to argue or to say that machinery abstractedly is an evil; I think it a great benefit; but I do think … that when it is introduced too rapidly, and runs into monopoly, so as to render the operation at all times of little value to his employer, frequently producing stagnations in trade, and thereby throwing numbers out of employ, then machinery becomes an evil…[203]

Interwoven into this essentially economic analysis of the operatives predicament were elements of an older analysis, incorporating traditional radical and biblical tenets – the stark contrast between rich and poor, the abuses of 'privilege' and 'monopoly', the scandal of poverty existing amidst plenty, the excesses of 'Mammon'. All were

---

Oastler Coll., 2, 9, pp. 70-2, Report on Halifax ten hours meeting, 6 Mar. 1832.

200 See, for example, Hanson, ibid., or Ralph Taylor's speech in, Oastler Coll., 2, 9, pp. 60-9, Report on Bradford ten hours meeting, 10 Dec. 1831.

201 For the economic arguments see, for example, John Hanson, *Humanity Against Tyranny* (Leeds, 1831) or Hanson's testimony, BPP 1831-2, XV, p. 402. For the moral improvements, see Leeds Operatives' letter to Hobhouse, *LM* 2 Apr. 1831. For the benefits to 'good' masters (also a theme of trade unionism), see *LP* 3 Apr. 1830, letter from 'A Labourer'.

202 For attacks on machinery, see Taylor's speech, Oastler Coll., 2, 9, pp. 60-9, Report on Bradford ten hours meeting, 10 Dec. 1831. Also the speech of an operative, M. Pickles, Oastler Coll., 2, 9, pp. 72-9, Report on Keighley ten hours meeting, 30 Jan. 1832.

203 For Hannam and Hanson on machinery, see BPP 1831-2, XV, pp. 289 and 200.

present or hinted at in the Leeds Operatives' Committee's letter to Hobhouse.[204] However, a key pamphlet of the early campaign, *Humanity Against Tyranny*, 'a striking document', written by John Hanson, provides some of the best examples of the old style of denunciation:

> while one part of the community is rolling in the most excessive luxury, nauseated even with variety, actually destroying itself by sensual gratification … starvation, yea destitution, in all forms, and in almost every degree, are the lot of the poor…

It also illustrates the fusion of old and new elements:

> How strange that machinery should have an invested and continually diverging effect upon society, rendering the condition of those attendant about it worse and worse while others are reaping its amazing productiveness in pernicious luxury.[205]

Increasingly the traditional radical vocabulary was being applied to a new context. Take, for example Hanson, speaking at Halifax in March 1832: 'Monopoly has created factories and competition has turned them into BASTILES … let us endeavour to bind down this cruel giant, who has placed our children under the most inhuman tyranny in the world'. Or Michael Pickles, an operative, arguing at Keighley that: 'The greatest danger from the factory system is, that the masters should be born and bred, and brought up tyrants, while at the same time it becomes so familiar to them they do not know that it is tyranny'.[206]

Also, this vocabulary was being extended by the coining and increased currency of terms like 'factory lord' and 'millocrat' which associated the new oppressors with the landed lords and aristocrats as part of an exploitative ruling class of non-producers. This new vocabulary, and the broader analysis it articulated, was given a sharper cutting edge, and a more specific political content, after the passing of the Reform Bill and the ensuing defeat of Sadler and the Ten Hour Bill. This crucial period of disillusionment and defeat helped to forge the agitational links and crystallize many of the ideas which were critical to the strength and coherence of early Chartism.

In a mood of growing bitterness, the opponents of the factory movement were increasingly identified as the very same people who had tricked the working class into supporting the Reform Bill. The factory question became a key issue in cutting off large sections of the working class and their leaders from the newly enfranchised middle class. The potential for disillusionment and conflict existed from the very start of the operatives' campaign. The Leeds Operatives' open letter to Hobhouse, with one

---

204 *LM* 2 Apr. 1831.

205 C. Driver, *Tory Radical*, pp. 105-6; these extracts are taken from, Oastler Coll., 2, 5, R. Oastler, *A letter to Mr Holland Hoole, in reply to his* (Manchester, 1832), p. 3.

206 For Hanson, see Oastler Coll., 2, 9, pp. 70-2, Report on Halifax ten hours meeting, 6 Mar. 1832; for Pickles, see Oastler Coll., 2, 9, pp. 72-9, Report on Keighley ten hours meeting, 30 Jan. 1832.

eye on Russell's first Reform Bill, contained a strong penultimate plea to local merchants and manufacturers:

> Let them not now trample in the dust those who made them great; but when they call for reform of abuses in State – when they call upon the sinecurist to relinquish his sinecure – the monopolist to give up his monopoly – the aristocracy to reduce its rents – the church to commute its tithes, and the government to reduce taxation – let them ask, is it not possible for us to sacrifice (if necessary) a little of our profits, to relieve a miserable and degraded poor?[207]

A number of local short time leaders opposed the Reform Bill or viewed its provisions with cynicism.[208] However, it was not until after the first reformed election and the first acts of the reformed parliament that disillusionment became more widespread and the attacks on the local Whig-liberal middle-class became more virulent. The appointment of a Royal Commission in 1833 was for many the last straw, the final proof of duplicity and deception. In a typically humorous, hard-hitting speech to mill delegates, (meeting indoors and at night to avoid victimisation), Cavie Richardson attacked the Commission and local mill-owners 'who used to send you to swell out the numbers at reform meetings, by which they intended to get you into their power, and leave you political nonentities [and who] now will not allow you to meet to state your wrongs, stay the effusion of blood, and solicit relief'.[209] William Rider also pointed out the wider significance in a pamphlet of May 1833:

> It will be remembered that some of the deceptive clique (with whom the Commissioners are often cheek by jowl) during the agitation of what some people call the 'Reform Bill' made a great noise about a 'full, free and fair representation' many were deceived with the words 'full, free and fair' but, however, it was soon discovered that what the denominated 'full, free and fair' excluded from the exercise of the elective franchise, nine out of every ten of the really useful classes of society. But it may be asked, what has this question to do with politics? inquire of Lord Althorp, is my answer.[210]

The bitter, resentful mood which characterised the massive Wibsey Moor meeting in July 1883 spilt over into internal recrimination and open hostility when Althorp published his Factory Bill and it became clear that the reformers had been 'outbidden in humanity'.[211] In what Oastler considered the closing event of a two-year long

---

207 *LM* 2 Apr. 1831.
208 See, for example, R. Taylor and J. Hannam, *To The Public* (Leeds, 1832); and Oastler Coll., 4, 8, C. Richardson, *Address to the Working Classes of Leeds*, both quoted in Ward, *Chartism*, p. 59.
209 Oastler Coll., 3., 22, C. Richardson, *A Speech Delivered April 19, 1833*, p. 7.
210 Oastler Coll., 3, 7, W. Rider, *Observations*, p. 7.
211 Ward, 'Leeds', p. 100.

campaign, James Hargreaves, a Hebden Bridge radical, asked a local meeting, 'But what have we had since the Whigs passed the Reform Bill? We have had nothing since but cruelty and hypocrisy, and this [Althorp's Act] is a sample of the Liberty-loving Whigs'.[212]

William Rider, in a letter to the *Voice of the West-Riding*, was even more pungent and provocative. Within a largely traditional rhetorical framework, he also attacks new enemies in urging,

> that some effectual, extensive and salutary measure must speedily be adopted to stem the torrent of misrule to curb the extravagances of the execrable oligarchy who grind the faces of the poor... let us not be cajoled by the lords of our own creation, by those who without us, would be as poor, as miserable, and as naked a set of beings as ever polluted the face of the earth. The voice of duty, the voice of STARVING INDUSTRY, and the voice of MURDERED INFANCY, all unite in commanding us to arouse and act the part of Britons, by evincing our determination to be free, and wear the galling chains of despotism no more; ... let us consider the power which we possess, let us concentrate that power in one Grand National Union ... [including 'men of influence and property' who will see that] instead of thirsting for blood, we ... are determined that the blood of patriots, as at Manchester, Clithero, and Calthorp-street shall not shed with IMPUNITY; and that the MURDER of childhood by the avaricious Millocracy and their underlings, shall NOT GO UNPUNISHED whether 'Honest' Althorp will it or nill it; or whether pretended friends be wishful to 'concede' or not. But, should the influential and wealth stand aloof, let us, the operation, do our duty; let UNION be the order of the day, and though we are disposed to show mercy to our Tyrants, which they show not us; yet let them beware how they conduct themselves to an united people a nation determined to be free, for our mercy may not endure forever, any more than their sway.[213]

This same bitterness is still evident in the letter of a Huddersfield operative six months later who urged that 'the labours of three years be not entirely lost, nor the cunning and undermining Knavery of Whig hypocrisy or Tory treachery sow the seeds of discord amongst us...' He bitterly recalled an agitation 'whose prayers and petitions have been scouted and laughed at, whose hopes have been blasted, whose ten hours bill has been dragged to the place of execution by whigs sycophants, and actually burked, in defiance of all justice and reason...'[214]

---

212 Hargreaves' speech and Oastler's assessment are in, Oastler Coll., 3, 3, Report on Hebden Bridge ten hours meeting, 24 Aug. 1833.

213 *VWR* 17 Aug. 1833.

214 *VWR* 15 Feb. 1834. The 'Tory treachery' possibly refers to Sadler's candidacy at Huddersfield in the divisive election of 1834.

The purpose of this letter was to advocate the Lancashire 'Eight Hour Plan' which was beginning to make an impact in the West Riding. The brief career of the National Regeneration Society – with its plan for an adult eight-hour day at full wages to be achieved by the mutual consent of masters and men, but if not then by the withdrawal of labour – illustrates the increasing convergence of radical, trade union and short time ideas, tactics and leaders in the winter of 1833-4.[215] In contrast to the extended factory campaigns of 1831-2 and 1833, which were Yorkshire-led, the Regeneration scheme was a Lancashire initiative; the idea coming in the aftermath of the defeats and disappointments of summer 1833 from their chief Parliamentary ally, the Radical MP for Oldham and large-scale cotton manufacturer, John Fielden. Writers on Lancashire movements and leaders have naturally provided the fullest accounts of the Regeneration Society, the only survey from the Yorkshire angle being Cecil Driver's.[216] The purpose of this brief *résumé* is not to rectify this justified imbalance but to relate the Regeneration episode to earlier and concurrent movements and to clarify the West Riding's response to, and relationship with, the 'Eight Hour Plan'.

The apparent slowness of the response in the West Riding was not due to the fact that radical, ten hours and trade union leaders were unprepared for such notions as an eight-hour day, 'National Regeneration', or a planned withdrawal of labour. Christopher Ellwand, a speaker, at a meeting of unemployed Leeds workers in July 1832 had recommended eight hours work, eight hours sleep and eight hours for recreation and meals as a cure for unemployment. At Huddersfield earlier the same year George Beaumont had applied William Benbow's 'General National Holiday' idea to the Ten Hour's agitation.[217] 1833 saw a closer and more formal identification of radical leaders and organisations with both the factory reform and trade union issues. At Leeds, William Rider and John Ayrey became leading figures in the local STC. A future Chartist, Robert Sutcliffe of Halifax is to be found chairing a Hebden Bridge ten hours meeting and even the hitherto lukewarm Bradford Political Union was moved to pass a resolution against the Factory Commissioners in June 1833.[218] A few months later radicals like Rider in Leeds were not merely citing Althorp's Factory Act as an example of Whig duplicity but were also reading about 'The Approaching Crisis' and becoming aware of the power and potential of the 'Trades' Unions', particularly in their co-operative and general unionism aspects, as an engine of change.[219]

Robert Owen imbibed this heady mixture of radical, trade union and co-operative aspirations when he met local working-class leaders during his visits to the West Riding towns in late October and early November 1833. After speaking at

---

215 The full title was 'The Society for Promoting National Regeneration'.

216 See Kirby and Musson, *Voice of the People*, pp. 272-301. John Foster, *Class Struggle and the Industrial Revolution* (London: Weidenfeld and Nicholson, 1974), pp. 108-14, gives a strikingly different account. For Yorkshire see C. Driver, *Tory Radical*, pp. 263-7 and Ward, 'Factory Movement', pp. 113-9.

217 *LP* 4 Aug.; 14 Apr. 1832.

218 Oastler Coll., 3, 3, Report on Hebden Bridge ten hours meeting, 24 Aug. 1833; *PMG* 24 Aug. 1833. Robert Sutcliffe (1808-1869?), a shoemaker, was a leading Halifax radical. A number of his children worked in factories in the 1840s.

219 See, for example, editorials in *VWR* 7 Oct., 9 Nov. 1833.

Huddersfield, where he had sought 'to enlist in our cause some leading men who had taken an active part in promoting the Ten Hour Bill', Owen travelled over to Todmorden where he stayed with Fielden, 'talking over all the measures that we can devise to change [the] condition in which he says all the workpeople are...'[220] The result was Fielden's 'Eight Hour Plan'. Given this indirect connection, it is not surprising that one of Owen's chief contacts in Huddersfield, Lawrence Pitkethly, quickly became a supporter of the scheme. On 23 November the local STC 'resolved to give a public dinner to Mr Fielden and other Friends of the measure' on 26 December, 'and on that day to flog Messrs Oastler Bill Wood Sadler etc into the 8 hours or regeneration society'. Pitkethly confidently predicted 'the Regeneration system will be firmly established on that day over the West Riding'.[221]

The fact that the dinner and the big launch of the Regeneration scheme never took place was not due to lukewarmness or hostility on the part of the West Riding operatives and their leaders.[222] It owed more to a combination of campaign fatigue, unfortunate timing, and the fact they had plenty on their plates at that particular time. Admittedly, Owen had received very little response when he read an outline of an eight-hour 'catechism' to a Leeds trades' union meeting on 18 November, but Leeds, as he noted, was a notoriously 'difficult place to make an impression on'.[223] The West Riding delegates had only recently established the pro-ten hours Factory Reformation Society at their Birstall conference. With the first local Factory Reformation meetings being held at the same time as Owen was in the area advocating the Regeneration scheme, the timing of the Lancashire initiative could hardly have been worse.[224]

The respectable wing of the West Riding ten hours' leadership, though cautious and somewhat sceptical, were far from hostile. Bull 'quite approve[d]' the Regeneration resolutions. William Stocks jnr. and Oastler, after first admitting that they did not 'thoroughly understand' the scheme, stood back partly through exhaustion, partly because of doubts about its practicability and its slogan, but largely because of what they perceived as their constitutional commitment to ten hours. Oastler stated his position clearly in a letter to Owen in late November: 'I shall never argue against an 8-hour Bill, I have often declared 8 hours long enough to the people at Public Meetings I still think so, and that children ought not to work at all – But the people must drive me by the majorities at Public Meetings from the 10 to the 8 hours Bill...'[225]

For their part, the operatives and their leaders had other preoccupations. At the inaugural meeting of the Bradford Factory Reformation Society in December, Joseph Brook, Grand Secretary of the Bradford Order, cited the case of a local master who when faced with a strike against 'excessive hours' presented his workmen with 'a sort of bond' binding them 'to join no association whatever, either for supporting wages or

---

220 *Crisis* 23 Nov. 1833.

221 O.C. No. 607, Pitkethly to Owen, 3 Dec. 1833.

222 Ward, *Factory Movement*, p. 115, is mistaken in saying that the dinner took place.

223 *Crisis* 7 Dec. 1833.

224 The Birstall delegate meeting was on 28 Oct. See *LT* 16, 23, 30 Nov.; 7 Dec. 1833, for the convergence of the two schemes.

225 O.C. No. 610, Bull to Owen, 27 and 30 Nov. 1833; O.C. No. 664, Stocks and Oastler to Owen, 11 Nov. 1833; O.C. No. 668, Oastler to Owen, 22 Nov. 1833.

shortening time'.[226] In such an atmosphere, with the local trades' union fighting wage reductions and supporting the striking Leicester workers, it is hardly surprising that the formal niceties of the Reformation or Regeneration societies had little immediate relevance or appeal.[227] The main winter focus was on survival.

In Huddersfield, the unexpected by-election campaign of late 1833 and early 1834 diverted energies and attention away from the Regeneration scheme. Important coordinating figures such as Pitkethly and Stocks quickly became caught up in the internal divisions and indecisions of the Huddersfield radicals.[228] The resulting acrimony delayed progress still further. Huddersfield in particular and the woollen textile district in general were key areas for the new scheme. Backwardness here led Fielden to recommend putting back the starting date of the eight-hour day beyond March 1834, and prompted the Lancashire men to urgently send forth missionaries.[229]

However, once a breakthrough had been achieved in early February progress was rapid. This may have owed something to the fact that the first Yorkshire branch, formed at Keighley on 4 February 1834 following a visit by two Lancashire missionaries, was established in the middle of a major half-yearly Trades' Union conference at which many delegates from the West Riding and beyond were present.[230] In Leeds the February by-election served as a catalyst rather than an inhibitor of development. Speaking at a Factory Reformation Society meeting on 6 February, William Rider and Thomas Bottomley successfully convinced the operatives to put questions about eight hours rather than ten hours to the election candidates.[231] A fortnight later, again in the presence of Lancashire delegates, the STC voted to discontinue with their efforts for the Ten Hours Bill and cooperate with other Regeneration committees in favour of the 'Eight Hours Plan'.[232]

The Huddersfield STC meeting at the White Hart Inn (the radicals' headquarters) followed suit – stressing the need, like their Leeds counterparts, for the postponement of the starting date until 1 June.[233] By the end of the month Pitkethly was reporting to Owen that in Huddersfield we had 'formed a committee and hope things will move on in the good way.'[234] However, his letter betrays a lack of real conviction, and even the *Voice*, which warmly supported the Regeneration scheme, was 'dubious' whether the proposed delay would be sufficient to allow all parties (both masters and men) to weigh things up, arguing that 'some time is requisite to move large bodies of people, even in a question like this'.[235]

Doubts and difficulties were also exposed when Manchester missionaries sought to float the scheme in Bradford. The first meeting attracted few operatives and no

---

226 *LT* 7 Dec. 1833.
227 *LT* 2 Nov. 1833.
228 See below, pp. 313-5.
229 O.C. No. 674, Fielden to Owen, 8 Feb. 1834.
230 Kirby and Musson, *Voice*, p. 286; *HG* 8 Feb. 1834.
231 *LT* 8 Feb. 1834, Bottomley, like Rider, was an ultra-radical. Together they defeated Cavie Richardson's 'Ten Hour' arguments.
232 *LT* 22 Feb. 1834.
233 *VWR* 22 Feb. 1834.
234 O.C. No. 677, Pitkethly to Owen, 26 Feb. 1834.
235 *VWR* 8 Mar. 1834.

masters.[236] The larger second meeting at William Hill's school-room, whilst it achieved a better response from the operatives, also brought a number of recurring divisions within and between the local radical and short time leadership to the surface. Both Bull, who chaired the meeting, and Oastler who was in attendance, voiced serious doubts about the scheme's practicability and the workers' unity and firmness of purpose. Two leading working-class radicals, John Jackson and Henry Rawnsley, were similarly sceptical; the former arguing that eight hours at full pay would lead to a general rise in all prices and the latter that eight hours was well enough, but only universal suffrage would permanently ameliorate their condition.[237] Peter Bussey also had serious practical reservations about possible victimisation and the feasibility of strike action in the current economic climate. He preached caution, urging the operatives,

> To wait patiently until 2nd of June. Then go [to the masters], and if trade is as it is at present, we must remain as we are, but if it stirs, then there will be a possibility of setting them at defiance... he really conceived that they could withdraw their labour for a month then better than they could for a fortnight now, and they would then be glad to take them on the eight hours plan and full wages.[238]

In spite of his reservations, Bussey, together with William Muff, proposed the formation of a Bradford Regeneration branch and played a full part in its short, unsuccessful, but not uneventful existence. The authorities were sufficiently worried by the Regeneration Society to keep an eye on its progress. In early January General Bouverie reported that the scheme 'is taking very much with the People' in Lancashire and 'might be dangerous'.[239] In March he hired a spy to visit various towns in the West Riding 'said to be the most excited by the Unions'. His report, however, paints a dismal picture of the society's progress and prospects. At Leeds 'Mr Mann the agent for the unstamped publications said that there had been two or three meetings of the Friends of the Regeneration scheme, but that he thought it was an impractical scheme and that Mr Owen's Plan for the exchange of Labour was better, the Regeneration Scheme is likely to be a total failure, many factories are working short-time'. At Dewsbury there was no society; whilst at Halifax 'there is one Regeneration Society, but it is little thought of, all complain of short work'. There had apparently 'been two public meetings on the Regeneration Scheme' in Huddersfield, 'but it makes no progress'.[240] Thus whilst the society's own unstamped publicity organ, the *Herald of the*

---

236 *BO* 27 Feb. 1834 gave the figure as 50. Also, *LT* 1 Mar. 1834.

237 John Jackson (1795-1875) worked as a child in a cotton mill before becoming a woolcomber. He later worked as a travelling salesman and gardener. A radical 'in the days of Henry Hunt and Cobbett', he became a moral-force Chartist and prominent opponent of Feargus O'Connor. See obituary in *BO* 17 Mar. 1875 and Koditschek, *Class Formation*, pp. 506-10.

238 *BO* 13 Mar. 1834; see also *LT* 15 Mar. 1834.

239 TNA: HO 40/32 f.9, Bouverie to Phillips, 5 Jan. 1834.

240 TNA: HO 40/32 f.49, Bouverie to Phillips, 19 Mar. 1834. 'Mr Mann' was presumably Alfred Mann (1816-?), son of James Mann, who espoused a more moderate radicalism than his father.

Rights of Industry, boasted agents and presumably readers in Leeds, Bradford, Huddersfield, Keighley and Featherstone,[241] the spy's assessment of the state of the West Riding Regeneration societies was probably correct. Indeed, a formal Huddersfield Committee only finally materialised after a visit by Oldham delegates on the last day of March.[242] Although it remained in existence, its focus soon shifted to more immediate concerns – namely Dorchester and the anticipated attack on local trade unions.

News from Oldham seemed to confirm these fears. Under the headline 'Disturbances at Oldham' the *Voice* of 19 April reported the chain of events whereby local police had broken into a meeting of the spinners' union, then in dispute with a number of masters, and arrested two of the committee. This had been followed the next day by a rescue attempt and disturbances, during which a local man, Bentley, was shot by an armed 'blackleg' from one of the 'turned-out' factories. Order was only restored after intervention by the military. The *Voice*'s interpretation was clear, 'the famous exploits of Exeter and Dorchester have been attempted at Oldham, and the men there have nobly and morally, firmly and quietly resented the aggressions'. Blame lay with 'the conduct of the Police! These conservators of the public peace and 'kickers-up' of riots…'[243]

By way of parenthesis, it is worth noting Oldham's strong connections with the West Riding textile district. Oldham was a thriving centre of radicalism and trade unionism in the early 1830s and had close political as well as geographical links with Huddersfield in particular.[244] The radical printer and publisher Joshua Hobson had apparently run away to Oldham in his teens. He obtained work as a cotton handloom-weaver and allegedly contributed 'revolutionary effusions' to the Lancashire press under the pseudonym 'The Whistler at the Loom'.[245] During the election campaign of late 1833 Oldham radicals printed and sent across posters urging the organisation of exclusive dealing in favour of Captain Wood.[246] And when 'Friends from Oldham' travelled across Standedge on Saturday 19 April to relate events in their town, five thousand people reportedly assembled in Huddersfield without placards to hear the latest news.[247]

---

241 Kirby and Musson, *The Voice of the People*, pp. 282-3 The *Herald of the Rights of Industry* started on 8 Feb. 1834. Interestingly the prospectus included a supplementary title 'and General Trades' Union Advocate'.

242 *VWR* 5 Apr. 1834.

243 *VWR* 19 Apr. 1834. For an account of events in Oldham, see Kirby and Musson, *The Voice of the People*, pp. 291-4.

244 Foster's *Class Struggle* traces the rise and fall of 'a revolutionary class consciousness' in Oldham and emphasises the strength and importance of the industrial and political organisations and agitations of the 1830s. See also John Foster, 'Nineteenth Century Towns – A Class Dimension', in H. J. Dyos (ed.), *The Study of Urban History* (London: Edward Arnold, 1970), pp. 281-90.

245 This story originates in *Death of Mr Joshua Hobson* (Huddersfield 1876) and has been repeated by historians ever since. I have not been able to discover any evidence to corroborate or disprove it.

246 TNA: HO 52/23, enclosure in Walker, Armitage and Batty to Melbourne, 17 Dec. 1833.

247 *VWR*, *LT* 26 Apr. 1834. The *Mercury* put the figure at 2,500, *LM* 26 Apr. 1834. Hobson chaired the meeting.

The Oldham delegates pressed strongly for a strike on Monday morning 'assuring them that their Oldham brethren calculated strongly upon the co-operation of their Huddersfield Friends; that if they did not meet with immediate support, some of their soft ones would be giving in'.[248] However, Samuel Dickenson of Almondbury and William Hill of Bradford questioned the policy of an immediate strike for eight hours and the release of the Dorchester men, wanting further consideration of the topic at the Wibsey Moor meeting. Eventually fairly tame compromise resolutions were passed supporting the Oldham men and recommending that their propositions be immediately taken into consideration in conjunction with 'Leeds, Halifax and Bradford operatives'.[249] Although Hobson and a few Huddersfield men walked across the Pennines to Bentley's funeral the next day, the Oldham people were generally 'disgusted at the want of support to them'.[250] The West Riding's caution must have been all the more galling to the Oldham men because the local cotton spinners union apparently had connections with the Yorkshire Trades' Union. Yorkshire forms and practices had certainly spread as far as Rochdale in late 1833. An Oldham connection in 1834 is, therefore, highly plausible and appears to be confirmed by the presence of a Bradford trade union delegate at the large protest meeting on Oldham Edge on 17 April, and by the subsequent events at Huddersfield.[251]

In a sense, the Huddersfield meeting marks the end of the Regeneration Society's brief public flowering in the West Riding. Remnants of local committees or sympathisers may have continued to meet. Letters from Halifax and Huddersfield were received by the delegate conference in Manchester on 16 May, which resolved to throw in its lot with the GNCTU and postpone the enforcement of the 'Eight Hour Plan' until 1 September.[252] Such a policy was recommended by a Huddersfield correspondent to the *Leeds Times* shortly after the conference. Commenting on the attack on local unions, he recommended co-operative production: 'I would advise that the people do immediately take their affairs into their own hands – that they become members of the Grand National Consolidated Trade's Union of Great Britain and Ireland – that they adopt the principles of the Regeneration Society…'; this meant not signing the bond until everyone was well clothed and fed and received the same wages as currently for eight hours labour.[253] Such advice, given at a time of stagnant trade, illustrates how the Regeneration scheme got its 'impractical' tag in Yorkshire. More generally, the context and content of the letter demonstrates how easily the Regeneration Society was washed away in the deluge of prosecutions, lock-outs, co-operative and general union schemes of late spring to early summer 1834.

---

248 *LM* 26 Apr. 1834.
249 TNA: HO 52/25, Walker to Melbourne, 21 Apr 1834, reports 'one of the old leaders' (Dickenson?) arguing that they were insufficiently prepared and that 'if not done simultaneously' – their object would be defeated as in Scotland. The episode in some senses pre-figures discussions on the Chartist 'Sacred Month'.
250 TNA: HO 52/25, Walker to Melbourne, 21 Apr. 1834; TNA: HO 52/24, Robert Sharp to Melbourne, nd 1834.
251 See, Kirby and Musson, *The Voice of the People*, pp. 291-2.
252 Ibid., p. 299.
253 *LT* 24 May 1834.

The Regeneration Society was never a major force in Yorkshire. It failed not just because the employers got their retaliation in first but because the Yorkshire operatives and their leaders were never in a fit state to put together an adequate 'foundation', let alone the 'superstructure', for a short hours strike.[254] Although diversions and divisions amongst radical and short time leaders at Huddersfield and Bradford did not help, the plain fact was that economic realities were against an offensive strike. Trade unionists had been on the defensive since the master's first attack in autumn 1833. They had neither the funds nor the will to ever seriously contemplate the Regeneration plan.

However, it is misleading to dismiss the episode as 'vague nonsense' as a 'ludicrous' Owenite scheme whose main function was a negative one: to kill off 'Oastler's Reformation Society and the remnants of the Factory movement'.[255] The Regeneration scheme evolved out of, and was a direct product of the defeat of, the mainstream factory movement. In Yorkshire, as in Lancashire, it included amongst its active participants a number of important ten hours' men. They were often independent-minded and pragmatic radicals, not blind adherents of an Owenite (or Oastlerite) faith. Also, given the local circumstances of late 1833 it is difficult to see where the Factory Reformation Society could have gone – save down the road of increasing involvement with, and defence of, trade unions.[256]

In a general sense the brief life of the Regeneration Society provides a good illustration of the impossibility of compartmentalising the multi-faceted movements of the early 1830s. More particularly, the episode marks the end of the first phase of factory campaigns and draws out and illuminates some of the key aspects of the early factory movement.

In the first place it highlights the continuing connection between the issues of adults' and children's hours. The Plan's initial starting date, 1 March 1834, was not plucked out of thin air but was the date on which the Althorp's eight hour limit on children's hours was due to be introduced. Factory reformers continued to cherish the hope that adults' terms and conditions of employment could be improved alongside those of the factory children. Secondly, the eventual adoption of the 'Eight Hour Plan' in the West Riding, without the active support of either Bull or Oastler, provides further evidence that the local leaders were quite capable of pursuing an independent line. Any doubts and divisions amongst local leaders were founded on pragmatic or political considerations rather a desire not to offend their respectable allies. Thirdly, the whole episode re-emphasises the existence of persisting, but often opaque, links between the early factory movement and both the trade unionism and popular radicalism. David Brook of Leeds, who personifies some of these links, was asked by one of the members of the 1834 Select Committee on Handloom Weavers' Petitions, in late June 1834, about his attitude to the Regeneration Society. His reply was that

---

254 O.C. No. 664, Oastler and Stocks to Owen, 11 Nov. 1833, used this metaphor in discussing the scheme.

255 Ward, 'Leeds', p. 102; Ward, *Chartism*, p. 65; and Ward, *Factory Movement*, p. 115.

256 Ward, 'Leeds', p. 101, quotes a *Leeds Intelligencer* report of the 1 August meeting of delegates of the West Riding STCs who resolved 'to maintain an organisation and to ask members to refuse to work more than ten hours per day'.

whilst he had always considered Ten Hours sufficient, he had 'no objection to work only 8 hours if I could get proper remuneration'.[257]

The overlap of personnel, the shared meeting places, the repetition of common themes and concepts all indicate that the connections which had existed from the start were welded more strongly together in the heat of the class antagonisms of late 1833 and early 1834. This fusion is illustrated by a Leeds Factory Reformation Society meeting held in early February 1834 at the Union Inn, (headquarters of both the Leeds STC and Trades' Union), to formulate questions to put at the imminent election hustings. William Rider, ultra-radical and former secretary to the STC, told his audience that whilst he belonged to a political party, they 'as unionists should not be distracted with political parties' and urged that question be put to the candidates about eight hours, factory children, machinery and trades' unions.[258] Rider had not sold out his radical beliefs, but was merely reflecting the concerns of his audience in the phoney war period of early 1834. They and he shared a common distrust and dislike of the 'Reforming Whigs' and their local mill-owning allies. The hope they briefly invested in the Regeneration scheme was one small manifestation of a wider frustration and sense of foreboding.

---

257 BPP 1834, X, p. 33.
258 *LT* 8 Feb. 1834.

6

Radicalism and Popular Movements, 1833–7

Gentlemen, I have now given you a brief sketch of Toryism; I will now, by your leave, tell you of some little thing which our liberal Whig Government has done for us. ("They have done nothing.") Yes, they have. (Loud cries of "What is it, then, sir.") I was going to tell you that, instead of our reforming Whigs alleviating those sufferings imposed upon us by the other oppressive tax-eating faction, their almost first act was passing a Coercion Bill for famishing Ireland (That's Whiggism.) Their next liberal and economical measure was, adding 10,000 men to the standing army, in time of general and perfect peace. (Shame). What comes next, think you? The humane Whigs felt so much for the poor black slaves (or else their masters) that they robbed the poor starving white slaves of twenty millions of their hard earned pittance, and gave it to the West India planters as a reward for their iniquity - iniquity of the darkest dye, traffic in human flesh and blood. (We will have it back yet). Gentlemen, have not the Whigs deprived us of the privilege of uniting to obtain and maintain reasonable wages. (The Dorchester labourers). Then, gentlemen, there is the poor law amendment bill, the joint production of Whig and Tory; I appeal to you, is that act not the most monstrous act ever decreed. (It is, and we will not have it). … Gentlemen, I believe that the ten pound reform bill was intended as a means of for ever riviting [sic] our heavy and galling chains, and, unless the productive classes exert themselves, and that immediately, that bill will have its intended effect. (It never shall.)[1]

The speaker is John Buckley, a radical greengrocer, addressing an audience of local operatives, mainly fancy weavers, at the Almondbury 'mock election' of summer 1837.[2] The views he expresses, in fairly traditional radical terms, are typical components of an analysis which summarised the perceived political experience of the working population and which gained widespread acceptance in the years leading up to emergence of Chartism.

If the agitational endeavours of 1829-32 aided the advent of an identifiable group of local leaders and the inception of independent working-class organisations, the multiple campaigns of the mid-decade years enabled these leaders to consolidate their position, practise their political skills and further develop a radical infrastructure. In addition, through the informal networks that blossomed and the more formal organisations that were set up, a number of new leaders emerged. These figures supplemented the cadre of town and village radicals who had come (or returned) to prominence in the Reform Bill era. Predominantly working-class in social class or origin, they were just as uncompromising in tone and outlook as the established leaders and, like them, often reserved a special hostility for the middle-class Whig-liberal 'reformers' of 1832.

The increasingly class-conscious and sophisticated analysis of political and social relationships which these new and established leaders voiced had its roots firmly embedded in the language and ideas of traditional radicalism and continued to emphasise the prime importance of political relations. However, the radical ideology of the 1830s was not simply Cobbett's attack on 'Old Corruption' writ large. The experiences of the 1820s, the 'decade of the silent insurrection', of early co-operation, of trades' unionism, of the factory campaigns and particularly the reform crisis helped to formulate an analysis, which whilst still using and drawing on the language and forms of an older critique, also incorporated elements of an alternative political economy.[3]

In the years following the passing of the Reform Act a special hostility was reserved for middle-class Whig-liberals and advocates of orthodox political economy who, personified in 'Neddy Baines', emerged as the chief political and economic enemies of the working class. A deep sense of betrayal pervades the speeches of many local leaders. After five months in prison as an 'unstamped' victim, Joshua Hobson, returning in January 1834 to a town (Huddersfield) riven by post by-election divisions and disappointment, gave full vent to his personal and class-based feelings of animosity to the 'patriotic and reforming ten-pounders'. Starting with the premise, which survived intact into the early Chartist years, that the government and their middle-

---

1   *LT* 19 Aug. 1837.

2   For further discussion of this event, with all the trappings of a real election, see John Sanders, 'The Voice of the "Shoeless, Shirtless and Shameless": Community radicalism in the West Riding, 1829 to 1839', *Northern History*, 58, 2 (2021), pp. 265-6; and see below, pp. 323-4.

3   Gwyn A. Williams' preface to Dorothy Thompson (ed.), *The Early Chartists* (London: Macmillan, 1971), p. x.

class allies were bent on provoking disturbances in order to attack the (working) people, he advised forbearance and self-help:

> 'Tis not by acts of petty outrage, or a blind attack upon persons or property, (hear, hear) that can give you redress for the many wrongs you are made to endure, but you must calmly and dispassionately use the moral power you possess, and take the management of your own affairs into your own hands... You must be fully convinced NOW, if you were not before, that all expectations of relief or help from a foreign source are in the highest degree delusive; – that to hope for the aid or support of any other class is all in vain; but that you yourselves must be the workers of your own emancipation. The aristocracy, it is needless to say, will render you no assistance, and the middle classes have by their conduct both recently and formerly proved themselves the greatest enemies you have to encounter in your fight for the rights and privileges of your own order. Yes! I emphatically repeat, the middle men are your greatest enemies – your most inveterate foes. They would grind you into dust beneath their feet, and even then not be content. You will have to come to close quarters with this mean-spirited but tyrannical crew before you obtain your just situation in society, for they will oppose your movements to the utmost of their power, and the sooner you let them feel and know your strength the better. Collect your forces, organise yourselves for the struggle – they have begun the attack – return them the compliment by abridging their profits, and then stand on your guard and wait for the result.[4]

Not all local leaders would have stated the case against the middle class so starkly and unforgivingly. Nor would all have gone along with his advocacy of co-operation and exclusive dealing.[5] Hobson was speaking after suffering personally, in the bitter aftermath of radical and factory reform defeats and with the spectre of the employers' counter-attack against trades' unionism looming ever larger. In places other than Huddersfield and in different, less charged, environments working-class radicals continued to work with middle-class 'liberals'. Their allies primarily comprised those on the radical wing of the Whig-liberal bloc (including a few avowed political economists) with whom, politically, they shared much in common. Such alliances might be limited and pragmatic, but the hope of an enduring popular, anti-establishment alliance was never quite extinguished. However, the story of popular movements during the five years from 1833 to 1837 is largely an account of the unfolding of a series of conflicts and campaigns whose collective result was to demonstrate the essential truth of Hobson's analysis, and to encourage its wider acceptance.

This chapter analyses the key campaigns and activities of the mid-1830s, and assesses their contribution to the development of radical leadership and organisation. Although a wide cross-section of movements are examined, it is not possible to cover every manifestation of popular endeavour, nor all local variations in the impact of these.

---

4   *VWR* 25 Jan. 1834.
5   Ibid. Hobson urges his audience to 'keep the proceeds of your own labour as much as possible within yourselves, by establishing co-operative stores, and dealing only with your friends...'

Some aspects of the incremental growth of working-class disillusionment and bitterness have already been covered in earlier chapters. Equally, a degree of artificiality is introduced by separating out and dissecting particular campaigns or events. In reality the agitations and organisations of the mid-1830s, like the leadership which they helped to develop, overlapped and fed off each other, and were merely the public expression of a far deeper radical culture and an increasingly class-conscious mindset.

The chapter seeks to overcome some of the inevitable dangers of compartmentalisation by examining the pervasiveness of this culture, by highlighting some of the points of overlap between movements, and by showing how working-class radicalism in the middle years of the decade was broadening its horizons and concerns. Although it argues that there existed a reservoir of latent support for radicalism, it does not pretend that this was always translated into formal support and activism. There were peaks and troughs. The multi-faceted conflicts which generated such bitterness and class antagonism in late 1833 and the first half of 1834 gave way to a period of relative quiet. This was partly the result of economic prosperity; but other factors – the recent trades' union defeats, the impasse which factory reform had reached, the relative lack of contentious parliamentary legislation, and the cooling of electoral fervour – were also important. The atmosphere changed in the second half of 1836 as radical organisation revived under the stimulus of Feargus O'Connor's tours, as the factory movement entered a more embittered phase, as the local economy faltered, and as the Poor Law Commission turned its attention to the north. The period of late 1836 and 1837 sees the convergence of a number of strands of working-class activity and the emergence of a more consciously independent and self-sufficient leadership and organisational framework. This provided the backbone of early Chartism in the West Riding.

The chapter has been divided into two halves which overlap in their chronology and concerns. The first part deals mainly with the 1833–35 period and looks at the key episodes in early disillusionment with the reformed Parliament and at the evidence for independent working-class political activity and organisation both during and outside election times. It emphasises the depth and breadth of popular radical culture and the importance of local political contests. It also examines in detail one key bridging agitation of the mid-decade: the 'struggle for a Free Press'.

The second half focuses firstly on the development of radical organisation in the 1835–37 period, particularly the growth of an independent working-class political presence. It then traces radical participation in the defence of trade unionism, from the continued support for the Dorchester victims to the agitation on behalf of the Glasgow cotton spinners, and investigates radical involvement in the handloom weavers' agitations of 1835 and 1837-38. A third section picks up the threads of the revived factory campaigns of 1835 and 1836 and follows these as they lead into the short–lived but highly-charged campaigns of the anti–poor law agitation.[6] This

---

6 Katrina Navickas, *Protest and the Politics of Space and Place, 1789-1848* (Manchester: Manchester University Press, 2016), p. 135 ff, accurately characterizes this as the 'anti-new poor law movement'. This book, however, uses the traditional, shorter designation used by contemporaries.

section is used to re-examine the existence and significance of Tory Radicalism and the transition to Chartism.

PART ONE

1: Political Unions and Popular Agitations, 1833-4

Formal radical activity and organisation subsided but did not totally die away after the excitement of the first reformed elections. The post–reform political unions in particular played an important role in keeping the machinery of local leadership and organisation in good working order in the hiatus between the 1832 election and the Dorchester agitation of spring 1834. Their concerns also testify to the growing distance between working–class radicals and their former Whig–liberal allies. Apart from the usual sprinkling of lower middle-class leaders and supporters, mainly shopkeepers and tradesmen who consistently advocated the people's cause, the political unions of 1833 were predominantly working–class bodies. They advocated 'real' radical measures – universal suffrage, vote by ballot, annual parliaments and the abolition of property qualifications – and took up topical issues – Irish coercion, the Calthorpe St. inquest, factory reform and the persecution of 'unstamped' victims.[7] 'Respectable' support, tacit or explicit, had now largely been withdrawn and the unions became looser popular forums without the consolidating reform focus of their predecessors.

The *Destructive*, organ of leading metropolitan radical Henry Hetherington, noted the general decline of political unions in July 1833: 'from all quarters we hear of nothing but divisions, disunion and consequent weakness among the Political Unions'.[8] However, General Bouverie, the Northern Commander writing at the same time, was a little premature in his assertion that 'there is scarcely a vestige remaining' of them in the northern towns. Formal organisations survived at Huddersfield, Bradford, Halifax, Hebden Bridge and Leeds. Indeed, Bouverie admitted a month later that Political Unions were still in existence, though 'their meetings are rare'.[9] The Bradford Political Union in fact met fortnightly, whilst the Huddersfield body held regular meetings at its Swan Yard Union room.[10]

With its infant press in the first exciting months of its existence, Huddersfield radicalism for a time positively buzzed with pride and purpose. John Cleave, of the National Union of the Working Classes in London, speaking at a local Political Union meeting in June, 'congratulated the Huddersfield Union that they had at length got a Press of their own' and 'friends' from Huddersfield helped to establish a political union

---

7   The inquest jury into the Calthorpe Street disturbances (when police allegedly attacked a National Union of the Working Classes rally in London) controversially returned a verdict of 'justifiable homicide' in relation to the death of a policeman who had been stabbed.

8   *Destructive*, 27 July 1833.

9   TNA: HO 40/31 f. 39, Bouverie to Phillips, 26 July 1833; f. 41, Bouverie to Phillips, 26 Aug. 1833.

10   *LT* 24 Aug. 1833. A. J. Peacock, *Bradford Chartism* (York: St. Anthony's Press, 1969), p. 7; *VWR* 8 June 1833.

in neighbouring Holt Head.[11] However, with employment tolerable and trade union concerns uppermost in people's minds, it was an uphill struggle. The Huddersfield radicals' paper, the *Voice of the West-Riding*, responded pugnaciously to reports in early October 1833 that political unions were dead by asserting, 'Yes the Unions still have signs of life; perhaps such numbers may not meet at any particular place as heretofore, but radicalism, is marching onwards, and assuming that ubiquity which constitutes PUBLIC OPINION.'[12]

The defiant tone, however, is married to a realistic appraisal of the difficulties of maintaining radical momentum in 1833. Bradford used prestigious visiting lecturers such as Richard Carlile, Robert Owen and Hetherington to stimulate interest and the Halifax Political Union was still meeting in late 1833.[13] The New Year Huddersfield by-election temporarily revived political excitement and organisation there. However, in the anti-climactic aftermath of the radicals' decisive and divisive defeat, and with the focus of working-class concern turning increasingly to the defence of trades' unions, formal political unions (but not their leaders, ideas or potential support) largely disappeared. A Home Office spy touring the West Riding in March 1834 reported that, though 'there is a strong radical feeling' in Huddersfield, 'there is no Political Union'. 'At Leeds there is one Political Union they have a meeting once a month, but this Union is very weak', whilst 'at Bradford there is a Political Union but it has only 88 members'.[14] This probably went out of existence shortly afterwards; and although isolated outposts, as at Hebden Bridge, may have survived it is likely that no major centre saw regular meetings of a political union in late 1834.[15]

However, formal political organisations were only the tip of the radical iceberg and their importance should not be exaggerated. As the spy noted of Bradford, 'political feeling is ... pretty strong, and the papers of Hetherington much talked of.'[16] This latent support for radicalism explains why even in the relatively dormant political years of 1833-5 radical leaders were able to invoke a substantial popular response to certain key issues. The resulting agitations and campaigns were particularly important in maintaining a radical presence, identifying fundamental points of differences with local Whig-liberals and in broadening the outlook and interests of radicalism.

The Irish Coercion Act of January 1833, the reformed Parliament's first major measure, rapidly became such an issue.[17] It provoked a number of rallies throughout

---

11 *VWR* 15 June, 20 July 1833. The Holt Head PU was still in existence later in the year, *VWR* 28 Dec. 1833. The Huddersfield radicals also tried to establish a political union at Penistone, *VWR* 10 Aug. 1833.

12 *VWR* 5 Oct. 1833. For reports of their decease, see *LM* 28 Sept. 1833.

13 Peacock, *Bradford Chartism*, p. 7. *LT* 7 Dec. 1833 for Halifax meeting. The speakers included William Thornton, woolcomber and Primitive Methodist preacher, and later a prominent Chartist who emigrated to the United States in 1840 after being implicated in insurrectionary planning.

14 TNA: HO 40/32 f. 49, Bouverie to Phillips, 19 Mar. 1834. The PU at Leeds is probably the Holbeck PU which had supported Joshua Bower in the 1834 by-election. The spy also noted the absence of a PU in Dewsbury.

15 See, for example, *PMG* 28 June 1834, for a meeting of the Hebden Bridge PU.

16 TNA: HO 40/32 f. 49, Bouverie to Phillips, 19 Mar. 1834.

17 On the nationwide response to this issue, see Dorothy Thompson, 'Ireland and the Irish in

the West Riding, beginning in Dewsbury where a public meeting was chaired by William Rhodes, a local gentleman on the radical wing of the Whig-liberal alliance.[18] At Leeds Thomas Bottomley, Huntite radical and future secretary of the Leeds Chartist Northern Union branch, chaired a sizable gathering which included speeches by the town's two leading working-class radicals, William Rider and John Ayrey.[19] According to the hostile *Halifax Guardian*, a Swan Yard meeting called at the Huddersfield operatives' request and chaired by Lawrence Pitkethley included a 'violent speech' from Mr Lalor, an Irish agitator; but was not numerously attended.[20] In Halifax the audience at a joint meeting on Irish coercion and the Repeal of Duties heard speeches from Thomas Wilson, the leading co-operator, Joseph Nicholson snr, Chair of the Halifax Political Union, and four future Chartists, Elijah Crabtree, Robert Wilkinson, Thomas Cliffe and W (in all probability, William) Thornton.[21] The Irish Coercion Bill was cited at a Bradford operatives' meeting on Eccleshill Moor as an illustration of the uselessness of the Reform Bill.[22] Indeed the spring campaign on Ireland provided a reason for the continued existence of local political unions and served as a channel through which working-class disenchantment with the Reform Bill was first voiced. For many local radical leaders Irish coercion remained the first entry in the catalogue of Whig deceit.[23]

The second key issue which helped maintain radical enthusiasm and an organisational framework in the months after the first reformed elections was the prosecution of sellers of unstamped newspapers. Local participation in the 'War of the Unstamped' will be examined in more detail later, but it is worth noting the extent of support generated for 'victims' such as Hetherington, Carlile and Rev. Taylor in the early and middle months of 1833.[24] Concern about the issue was not new. The Huddersfield radicals, including many prominent leaders and future Chartists, had held a public meeting on the 'Liberty of the Press' in August 1831.[25] However, this campaign gained added resonance in early 1833 now that it was a reformed Parliament condoning prosecutions and perpetuating 'taxes on knowledge'. The Leeds contributions to the 'Victim Fund' included familiar radical names as well as 13s.5d

---

English Radicalism', in James Epstein and Dorothy Thompson (eds.), *The Chartist Experience: Studies in Working-class Radicalism and Culture, 1830-60* (London: Macmillan, 1982), pp. 126-8.

18 *HG* 23 Feb. 1833. Rhodes was denounced as a 'Whig' by local Chartists in the late 1830s, *NS* 8 June 1839.

19 *LT* 14 Mar. 1833. Little is known about Thomas Bottomley (1796?-1859+).

20 *HG* 2, 9 Mar. 1833.

21 *HG* 16 Mar. 1833. The unpopular duties were on malt, hops and soap. 'Radical Bob' Wilkinson (1793-1855), a shoemaker, became a prominent local leader.

22 *LT* 14 Mar. 1833.

23 See, for example, Thompson, 'Ireland and the Irish', p. 127; and the prefacing quote from John Buckley.

24 See below, p. 291.

25 *PMG* 17 Sept. 1831.

from 'the haters of tyranny at Gott's manufactory' and 3s.6d from 'Friends wishing all Tyrants heads smouldering in the dust'.[26]

The blood-curdling epithets in this and other lists is a reminder of the persisting influence of a traditional radical invective and the Paineite ideas it conveyed. For many the chief enemy remained 'Old Corruption' – Church and State, tyranny and taxation. This familiar vocabulary was shared by radicals of all persuasions – whether 'Huntite', 'Cobbettite', Carlileite republican or lower middle-class radicals and freethinkers who had supported 'first-step' reform. The extent to which specific strands of radicalism can be separated out in the local context is strictly limited.[27] Certainly identifiable 'Huntite' and 'Carlileite' factions had repeatedly clashed in Leeds in the late 1820s and early 1830s.[28] Tellingly, a Honley correspondent to Carlile's Gauntlet spoke in May 1833 of the Reformers' 'aptitude to divide themselves into sects and parties, such as Political Unionists, Trade Unionists, co-operatives, Cobbettites, Huntites etc, having each and all a separate nostrum for the cure of Church and State and letting name and not principle be their guide'.[29] However, it is likely that he is overstating the extent of local divisions. Radicals of varying shades of belief, dined to celebrate Paine's birthday, drank the health of both Cobbett and Hunt and supported Carlile's fight for a free press.[30] Indeed, the subscriptions and lists of volunteers which were sent into Hetherington's Guardian and Carlile's Gauntlet in 1833 indicate that the 'Liberty of the Press' issue was one which united a wide cross-section of radical support.[31] Whilst local radicals may have had different priorities and emphases, it is doubtful whether the constant quarrels and splits which marked the national leadership were automatically translated into the local context. Here common ground and shared enemies meant that collaboration between different shades of radicalism was just as evident as the 'wrangling and ill-will' that the Honley correspondent cited.[32]

---

26 PMG 20 Apr. 1833. Contributors included William Rider, Thomas Bottomley, J. B. Walker (Secretary of the Radical Reform Union in late 1831), and James Halliwell (a publican and soon to be treasurer of the local 'Hobson' fund).

27 For the eclecticism of radical followers, particularly outside the major centres of population, see Edward Royle, Victorian Infidels: The origins of the British Secularist Movement, 1781-1866 (Manchester: Manchester University Press, 1974), p. 10.

28 See above, pp. 135-6 and 158.

29 Gauntlet 9 June 1833. If anything, the evidence points to the 'Carlileites' being more sectarian than other radical groups.

30 On the radical convivial culture of the 1830s, see below, p. 320.

31 Gauntlet 31 Mar. - 28 July 1833. PMG 20 Apr. - 29 June 1833. The subscriptions and lists of volunteers (to work for a reduction in taxes) were sent in by local 'network' figures such as Alice Mann and Charles Mayne in Leeds, Christopher Tinker in Huddersfield, Peter Bussey and Squire Farrar in Bradford. They include many familiar leaders as well other local activists and adherents.

32 Although there were later divisions in Huddersfield, the only general exception appears to have been Leeds where the Carlileite Republican radicals remained distinct from the ultra-radicals, and with middle-class 'Cobbettites', tended to be absorbed into the class-collaborationist Holbeck PU and later the Operative Radical Association. The influence of Carlile's narrow branch of individualistic radicalism, with its hostility to formal organisation, declined in the 1830s; E. P. Thompson, The Making of the English Working Class

The third issue which evoked considerable radical interest and engagement in 1833 – factory reform – has been discussed at length earlier.[33] Radicals addressed themselves to the issue not just in Huddersfield and Keighley where connections had always been strong, but also in Bradford, where the local political union met to protest against the Factory Commission.[34] The meeting provides important evidence of formal radical participation in the ten hours issue and also an insight into their reasons for engagement. They opposed the Commission on the grounds that, firstly, the injustice of employing children was self-evident, secondly, it was a waste of public money, thirdly, child labour was caused by poverty and, fourthly, the only remedies for popular distress were the abolition of pensions and excessive taxation and the extension of the suffrage. In adopting this stance, the radicals were not merely extending the range of their interests to include factory reform, they were also seeking to expose the broad mass of people who supported this cause to a deeper understanding of its wider political and economic significance.

This same approach – the stressing of the broader political context of immediate struggles – is also noticeable in radical responses to a fourth major issue which moved sharply into focus in the second half of 1833: the attack on trades' unionism. In general, working-class radicals had supported the growth of the trades' unions. Many radicals were members themselves and a few, as at Bradford, were active leaders.[35] Political unions and trades' unions were not necessarily alternatives, but shared many common concerns, perceptions and members. The authorities certainly saw and feared connections.[36] General Bouverie, writing in early 1834, voiced the widely-held opinion that 'the regulation of trade and wages is not their ultimate object, but that there is a strong Republican spirit pervading all their discussions, and that although in name Political Unions have almost ceased to exist, the so-called Trades Unions are in fact Political Unions to all intents and purposes'.[37] The Huddersfield Trades' Unions certainly co-operated closely with the Huddersfield Political Union in the 1832 and 1834 elections, and in late 1833 the radicals' admiration for the trade unionists' unity and organisation was expressed in an address to the non-electors.[38]

However, it is clear that many leading radicals saw trades' unions in general and the strike weapon in particular as limited engines of change. Writing in November 1833, William Rider stressed that as an individual he had always tried to get a fair return for his labour from a master, but argued that it was equally important to 'secure the enjoyment of the reward of our industry ... and I contend that we shall never obtain this security so long as an overbearing oligarchy are permitted to load us with onerous exactions'.[39] Even when there were signs that the trades' unions were turning to co-operative production (through 'commercial orders'), and the replacement editor

---

(Harmondsworth: Penguin, 1968 edn), p. 844 and Royle, *Victorian Infidels*, p. 42

33 See above, pp. 278-82.

34 *VWR, HG* 15 June 1833.

35 For example, Peter Bussey, Joseph Brook, John Douthwaite.

36 See, for example, TNA: HO 40/31 f. 41, Bouverie to Phillips, 26 Aug 1833.

37 TNA: HO 40/32 f. 35, Bouverie to Phillips, 25 Feb. 1833.

38 *PMG* 7 Dec. 1833.

39 *VWR* 2 Nov. 1833.

of the *Voice of the West-Riding* was predicting that 'Co-operative and political knowledge are about to give a glorious emancipation to the producers of wealth and really conduct us into the "new age"', the primacy of political change was always stressed.[40] The same author, commenting in October 1833 on the 'Crisis' in Leeds brought about by imminent industrial conflict, strongly recommended co-operative production but 'only upon the principal of Expediency – under a well-regulated state of society it would be unnecessary, we are for Political Equality, and then every man for what he is worth.'[41]

Not all radicals would have defined their political philosophy so individualistically, but it is clear that a number had strong reservations about secret oaths and the quasi-religious procedures of the unions.[42] Others were frustrated by what they perceived as the unions' blinkered political perspectives and the pro-Reform Bill sympathies of some of their leaders. The 1832 obituary of Thomas Roberts, President of the Leeds Trades' Union, had characterized him as 'one of the warmest friends of Reform' and allegations had circulated that leading members of the Union had been given tickets for one of Baines' election dinners.[43]

However, in the increasingly bitter and class-conscious atmosphere of late 1833 such reservations began to count for little. Although Rider admitted, the Trades' Unions in Leeds 'in a political point of view comprised of Radicals, Whigs and Tories', he nevertheless asserted that 'no man ought to find fault with the Institution on that account'. It was obvious to him 'that the Trades' Union have no other object in view than the removal of those accumulated grievances which are inflicted upon the working classes'. That being the case, he concluded in typical cliff-hanging fashion:

> It behoves every friend of justice to be on the look out, and to take care
> and let the adversaries strike the first blow, and when it is struck, let it
> be the signal for – but I must conclude until another week.[44]

The following weeks simply provided more evidence of what Peter Bussey termed the 'struggle of might against right' in a society suffering from 'the effect of excessive wealth in one part of the community which never fails to produce excessive misery in the other' and divided, in the *Voice's* words, 'into the governed and the governing'.[45] Locally, enemies were more easily identifiable. Under the headline 'CONFOUND

---

40 *VWR* 28 Sept. 1833. This may have been John Francis Bray, the early socialist writer. For fuller discussion, see below, p. 331 (fns. 197 and 198).

41 *VWR* 12 Oct. 1833.

42 *BO* 17 Mar. 1875. This summary of the political career of Bradford woolcomber John Jackson recalled that he had 'opposed the secret lodges in connection with trades unions in 1834, maintaining that they would be nothing but a nest of spies and informers'.

43 *LM* 8 Dec. 1832; 25 Aug. 1832. Roberts had been a signatory (intriguingly just below the name of the mythical 'John Powlett') of a Leeds requisition for a public meeting to petition the House of Lords in favour of the Reform Bill (*LP* 24 Sept. 1831).

44 *VWR* 2 Nov., 26 Oct. 1833. The anticipation of conflict being provoked by the radicals' enemies was an established part of the radical conception of violence and was carried through into Chartism.

45 *VWR* 16 Nov.; 9 Nov. 1833.

THOSE UNIONISTS! THEY WONT LET <u>US</u> DO WHAT WE LIKE WITH THE <u>SWINE</u>', the *Voice* reported the posting of a scurrilous note 'upon the corner of a street at Lindley [near Huddersfield] the morning after "John Powlett" had been with a strike to a Card-maker who wants to pull his workmen down from Fifteen shillings a week to about Eleven shillings: he is building a large factory and the money must come from some where'.[46] Meanwhile, 'the labouring classes' new-found spirit and 'determination to aid each other' had 'already caused no small amount of alarm in the ranks of those who are always hostile to the emancipation of the many from the unnatural thraldom in which they have been held so long'.[47]

In such a confrontational atmosphere, with the *Voice* presciently predicting, 'that if the union discover any symptoms of weakness the Government will give it a cowardly kick, as bystanders sometimes do in a village fray when the parties are down', labels such as 'radical' or 'trade unionist', 'co-operator' or 'factory-reformer' became increasingly irrelevant.[48] Local leaders of all persuasions used the public platform and the columns of the press to proclaim workers' right to organise to defend their living standards. In Bradford, for example, Peter Bussey, Joseph Brook, William Hill, John Jackson and William Thornton participated in a series of trade union meetings in the winter of 1833-4, whilst in Huddersfield the local trades' union was heavily engaged in the political manoeuvring around the Huddersfield by-election.[49]

After a midwinter lull, with employers and unions both resting 'on their oars', and trades' unionists' efforts focused on support for the Leicester and Derby disputes, industrial conflict re-emerged with a vengeance in the spring of 1834.[50] Rumours were already circulating about local magistrates' attempts to break the unions' barrier of secrecy and news of the arrests of trade unionists in, first, Exeter and then Dorchester ramped up tensions. Despite impressive shows of strength and solidarity at the funerals of prominent members, the West Riding unions were now increasingly on the backfoot, fearful of both prosecution and an employers' counter-attack.[51]

The news from Dorchester inspired a resolution at a Leeds meeting of 'distressed operatives' in April 1834 'to resist every attempt which may be made to suppress the Trades' Unions'.[52] Chaired by Thomas Bottomley, a leading radical, and addressed by William Rider, the gathering also condemned excessive competition, the abuses of machinery and long working hours. Meanwhile, in Huddersfield, Joshua Hobson located the Dorchester case within a broader economic and political context. The lesson for the working class was that they

---

46 *VWR* 2 Nov. 1833.

47 *VWR* 9 Nov, 1833.

48 *VWR* 12 Oct. 1833.

49 *LT* 2 Nov., 21, 28 Dec. 1833, 18 Jan. 1834 (for Bradford). See *LM* 28 Dec. 1833 and Alan J. Brooke, 'Labour disputes and Trade Unions in the Industrial Revolution', in E. A. Hilary Haigh (ed.), *A Most Handsome Town: Aspects of the History and Culture of a West Riding Town* (Huddersfield: Kirklees Cultural Services, 1992), pp. 228-9 (for Huddersfield).

50 *LT* 19 Oct, 2, 9 Nov. 1833; *LM* 2 Nov. 1833; *LT* 29 Mar.1834.

51 For Derby, Exeter, Dorchester, the funerals and the local 'spies', see *VWR* Feb. - Apr. 1834.

52 *LT* 12 Apr. 1834.

must be the workers of their own emancipation. To depend on the exertions of any other men or any class, is to lean on a broken reed… Society must be completely revolutionised, completely changed; and this too must be the work of the workers. But in order to do this, they must work for themselves. They must intercept profits – they must accumulate Capital – they must obtain property – and, above all, they must become possessed of their political rights. They must, as Mr Owen justly said the other day, become a fourth estate in the realm, and if the other three will not give way, they must be superseded…[53]

For radicals in general 'the cruel the vindictive, the blood-thirsty, the MONSTROUS sentence' passed on 'the poor Toll-Puddle men' was, as argued elsewhere, 'the last straw, the final confirmation of the reformed Parliament's vendetta against the working class'.[54] William Hill in Bradford characterised it as 'to all intents and purposes a trial of the strength of the working-classes, as well as of their spirit'.[55] A frenetic editorial in the *Voice* put the situation facing 'the people' (now equated unequivocally with the working class) in more fundamental terms:

Will this fresh indignity – this additional insult––– this *one lash* more, be borne with patience? … PATIENCE? … What when the assassin's knife is at our throat - when our very existence is at stake … when our very heart-strings are being torn asunder by the rude grasp of our relentless oppressors? PATIENCE!! Good God! Patience under circumstances like these? The idea is enough to drive one mad! Vile slave, thou that dar'st to talk of *patience*. Scourge him, aye, scourge him Tyrant, to his heart's content ––– tread him into the dust ––– trample on his spiritless carcase ––– whip him, whip him, aye whip him, he can't complain.[56]

A casual sentence in a late nineteenth century account of the early political career of Chartist leader William Armitage of South Crossland (near Huddersfield) provides confirmation of the close West Riding connection to 'the Dorchester case' and the reason why, in the *Poor Man's Guardian's* words, local people treated it 'as personal to themselves'. A 'Retrospective' of Armitage's 'Radical life' notes that the Tolpuddle men were prosecuted 'for being connected with the John Poulett [Powlett] movement which was a trades union organisation, a branch of which was established in Dorsetshire among the agricultural labourers that wanted to better their condition by an advance of wages'.[57]

---

53 *VWR* 29 Mar. 1834.

54 *VWR* 12 Apr. 1834; John Sanders, 'John Douthwaite and "John Powlett": Trades' Unionism and Conflict in Early 1830s Yorkshire', *Labour History Review* 86, 1 (2022), p. 27.

55 *LT* 12 Apr. 1834.

56 *VWR* 12 Apr. 1834.

57 *HDE* 26 Dec, 1885; *PMG* 11 July 1835. On the links between Yorkshire and Tolpuddle, see Sanders, 'John Douthwaite and "John Powlett"', p. 26.

The 1834 campaign against the Dorchester sentences revived popular radicalism. At Halifax a large public meeting on Skircoat Moor chaired by Thomas Wilson, the leading local co-operator and radical, heard speeches from future Chartists Benjamin Rushton, William Thornton, Thomas Cliffe, Thomas Howarth, and Robert Wilkinson. Isaac Haley, a 'working man', endorsed the merits of 'one grand union' and urged 'all who had not joined ... immediately to become members'. The meeting ended with three cheers for the Dorchester labourers and three for the 'national consolidated Trades Union.'[58] The Bradford platform on the same day included William Hill (later editor of the *Northern Star*) in the chair, Peter Bussey, James Ibbetson, the local unstamped seller, Joseph Brook, secretary of the Bradford Trades' Union, John Bowden, another prominent trade unionist, plus John Hanson and Joshua Hobson from Huddersfield.

Hobson, himself a recent victim of Whig 'persecution', was the natural choice to chair the Huddersfield protest meeting where again the radical presence was particularly strong.[59] A few days earlier a deputation headed by Hobson and Lawrence Pitkethly had interrupted a dinner in honour of John Blackburne, the new Whig MP for Huddersfield, to present a petition against the Dorchester sentences. The gathering had already achieved a degree of notoriety on account of Blackburne's anti-union views and its alleged exclusion of Richard Oastler, prompting a correspondent to the *Voice* to ponder,

If the appearance of one unwelcome guest creates such fear and trepidation amongst them, how would the "party" like to be visited by a few thousand of the Almondbury Bludgeon men (as the *Mercury* calls the operatives of this district) on the evening of their festivities and prove to their good friend Mr. Blackburne they are what designated them – "Bulls, Tigers and serpents"[60]

Leeds as always lagged somewhat behind other centres. An initial meeting on 7 April had focused on distress and was primarily an ultra-radical affair to which none of the respectable press sent reporters.[61] In contrast, a meeting held on Hunslet Moor the following Monday attracted a vast crowd. Speakers included prominent Leeds Trades' Union officials (for example, Simeon Pollard, Major Scholefield and Thomas Buckley) and sympathisers (including Thomas Barlow, a local hatter) as well as prominent radical-liberals from the 'Holbeck' Political Union (such as Joseph Lees and Zachariah Orrell). The only recognisable ultra-radical is John Ayrey and by this time he may

---

58 *LT* 12 Apr. 1834. Thomas Howarth (1788? - 1851+) was a carpet weaver. Isaac Haley's occupation is not known.

59 *LT, VWR* 12 Apr. 1834. Speakers included, Pitkethly, Bray and Green and Sykes. 'Bray' (J.F.?) and 'Green' (David?) are particularly intriguing.

60 *VWR* 29 Apr. 1834, quoted in Alan J. Brooke, 'Radicalism, Reform and Class Conflict in Huddersfield 1831-1834', p. 25, in 'Dangerous Societies', available at: https://undergroundhistories.wordpress.com/dangerous-societies/ (accessed 14 May 2022). Blackburne had referred to trades' union members in these terms the previous December.

61 *VWR* 12 Apr. 1834

well have split with his former colleagues.[62] The composition of the platform suggests both that the Huntite radicals were weak, and that the Trades' Union which encompassed a wide cross-section of political opinion, enjoyed closest links with the 'moderate' radicals.

Bradford, however, remained the centre of the agitation and, in an atmosphere of imminent confrontation, hosted another large outdoor meeting on Monday 21 April.[63] Speakers from across the textile district vilified the Whigs and 'the cruel and unjust sentence pronounced upon the Dorchester Unionists'. Peter Bussey lauded the trades' unionists' moral power, whilst refuting Lord Howick's prediction of bloodshed and class war. Joseph Crabtree, a leading Barnsley radical and trade unionist, asked the meeting what they would do if petitioning failed: '*(Cries of, "give over working, and go to London together".)*'; John Bowden urged universal suffrage, and John Hanson endorsed co-operation in a strong speech attacking the government and the middle class. He admitted to having 'many doubts as to the utility of strikes, which he began to think were only an accommodation to the markets. But a general strike, a reduction in the hours of labour, would regulate the markets, and call them all into work'. The meeting also marked the emergence of one particularly significant new speaker: woolcomber and future Chartist leader, George White. He told the meeting that the Whigs 'were making many spouters amongst the working-classes *(laughter)*, and he was one of them, *(cheers)*, he was making his first speech, they should by and by have a House of Commons of their own to speechify to *(Laughter.)* ... They saw that the profit mongers – the people who were living on their capital – were getting rich out of them, for the less the working-classes got, the more these men put into their pockets *(Hear, hear.)*'.[64]

By this time, the feverish local atmosphere had been ramped up still further with the news from across the Pennines in Oldham, where disturbances following a police raid on a union lodge had resulted in a unionist being shot dead. Delegates from Oldham, addressing a meeting of over five thousand people in Huddersfield on 19 April, had urged a general strike until the Dorchester unionists were repatriated and an eight-hour working day implemented. Perhaps fearing prosecution themselves, and aware of potential 'snakes in the grass', local leaders were more cautious and pinned their hopes on the power of a mass meeting.[65]

---

62 *LT* 19 Apr. 1834. The crowd was estimated at between 20-30,000.

63 For example, Keighley urged Bradford to call a delegate meeting and a Bradford man co-ordinated the eventual West Riding meeting, *VWR* 19, 26 Apr. 1834.

64 *VWR* 26 Apr. 1834. The talk of a general strike 'until all the grievances complained of by the labouring classes are redressed' is mentioned by George Beaumont (now an informer) in his letter to Melbourne, 21 Apr. 1834, in TNA: HO 52/25. On White (1813-1868?), an Irish-born woolcomber and Chartist stalwart, see J. T. Ward, *Chartism* (London: Batsford, 1973), p. 243, and Dorothy Thompson, *The Chartists: Popular Politics in the Industrial Revolution* (London: Breviary Stuff, 2013 edn.), pp. 161-2.

65 Brooke, 'Labour disputes and Trade Unions in the Industrial Revolution', in E. A. Hilary Haigh (ed.), *A Most Handsome Town: Aspects of the History and Culture of a West Riding Town* (Huddersfield: Kirklees Cultural Services, 1992), p. 229; *VWR, LM* 26 Apr. 1834; *VWR* 29 Mar, 1834.

The proposed climax of the agitation the following week, a major regional rally organised by Samuel Bower jnr. and a West Riding delegate committee, attempted to replicate the ten hours success of the year before.[66] The outdoor gathering on Wibsey Moor was stymied by foul Yorkshire weather, but, nevertheless, attracted a respectable turnout of over ten thousand people. Chaired by Capt. Wood of Sandal, the meeting heard unusually brief speeches from leading local figures such as Thomas Cliffe, William Thornton, John Hanson, Joshua Hobson and Peter Bussey, who declared that 'they were in the midst of a revolution; it was not a revolution of swords and knives, but a revolution of moral principle'. However, the absence of any significant Leeds participation, allied to rumours of trades' union difficulties and fears of imminent attack may all have dampened enthusiasm. The meeting adjourned to Whit Monday after delegating Bussey and Hobson to present a memorial to Lord Melbourne.[67] The delegates duly journeyed down to London, lodging at the headquarters of the GNCTU, but were unsuccessful in their efforts to meet Melbourne: a snub that only confirmed their already low opinion of the Home Secretary and his Whig colleagues.[68]

The planned report-back meeting never happened.[69] Dorchester proved to be but a well-timed prelude to the West Riding masters' concerted and completely successful attack on local trades' unions. The final struggle was waged throughout the textile district with extreme ferocity in an atmosphere of class antagonism and bitterness. In Leeds textile workers were locked out, poor relief was refused to strikers and their families, and trade union pubs were victimised.[70] The middle-class sponsored Mechanics Institute judged it prudent to postpone their AGM for a year, 'on account of the Trades Union'. In Bradford a trades' union committee man who sought to negotiate with a local manufacturer about weavers' wages was unceremoniously seen off the premises.[71]

Radicals such as Hobson and Rider gave what support they could and suggested wider radical or co-operative remedies but were literally often mere spectators of the conflict. Hobson's *Voice* provided 'NEWS FROM THE THEATRE OF WAR' and printed Rider's letter on the contest citing Lord Howick's view that the 'war at present waging between industry and capital, "was a struggle CLASS v CLASS, and whichever proved the master blood must flow"'[72] Rider spoke at just one of the Leeds unionists' regular outdoor meetings, in early June, when he gave a rousing address

---

66 *VWR* 26 Apr. 1834; Beaumont's letter (above). The marshalling arrangements were very similar to 1833.

67 *LT* 3 May 1834. The *Leeds Times* estimated the crowd at 15,000; the authorities gave the figure as 8-10,000, TNA: HO 52/25, Harewood to Melbourne, 2 May 1834; TNA: HO 40/32, f. 89, Bouverie to Phillips, 29 Apr. 1834.

68 *VWR, PMG* 10 May 1834 (Bussey and Hobson's letter to Melbourne).

69 *LT* 17 May 1834 for notice of the postponement.

70 See, *LT* 10, 17, 24, 31 May 1834; also 'Address to the Labouring Classes' in *PMG* 31 May 1834.

71 *LM* 28 Nov. 1835, cited in R. J. Morris, 'The Rise of James Kitson: Trades Union and Mechanics Institution, Leeds 1826-51', *Publications of the Thoresby Society*, 53 (1973), p. 104; *HHE* 22 May 1834.

72 *VWR* 17 May 1834.

which ended with a plea to the operatives not to sign 'the infernal document' and to adopt a 'real' radical approach:

> If they … signed this document; they might rest assured, a fair day's wage for a fair day's work would become unknown in the market of labour (*Cheers.*). He would conclude by giving it as his opinion, that unless the working classes of England did embrace real radical principles, and demand more wage for less work, they would never do any good. And while he said go on and persevere, he also said, probe the evil to the bottom, let the plaster be as large as the wound, and then restoration would not be far hence. (*Cheers.*)[73]

By this time the trades' union's non-political mask had slipped and Rider was not alone in drawing political conclusions from the contest. George Hodgson, woollen weaver of Wortley, near Leeds, and prominent union supporter, commenting on 'the existing struggle between capital on the one hand, and labour on the other', recalled how the operatives had helped the middle-class reformers carry the Reform Bill, but were being turned out by these very same people.[74] The *Voice*, for its part, gave the political colours (mainly Whig yellow) of the masters who had dismissed their workmen.[75]

The political lessons of the trades' union defeat were pivotal in framing the mindset of key radical figures. As argued elsewhere, 'the co-partnership of Whigs and local middle-class manufacturers in the harsh Dorchester sentences and the decimation of Yorkshire trade unionism had immense psychological impact on the early Chartist movement and the local leaders who orchestrated it'.[76] Their defence of trades' unions linked them to a broad-based and popular instrument of working-class endeavour, and provided them with valuable platform and organisational experience. It also sharpened their awareness of the power and the intransigent nature of their opponents and heightened their anticipation of government repression which continued to inform their later tactics. Above all, though, it emphasised the primacy of political reform as the most effective way of protecting working-class living standards. As Rider wrote in the early weeks of the strike, dismaying at the 'industrial' perspective of one Woodhouse Moor speaker:

> If men imagine that Jack Strike will work out their salvation, they will eventually find themselves labouring in vain, and spending their strength for naught while urging him on. The axe must be laid to the

---

73 *LT* 14 June 1834.

74 *LT* 24 May 1834. Hodgson (1790-1869) was a prominent speaker at the Leeds Trades' Union meetings in the summer of 1834. He gave evidence to the Handloom Weavers' Commission in 1838 and later the same year acted as a 'second' to Owenite socialist missionary, Lloyd Jones, in a public debate on the merits of 'Socialism' (*LT* 4 Aug., 10 Nov. 1838)

75 *VWR* 17 May 1834.

76 Sanders, 'John Douthwaite and "John Powlett"', p. 37

root, it is the <u>fellers</u> not the <u>pruners</u> that are wanted at corruption's tree...[77]

2: Local and National Politics in the Mid-1830s

The incremental growth of hostility to the Whigs and their middle-class supporters was a distinctive feature of the post-reform period. It happened despite plentiful instances of alliances between working-class radicals and middle-class elements of the predominantly Whig-liberal local elites in both parliamentary elections and in contests for the offices of local government. If the popular radicals were so embittered by their experiences in 1832 and immediately afterwards, why did they continue to work with their enemies?

This dilemma can be answered from a number of common-sense standpoints. In the first place the working-class radicals were practical politicians. The alliances they forged were often limited in duration and tactical in nature. Equally, memories of post-war Tory repression remained strong and the instinct to support the most radical candidate or option on offer remained strong.

Secondly, the very nature of the ideological framework within which most radicals were operating gave rise to ambiguous attitudes to the middle class. The persistent power of the notions of 'Old Corruption' and of the essential division in society being politically determined – with a fundamental dichotomy between governors/governed, rich/poor, oligarchy/people – meant that many radicals, and later Chartists, continued to hold out the hope that the middle classes would reject their new aristocratic allies and return to the popular fold.

Thirdly, the Whig-liberal bloc was not a monolithic entity. Working-class bitterness was primarily directed towards the old aristocratic Whigs and the mill-owning Whig-liberals (such as John Marshall in Leeds, or Jonathan Ackroyd who had led the attack on the Trades' Union in Halifax) and their allies in the press and professions. Lower middle-class small masters, tradesman and shopkeepers, though tarnished and not to be trusted after 1832, were a different case. For a start, a number of small shopkeepers and tradesmen were active radical leaders or sympathisers, and it was on this social group that hopes of an enduring alliance were primarily focused. After 1832 they were an important political force. They possessed the vote and their existence on the class borderline gave rise to hopes that through the lessons of hard experience, or via persuasion or exclusive dealing, they could be drawn into a broad radical alliance for further reforms and the extension of the suffrage.

Disillusionment with the reformed Parliament was not confined to working-class 'real' radicals.[78] Some of the better-paid working-men and lower middle-class elements

---

77 *VWR* 24 May 1834.

78 It is important to note that class labels should not be applied too inflexibly or interpreted too rigidly in relation to the loose but still identifiable political groupings which evolved in the mid-1830s. The 'real' (ultra) radicals who advocated the enfranchisements of the labouring-classes included 'lower' and 'middle' middle-class leaders and supporters and also some gentlemen-leaders. Equally working men supported all political parties, and amongst some groups of workers (for example better paid factory workers and the independent clothiers weaving high quality cloths in the villages outside Leeds) the limited reform programme

who had strongly supported the Whigs in 1832 alliances also voiced disappointment in the new legislators. By May 1833 the 'Holbeck' Political Union, the popular arm of Baines' Whig-liberal alliance, was criticising Macauley, one of the victorious Liberal candidates in Leeds in 1832.[79] Indeed the union's very existence, under the increasing influence of Joshua Bower, a popular local glass manufacturer, is an indication of the increasingly independent stance taken by the 'radical-liberals' in Leeds.[80]

A number of the issues which roused working-class radicals in the mid-1830s also won support on this radical wing of the Whig-liberal alliance. Many middle-class radicals opposed 'taxes on knowledge' and supported unstamped victims. They also shared common ground with working-class radicals on particular measures like the compensation and apprenticeship clauses of the government's slavery legislation or in their opposition to local church rates. More generally a common abhorrence of all manifestations of 'Old Corruption', both local and national, a mutual desire for cheap government and a shared list of desirable reforms united both camps. The extent of this common ground should not be exaggerated: the radical-liberals did not go far enough on many key issues and their endorsement of the tenets of political economy remained a major stumbling block to full collaboration. Nevertheless, the existence of important areas of overlap, based on a shared vocabulary, common interests and joint enemies, helps to explain the working-class radicals' often ambivalent attitude to this pivotal political grouping. The ambiguity of the radicals' position and local variations in the timing and extent of alliances can be illustrated by looking at both local politics and the parliamentary elections during the middle years of the decade.

Derek Fraser's adage, that 'Politics for Victorians began not at Westminster but at their own front gates', was equally true in the immediately preceding period, when, as Simon Morgan argues, 'popular politics was primarily *local* politics'.[81] The mainsprings

---

(ballot and/or extension of the franchise, Corn Law repeal, cheap government and religion) espoused by the radical wing of the Whig-liberal bloc had great appeal.

79 *LI* 4, 25 May 1833.

80 The composite term 'radical-liberals' is used here and elsewhere to try and overcome the problem of adequately describing advocates of moderate programme of radical reform. These were sometimes described by contemporaries as 'Whig-Radicals' or later more disparagingly by Chartists as 'sham Radicals'. Politically they were very close to the 'real' or 'ultra' radicals (and later Chartists). Joshua Bower in Leeds, for example, advocated the ballot, annual parliaments and universal suffrage (*LT* 29 Dec. 1831). But his emphasis was different; the ballot was the *sine qua non*, the suffrage could be extended by stages, and he described himself as a Whig. 'Radical-liberals' differed and clashed with the 'ultras' particularly in their stress on class collaboration and in their certainty that the working class was not yet ready or sufficiently educated for the franchise. Their acceptance of the main teachings of political economy and their indifference or hostility to the ten hours and trade union movements was also a major point of incompatibility. Although Bower was a major (self-made) manufacturer, the 'radical-liberals' were drawn predominantly from lower middle-class tradespeople and shopkeepers and from the more skilled, highly-paid workers. Normally, though not in 1834, they worked closely with the established Whig-liberal leadership, especially when a Tory victory threatened.

81 Derek Fraser, *Urban Politics in Victorian England: The Structure of Politics in Victorian Cities* (Leicester: Leicester University, 1976), p. 9; Simon Morgan, *Celebrities, Heroes and*

that underpinned the micro-political contests in the various townships of the textile district are often hard to discern. The precise personal and politico-religious dynamics of local power struggles could be very different in contiguous communities. Equally, with notable exceptions such as Derek Fraser's work on Leeds, the 'unglamourous' territory of local governance has been relatively under-researched during this period.[82] However, forays by Malcolm Chase and Katrina Navickas into the workings of the 'local state' in Regency Britain and the contested 'new administrative geographies' created by the Whig-liberal legislation of the 1830s and 1840s have emphasised that 'Local power was important in and of itself, as well as being a step towards accessing national power'.[83] The intertwined strands of one-off campaigns, sustained agitations, and contests for the offices of local governance made up a powerful thread of radical and later Chartist endeavours which sought to challenge the power of local notables and promote an alternative vision of democracy in action.[84]

This democratic crucible contained a number of different elements. In the first place, the open and participatory nature of the vestry, 'the basic unit of local government', made it an arena in which popular influence could be mobilised and where radical victories were feasible. All ratepayers (male and female) potentially had an opportunity to voice their opinions and select their representatives at the parish meeting.[85] Malcolm Chase's advice that 'local historians … ignore the vestry at their peril' applied equally to local elites. In the aftermath of disturbances at the 1832 election in Huddersfield, where radicals controlled the vestry, a local magistrate warned the Home Office that 'Should any Police be established the appointment and remuneration *should not on any account* be under the control of the vote of Rate payers of Parish Meetings or Vestry (otherwise it would be totally insufficient – should the vote of numbers influence the arrangements)'.[86] Local power mattered. For example, in Holmfirth the radical vestry was successfully able to resist attempts by the dominant Whig elite to remove the incumbent constable in 1833 on account of his allegedly lenient attitude to 'John Powlett's men' during the previous year's bitter strike.[87] Later in the decade, as Katrina Navickas argues, 'the vestry gained even more political

Champions: Popular Politicians in the Age of Reform, 1810-67 (Manchester: Manchester University Press, 2021), p. 2.

82 For Derek Fraser's series of articles on the main areas of local political conflict in Leeds – churchwardens, poor relief, water and improvement – see *Publications of the Thoresby Society*, 53 (1970), pp. 1-81; Malcolm Chase, 'The "local state" in Regency Britain', *Local Historian*, 43, 4 (2013), p. 266; Malcolm Chase, *Chartism: A New History* (Manchester: Manchester University Press, 2007), p. 23.

83 Chase, 'The "local state"', pp. 266-78; Katrina Navickas, *Protest and the Politics of Space and Place, 1789-1848* (Manchester: Manchester University Press, 2016), Ch. 5 and pp. 154-5.

84 On this see John Sanders, 'The Voice of the "Shoeless, Shirtless and Shameless": Community radicalism in the West Riding, 1829 to 1839', *Northern History*, 58, 2 (2021), p. 262.

85 See Chase, 'The "local state"', pp. 272-6 on vestries, select vestries and other attempts to place more powers into the hands of local oligarchies.

86 TNA: HO 52/23, Walker to Melbourne, 31 Jan. 1833; *NS* 12 May 1838.

87 *WDJ* 25 Oct. 1833; *LT* 26 Oct., 2 Nov. 1833. 'John Powlett' was the personification of the powerful local trades' union.

significance as the point of conflict for and often the administrative centre of resistance to the 1834 Poor Law Amendment Act'.[88]

Secondly, though the prestige and practical clout of the offices of parochial administration should not be exaggerated, control over them at least gave radicals a modicum of local leverage and access to minor powers of patronage.[89] Indeed some of the vehemence and persistence of opposition to the new poor law arrangements in Huddersfield and Keighley can be explained by the fact that they threatened an area of community life where radicals had established a bridgehead of power and influence. Control over the administration of poor relief, the costliest item of local expenditure, through poor overseers elected by and accountable to the vestry offered the opportunity to establish a minor network of patronage by the selective granting of jobs, contracts and relief. The other key office that radicals sought to control, that of local parish constable, offered a potentially valuable oversight of local mechanisms for the enforcement of law and order and for the granting of permission to hold public meetings.[90] Constables were nominated by the vestry and their quarterly accounts also had to be approved by the ratepayers. However, their appointment was subject to confirmation by the manorial court leet, a feudal survival often controlled by local landowners and notables.

Thirdly, contests for local offices provided a public arena in which leaders could voice and protect the interests of their unofficial constituents and embarrass or attack established power-blocs, whether Tory-Anglican or Whig-liberal-dissenting. No office, issue or incident was too minor to turn to the radicals' advantage. Local leaders such as Lawrence Pitkethly and William Stocks jnr. in Huddersfield, hailed by the *Leeds Times* in 1836 as 'the people's advocates and exposers of public abuses and swindling', could be relied upon to articulate a radical perspective on any local issue. For example, Pitkethly alongside another stalwart, John Hanson, opposed the proposed removal of the assizes from York to Wakefield in November 1833 on the grounds that it 'was intended for the rich and not for the poor, as the former would be the savers by it'. Both formed members of what the *Halifax and Huddersfield Express* called 'the usual sagacious and eloquent clique' who amidst the fallout from the 1832 election riots had effectively torpedoed proposals for the town to accept a £2,000 government grant to support the establishment of a volunteer corps of yeomanry for Huddersfield.[91] This willingness of local leaders to serve as advocates of the poor

---

88 Navickas, *Protest*, p. 159.

89 Some offices had material attractions; the Halifax deputy constable received £50 p.a. plus a rent-free house and other perks, *HG* 21 Feb. 1835. Also see *NS* 2 Feb. 1839 for James Brook on the political usefulness (for registration purposes) of the offices of poor rate collector and assistant overseer.

90 On the role of constables, see F. C. Mather, *Public Order in the Age of the Chartists* (Manchester: Manchester University Press, 1959), pp. 75-80. Constables were unpaid but in the northern industrial towns were able to delegate duties to paid deputies. In the late 1830s Halifax had two constables and two deputies; in the Dewsbury area each township had just one constable (plus paid deputies); and Bradford had a chief constable, two assistants and a constable for each township.

91 *LT* 30 July 1836; *LT* 12 Oct. 1833; *HHE* 11, 25 May 1833.

remained an important part of their radical identity and a major factor in the mass support they continued to enjoy.

Fourthly, their engagement in local contests and parochial politics tied in with their conception of active democracy, their belief in localism and their detestation of 'centralised despotism'. This included ground that they shared with potential lower middle-class allies: deep-rooted opposition to church rates, long-standing hostility to local elites, and an ingrained belief in cheap, economical government and local accountability. This common territory, however, did not always guarantee collaboration; other affiliations and enmities could get in the way. In Huddersfield, leading Whig-liberals, in conjunction with respectable Tories, fought back when the vestry decided to establish a committee to value all property liable to poor-rates. They successfully cleared all non-ratepayers from a stormy meeting in March 1833 and narrowly defeated the radical list submitted by James Brook 'secretary of the operatives [the STC]'. Six months later when the surveyors reported that they had appointed their own committee to audit their accounts, the radicals responded vigorously. Minor scuffles broke out after the respectable chairman refused to put radical bookseller Christopher Tinker's resolution for an adjournment to the meeting. The *Voice of the West-Riding*'s condemnation of 'Whig and Tory in jobbing alliance' puts into perspective the limits of any supposed local Tory-radical alliance at the time.[92]

Fifthly, within the new agitational landscape following the passage of the Reform Bill, local contests provided a ready-made arena for leaders to hone their political skills and rehearse confrontational tactics. Sometimes their success was predicated as much on the opting out of 'respectable' middle-class elements as on their effective mobilisation of the vestry. A number of Dewsbury notables, having been 'so often and so grossly insulted', withdrew from active participation in the vestry, disparaging 'those shoeless, shirtless and shameless persons who form the greater part of such meetings'.[93] In Keighley, the parochial assemblies were allegedly 'such as no gentleman would disgrace himself by attending; being conducted in a most disorderly manner'.[94] The resulting vacuum was readily filled by radical political enthusiasts. In Bradford, for example, Peter Bussey was active in the local vestry alongside operatives such as Moses Watkins and James (?) Ibbetson in securing a reduction in the churchwardens' salaries in 1834.[95]

How these radical enthusiasms played out in different localities varied and much work remains to be done to unravel the complex micro-politics of local government in the West Riding textile towns and villages.[96] In Bradford, Halifax and Dewsbury

---

92 *HG* 30 Mar.; *VWR, HG* 19 Oct. 1833. Memories of the role of the yeomanry at Peterloo remained strong.

93 A *Leeds Intelligencer* report cited in *LM* and *NS* 6 Oct. 1838

94 *NS* 12 May 1838.

95 *BO* 10, 24 Apr. 1834. Watkins (1781-1835), 'an exceedingly sensible man', died suddenly the following year (*BO* 19 Feb. 1835). Bussey was active in 1836 scrutinizing the poor overseers' and churchwardens' accounts, *BO* 7 Apr., 26 May, 2 June 1836.

96 It is clear from Derek Fraser's pioneering work on the parochial and township institutions of the town that Leeds, with its more advanced administrative infrastructure and diverse occupational profile, was not representative of other major centres of the textile trade; see

where radicals had engaged in parliamentary election alliances with radical-liberals, the co-operative spirit often carried over into local affairs during the 1830s. In Halifax, for example, the key posts of churchwardens and poor overseers remained in the hands of predominantly lower middle-class radical-liberal shopkeepers and tradesmen. A broad 'Whig-Radical' alliance, already evident in 1829, held firm throughout the 1830s.[97] In Dewsbury a similar configuration dominated until April 1838 when the local RA flexed its muscles, with the *Leeds Intelligencer* subsequently alleging that the constable of Dewsbury, Mr. Newsome, had in reality been 'appointed by the Radical Association' rather than elected by the vestry.[98]

Radicals in Huddersfield and Keighley, by contrast, had managed to attain and sustain significant control of the 'local state' significantly earlier.[99] A succession of radical activists or sympathisers held the post of Head Constable in Huddersfield; and radicals regularly succeeded in electing their nominee to chair ratepayers' meetings.[100] Their political potency was, however, always provisional and subject to challenge, as in 1836 when opponents used their power in the Court Leet to ensure the rejection of the radical choice, Abram Walker, a cloth-dresser, in favour of George Mallinson, a cloth merchant. As the *Bradford Observer* noted, 'This is the first time, for many years, that the Court Leet has rejected the candidate chosen by a town's meeting'.[101]

Just as it may be misleading to posit a transition from national to municipal concerns after the Chartist defeats of 1839-40, so it would be wrong to assume a simple switch of attention from national to local politics earlier in the decade following the disappointments of the Reform Bill. Radical engagement in contests for local power and influence was long-standing and an integral part of leaders' role as *de facto* representatives of their constituents.[102] Rather than being alternative calls on their attention, their involvement in local and national campaigns was complementary and mutually reinforcing.

For all the heat and fervour occasionally generated by local conflicts, the national political sphere remained significant, particularly at election times. Even though very few working men actually possessed the vote, parliamentary contests were important occasions for working-class radicals and their leaders. In the first place, elections were hugely popular local events, often combining elements of carnival and crusade, melodrama and farce. They provided a break from the humdrum routine of everyday life and opportunities for working people to jeer, ridicule and occasionally intimidate the representatives of their 'respectable' neighbours. Secondly, the hustings allowed

Fraser's articles in *Publications of the Thoresby Society,* 53 (1970), pp. 1-81.

97 *HCC* 11 July, 31 Oct. 1829; 20 Mar. 1830; *HG* 21 Feb., 7, 21 Mar. 1835; *LI* 18 Mar. 1837.

98 *LM* 28 Apr. 1838; *LI* quoted in *LM, NS* 6 Oct. 1838.

99 See Felix Driver, 'Tory Radicalism? Ideology, Strategy and Locality in Popular Politics during the Eighteen-Thirties', *Northern History,* 27 (1991), p. 124, on radical control in Huddersfield.

100 *LM* 6 Oct. 1832; *LT* 4 Apr., *VWR* 28 Sept. 1833; *LT* 21 Nov. 1835; 13 Feb. 1836, 2 Sept. 1837.

101 *BO* 7 Apr.; 3 Nov. 1836.

102 On municipal Chartism, see J. F. C. Harrison, 'Chartism in Leeds', in Asa Briggs (ed.), *Chartist Studies* (London: Macmillan, 1959), pp. 85-93.

them to publicly air their views, and the show of hands (which almost invariably went in favour of the most radical candidate only to be reversed in the actual poll) both reaffirmed their sense of moral indignation and vividly illustrated the unfairness of the franchise. Finally, the elections stimulated organisation – usually in the form of non-electors' or radical committees, which arranged public meetings, exclusive dealing and the marshalling of popular forces – and confirmed radical leadership through the choice of spokesmen to question candidates on behalf of the non-electors.

A near constant stream of electoral activity during the middle years of the decade heightened tensions and exposed fault lines in political allegiances in a number of the communities of the textile district. The Huddersfield by-election of early 1834, for example, was a particularly convoluted episode, generating a wealth of polemical publications and no little confrontational heat.[103] The contest, caused by the sudden death of Captain Fenton, the unpopular Whig victor in 1832, brought to the surface pre-existing fissures within the radical ranks. Capt. Wood of Sandal, the defeated Radical candidate the previous year, referred to these in a letter to William Stocks the day after Fenton's death and initially refused the nomination. He recommended instead that one of the two factory reformers, Michael Sadler or Richard Oastler, should stand, pledged to a Corporation Bill and the extension of the suffrage, on an independent, anti-Ramsden ticket. This refusal by the obvious radical candidate however only complicated matters. On 3 December, Lawrence Pitkethly summarised the situation in a letter to Robert Owen:

> The Radicals are resting on their oars till Fenton is buried and they receive answers from friends they have wrote to Capt. Wood is the favourite with the people. Some voters object to him turning catholic. General Johnson is the most likely for us at present.[104]

A hastily convened public meeting of radicals the following evening duly proposed the veteran Lincolnshire gentleman-radical General W. A. Johnson in the belief that the voters would not vote for Wood, but because of the sparse attendance the meeting was adjourned for a night to decide between Johnson and Wood. The reconvened meeting eventually decided on the latter and asked Stocks and Oastler to approach him. Oastler refused and Stocks, finding that there was no proper committee or funds, also did not go to Sandal. Eventually the radical committee decided to formally invite Sadler to stand as an independent candidate. Despite this, and also letters from Johnson and Wood backing Sadler as the best man to represent a united anti-Whig front, the chief Wood supporters continued to campaign on his behalf.

103 This account draws on Cecil Driver, *Tory Radical, The Life of Richard Oastler* (New York: Oxford University Press, 1946), pp. 255–9; Richard Oastler, *Huddersfield Election. The Pearking or (If you will have it so) The Biter Bit in answer to the Question who is to Blame?* (Huddersfield, 1834); Vivienne W. Hemmingway, 'Parliamentary Politics in Huddersfield, c.1832–53', in Hilary Haigh (ed.), *Huddersfield*, pp. 481–500; Brooke, 'Radicalism, Reform and Class Conflict'; *VWR* Dec. 1833 - Feb. 1834 and local stamped newspapers.
104 OC No. 607, Pitkethly to Owen, 3 Dec. 1833.

The precise lines of division within the radical ranks are not always clear. The divergence of opinion was not simply between 'blue-tailed' radicals and radical republicans of the old school. Nor it is likely, as Cecil Driver suggests, that the presence of Irish Catholic voters was significant factor in favour of Wood. The split appears to be between those radicals like William Stocks, John Hanson and James Brook (the STC secretary) who for tactical rather than ideological or personal reasons favoured Sadler's candidature and the majority of local radicals, both working class and lower middle class, who supported Wood.[105] In late December relations between the different camps became more embittered.[106] The 'Woodites' continued to solicit their candidate who began now to back down from his previous high-minded refusals. He alleged that 'misapprehensions' had first led him to stand back and accused Oastler of seeking 'to win over the [Trades'] Unions to Mr Sadler!!'

Eventually Wood decided to run on a platform which condemned the Reform Bill as a 'delusion' and advocated triennial parliaments, household suffrage, secret ballot, the reduction of taxation, the abolition of sinecures, Church reform and the liquidation of the national debt. This was sufficient for most working-class and lower middle-class radicals in the town; and they rapidly set up an extensive organisation of local and central non-electors' committees which began to organise exclusive dealing in favour of Wood. William Moore, the hated Whig postmaster, complained of 'a system of uncontrolled intimidation' organised by 'a few unruly spirits who have long agitated this locality… They have gone out as Missionaries into the villages and have succeeded in influencing the minds of a great part of the population'. The Almondbury leader George Beaumont was apparently waited on by two of Wood's Committee to help agitate and organise the villages.[107] However, it is unlikely that the system of 'exclusive dealing at first remove' – with non-electors in the villages pressurising their local 'Shopkeepers, Shoemakers, Tailors, and others' to persuade the Huddersfield wholesalers with whom they dealt to vote for Wood – had anything but a limited impact.[108] Equally, the intimidation implicit in exclusive dealing could be a double-edged sword. It not only risked a backlash from freedom-loving shopkeepers, but also allegedly stimulated retaliatory actions by both Whigs and Tories against their workpeople and tenants.[109]

The poll itself and its immediate aftermath shed light on the internal divisions within local radicalism and bring into question the reality of a widespread 'Tory-Radical' alliance. Expectations of trouble never materialised despite, or perhaps because

---

105 These included important local working-class leaders; for example, Thomas Vevers, Christopher Wood, Stephen Dickinson and Christopher Tinker. The lower middle-class radicals included figures such as John Machan, Richard Foss, John Liddle. Wood had secured substantial support from elements of the 'shopocracy' particularly food and drink retailers in the 1832 poll, Hemmingway, 'Parliamentary Politics', p. 493.

106 On the suspension of the pro-Sadler editor of the *Voice*, see below, p. 331 (fn. 198).

107 TNA: HO 40/31 f. 223, Moore to Francis Fielding (GPO) 30 Dec. 1833; HO 52/25, Deposition of George Beaumont, 2 Jan. 1834.

108 See, for example, placards from Almondbury and Slaithwaite meetings, TNA: HO 40/31 f. 222 and 224.

109 Hemmingway, 'Parliamentary Politics', pp. 493-4; see *VWR* 28 Dec. 1833 for alleged intimidation of workers at the Starkey's factory at Longroyd Bridge.

of, the swearing in of 150 special constables and a significant military presence nearby.[110] Wood easily won the show of hands, but came bottom at the poll with 108 votes to Sadler's 147 and the Whig Blackburne's 234. Afterwards the crowds, managed throughout by local radical leaders, dispersed peacefully and magistrates and operatives exchanged placatory placards.

Both camps drew obvious lessons from the fact that Blackburne was elected on a minority vote. Oastler, who engaged in an extremely acrimonious pamphlet war with Captain Wood, argued that the 'Radicals' had put party first and had betrayed the interests of the people. The pro-Wood *Voice* which gave out a 'likeness' of their unsuccessful candidate with the paper in mid-January, attributed Captain Wood's defeat 'to the intrigues of certain characters who, after all, profess to be his staunch friends'. Some weeks later 'a few Radicals' writing to the *Voice* put the blame squarely on Oastler and Sadler. Oastler summarised the extent of internal recrimination in one of his pamphlets:

> Some lay blame on Sir John Ramsden: some say Mr Stocks had 'deluded' Capt. Wood: whilst others declare that Mr Oastler has been the great deceiver: even Mr Pitkethly himself does not escape from censure...'[111]

Others apparently blamed Capt. Wood, whilst Wood himself pointed to Sadler and his friends. The indefatigable Pitkethly, 'one of the most noble souls in existence' in O'Connor's effusive later assessment, saw his role as mediator between the different factions.[112] He was partly successful, but his eventual decision to vote for Wood temporarily soured his relationship with Oastler. He reported in late February that 'our political agitation has in a great degree subsided'. Despite his hopes that 'we can all be bro[thers] to work cordially for the public good in a short time', it is likely that the 'bad spirit', fanned by rival post-election dinners, lingered and weakened local radicalism in 1834 and perhaps beyond.[113]

The Leeds by-election of February 1834 did not generate the same widespread interest and excitement as the 1832 contest.[114] Working-class radicals played little part in the campaign and it is doubtful whether they took up the Huddersfield non-electors' call to organise exclusive dealing.[115] The official Whig and Tory candidates, Baines and Beckett, had little appeal and the non-electors eventually fell in behind the third candidate Joshua Bower, now standing as an outright Radical, whose power base, the 'Holbeck' Political Union, had drifted away from Baines' Whig-liberal alliance. Although Huntite radicals like Rider and Bottomley stayed uncommitted (merely urging the close questioning of candidates on eight hours and factory reform),

---

110 See, for example, TNA: HO 52/25, letters from local magistrates to Lord Melbourne, 2, 6, 8, 9 Jan. 1834.

111 Oastler, *Pearking*, p. 3.

112 *NS* 27 Apr. 1839.

113 OC No. 677, Pitkethly to Owen, 26 Feb. 1834.

114 For an account of this election, see Derek Fraser, 'Politics in Leeds, 1830-52', Unpub. Ph.D Thesis, University of Leeds, 1969, pp. 96 ff.

115 *LT* 28 Dec. 1833.

other prominent leaders like John Ayrey and (after Sadler's withdrawal) Cavie Richardson supported Bower.[116] The essentially limited and temporary nature of any Tory-radical alliance is again thrown into relief. As Derek Fraser writes, referring to J. T. Ward's account of the election, 'It is misleading to claim that Sadler's former friends lined up behind Beckett as they had done behind Sadler'.[117] Radical leaders and non-electors as a whole again showed their propensity to support the most radical candidate on offer. Although Bower polled few votes, his incursion rocked the Whig-liberal boat and very nearly let in the representative of old-fashioned political Toryism.

The general election of January 1835, coming in the aftermath of the defeat of trades' unionism, when working-class organisation was practically non-existent and local leadership temporarily demoralised and quiescent, marks a low-point in the fortunes of working-class radicalism. The Huddersfield election, the third poll in just over two years, was a relatively low-key affair. Radical exhaustion and despondency after the defeats and recriminations of the past twelve months played a large part in the prevailing apathy. The radicals sought to unite all reformers behind the slogan 'Reform and Durham' and finally chose General Johnson of Lincolnshire as their candidate.[118] He arrived at the hustings accompanied by Capt. Wood (the defeated candidate twelve months earlier), Pitkethly and Thomas Vevers and was nominated by two of Capt. Wood's former committee, Machan and Scholes. He won the show of hands but was easily defeated by the sitting Whig candidate, Blackburne, in a small poll. The defeat served to confirm the impossibility of a straight radical victory in a Whig-dominated town.[119]

At Leeds the two rival political elites had initially thought in terms of an uncontested election. Only the late nomination of William Brougham and the putative candidacy of George Wailes, a radical lawyer, cut through the prevailing apathy. Beckett the narrow loser in 1834 headed the poll and became the first out and out Tory elected by an industrial borough. It is likely that local working-class radical leaders followed the *Leeds Times* in supporting Wailes' candidacy, but his withdrawal left them without a popular candidate to support and they played little part in the election proceedings.[120]

The middle-class radicals' dissatisfaction with the Whig Government and particularly the voting of John Hardy, a Whig victor in 1832, dominated the Bradford election.[121] They brought forward a radical Manchester solicitor, George Hadfield, who advocated disestablishment of the Church and other favoured reforms of middle-class radicalism – triennial parliaments, the ballot, cheap law and government, free

---

116 *LT* 4, 11 Jan. 1834.
117 Fraser, 'Politics in Leeds' , p. 110.
118 Lord Durham was an advocate of the secret ballot.
119 *LM* 22 Nov.; *LT* 6 Dec. 1834; 10 Jan. 1835, *HG* 10 Jan. 1835.
120 This summary draws on Derek Fraser, 'The Fruits of Reform: Leeds Politics in the 1830s', *Northern History*, 7, (1972), pp. 99-101; Fraser, 'Politics in Leeds', pp. 133-5 and local newspapers (*LM, LT, LI* Dec. 1834 - Jan. 1835)
121 For an account of the 1835 election, see D. G. Wright, 'A Radical Borough: Parliamentary Politics in Bradford 1832-41', *Northern History*, 4 (1968), pp. 140-2.

trade, municipal reform, Corn Law repeal, and reduction of the pension list.[122] Although Hadfield was totally opposed to universal suffrage (one of the fundamental props of their former Political Union), Bussey and the Bradford working-class radicals joined with the middle-class radicals in supporting him. The questions which Bussey posed Hadfield on the election hustings in December 1834 were not, as Dorothy Thompson believed, a statement of 'the programme of working-class political radicalism, soon to be absorbed into the wider movement of Chartism' but a compromise programme designed not to cause a middle-class radical too much embarrassment.[123] Only triennial not annual parliaments were mentioned and household not universal suffrage, but even this went too far for Hadfield. The radical non-electors' willingness to support Hadfield and the radical-liberal ticket is not surprising. The morale and enthusiasm of the working-class radicals was at a low ebb, Hadfield was the most radical of the three candidates and he was opposing Hardy, son of the local iron magnate, who had incurred deep working-class hatred for his attitude to the Dorchester sentence and his virulent speeches against trades' unions, and who now was being supported by many of the town's leading Tories.[124]

Much to the radicals' chagrin Hardy headed the poll and Hadfield was well beaten, mainly because the alliance between radical and moderate Whig voters failed to operate, with many of the latter group continuing to support Hardy. The election did, however, provide the stimulus for a revival of working-class organisation. The non-electors' committee, with Peter Bussey and two experienced radical woolcombers and trade unionists, George Hopkins and John Atkinson, prominently involved, became the basis for an 'Association of the Working Classes' formed in January 1835. This organisation and its off-shoot branches at Bowling aimed to provide a forum 'for the mutual discussion and communication of knowledge, and for assisting and protecting the political rights of the labouring classes'.[125] The Association was initially very popular and continued in existence until at least May 1835 and possibly provided a thread of organisational continuity through to the formation of the Radical Association later in the year.[126] However, some links with their lower middle-class electoral allies were also maintained through the choice of William McKay, an important radical-liberal leader, as president.[127]

In Halifax, where the middle-class radicals also fielded a radical candidate, Edward Protheroe, in an anti-Tory alliance with local Whigs, working-class support fell in solidly behind Protheroe. His defeat by one vote, amidst allegations of bribery and bias resulted in attacks on the property of leading Tories in which the local radicals were

---

122 *LM* 29 Dec. 1834.

123 D. Thompson (ed.), *Early Chartists*, pp. 6-7; *LM, LT* 6 Dec. 1834.

124 See, for example, *VWR* 29 Mar. 1834. On the Tories joining his election committee, see *BO* 27 Nov. 1834 and D. G. Wright, 'Politics and Opinion in Nineteenth Century Bradford, 1832-1880, with special reference to Parliamentary elections', Unpub. PhD thesis, University of Leeds, 1966, p. 120.

125 *LT* 24, 31 Jan.; *LM* 31 Jan.; *LT* 14 Mar. 1835.

126 *LT* 14 Feb., 31 May 1835. The Association met at William Hill's School-room.

127 *LT* 14 Feb. 1835. McKay was simultaneously trying to repair bridges between 'radical' and 'moderate' Liberals through the Bradford Reform Society.

implicated. Middle-class radicals drew the same lessons as at Bradford from the failure of the Whig-Liberal-Radical alliance to operate effectively. They sought to repair bridges with moderate Whigs, improve registration procedures, but also to maintain links with radical electors and non-electors.[128]

No clear pattern emerges from the 1835 election. Working-class radicals everywhere supported the most radical candidate but failed to secure a single victory. In Bradford and Halifax they continued in electoral alliance with the radical elements of the Whig-liberals. In many ways this was a sign of weakness rather than strength. The surprise is perhaps that the radical-liberals spent so much time and effort courting them. The special features of the Huddersfield constituency ensured the continuation of radical-Whig antagonism, but even a broad radical alliance made no headway. With trade unions smashed and key politically-conscious groups like the handloom weavers and combers under increasing economic pressure, formal radical organisation and activity had reached rock-bottom. Although a working-class association was formed at Bradford, the election gave only a temporary boost to organisation. The lessons drawn by their lower middle-class allies on the need for continuing and effective organisation, though absorbed by working class radicals, were not yet widely acted upon.

3: Radical Culture in the Mid-1830s

Formal permanent organisation was never a particular strong point of working-class radicalism, and a true indication of its vitality and pervasiveness should not be sought in this alone. It is important to look beyond political unions and public meetings in order to adequately examine the roots of radical and future Chartist leadership and organisation and the fertile soil which sustained them. To do this it is necessary to focus on aspects of the radicals' daily existence: the informal network of radical pubs, beerhouses and bookshops, the mutual instruction groups and newspaper reading circles, the convivial occasions, and the personal ties and friendships. A number of studies have explored elements of this infrastructure and other scholars have examined radical material culture and ritualistic practices.[129] However, as Tom Scriven notes,

---

128 This brief summary of the Halifax election draws on Benjamin Wilson, *The Struggles of an Old Chartist* (Halifax: John Nicholson, 1887), p. 2; J. A. Jowitt, 'Parliamentary Politics in Halifax, 1832-47', *Northern History*, 12 (1976), pp. 182-3; *HHE* 18 Dec., *LT* 20 Dec. 1834, 10 Jan. 1835.

129 For example, James Epstein, 'Some Organisational and Cultural Aspects of the Chartist Movement in Nottingham' in Epstein and D. Thompson (eds.), *The Chartist Experience*, pp. 221-268.; James Epstein, *Radical Expression: Political Language, Ritual and Symbol in England 1790-1850* (London: Breviary Stuff, 2014 edn.); James Epstein, 'Radical Dining, Toasting and Symbolic Expression in Early Nineteenth-Century Lancashire: Rituals of Solidarity', *Albion* 20, 2 (1988), pp. 271-91; Matthew Roberts, '"God Save the Paddock Flag": Anti-Poor Law and Chartist Banners, 1837-1844', in J. A. Hargreaves (ed.) *The Charter our Right! Huddersfield Chartism Re-considered* (Huddersfield: Huddersfield Local History Society, 2018); Peter Brett, 'Political dinners in Early Nineteenth Century Britain: Platform, Meeting Place and Battleground', *History* 81, 264 (1996), pp. 527-52;

most have focussed on the exceptional or the symbolic rather than the more mundane, everyday ways in which activists interacted with their communities.[130] This is perhaps not surprising. By their very nature, these aspects of a popular radical culture are rarely recorded. But the relative silence of our sources should not be taken as an indicator of absence or apathy. Just occasionally, as in recollections of Abram Hanson's quasi-medical and thespian activities or John Bates' memoirs of his mutual instruction group, we are able to get a glimpse of the strong bonds that bound radical leaders to their communities and companions.[131]

Popular radical feeling did not wither away in 1832 only to reappear in a more striking form in early Chartism. It was always there, even though not always fully visible. It pervaded the day-to-day life of its adherents and remained a point of reference for the many thousands of its sympathisers and supporters. This culture can be examined from a number of standpoints.

In the first place it can be seen in the way the radicals assuaged their 'almost inexhaustible desire for knowledge' in the provision of a variety of formal or informal means of mutually instructing themselves.[132] The operatives and their leaders had long recognised the educational and class limitations of the Mechanics Institutes with their restricted curricula and libraries and their lack of outlets for political or religious discussion, the subjects which really interested working people. As the *Voice* commented sarcastically in August 1833, 'we do not conceive that the 'mutations of forms in the Laboratory' or the properties of the 'deep triangle' are the best adapted studies for the great majority of the working classes in their present condition'.[133] Perhaps for this reason, the Huddersfield radicals attempted to run, first, a day school and then a Sunday school at their Swan Yard Union Room.[134] Their other great educational achievement was the production of the *Voice*, a paper whose columns were a quarry of political information and whose editorials and leading articles occasionally adopted the schoolmasterly tone so familiar in the later *Northern Star*.

The recurring theme of early working-class radicalism, of responding to defeat or despondency by stressing the need for education and political knowledge, can be seen in the educational aspirations of the Bradford Association of the Working Classes in early 1835. With the 'popular and talented' William Hill, radical schoolmaster and reporter, providing accommodation (in his school room) and educational input (for example, he opened the discussion on the 'Church and State' at the 10 February

Robert G. Hall. 'A Bookshop of Their Own: Reading and Print in Chartism 1838-1850', *EHR*, 136, 581 (2021) pp. 894-917.

130 Tom Scriven, 'Activism and the Everyday: The Practices of Radical Working-Class Politics, 1830-1842', Unpub. Phd thesis, University of Manchester, 2012, p. 13.

131 *Boot and Shoemaker*, 8 Feb. 1879; A. C. Carter, *John Bates, of Queensbury, the Veteran Reformer*, (Queensbury, 1895), p. 2.

132 *VWR* 3 Aug. 1833. On the importance of mutual-improvement societies in fostering local leadership, see Emma Griffin, 'The making of the Chartists: Popular Politics and Working-class Autobiography in Early Victorian Britain' *EHR*, 129, 538 (2014), pp. 583-7.

133 *VWR* 17 Aug. 1833. See also, the proposal at the Halifax M.I.'s annual meeting to 'institute a class for the study of political economy', *HHE* 12 Jan. 1833.

134 *VWR* 21 Sept. 1833, 1 Feb. 1834.

meeting), the Association proved very popular. Money was donated for a library and by the middle of May a news and reading-room had been established. But the working-class promoters of educational activity like their middle-class counterparts in the Mechanics Institutes soon experienced some of the difficulties of maintaining interest and motivation when 'the minds of the working-classes are too much disturbed with the uncertainties of their position; the continual depreciation of the value of their labour...'[135]

Secondly, popular radical culture had a strong convivial aspect. 'Educational' and 'social' functions and institutions often overlapped. Reading rooms and mutual instruction groups were a cheap means of access to the printed word, but also a source of friendly discussion and banter. The Huddersfield radicals supported their day school with the proceeds of occasional 'Radical Balls'.[136] These were aimed at couples and serve as a reminder that radicalism, like co-operation with its tea parties and festivities, was a family affair. Women played a vital role in the informal networks and activities of popular radicalism.[137] They shared and sometimes outstripped their husband's, brother's or son's radical fervour and involvement. However, only occasionally are their names and contributions recorded. Exceptions include the list of Huddersfield republican 'volunteers' which Christopher Tinker sent to the *Gauntlet* in April 1833, headed by two women bearing familiar radical surnames (Mary Tinker and Mary Vevers), and the Victim Fund in support of Joshua Hobson.[138]

Radical dinners with their accompaniments of toasts, glees and songs, roast beef and plum pudding comprised a particularly male aspect of this convivial dimension of radicalism.[139] They were special and quite costly occasions: held to celebrate victories or commiserate after defeat, to remember the birthdays of radicals-past such as Paine, or to welcome present-day champions heroes such as O'Connor, or merely to commemorate the founding of an institution. Whatever their precise rationale they

---

135 *LT* 2 May; 14 Feb.; 14 Mar.; 20 May 1835; *VWR* 17 Aug. 1834.

136 *VWR* 21 Sept. 1833; 1 Feb.; 10 May 1834.

137 See above, pp. 47-8.

138 *Gauntlet* 5 May, 28 July 1833. The precise family relationships require further specialist investigation in both cases. Mary Tinker may have been Christopher Tinker's mother or sibling. Mary Vevers was possibly the sister of William Vevers, another key network figure. A later list of local 'volunteers' (published 28 July) included the names of six other female radicals. The Hobson Victim Fund contributions are listed and analysed by John Halstead in 'The Voice of the West Riding: Promoters and Supporters of a Provincial Unstamped Newspaper, 1833-34', in Chris Wrigley and John Shepherd (eds.), *On The Move: Essays in Labour and Transport History Presented to Philip Bagwell* (London: Hambleton Press, 1991), pp. 33-57. The lists provide the names of at least 26 women, including Elizabeth Vevers (either the wife or daughter of radical stalwart, Thomas Vevers, or 'Betty', the spouse of William Vevers); and, listed separately in the *VWR* of 10 Aug. 1833, Mary Tinker and Mary Ann Tinker (the designation of Christopher's wife in the 1841 census). There were strong connections between the two families. In July 1833 Christopher Tinker took over the bookshop in Market Walk that William Vevers ran before he moved to the Albion tavern.

139 On radical dinners, see Brett, 'Political dinners'; and James Epstein, 'Radical Dining'.

served as both a reward for and a re-affirmation of the position of the inner circle of local leaders.[140]

The venues for public dinners provide a good indicator of the key locations of a third element in the vital informal aspects of popular radicalism: the network of safe, favoured radical pubs, taverns and beerhouses. These focal points also often served as centres where the various facets of working-class agitational activity converged. A number of locations stand out.[141] Here the landlord or landlady was often sympathiser or active official as well as host, and the pub served as meeting place, committee room, collection centre for subscriptions and ticket agency for radical events.

Newly established beershops augmented the network of drinking and meeting places. A number of radicals took the opportunities offered by the 1830 Beer Act and became in effect full or part-time activists by setting themselves up as beersellers. Chief among these was Peter Bussey of Bradford whose home, converted into a beershop, became an important radical centre. Other notable leaders who were linked to the trade included Thomas Cliffe of Halifax, William Muff of North Bierley and William Vevers of Huddersfield. The beersellers' livelihood, especially if they were prominent radicals was often precarious, subject to strict and often petty local control. A radical pamphlet in the aftermath of the 1832 Huddersfield election, referring to the recent prosecution of William Vevers of the Albion Tavern, commented that 'the Albion is one of the best conducted Beer Shops in Town; Drunkenness and other immoralities are discountenanced; but the great crime is, Politics'.[142]

The beersellers organised themselves to fight harassment and their second-class status. Peter Bussey led 'the beersellers' party' in Bradford. In 1835 he spearheaded the opposition to a respectable public meeting which sought to curb the number of beershops. In a deliberately provocative amendment to the petition against beer and spirit drinking he suggested that beer shops should be 'more unshackled', that the tax on malt should be repealed, with the deficit coming from the revenues of the Church of England.[143] In the resulting controversy Bussey's analysis differed from the high moral tone adopted by William Hill. He used the occasion to attack both Whigs and Tories, but reduced the issue to one of basic class interest, 'The licensed victuallers are generally capitalists; aye, capitalists – there's the rub – while the beerseller is only a poor man.'[144] Not surprisingly the radical connection persisted into the Chartist era,

---

140 Tickets were often in the range of 1s to 1s.6d. Paine's birthday in January was regularly celebrated in all the major centres. For a good example of a convivial dinner, see the Bradford dinner to O'Connor *LT* 14 Jan. 1837.

141 For example, Union Inn, Saddle Inn, Brewers Arms, Lloyds Arms (Leeds); White Hart Inn, Ship Inn (Huddersfield); Commercial Inn, Roebuck Inn and Black Bull Inn (Bradford); Union Cross Inn, Talbot Inn, and John Tiffany's 'Labour and Health' (Halifax) Hope and Anchor, Stag and Pheasant (Dewsbury), Woolpack Inn (Almondbury). For discussion of the roles of a multi-purpose working-class pub, see Morris, 'James Kitson', pp. 182-3.

142 *LT* 18 July 1835 (for Bussey's as a radical centre); *BO* 6 Sept. 1838 (Cliffe and Muff); *VWR* 6 July 1833 and *Woodites*, p. 16 (Vevers).

143 *BO* 25, *LT* 27 June 1833. For an unsuccessful attempt to prosecute Bussey, see *BO* 27 Feb. 1834.

144 *BO* 2 July 1835.

with Thomas Cliffe writing from the World's End Inn, Bradford, serving as secretary of the 'Beersellers' Association'.[145]

For temperance, security or prestige reasons radicals in a number of places also set up their own independent meeting rooms. In the early 1830s the Leeds Radical Political Union established its own Union Room at the top of St Peter's Square, Leeds; Huddersfield Political Union's 'Radical Union Room in the Swan Inn Yard' served as a meeting place, a printing house, newsroom and dance hall; the Bradford radicals and trade unionists in 1833-4 used the Jumping Ranters meeting house in the backyard of the Commercial Inn; and in the mid-1830s the Leeds RA took over the Independent Methodist's chapel as a Union room. Rooms and meeting places directly under the control of radicals were particularly useful. William Hill's school-room fulfilled a crucial role in Bradford in 1834-5; but it was not until the early Chartist period that a wider network of radical newsroom and 'union' rooms became more firmly established.[146]

Such venues could often accommodate routine monthly gatherings or even small public meetings, but were inadequate for more popular events. The radicals' large-scale public meetings had to be held outside, which in winter effectively curtailed their appeal and effectiveness. In addition, as Katrina Navickas has shown, control of public spaces was highly contentious. Radicals throughout the north fought rearguard actions in response to their adversaries' attempts to restrict access to traditional outdoor venues, but were gradually forced to use more remote locations for their mass meetings.[147] This at least left them less vulnerable to surveillance and confrontations with landowners.

It was the need for secure indoor accommodation which led to the floating of ambitious plans for working-class meeting places in Huddersfield and Bradford in the winter of 1833-4. The Bradford scheme which involved selling 5s shares to local friendly societies and trade unions can be traced directly to a rain-sodden union meeting in late October 1833. The plans for 'erecting a Working-man's Guildhall' in Huddersfield, probably foundered like those of Bradford on the trades' union defeat of the following summer.[148] However, links with friendly societies bore fruit later in the decade with the opening in 1836 of the spacious Odd-Fellows Hall on Thornton Road, Bradford, which became a venue for public meetings in the early Chartist years.[149] O'Connor commended the Halifax radicals in early 1837 for their attempt to establish a Working Man's Hall; and in the other main centres radicals sought to use accommodation provided by socialists or sympathetic nonconformist sects or

---

145 See NS 31 Mar. 1838 for a meeting at which Bussey and O'Connor spoke; and BO 6 Sept. and HHE 8 Sept. 1838 (Cliffe). It is not clear why Bradford beersellers selected Thomas Cliffe of Halifax as their spokesperson.

146 See F. Driver, 'Tory Radicalism?', p. 123, for the dense network of meeting places in Huddersfield.

147 Navickas, Protest, pp. 223-47.

148 LT 2 Nov.; 14 and 28 Dec. 1833; VWR 1 Mar., 12 Apr. 1834.

149 LT 30 June 1836; 16 Nov. 1837. Plans for erecting their own building revived in late 1839 after further harassment. NS 26 Oct. 1839.

benefactors.[150] The problem of accommodation, both large and small-scale, remained a perennial one and, if anything, became more acute in the antagonistic atmosphere of the early Chartist years.

This constant deficit was partly offset by the strength of the often hidden final dimension of popular radicalism, the informal network of personal acquaintances and friendships which bound together the regional and local movements. Lloyd Jones, in later years, recalled visiting Huddersfield as an Owenite socialist lecturer in the December 1837, and encountering a knot of 'the most thorough Radicals' in the room above Lawrence Pitkethly's shop and enjoying 'the many warm discussions held by the parties assembled'.[151] We rarely see this network in action, but it is clear that there were well-established routes and pathways, eased by letters of introduction, for visiting speakers and radical friends. A chance reference to the prosecution of George Bready, Salford cotton-spinner and itinerant radical orator, in November 1830 for not paying the bill for his accommodation at the Brewer's Arms reveals that he had been recommended to that inn by Midgley, the radical Deputy Constable of Huddersfield.[152] Although largely invisible, this intricate web of sympathetic publicans and shopkeepers, safe-houses and contact points developed throughout the 1830s and ensured that when open Chartist activity became dangerous in late 1839 the movement was able to go underground and still function.

This radical infrastructure was built on a common culture, shared beliefs and sometimes playful exchanges between leaders and 'constituents'.[153] As Tom Scriven has noted, 'humour was a major aspect of Chartist culture and a means of interaction between leadership and rank-and-file.'[154] It is equally evident in the preceding period and often manifested itself in performative radical vignettes: such as when the Hebden Bridge RA employed the local bellman to publicise the expulsion of a member who had 'plumped' for Wortley in the 1837 West Riding elections; or when Keighley local radicals subverted a respectable procession to proclaim the new Queen Victoria by placing someone in a 'curious dress' and wearing a fool's cap decorated with radical colours on an ass at its head.[155] Other special occasions, such as customary rush-bearing celebrations, were similarly appropriated to the radical cause. The impressively organised Almondbury 'mock election' held on the local feast day in August 1837

---

150 *LT* 14 Jan. 1837. The Halifax scheme eventually had to be abandoned. Huddersfield radicals, for example, used the Social Institution in 1838. Keighley radical, David Weatherhead later spent nearly £300 of his own money 'on behalf of the Radical Association' to buy an old Primitive Methodist Chapel to act as a 'Working Men's Hall', *NS* 27 Apr. 1839.

151 *HWC* 19 July 1879, quoted in F. Driver, 'Tory Radicalism?', p. 125.

152 *LI* 4 Nov. 1830.

153 For a fuller discussion (drawing on Tara Yosso's 'Community Cultural Wealth framework') of how local leaders tapped into and contributed to the development of community cultural capital, see John Sanders, 'Out of Obscurity: Local Leadership and Cultural Wealth in the Radical Communities of the West Riding Textile District, 1825-40', *History Workshop Journal*, 94 (2022), pp. 1-23.

154 Tom Scriven, 'Activism and the Everyday', p. 19.

155 *LT* 12 Aug.; 1 July 1837. See Sanders, 'The Voice of the "Shoeless, Shirtless and Shameless"', pp. 6-7 for further discussion of radical interactions with royal celebrations.

featured all the paraphernalia of a real election (posters, election committees, a returning officer, processions with bands and flags, formal nominations and speeches from the candidates, a show of hands and a polling booth housed in an unoccupied cottage), and resulted in the unsurprising landslide victory for the Radical candidate John Buckley, a greengrocer, over the putative Tory candidate Joseph Broadbent, a weaver. The carnivalesque event, though, carried a serious political message, as a *Leeds Times* report recognised:

> This mock election did not arise out of the frolic of a feast; it was previously agreed upon; the cottagers of Almondbury believing that they have as clear a right to vote for representatives as their ten pound neighbours, but as want of intelligence is the pretext for withholding that right, and knowing that argument is no use, they agreed to prove to the privileged few, that poverty is as capable of conducting an election as wealth; ...[156]

This 'village recreation', witnessed by the touring missionaries, Vincent and Cleave in 1837, was repeated the following year, when 'J. Buckley, Esq., M.P. and G. G. ... was drawn through the village in a carr preceded by a band of music and a white flag ...' Rush-bearing festivities were similarly commandeered by another mock election outside Halifax. Here, the proceedings overseen topically by 'Nicholas Nickleby, Esq., returning officer for the ancient and independent borough of Ovenden' and witnessed by over seven hundred people, resulted in another sweeping Radical victory.[157]

Radical sympathies were equally evident in everyday transactions: the pooling of community resources to support 'victims', interactions with neighbours and work companions, the popularity of radical poems and songs, and the speed and extent of mobilisation to counter perceived challenges or threats, whether poor law commissioners or metropolitan police.[158] As Tom Scriven argues, 'studying Chartist politics on the formal level of Associations, unions, newspapers and public meetings needs to be complemented by informal day-to-day social, convivial, sexual, gender, familial and financial relationships'.[159] Thus, the *Leeds Times*' accurate but formal reportage of 'Radical Missionaries at Almondbury' when 'Messrs. Cleave and Vincent, from London, accompanied by Messrs. J. Hanson (from Huddersfield), John Buckley, S. Midgley, J. Lodge, and others from Almondbury' met to set up a WMA in late

---

156 *LT* 19 Aug. 1837. The contest was conducted on the basis of household suffrage. The returning officer, Abraham Donkersley, was a radical fancy weaver who had been a member of the council of the Almondbury PU council in 1830, as had Joseph Broadbent the 'Tory' candidate. For a reference to John Buckley 'MP and GG [Green Grocer] for Almondbury', see *NS* 31 Mar. 1838. Almondbury radicals felt doubly excluded since the village and its environs did not fall within the narrow boundaries of the Huddersfield constituency.

157 Alan J. Brooke, 'The Roots of Chartism in the Huddersfield Area *c.* 1826 to *c.* 1838', in Hargreaves (ed.), *The Charter our Right!*, p. 30; *NS* 18 Aug.; 8 Sept. 1838. Dickens had published the first instalment of his third novel the previous March.

158 Mike Sanders, *The Poetry of Chartism: Aesthetics, Politics, History* (Cambridge and New York: Cambridge University Press, 2009); Navickas, *Protest*, pp. 135-42.

159 Scriven, 'Activism and the Everyday' p. 20;

August 1837 contrasts starkly with Henry Vincent's vivid if patronising account of the same outdoor meeting on Almondbury Bank:

> We were ... conducted through the town amidst delightful scenes of excitement. The townspeople, cottagers and farmers, with their wives and daughters, all came out of their little houses and flocked with us to the meeting ... the men stood in the hollow, whilst the pretty lasses and women with white aprons and caps trimmed with green, sat around the sides of the hill. I never witnessed a more gratifying sight in my life.

Equally, his flirtatious private recollection of 'a profusion of bright eyed Yorkshire Radical lasses' on his first northern tour is not even hinted at in the newspaper reports which fails to mention the presence of any women at the Almondbury meeting.[160]

4: Joshua Hobson, the *Voice* and the Struggle for a Free Press, 1833-4

A vital link in the informal network of local radicalism – the booksellers, printers and newsagents whose shops, offices and houses served as informal meeting places, reading rooms, and staging posts in a wider provincial and national circuit – has merited extensive scholarly attention.[161] Such figures played a vital role in the development of local leadership and organisation. They acted as a focus, giving coherence to the wide range of agitations and activities which they served and serviced.

The struggle for a free press – the so-called 'War of the Unstamped' – was perhaps the key radical issue of the mid-decade. As Robert Hall has noted, 'a deep and principled opposition to the taxes on knowledge remained an article of faith' among leaders and activists, and the ensuing campaign served as a bridge between the agitations and leadership of 1829-34 and those of early Chartism.[162] It provided early Chartist leaders with journalistic and organisational experience, a ready-made network of book and newspaper sellers and a truly national perspective. It also did much to develop the inter- and intra-regional links and the fusing of traditional and new strands of radical analysis which were so important to the blossoming of the initial agitation for the Charter. Finally, involvement in this network was the means by

---

160 *LT* 9 Sept. 1837; Vincent to Minikin 4 Sept. 1837, quoted in Brooke, 'The Roots of Chartism', p. 30; Scriven, *Politics and Everyday Life*, p. 61. Joseph Lodge (1808-1880) was a fancy weaver. Samuel Midgley (1785-1859?), like John Buckley, was an Almondbury shopkeeper.

161 Patricia Hollis, *The Pauper Press: A Study in Working-class Radicalism of the 1830s* (Oxford: Oxford University Press, 1970); Joel H. Wiener, *The War of the Unstamped: The Movement to Repeal the British Newspaper Tax, 1830-1836* (Ithaca: Cornell University Press, 1969); R. G. Kirby and A. E. Musson, *The Voice of the People: John Doherty, 1798-1854, Trade Unionist, Radical and Factory Reformer* (Manchester: Manchester University Press, 1975); Halstead, 'Voice of the West Riding'; Simon Cordery, 'Joshua Hobson and the Business of Radicalism', *Biography*, 11, 2 (1988), pp. 108-123; Hall, 'A Bookshop of Their Own'.

162 Hall, 'A Bookshop of Their Own', p. 897.

which a number of key local leaders became full or part-time radicals. This section will concentrate on one such figure, Joshua Hobson, and his sorties in the local campaigns of the war of the unstamped.[163] However, before looking at Hobson and his first paper, *The Voice of the West-Riding*, it is necessary to trace something of the local background to the struggle and the evolution of this pivotal radical network.

West Riding interest in a free press was long-standing. Illegal unstamped radical papers circulated extensively in the post-war period in Leeds and the other major towns, and there were strong links with London-based agitations and distribution networks.[164] Throughout the early 1830s the packages which journalists such as James Watson, Henry Hetherington and John Cleave sent north served as a major channel of communication between metropolitan and provincial radicalism.

Another key figure in the evolution of this network was James Mann, the former cropper whose bookselling business in Leeds dated from his radical involvement in the post-war period. His shop became the chief 'radical depot' in Leeds and a focus for the West Riding. After his death in 1832 his widow, Alice, and son, Alfred, carried on the business and their Duncan Street premises retained its primacy in the local and regional movement.[165] Mann was one of the chief local handlers and sellers of the early unstamped papers which began to multiply in 1831 and which helped to make the questions of the 'Taxes on Knowledge' and press freedom into major radical concerns. Hobson's first recorded public speech was appropriately at a 'Liberty of the Press' meeting reported in the *Poor Man's Guardian* in September.[166] Hetherington's paper was highly thought of in Huddersfield, and Hobson along with Hanson and Leech recommended it in November as the 'centre of communication' for their National Convention idea 'it being the most valuable and cheapest paper in circulation'.[167] It is not certain whether John Doherty's early papers reached the textile district, but his unstamped *Voice of the People*, which included James Mann amongst its agents, and which circulated throughout the West Riding, may have been the inspiration for the title of Hobson's later paper.[168]

After a peak of radical optimism and interest in 1831, the next big stimulus to the creation of an independent working-class press and the network of radical booksellers and newspaper agents came in late 1832 and early 1833 when the 'war of the unstamped' was stepped up. In response, Victim Funds were raised in the West Riding and people such as Christopher Tinker of Huddersfield, James Ibbetson of Bradford

163 John Sanders, 'Joshua Hobson: "One of Freedom's Boys", 1829-37', Unpub. BA thesis, University of Manchester, 1973; Simon Cordery, 'Joshua Hobson, 1810-1876' in Joyce M. Bellamy and John Saville (eds.), *Dictionary of Labour Biography*, 8 (London: Macmillan, 1987), p. 113-19; and Halstead, 'The Voice of the West Riding'.

164 See W. J. Linton, *James Watson, A Memoir... etc* (Manchester: Abel Heywood and Son, 1880); also Patricia Hollis, *Pauper Press*, p. 110.

165 Malcolm Chase, 'Alice Mann [*née* Burnett] 1791-1865', *Oxford Dictionary of National Biography*, https://doi.org/10.1093/odnb/9780198614128.001.0001 (accessed 4 May 2021).

166 *PMG* 17 Sept. 1831. In an earlier 'public appearance' Hobson is to be found proposing a toast to John Foster, editor-proprietor of the radical *Leeds Patriot*, *LP* 22 Jan. 1831.

167 *PMG* 5 Nov.; *LM* 10 Dec. 1831.

168 On Doherty's paper, see Kirby and Musson, *Voice of the People*, p. 260 ff.

and John Bible Aked of Keighley emerged as specialist agents for the unstamped.[169] As the political temperature rose in late 1832, it became increasingly difficult for working-class radicals and factory reformers to get their propaganda printed. The prospectus for the *Voice* complained vigorously that 'Every kind of production, from the letter to the placard had to undergo the odious ordeal of ... an arbitrary, yet petty kind of censorship!', and that they had even gone as far as Manchester to engage a sympathetic printer.[170] An independent press gave Huddersfield radicals and their ten hours friends a means of producing the pamphlets, handbills, posters and placards essential to any mass agitation.

The origins of this independent press and the *Voice* itself can be traced back as far as January 1833 and perhaps much earlier.[171] From the start it appears that the Huddersfield initiators' ideas went beyond a mere printing press to more ambitious plans for their own newspaper. The Tory *Halifax Guardian* of 19 January 1833 sneeringly mentions that the radicals are talking of setting up a rival weekly journal, 'theirs, too, is not to be merely the 'Guardian' of two or three paltry towns but the 'Voice' (quere Vice?) of the West Riding'. The paper was indeed always more than just a local initiative. It relied on the 'pledged assistance of many friends in all the principal towns in the West Riding'; one of whom, Thomas Cliffe of Halifax, in a letter to the *Halifax Guardian* apparently threatened the use of 'our press at Huddersfield' against the *Guardian*.[172]

Hobson was not exaggerating when he later recalled that the project as a whole only got off the ground after 'the most extraordinary and the most praiseworthy exertions', 'a great outlay of capital (or at least 'great' for working men) was necessary, and they in these days of grinding taxation and low wages have not much superfluous cash at their command'.[173] The projectors attempted to solve this problem by appealing for donations and issuing five-shilling shares; but they appear to have been only partially successful.[174]

Eventually sufficient money was raised to buy type, but Hobson allegedly had to use his joiner's skills to build a wooden hand-press himself.[175] One of the first productions was probably *The Woodites' forget-me-not,* an account of the 1832 election campaign 'Printed and Published at the Union Free Press, by J Hobson, Swan Yard, 1833'; and it is likely that radical and short time handbills placards and pamphlets

---

169 *Gauntlet* 7, 21 Apr.; 23 June 1833, *PMG* 4 May 1833.

170 *VWR* 1 June 1833, the death of James Mann and Thomas Inchbold in the cholera outbreak of 1832 was an additional blow in Leeds.

171 Wiener, *War of the Unstamped*, p. 226, fn. 4, dates the Huddersfield men's first 'Address' 6 Jan. 1833. For evidence of earlier co-operative/radical printing activities, see Thomas Hirst's remarks, p. 212 above.

172 *HG* 19 Jan. 1833; *VWR* 1 June, 10 Aug. 1833; *HG* 9 Feb. 1833.

173 *VWR* 25 Jan. 1834; 1 June 1833;

174 For the origins of the *Voice*, and an analysis of its managing committee, shareholders and supporters, see Halstead, '*The Voice of the West Riding*', pp. 29-33.

175 *VWR* 25 Jan. 1834; 1 June 1833; *Death of Mr Joshua Hobson* (*HWN* 13 and 20 May 1876). Cordery, *DLB,* p. 114, however, suggests that the press was second-hand.

provided the bulk of the early work. It was only in June, nearly six months after the idea was first mooted, that the first edition of the *Voice* was printed.[176]

J. F. C. Harrison is correct in saying that the *Voice*'s 'history draws together many aspects of the working-class struggle'. However, he is mistaken in suggesting that the paper was originally intended as the organ of the local STC. Equally, it is misleading for Joel Wiener to call it a 'factory journal' which absorbed the issues of political radicalism and trade unionism.[177] In origin, content and tone it was above all radical. The early issues carry a heavy proportion of 'factory news' but this is merely a reflection of current local interest in the Factory Bill and the activities of the Factory Commissioners. The same issues also contain reports on Political Union meetings as well as articles on the 'Portuguese Question', Church-rate refusal at Gateshead and attacks on Whigs, both local and national.[178]

The *Voice* was never intended to be merely the mouthpiece of the local STC. The very publishing of an unstamped paper was a conscious act of political defiance.[179] Indeed, the initial location of Hobson's press in Swan Yard, and John Cleave's remarks to local radicals, congratulating 'The Huddersfield Union that they at length got a press of their own', both confirm that the Political Union was the prime motive force behind the project.[180] The establishment of the *Voice* was an attempt to redress an obvious imbalance. The *Leeds Mercury* (the leading West Riding paper) was a consistent opponent of 'Ultra-Radicalism' and factory reform, whilst the Tory *Leeds Intelligencer* supported the operatives only on the factory issue. Worse still, the radical *Leeds Patriot* and the Rev. G. S. Bull's *Protector* (the organ of the factory movement in Yorkshire) had ceased publication in February and April 1833 respectively. The *Patriot*'s successor, the radical *Leeds Times* (published and printed by Frederick Bingley) was still a largely unknown quantity; whilst outside Leeds the *Wakefield and Halifax Journal* pursued an independent Tory line; the *Halifax and Huddersfield Express* was a solidly Whig-liberal paper and the *Halifax Guardian*, although sympathetic to the factory cause, remained resolutely Tory. Bradford at this time had no paper of its own. With letters often ignored, meetings inadequately or inaccurately reported and leaders frequently vilified, the voice of local working-class protest was muted. Hobson declared at his trial in August:

> I was induced to publish the "Voice of the West Riding," because a paper was wanted to support the rights and interests of the order and class to which it is my pride and boast to belong, It being notorious that their just privileges were not only left unadvocated, but absolutely

---

176 *VWR* 1 June 1833.

177 Harrison, *Chartism in Leeds*; p. 67; Wiener, *War of the Unstamped*, p. 190.

178 *VWR* 1, 15, 22 June; 27 July 1833. Portugal was embroiled in a civil war between liberals and absolutists.

179 *Death of Mr Joshua Hobson*. The war of the unstamped was perhaps the 'purest' political campaign of the decade.

180 *VWR* 15 June 1833.

denied, and they, made the object of abuse and misrepresentation, by the majority of those who have the public Press under controul [*sic*].[181]

The *Voice* was printed on both sides of 'single crown' (20" x 15") paper folded twice to produce an eight-page quarto (10" x 7½"). Hobson and his colleagues were inexperienced as printers and the first number took over a week to produce.[182] Even then it was barely legible due to the poor quality of the paper. The following number contained an apology from Hobson and praise from John Cleave of the NUWC: 'they must not be discouraged by small beginnings', he was sure that the *Voice* was 'as good as many of the provincial stamped newspapers.' Not unnaturally, William Rider preferred it to the Whig *Leeds Mercury*: 'it is fraught with more truth in one week, than a waggonload of Baines's bagatelles, alias bag of tales, alias bag of lies...'[183]

The early struggles of the V*oice* are well attested.[184] In Hobson's words, the paper soon 'laboured under great and almost unsurmountable difficulties'. After three issues he was desperately urging that it was '[the people's] imperative duty ... to support us'. By the end of July he was confiding that 'the sale does not cover the expense, and if our friends and shareholders do not exert themselves a little more, we shall be obliged to discontinue the Voice for the present'. Yet at this critical time 'a friend appeared in the shape of an enemy' and all the *Voice's* immediate problems were solved by a Stamp Duty prosecution, initiated by the local postmaster and leading Whig, William Moore.[185]

Hobson and his supporters welcomed the prosecution, whose cause was obviously 'the Politics and Principles of the paper': 'this warfare is not for revenue – it is with intellect'.[186] 'Great excitement pervaded the whole town' on the day of the trial, and Hobson was given a hero's reception.[187] His line of defence mirrored that of previous 'victims' such as 'Hetherington, Watson and many others', emphasising the partiality of the Stamp Laws and the political, class-based nature of his prosecution.[188] Hobson maintained a consistently defiant attitude throughout the trial and martyrdom was finally assured when his inability (not to say unwillingness) to pay a £20 fine meant the

---

181 *VWR* 10 Aug. 1833.

182 *VWR* 1 June 1833 (the editorial is dated 8 June), *Gauntlet* 18 Aug. 1833.

183 *VWR* 15, 22 June 1833.

184 Hollis, *Pauper Press*, p. 117; Sanders 'Joshua Hobson', pp. 48-9; Halstead, 'The Voice of the West Riding', pp. 23-4.

185 *VWR* 25 Jan. 1834; 29 June; 27 July; 3 Aug. 1833; see also Hobson's letter, *True Sun* 20 Aug. 1833. The immediate cause of the prosecution appears to have been a scurrilous attack on Rev. Franks, vicar of Huddersfield parish church and pillar of the local establishment (*VWR* 22 June 1833).

186 *VWR* 3, 10 Aug. 1833.

187 Stanley Chadwick, *'A Bold and Faithful Journalist': Joshua Hobson 1810-1876* (Huddersfield, Kirklees Libraries and Museums Service, 1976), p. 19 ; *VWR* 10 Aug.; *Cosmopolite* 17 Aug. 1833.

188 *VWR* 10 Aug. His impressive speech to the magistrates was widely reported.

enforcement of a six-month prison sentence. The new hero was accompanied by a large procession headed by bands on his way to Wakefield House of Correction.[189]

The 'persecution' of young Hobson exacerbated anti-Whig feeling and ensured that the *Voice* was 'rescued from oblivion'. By the end of the week a formal Victim Fund was already raising money in Huddersfield.[190] Elsewhere in the Riding, committees were quickly established to collect subscriptions for the Fund and to promote the *Voice*. Supporters in Bradford, Halifax, Leeds, Wakefield and many of the Huddersfield out-townships subscribed regularly. Four months after the trial was over £20 had been collected – a respectable figure considering that formal radical activity was at a relatively low ebb.[191]

Hobson's imprisonment excited considerable local interest. This benefited the network of unstamped sellers which had been growing up in the textile district.[192] The prosecution also boosted sales and the area of circulation. As an editorial commented, 'we hardly expected being able to walk above a week or two longer; but our bitter enemies in the excess of their hostility have not only lent us crutches but stilts, and now we call at many more places than before'.[193] The prosecution made Hobson a working-class martyr and temporarily a national personality. As he recalled, 'in all the wildest of my ambitious hopes and thoughts, I never dreamed of the fame and renown of a government prosecution until they literally sought me out'.

Hobson's trial and subsequent allegations of ill-treatment in prison were widely reported by the London unstamped papers, who used it as propaganda in the Stamp Duty campaign. In addition to a public meeting in Huddersfield about his incarceration, petitions were also raised in Wakefield, Nottingham and London. These were presented to Parliament by Col. De Lacy Evans, the Radical MP for Westminster, and William Cobbett – both of who repeatedly sought admissions that Hobson's treatment was illegal.[194] Cobbett even wrote Hobson a short letter which contained hope and a fatherly reprimand:

---

189 *VWR* 10 Aug. 1833 (resolutions of Holt-head PU); *Death of Mr J Hobson*; *HDE* 8 May 1876.

190 *VWR* 10 Aug. 1833.

191 *VWR* Aug.- Oct. 1833; 30 Nov 1833. The subscription lists read like a 'Who's Who' of local radicalism. John Halstead's detailed analysis of subscribers suggests an abundance of small contributions from mainly working-class sources, 'The Voice of the West Riding', p. 34.

192 For example, Alice Mann (Leeds), James Ibbetson (Bradford), Christopher Tinker (Huddersfield), J. B. Aked (Keighley). Other vendors of the *Voice* included established booksellers such as Benjamin Barker of Halifax, and radical activists or sympathisers who sold the paper as an 'extra line' on a part-time basis, such as Richard Scholes, a corn-dealer and town-radical in Huddersfield, or John Barker, a radical activist from Huddersfield who was set up as an unstamped seller in Leeds following his release from prison (he had been prosecuted for his part in the 1832 election disturbances).

193 *VWR* 17 Aug. 1833. After the trial Sheffield, and more importantly Abel Heywood in Manchester, began taking the paper.

194 *True Sun* 13 Aug. 1833, reprinted in *VWR* 17 Aug. 1833; *Cosmopolite* 23 Aug.; *VWR* 31 Aug.; *Destructive* 17 Aug. 1833; Hansard, Parliamentary Debates 3rd Series (20), 1833, p. 582.

I have good reason for believing that your release, and a remittal of your fine will speedily be ordered by the government. You have been unlawfully treated in prison, but I beg you to bear in mind, that you violated the law, and I advise you most strongly not to do it again. As long as it exists, one must obey it.

Hobson kept the letter, but ignored and later repudiated the advice.[195]

The fact that he had endured martyrdom gave Hobson immense personal prestige in the textile district. He became a popular 'folk hero'. On the day of his release, in January 1834, crowds gathered in Huddersfield amidst popular rejoicing for a celebratory meeting attended by over five thousand people. The whole ritual of trial, imprisonment and freedom gave Hobson a lasting eminence in West Riding radicalism.[196]

When Hobson returned the paper was in a healthier state than when he left it, but only just.[197] Political radicalism was at a low ebb and the *Voice* had become caught up in the bitterness surrounding the Huddersfield by-election.[198] Accordingly, in the middle of February Hobson went on a tour of the Riding, speaking about his imprisonment and trying to boost the circulation by establishing or reviving local committees 'to see after the interests of the Voice'. By the end of March the *Voice* was looking stale, with little original material or comment.[199] However, Hobson's involvement in the Dorchester case and the excitement caused by attacks on trade unionists added a new dimension; and by the middle of April Hobson had a wide choice of 'communications' for insertion. The journal increasingly identified itself with the trade union struggle; yet as defeat loomed towards the end of May, so the problems of the paper multiplied. A week after a leading article on the death of Lafayette, whose motto ('for a nation to be free it is sufficient that she wills it') had always headed the front-page, the *Voice* too breathed its last.[200] The paper had run for a little over a year and had just started a second volume.

---

195 Tolson Memorial Museum, Huddersfield, Cobbett to Hobson, 24 Aug. 1833; *LT* 1 Feb. 1834.

196 *VWR* 25 Jan. 1834; *Death of Mr J Hobson.* Hereafter Hobson frequently chaired public meetings.

197 On the struggles to keep the paper afloat after Hobson's imprisonment, see *VWR* 17 Aug. 1833 (to Readers and Correspondents). The early socialist theorist, John Francis Bray, a qualified printer, left Leeds at the end of August to print the paper and run the *Voice* office. There is no hard evidence that he actually edited the paper, though the style and content editorials in October and November suggest this. William Rider is also mooted as a possible interim co-editor (F. Driver, 'Tory Radicalism?', p. 128).

198 *VWR* 14, 21, 28 Dec. 1833. Many regular customers refused to buy the paper because of the editor's support for Sadler and he was eventually suspended. Bray's recollections suggest that he only gave up his role after Hobson's return, H. J. Carr, 'John Francis Bray', *Economica*, 1940, p. 399 ff.

199 OC No. 677, Pitkethly to Owen, 25 Feb. 1834; *VWR* 22 Feb.; 15, 22 Mar. 1834.

200 *VWR* 12 Apr.; 3, 10, 17, 24 May; 31 May; 7 June 1834. There were three shareholders' meetings in five weeks in May and early June.

There is no need to look too deeply into the reasons for this 'radical mortality'.[201] The defeat of the Yorkshire trades' unions and cumulative radical exhaustion after four years of almost continuous activity must together provide a large part of the explanation. With its working-class core support under pressure and in retreat, the penny quarto was no longer viable. Any estimation of the *Voice*'s success or impact depends upon the criteria adopted for judgement. In terms of survival, it was a qualified success. Certainly, the Huddersfield projectors, contemplating the possible demise of the paper after only eight issues thought that 'it is a miracle that we succeeded so well'. The *Voice* survived for over a year without change in title or price; a feat shared by only fourteen London and two provincial unstamped papers throughout the whole unstamped war, 1830-36.[202]

Yet longevity is not necessarily a sure indicator of a paper's vitality or influence. The *Voice* was always a 'little paper' competing with numerous rival cheap publications. Not least of these were the other radical unstamped papers.[203] However, within its own area it more than held its own and became, in Joel Wiener's words, 'one of the liveliest and most controversial of the illicit provincial journals'.[204]

Journalistically, the *Voice* was not a very ambitious project. The layout was simple, the style repetitive and the content uneven. To some contemporaries it was a 'London paper edited at Huddersfield'. Others criticised its lack of humour; and the Leeds 'Friends' desired more foreign and parliamentary news.[205] But within its own terms of reference the *Voice* was a fairly successful newspaper. It consistently explained and supported the rights and interests of the working class. The aim to expose 'Local as well as National abuse' was achieved by attacks, for example, on the local clergy, magistracy and the allegedly all-powerful 'Ramsden interest' in Huddersfield.[206] Within the wider region the paper reported trade union activity in Barnsley, co-operation in Halifax, ten hours protest in Bradford, radicalism in Wakefield and meetings on a range of issues in Leeds. The coverage of 'national abuse' was often dependent upon what the London papers printed, nevertheless the *Voice* managed to

---

201 *LM* 21 June 1834, for the *Mercury*'s obituary on 'an organ of the lowest radicalism'.

202 *VWR* 27 July 1833; figures taken from Joel H. Wiener, *A Descriptive Finding-List of Unstamped British Periodicals, 1830-36* (London: Bibliographical Society, 1970).

203 VWR 27 July 1833. Sales must have run into hundreds rather than thousands. For example, in March 1834 the *Herald to the Rights of Industry* was selling 800 copies in Lancashire. However, Patricia Hollis, *Pauper Press*, p. 119, suggests a 20:1 readership to sales ratio, and unstamped papers' listening audience must have been even greater. See *VWR* 6 July 1833 for the range of other unstamped papers offered by Christopher Tinker when he took over William Vevers' shop.

204 Wiener, *War of the Unstamped*, p. 190.

205 *VWR* 17 Aug. 1833.

206 As the principal landowners in the town, and lords of the manor of both Almondbury and Huddersfield, the Ramsden family exercised significant local political and economic control. For an assessment of the extent of the influence of the 'Ramsden interest' see, Edward Royle (ed.), *Power in the Land: the Ramsdens and their Huddersfield Estate, 1542-1920* (Huddersfield: Huddersfield University Press, 2020).

cover the topical issues of the day through reprinted reports or wide-ranging editorials.[207]

In terms of ideology, the 'old' and 'new' radical analyses existed side by side in the paper.[208] This is evident in the founders' stated intention to advocate, 'the Rights of Man against the "exclusives," the rights of labour against the "competatives," [sic] and the "Political Economists"'. The influence of the French Revolution is evident in the Jacobin-like stress on political equality in the first issue, 'let the basis of society be equal, the superstructure will be sufficiently diversified by various degrees of Talent and Industry.'[209] Similarly, the tradition of Paine and Cobbett is echoed in repeated attacks on various aspects of 'Old Corruption' – the monarchy, the Church, the national debt, and the 'execrable oligarchy'.[210] But the ideas of 'labour as the source of all wealth' and the division of society into the 'productive' or working-classes and the non-productive 'middlemen' and capitalists are taken for granted in numerous editorials and articles.[211] At the time of the attacks on trades' unions, for example, we find Hobson declaring that, 'the Trades' Unions were formed for no other earthly purpose than to endeavour to put a stop to the ruinous depreciation and continual reduction of wages – to protect the workman's PROPERTY – his labour – from the encroachment of capital and capitalists'. Similarly, political economy, with its propensity to reduce Man to 'a mere secondary consideration… an engine to be worked for the good of trade' was regularly attacked in the paper.[212]

Whether speaking in the terms of the new or the old radical analyses, the *Voice* had an unmistakable tone of class hostility.[213] Hobson expresses this most starkly after his release from prison when he rejects all association with the middle class.[214] This tone may partly be explained in terms of the paper's geographical location. The consequences of competition and political economy were plainly visible to the working-class radicals of the manufacturing districts, in the distress of local operatives and in the abuses of the factory system that were evident around them. But the chronological context was equally important.[215] The *Voice* was published at a time

---

207 For terms of reference, see *VWR* 1 June, 10 Aug. 1833.

208 The ideological content of the unstamped papers was the subject of historical controversy in the early 1970s, with Patricia Hollis stressing continuity with the earlier radicalism of post-1817 and playing down the 'class component' of the 1830s popular press; and with Joel Wiener emphasising the generality of attacks on private property and political economy in the unstamped, the consciousness of the working-class readership and the symbolic fact of illegality.

209 *VWR* 1 June 1833.

210 See, for example, *VWR* 27 July (National Debt); 17 Aug. (oligarchy) and letters from Hobson, Bussey and Rider 14 Sept.; 2 Nov.; 6, 28 Dec. 1833.

211 See, for example, *VWR* 3 Aug., 28 Sept., 5 Oct. 1833.

212 *VWR* 24 May 1834; 13 July 1833. See also *VWR* 3 Aug., 9 and 16 Nov. 1833.

213 This tone and the analysis which underpinned it were not particularly sophisticated and owed much to fairly traditional motifs: rich/poor, tyrants/slaves, oligarchs/the people. But the paper also incorporated more recent political and economic developments into its analysis, like the Reform Bill, ten hours and local industrial conflicts.

214 *VWR* 25 Jan. 1834.

215 The time factor – the change of emphases in unstamped papers generally from political issues

when the full implications of the Reform Act were beginning to be understood – thus the paper's verdict, that 'it was intended to crush the people forever, to be final'.[216] It was also an era of bitterness and frustration following the humiliating defeat of two years' efforts in favour of a Ten Hours Bill. The prosecution of Hobson and the attack on the trades' unions only served to confirm the validity of class attitudes. The oppressors in all cases were the corrupt tyrannical Whigs, the political exploiters of the working class, allied to the idle capitalists and 'millocrats' who were their economic exploiters. Radicals expected and received no assistance from the aristocracy, the traditional enemy, but the perceived desertion of the middle-class – now including factory employers, middle men and shopkeepers – was felt particularly bitterly. The close overlap and interconnection between these groups and the politically-endorsed basis of their ascendency was seen as being crucial; and although the *Voice* urged workers to 'intercept profits' and set up co-operative retailing and self-production, the ultimate solution to their predicament was seen as being political through their attainment of the vote.[217]

This fusion of old and new analyses is essential to any understanding of Hobson and his paper. Their middle-class enemies had seized the political and economic opportunities offered by the Reform Act and now opposed all the working-class movements 'to the utmost of their power'.[218] Although not universally accepted, it was an analysis which gained credence in the following years and came of age, like Hobson and the radical press itself, in early Chartism.[219] The *Voice* was an important contributor to this process. While it never attained the range or sophistication of some of the London unstamped papers in content or ideology, this 'spirited little journal' nevertheless merits Malcolm Chase's assessment as 'the greatest of the provincial radical papers of the early 1830s'.[220]

5: The War of the Unstamped, 1834-6

The cessation of the *Voice* in early June 1834 was not the end of Hobson's involvement in the war of the unstamped. Within a couple of months he surfaces again as editor, publisher and printer of another weekly penny journal, the *Argus and Demagogue*. The paper had its origins in Leeds where, in the aftermath of the defeat of the trades' union, William Rider started the *Demagogue*, a penny weekly edited by himself and printed by Alice Mann. The paper ran to only two numbers and confined itself to attacks on 'Aristocrats', 'Baines-ocrats' and the elder Baines himself, for their opposition to

---

and news in 1831-2 to proportionately more economic concerns in 1833-4 – may also help to explain how Hollis and Wiener arrived at their different interpretations.

216 *VWR* 26 Oct. 1833.

217 See, for example, *VWR* 24 Aug. 1833; 25 Jan. 1834.

218 *VWR* 25 Jan. 1834.

219 Another prefiguration of early Chartism can be seen in the attitude of Hobson and the *Voice* to violence and the stress on defensive rather than revolutionary arming; see, for example, *VWR* 29 June; 26 Oct. 1833; 12 Apr. 1834.

220 *VWR* 30 Nov. 1833 (Bready's letter); Malcolm Chase, 'Chartism in Huddersfield, the cultural dimension', in Hargreaves (ed.), *The Charter our Right!*, p. 71.

factory reform. Baines senior apparently took exception to the paper, not least for a spoof biography of himself which claimed that he was both illegitimate and immoral. The last issue contains allegations that Baines' eldest son had taken various measures, including assaulting Rider, starting a fire in Mann's shop, and threatening to prosecute Mann in order to suppress publication of the paper. The latter threat appears to have been carried out, for in early August the *Leeds Times* reported the trial and imprisonment of Alice Mann.[221] The fact of impending prosecution may explain why attempts to revive the project centred on an alternative radical printer: Hobson in Huddersfield.

The first edition of Hobson's new paper came out on 2 August 1834, with the enlarged title of the *Argus and Demagogue*.[222] Although the paper only survived for another three issues, its content reflects a certain degree of continuity with the *Voice*. There is support for universal suffrage, advocacy of factory legislation and letters from Oastler.[223] The reason for its short life was probably the same exhaustion of popular radicalism which had played a decisive role in the demise of the *Voice*. Disappointment over the failure of the new venture may have played some part in Hobson's decision to move to Leeds in the autumn of 1834. However, the precise timing and motivation for this relocation are unclear.[224] Whatever its rationale, the transfer was a blow to the Huddersfield radicals, who now closed their printing establishment and allowed Hobson to buy the equipment from the shareholders.[225]

Although he did not bring out any more illegal papers, Hobson's involvement in the war of the unstamped was in no way diminished by his move to Leeds. His principal contribution now was as an unstamped seller and martyr. His bookselling and printing business had a wider significance to both local and national radical movements. On the local level the bookshop was a focus for all forms of radical activity, both formal and informal. As Robert Hall notes, 'Most booksellers dealt in a range of goods and services, from stationery and patent medicines to insurance and postal addresses, and often ran a circulating library and sometimes a coffee house as well'.[226] Even though mass campaigns were dormant, radical literature was still

---

221 *Demagogue* 29 June, 5 July 1834; *LT* 9 Aug. 1834; Chase, 'Alice Mann', *ODNB*.

222 'Demagogue' was Rider's *nom-de-plume*, and Hobson at his first trial had equated the People with the Argus, the hundred eyes of the mythical monster acting as 'the great moral corrector', Halstead, '*Voice of the West Riding*', pp. 25-6.

223 J. T. Ward, *The Factory Movement, 1830-1855* (London: Macmillan, 1962), p. 123; R. Oastler, *A letter to the Editor of the 'Argus and Demagogue'* (Huddersfield, 1834).

224 J. F. C. Harrison, *Robert Owen and the Owenites in Britain and America: The Quest for the New Moral World* (London: Routledge and Kegan Paul, 1969), p. 226, fn. 2 suggests that Hobson went to Leeds to run Alice Mann's bookshop while she was in prison and entered into a business partnership with her. John Halstead's chapter, '"The Charter and Something More!" The Politics of Joshua Hobson, 1810-1876', in Hargreaves (ed.) *The Charter our Right!*, p. 92 examines doubts about this explanation.

225 *Death of Mr Joshua Hobson*; Letter from Hobson to the *Manchester Examiner*, 10 Nov. 1847. This episode is discussed by Halstead, '*Voice of the West Riding*', pp. 30-1.

226 Hall, 'A Bookshop of Their Own', p. 896. See also, Harrison, *Robert Owen and the Owenites*, pp. 229-30.

popular. The lifting of duties on almanacs and pamphlets in 1834 caused a boom in this branch of publishing, which benefitted Hobson and other radical booksellers in the West Riding. For example, James Ibbetson, who moved to more spacious premises in New Street, Bradford in August 1834, now advertised a host of periodicals (including the *Argus and Demagogue*) and a variety of cheap penny novels; and in summer 1835 Hobson was selling some of Oastler's pamphlets 'like wild-fire'.[227]

With a wide range of radical, Owenite and freethinking tracts on offer, in addition to the staple 'non-political' fare (like Ibbetson's penny dreadfuls), the commercial side of the local radical bookshops developed substantially in the mid-1830s. The very success and broad range of publications offered also caused some tensions. The Huddersfield Radical Association sought to curtail support for more opportunist vendors in April 1836 by passing a resolution that only those devoted to the cause of the unstamped should receive subscriptions as sufferers. The source of the resolution was apparently their disgust at seeing a 'filthy tory publication emanating from Mrs Alice Mann's, Leeds'. They warned 'A villain can do mischief when hid beneath the robe of sanctity or liberty... there is a lynx eye upon <u>the radical depot of Leeds</u>, ... let them look to themselves!!'[228]

As well as fulfilling important local functions, the radical bookshops also formed part of the informal network of a wider national movement. This can be seen in action during the sequence of face-to-face and written communications between Hobson in Leeds, John Cleave in London, George Pilgrim in the Potteries and Mr A. Yates, a canvasser for one of Clements' papers, which led to Charles Clements (former publisher of *Cobbett's Political Register*) being denounced as a Stamp Office spy.[229] This extended intimate web acted as an intelligence network and helped to give the working-class repeal campaign its self-consciously national character.

Hobson had reason to be worried about Stamp Office spies, for he had already been prosecuted once for selling unstamped papers in Leeds. The court case, heard early in February 1835, was less spectacular than his first brush with the Stamp Duty laws. In contrast to the Huddersfield bench, the Leeds magistrates appear to have had some sympathy with Hobson, a fact which did not altogether suit his aspirations for renewed martyrdom, and they gave him the most lenient sentence.[230] In general, the prosecution generated little public interest in Leeds. Ten days after the trial a Victim Fund was still being contemplated, though the Huddersfield men had already started a 'liberal subscription'. The *Leeds Times* and William Rider railed against this 'climax of outrage' but the fact that it caused only a brief stir reflects the low ebb of popular agitation in Leeds.[231]

This lack of response does not appear to have dulled Hobson's dedication to the cause of 'Repeal'. In August we find him issuing handbills bitterly condemning the

---

227 *BO* 14 Aug. 1834; Ward, *Factory Movement*, p. 137.

228 *LT* 16 Apr. 1836; Hobson and Mann were both in jail at this point.

229 Full details are in *London Dispatch* 4 Dec. 1836, the initial discovery was probably made in late 1835. Pilgrim was originally one of the publishers of *Cosmopolite* in London and a well-known 'victim' who set up shop in the Potteries.

230 *LT* 14 Feb.; 7, 28 Mar. and 5 Apr. 1835 (for his surprise early release).

231 *LT* 21 Feb.; 14 Mar. 1835.

impounding of Cleave's and Hetherington's presses. This action marked the start of an enlargement of the government attack on the unstamped infrastructure. In the winter of 1835 the Stamp Office took over direct responsibility for prosecutions and issued a circular urging all local distributors of stamps to press forward with the conviction of unstamped vendors. This hardening of the government response, allied to the propaganda of Feargus O'Connor's 'Great Radical Association', helped revive the working-class 'Repeal' agitation as a popular movement in the winter of 1835-6.[232]

The bitter resentment of 1833 was re-awakened in the West Riding by a spate of prosecutions in early 1836. The first of these, early in January, saw Hobson prosecuted once more, with Alice Mann, for selling unstamped papers. In a planned court-room oration, which magistrates prevented him from delivering but the *Leeds Times* printed in full, Hobson reaffirmed the special nature of his occupation 'as a vendor of the unstamped', his consciousness of being directly involved in 'warfare' for 'the freedom of the press' and his complaints about the biased administration of the law. Contrasting the treatment of unstamped papers to that afforded to the unmolested *Penny Magazine* he argued scathingly that,

> Dame Justice has got the bandage removed from that eye which looks upon the golden heap; on those who own it she smiles; on those who own it not she frowns… But this is easily accounted for. They are rich - I am poor. They are the messengers of corruption - I only aim to become one of freedom's boys. Their business is to perpetuate evil - mine to extirpate it. They labour to propagate error - I to uproot it. Their reward is pelt - mine a prison…[233]

The prosecution of 'one of freedom's boys', as the *Leeds Times* rightly guessed, signified that the government was widening its campaign. In February other key network figures, James Ibbetson of Bradford and Christopher Tinker of Huddersfield, were also convicted under the Stamp Acts, stimulating an upsurge in popular radicalism.[234] Public meetings on Stamp Duty repeal in Halifax, Bradford and Leeds claimed the support not just of working-class radicals, but also respectable middle-class radical-liberals, and for a time 'Repeal' became the chief radical issue of the day.[235]

With pressure increasing on all sides, the government decided in March to introduce a Bill that sought to tie the reduction to the Stamp Day to a penny to clauses for stricter enforcement of the law.[236] This compromise pleased the stamped newspaper

---

232 Hollis, *Pauper Press*, p. 115; Wiener, *War of the Unstamped*, pp. 207-8; *LT* 19, 26 Dec. 1835 for O'Connor on a 'Free and Untaxed Press'.

233 *LT* 16 Jan 1836.

234 *LT* 16 Jan., 6, 20, 27 Feb., 12 Mar, 1836; Peacock, *Bradford Chartism*, p. 11. Meetings were also held in smaller townships such as Heckmondwike and Idle, *LT* 5 Mar. 1836.

235 *LT* 6 Feb. (Halifax) 20 Feb. (Leeds) *BO* 3 Mar. 1836 (Bradford). The Leeds meeting chaired by the mayor included speeches from Joshua Bower, Smithson and Lees (of the old Holbeck PU). See *BO* 21 Jan. and *LT* 6 Feb. 1836 for the reactions of liberals in Bradford and Halifax.

236 *LT* 5 Mar. 1836; Hollis, *Pauper Press*, p. 85.

interest, but only alienated the unstamped proprietors and many of their working-class supporters. Bradford radicals met under John Douthwaite in May to press for the abolition of the remaining penny which, though it 'may appear small, yet it is in fact too great, because it presses too much upon the working-classes'. Many agreed with Bronterre O'Brien's denunciation of this new 'Gagging Bill' as a 'declaration of war against the working-classes.'[237] Like the earlier Reform Bill 'compromise' of 1832, it was seen as a betrayal, depriving the working class of yet another means whereby they could express their political and economic grievances.

The events of the late summer did little to soothe tensions. Despite the imminence of legislation, the governmental campaign against the unstamped press continued unabated. Hobson, who had been released with Alice Mann in late June, prosecuted again in early September, was to become one of the last martyrs of the unstamped agitation.[238] His close collaborator, Richard Oastler concluded a letter to the Mayor of Leeds, by contrasting Hobson's six-month sentence with the lenient fines given to Factory Act offenders:

> Call you this Justice, Sir? Blind 'respectability' trampling upon Law. It is murder hurling defiance at justice... The people are tired of seeing unstamped sellers and poachers sent wholesale to prison and then five shilling and ten shilling and twenty shilling allowed to be paid of 'Child Murder' ... Be warned in time - prevent the laws no more in favour of the 'respectables' ... you cannot keep labour down, if you try, much longer; and if some must be 'bulletted' by these hateful monsters, we shall soon have bloody times'.[239]

The reduction of the Stamp Duty on 15 September gained a reprieve for existing offenders, including Hobson, and almost immediately ended the war of the unstamped. The working-class press hereafter concentrated on producing cheap radical pamphlets and tracts. Hobson followed this trend and became 'the chief publisher of Radical material in the West Riding'. His personal involvement in radical journalism, however, was far from over.[240] More generally, after a campaign lasting six years, the working-class 'Repeal' movement had only managed to secure a concession which appeared to benefit everyone but themselves. The widespread sense of alienation and bitterness generated amongst radical leaders in the spring and summer of 1836 gave an impetus to attitudes which were to emerge more openly in the anti-poor law and radical agitations of the following year.

---

237 *BO* 19 May 1836; O'Brien is quoted in Wiener, *War of the Unstamped*, p. 269.

238 BPP, Report of the Select Committee on Newspaper Stamps, 1851, XVII, Hobson's name occurs twice in the list of prosecutees for 1836; the second mention is at the end of the list.

239 Oastler, *The Unjust Judge* (Leeds, 1836).

240 Wiener, *War of the Unstamped*, p. 277; Harrison, 'Chartism in Leeds', p. 68.

PART TWO

6: Radical Organisations, 1835-7

The local Radical Associations and, later, the Working Men's Associations, which kept the green flag flying in the mid-1830s, prefigured many aspects of later Chartist organisation and leadership.[241] It was through these key bodies that many main early Chartist leaders became personally acquainted with Feargus O'Connor and helped to nurture a sense of national unity and organisation. A list of local people who spoke at or organised the meetings which mark O'Connor's first major northern tour in December 1835 reveals a solid core of future Chartist leaders, as well as a number of established town-radicals and 'liberals' who never quite made the transition to Chartism. O'Connor's further tours in 1836 and 1837 stimulated or revived local organisations and reinforced links with an increasingly coherent group of key working-class leaders. By 1837 these activists were putting into practice earlier plans to speed up 'the furtherance of the objects and principles of the Radical Association – by extended organisation in the form of new branch associations – the diffusion of sound political knowledge – and to rally round our acknowledged champion, Feargus O'Connor' and were acting as the voice of the unenfranchised at the election hustings.[242]

As well as being in obvious line of succession to the radical remnants of the old Political Unions, the Radical Associations also followed on from more recent *ad hoc* entities, such as the non-electors' committees of late 1834, and more formal bodies, for example the Bradford 'Association of the Working Classes', or a similar working-class association for mutual improvement and the dissemination of political knowledge which appeared in Heckmondwike in June 1835. This latter entity was flourishing in early October, unlike the Bradford Association the 'desertion' of which left John Jackson, the Bradford radical, pessimistic about the prospects for a new Radical Association: 'I must confess I have no great expectations of the labouring man of Bradford attending to their political interests as they ought', he wrote in late December 1835.[243]

The fact that a RA was successfully floated at Bradford but not at Heckmondwike in late 1835, illustrates the importance of the interaction of national and local leadership in stimulating radical organisation. The first West Riding Radical Associations were formed as a direct result of Feargus O'Connor's whistle-stop northern tour undertaken on behalf of the Marylebone RA, at the instigation of several provincial radical groups, including Leeds.[244] Wherever O'Connor appeared, (and he

---

241 Their role in the pre-Chartist revival of radicalism in the West Riding has been touched upon in a range of local studies, (for example, see Harrison, 'Chartism in Leeds', p. 68; Peacock, *Bradford Chartism*, pp. 10-17; Brooke, 'The Roots of Chartism in the Huddersfield Area', pp. 20-31), however, their collective contribution has not been systematically investigated until now.

242 *LT* 26 Nov. 1836.

243 *LT* 27 June, 11 July; 3, 10 Oct. 1835 (Heckmondwike); *BO* 31 Dec. 1835.

244 For an account of the tour, see James A. Epstein, 'Feargus O'Connor and the English Working-class Movement, 1832-41: A study in national Chartist leadership', Unpub. PhD

spoke, often more than once, at all the major West Riding textile centres except Dewsbury), 'branch associations' were established on the Marylebone model and the 'sound radical principles' of universal suffrage, annual parliaments, vote by ballot, equal representation and no property qualifications. However, the predominantly working-class audiences also heard O'Connor and other speakers voice the importance of labour as the source of all wealth, radical critiques of machinery and competition, attacks on both Whigs and Tories, the injustice of the Dorchester sentence, the Poor Law Amendment Act, Irish coercion and distress, the need for a free press, an effective Ten-Hour bill and other radical concerns.

As well as these recurring themes, the inaugural and early RA meetings also throw up some important and recurring radical names – Joshua Hobson, William Rider, David Green, Francis Phillips, Thomas Bottomley at Leeds; Lawrence Pitkethly, John Hanson, Stephen Dickinson, Thomas Vevers, Christopher Wood, John Leech and Christopher Tinker at Huddersfield; Peter Bussey, James Ibbetson, John Jackson, John Douthwaite, Christopher Wilkinson at Bradford; Joseph Firth, James Bedford, D. W. Weatherhead, Joseph Vickers and John Thornton at Keighley; Henry Dixon, Elijah Crabtree and Abram Hanson at Halifax.[245] These radicals who invited and spoke with O'Connor became the backbone of the new associations. Nearly all were established radical leaders who had been agitating for universal suffrage and on a range of other issues for four years and more. The value to O'Connor's leadership and the future shape of the Chartist movement of his early contact with such key radical 'brokers' in the West Riding cannot be over-stressed. Equally, the boost which O'Connor's presence and popularity gave these local leaders was important in helping to drag popular radicalism out of the trough of depression and inactivity into which it had subsided in 1835.[246]

The early meetings of the associations displayed an impressive vitality and breadth of interest. Activities focused particularly on the Stamp Duties issue, but Bradford also discussed the Poor Law Amendment Act and Irish distress, whilst the Huddersfield adherents attended lectures and composed an address commending the electors of Glasgow for having chosen O'Connor as their radical candidate.[247]

Although the Huddersfield Radical Association flourished for a time, associations elsewhere quickly began to run out of steam. By March the Leeds Radical Association was contemplating a change of venue and proposing to meet every second and fourth Wednesday of the month instead of every Monday. Little is heard of either the Halifax or Bradford associations, though both probably maintained a fairly small-scale, low-

---

Thesis, University of Birmingham, 1977, p. 43 ff. See also O'Connor's note to William Rider, *LT* 12 Dec. 1835. Reports of the meetings are in *LT, BO* and *LM* Dec. 1835 - Jan. 1836.

245 Joseph Vickers/Vicars (1810-1852) was a shoemaker; John Thornton (1803-1875?) was a woolcomber.

246 For O'Connor's popularity, see Epstein, 'Feargus O'Connor', pp. 47-8.

247 For example, *LT* 23 Jan. (Leeds); 16, 30 Jan. 6, 13 Feb. (Huddersfield); 6 Feb. (Bradford); 20 Feb. 1836 (Keighley). Subscriptions were collected, petitions organised and committees formed on the Stamp Duties issue.

key sort of existence.[248] In Keighley, where, as always, the newspaper sources tell us little, we can only speculate that enthusiasm waned after the initial stimulus and energies were diverted into the renewed factory reform campaigns. However, although the flowering was in most cases short-lived, the radical perennial did not die and could easily be revived by further tours or pressing issues.

O'Connor's tour and the ensuing burst of radical activity and organisation marked out the path for future developments. The RAs themselves had a clearly defined organisational structure, comprising a committee of management (ten people) elected every three months, with a secretary and treasurer chosen annually. Subscriptions were 1d a week plus 6d entrance fee. They also had membership cards.[249] The need for wider organisation and the establishment of a formal political presence, independent of both Whigs and Tories, became one of the dominant themes of the early meetings. In Leeds, for example, a committee was formed to look into ways of getting as many radicals as possible onto the electoral registers.[250]

Talk of registration committees, taken with O'Connor's praise for Joshua Bower and the Leeds radical-liberals' local government successes, demonstrates that the local Radical Association often included a broad spectrum of opinion.[251] One of the stated general objects of the associations was to promote unity of all classes and unified political action. In practice this meant a broad alliance. Some of O'Connor's inaugural meetings were chaired by respected middle-class radicals (John Sugden at Keighley, William Cook at Huddersfield, Henry Rawson at Halifax) and attracted a wide spread of local interest and support.[252] At Leeds lower middle-class radicals like Joseph Lees, Hamilton Richardson, G. M. Bingley and Frederick Hobson (the latter three all associated with the radical-liberal press) participated in the meetings and activities of the Leeds Radical Association, and the body was reported to be making slow advances amongst both electors and non-electors in early 1836.[253] At a Halifax dinner to form a Radical Association 'the Old [Radical-Whig] Union for household suffrage was ... formally united to the new association, and its books, flags etc given up'. Even at Bradford, where the *Halifax Guardian* predicted the imminent demise of the Whig/Whig-radical/Radical electoral alliance because of dissatisfaction with E. C. Lister (one of the town's Whig MPs), relations between the working-class radicals and the lower middle-class radical-liberals remained sufficiently cordial for them to co-operate in the Stamp Duty repeal agitation.[254]

---

248 *LT* 26 Mar., 16 Apr. 1836. John Bell, late editor of the radical *Weekly True Sun*, for example, referred to the existence of a RA in Bradford, *BO* 4 Aug. 1836.

249 *LT* 26 Dec. 1835.

250 *LT* 2 Jan. 1836 (O'Connor at Leeds), also Epstein, 'Feargus O'Connor', p. 46; *LT* 13 Feb. 1836 (for Leeds registration committee and the moves to organise radical representation at all levels). See also John Hanson, on a possible national convention of radical delegates, *LT* 19 Dec. 1835.

251 *LT* 2 Jan. 1836.

252 *LT* 2 Jan. 1836 (for the breadth of interest at Halifax).

253 *LT* 23 Jan. 1836. See also *LT* 5 Mar. 1836 for co-operation on the Stamp Duties issue.

254 *LT* 9 Jan.; *HG* 16 Jan.; *BO* 3 Mar. 1836.

If the Stamp Duty issue was the chief cement between the two main radical camps in early 1836, they also shared common ground on other issues, notably Ireland.[255] Radicals, for example, spoke with 'respectable' Whig-liberals at meetings on the Irish Corporation Bill; and in June a Bradford placard advocating a subscription for O'Connell was printed on yellow and green paper to 'signify union of the Whig and Radical parties in effecting the common object'.[256] Such instances indicate once more the equivocal position of many working-class radicals in places like Bradford and Halifax in relation to potential lower middle-class radical-liberal partners.

Although local alliances and common platforms continued, and O'Connor himself never totally let go of the notion of an accommodation with middle-class radicals, late 1836 and early 1837 saw the emergence, in places like Bradford and Halifax, of more and more issues on which working-class radicals diverged appreciably from their recent allies. O'Connor's further tours in August 1836, November 1836 and January 1837 not only revived flagging local organisation and enthusiasm, but also helped local radicals to define where they stood in relation to local radical-liberals.[257] O'Connor's final split with O'Connell in the autumn sharpened the focus still further and helped to identify contentious issues.[258] Gradually areas of incompatibility came to outweigh areas of common interest and support.

The precise timing and context of this change of emphasis – away from limited alliances with lower middle-class radical-liberals to an independent, predominantly working-class organisational presence – varied from place to place and is sometimes hard to pin down. In Huddersfield, for instance, where the radicals were a proverbially 'strong body' and opposition to the pervasive 'Ramsden interest' served as a strong radicalising factor, a fundamental split with main body of local 'Liberals' had occurred even before the 1832 election. Lower middle-class radical-liberals had the choice of supporting either the radicals or the Whigs. They tended to choose the latter. Not surprisingly, a Huddersfield radical writing to the *Leeds Times* in September 1836 had little sympathy for the Whig-Radical alliance in Halifax. His view, which was apparently shared by a group of Halifax radicals, was that 'the Radicals have been leaning too much upon the Whigs' and that they had been deceived over Protheroe's candidature in 1835. However, he now believed that their eyes were open.[259]

The cause of this new insight, which saw the final untwining of the strands of popular radicalism and middle-class radicalism in Halifax, was the contentious issue of

---

255 See *LT* 20 Feb. 1836 (Leeds); *BO* 10 Mar. 1836 (Idle)

256 *LT* 26 Mar., 28 May, 11 June 1836 (meetings on Ireland); *LT* 25 June 1836 (O'Connell). This support for O'Connell had a wider significance since he was widely attacked at this time for his support of Poulett Thomson's factory legislation amendment, see Ward, *Factory Movement*, pp. 156-7.

257 See Epstein, 'Feargus O'Connor', p. 62 ff. O'Connor was accompanied by John Bell, former editor of the radical *True Sun*, on the first of these tours; see *LT* 6, 13 Aug. 1836 for Bell's meetings.

258 For O'Connor's split with O'Connell, see Epstein, 'Feargus O'Connor', pp. 56-61. For radical support for O'Connor, see *LT* 5, 12 Nov., 31 Dec. 1836, 14, 21 Jan. 1837. For 'Erinensis' of Huddersfield defending O'Connell, see *LT* 5 Nov. 1836.

259 *LT* 5 Nov. 1836 (attacks on the Ramsden interest); 10 Sept. 1836 (Halifax).

O'Connor's attendance at a Whig-liberal joint dinner to Wood and Protheroe (the 'liberal' candidates). The Radical (presumably RA) committee were incensed when an invitation they had secured from the official joint dinner committee was withdrawn under pressure from the local pro-Whig Reform Association. They decided to hold a rival dinner as a protest against the influence of 'masses of property and superior intelligence', alleging that, 'Whiggism in Halifax is the same as Whiggism in London'.[260]

The Radical dinner was a huge success and although Protheroe attended both events, the cracks were too fundamental to be papered over.[261] O'Connor was welcomed by large crowds; and in a speech addressed directly to the non-electors, he demanded universal suffrage and a Ten Hours' Bill, and attacked the new poor law and the state Church. In a sense, the story of Halifax Chartism begins here. Although the RA threw its weight behind Protheroe in the 1837 election and a number of middle-class radicals continued to take an active part in its proceedings, the local leadership increasingly fell into the hands of a group of artisans, outworkers and shopkeepers who represented a different, predominantly working-class tradition. These people – 'Radical Bob' Wilkinson (a shoemaker), Benjamin Rushton (handloom weaver), Abram Hanson of Elland (shoemaker), William Thornton (woolcomber), Robert Sutcliffe (shoemaker), William Thorburn (shopkeeper) and Robert Tetley (book-hawker) – all became prominent early Chartists. By the beginning of 1837 the RA was reported to be 'increasing both in numbers and "respectability" as the world has it' and was contemplating establishing its own newsroom and meeting-room. By this time it was also clearly differentiated from the Whig-liberal Halifax Reform Association.[262]

In Halifax it is possible to isolate a decisive turning point in relations between working-class radicalism and middle-class radicalism. Elsewhere this shedding of former allies or supporters was more gradual, or it pre-dated the establishment of a RA. The sparse evidence from Keighley where a RA was still nominally in existence in August 1836, when metropolitan radical John Bell spoke at the RA room and where radicals were also active in local politics, suggests parallels with Huddersfield. The existence of a well-established Whig-liberal elite in the town allied to strong tradition of independent working-class activity and organisation contributed towards the formation of a well-integrated and locally quite powerful radical caucus, predominantly working-class in outlook and composition, but also including 'respectable' lower middle-class elements.[263]

In the Dewsbury area, where formal political organisations were slow to develop, it is likely that an informal and possibly unstated Whig-Radical alliance continued in existence and that radical leadership remained in the hands of respectable town-radicals. At one of the few reported local public meetings in May 1836, on the

---

260 This section draws on *LT* and *HG* Aug. – Nov. 1836 and Dorothy and E. P. Thompson, 'Halifax as a Chartist centre', in Stephen Roberts (ed.), *The Dignity of Chartism: Essays by Dorothy Thompson* (London: Verso, 2015), pp. 85–6.

261 *LT* 5 Nov. 1836, a quarter of the surplus £20 raised went to the Dorchester fund.

262 *LT* 14 Jan. 1837; *BO* 22 Dec.; *LT* 31 Dec. 1836.

263 *LT* 6 Aug. 1836. Also, *LT* 4 Mar. 1837.

mutilation of the Irish Municipal Reform Bill, town-radicals and future Chartists such as Morritt Matthews and Titus Senior Brooke (a druggist) shared the platform and much common ground with middle-class radicals William Rhodes and Thomas Todd and mainstream 'Liberals' such as John Halliley, a local manufacturer. The final break with middle-class radicalism did not come until 1839.[264]

In Leeds, the RA of early 1836 contained a wide spectrum of political opinion. After an initial flourish it lost momentum and possibly some of its radical-liberal working-class and lower middle-class adherents. Although still in existence in January 1837 when it suggested O'Connor as candidate for Leeds, it never fulfilled O'Connor's hopes that it would 'serve as a rallying point for the Radicals of Yorkshire'. Indeed, it was rather over-shadowed in its twilight by the Holbeck Operative Reform Association, formed in December 1836, which stood in direct line to the Leeds (Holbeck) Political Union of 1831-4, and which advocated a more gradual and limited radical programme. Comprising mainly well-paid factory workers, skilled craftsman and tradesmen, the Association consistently sided with the more radical wing of the local middle-class liberalism and came to represent 'the sort of Radicalism which the Leeds Times stood for in 1836'.[265]

In Bradford, where formal contact and co-operation with the radical-liberals appears to have been minimal, the local RA of late 1836 and early 1837 was far from being a slavish vehicle for O'Connor or ultra-radicalism. The local leaders included John Jackson, an avowed political economist and advocate of the new poor law; two leading Owenite socialist radicals, John Douthwaite and Samuel Bower jnr.; Squire Farrar, noted radical and infidel, and apologist for political economy; and Christopher Wilkinson, a moderate radical bookseller. When all five spoke at a public dinner to welcome O'Connor in January 1837, Peter Bussey was a notable absentee and there were reports that some radicals were unhappy about the arrangements.[266] In the early months of 1837 the 'moderates' appear to have held the upper hand and many of the same speakers (plus Henry Rawnsley, William Fox and the veteran John Burrows) appeared on a radical platform in March to support Joseph Hume's motion for household suffrage. Farrar, quoting letters from Radical MPs, argued that universal suffrage was impolitic at the present time and other speakers echoed this gradualist line. Significantly, Bussey again did not appear at this meeting, and this fact, taken with John Jackson's letter in August 1837 with its references to 'ill feeling and retaliation' and its plea to the non-electors to 'cease their strife one amongst another', indicates that divisions within the radical ranks went fairly deep at this time.[267]

Jackson's plea for internal peace and friendship came in the aftermath of the July 1837 General Election. The election not only aided the resolution of radical

---

264 *LT* 28 May 1836; *NS* 8 June 1839.

265 *LI* 17 Jan. 1837; *LT* 7 May 1836; Fraser, 'Politics in Leeds', p. 265. On the Holbeck Operative Reform Association, see Fraser, 'Politics in Leeds', pp. 261-65. The leading figures comprised a newsagent, a book-keeper, a paperhanger and a wood-turner, *LT* 24 Dec. 1837.

266 *BO* 5, 12 Jan., *LT* 14 Jan. 1837. William Hill a key figure of the mid 1830s had left Bradford (to go to Hull) by this time. Wilkinson (1805-1888) was also an Owenite socialist.

267 *BO* 23, 30 Mar.; 10 Aug.; and also, 26 Aug. 1837 (Bussey). See Epstein, 'Feargus O'Connor', p. 69, for O'Connor's, Bell's and O'Brien's opposition to Hume's 'Whig-Radical' initiative.

differences at Bradford but also gave a general boost to popular radicalism. With economic recession beginning to bite and the poor law issue starting to arouse widespread indignation, the apathy about which local radical leaders had frequently complained in the previous eighteen months began to dissipate. As O'Connor had predicted, the groundwork done in the relatively quiescent years of 1835 and 1836 began to bear fruit.[268]

One of the first fruits was the extension of formal radical organisation beyond the main textile towns. In November 1836 a meeting of 'friends from Bradford, Halifax, and Huddersfield, and surrounding villages' had urged the spread of RAs 'by extended organisation in the form of new branch associations' and 'the diffusion of sound political knowledge'.[269] By the middle of 1837 local leaders at Halifax and Huddersfield were putting these earlier plans into operation. A RA probably already existed at Hebden Bridge, and between June and August 'friends from Halifax' helped to establish new RA branches at Southowram, Ambler Thorn and Northowram.[270] Meanwhile the chief Huddersfield radicals were all involved in a Honley public meeting which set up an 'Association for universal suffrage'. The Halifax men, though, were particularly active and by the end of the year there were said to be twelve RAs in the area.[271] The spread of formal organisation to the outlying villages confirmed the district stature and importance of the key town leaders and also signalled the emergence and wider involvement of a number of important village leaders.

This development of organisation tied in closely with developments in the anti-poor law agitation, and also owed much to the political interest generated by a Huddersfield by-election in May and a general election two months later.[272] A contest had been in the offing a long time and many places had their candidates ready well before the summer poll. In Leeds, the radical *Leeds Times*, through its editor Robert Nicholl and proprietor-printer Frederick Hobson, successfully pressed for the candidature of Sir William Molesworth 'a Radical aristocrat, a levelling peer'.[273] An uneasy and pragmatic alliance with the local Whig-liberal hierarchy was maintained only with some difficulty, but it held sufficiently firm to ensure Molesworth's successful return. According to Derek Fraser, the 'most distinguished Molesworth plumper' was Joshua Hobson.[274] The victory, however, was not that of the working-class supporters of O'Connor and universal suffrage, like Hobson, but of the more

---

268 See, for example, Bussey, *LT* 27 Aug. 1836; on O'Connor's predictions see Epstein, 'Feargus O'Connor', p. 65.

269 *LT* 26 Nov. 1836.

270 *LT* 3, 17 June, 12 Aug. 1837.

271 *LT* 15 July 1837 (the speakers were Pitkethly, Stocks, Hanson and Buchanan); *NS* 6 Jan. 1838.

272 The Huddersfield by-election was triggered by another untimely death, that of the incumbent MP, Blackburne. The general election resulted from the death of King William IV.

273 On the Leeds election, see Fraser, 'Politics in Leeds'; p. 213 ff; Fraser, 'Fruits of Reform', p. 103.

274 *LM* 7 Jan. 1837; *LT* 8 Apr. 1837, Fraser, 'Politics in Leeds', p. 218 (for alliance); Fraser, 'Fruits of Reform', p. 104 (for quotation).

limited radical programme favoured by the *Leeds Times*, its lower middle-class supporters and their allies in the Holbeck Operative Reform Association.

The Huddersfield elections of 1837, which in some ways represent the apogee of co-operation between radicals and Tories in the 1830s, also illustrate the need for caution when dealing with the concept of Tory Radicalism.[275] There is no doubt that all the major leaders of local working-class radicalism were firmly committed to the candidature of Oastler, an avowed 'ultra-Tory'. The *Leeds Mercury* feigned shock and horror at seeing, 'Mr Whitacre [a leading Tory] hand in hand with Mr Pitkethley ... [and] Huddersfield Blues hallooing on the Almondbury Radicals'. It portrayed the alliance as a 'union of opposite extremes, in support of one candidate, whose chief recommendation seems to be this, that he professes violence enough for both Ultra Tories and Ultra Radicals together'[276]. Many radicals outside Huddersfield were unhappy about the union. The Bradford radicals' reservations about close co-operation with Oastler were long-standing and spilt over into an acrimonious controversy with their Huddersfield 'friends' after the election.[277] But perhaps more surprising is the post-election attitude of the Almondbury radicals, who took pains to disassociate themselves from 'many in this district who call themselves Radical reformers, have lately formed an inconsistent and unholy collision, if not with the men, with the principle which has brought us into our present deplorable state... the Radical reformers of Almondbury are Radical reformers still'.[278]

Radical support for Oastler was not new, nor was it confined to Huddersfield. During 1835 and early 1836 Oastler had become a regular contributor to the unstamped press, and more recently he had shared many platforms with O'Connor. The Huddersfield radicals' adoption of Oastler as their candidate jointly with the Tories in the May 1837 by-election does not damn them as inveterate Tories in radical clothing, or, as the *Bradford Observer* put it, 'blue-tailed Radicals'.[279] Leaving aside important personal bonds and years of shared activity and the particularly urgent context of the new poor law, radical support for Oastler also had a severely pragmatic

---

275 The fullest account of the two elections is in C. Driver, *Tory Radical, The Life of Richard Oastler* (New York: Oxford University Press, 1946), pp. 344-50 and 357 ff. For discussions of the use and misuse of the 'Tory Radicalism' label, see F. Driver, 'Tory radicalism?', pp. 120-2 and Epstein, 'Feargus O'Connor', pp. 184-7.

276 *LM* 13; 6 May 1837.

277 On the long running dispute between Bussey (later supported by the Bradford radicals) and the Huddersfield radicals (for whom John Hanson and Robert Buchanan replied) see *LT* Aug. – Oct. 1837 (the contest lasted five rounds). For the background see *LT* 16 Apr., 6 Aug. 1836 (Bussey's dispute with Oastler and Cleave). At the heart of the dispute lay the Bradford radicals' hatred of Toryism and their distrust of Oastler's links with the Tory party. The Huddersfield men stressed reasons for supporting Oastler which were both pragmatic ('we know of no other man, with whom we have so good a chance of success whose views are in accordance with the interests of the people') and ideological (Oastler's hatred of political economy and his commitment to 'social reform').

278 *LT* 19 Aug. 1837. See also the Gomersal radicals' disapproval, *LT* 7 Oct. 1837. It is possible that the Almondbury response was initiated by George Beaumont (the *Leeds Times* local correspondent) as payback for his outing as a turncoat three years earlier.

279 *BO* 11 May 1837.

side. As Felix Driver concludes, 'strategic rather than ideological considerations were dominant'.[280]

The lesson of the previous three elections was that the borough could only be rescued 'from the degrading influence of mere Whiggery' with some Tory support. As the radicals stated in their manifesto, they realised 'after much deliberation that neither of their former Candidates have the slightest chance, under present circumstances, of being returned'. They, therefore, supported a man who 'is a strenuous advocate for equal rights and equal laws, which are the very essence of the Radical creed'.[281] Such assertions of ideological affinities, though flimsy, did not entirely stretch the bounds of credibility since, as Matthew Roberts has argued, Oastler's brand of toryism 'was in fact closer to Cobbettite radicalism than it was to the new conservatism of Peel and Wellington, or even to the evangelical toryism associated with his mentor, Sadler'.[282]

The by-election was an extremely animated affair. Oastler held nightly meetings and the radicals organised extensive exclusive dealing. The Whig candidate, Edward Ellice, was stoned on his entry into town and endured a rough ride at the hustings where John Hanson, Reuben Earnshaw, Robert Buchanan and J. N. Reid acted as voice of the radical non-electors.[283] Oastler's narrow defeat, though disappointing, at least gave hope that Whig dominance could be overturned. As Cecil Driver notes, 'he polled more than the combined votes of Sadler and Wood in 1834'.[284]

Oastler and the radicals got a second chance less than two months later when King William IV's decease brought about the automatic dissolution of Parliament. With anti-poor law sentiments running high, it proved another bitterly contested election. The radicals again organised extensive exclusive dealing and massive popular demonstrations that kept the nearby troops on high alert. At times on polling day Oastler led his new Whig opponent Stansfield, but after the poll began to swing against him his cause was not helped by a boisterous crowd which began intimidating Whig latecomers and, after seeing off the 'blue jackets and cutlass-armed Police', was only chased off by the arrival of the cavalry. The temporary abandonment of the poll, which may have given some Tories cold feet, together with the loss of some crucial Irish votes (due to the 'Factory King's' intransigence on the emancipation question) cost Oastler dear and he lost by just twenty-two votes.[285]

---

280 F. Driver, 'Tory Radicalism?', p. 138.

281 See the radicals' election manifesto, quoted in C. Driver, *Tory Radical,* pp. 345-7.

282 Matthew Roberts, 'Richard Oastler, Toryism, Radicalism and the limitations of Party, c.1807-1846', *Parliamentary History,* 37 (2018), p. 252.

283 *LM* 6, 13 May 1837; C. Driver, *Tory Radical,* pp. 347-8. Brooke, 'The Roots of Chartism', p. 25. Ellice was the 26 year-old nephew of Lord Grey. Buchanan, a young Owenite tailor, was by this time well-established in radical circles through his involvement in press freedom, anti-poor law and factory reform campaigns. He may well have been the 'Mr. Buccan' who chaired a Huddersfield meeting on the Dorchester labourers and Stamp Duty repeal (*LT* 25 July 1835).

284 C. Driver, *Tory Radical,* p. 349. Ellice's majority was 50 out of a poll of 630.

285 C. Driver, *Tory Radical,* pp. 359-60; *LM* 5 Aug. 1837 (on local bitterness). This election, the fifth in five years, made the radicals' dream of annual parliaments a reality locally. For exclusive dealing and the bitterness aroused by the election, see the placard 'Villagers! Awake: Arise!', from a 'Hand-Loom Weaver', 25 July 1837, in TNA: HO 52/35.

The sense of loss was exacerbated by another defeat three days later; this time at the hands of alleged 'Whig-hired thugs' who attacked the Huddersfield radical contingent as they made their way to Wakefield to attend nomination day for the West Riding constituency held in Wakefield. Their aim was to proclaim the full radical programme, nominate O'Connor and win the show of hands, 'thereby exhibiting Radicalism in the ascendent throughout the West-Riding'. However, with the hustings already full and unable to secure a ticket for his seconder, Samuel Midgley, a leading Almondbury radical, O'Connor struggled to make himself heard. His speech was greeted with a hail of stones from the 'yellows', in what radicals later alleged was a planned attempt to 'destroy their white flags and especially the Paddock Poor Law flag'. In the ensuing carnage two people died and many were injured, including Oastler. The efforts to defend the Paddock flag entered local radical folklore; but more generally the episode became another opportunity for critics like Bussey and the Bradford radicals to berate their Huddersfield counterparts on the folly of their dalliance with Oastler.[286]

As earlier in the decade, the Halifax and Bradford contests followed a different pattern. At Halifax, where O'Connor had considered entering the contest, a proposal by a radical elector that Protheroe should pledge himself to household suffrage in order to get the radical vote was narrowly defeated. In the face of a strong Tory challenge the RA reverted to their old alliance with the 'Liberals' and swelled the popular fervour behind Protheroe, the eventual victor.[287] Despite reservations, the working-class radicals had few options but to support the most radical candidate on offer.

This pattern was repeated in the bitterly contested Bradford election, where the organised non-electors of the Bradford RA eventually came down in favour of supporting 'the most Liberal candidates'.[288] At the poll both of the Whig-liberal candidates easily defeated Hardy, one of the sitting MPs, and William Busfeild, a Tory ten-hour and anti-poor law sympathiser. However, what is most interesting and significant is the growing confidence and influence of the organised non-electors. They can be seen moving to a more independent position and towards the more systematic use of the election excitement and hustings to highlight their 'exclusion from civil rights'. As Peter Bussey told an audience of non-electors before the contest, 'In a very short-time will come the tug of war. We have hitherto assisted, in these struggles, the contending parties have made use of us to answer their own end. We have been cast on one side by both factions when they had no further need for us'.[289] This time would be different.

Novel radical strategies were debated in the weeks preceding the election. John Jackson proposed a totally independent working-class position with non-electors

---

286 Roberts, 'God Save the Paddock Flag', pp. 39-40; Brooke, 'The Roots of Chartism', pp. 27-8; *LT* 2 Sept. 1837 (Hanson and Buchanan's letter); *LM* 5 and 26 Aug.1837 (on subsequent radical retaliation).

287 *LT* 8 July 1837; Wilson, *Struggles*, p. 2.

288 On the Bradford election see Wright, 'Bradford Politics', p. 170 ff and 'Radical Borough'. The *Bradford Observer* had urged Whig-Radical unity, *BO* 6 July 1837.

289 *LT* 15 July 1837 (C. Wilkinson and P. Bussey). According to Wright, 'Bradford Politics', p. 187, the non-electors dictated the shape and substance of the contest.

supporting neither candidate and instead presenting a radical hustings candidate. However, the Bradford radicals preferred Samuel Bower's proposed 'radical tactics'. This involved non-electors calling public meetings when excitement was at its height to pass Protests about their exclusion. A resulting address would be read and presented to the returning officer on nomination day. By this means the non-electors, instead of being led away by either party or standing neutral, would be seen to be doing something positive.[290] Bower's plan was adopted and put into practice at the Bradford election. At an outdoor public meeting of the 'unrepresented', Bussey from the chair gave a detailed history of the demand for universal suffrage; Bower read the Protest and stressed the need to keep 'distinct from the two great parties'; and an impressive array of local speakers reiterated the theme of the fundamental iniquity of the ten pound franchise. The independent line adopted, and the Protest which Bussey read out on Nomination Day, were important steps on the road to creating a separate political party.[291]

The election drove home the lesson of the need for effective organisation and unity. According to Bussey 'the reason that the Radicals were so weak, was not on account of their numbers ... but for want of discipline and unity and purpose'.[292] However, Bussey's proposed re-organisation of the RA, into local sections of twenty-five people each under a class leader affiliated as a branch of the Central National Association (CNA), threatened the recently acquired post-election unity.[293] His plans were opposed by Christopher Wilkinson as premature and the proposed re-organisation only went ahead after a special committee had investigated various options and the idea of joining the CNA had been dropped.[294] For a time unity was restored within the local radical leadership. All agreed on the primacy of the suffrage question and although the 'moderates' like John Jackson still hoped and urged that the middle-class would give the lead for 'Universal, or at least Household Suffrage, and three year's Parliaments and not to take the Ballot except the two former points be granted along with it'; he acknowledged that 'If this step be not taken by the Liberals, Whig-Radicals, and the dormant, and Neutrals, then let the Ultra-Radicals confide no more in any but themselves...'[295]

Radicals elsewhere were coming to the same conclusion. Leading working-class radicals in Halifax adopted Samuel Bower's plan, held a non-elector's meeting and delivered a Protest to the Returning Officer. In all the main manufacturing centres the rigorous cross-examination of local or West Riding candidates provided an

---

290 *BO* 29 June; *LT* 1 July 1837.

291 *LT* 15, *BO* 13 July; 27 July 1837.

292 *LT* 26 Aug. 1837.

293 On the CNA, an attempt to link small farmers, agricultural labourers and the urban working class in a national organisation to press for universal suffrage as a means towards a mixture of radical and ultra-Tory protectionist ends, see Epstein, 'Feargus O'Connor', pp. 70-7. It vigorously opposed the new poor law and Bussey and Pitkethly attended its early meetings. After flourishing briefly, it collapsed in late summer 1837 (Chase, *Chartism*, pp. 14-15).

294 *LT* 12, 26 Aug., 2 Sept. 1837. See also Huddersfield radicals' letter, *LT* 19 Aug. 1837, seeking to exploit divisions in Bradford.

295 *BO* 5 Oct. 1837.

opportunity for working-class radicals to assert an independent stance and establish or confirm their position as the voice of the unenfranchised.[296] Robert Wilkinson and William Thornton questioned the Tory Wortley at Halifax, and Titus Brooke performed the same function at Dewsbury. The Keighley non-electors chose 'Joseph Firth, James Bedford and Thomas Walton, three respectable and intelligent working-men', to tell the Whig candidates (Morpeth and Strickland) of their dissatisfaction with their conduct.[297] At Elland Morpeth was 'pinned by the questions of an old veteran in the Radical cause, of the name of [Abram] Hanson' and at Bradford Bussey quizzed the Whig duo on every conceivable radical topic.[298] The choice of questioners is significant – all were future Chartist leaders and all, except Titus Brooke, originally working-men. It indicates that moves towards the evolution of an independent working-class political stance were accelerating rapidly and that popular radicals were placing more emphasis on their own leaders and organisations.

The final stimulus to what might be termed the pre-Chartist phase of development came with the arrival in the north of John Cleave and Henry Vincent in late August 1837 as delegates of the London Working Men's Association. Formed in 1836, the LWMA had hitherto been a rather exclusive London body expressing 'many of the traditional artisan attitudes'. It achieved national attention in 1837 through a series of addresses (written by Lovett) and public meetings (on the 'five points' and Canada).[299] The first West Riding WMAs were formed in late June to early July 1837, well before Cleave and Vincent's tour. In fact, the direct effects of their speaking tour were negligible as they largely built upon and fed off existing radical networks and enthusiasm. The tour was important, however, as a part of a wider late 1837 radical campaign and for developing a sense of a national co-ordinated movement.

The early West Riding WMAs owed more to the general stimulus of the 1837 election. One of the first tasks of the Dewsbury WMA, formed by local operatives in late June 1837, had been to decide upon what questions to put to the West Riding candidates. With future Chartist Jeremiah Marsden in the chair, they launched themselves publicly in July with a meeting whose only disappointing aspect was the poor response from neighbouring radical speakers. In nearby Gomersal the intention to form a WMA was announced at a Whig dinner (to celebrate the election of Morpeth and Strickland) which George Crowther used as a platform to proclaim the rights of the working-classes and to urge non-electors and electors alike to press for universal or household suffrage, the ballot and repeal of the Corn Laws. In Lepton, near Huddersfield, the election was one of the early concerns of a WMA formed after

---

296 The 1832 Reform Act created parliamentary constituencies in Leeds, Bradford, Halifax (each with two MPs) and Huddersfield (with one MP), and two new 'county' MPs for the West Riding. Accordingly, candidates for the county election presented themselves at meetings across the textile district and beyond.

297 *LT* 29 July, 5 Aug. 1837. James Bedford (1801-1871?) was a shoemaker; and Thomas Walton (1807-1874?) a woolcomber.

298 *LT* 5 Aug.; *BO* 27 July 1837.

299 On the LWMA, see Iorwerth Prothero, *Artisans and Politics in Early Nineteenth-Century London, John Gast and His Times* (Folkstone: Dawson, 1979), pp. 310-24. There was widespread radical criticism of the Whig government's handling of the 1836 Canadian rebellion.

a series of meetings in late June and early July. Again, the choice of local chair is significant: John Smith jnr., a key figure in many of the overlapping agitations which merged into Chartism. The origins of the Leeds WMA, which have been amply described by J. F. C. Harrison, also pre-dated the arrival of the metropolitan missionaries.[300]

The decision of the West Riding associations to adopt the LWMA rules and nomenclature may have reflected a desire to include a wide spectrum of radical opinion (as at Leeds) and a stress on respectability and the moral educative side of radicalism. However, there is a danger in reading too much into titles. The West Riding WMAs tended to be formed either in places like Leeds, where the earlier RA had languished, or in towns and villages where O'Connor had not visited. Cleave and Vincent were also welcomed and spoke at meetings organised by the RAs in Halifax, Bradford, and Huddersfield.[301] Indeed, it is not clear how far people bothered to distinguish between RAs and WMAs. In Almondbury the existence of both a WMA and RA in 1839 represented either different emphases in the activities of the same leaders or just an excuse for bi-annual festivities.[302] At Dewsbury Feargus O'Connor, who continued to play his part in the general agitational upsurge, was instrumental in forming an RA which, rather than being a rival, probably inherited the remnants of the ailing or quickly defunct WMA.[303] When Henry Hetherington, also a WMA missionary, toured the north in late 1837 he spoke to RAs and WMAs alike.[304] He must have been impressed, for radical organisation was spreading rapidly.

The Halifax leaders were particularly active, servicing existing branch associations and establishing new branches in small (mainly handloom weaving) hamlets such as Mixenden Stones. In September they co-operated with delegates from another prospering radical centre, Bradford, in stimulating a RA in Thornton, (a worsted manufacturing and stone quarrying village, five miles west of Bradford), and were rewarded with an 'excellent supper'. Autumn 1837 abounds with similar examples of missionary activity.[305] Whilst precise titles and activities might vary, by the end of 1837 distinct working-class radical organisations existed in all the main woollen textile towns and in numerous villages and out-townships.

Local radicals were not alone in their evangelical endeavours. In the west end of Leeds, and in the clothing villages between Leeds and Bradford, pro-reform, radical-

---

300 *LT* 8 15 July (Dewsbury); 26 Aug (Gomersal); 29 July 1837 (Lepton). For the Leeds WMA see Harrison, 'Chartism in Leeds', pp. 65-72. The only place where Cleave and Vincent's visit led directly to the formation of a WMA was at Almondbury, *LT* 9 Sept. 1837. Interestingly a 'Mr Marsden representative of the Operatives of Dewsbury' went to Bradford during the 1825 strike, *LI* 6 Oct 1825. Crowther became an anti-poor law Guardian.

301 *LT* 9 Sept. 1837. A WMA had also been formed at Stanningley/Pudsey, *LT* 14 Oct. 1837.

302 *NS* 16 Oct.; 3 Nov. 1838, 16 Mar., 18 May, 16 Nov. 1839. For a similar dual at New Pellon near Halifax, see *NS* 30 June 1838; 5 Jan., 29 June 1839.

303 *LT* 30 Sept., 14 Oct. 1837. He also spoke at Hebden Bridge, *LT* 19 Aug., and Keighley, *LT* 23 Sept. 1837.

304 *LT* 28 Oct., 4 Nov. 1837.

305 *LT* 9 Sept. (Mixenden Stones); 23 Sept. (Thornton); see also *LT* 2, 30 Sept., 7, 28 Oct., 30 Dec. 1837.

liberal working-class associations were developed; and operative conservative societies were already active in some of the main urban centres and their outlying townships.[306] However, John Bates' 1895 recollections of the politics of his youth in Queenshead ('there was no such thing as a working man Conservative as there is now'), though not strictly accurate, contained more than a grain of truth when applied to the extensive radical heartlands.[307] Here, any rival efforts were overshadowed by the sheer scale and spread of radical organisation. The resulting associations, with their independent tone, uncompromising programme, their national connections and their extensive district and regional links, not only provided early Chartism with its organisational base, they also served to facilitate the training of a mature, experienced and, above all, articulate local leadership.

The existence of this organisational framework and ready-made cadre of experienced leaders could not alone have created the Chartist take-off – similar organisations had existed before and many of the same leaders had been active previously – other conditions were also necessary.

The widespread acceptance of the radicals' political analyses and nostrums amongst the working population was also not new, but because it reached a greater level and depth in 1837-8 it is perhaps worth re-emphasising. It is easy to overlook or ignore just how deeply radicalism was embedded in the popular culture of the West Riding textile district. Peter Bussey was largely correct in his assertion that 'the great masses of the people were, in the nature of things, Radicals'.[308] A speaker at a meeting of unemployed Leeds workers in late June 1837, which sought merely to enlist respectable help to alleviate distress, declared that 'Politics would do nothing for them; except they had the suffrage, then they might be able to turn the scale'.[309]

The second key factor in the Chartist lift-off was the multi-layered context in which radical sentiments and organisation flourished. The economic impulse was not the only factor here. Unemployment, short time working and poverty were undoubtedly on the increase in 1837, but the depths of the depression do not readily match with the surges of radical activity. The psychological and financial burden of the beginning of winter after a stagnant and ill-rewarded spring and early summer was as important as the actual state of trade. The political and agitational context should also be stressed. The spring campaign for household suffrage had come to nothing. After the July election the Whigs were seemingly entrenched in power and their actions and attitudes – their indifference to the plight of the handloom weavers; their enforcement of the poor law and continued hostility to factory reform; the prosecution of Glasgow cotton spinners; their attitude to Canada and Ireland – all seemed to confirm the lessons of 1833-5: that the working class had no hope of

---

306 For the development radical-liberal associations, see *LT* 2 Sept. (Leeds W. End), 30 Sept. (Yeadon), and *LM* 27 May 1837 (Pudsey). On the development of Operative Conservative Associations (beginning with Leeds in February 1835), see Jörg Neuheiser, *Crown, Church and Constitution: Popular Conservatism in England, 1815-1867* ((New York and Oxford: Berghahn, 2016), pp. 69-78.

307 *Bradford Weekly Telegraph* 9 Mar. 1895 ('A chat with a Chartist').

308 *LT* 26 Aug. 1837.

309 *LT* 8 July 1837; also *LM* 1, 8 July and 5 Aug. 1837.

restitution from this source. By the end of 1837 popular radicalism in the West Riding, with its independent organisations and local leaders and its own fledgling newspaper (the *Northern Star*), was at a stage of development whereby it was both possible and natural to focus the bitterness and resentment of five years of betrayal and to channel the energies of a flourishing radical culture into a movement for fundamental political reform. However, before tackling the emergence and main features of the early Chartist movement it is necessary to untangle a few more of the agitational threads which came together in 1838.

7: Dorchester, Glasgow and the Handloom Weavers' Campaigns, 1835-8

The issues discussed and taken up by local leaders of the radical organisations of 1835-8 reflected a catholic concern with the rights and welfare of labour. Indeed, in the days before the formal establishment of political associations popular radicalism had, in part, been kept alive by their continuing preoccupation with the fate of the 'Dorchester Victims'. This issue, like that of the unstamped press, acted as a key bridging agitation in the relatively stagnant mid-1830s.

The same local radicals who had voiced their disgust at the sentences in 1834, strove to keep the issue before the public eye in 1835 by holding public meetings, organising petitions for repatriation and collecting subscriptions on behalf of the victims' families. With radicalism at a low ebb they were fighting an uphill battle.[310] However, local petitions and subscriptions organised in Leeds, Bradford, Dewsbury, Heckmondwike, Halifax and Huddersfield achieved a good response.[311] The 'people of Huddersfield' led the way and on the anniversary of the first protests were commended by the *Leeds Times* for their continued financial support for the 'Dorchester Unionists'. A committee which sat three evenings a week at the White Bear Inn had collected nearly £30 by the middle of the month. In addition, local radicals held two public meetings, addressed by many familiar speakers. It was presumably the strength of the Huddersfield effort that moved the *Poor Man's Guardian* to praise the 'men of Yorkshire' for treating the case 'as personal to themselves' and as 'a blow at the entire body of the working classes'.[312]

The Dorchester campaign, like the Stamp Duties issue, was one on which working-class and some middle-class radicals shared common ground.[313] As well as familiar names like Ibbetson, Bussey and Joseph Brook (and intriguing ones like G.

---

310 See, for example, *LT* 16 May 1835 (Joshua Hobson's complaints about the lack of public meetings and his idea for a Whit Monday meeting). The plan for a gathering was abandoned and the petitioning committee had to plead with local workers to disprove allegations of 'apathy to their own interests and rights', *LT* 30 May, 13 June 1835.

311 *HG* 6 June, *LT* 13 June, 11, 18 July, 3 Oct.; *LM* 22 Aug. 1835. After a slow start, the Leeds petition gathered over 12,500 signatures, *LT* 20 June 1835.

312 *LT* 4 Apr.; 4, 11 July; 27 June; 25 July; *PMG* 11 July 1835. New speakers on the Huddersfield platform included Robert Buchanan, a tailor and future Owenite socialist missionary, and J. N. Reid, 'a co-operative tailor' formerly of London and now a leading local Owenite socialist.

313 See, for example, the speeches of John Ratcliffe and Luke Bradley at Huddersfield, *PMG* 11 July 1835.

Hopkins), the 1835 subscription lists from Bradford also contain the names of leading lower middle-class radical-liberals. At Halifax local 'Liberals' apparently subscribed forty guineas for the education of the Dorchester labourers' families and the Heckmondwike petition included the names of 140 freeholders.[314] In addition, the campaign's links with the London Committee helped to imbue popular radicalism with a wider national perspective. Feargus O'Connor's first contact with the local radical leadership in Huddersfield came when he made a brief appearance at their second Dorchester meeting in July 1835;[315] and the return of the 'Dorchester Men' became one of the prime objectives of the RAs which O'Connor helped to set up during his first Northern tour in December 1835. It is likely that the Dorchester petitioning and subscription committees became the nucleus around which wider, more permanent organisations were later formed in the major West Riding towns and in places such as Heckmondwike which O'Connor never visited.

The Dorchester agitation and subscription lists also indicate that trade unionism in the West Riding was not totally destroyed by the defeats of summer 1834. A Huddersfield radical, citing the many workers in 'factories, and in bodies too' who had agreed to subscribe at least 6d each to the families, urged 'members of the late and present unions' to follow suit. The Bradford list included £2.10s from the Stonemasons' Society and 6s.6d from members of the Cabinet Makers' Society.[316] Trades' unionism might have been dead, but small-scale local trade unionism continued to flourish in the mid-1830s. Favourable economic conditions provided plenty of opportunities for well organised 'lower' artisan trades (for example, carpenters and joiners, tailors, shoemakers, cabinet-makers, stonemasons and basket-makers) as well as the rising new trades (for example, machine makers and iron workers) to gain advances.[317]

Even within the textile industry there were a few signs that the associative spirit had not totally died out. The Earlsheaton blanket-raisers (finishers) and blanket weavers both secured minor wage rises by separate actions in April 1836; and the canvas and sacking weavers in the small Leeds linen-weaving industry also sought an advance in June 1836. *Ad hoc* combinations such as these, or the Keighley female power-loom weavers who struck against 'tyrannical rules' in 1836, might win temporary concessions but were easy to defeat in the long-term.[318] The real strength of

---

314 *PMG* 11 July (Bradford); *LT* 5 Dec. (Halifax); 3 Oct. 1835 (Heckmondwike). Hopkins, 'an operative woolcomber', spoke at radical and trade union meetings in 1831, served on the non-electors' committee in 1835 and was a *NS* agent in 1839.

315 *LT* 25 July 1835. On the Dorchester Labourers Committee in London, see Prothero, *Artisans and Politics*, pp. 306-12.

316 *LT* 4 July; *PMG* 11 July 1835. Bradford combers (presumably) at 'Wood's New Shops' also contributed.

317 For example, on the joiners see *LT* 20 June 1835 (Halifax), *LM* 10 Apr 1836 (Bradford). These trades are taken from *LT, LM, HG, BO* 1835-6 but they may only be the tip of the iceberg – the papers generally only reported advances when a strike broke out or was threatened.

318 *LT* 26 Mar.; *LM* 18 June; *LT* 18 June 1836. The linen merchants in Leeds contemplated presenting 'the document'.

trade unionism tended to be amongst the relatively well-paid skilled trades who could afford to maintain a continuous existence and a strike fund. When STC delegates appealed to the West Riding operatives in March 1837 to send representatives to meet and discuss the ten hours and poor law questions the 'associated trades' they specifically mentioned ('slubbers, overlookers, mechanics, masons, joiners') were clearly recognised as being in the vanguard of organised labour.[319]

Many of these same trades no doubt felt under renewed threat in autumn 1837 when members of the Glasgow Cotton Spinners Committee were arrested and put on trial on charges of conspiracy, administering unlawful oaths and secret transactions of union business.[320] The resulting campaign in the West Riding, though not quite as widespread or as deep-felt as that of Lancashire, was nevertheless important in once more bringing together radicals and trade unionists. As Robert Sykes rightly maintains, its importance in the constellation of pre-Chartist agitations and activities has been generally underestimated.[321]

Parallels with the Dorchester case were not lost on local radical leaders. John Hanson told an early Huddersfield meeting that they were gathered to stop the 'Whigs from perpetuating in Glasgow, a similar atrocity to that practised on the Dorchester Labourers'. Early the following year Pitkethly declared the sentence of seven years transportation to be 'in perfect consonance with Starvation Law, the Rural Police Law, and the transporting of the Dorchester Labourers … the coercing of the Irish and the Canadians'. Pitkethly, himself a Scot, became a key coordinating figure in the Glasgow agitation. In a chance insight into the informal networks of early working-class movements we find him urging a radical friend at Sutton in Ashfield (Nottinghamshire) to organise a meeting on the issue and stating his belief that 'this case is far worse than the Dorchester labourers'.[322]

In spite of hesitancy in some quarters, the Glasgow issue became the focus of one of the most important pre-Chartist campaigns. It brought together established radical leaders, trade unionists and new local leaders on a well-supported platform. The first phase of activity in late 1837 saw meetings held and subscriptions started in most of the major West Riding towns.[323] However, after the trial and conviction of the Glasgow men in early 1838, the second phase of the campaign became more urgent and embittered. As Templeman (a *Northern Star* reporter) told a meeting called by the Dewsbury RA in late January 1838, 'this sentence is intended as a blow to every attempt of working men to protect themselves from the oppression of those whose

---

319 *LT* 4 Mar. 1837.

320 The Carpenters and Joiners' Society, for example, contributed £5 to the Halifax 'Glasgow' fund. On the Glasgow Spinners case, see W. H. Fraser, 'The Glasgow Cotton Spinners, 1837', in John Butt and J. T. Ward (eds.), *Scottish Themes: Essays in honour of Prof. S.G.E. Lythe* (Edinburgh: Scottish Academic Press, 1976), pp. 80-97.

321 Robert Sykes, 'Early Chartism and Trade Unionism in South-East Lancashire', in Epstein and D. Thompson (eds.), *The Chartist Experience,* p. 156.

322 *LT* 7 Oct. 1837; *NS* 27 Jan. 1838; TNA: HO 40/47 f. 530, Pitkethly to Broyen, 6 Oct 1837. On Pitkethly's role see, D. Thompson (ed.), *Early Chartists*, p. 9. Robert Buchanan, a Glaswegian by birth, was also prominent in the West Riding agitation.

323 *LT* 7, 21 Oct., 4, 11 Nov. 1837; *NS* 6 Jan. 1838.

God is their gold...' Or in John Hanson's words, at a Huddersfield protest meeting a week earlier, the cotton spinners' crime was 'treason against the Majesty of capital – capital sits on the high place, and with a sceptre of iron crushes to the earth the industrious classes...' Other speakers at Huddersfield and Dewsbury attacked 'middle-class Government', 'shopocrats' and 'profit-hunters' and sought to incorporate the prosecution into the gradually unfolding master plan of Whig tyranny.[324] Joshua Hobson, speaking at Dewsbury, used the case to warn of imminent government repression. His theme was the connection between the new poor law and the Dorchester prosecution in 1834:

> If they reflected for a moment, they would remember that, at that time, the Whigs were about introducing in Parliament, the most famous of all their famous measures, the Poor Law Amendment Act. If they reflected again, they would also remember that Trades' Unions were rife in every part of the Kingdom. The Whigs, daring as they were, dared not to propose the New Poor Law in the face of the Trades' Unions – (hear, hear) – because they knew that if they did so, working men, by means of these Unions and Associations ... would have swept the Whigs and their law from off the face of the earth. (Cheers.) They transported the Dorchester labourers, therefore, for the purpose of breaking up Trades' Unions. That transportation answered its purpose. They all knew that Trades' Unions crumbled to nothing before it; and while working men were thus paralysed, the Poor Law Amendment Act was passed by the Whigs, with such shameless haste...

The Glasgow case merely marked the final stage of the attack on 'The Unions':

> And *why* was all this done? In order to enable the Whigs to re-enact the hateful combination laws: in order to pave the way for another Green Bag Conspiracy, and the passing of another Gagging Bill. (Hear, hear.) Yes, yes, these transportings were but a prelude to more despotic measures.[325]

This belief that repression was just around the corner, an important ideological element of the early Chartist movement, was greatly strengthened by the Glasgow prosecution. Indeed, the agitation, rather than being a narrow defensive campaign on behalf of trade unions, became part of a wider radicalising process. Like the anti-poor law agitation, which likewise engaged much public attention in early 1838, it provided an issue which local leaders were able to relate to the suffrage question and on which could rehearse their rhetoric justifying defensive arming and in favour of 'physical force' as a last resort.[326]

---

324 *NS* 3 Feb.; 27 Jan. 1838.

325 *NS* 3 Feb. 1838.

326 See, for example, *NS* 3 Feb. 1838 (J. Newsome at Dewsbury) also *BO* 25 Jan. 1838 (for talk of selling coats to buy swords). On this trend in Lancashire see Sykes, 'Early Chartism and

Despite some variations in the level of response the Glasgow agitation played a central role in the emergence of a concerted working-class political movement in the first half of 1838.[327] The West Riding protest meetings, with their emphasis on the right of the worker to protect his labour, not only dovetailed neatly with contemporaneous poor law, suffrage and handloom weavers' agitations, and emphasised local radicals' common ground with trade unionists, they also brought a number of important working-class leaders such as Samuel Binns, and William Cunningham in Huddersfield and Samuel Healey of Dewsbury to the radical platform for the first time.[328] These new leaders and their established counterparts increasingly fused a class perspective onto the traditional framework of popular radical rhetoric. Samuel Healey at Dewsbury, for example, proposed a resolution that 'juries composed of the middle-class, or masters, sitting on the trial of the Glasgow Cotton spinners, is unconstitutional, in as much as Magna Carta expressly declares that no man shall be tried but by a jury of his Peers'. Stephen Dickinson meanwhile asked the Huddersfield protest meeting, 'when did any of the ten-pounders attend any of their meetings, or do any thing for the working classes'.[329]

As in Lancashire, the issue was used to differentiate 'real' from 'milk and water' radicals. It posed the fundamental question of how far were middle and lower middle-class radical-liberals prepared to travel with local working-class radicals. The answer seemed to be Canada. For whilst 'moderate' radicals at Leeds and Bradford were able to share the platform with local working-class leaders on the Canadian question, no alliance was possible on the Glasgow case.[330] It exposed and clearly delimited two incompatible philosophies and mindsets.

Support for the Glasgow trade unionists was but one of a number of co-existing, mutually reinforcing agitational endeavours which kept local working-class leaders busy in the cold and economically harsh winter of 1837-8. In another, less well-known campaign the distressed handloom weavers diligently organised the collection of evidence to present to the recently appointed 'Royal Commission on Hand-Loom Weavers'. Many were suspicious of its intentions and pessimistic about any improvement in their condition. A Keighley weavers' meeting at the local RA room, for example, was sparsely attended, and after literally going through the motions broke up 'in almost hopeless despair' of any amelioration without parliamentary representation.[331] The handloom weavers had reasons for their pessimism. Trades'

Trade Unionism', p. 157.

327 Huddersfield and Dewsbury were particularly active; Halifax contributed generously in late 1837; Bradford held meetings; Leeds as always was 'in the rear' but roused itself to receive three Glasgow delegates in March, see *NS* 17 Feb. (letter of 'Observer') and 17 Mar. 1838; in Keighley, which had a poor record on Dorchester (*NS* 16 June 1838), the response may have been muted.

328 Cunningham may well have been victimised for trade union activity in Ireland, see *NS* 27 Jan. 1838.

329 *NS* 3 Feb., 27 Jan. 1838.

330 Sykes, 'Early Chartism and Trade Unionism', p. 158. For example, the 'Canada' platform at Bradford included William Byles, editor of the Whig-liberal *Bradford Observer*, William Carlile (tailor) and Thomas Hill (maltster), both radical-liberals.

331 *LT* 25 Nov. 1837.

unions and political unions had both failed to improve their situation and their subsequent 1835 agitation had demonstrated the futility of petitioning parliament.

The short but impressively organised 1835 campaign had involved just one branch of the trade: worsted or stuff weaving. Centred on Bradford, the capital of the worsted trade, it had close links with the Rev. G. S. Bull and the factory movement and spawned a dense network of local and district committees operating under the direction of a 'Central Committee' drawn from a 'General Committee' for the West Riding, comprising between forty and fifty delegates from the different townships.[332] The deputies produced figures in March 1835 to show a general reduction in actual wages of forty per cent since 1828. Handloom weavers' grievances and sense of foreboding were not helped by a notable spurt of investment in power-looms in worsted centres such as Keighley.[333] In Benjamin Rushton's words, their condition was 'so ruinous that if matters are suffered to go on as they have done, and are doing... that useful body will very soon be annihilated or they must degenerate into paupers, poachers and thieves'.[334]

Whilst the surplus and cheapness of labour and the low skill level needed in many branches of the trade can be identified as the underlying difficulties, the handloom weavers themselves saw the 'unequal competition between the power-loom and the handloom' as the major immediate factor in their decline. They bitterly resented

> ... the unrestricted use (or rather abuse) of improved and continually improving machinery... the neglect of providing for the employment and maintenance of the Irish poor, who are compelled to crowd the English labour market – for a piece of bread. The adaptation of machines, in every improvement, to children and youth, and women, to the exclusion of those who ought to labour – the MEN.[335]

However, the weavers' leaders could not agree on the way forward and sometimes disagreed vehemently about preferred solutions.[336] 'First-line' solutions included a

---

332 Oastler Coll., Vol 9, Item 12, *The Report and Resolutions of a Meeting of Deputies from the Handloom Worsted Weavers residing in and near Bradford, Leeds, Halifax etc Yorkshire* (Bradford 1835). See also *LT* 25 Mar., 1 Aug. 1835. Rev. G. S. Bull apparently wrote much of the General Committee's official correspondence and William Muff, the secretary who saw ten hours as 'twin sister to that which we have in hand', lived in Bull's parish.

333 On Parliamentary interest, see P. Richard, 'The State and Early Industrial Capitalism: The Case of the Handloom-weavers', *Past and Present*, 79, 1 (1979), pp. 91-115. On power looms, see *PMG* 18 Apr. 1835; for Keighley, see John Hodgson, *Textile Manufacture and Other Industries of Keighley* (Keighley: A. Hey, 1879), p. 30 ff.

334 *PMG* 18 Apr. 1835. For Joseph Brook's calculations for the Bradford area, see *BO* 30 Apr. 1835. *LT* 11 Apr. 1835 (Rushton).

335 *Report and Resolutions*, p.12, quoted in Thompson, *Making*, p. 335. See also, *LT* 11 Apr., *PMG* 18 Apr. 1835.

336 The Leeds stuff-weavers (or at least some of them) disapproved of Fielden's 'Boards of Trade' plan. For the long-running controversy between Sunderland, Hutton and Mahoney (who advocated Corn Law repeal and favoured working with Leeds MPs) and William Rider (who

graduated tax on all looms (hand or power) to keep establishments small; local 'Boards of Trade' to fix wages; and a 25% tax on power-looms. A 'second line' of back-up measures took in a Ten Hours Bill; abolition of the Corn Laws; and the scrapping of duties on soap, malt and tea. The variety of proposals serves as a reminder that 'distressed handloom-weavers', even within one branch (worsted), were not an undifferentiated mass on the verge of revolutionary insurrection. They included a variety of opinions and affiliations.[337]

Indeed, though local radical leaders such as Benjamin Rushton, Joseph Brook (of Little Horton) and William Rider were active in the campaign, their role was fairly constrained. For example, Rider's attempts to emphasise the primacy of universal suffrage and to situate the weavers' predicament within a wider radical analysis largely fell on deaf ears. In general, the leadership, including community figures such as William Muff and Jeremiah Dewhirst who later re-emerge in the anti-poor law agitation, modelled their campaign on the factory reform movement's cross-party approach and its aspiration to attract respectable, philanthropic support. The emphasis of the 1835 agitation was on limiting 'the time of working machinery' rather than an 'enlargement of political privileges, however desirable'.[338] Their efforts, however, came to nought.

By late 1837 this gradualist, consensual ethos had given way to a more vigorous, politicised approach. With distress worsening and memories of recent failures to gain legislative help still fresh it is remarkable that so many localities roused themselves to furnish information for the recently inaugurated Royal Commission. Ingrained organisational habits and strong radical instincts possibly prevailed. It was often the weaving villages which had recently established political associations that took the lead. At Lepton, for example, the decision to collect evidence for the commission emerged after a long discussion at the end of a WMA meeting. Great Horton, with its strong radical traditions, set up a committee of nine to collect information to feed into Bradford's district committee. Huddersfield also established a central committee, chaired by agitational stalwart William Stocks jnr. and with fellow radical John Hanson as secretary. In Halifax shoemaker Bob Wilkinson, chair of the RA, likewise urged weavers in the outlying townships and villages to meet to co-operate and collect information.[339]

Unlike the earlier 1835 campaign, this burst of activity was very much led by key town and village figures who had played a prominent role in the anti-poor law agitation earlier in the year and who were central to the new formal political organisations that were emerging. Correspondingly, their analysis of the weavers'

---

recommended Fielden not Baines, and argued for universal suffrage and ten hours) about the true opinions of the Leeds stuff-weavers see, *LT* 9 May - 1 Aug. 1835.

337 On remedial measures proposed see *LT* 18 Apr., 30 May, 6 June 1835; BPP, Report from the Select Committee on Handloom Weavers' Petitions, 1834, X, p. 290; 1835, XIII, pp. 230-1. See also Thompson, *Making*, pp. 335-7.

338 See, for example, the meeting of 'masters and men' at Bradford, *LT* 11 Apr. 1835. *Report and Resolutions*, p. 12.

339 *LT* 28 Oct.; *BO* 9 Nov.; *LT* 18 Nov.; 2 Dec. 1837. Also, *NS* 9 June 1838 (for Hanson as secretary).

plight linked pressing issues like wages, conditions and the erosion of established ways of life to fundamental political questions such as the suffrage. They incorporated contemporary questions like Glasgow and the new poor law and located the weavers' struggles in the context of a wider critique of the Whig government and its allies. For John Smith jnr. of Lepton the Dorchester prosecution and the broader attack on trades' unions in 1834 had merely encouraged 'underselling manufacturers' to 'pursue the old course of competition'. It was the ultimate proof that the government would not 'protect the weavers nor let them protect themselves'.[340]

Another feature that distinguished it from the previous agitation was the fact that the 1837-8 campaign included handloom weavers in all branches and not just the stuff weavers. Traditionally better paid groups like the woollen weavers of the villages between Leeds and Bradford and the fancy weavers of the Huddersfield district participated this time. Both were suffering from the short time effects of deep recession and the long-term impact of a surplus of labour caused partly by the displacement of handworkers in other branches. Handloom weavers as a whole never articulated a single, simple narrative of their plight. However, shared perceptions and experiences undoubtedly helped to shape a convergence of views and a more overtly political analysis.

This reflected the changed political climate. Many of the grievances voiced in 1835 remained intact: the unnatural competitive system causing undercutting by unscrupulous masters, or the deployment of 'steam looms' leading to reduced wages and demand for labour. Proposed remedies, including the repeal of the Corn Laws and the adoption of Fielden's board of trade plan, had similarly not changed. However, there was an increasing realisation that even if limited concessions were extracted reluctantly from an unrepresentative parliament, these measures were unlikely to provide lasting solutions. As Lepton's John Smith jnr. told his fellow weavers, 'however you may be temporarily relieved by boards of trade, etc nothing will give you permanent relief until you obtain universal suffrage, which is the cause of universal freedom'. A fellow fancy-weaver, 'GB' of Almondbury, who lambasted the total ignorance of the 'representatives of shopocracy' regarding their situation, viewed the Royal Commission cynically, '… it is all humbug, I know it is humbug; but any [a?] scheme or plan, to amuse us, and prevent us demanding that measure which alone can give us real and permanent relief – an extension of the elective franchise'.[341] Other correspondents and speakers repeated the same theme. Whereas Rider in 1835 had often been a relatively isolated voice, by 1837 many of his fellow weavers had joined the chorus.

This new politically charged atmosphere fostered numerous instances of class antagonism. Although it was still feasible for small master manufacturers and journeymen handloom weavers to form a joint committee to produce correct accounts of earnings in places outside Leeds, such as Armley, where small, independent clothiers still predominated; similar collaboration was impossible in more distressed and divided

---

340 *LT* 9 Dec. 1837. See also letters from 'GB' in the same paper; and 'JA', possibly John Ambler, *LT* 16 Dec. 1837.

341 *LT* 9 Dec. 1837. 'GB' was probably George Beaumont, the radical and trade union leader of the early 1830s who 'turned coat'; see also, *NS* 4 May, 17 Aug. 1839.

communities.[342] In Lepton, for example, John Smith jnr. voiced his lack of confidence in the masters' figures and advised the fancy weavers to produce their own wage calculations. The Bradford Central Committee similarly decried the misrepresentation of wage levels and the haughty stance of local masters; whilst a small gathering of Keighley weavers entertained few hopes of assistance from their employers. The 'muttered curses' that large groups of Hebden Bridge weavers directed towards local master manufacturers, after the latter had refused to sign a paper which urged them to give up business or increase wages, provided the aural backcloth to the toxic atmosphere of the time.[343]

Reports that the Commission would arrive in November proved to be false, causing John Smith to remind his fellow fancy weavers that it was 'not the first time that you have been deceived by the government'. When Chapman and the commissioners eventually appeared in the West Riding in late summer 1838 they ignored the fancy and heavy woollen areas and focused on the woollen and worsted villages in the hinterlands of Leeds and Bradford.[344] When their report finally appeared in 1840, it provided another indication of the distance between rulers and ruled, by pointedly rejecting the weavers' proposed solutions and reiterating instead a *laissez-faire* endorsement of the freedom of labour.[345] By then, however, weavers and their leaders had long given up hope of any amelioration from a seemingly hostile state.

The ultimately abortive handloom weavers' agitation of winter 1837-8 had nevertheless served a useful purpose. It reinvigorated delegate structures, strengthened links between the main radical centres and the outlying townships and promoted a more explicitly political analysis of the weavers' predicament. Alongside the radicalising effect of the anti-poor law agitation, it served to draw the weavers and their leaders more firmly into the suffrage campaign.

8: Factory Reform and Anti-Poor Law Agitations, 1835-8

The vast chasm between the Malthusian political economists and the defenders of the rights of labour is nowhere better illustrated than in attitudes to the new poor law. The Poor Law Amendment Act, 'the most contentious piece of social legislation passed by any nineteenth-century Parliament', met with its most vigorous opposition in the textile districts of the West Riding.[346] The Act, the embodiment of orthodox political economy, was assailed from many quarters and for a range of different reasons. At the heart of popular hostility lay the perceptions that it directly attacked workers' financial security and familial integrity. Particularly in the industrial north the locally

---

342 *LT* 2 Dec.; 11 Nov. 1837.

343 *LT* 28 Oct. (Smith); 18 Nov., 2 Dec. (Bradford); 25 Nov. (Keighley); *BO* 23 Nov. 1837 (Hebden Bridge). This reverse 'document' echoed the conflicts of 1833-4.

344 *LT* 9 Dec. 1837; for the collecting of evidence in Bradford see *BO* 27 Sept., 4, 11 Oct. 1838; for Leeds see *NS* 4 Aug. 1838.

345 BPP 1840, XXIII, pp. 587-90. On this see, Thompson, *Making*, p. 333.

346 D. Thompson, 'Chartism, Success or Failure', in David Rubenstein (ed.), *People for the People: Radical Ideas and Personalities in British Social History* (London: Ithaca Press, 1973), p. 91.

administered old poor law had buttressed the domestic economy by being a mechanism of last resort against the threat of destitution. The provision of 'outdoor relief' (in cash or kind) for the able-bodied had allowed them to survive periods of intense distress. The proposed replacement of outdoor with 'indoor relief', via a strictly administered regime overseen by amorphous Poor Law Unions, was viewed as an abomination and a fundamental attack on the family and the dignity of labour. The Act's assumption that poverty was the result of moral failings underpinned the proposals for large-scale, regimented workhouses (the dreaded new, prison-like 'Bastiles') in which families were split up and inmates were forced to wear uniforms.

Working families were not alone in rejecting the Act's ostensible purpose, which was, in John Knott's words, 'to save the labouring population from pauperism, and save the property-owning class money'. The creation of a centralized bureaucracy in the form of the Poor Law Commission and the replacement of parish administration by that of conglomerated Poor Law Unions, governed by elected Boards of Guardians, offended local pride and ignored improvements in poor relief mechanisms that has already been undertaken. This, and the removal of local accountability and minor powers of patronage, lay behind some of the 'respectable' and cross-party support that opposition to the new law initially enjoyed. However, the raw passion which fuelled effigy-burning, physical attacks on Assistant Commissioners and violent confrontations with the military came directly from the working communities of the textile district and their belief that the new legislation was both unchristian and unconstitutional, undermining the social compact implicit in the original Elizabethan poor laws.[347]

Although bitterness from a wide range of interlocking and mutually reinforcing campaigns was channelled into the early Chartist movement, the characteristic defiant, enraged tone of northern Chartism came directly from the anti-poor law movement. The local leadership which conducted the campaigns and articulated the deep-felt, communal hatred of the 'starvation law', its murderous 'bastiles' and the overriding concept of centralism, included many factory and political reformers who later went on to become Chartists. Indeed, often they were the medium through which the fervour of local opposition to the new poor law was transmitted to the early Chartist movement. However, it also needs to be emphasised that the anti-poor law campaign was one amongst many. It had periods of brilliant incandescence in the spring and early summer 1837 and in winter 1837-8. However, even in its heartland, the West Riding textile district, it was a relatively short-lived and geographically limited agitation.

The best general accounts of the movement in the West Riding remain those of Cecil Driver and Mike Rose, to which Nicholas Edsall, John Knott and Felix Driver have added much valuable and informative local detail.[348] J. T. Ward's pioneering

---

347 John Knott, *Popular Opposition to the 1834 Poor Law* (Beckenham: Croom Helm, 1986), p. 59; on the Christian dimension of opposition, see Roberts, '"God Save the Paddock Flag"', pp. 42-4.

348 C. Driver, *Tory Radical*, pp. 269-86 and pp. 331-377; Michael Rose, 'The Anti-Poor Law Movement in the North of England', *Northern History* 1 (1966), pp. 70-91; and 'The Anti-Poor Law Agitation', in J. T. Ward (ed.), *Popular Movements c.1830-1850*, (London:

work on the factory movement is also useful for showing 'how the anti-Poor Law Movement in Northern England emerged out of the Ten Hours movement and was in turn swallowed up by Chartism'.[349] But, as in his later writings on the agitation for the Charter, a stress on the importance of Tory-radicalism overlooks the fundamental point that this easy transposition of personnel and energies could only have happened because a strong thread of radical leadership, ideas and support ran through all three movements. Before looking at these connections and the transfer of ten hours leadership and support to the anti-poor law cause in early 1837 it is first necessary to trace the resurgence of the factory movement in the mid-1830s.

The timing of the 1835 revival, (a largely defensive affair inspired by a *Leeds Mercury*-led campaign which sought to amend the Factory Act so that it allowed children under ten to work eleven hours), was governed by the extension of the eight-hour provisions to eleven-year-old children, due to take place on 1 March. Most of the meetings in Leeds, Huddersfield, Bradford, Dewsbury and Gomersal which opposed the implementation of this clause were stage-managed by master-manufacturers hostile to factory legislation and dominated by overlookers including some such as John Hannam of Leeds who had taken an active part in the ten hours campaign three years earlier.[350]

Local factory reformers found themselves in the invidious role of 'defending the 1833 Act against its authors'.[351] Their position was not an easy one. They sought to disclaim responsibility for the Act and argue that only a proper ten hours measure would permanently improve matters; whilst simultaneously asserting that, in the absence of such legislation, Althorp's Act was better than the alterations proposed by the factory owners.[352] They put over this message in a series of meetings at Keighley, Bradford and Huddersfield, organised by quickly resurrected STCs. The platforms contained some familiar figures from the earlier campaigns, including radicals such as Weatherhead, Wildman and Bedford of Keighley, Hanson, Glendinning, and Stocks

---

Macmillan, 1970), pp. 78-94. The fullest narrative account is in N. C. Edsall, *The Anti-Poor Law Movement, 1834-44* (Manchester: Manchester University Press, 1971). This has been augmented by John Knott's *Popular Opposition to the 1834 Poor Law* and Felix Driver's *Power and Pauperism: The Workhouse System, 1834-1884* (Cambridge: Cambridge University Press, 1993).

349 Ward, *Factory Movement*, pp. 121-4 and 158-185, and *Chartism* (London: Batsford, 1973), pp. 68-70 and 87ff; Rose, 'Anti-Poor Law Agitation', p. 93.

350 *LM* 14 Feb. 1835 (for allegations that the provisions of the Factory Act were threatening employment). For the meetings see *LT, LM* Feb-Mar 1835, Ward, *Factory Movement,* p. 132 and C. Driver, *Tory Radical*, p. 310. On Hannam see *LT* 28 Feb. 1835. He was chair of the flax overlookers' committee which had thanked a firm which reduced maximum working hours by three hours (*LT* 22 Nov. 1834). The Leeds overlookers had pressed for an eleven-hour Act in November 1833. (*LT* 16 Nov. 1833) and their campaign for a lower age limited reflected a concern shared with many parents of factory children about loss of income.

351 Ward, *Factory Movement*, p. 132.

352 Althorp's 1833 Act had prohibited child working under the age of nine, limited those aged 9 to 13 to working 48 hours a week (and a maximum of eight hours per day) and restricted juveniles between 13 and 18 to twelve hours' work a day. The Act also included educational provisions and the establishment of a factory inspectorate.

of Huddersfield, and Rider of Leeds. The wider radical influence is also apparent in the passing of resolutions for the return of the Dorchester men at the second Huddersfield meeting. As before, however, respectable and clerical support is evident in Bradford and Huddersfield; and the Bradford radicals are again notable for their absence from the local platform or STC. The only exception was a newcomer, William Hill, who together with John Reid, the Huddersfield co-operative tailor, comprised the most prominent recent adherents to the campaign.[353]

The ten hour riposte to the masters' counter-offensive was not totally convincing, nor was it universal. Leeds, with Hobson in prison, was 'dis-organised' and Halifax and Dewsbury did not hold meetings. Nevertheless, at least the factory reformers demonstrated the ease and speed with which organisation could be resurrected and were able to alert people to the fact that, as William Rider put it in his inimitable way, 'the hydra-headed monster was still alive, the monster still raised his hideous crest, it still sucked the infant's blood'.[354]

The stimulus for the 1836 campaign came from the actions of Poulett Thomson, President of the Board of Trade, who took up the masters' case against the full implementation of the eight hours provisions of Althorp's Act.[355] Although the initial challenge to this threat came from Lancashire, the response in Yorkshire was vigorous and widespread. A revived Leeds committee organised meetings, first at the 'Radical Union room', then at the Court House. The Huddersfield, Bradford and Keighley reformers, as expected, were quick off the mark, with William Hill speaking at all the meetings they organised. Rallies were also held at Halifax, Dewsbury and, more surprisingly, Whig-dominated Pudsey where John Bateman, an old clothier and long-standing secretary to the 'Ten-Hours' Bill Committee', took the lead. A meeting held in Bingley in mid-April was reckoned to be the thirteenth in the West Riding since February.[356] This meeting is also notable for including a Bradford radical, John Jackson, on its platform but, with the exception of the ubiquitous William Hill, the town's main radicals kept their distance. The movement's connections, with Toryism in general and Oastler in particular, appear to have been a continuing stumbling block, In April, for example, Peter Bussey wrote a letter to the *Leeds Times*, in which he attacked Oastler's old fashioned Tory principles (particularly his preference for the 'ancient and varied' suffrage and opposition to the new-fangled 'ten-pound plan'), reminded readers that it was a Tory yeomanry which attacked at Peterloo, and requested assurances from Oastler that he really was 'a friend to the working classes'.[357]

Bussey's fellow official in the Bradford Trades' Union of 1833-4, Joseph Brook, cared less about the political complexion of his platform companions, and spoke together with fellow operative John Robertshaw at a Great Horton meeting which

---

353 *LT* 7 Feb. (Keighley); 21 Mar. (Bradford); 28 Mar. and 18 Apr. 1835 (Huddersfield).

354 On Leeds, see J. T. Ward, 'Leeds and the Factory Reform Movement', *Publications of the Thoresby Society*, 46 (1961), p. 104; *LT* 21 Mar. 1835 (Rider).

355 The early campaign was for Hindley's Bill and against any modification of the Act. A meeting was held in Bradford on this in February; see Ward, *Factory Movement*, p. 148.

356 *LT* 26 Mar. (Huddersfield); 2 Apr. (Leeds); 9 Apr. (Leeds, Bradford, Keighley, Dewsbury); 23 Apr. (Halifax); 16 Apr. (Pudsey); *HG* 23 Apr., *BO* 21 Apr. 1836 (Bingley).

357 *LT* 16 Apr. 1836.

also included three local clergymen. This 'respectable' presence remained a feature of the first phase of the 1836 campaign, which also included related meetings to promote religious education by making the Act's education clauses more effective. However, an important and seemingly growing, radical presence was evident in many of the main centres.[358]

Factory reformers maintained their momentum after Poulett Thomson withdrew his Bill having only narrowly won a division on the second reading. They channelled their renewed energies into pressing for Hindley's Ten Hour Bill, holding meetings at Halifax, Bradford and Leeds.[359] The Dewsbury area was also particularly active. Petitions were prepared and meetings held in Heckmondwike and Ossett. Meanwhile, the Dewsbury committee collected twenty petitions (in favour of ten hours) from local mills, and, in July, organised a prestigious meeting with some notable outside speakers. In all places the bulk of the orators were ten hour veterans and included some 'respectable supporters', but the platforms also blooded some new radical 'speechifying' talent.[360]

With the failure of Hindley's Bill and the end of the spate of public meetings, the local committees settled down to the more mundane work of reporting evasions of the Act. Enforcement became the theme of the second half of the year; but the frustrations and disappointments of the summer and of earlier attempts to win a Ten Hours' Bill were not forgotten. In an atmosphere of growing antagonism and hostility, local leaders added another entry to the catalogue of working-class grievance and articulated a growing sense of injustice.[361] At the same time, Oastler. dubbed by opponents 'the Danton of the Factory movement', was stretching the language of rhetorical violence and bitter invective to the limits, notably in his 'The Law or the Needle' speech in which he seemingly endorsed industrial sabotage, urging factory children

> to ask their Grandmothers for a few of their old knitting-needles, which I will instruct them how to apply to the spindles in a way which will teach these law-defying mill owner magistrates to have respect even to "Oastler's law", as they have wrongly designated the factory law.[362]

---

358 *LT* 30 Apr. 1836 (Horton). Sympathetic vicars sometimes chaired meetings, and were important figureheads, but a closer look down the list of speakers usually puts their role into perspective. On the 'education clause' meetings see, Ward, *Factory Movement*, p. 152.

359 *LT* 4 June; *BO* 26 May; *LT* 28 May 1836.

360 On Dewsbury, a thriving ten hours district, see *LT* 7, 28 May, 4, 11 June, 30 July 1836. The leading local figures were Mark Crabtree 'a Radical operative', (Ward, 'Leeds', p. 105), George Crabtree, John Tweedale and Robert Dibb. Few prominent 'town-radicals' appeared on the platform. At Heckmondwike speakers included Charles Etherington (a leading figure in 1832-3), Samuel Newsome (radical) and possibly Joseph Whiteley, a radical and future Chartist.

361 See Ward, *Factory Movement*, pp. 160-7 and C. Driver, *Tory Radical*, pp. 325-30.

362 C. Driver, *Tory Radical*, p. 4. For an assessment of Oastler's rhetoric and quasi-revolutionary status, see S. A. Weaver, 'Richard Oastler', *Oxford Dictionary of National Biography* (Oxford: Oxford University Press, 2004), and John A. Hargreaves, "'Treading on the edge of

The factory movement did not entirely die away in the autumn and winter of 1836-7. The Dewsbury STC was still active in September, and in October William Hill chaired a Bradford meeting to form an association to protect juvenile labour. Joseph Rayner Stephens, the radical firebrand from Ashton-under-Lyne, was present here and also preached sermons (with collections for the factory cause) at Huddersfield and Dewsbury in November. In early January Squire Auty, a Tory printer, tried to revive the ten hours agitation in Bradford.[363] However, by this time interest had already turned to the new poor law, which was now beginning to be applied in the industrial north. A working-class meeting at the STC room, Butterworth Buildings, later in the month considered steps to oppose the establishment of the Bradford Poor Law Union and formed a committee to collect information and call meetings. They were not the first in the field, however. Keighley led the way with a public meeting on 'the merits and demerits of what is falsely called the Poor Law Amendment Act' in November 1836.[364] Held in the RA room and chaired by David Weatherhead, the town's leading radical and ten hours supporter, this well-attended gathering indicates the strong and early radical engagement with the issue.

Nor was this interest new.[365] Working-class radicals had opposed the 'Poor Law Bill' from the start. In June 1834 the final issue of the *Voice of the West-Riding* had declared the new proposals 'most obnoxious and unconstitutional'; and in the first edition of Hobson's short-lived paper, the *Argus and Demagogue,* Oastler had penned a strong attack on the new act. On this question, at least, Oastler shared much common ground with Bussey and some of the radicals who had held back from direct involvement in the factory campaigns. Both hated centrally-constituted bodies, whether they be the factory inspectorate, the Poor Law Commission or the new police. Peter Bussey giving 'An Operatives' Opinion on the Poor Law Bill' penned a detailed, passionate attack on the Act's centralising, unnatural and punitive aspects: 'for you must understand we are to have a prison in every workhouse that punishment may be added to disgrace'. His analysis incorporated many traditional radical arguments (on the national debt, emigration, and the cultivation of wastes) and anticipated many of the planks of the anti-poor law movement's platform.[366]

Radicals continued to condemn its provisions over the next two years.[367] However, it was only when the Poor Law Commissioners turned their attention to the industrial north in late 1836 and early 1837 that the well-rehearsed rhetoric was converted into a

---

revolution?" Richard Oastler (1789-1861) a reassessment', in Hargreaves and Hilary Haigh (eds.), *Slavery in Yorkshire*, pp. 201-28.

363 *LT* 3 Sept.; *BO* 27 Oct.; *LT* 5 Nov. 1836; Ward, *Factory Movement*, p. 168. The Bradford STC contained a number of Tory Anglican tradesmen and operatives and met at John Wade's New Inn, later a venue for Operative Conservative meetings.

364 *BO* 26 Jan. 1837; *LT* 26 Nov. 1836.

365 Radical concern with the poor and poor relief was long-standing. It showed itself in the exposure of local distress, participation in meetings of the unemployed, concern about Ireland and its Poor Law, participation in local poor relief politics and control of local offices.

366 *VWR* 7 June; *Argus and Demagogue* 9 Aug.; *LT* 15 Nov. 1834.

367 It formed part of O'Connor's and the RA's platform in 1835-6. The wage-cutting effects of the Act's migration proposals were also emphasised.

coherent campaign. This ensuing agitation built on existing radical and short time networks and ideas and included a substantial radical leadership component.

This is not to deny that the West Riding anti-poor law movement contained a wide cross-section of local political opinion and social groupings, including Anglican clergymen, Tory and even some Whig-liberal magistrates, and 'a considerable number of respectable and influential persons', in addition to parish officials fearing for their posts and privileges, and virtually the whole of the local working community.[368] So when the Bradford radical John Jackson, a 'working man', admitted his conversion to the arguments in favour of the new act in December 1835 he was denounced as a tool of the political economists and endured great unpopularity amongst his fellow workers.[369] Working-class hostility was hardening appreciably in the winter of 1836-7 as a harsh trade depression, bringing unemployment in its wake, made for a hungry, embittered population who felt personally threatened by the prospect of 'Poor Law bastilles'. Factory workers on short time, artisans without work and underemployed textile outworkers all lived with the spectre of the degradation of the workhouse and the separation of their families. It did not help that the commissioner appointed to implement the act in the West Riding was Alfred Power, already hated for his role in the Factory Commission in 1833. When he came to Huddersfield in January 1837 to meet the overseers and make arrangements for Board of Guardian elections he was faced by a hostile crowd. 'Mr C. Tinker then declared that he was a poor man, and that if all the poor men were of his opinion, he would take a rifle and lodge a ball in the heart of every Commissioner who came into the town'. This caused the meeting to break up and Power soon left.[370]

Local radical leaders both nourished and fed off this communal hostility. They were the natural leaders of the opposition to the new poor law. Not only did they provide a thread of continuity with earlier movements, they also had the experience, the analysis and the agitational energy to carry a large part of the working population with them. In Huddersfield, as John Knott notes, local radicals continued to campaign 'with wit and style' into the early 1840s, employing amusing visual stunts incorporating evocative emblems and symbols. This performative strand had its origins in the earlier period when, for example, radicals had used the holiday to mark Victoria's birthday in May 1837 to parade the town with bands and flags and to drown out the national anthem with a rendition of 'Paddy Whack'.[371] Radical leaders played vital roles in the two main bursts of anti-poor law activity – first in early 1837 and then in the winter of 1837-8 – speaking at local and regional gatherings, agitating the out-townships, co-ordinating information, publicity and propaganda, contesting Board of Guardian elections, organising direct action, and generally mobilising and

---

368 See Knott, *Popular Opposition*, pp. 94-100.

369 See Rose, 'Anti-Poor Law Movement in the North', pp. 83-4 and Rose, 'Anti-Poor Law Agitation', pp. 84-5 (for respectable and 'Liberal' reservations); *BO* 31 Dec. 1835, 21 Jan. 1836 (Jackson).

370 *LM* 14 Jan. 1837. Tinker, a republican and Owenite socialist, and the town's leading unstamped seller, had recently served a six-month sentence for Stamp Duty offences.

371 Knott, *Popular Opposition*, p. 140; Brooke, 'The Roots of Chartism', p. 26.

managing discontent in their areas. In many of these functions they anticipated their later roles in the early Chartist movement.

Initial opposition to the new arrangements was most highly organised in Keighley and Huddersfield, where radicals had traditionally exercised significant influence on the administration of poor relief. The Huddersfield Workhouse Board in 1833 contained a radical majority, and in Keighley radicals filled a number of minor poor relief offices.[372] A major Keighley meeting in February 1837 included contributions from Abraham Wildman, Joseph Firth, James Walton, Archibald Leighton (of Haworth), Mr (probably Thomas) Knowles and David Weatherhead – all of whom, except Wildman, went forward into the early Chartist movement.[373] Its Huddersfield counterpart, chaired by Pitkethly, included contributions from many established radical speakers. The radicals also successfully captured the existing poor law machinery when John Leech's list (of overseers of the poor) – nearly all recognisable as radicals – was carried by a large majority and defiantly continued to administer poor relief.[374] In Huddersfield a skilfully orchestrated outdoor campaign of numerous small meetings, demonstrations and effigy-burning was matched by the systematic application of popular pressure at Board of Guardian meetings in spring and summer.[375] Both places returned anti-poor law majorities in the Board of Guardian elections of early spring.[376]

Elsewhere the picture was more complex. At a Halifax ratepayers meeting to nominate guardians in February, Robert Wilkinson and William Thorburn (two leading radicals) moved a resolution denouncing the Bill and caused the meeting to end in chaos. The nomination of Jonathan Ackroyd, a local Whig mill-owner, was met with cries of 'the greatest tyrant in the town' and 'we want no grinders – no enemy of the Ten Hour Bill'. Local middle-class radical-liberals like Michael Stocks, who favoured contesting the elections, were shouted down as 'renegades' and the hard-line radicals resolved to return their voting papers unsigned. The town's first big public meeting on the issue was chaired by Robert Wilkinson (recently elected chair of the local RA) and had a distinctly radical flavour.[377] Nevertheless, Halifax, where Power had cultivated strong connections with local worthies, returned a large 'Liberal' majority in the subsequent Board of Guardian elections. The position was similar in

---

372 *LT* 4 Apr. 1833; 9 Apr. 1836 (S. Sunderland, collector); *LM* 4 Feb. 1832 (Gillet Sharp, overseer).

373 James Walton (1803–1875?) was a woolcomber. Archibald Leighton (1800–?), another woolcomber, was later prominent as a Chartist and teetotaller.

374 *LT* 11 Feb.; 25 Mar. 1837.

375 See Edsall, *The Anti-Poor Law Movement,* pp. 93–4. Also, TNA: HO 52/35, W. Moore to Lt. Col. Maberley, 16 June 1837. Huddersfield also made the ultimate gesture of opposition by refusing to elect a clerk. On this see, Edsall, *The Anti-Poor Law Movement,* p. 91.

376 Ibid., p. 98. There was 'extensive cooperation between Radicals and Tories'. The majority of Guardians were radicals according to Ellice to Lord John Russell, 8 June 1837 in TNA: HO 52/35.

377 *HG, LT* 4 Feb.; 1 Apr. 1837. The meeting included many future Chartists, plus Francis Crossley, a radical and later the town's leading carpet manufacturer, and some ten hours stalwarts

Bradford and Dewsbury, where attempts to vote in anti-poor law candidates were unsuccessful.

These results, however, do not necessarily indicate a lack of anti-poor law feeling on the part of the wider community or an absence of endeavour on the part of the local radical leadership. The 1837 board elections were of limited importance. Voters comprised only ratepayers, who possibly instinctively followed existing political allegiances and who, for religious and ideological reasons, were reluctant to jeopardise the implementation of the Registration Act, which was the first task of the commissioners.[378] For example, in Dewsbury, which elected a 'comfortable pro-Poor Law majority', there was nevertheless formidable opposition to the act which voiced itself at a respectable meeting in mid-February. This included some important town-radicals – Titus Brooke and Thomas Todd of Dewsbury, and Morritt Mathews of Liversedge – who had never publicly taken up the factory issue, as well as a few established factory reformers.[379]

In Bradford the radicals were divided. The strong Tory presence at the early 'respectable' meetings on the issue may have put off some radical leaders. A few certainly approved of the act and others may possibly have considered other issues (like household suffrage) more pressing. John Jackson, a supporter of the act, blamed all the 'excitement and alarm' on Bull and voiced the traditional radical objection to single issue campaigns:

> Here is that grand point, which, above all others, should never be lost sight of; for should you (the unrepresented) succeed in getting the Amendment Act amended, what guarantee have you that you will not be as you hitherto have been, loaded most unmercifully with taxation and aristocratic monopolies, various and vexatious.[380]

For others the poor law issue was more central to their radicalism. John Douthwaite, president of the Bradford RA, and Bussey, its secretary, spoke at a Great Horton meeting in early February alongside Henry Rawnsley (a radical weaver), Joseph Brook and William Fox, 'a labouring man' and future Chartist.[381] At other meetings William Muff (leader of the handloom weavers in 1835), Samuel Bower and possibly John Burrows, a radical veteran, also took to the anti-poor law platform.[382] However, radical engagement in an issue which also enjoyed widespread support from many Tories should not be read as evidence for local Tory-radicalism. John Douthwaite, somewhat tongue-in-cheek, referred to the different names by which the radicals were called: 'they had got the appellation of Tory-Radicals. He had no

---

378 The passage of the 1836 Births, Deaths and Marriages Act placed administrative responsibility for the new legislation in the hands of the Poor Law Unions.

379 *LT* 25 Feb. 1837. The meeting was also addressed by Rev. G. S. Bull and ten hours veteran George Crabtree.

380 *LT* 11 Mar. 1837 (respectable meeting); *BO* 16 Feb. 1837 (Jackson). For an attack on some Bradford radicals' support of the Act, see *LT* 2 Sept. 1837 (letter of Hanson and Buchanan).

381 *LT* 11 Feb. 1837.

382 *LT* 4, 25; *LI* 25 Feb.; *LT* 4 Mar. 1837.

objection to the name, but he had rather have it Conservative-Radicals; then he could call himself so, and preserve those principles on which he based himself'. His principles indeed were unashamedly radical. Similarly, Bussey had no intention of formally supporting any Tory and reminded an audience of non-electors in July of Tory culpability on this issue and others.[383]

Derek Fraser has provided a detailed account of the intense micro-politics in Leeds, where poor law administration had traditionally been a political football contested by the two main parties.[384] Things changed very little as a result of the Commissioners' arrival. It remained an arena in which working-class radicals had little involvement or influence; a fact which may help to explain why Leeds attained a reputation for being notoriously sluggish on the poor law question. The local STC converted itself into an anti-poor law organisation in early April but few Leeds operatives attended the West Riding Peep Green meeting, and in June Robert Buchanan of Huddersfield condemned the Leeds men to their faces for their apathy on the issue.[385]

Elsewhere, the main town leaders played an important role in agitating the outlying villages of their districts during the campaigns of spring 1837 and winter 1837-8.[386] Some localities, notably the fancy-weaving area to the south and east of Huddersfield, were fairly well stirred up already and had long traditions of radical and trade union organisation. But in townships like Golcar, 'a very Whig place', which the Huddersfield orators visited in March, or Morton (near Bingley) where the Keighley leaders led the township's first ever public meeting, the outside input was crucial.[387] These local meetings to establish and coordinate resistance saw the emergence or reappearance of a number of important village-leaders – people such as Michael Scholefield of Clayton, John Smith jnr. of Lepton, Samuel Midgley, brothers John and James Buckley and John Heaton of Almondbury, and Archibald Leighton of Haworth – many of whom are recognisable later as Chartists.[388] The anti-poor law agitation was important for providing them with a popular platform and for initiating or re-establishing a dialogue with radicals in the main urban centres. It is clear that in a number of places the anti-poor law revival of public meetings and associative bodies paved the way, and provided the initial stimulus for, later radical organisation.[389]

The formal organisational structure of the anti-poor law movement built on short time precedents and pre-figured some later Chartist patterns. A co-ordinating West Riding Central Committee was formed after a gathering of STC and trade union delegates at Bradford in early March. The meeting convened by the four most active

---

383 *LT* 14 Jan.; 15 July 1837. See also, *LT* 16 Dec. 1837.

384 Derek Fraser, 'Poor Law Politics in Leeds, 1833-1855', *Publications of the Thoresby Society*, 53 (1970), pp. 23-49.

385 *LT* 4 Mar.; 1 Apr.; 10 June 1837.

386 Edsall, *The Anti-Poor Law Movement*, p. 72, says that this missionary work was done by reconstituted STCs and that organisers, 'in some cases full-time paid professionals', went out to build up local committees.

387 *LT* 25 Mar. (meetings in 'fancy' area); LT 27 Apr. (Golcar); *LT* 25 Feb. 1837 (Morton).

388 Michael Scholefield (1802-1870?) was an Irish-born shoemaker.

389 See, for example, Southowram *LT* 6 May and 3 June 1837.

local STCs – Huddersfield, Halifax, Bradford and Keighley – formally converted the existing structures and committees into anti-poor law bodies and decided to abandon all agitation for factory reform in favour of concentrating on the single poor law issue. The new Central Committee appointed two experienced and respected radical organisers, William Stocks jnr. and Samuel Bower, to the key posts of Treasurer and Secretary and, as its first task, set about organising the proposed West Riding meeting at Peep Green.[390] This, like its 1833 predecessor, was an organisational and propaganda triumph.[391] A number of key West Riding leaders – Samuel Bower and John Douthwaite of Bradford, William Thornton and Thomas Cliffe of Halifax, Titus Brooke of Dewsbury, James Penny of Millbridge, and Robert Buchanan, John Leech and Lawrence Pitkethly of Huddersfield – added a local and distinctly radical flavour to the heady concoction of speakers at the May meeting.[392] The rally was exceedingly well-managed, massively attended and provided ample evidence of the region's visceral and deep-seated hostility to the new poor law and its commissioners.[393]

It also spawned a number of organisational off-shoots. In some areas district committees covering the proposed Poor Law Union boundaries were formed. This was the case in the Huddersfield area where delegates from the local committees met in June with John Hanson in the chair; and Keighley may have had a similar district body. The precise relationship between the different organisational levels is probably not such a 'mystery' as Edsall suggests. Like the STCs before them, the permanence and penetration of anti-poor law organisations was patchy, with variation within and between areas. In most places the main town committees served as both town and district foci, whilst in a few places a proper district delegate structure evolved and dovetailed into the regional framework.[394] It was through such structures that administrative resistance to the new poor law entities was organised.

Equally, these bodies – and the local (particularly radical) leaders who served on them – formed the vehicle through which the mobilisation and orchestration of the campaigns of communal resistance took place. Typical activities included the posting of blood-thirsty handbills and placards and the holding of regular outdoor meetings incorporating processions and bands, effigies and banners. One of the large black flags displayed at a Huddersfield anti-poor law rally on 5 June 1837 showed an image of three men hanging from a gibbet with the slogan 'The Kings of the bastiles drawing their wages'. The Home Office's 'Municipal and Provincial' papers for 1837 are replete with letters from worried local 'respectables' forwarding inflammatory placards and

---

390 *LT* 4 Mar. 1837. The establishment of this body was anticipated at a Keighley meeting, *LT* 11 Feb. 1837. It is not clear how regularly the West Riding committee met after this.

391 For an appreciation of the meticulous organisation of this event, see Knott, *Popular Opposition*, pp. 114-5.

392 *LT, LI* 20 May 1837. The platform included a wide spectrum of speakers (of national and regional repute) – Oastler, Stephens, O'Connor, O'Brien, Bell, Bernard, Owen, Hetherington, G. A. Fleming, John Fielden, and a few other mainly 'respectable' local activists. A meeting in favour of universal suffrage was held after the main anti-poor law proceedings.

393 Estimates of the attendance varied between 150,000 (*Times*) and 60-70,000 (*Leeds Mercury*).

394 *LT* 24 June; *LT* 11 Feb. 1837 (for proposed Keighley committee); Edsall, *The anti-Poor Law movement*, p. 72.

reporting instances of harassment and mass intimidation. William Moore, the jumpy Huddersfield postmaster, bemoaned the 'anarchical state of the population' in mid-June, complaining that 'It is perilous to stir out in the villages. Night after night effigies are burnt, individuals grossly insulted and shopkeepers actually prevented pursuing their business'. Meanwhile a local magistrate forwarded to the Home Secretary a rough hand-written placard addressed to the 'Men of Paddock' proclaiming them as 'Heroes' and urging that it would take more than 'a Butchers Bull Dog and Three men with glazed hats and shining buttons and a few snotty nosed constables' to frighten them off.[395] As Katrina Navickas notes, many localities had a long history of 'enforcing community justice against state compulsion' and violence, whether bodily or psychological, was often 'a carefully chosen tool in the repertoire of protest', a considered adjunct to other options such as petitions or engagement in contests for local power. This is evident in Keighley in March 1837, where direct action, including the storming of poor law meetings and physical attacks on Alfred Power, the Assistant Poor Law Commissioner, operated in tandem with administrative resistance to the new poor law.[396]

In Huddersfield, opposition to the poor law, given an extra dimension by Oastler's candidature in the elections of May and July, reached an early peak in mid-summer. An estimated 10,000 people 'whipped up by almost a month of unceasing agitation' turned out for the 5 June Board of Guardians meeting. For an hour before the assembly Oastler and the radicals held a meeting on the 'distressed state of the country', then, according to a hostile observer, 'the mob went directly in thousands (with bands of music and flags displaying the three commissioners suspended by the neck from the gallows) to the Poor House and there broke open the gates...' The Guardians escaped by the back door to the Albion Tavern, but the crowd searched the building for Power, who the local overseer believed would have been killed had he been found. Virtually imprisoned in their new venue, the majority of Guardians voted against electing a clerk. The result was announced to the cheering crowd outside by Oastler, after which 'Mr Pitkethly (the Radical Infidel) announced from the same window we shall be able to tell the Mob the names of the 11 Whig Guardians who had voted for a clerk (and for sending you the people into the Bastiles) so that you can then know your friends from your enemies'.[397]

Local Whig 'respectables' blamed Oastler and 'our unworthy bunch of Magistrates (who are all Torys...)' for using the issue 'to serve their own and their party political purposes... it is now no uncommon thing to see our magistrates associating with and currying favour with Hobson and Tinker the printer and sellers of unstamped publications and others of their revolutionary fraternity'. The magistrates were taken to task for not reading the Riot Act, but one, Armitage, referred to the difficulties

---

395 Knott, *Popular Opposition*, p. 152; TNA: HO 52/35, Moore to Maberley, 16 June 1837; Armitage to Russell, 17 June 1837. On Paddock (a fancy weaving township) and its famous flag, see Roberts, "'God save the Paddock flag'".

396 Navickas, *Protest*, pp. 131 and 136-8.

397 Edsall, *The Anti-Poor Law Movement*, p. 95; TNA: HO 52/35, Ellice to Russell, 8 June 1837 also testimony of Thomas Shepherd enclosed in Ellice's letter. Edsall, pp. 91-9 gives a full account of events in Huddersfield. See also, Knott, *Popular Opposition*, pp. 149-57.

posed by 'an organised system of opposition to the Bill'. When the Guardians (or at least those who had not resigned or stayed away) met the following week, not even three could be found to push through the election of a clerk. The Poor Law Commission tried once more to force the election. In a placard headed 'Now for the Tug of War. The Commissioners against the People' the local anti-poor law committee replied in typical style:

> Is this not Despotism – despotism of the most daring description …
> [your elected Guardians] are to be coerced by these Vampire Despots,
> who suck their luxuries from your blood and bones – because they will
> not bring God's terrific curse upon the land - because they will not
> consent to oppress the poor and needy, and support Tyranny and
> Dictation... Is there a man in the Union fool enough to accept the
> office? – if so – let them be Anathematised by the whole community –
> yea Woe! Woe! be upon them!!!![398]

In the event, despite the ample protection provided by Metropolitan police, the 17 July meeting ended in 'the most humiliating defeat suffered by the Poor Law Commissioners in Huddersfield'. A clerk was not even nominated, the reason being as one Whig Guardian 'frankly confessed', 'No person dare name one!' The mobilisation of popular opposition backed up by the threat of violence, and its controlled use, alongside the strategic use of administrative resistance effectively delayed the implementation of the Act in Huddersfield.[399] In Felix Driver's assessment, the local anti-poor law campaign 'proved remarkably successful', and although there are dangers in interpreting the reports of local Whig correspondence to the Home Office too literally, it is clear that the chief local radicals played a central role in orchestrating both strands of oppositional activity.[400] This continued into 1838, when the ratepayers made interim arrangements to collect poor rates and keep the town's accounts.[401] Indeed, Katrina Navickas suggests that such 'Administrative resistance … was arguably much more important, and actually more effective, than popular violence against "bastilles".[402]

Events in Bradford the previous year had thrown into focus some of the dilemmas faced by radical leaders in relation to direct action and reopened earlier divisions. When Power met the Guardians in late October 1837 with a view to introducing the Act in Bradford he was faced with a hostile crowd, aware of the Huddersfield victory,

---

398 TNA: HO 52/35, Ellice to Russell, 8 June 1837, (see also J. Sutcliffe to Joseph Hume, 7 June 1837); Armitage to Russell, 17 June 1837; Edsall, *The Anti-Poor Law Movement*, p. 96; placard in TNA: HO 52/35, W. Moore to Home Office, 5 July 1837.

399 Edsall, *The Anti-Poor Law Movement*, p. 98; TNA: HO 52/35, Wrigley to Harewood, 17 July 1837.

400 F. Driver, 'Tory Radicalism?', p. 134. It took the autumn intervention of the Home Secretary to ensure that the minimum requirements of the 1834 Act were finally met.

401 *LT* 4 Apr. 1833; 9 Apr. 1836 (S. Sunderland, collector); *LM* 4 Feb. 1832 (Gillet Sharp, overseer); *LT* 25 Mar. 1837, *NS* 7, 21 July 1838.

402 Navickas, *Protest*, p. 159.

who refused to allow the meeting to proceed. After being confronted by Peter Bussey urging him to go home: 'we don't want you', Alfred Power was pelted with mud and stones and forced to run. For the next meeting, on 20 November, the magistrates took elaborate precautions but could not prevent, or perhaps helped to cause, a major riot which ended in a pitched battle between the crowd and the Guardians' military escort.[403]

Reactions to the violence are revealing. The Whig-liberal *Bradford Observer* alleged that there was no evidence of any deep-rooted opposition to the poor law before the disturbance and insinuated that the soldiers had been partly to blame. Certainly, the military commanders were unhappy about billeting arrangements in the town and displayed some uncharacteristic uncertainty about their troops' morale and equanimity. The moderate elements within the local radical leadership appeared genuinely shocked by the disturbances. Thomas Cliff, writing from the World's End Inn in Bradford, deprecated the violence and urged people to concentrate on their moral power. Similar sentiments were voiced by other leading figures at a major public meeting in mid-December.[404] However, radicals who had been most prominent in anti-poor law activities earlier in the year were more equivocal. Bussey, for example, interpreted the unnecessary introduction of the military by the authorities as provocative, and Joseph Brook who 'was present during the whole of the disturbances' argued that the Riot Act should not have been read, that the military presence had provoked the confrontation and that, in any case, 'the chief part of the mischief … had been by boys'. John Douthwaite, a leading Owenite and an 'operative well known in the ranks of Radicalism', 'exhorted them to assert their rights morally and not physically, unless they were forced to it'. Significantly, when Feargus O'Connor praised the 'heroism' of the Bradford men and argued 'in the name of Justice, common sense and the five Radical principles', 'that part of the petition which expressed contrition for the late 'Battle of Bradford' should be expunged', he was supported by Bussey and the majority at the meeting.[405]

This may have been the final straw for Bull, who had helped to draw up the petition. In January the *Mercury* was reporting that he had written to Bussey saying that he was no longer willing to act with the radicals because they had turned all anti-poor law meetings into universal suffrage gatherings.[406] The radicals, however, were scarcely united. When Bussey wrote to the chair of the Bradford Guardians in early December requesting that two delegates attend their deliberations (as observers and reporters) he was publicly reprimanded by Samuel Bower and John Douthwaite who asked 'when and where he (Mr Bussey) received his authority from the working-classes of Bradford, to make such a proposition to the Board of Guardians?' Relationships within the radical camp were clearly becoming strained and when Squire Farrar spoke at radical meetings in early January he defended the 'Malthusian

---

403 On the Bradford riots, see Edsall, *The Anti-Poor Law Movement*, pp. 109-12; Peacock, *Bradford Chartism*, pp. 12-13; *BO* 2, 23, 30 Nov. 1837; Correspondence in TNA: HO 40/35 f. 51 ff.

404 *BO* 23 Nov.; *LT* 16 Dec. 1837. It is not clear whether this is the Thomas Cliffe (of Halifax).

405 *BO* 7 Dec.; *LT* 16 Dec.; *BO* 14 Dec.; *LT* 16 Dec. 1837.

406 *LM* 20 Jan. 1838; Knott, *Popular Opposition*, p. 163.

Radicals', urged minor differences to be forgotten, and recommended 'a union for all'. Support for the Canadians temporarily united all shades of radicalism, but fundamental differences of approach and emphasis remained within the radical leadership and may help to explain why opposition to the new poor law petered out earlier than in neighbouring areas.[407]

The Bradford evidence clearly demonstrates that the traditional radical agenda was never forgotten amidst the anti-poor law excitement. Throughout the campaign O'Connor and his network of local West Riding contacts continued to strengthen and develop the radical base and keep the suffrage question in the public mind. At the height of the early anti-poor law upsurge in spring 1837, the Keighley radicals met under David Weatherhead to petition for the full radical programme and a small but significant radical reform meeting was held at the end of the May Peep Green rally. By the end of the year, at the height of the petitioning campaign against the Poor Law Amendment Act, the 'Anti-Poor Law' and suffrage issues were often agitated in tandem.[408]

The analysis expressed at these meetings frequently tied the poor law issue into a far broader radical critique. Robert Sutcliffe, speaking at a Halifax 'Great Radical and Anti-Poor Law Meeting' in January 1838, believed that the Whigs stood in direct lineage with the oligarchic factions of 'times past' who had waged reactionary wars, compiled an enormous tax-eating debt and imposed the harsh Corn Laws. Their record spoke for itself:

> Their first act was the Reform Bill, by which the people were led to expect a redress of all their grievances, and after that, the next step of the Whigs was the passing of the Irish Coercion Bill. Next came the misnamed Poor Law Amendment Act... That was followed by the Combination or Conspiracies Act. The money monger, said he, could legally conspire as they pleased to undervalue labour, and crush the working-classes; but if they united for the protection of their labour, they were subject to transportation, as might be seen in the cases of the Dorchester Labourers, and the Glasgow Spinners.[409]

Purely anti-poor law meetings continued to be held, but in many of these the radical presence was often pronounced and throughout the area existing pockets of radical organisation and activity continued to develop.[410] Given this background, it is easy to see why and how, when the poor law agitation reached an impasse in early spring 1838, energies were readily re-directed towards attainment of the radical reform programme. Although it had special features, the anti-poor law campaign was

---

407 *BO* 7; 14 Dec. 1837; *NS* 13 Jan. 1838; Peacock, *Bradford Chartism*, p. 13.
408 *LT* 4 Mar.; 20 May 1837; see, for example, the Dewsbury RA, *LT* 25 Nov., 2 Dec. 1837.
   'Two-in-one' meetings were also held at Halifax, Almondbury, Elland and Stainland in early 1838.
409 *NS* 27 Jan. 1838.
410 See *NS* 6 Jan. (Gawthorpe, Clayton), 20 Jan. (South Crossland) and 27 Jan. 1838 (Holmfirth).

never an autonomous movement which was 'captured' by O'Connor and the radicals; it had always, partly at least, been theirs from the start.

Nor did these same radicals give up their interest in the poor law and factory reform issues when Fielden's motion in February 1838 was defeated and political radicalism assumed primacy. In Huddersfield, Dewsbury and Halifax the radicals took the lead in selecting and attempting to secure the election of anti-poor law Guardians. Four out of the five Huddersfield Guardians were radicals and the four successful Dewsbury Guardians had all been chosen by the local RA.[411] Both places became the focus of anti-poor law activity in the West Riding during spring and summer of 1838. Elsewhere the radicals were less successful. At Halifax and Bradford the pro-poor law majority was retained, and generally results were 'disappointingly inconclusive'. Bussey at Bradford, despairing of the futility of petitions, sought to instigate a new tactic – the mass refusal of poor rates; but his campaign met with a weak response. A major town anti-poor law meeting three weeks later, including an 'impressive array' of radical talent, failed to attract a large turn-out and led the hostile *Bradford Observer* to comment on the weakness of the opposition to the poor law in the area.[412]

The *Observer's* judgement, that this lack of response stemmed from the fact that the workings of the new poor law had been seen not to be oppressive, may have been premature. However, the fact that the new legislation was not living up to its advance publicity, and the lack of any real progress by opponents or provocative actions by advocates, certainly helped to deprive the issue of some of its urgency. The increasing absorption of radical energies in a variety of campaigns, both local and national, also took away some of the driving-force behind the movement. For a year or more the poor law question had been the most important single issue upon which O'Connor and many local radical leaders agitated. However, other concerns and the traditional radical programme had never been forgotten. Increasingly after the short, bitter winter campaign of 1837-8, the poor law became just one of a number of evils which could only be remedied by the achievement of parliamentary reform. As a *Northern Star* editorial put it in June 1838:

> The London Journals are in error when they suppose that, in the North, all agitation is directed against the New Poor Law Amendment Act. No; but it is the basis of a new Constitution, and therefore do we work the Battering-ram of discontent against it... The auxiliaries to this infernal law are the Factory system, the Rural Police, and the complete destruction of Trades' Associations which was the last remnant of power in the hands of the working-classes.[413]

The poor law issue provided the final proof, if such were needed, of the irreconcilable gulf between popular working-class radicalism and middle-class Whig-liberalism. The Whigs, particularly the 'Malthusian Radicals', were now, in Lawrence

---

411 *NS* 31 Mar. 1838.
412 Edsall, *The Anti-Poor Law Movement*, p. 171; *NS* 14, 28 Apr., 12 May 1838 (for Bussey and his complaints); *NS* 9 June, *BO* 7 June 1838.
413 *NS* 23 June 1838.

Pitkethly's view, more dangerous because they were more deceitful than the Tories. Despite their professions of liberality, they still passed 'hateful and diabolical' laws. The opposition which Pitkethly and fellow radicals encountered locally from Whig-liberal apologists for the new law only served to provide a final twist to the spiral of bitterness and class antagonism which had been set in motion during the reform crisis.[414]

West Riding Chartism inherited something of its distinctive tone and direction from the anti-poor law movement. The abject failure of the campaign's mass petitioning efforts of late 1837 and early 1838 to achieve so much as an echo in parliament helps to explain why few West Riding leaders ever held out much hope for the Chartist National Petition and why some were early advocates of 'physical-force' sentiments. The first recommendations for the people to arm came from the anti-poor law platform; and, as late as summer 1838, Bradford discussions about friendly societies' participation in Queen Victoria's coronation celebrations were thrown into turmoil by Michael Scholefield's (Ancient Forester and Chartist) assertion that the people of Clayton were arming themselves against the Poor Law Amendment Act.[415]

The threats of direct action and the sense of imminent confrontation which marked Chartism's early years also owed much to the anti-poor law campaigns. Strong threads of moral righteousness and of communal solidarity, and a violent, menacing rhetoric, were also shared by both movements. This last area of overlap was not solely the result of Joseph Rayner Stephens' adherence to the early Chartist cause; it also had a strong radical dimension. The constitutional right to resist unjust impositions was part and parcel of the radical tradition. Although orators such as Oastler and Stephens, with their religious imagery and appeals to traditional rights, extended the scope and vocabulary of violent rhetoric, the language they spoke shared much in common with the overtly threatening, blood-curdling discourse of the Jacobin tradition, expressed in the speeches of local working-class leaders such as William Rider, Peter Bussey and George White.

For them, the poor law agitation was merely the latest, most intensively organised and supported of a series of overlapping campaigns which they had orchestrated since the passing of the Reform Bill. It provided a further sphere in which they might exercise their speaking talents, expand their network of contacts, refine their models of organisation and sharpen their political analysis. This critique was informed by a lingering perception of betrayal and, increasingly, a shared sense of separate class identity. In the later words of a Bradford operative, Edmund Whitney: 'When they (the Radicals) had attended Whig meetings, Mr. Byles [editor of the liberal *Bradford Observer*] had called them "gentlemen", but when they held meetings of their own, Mr. Byles called them "the shirtless, shoeless, penniless portion of the community".[416]

Working-class leaders increasingly weaponized such alleged slurs in local conflicts. The fight for the vote, drawing some of its early passion and support from the anti-poor law struggle, became the most important of these. As Frederick Engels

---

414 *NS* 6 Jan. 1838; for local antagonism see, TNA: HO 52/35, Ellice to Russell, 8 June 1837;
   W. Moore to Lt. Col. Maberley, 16 June 1837.

415 *BO* 21 June 1838.

416 *BO* 14 Feb. 1839. Edmund Whitney (1792?-1855?), born in Leicestershire, was probably a woolcomber, at this time.

retrospectively noted, 'there is but one voice among the workers – the voice of hatred against the new [poor] law. The bourgeoisie has formulated so clearly in this law its conception of its duties towards the proletariat, that it has been appreciated even by the dullest... Hence it is that this new Poor Law has contributed so greatly to accelerate the labour movement, and especially to spread Chartism'.[417]

---

417 F. Engels, *The Condition of the Working Class in England* (first published Leipzig, 1845; Panther Books, London, 1972 edn.) p. 316, quoted in Knott, *Popular Opposition*, p. 129.

7

Early Chartism

He was charged by his mill-master with having a little more knowledge than most of his fellow workmen; and in the eyes of a mill-master that is a crime of no small degree. Well, how was he situated in order to get this knowledge? He lived in a cellar, nine feet by seven. *This dwelling was his workshop, his bed-room, his kitchen, his study*; AND NOT UNFREQUENTLY HIS HOSPITAL. Could any man live thus and not 'acquire knowledge'. Was he to close his eyes to the fact, that while he was obliged to toil in such a position, the fruit of his labour was filched from him, and splendid mansions arose in every direction around him, inhabited by those that mock him with their expressions of sympathy?[1]

The recollections are those of George Flinn, a Bradford woolcomber and leading conspirator in the Chartist rising of January 1840, reflecting half a decade later on the physical environment in which he lived, worked and cogitated. Such testimony serves as a reminder of the social awareness, sense of injustice and raw passion, which fired the ideas and actions of early Chartist leaders. Its clarity and immediacy also help to explain why, in Gregory Claeys' words, 'Chartism remains one of the best studied – and controversial – areas of British labour history'.[2] Although the volume of scholarship has not regained the 'industrial' levels of the 1970s and 1980s, Chartist

---

1   *NS* 3 May 1845, George Flinn, quoted in Malcolm Chase, *Chartism: A New History* (Manchester: Manchester University Press, 2007), p. 22. On Flinn, see A. J. Peacock, *Bradford Chartism, 1838-40* (York: St Anthony's Press, 1969), pp. 42 and 48.

2   Gregory Claeys, *Citizens and Saints: Politics and Anti-Politics in Early British Socialism* (Cambridge: Cambridge University Press, 1989), p. 208.

history continues to be refreshed and extended by new avenues of research.[3] Meanwhile, Chartist historiography retains a niche interest, not least because of its stint on the frontline of skirmishes between structuralists and postmodernists during the latter years of the twentieth century.[4]

This initial overview does not seek to go over that well-tilled ground in any detail, but rather to summarise some of the different approaches which have informed interpretations of Chartist endeavours. First among these are the 'trade cycle' narratives which view Chartism primarily as a response to hunger and socio-economic dislocation. These formed a mainstay of early Chartist historiography and also influenced some later writing.[5] The second category comprises the host of local studies that have been the bedrock of Chartist scholarship ever since Asa Briggs nudged research in that direction in 1959.[6] Sustained by the enthusiasms of local heritage organisations and part-time researchers, as much as by full-time academics, they remain a pivotal component of our understanding of the movement and its wider connections.[7] As Katrina Navickas has noted much of the methodology of the new research on popular protest and collective action is 'predicated on regional or local studies'.[8]

The third element takes in both thematic overviews and the diverse collections of essays that have been a notable feature of the movement's historiography. Many of these consciously sought to move away from a primarily local focus and provide a 'newer and more flexible picture of Chartism'. Though often still drawing extensively

---

3   Tom Scriven, 'Slavery and Abolition in Chartist Thought and Culture, 1838-1850', *Historical Journal*, 65, 5 (2021), pp. 262-84; Emma Griffin, 'The Making of the Chartists: Popular Politics and Working-class Autobiography in Early Victorian Britain', *EHR*, 129, 538 (2014), pp. 578-605; Mike Sanders, *The Poetry of Chartism: Aesthetics, Politics, History* (Cambridge: Cambridge University Press, 2009).

4   Accounts of these controversies can be found in Miles Taylor, 'Rethinking the Chartists: searching for synthesis in the historiography of Chartism', *Historical Journal*, 39, 2 (1996), pp. 479-95; Katrina Navickas, 'What happened to class? New histories of labour and collective action in Britain', *Social History*, 36, 2 (2011), pp. 192-204; Andrew Messner, 'Land, Leadership, Culture, and Emigration: Some Problems in Chartist Historiography', *Historical Journal*, 42, 2 (1999), pp. 1093-4; Matthew Roberts, *Political Movements in Urban England, 1832-1914* (Basingstoke: Palgrave Macmillan, 2009): Peter J. Gurney, 'The Democratic Idiom: Languages of Democracy in the Chartist Movement', *Journal of Modern History*, 86, 3 (2014), pp. 568-70.

5   Mark Hovell, *The Chartist Movement* (Manchester: Manchester University Press, 1966, 3rd edn.); G. D. H. Cole, *Chartist Portraits* (London: Macmillan, 1965). It also informed Asa Briggs (ed.), *Chartist Studies* (London: Macmillan, 1959); and J. T. Ward, *Chartism* (London: Batsford, 1973).

6   Briggs (ed.), *Chartist Studies*. See also, Peacock, *Bradford Chartism*; Peter Searby, *Coventry Politics in the Age of the Chartists, 1836-48* (Coventry: Coventry Historical Association, 1964); David. J. V. Jones, 'Chartism in Welsh Communities', *Welsh History Review*, 6 (1972-3), pp. 243-61; Iorwerth Prothero, 'Chartism in London', *Past and Present*, 44, 1 (1969), pp. 76-105.

7   For example, Robert G. Hall, *Voices of the People: Democracy and Chartist Political Identity, 1830-1870* (Monmouth: Merlin Press, 2007); John A Hargreaves (ed.), *The Charter Our Right! Huddersfield Chartism Re-considered* (Huddersfield: Huddersfield Local History Society, 2018).

8   Navickas, 'What happened to class?', p. 197.

on local material they sought to utilise this to highlight particular aspects of Chartist ideology and culture, organisation and activity.[9] A pivotal contribution was Gareth Stedman Jones' exploration of 'The Language of Chartism'. With an emphasis on the primacy of language and its crucial role in shaping political ideas and identities, it is 'widely credited as the progenitor of the much discussed "linguistic turn" in social history'.[10] Its stress on continuity and the autonomy of politics from society posed a challenge to the grand narratives of many leading Chartist historians who 'interpreted radicalism and Chartism as the political expression of a working class that was conscious, in E. P. Thompson's words, of an "identity of … interests as between themselves, and as against other men"'.[11] In response, writers from a Marxian tradition, who emphasised the class-based nature of the movement, warned of an over-reliance on the printed word and argued for the fuller appreciation of the importance of visual, oral and symbolic elements within agitations and for a greater focus on the lived experience of communities.[12]

There followed what Peter Gurney called 'a protracted, often acrimonious controversy in which positions tended to become more and more ossified into simple choices between language and structure, consciousness and being, postmodernism and Marxism, the new and the outdated'.[13] The resulting impasse was partly resolved by attempts to reconcile these differing approaches through emphasising elements of commonality, notably the political rather than social or economic underpinnings of the movement and its national dimensions.[14]

A fourth component includes a range of newer studies that locate Chartism within the broader context of protest and popular politics or seek to reconnect Chartist

---

9   Thematic overviews include: Dorothy Thompson, *The Chartists: Popular Politics in the Industrial Revolution* (London: Breviary Stuff, 2013 edn.); Jutta Schwarzkopf, *Women in the Chartist Movement* (London: Macmillan, 1991). Key collections of essays include: James Epstein and Dorothy Thompson (eds.), *The Chartist Experience: Studies in Working-class Radicalism and Culture, 1830-60* (London: Macmillan, 1982); Owen Ashton, Robert Fyson and Stephen Roberts (eds.), *The Duty of Discontent: Essays for Dorothy Thompson* (Leicester: Leicester University Press, 1995); Owen Ashton, Robert Fyson and Stephen Roberts (eds.), *The Chartist Legacy* (Woodbridge: Merlin Press, 1999); Stephen Roberts (ed.), *The People's Charter: Democratic Agitation in Early Victorian Britain* (London: Merlin Press, 2003); Stephen Roberts (ed.), *The Dignity of Chartism: Essays by Dorothy Thompson* (London: Verso, 2015); Malcolm Chase, *The Chartists: Perspectives and Legacies* (London: Merlin Press, 2015).

10 Gareth Stedman Jones, 'The Language of Chartism', in Epstein and D. Thompson (eds.), *Chartist Experience*, pp. 3-58; Messner, 'Land, Leadership, Culture, and Emigration', *Historical Journal*, 42, 2 (1999), p. 1093.

11 M. Roberts, *Political Movements*, p. 45.

12 D. Thompson, 'The Languages of Class', *Bulletin of the Society for the Study of Labour History*, 52, 1 (1987) pp. 54-7; Neville Kirk, 'In defence of class: a critique of recent revisionist writing upon the nineteenth-century English working class', *International Review of Social History*, 32, 1 (1987), pp. 2-47; Paul A Pickering, 'Class Without Words: Symbolic Communication in the Chartist Movement', *Past and Present*, 112, 1 (1986), pp. 144-62; James Epstein, *Radical Expression: Political Language, Ritual and Symbol in England 1790-1850* (London: Breviary Stuff, 2014 edn.).

13 Gurney, 'The Democratic Idiom', p. 569.

14 Taylor, 'Rethinking the Chartists', pp. 482-6.

ideology, organisation and activism to the everyday social networks and culture of the working class in radical locales.[15] These approaches emphasise the significance of particular spaces and places to the history of protest and explore under-researched areas such as family, gender, morality and the practical politics of daily life. Equally they recognise the importance of studying 'what people did as well as what they said or wrote'.[16] In doing so they often foreground the private over the public, the informal over the formal, the intimate over the performative, the quotidian over the exceptional. Such bottom-up community-based perspectives provide a valuable corrective to text-rich metropolitan accounts.

A fifth element comprises the range of syntheses which sought to provide an overarching view of the movement. Whilst some of the best overviews and most valuable insights into Chartism traditionally came in short introductions to collections of documents, an 'all-embracing' narrative account was always lacking – a gap identified by Dorothy Thompson in her wide-ranging exploration of *The Chartists* in 1984.[17] It was not filled, however, until the publication of Malcolm Chase's nuanced and magisterial *New History* of Chartism in 2007.[18] Suitably updated, this provides a valuable synthesis of much of the material discussed above and has become an essential reference point for all students of Chartism.

The chapter which follows, though finite in its geographic and chronological scope, seeks to make a contribution to the wider debate about the nature and importance of Chartism. It argues that whilst Chartism came together as an identifiable entity in the summer of 1838, it was in fact a re-invigoration on a massive scale of a style of community-based radicalism and drew extensively on previous struggles and campaigns and on the leadership, organisational patterns and tactics which had been refined therein. However, it also developed new ways of organising and agitating. Combining these dual elements, it became the defining movement of a politically articulate and self-aware working class: the culmination of a decade of agitation and endeavour and the forerunner of later forms of political and industrial organisation.[19]

---

15 Katrina Navickas, *Protest and the Politics of Space and Place, 1789-1848* (Manchester: Manchester University Press, 2016); Hall, *Voice of the People*; Tom Scriven, *Popular Virtue: Continuity and change in Radical moral politics, 1820–70* (Manchester: Manchester University Press, 2017).

16 Iorwerth Prothero, *Radical Artisans in England and France, 1830-1870* (Cambridge: Cambridge University Press, 1997), p. 4.

17 For short introductions to Chartism, see Dorothy Thompson (ed.), *Early Chartists* (London: Macmillan, 1971), pp. 1-41; A. Wilson, 'Chartism', in J. T. Ward (ed.), *Popular Movements c.1830-1850*, (London: Macmillan, 1970), pp. 116-134; Edward Royle, *Chartism* (London: Longman, 1980), pp. 1-87; and Malcolm Chase, 'Chartism' in Mike Childs *et al.*, *Campaigning for Change: Lessons from history* (London: Friends of the Earth, 2017), pp. 41-52. One of the liveliest, impressionistic accounts of the movement, David J. V. Jones, *Chartism and the Chartists* (London: Allen Lane, 1975), evolved from an introduction to Chartist documents. D. Thompson, *The Chartists*, pp. 1-2.

18 Chase, *Chartism*.

19 Chase, 'Chartism' in Mike Childs *et al.*, *Campaigning for Change*, p. 52.

The West Riding textile district was always a Chartist stronghold. In the 'early' period it was arguably the pre-eminent Chartist region. During these years, when the aggregate of energies and experiences built up during a decade of near-constant activity was channelled towards the attainment of one prime objective, Chartism in the area enjoyed a potency and primacy which it never quite recaptured. This chapter seeks to build up a rounded picture of the various levels and forms of Chartist leadership, organisation and activity in this key Chartist region during the vital early years when the movement 'was characterised by a high degree of spontaneity along with a sense of imminent and decisive class confrontation.'[20]

After first mapping out the key landmarks of the early Chartist landscape, the chapter begins by looking at the emergence of Chartism and how the movement matted together various agitational and organisational strands. The central core of the chapter – a series of local studies – draws on and supplements existing accounts, and describes the distinctive features of early Chartist leadership, organisation and activity in each of the main textile centres.[21] It also seeks to present a more rounded picture by stressing the importance of Chartist activity in the numerous manufacturing villages and townships which dotted each locality.

The third section takes an overview of Chartist leadership and support in the West Riding. It identifies different levels of leadership and argues that whilst Chartism included a number of lower middle class leaders and in a sense became more 'professional', its cohesive strength resulted from the close identification which both 'established' and 'new' working-class leaders enjoyed with their local communities. The extent, variety and pervasiveness of Chartist support is also emphasised and illustrated by examining links with areas of working-class life (factories, trade unions and friendly societies) with which Chartist contact has traditionally been assumed to be fairly limited.

A number of writers have stressed the danger of too much attention being given to local differences and peculiarities, obscuring one of Chartism's most vital and distinguishing features – its regional and national dimensions.[22] The remaining sections seek to highlight the wider perspectives and common experiences around which this prototype national working-class party coalesced. Section Four looks at the informal and formal mechanisms which tied regional activities together and linked them to the wider national movement. Section Five explores, in the regional context, a number of early Chartist themes, relating to 'ulterior measures', the rhetoric of resistance, arming and insurrection; and to Chartist culture, class identification and

---

20 J. Epstein, 'Some Organisational and Cultural Aspects of the Chartist Movement in Nottingham' in, Epstein and D. Thompson (eds.), *Chartist Experience*, p. 221.

21 Particularly Peacock, *Bradford Chartism*; J. F. C. Harrison, 'Chartism in Leeds' in Briggs (ed.) *Chartist Studies*; G. R. Dalby, 'The Chartist Movement in Halifax and District', *Transactions of the Halifax Antiquarian Society* (1956), pp. 92-110. Dorothy and E. P. Thompson, '"The Dignity of Chartism": Halifax as a Chartist Centre', in Roberts (ed.), *The Dignity of Chartism*, pp. 73-124; Hargreaves (ed.), *The Charter our Right!*

22 For example, Gareth Stedman Jones, 'The Language of Chartism', in Epstein and D. Thompson (eds.), *Chartist Experience*, p. 9; D. Thompson, *Early Chartists*, p. 28; Phillip Howell, 'The local background of Chartism revisited: a note on the geography of popular politics in early Victorian Britain', *Area* 28, 2 (1996), pp. 150-9.

conflict with the middle-class. These are used to highlight the futility of using simple divisions like 'moral force' and 'physical force' to label Chartist leaders; to show the process whereby a movement which stressed open constitutionalism should become involved in arming and plotting; and to stress that 'insurrectionist' and 'cultural' endeavours were not necessarily incompatible alternatives for local Chartists. Finally, the last section emphasises that the early movement, drawing from its constituent strands and influences, was permeated by a strong sense of class. This involved a positive identification of common working-class interests, experiences and perspectives, but was also a product of the hostility shown to, and reciprocated by, an increasingly antagonistic middle-class.

The chapter as a whole argues that despite local variations in the level of support and activity and its failure to achieve its declared ends, early Chartism provided a vivid illustration of the capabilities of an increasingly confident and self-aware working class. Although the movement after 1840 lost some of its established local leaders and its earlier spontaneity, the tradition of community radicalism which the early movement built on and extended, and the experience of leadership and organisation which it provided, left a firm foundation for independent working-class political activity into the 1840s and well beyond.

Overview

The main contours of early Chartism in the West Riding can be mapped out briefly. The establishment of the *Northern Star* newspaper in Leeds in November 1837 was a major landmark. Printed and published by Joshua Hobson and edited by William Hill, it fulfilled a vital co-ordinating role in the regional and national movement and, whilst reporting on a wide range of campaigns, it always gave primacy to the radical programme. In the early months of 1838 this popular agenda was articulated in the localities by a number of Radical Associations and Working Men's Associations, many of which had maintained a continuous existence since the tours by O'Connor, Vincent and Cleave and the visits of local 'missionaries' in the preceding three years.[23] Many also stood in direct, if broken, line with radical political unions of the reform crisis era.[24] However, as Malcolm Chase has noted, 'In the spring and early summer of 1838 Chartism was a *mood* rather than a movement'.[25]

With the *Northern Star* firmly established as 'a major force in radical journalism' any sense of transience, however, soon dissipated.[26] The formation of the Great

---

23 Approximately twenty-five local associations were, or had recently been, in existence at the time of the floating of the GNU in early June 1838. The largest and longest-lasting were in the main towns of the region, but there were a number of smaller branch associations, especially in the Halifax area.

24 For example, a line can be traced from the Huddersfield PU of the early 1830s to the RA and NU branch of the middle and later years. Similarly in Leeds from the RRA (1830) to the RPU (1831-3), RA (1835-6), WMA (1837-8) and NU (1838-40); or in Bradford from the PU (1831?-3) to the Association of the Working-classes (1835), the RA (1835-8) and NU (1838-40). For continuity at Almondbury see below, p. 415.

25 Chase, *Chartism*, p. 35.

26 Ibid., p. 16.

Northern Union (GNU) in June 1838, though never more than a 'loose affiliation' and slow to catch on, was a significant turning point, with most of the major West Riding towns eventually adopting its designation and organisational framework.[27] By the end of summer and beginning of autumn 1838 a number of important strands had come together: the expansion of the GNU; the adoption of the Birmingham Political Union's National Petition and the London Working Men's Association's People's Charter at a series of meetings and dinners; the discussion of the 'forty-nine' (the 'National Convention') and a general quickening of the pulse of radical activity.[28] Serious anti-poor law disturbances in Dewsbury, victimisation of cotton spinners in Stalybridge and Oastler's emotional departure from Fixby Hall all added to an impassioned local atmosphere.[29] With talk of arming and physical force in the air and the first regional delegate meeting about to be called, many of the distinctive aspects of early Chartism in the textile district were already apparent.

The great West Riding rally held on Peep Green on Monday 15 October 1838 provided the *raison d'être* for this initial delegate meeting and a focus for much intensive local activity in the weeks which preceded and followed it.[30] Although some notable outside speakers, such as Feargus O'Connor, John Fielden and Joseph Rayner Stephens, addressed the gathering, the meeting itself was a proudly West Riding affair and included contributions from a number of established local leaders representing their radical associations and communities. These included Lawrence Pitkethly and George Barker (Huddersfield); Abram Hanson (Elland); Peter Bussey (Bradford); George White (Leeds); Thomas Todd (Dewsbury); Samuel Dickenson (Almondbury); Robert Wilkinson and William Thornton (Halifax); and Joseph Crabtree (Barnsley). As Malcolm Chase notes, the majority of the twenty-one speakers were working men. The meeting also elected five West Riding delegates – O'Connor, James Cobbett (son of William), Pitkethly, Bussey and William Rider – to represent the region at the 'General Convention of the Industrious Classes' in London.[31] With torchlight meetings commonplace in Lancashire (but less so in Yorkshire), arming openly

---

27 Ibid., p. 18; *NS* June–Sept. 1838.

28 The National Petition for universal suffrage and the six points of the Charter became the twin pillars of early Chartism. See Chase, *Chartism*, p. 19, for the adoption of the Charter in Dewsbury in July 1838. The limit of forty-nine delegates was in order to avoid prosecution under the Seditious Meetings Act of 1817,

29 On Oastler's departure and imprisonment for debt, see Alan J. Brooke, 'The Roots of Chartism in the Huddersfield Area *c.* 1826 to *c.* 1838', in Hargreaves (ed.) *The Charter Our Right!*, pp. 32-4; and Janette Martin, '"Oastler is welcome": Richard Oastler's triumphant return to Huddersfield, 1844', in John A. Hargreaves and E. A. Hilary Haigh (eds.) *Slavery in Yorkshire: Richard Oastler and the Campaign against Child Labour in the Industrial Revolution* (Huddersfield: University of Huddersfield Press, 2012), pp. 176-8.

30 See, for example, activity in the Bradford area, *NS* 13 Oct. 1838. In the month before and the two months after the Peep Green meeting NU branches were established (or planned) in seventeen localities in the Bradford area.

31 *NS* 6, 13, 16 Oct. 1838. Chase, *Chartism*, p. 30. The West Riding delegates decided in favour of having a local man, Robert Wilkinson of Halifax, to chair, in preference to a joint chair of Col. Thompson, John Fielden and Sharman Crawford. The choice of five West Riding delegates indicates early regional unity and organisation. The 'General Convention of the Industrious Classes' was most often referred to as the 'National Convention'.

advocated and government repression anticipated any day, the year ended on a peak of excitement and expectation.[32]

The Convention, the collection of signatures for the National Petition, and the raising of money for the 'National Rent' (a small levy to support the Convention) and for the defence of J. R. Stephens (arrested in late December 1838), provided the main foci of Chartist activity in the early months of 1839. Skirmishes with local Corn Laws repealers, further arming and fears of imminent repression occasionally injected heat into the local movement, and the West Riding Peep Green meeting on 21 May 1839, once again provided a major stimulus and focal point for organisation.[33] However, by this time attention and interest had moved back to the Petition, the Convention, and talk of what 'ulterior measures' to adopt if, as expected, Parliament rejected the Petition. Some time-honoured tactics such as exclusive dealing had already begun to be put into practice, and renewed efforts to spread the Chartist message and tighten up organisation nationally resulted in what Malcolm Chase called 'a remarkable flowering of popular political awareness unparalleled in any previous radical agitation'.[34]

Following disturbances and arrests in Lancashire and Birmingham (to where the Convention had moved in mid-May), and with supplementary delegates being elected in the West Riding in the expectation of further detentions, a new peak of excitement and intensity was reached in the middle of summer 1839.[35] The adoption of the 'Sacred Month', a general cessation of labour until the Charter became the law of the land, following Parliament's summary rejection of the Petition, added to the sense of expectation and imminent deliverance. Dewsbury radicals for a time met nightly at the Market Cross to read the latest newspapers and discuss grievances; whilst at Bradford local Chartists allegedly expected that the 12 August general strike 'would put them in possession of the fair share of everything the land produced'. The late abandonment of the sacred month and its replacement by a token three-day 'National Holiday' came as 'a sickener' to ardent supporters 'anxiously awaiting the arrival of the day of deliverance'.[36] A programme of activities was carried out on the designated days in areas of strong support or where labour was not under the direct supervision of local

---

32 On the 'profound sense of contemporary social bifurcation', the extent of arming and the unprecedented scale and profound impact of nocturnal meetings at this time, see Chase, *Chartism*, pp. 36-40.

33 *NS* 25 May 1839. Local speakers were Samuel Dickenson (Almondbury) in the chair, Thomas Vevers, Pitkethly, George Barker (Huddersfield); Samuel Healey (Dewsbury); Abram Hanson (Elland); Robert Sutcliffe, Benjamin Rushton, (Halifax); George White (Leeds); Joseph Crabtree, Peter Hoey, William Ashton (Barnsley), Peter Bussey, William Thornton, John Arran (Bradford).

34 Chase, *Chartism*, p. 65.

35 Six candidates contested the three possible vacancies (in case of the arrest of O'Connor, Bussey and Pitkethly) – Rushton of Halifax, Healey of Dewsbury, Vevers of Huddersfield, White of Leeds, John Jackson of Bradford and Peter Hoey of Barnsley – the first three were successful, *NS* 27 July 1839.

36 *NS* 20 July 1839; John Jackson, *The Demagogue Done Up: An Exposure of the Extreme Inconsistencies of Mr Feargus O'Connor* (Bradford, 1844) pp. 3 and 16, quoted in Chase, *Chartism*, p. 104.

employers; but the prevarication on the sacred month and the failure of the Convention were major blows to Chartist credibility and confidence.

Amidst continuing fear of arrest and, in a few places, planning for insurrection, parts of the movement went underground. Whether they still held out hopes of a single decisive blow for the Charter or whether they had accepted that its attainment would require a longer timescale and a more systematically organised movement, local leaders throughout the textile district continued to be involved in a broad range of local agitational endeavours, some visible others more shadowy. The general impression of decline and despondency in the autumn and early winter of 1839, however, is not totally a deception of the sources. The failure of the sacred month was undoubtedly a turning point, and in a few localities the Chartist flame all but went out. Ironically, one of the key factors in the re-emergence of mass political engagement was the tragic outcome, in early November, of the 'Newport Rising' in Wales; an event which in Malcolm Chase's words, 'culminated in the largest number of fatalities of any civil disturbance in modern British history'.[37] The campaign to save Frost and the other Chartist insurgents arrested after the failed rising re-kindled radical enthusiasm, re-activated local organisation and re-opened the channels of constitutional protest. The Newport affair, however, had other echoes in the West Riding. Simultaneous risings had been expected on 3-4 November in a number of West Riding localities and plotting continued into the harsh winter months.[38] The eventual insurgencies in two of the strongest early Chartist districts – Dewsbury on the night of 11-12 January and Bradford on 26-27 January – soon fizzled out and their failure can be taken as a convenient finishing point for the early phase of Chartism in the West Riding.

1: The Emergence of Chartism

As Malcolm Chase notes, the emergence of Chartism 'cannot be explained without reference to economic conditions at the time'.[39] However, it is difficult to synchronise precisely the deepening economic depression and the growth of radical activity or organisation. Even within a small region like the West Riding textile district there were important seasonal and local variations in the economic cycle. Equally, as Chase has argued, 'Hunger ... does not readily translate into a sustained political movement, supported by a dedicated press and its own professional agents and lecturers, and for the most part distinguished by self-restraint and discipline. Yet this exactly is what Chartism was.'[40] Clearly the existence of widespread distress, particularly amongst key groups like the textile outworkers helped rather than hindered the spread of radical sentiments in 1837-8, but it does not provide a comprehensive explanation. Political radicalism was far more than just a 'gut' response to economic stimuli. It had a rationale, a rhythm and a momentum of its own.[41]

---

37 Chase, *Chartism*, pp. 109-110.
38 Saving Frost, as well as gaining the Charter, became an object of all subsequent plots, see Peacock, *Bradford Chartism*, p. 35.
39 Chase, *Chartism*, p. 20.
40 Ibid.
41 The development of campaigns for the suffrage and other points on the radical political

This can be seen by looking more closely at the economic and political indicators during 1837-38. For example, the severity of the depression of spring 1837 did not immediately or directly invigorate radical organisation, though it may well have added extra urgency and support to the early anti-poor law protests. Equally, whilst the lingering impact of poor trade may have aided the radical advance of the summer, the main stimulus came from the General Election of July and August 1837, when the local economy was beginning to look up again.[42] The recovery of late summer and early autumn however was only partial, and by November the *Mercury* was reporting that all mills in the Bradford-Dewsbury district were again working short time and that weavers' wages were very low.[43] It is likely that the gloomy prospects for the winter ahead, coming on top of an unremunerative year, gave a boost to the spread of radical activity and organisation in the hard-pressed textile villages. Although there was some diminution of activity in some of the main centres, this radical base did not fade away in the relative recovery of spring and early summer 1838. West Riding Chartism was, in fact, floated at a time when the *Mercury* was reporting full-time working in Leeds and busy markets in Huddersfield.[44] The early expansion of autumn and early winter 1838 took place against a backcloth of tolerable employment and steady demand in many places. Economic factors played a significant part in the genesis of Chartism, particularly the cumulative effect of increasingly severe slumps and the dislocations caused by new technology and productive relationships. But a simple causal connection between economic hardship and political agitation is hard to demonstrate and obscures the important point that Chartism was the product of an increasingly literate, articulate and self-conscious working class.

The *Northern Star* provides ample evidence of the richness of oppositional culture and the diversity of radical concerns in the first half of 1838. Rather than being rivals competing for a limited amount of popular interest and support, the movements generated at this time tended to nurture and feed off each other. The Dewsbury area, for example, emerged as a centre of multi-faceted working-class activity. The 'Glasgow' protest meeting called by the local RA in late January 1838, chaired by David Sharpe, 'an intelligent working man', and held in the Methodist New Connexion school-room, was addressed by a range of speakers who may be classified in shorthand as 'radicals', 'socialists' and 'trade unionists'. In reality, however, they shared common attitudes to the 'protection of the working man's property', mutual antipathy to 'middle-class Government' and a shared belief in the necessity of universal suffrage to end such persecutions. The speakers related the Glasgow issue to the Poor Law Amendment Act, Dorchester and the destruction of the trades' unions, and the

---

programme were often linked to parliamentary or electoral factors, to perceptions of possibilities and to the failure of specific issue campaigns.

42 On the effects of the depression on trade on Dewsbury, Halifax and Leeds see, *LM* 6, 13, 20 May 1837. There are good reasons for allowing for a time-lag between the onset of short time working or unemployment and any 'political' responses. Because of the exhaustion of any savings or credit facilities individual families' distress might be at its height when general economic indicators were becoming more favourable again.

43 *LM* 4 Nov. 1837.

44 For example, *LM* 21 July 1838. As always, though, generalisation is difficult; trade in Dewsbury was very flat at this time.

meeting did not break up before Joshua Hobson had given a first-hand account of events that day at the Huddersfield Board of Guardians' meeting.[45] The Dewsbury RA, in fact, took a leading role in the local Board of Guardian elections in March and in popular demonstrations against the new poor law later in the year, though it never lost sight of its founding principles. At Easter, for example, it organised a public meeting and dinner in favour of the five radical points attended by many major local and regional leaders; an event which confirmed its role as the focal point of radicalism in the district.[46]

In the coarse woollen-weaving centre of Elland, where 'the Radical cause' was reported to be 'in a very flourishing way' in April 1838, local activity included formal RA meetings on the new poor law and Glasgow; the establishment of a radical school and a female Radical Association; and the holding of religious services and debates with local 'socialists'.[47] Elsewhere, though not quite as vigorous, political activity and organisation made steady progress in the first half of the year. New Associations were formed in Queenshead (January), Crossland Moor, Mirfield, Birstall (March) and Heckmondwike (May).[48] The Bradford and Halifax RAs continued to meet, though fairly infrequently, and a number of the outlying branches like Midgely, Mount Pellon and Ovenden were reported to be flourishing. At Mount Pellon in April, for instance, three sermons preached by Benjamin Rushton, William Thornton and Jonathan Bairstow of Queenshead raised money for the RA's adult school.[49] Even in apathetic Leeds the WMA was reported to be doing well and combining all the useful features of Mechanics' Institutes and Political Unions. When the town finally stirred itself to receive the Glasgow delegates, O'Connor took the opportunity to announce his Great Northern Union scheme.[50]

Yet, as well as new radical plans, older concerns also re-emerged in early 1838. Handloom weavers' committees in Keighley and Hebden Bridge reported on areas of extreme distress, and in Leeds and Dewsbury committees were formed to collect evidence for the Royal Commission.[51] The return of the transported 'Dorchester victims' was celebrated by Addresses produced by Eli Crabtree in Halifax and the female radicals of Elland. Their repatriation also stimulated plans for a large-scale tour to publicise the Glasgow case.[52] With a Parliamentary Select Committee of enquiry imminent, trade union matters were particularly prominent.[53] In Dewsbury a meeting

---

45 NS 3 Feb. 1838.
46 NS 24, 31 Mar., 21 Apr. 1838. The sixth radical point incorporated in the Charter was equal electoral districts.
47 On radical activity in Elland, see NS Jan. - Apr. 1838.
48 NS 20 Jan., 24, 31 Mar., 9 June 1838.
49 NS 21 Apr., 5 May 1838.
50 NS 3; 17 Mar. 1838.
51 NS 27 Jan.; 17, 24 Mar.; 21 Apr. 1838.
52 NS 31 Mar., 14 Apr. 1838. On the tour plans, see James Epstein, 'Feargus O'Connor and the English Working-class Movement, 1832-41: A study in national Chartist leadership', Unpub. PhD Thesis, University of Birmingham, 1977, p. 193.
53 See, for example, NS 24, 31 Mar., 14 Apr. 1838 (particularly discussion of the Bury 'Trades' Council' scheme). On fears that the Select Committee would lead to a new attack on unions, see Malcolm Chase, *Early Trade Unionism: Fraternity, Skill and the Politics of Labour* (London:

of 'handloom weavers and others' which formed a committee to collect information for the Handloom Weavers' Commission also established a 'Trades' Union ... to be called the Dewsbury United Trades' Society. A Committee was appointed to manage the business of the society, and to correspond with the Trades' Committee of London, that is appointed to conduct the enquiry into Trade Combinations'. Although it is unlikely that the United Trades' Society attained any permanency or strength, the floating of the scheme – probably on the wave of enthusiasm generated by the crowded meeting which received the Glasgow delegates the previous Tuesday – serves as a caution against underestimating the trade union component in the Chartist take-off.[54]

When the factory question revived briefly in late spring and early summer, radicals were everywhere to the fore. The *Star* reported prosecutions for overworking, and amidst rumours of a new Factory Bill to repeal Althorp's Act, urged the operatives to, 'agitate! agitate! agitate! for short hours, and a moderate day's work for a good day's wages!'[55] The Bradford men unfurled the ten hours banners once more and elected a new STC. Their public meeting included familiar Anglican and Tory supporters but also some notable radicals in Joseph Brook, a 'humble operative', who urged an eight-hour-day, William Hill and, most interestingly, Peter Bussey, whose accession to the factory reform platform was greeted with very loud cheers. His speech connected the issue to the new poor law and resurrected the themes of over-production and adult hours:

> I suppose it will be desirable, if we can manage a Ten Hour Bill for the children, to look after a Ten Hour Bill for you weavers and combers? (hear, hear.) You work too long ... If we could effect this for children, and then obtain a Ten Hour Bill for you adults (hear, hear), you would ... work less and be better paid, and the market would never be overstocked, for you would consume three times as much as you do now if you were in a proper condition [56]

Elsewhere the radical complexion of the agitation was even more pronounced. Meetings at Keighley and Elland were held in RA rooms and comprised radical speakers only. At Huddersfield familiar figures such as William Stocks jnr., Lawrence Pitkethly, James Brook and Robert Buchanan were also prominent, and at Leeds William Rider, George White and Fergus O'Connor gave the keynote speeches.[57]

Breviary Stuff, 2012 edn.), pp. 151-2.

54 *NS* 24 and 17 Mar. 1838. There is no mention of the society after *NS* 31 Mar. 1838, though it may have formed the basis of a blanket weavers' union which flourished in the summer, *NS* 18 Aug. 1838. Chase, *Chartism*, pp. 1 and 5, highlights the role of trade unions in the pivotal Glasgow Green meeting of 21 May 1838.

55 For example, *NS* 21 Apr. 1838 (it is likely that these resulted from information laid by still active STCs or ten hours caucuses); *NS* 28 Apr. 1838.

56 *NS* 5 May, *BO* 3 May 1838.

57 *NS* 5 May; 12 May; 23 June 1838. J. T. Ward, *The Factory Movement, 1830-1855* (London: Macmillan, 1962), p. 203, hardly mentions these meetings.

Radicals also used Queen Victoria's coronation in June 1838 as an opportunity to put across their message and ruffle the feathers of their local middle-class adversaries. A 'numerous body' of Huddersfield radicals carried out their intention to disrupt the singing of the national anthem with alternative anti-poor law verses.[58] Peter Bussey attended the respectable public meeting to plan celebrations in Bradford, but his proposals for any Address to be approved by the town's inhabitants and for a general subscription to erect almshouses for orphans and widows were both defeated. Michael Scholefield of Clayton, attending a friendly societies' delegate meeting in Bradford as a representative of a local Ancient Foresters' Court, fared little better. He attacked the absurdity and wickedness of celebrating the coronation whilst poverty was so prevalent but only succeeded in getting himself disowned and expelled from the meeting.[59] At Halifax radical delegates planned to celebrate the coronation with a meeting on national distress and the resolutions of the Great Northern Union.[60] At Dewsbury and Keighley local radicals disrupted respectable planning meetings – and the resulting procession in Keighley was allegedly 'pitiful'.[61] The new Leeds NU branch contented itself with resolutions against the processions, and the Huddersfield Socialists put on a rival tea-party and meeting.[62] Here as elsewhere, though, it is likely that they were fighting an uphill battle in seeking to achieve working-class abstinence from popular celebrations and conviviality. Evidence from Elland, and possibly Bradford, points to the likelihood that a number of radical sympathisers within friendly societies took a full part in the coronation festivities.[63]

The radicals were able to carry more of their natural supporters with them in their adoption of the case of Bridget Cone, a pregnant young Irishwoman who was allegedly beaten up by a Leeds policeman and dealt with harshly by Justice Clapham in the Leeds courts. The issue quickly evoked a substantial local and regional response and helped to maintain radical interest and organisation in the comparative lull between the withering of the anti-poor law and factory agitations and the floating of the GNU. Following O'Connor's lead, radicals throughout the Riding held meetings, passed resolutions, formed committees and started subscriptions for the 'Clapham Justice Fund'. By the middle of July subscriptions were still coming from as far away as Manchester and Nottingham. Indeed, it was not until the following summer that the case was declared lost and the monies redirected into the Stephens Fund.[64]

---

58 *LT* 30 June; *HG* 23 June 1838 cited in Brooke, 'The Roots of Chartism', p. 30.

59 *BO* 7, 21; *NS* 23 June 1838. Michael Scholefield (1802-1870?) was an Irish-born shoemaker.

60 *NS* 9 June 1838.

61 *NS* 23 June; 7 July 1838. There were also disruptions at Horbury near Wakefield, where local radical banners proclaimed universal suffrage.

62 *NS* 23 June; 7 July 1838.

63 *NS* 21 July 1838 (Richard Grassby's letter). Popplewell, the chairman of the Bradford friendly societies' meeting (*NS* 23 June 1838), may have been a radical, see *LT* 2 Dec. 1837.

64 For details of the case and early meetings at Stainland, Elland and Dewsbury see *NS* 2, 16 June 1838. The cause was also taken up by radicals at Halifax, Keighley, Paddock, Honley, Hebden Bridge and Ambler Thorn. *NS* 9-30 June 1838. For Manchester and Nottingham, see *NS* 21 July 1838 ('To Readers'). The recommendation to transfer the money to the Stephens Fund is in *NS* 6 Apr. 1839.

As well as showing his concern for the welfare and support of a compatriot, O'Connor's adoption of the Bridget Cone case also demonstrates the sureness of his political touch. The episode, with its potent combination of elements – police brutality, class bias, injustice and an Irish dimension – provided just the right sort of issue to act as a temporary focus and stimulus for radical activity and organisation. It also again illustrates the breadth of O'Connor's and local radicals' concerns in the first half of 1838.[65]

O'Connor in particular was the epitome of radical energy and creativity during this period. Not content with his *Northern Star* outselling all other West Riding papers, he planned to start a new radical daily paper, the *Evening Star*. He also appeared frequently at radical dinners and anti-poor law meetings and was the source of a stream of agitational initiatives and ideas.[66] At the local level the catholicity of his approach is demonstrated by his appearance at a meeting of the beersellers of Leeds and the surrounding towns and his attendance at a joint meeting of the Leeds stuff-weavers and their masters to organise evidence for the Handloom-weavers Commission.[67] As well as the commercial and leadership benefits to be derived from simply showing his face and widening his circle of contacts, both instances also demonstrate O'Connor's concern to broaden the base and appeal of popular radicalism in Leeds.

West Riding radicals were always worried about Leeds. The *Northern Star* of September 1838 spoke of 'those reproaches so frequently and so justly heaped upon' 'the heretofore enslaved men of Leeds'. Throughout the 1830s the town's radicalism was notorious for being weak and divided.[68] O'Connor, speaking at a 'Great Political Meeting' on universal suffrage and the Canadians in early January 1838, mentioned how 'a very short time ago, the men of the west ward had one political creed – the men of Holbeck another – and the men of Leeds another'. With Leeds now his West Riding base, O'Connor sought to change this situation. He claimed at the meeting that 'the three dimensions are now united, and we have only one political creed'.[69] Although a large dose of wishful thinking played a part in this assertion, he made strenuous efforts to placate and unite the different strands of working-class and lower middle-class radicalism. In April 1838, for example, both the *Star* and the Leeds WMA praised 'the good men of Holbeck' who 'have at length discovered the treachery of their Whig leaders'; and the *Star*'s selection (which was criticised in some quarters) of William Molesworth, the 'radical' victor in Leeds in 1837, as a subject for one of its giveaway miniature portraits in July 1838 can also be interpreted as part of a continuing attempt to woo the Holbeck operatives and some of their lower middle-class allies.[70] The vigorous early life of the Leeds Great Northern Union (GNU) branch suggests a degree of temporary success for this strategy. However, as the

---

65 Anti-police sentiment remained strong throughout the early Chartist period and beyond; see Chase, *Chartism*, pp. 81-3 and 99 and Navickas, *Protest*, pp. 141-8.

66 See Epstein, 'Feargus O'Connor', pp. 173 ff.

67 *NS* 31 Mar.; 21 Apr. 1838. Bussey also spoke at the beersellers' meeting.

68 *NS* 15 Sept. 1838; *LT* 13 June 1835; *NS* 17 Feb. 1838.

69 *NS* 13 Jan. 1838.

70 *NS* 21 Apr., 4 Aug. 1838.

disappointing turn-out for the October Peep Green meeting was soon to demonstrate, Leeds still had a long way to go to kill off its reputation for apathy and disunity.

The 'Great Northern Union' title adopted in Leeds was itself far from new.[71] Its resurrection in the early Chartist period can be traced back to late 1837 when O'Connor first mentioned a scheme for establishing 'a great political union' in Yorkshire and Lancashire. The idea began to take firm root in Spring 1838 after O'Connor had pledged himself to set up a 'great Northern Union' in Leeds. He spoke to the Leeds WMA about the scheme in April and suggested a four-day Conference of Lancashire and Yorkshire delegates in Leeds. Nothing came of this suggestion but a local committee was established to draw up the objects, rules and regulations of the union. This worked quickly and in early June, with George White and William Rider having done much groundwork, the union was launched in Leeds.[72]

Although the inaugural Hunslet Moor meeting to launch the new organisation was a success, the GNU concept and moniker did not immediately catch on. It was six weeks before the Leeds WMA and GNU formally decided to join together under the GNU title and no other associations had affiliated in this time.[73] The first area to move was Halifax, which established a GNU branch and adopted the Birmingham petition at a meeting in late July. Barnsley and Stalybridge followed suit, but the *Star* was certainly indulging in chicken-counting when it claimed in early August that the GNU had 50,000 members.[74] For example, it was not until September that branches were formed in Bradford and Huddersfield. Some areas never embraced the new title and retained their old nomenclature; but they nevertheless felt themselves part of the same wider movement and it is likely that their members were included in the *Star*'s more realistic estimate of 56,000 GNU members in December 1838.[75]

On the surface the GNU was not an outstanding success. It lasted a relatively short time and never really established itself beyond its West Riding heartland. As Epstein has rightly said, 'to some extent the GNU merely superimposed a new label upon existing radical and anti-Poor Law associations'. However, its general significance and influence outweighed its actual membership or affiliations. In the first place, it helped to consolidate O'Connor's leadership in the north. Secondly, it tied the northern associations more closely and formally to the National Petition, the Charter and the plans for the Convention. Thirdly, and perhaps most importantly, it 'fostered a sense of identity and allegiance which went beyond the immediate Chartist locality…'[76]

In the West Riding the timing of the new organisational framework was particularly important. It gave a boost, a sense of direction and purpose to existing

---

71 For Henry Hunt's 'GNU' plan and its adoption in 1831-2 see John Belchem, 'Radicalism as 'Platform' Agitation in the periods of 1816-21 and 1848-51: with special reference to the leadership of Henry Hunt and Feargus O'Connor', Unpub. D.Phil thesis, University of Sussex, 1974, p. 173 ff. Leeds, under James Mann, was one of the strongest supporters of what was essentially a money-raising scheme to get a Radical elected to Parliament.

72 On the establishment of the GNU see Epstein, 'Feargus O'Connor', pp. 191-5 and *NS* 17 Mar., 25 Apr., 5 May, 9 June 1838.

73 *NS* 14 July 1838.

74 *NS* 28 July; 4 Aug. 1838.

75 *NS* 8, 15, 29 Sept.; 22 Dec. 1838. Places such as Halifax always retained their RA title.

76 Epstein, 'Feargus O'Connor', p. 194.

organisations at a time when energies were flagging or were being dissipated in a profusion of concerns. Radical organisation was hardly flourishing in many of the main West Riding towns during the early summer of 1838. In Leeds the *Star* admitted that before the GNU meeting 'we had nearly despaired'.[77] In Bradford the splits between the ultra-radicals (including Bussey) and the socialist-radicals (for example, Samuel Bower and John Douthwaite), which had been exposed at the turn of the year, appear to have widened. The socialists went from strength to strength as the RA declined. Whilst denying the *Mercury*'s claim that the RA was almost defunct, the *Star* admitted in May that 'the members of the association have, to a considerable extent formed themselves into a branch of the Socialists ... [who] proclaim themselves to be the true Radicals; they strike at the root of all the evils, political and otherwise'.[78]

The story of the relationship between Owenite socialists and Chartists is complex and at times obscure. As Gregory Claeys observed in 1989, 'Owenite Studies' have never matched the vigour and scope of their Chartist equivalent.[79] Detailed local investigations remain thin on the ground.[80] The evidence that is available for the late 1830s suggests that the tensions occasionally evident in Bradford and Huddersfield were not widely replicated. Relations between the two groups were often cordial and close. There are dangers of projecting back into the preceding era the mutual suspicion and outright hostility that often characterised high-level interactions between the two bodies in the 1840s. At the grassroots level, as Edward Royle has stressed, things could look and feel very different.[81]

This was certainly the case in the period covered by this book. As we have seen, Owen's co-operative and economic ideas, suitably mediated and, in some cases, moderated by a number of key local radical and trade union leaders, found a ready audience in a number of the main centres of the district during the early 1830s.[82] This cross-over continued in the later part of the decade. Chartists and Owenites shared many cultural forms and associational practices: lectures, tea-parties, dances and debates.[83] Socialists provided Chartists with safe meeting places in Leeds, Halifax and Bradford, and, in Malcolm Chase's words, 'relationships between them in Huddersfield were close and mutually supportive'.[84] Huddersfield co-operators, meeting for the annual festival at their Social Institution on New Year's Eve 1837, toasted 'Feargus O'Connor and may the Principles of Radicalism advance'. Ten months later they

---

77 *NS* 9 June 1838.

78 Peacock, *Bradford Chartism*, p. 15; *NS* 12 May 1838.

79 Claeys, *Citizens and Saints*, p. 208.

80 Notable exceptions include, Simon J. Cross, 'The experience of Owenite Socialism and Anti-Socialism in Halifax, 1829-1845', *Transactions of the Halifax Antiquarian Society*, 15 (2007), pp. 91-111; and Alan J. Brooke's detailed account of the 'Huddersfield Hall of Science', available at https://undergroundhistories.wordpress.com/huddersfield-hall-of-science/ (accessed 1 Mar. 2023).

81 Edward Royle, 'Chartists and Owenites – many parts but one body', *Labour History Review*, 65, 1 (2000), p. 2.

82 See, for example, pp. 223-35.

83 *NS* 9 June 1838 (Halifax); 7 July 1838 (Huddersfield).

84 Chase, *Chartism*, p. 142; and 'Chartism in Huddersfield, the cultural dimension', in Hargreaves (ed.), *The Charter our Right!*, p. 68.

helped to defray the costs of the great Peep Green Chartist meeting. The following year, leading co-operators such as George Barker (a founder member of the Huddersfield NU) and James Matthewman were prominent speakers at an illegal Chartist meeting on 10 August, urging exclusive dealing and arguing that 'There was only one society in that town that had carried out the recommendations of the [Chartist] Convention'.[85]

At the leadership level the linkages were even more striking. A number of prominent figures, such as Samuel Bower and John Douthwaite in Bradford and Lawrence Pitkethly, Robert Buchanan and John Hanson in Huddersfield, initially straddled both camps without any difficulty or sense of incompatibility. According to Gregory Claeys, Pitkethly 'was recorded as advocating the Charter in order to gain the advantage of Socialism with political security, and noting that this was the only difference he and many other Chartists had with Owen'.[86] Connections were equally strong in Leeds. The wide range of radical activity (including socialism, co-operation, trade unionism and Christian radicalism) that the *Northern Star* reported may in part have been due to the eclectic interests of its editor (William Hill) and the Owenite sympathies of its publisher (Joshua Hobson) and bookkeeper (John Ardill).[87]

In general, the local evidence supports Gregory Claeys' provisional conclusion that 'In some towns, the Owenites and Chartists met on the same premises, and sometimes shared lecturers, social functions, and even leaders'.[88] They were, in the biblically-inspired phrase adopted in Edward Royle's account, 'many parts but one body'.[89] However, a few notes of caution may be in order. First, it is possible to exaggerate the influence of a few key leaders and the reach of Owenite organisation. Claeys estimates that the number of branches (thirty-three) and paying members (1,700) in 1838 had scarcely doubled nationally by the movement's highpoint two years later. Although West Riding towns, with Huddersfield pre-eminent, featured in the rapid expansion of Owenite socialist branches in this period, total numbers were generally not large and, as at Bradford, soon dwindled. The *Northern Star*, perhaps accurately, described it as a 'new sect'.[90] Second, notwithstanding the example of Queenshead, where a Socialist organisation flourished briefly in the summer of 1838, despite or perhaps because of a concerted Christian offensive, the main urban centres rather than the outlying manufacturing villages and out-townships formed the chief bastions of

---

85 *NS* 6 Jan. 1838, 5 Jan 1839; Robin Thornes, 'The origins of the co-operative movement in Huddersfield: the Life and Times of the 1st Huddersfield Co-operative Trading Association', in E. A. Hilary Haigh (ed.), *Huddersfield, A Most Handsome Town: Aspects of the History and Culture of a West Riding Town* (Huddersfield: Kirklees Cultural Services, 1992), pp. 183-4.

86 Claeys, *Citizens and Saints*, p. 233, citing *New Moral World*, 21 Dec. 1839. Pitkethly's son of the same name was a leading local Owenite. See, Brooke, 'Huddersfield Hall of Science', for a detailed discussion of the respective roles of father and son.

87 D. Thompson, *The Chartists*, p. 33; *NS* 21 July 1838 (for the allegation that 'Mr Hobson ... is a Socialist'). Not all *Northern Star* staff were sympathetic, Templeton, the paper's reporter, declared 'I am not a Socialist. I detest the principles of the system', *NS* 27 Oct. 1838

88 Claeys, *Citizens and Saints*, p. 241.

89 Royle, 'Chartists and Owenites'.

90 Claeys, *Citizens and Saints*, p. 250; p. 242 (citing Samuel Bower's testimony); *NS* 25 Apr. 1838.

Owenite socialism.[91] It is likely that Owen's views on marriage, religion, and property alienated many potential adherents in the Chartist heartlands. Here, communities that had recently rejected the new poor law as an attack on traditional family ties, associated Owenism with infidelism and looser familial bonds, and were fighting to protect the value of their labour, their only property. The fault lines were clear. As Edward Royle notes, 'socialists looked to communal ownership, radicals to individual property rights'.[92]

None of these potential barriers prevented local magistrates, such as Joseph Walker in Huddersfield, responding to the socialist advance in 1838 with habitual confusion and apprehension. Noting 'great dissatisfaction amongst the lower orders' he surmised that 'since Socialism has become so prevalent amongst them – they have become more reckless'.[93] The reverse is a more likely scenario. Gregory Claeys suggests that 'the events of 1839 – the spectre of revolution – led many Owenites to withdraw abruptly from politics'.[94] The limited evidence from the West Riding suggests that, while the growing influence of physical-force rhetoric may have put off potential allies amongst the socialists, the unmooring was more gradual and not total, and that specific local ruptures in leadership cadres had their origins well before the discussions of the sacred month and insurrection.[95]

Reciprocally, it is likely that the socialist upsurge following a spring and summer of proselytising in 1838 temporarily weakened radicalism in Bradford, and possibly elsewhere. Samuel Bower, writing in 1838, spoke of 'the friendly section' and the 'anti-Socialist section' amongst the Bradford Chartists.[96] Thomas Cliffe in Halifax, for his part, disparaged the 'new start-up sect' as a distraction from 'the glorious cause of Radicalism'.[97] Some tensions were inevitable, for as well as the evident free exchange of ideas, speakers and resources, Chartism and Owenism were also rivals competing for popular primacy and support.[98] Possibly as a result of these tensions or simply agitational fatigue, in Bradford and other centres, such as Halifax, Huddersfield and Leeds, a number of important working-class leaders who had been prominent in previous agitations withdrew or maintained a low profile as Chartist momentum built up from the autumn of 1838 onwards.[99]

The other key issue competing for radical attention was the implementation of the new poor law. Here the evidence is ambiguous. In Huddersfield and Keighley, for example, it is likely that the continuing anti-poor law activities significantly sapped

91 *NS* 21 July; 26 May 1838.
92 Royle, 'Chartists and Owenites', p. 4.
93 WYAS: HP, Box 1, Walker to Harewood 30 Dec. 1838.
94 Claeys, *Citizens and Saints*, p. 242.
95 See, for example, p. 486 below, for evidence of Chartists and Socialists collaborating in Leeds (Dec. 1839).
96 S. Bower, *The Peopling of Utopia* (Bradford, 1838), p. 4, quoted in Claeys, *Citizens and Saints*, p. 242.
97 *LT* 6 Jan. 1838.
98 Chase, 'Chartism in Huddersfield', p. 67.
99 See discussion of individual districts in Section 2 below.

radical energies.[100] The reverse, however, may have been true at Dewsbury where the previously flourishing Radical Association was near to collapse in early July 1838. It revived with new working-class members and leaders who discussed the People's Charter later in the month and received a great boost from the August anti-poor law disturbances and the wrongful arrest of one of its members the following month.[101] As so often, perceived persecution stimulated a vigorous response, and as radical momentum increased in the late summer and early autumn of 1838, the district became one of the strongest centres of Chartist support in the region.

The fact that the association of the Dewsbury district never formally adopted the NU title is unimportant.[102] The GNU initiative, through focusing concerns back on to the radical programme and the Charter, could not have been better timed. It facilitated the opportunity for a revival or fresh start where formal organisation had withered or had never got off the ground, and together with the Charter and the National Petition it provided an attractive and ready-made framework to draw outlying townships and villages into the agitational mainstream. This process of co-ordination and consolidation, so crucial to the emergence of Chartism, is confirmed by the reminiscences of John Bates, a local Queenshead Chartist who, sometime in the 1830s (probably 1837), had joined the Ambler Thorn RA, later to become the Queenshead RA. He recalls that 'we were then practically a branch of the Halifax Radical Association. There were similar associations all over the country but there was a great lack of cohesion. One wanted the ballot, another manhood suffrage and so on. We saw there was a great necessity for the formation of a national organisation'. With the publication of the Peoples' Charter in 1838, which clearly defined 'the urgent demands of the working classes, we felt we had a real bond of union; and so transformed our Radical Associations onto local Chartist centres'. This formality was gone through in early November 1838 when a torchlit meeting addressed by three Bradford leaders officially adopted the National Petition and enrolled members in the GNU.[103] Such meetings, held in the aftermath of the October Peep Green rally, were indicative of the broad direction of travel in the localities as the emergent Chartist movement gathered force in late 1838. However, to fully appreciate the contours of this upsurge it is necessary to examine developments in each of the main districts of the region.

---

100 See below, pp. 417-8.

101 *NS* 30 June, 7, 14 July, 18 Aug. 1838. There appears to have been conflict with local Whig-liberal former allies. On the Dewsbury disturbances, see *NS* 28 July - 15 Sept. 1838; N. C. Edsall, *The Anti-Poor Law Movement, 1834-44* (Manchester: Manchester University Press, 1971), pp. 155-7; and WYAS: HP, Box 1, 'Dewsbury Poor Law Riots, 1838'. On the case of Frank Dews, the arrested RA member, see *NS* 8 Sept. 1838 and 10 Mar. 1839, TNA: HO 40/51 ff. 17-21, Oldroyd to Russell, 4 Mar. 1839.

102 For the various titles used at the time of the Peep Green meeting, see *NS* 13 Oct. 1838.

103 Bates' account is taken from, 'A Chat with a Chartist', *Bradford Daily Telegraph* 7 Mar. 1895, and A. C. Carter, *John Bates, of Queensbury, the Veteran Reformer* (Queensbury, 1895), pp. 2-3; *NS* 10 Nov. 1838.

2: Local Studies

Chartism in many senses reflected the equivocal age in which it emerged: the widespread implementation of new technologies alongside expansion of traditional handicrafts; the advent of new means of communication in tandem with the proliferation of customary modes; fervent religiosity alongside widespread indifference and pockets of agnosticism; the articulation of new political and economic ideologies juxtaposed with the defence of traditional ideas and practices. It was also an era of rapid urban and industrial expansion fuelled by growing local and regional specialisation. For all its emerging national features, Chartism was still, in the words of Malcolm Chase, 'a movement wherein local and regional identities and particularities carried such force'.[104] It is important therefore to pay attention to the variations that existed within the textile district.

a) Leeds

Leeds Chartism has already been the subject of an extensive study.[105] The purpose of this section is not to go over the same ground, but to fill in some of the inevitable gaps in the narrative treatment of early Chartism and to suggest a more rounded interpretation of events in 1839.

Leeds, with its diverse occupational structure and its tradition of sectionalism in radical politics, was a relatively backward early Chartist centre. The town's reputation for apathy, which had haunted working-class leaders throughout the 1830s, was apparently confirmed by the poor turnout for the Peep Green meeting of October 1838.[106] All was not gloom, however. In late November the collection of the National Rent and the calling of the National Convention gave local Chartism a boost. The Leeds NU Branch, its numbers increasing rapidly, moved to the large School Room, on York Street where it held weekly meetings. After another good attendance at a branch meeting in mid-December the *Star* speculated, tongue-in-cheek, that Leeds might even become the leading democratic town in the West Riding![107] Collections for the National Rent continued but Leeds was never a large contributor, a fact noted by the more generous Barnsley radicals.[108] Local Chartists were also neither sufficiently numerous or strong to prevent a Whig-liberal meeting passing resolutions against the

---

104 Malcolm Chase, 'Building identity, building circulation: engraved portraiture and the "Northern Star"', in Joan Allen and Owen Ashton (eds.), *Papers for the People: A Study of the Chartist Press* (London: Merlin Press, 2005), p. 30.

105 Harrison, 'Chartism in Leeds' covers the whole Chartist period and focuses in particular on post-1842 municipal Chartism. His main source for the 'early' period is the radical *Leeds Times*. The study below draws chiefly on the *Northern Star*.

106 *NS* 13 Oct. 1838. According to the hostile *Leeds Mercury* 20 Oct. 1838, the factories stayed in and the Leeds contingent numbered just 500. The '200 people' who Harrison refers to, (in 'Chartism in Leeds', p. 76), attended a torchlight meeting on Hunslet Moor on the preceding Saturday.

107 *NS* 24 Nov., 1, 15 Dec. 1838.

108 *NS* 16 Feb. 1839. Only £3 had been collected by this time. The rebuke had had the desired effect for a further £20 was forwarded in early March.

Corn Laws in January 1839.[109] After William Rider had 'tramped it' down to London as one of the West Riding delegates, the proceedings of the Convention temporarily rekindled interest; and a major public meeting, held on Easter Monday and chaired by William Hill, editor of the *Star*, heard forceful speeches from O'Connor, George White, Rider and Dr. John Taylor of Scotland.[110] The event, though well attended, included numerous references to the previous apathy in the town. O'Connor sought to explain this 'appearance of indifference' in terms of the town's occupational structure. He had informed Dr Taylor:

> that though there were thousands of genuine Radicals in Leeds, the circumstances attendant on their respective employments, rendered it not so easy for them to make large displays at public meetings as could be done by smaller bodies of population who were not so thoroughly trammelled by social and commercial tyranny.[111]

Although disingenuous and optimistic, O'Connor's assessment was not without an element of truth. Certainly, in the weeks after the meeting Chartism in the town began to blossom. A burst of agitational activity in late spring and early summer in preparation for the May 1839 Peep Green meeting saw NU branches formed in many of the out-townships of the area. Although the *Mercury* asserted that there was no arming and that Chartism was ineffectual in Leeds, the authorities took the precaution of enrolling special constables and assembling the local yeomanry cavalry.[112] The Leeds response to the West Riding meeting, however, was again disappointing.

Hereafter the tempo, if not the temperature, of activity declined, leading the *Mercury* to allege that 'Chartism in Leeds, if ever it existed is rapidly dying away'.[113] The news of Chartists arrests and related disturbances in Birmingham and the presence of Bronterre O'Brien in Leeds temporarily aroused great interest and excitement in mid-July; and the arrest of two 'National Rent' collectors added to the 'atmosphere of rising tension'.[114] However, the local leadership was unable to maintain momentum and convert this energy into consistent support or manifestations of formal allegiance, such as paying regular subscriptions or attending branch meetings. William Rider admitted as much in July when he opposed the idea of a replacement National

---

109 *NS* 19 Jan. 1839.

110 *NS* 2, 16 Feb. 1839 and, editorial headed 'Leeds Shaking off her Slumber', *NS* 30 Mar. 1839. Dr John Taylor, one of the main architects of Scottish Chartism, was afterwards heavily implicated in insurrectionary plotting.

111 *NS* 6 Apr. 1839. O'Connor appears to be referring to the direct control wielded over their employees by the large, predominantly Whig-liberal manufacturers in the town, through the exercise of strict time and work discipline. Victimisation was also a constant threat; George White attributed the poor turn-out for the May Peep Green meeting to the operatives' fear of the sack, *NS* 29 June 1839.

112 *LM* 18, 25 May 1839; Harrison, 'Chartism in Leeds', p. 78.

113 *LM* 22 June 1839.

114 *NS* 13 July 1839. On the arrest of George White and John Wilson, see Harrison, 'Chartism in Leeds', pp. 78-9. Other local leaders feared arrest, see Illingworth's speech *NS* 29 June 1839. On the 'Bull Ring Riot', see Chase, *Chartism*, pp. 81-4.

Convention delegate for Leeds, because 'I know that the Chartists of Leeds are too poor, and too few in number to support a delegate'.[115]

The same inability to translate potential support into firm commitment, and the persisting residue of inertia and indifference, is also revealed in the local attitudes to the sacred month. Although placards advocating 'ulterior measures' had appeared on the town's walls in July, and the NU attempted unsuccessfully to organise exclusive dealing, in the event the Leeds Chartists contented themselves with marking the proposed start of the national holiday with a major public meeting on St Peter's Hill.[116] After the damp squib of the sacred month, local Chartism takes on a more sober and sect-like character and familiar jibes re-appear. A *Star* editorial commenting on the trial of the Welsh 'patriots' in December noted that, 'Even Leeds which is always a hundred miles behind every other place, is moving'.[117] The early history of the local movement ended as it had begun, with question marks against the town's commitment to the radical cause.

If the story of early Chartist endeavour in Leeds is fairly unspectacular and revolves around a constant battle to arouse and maintain a response, it nevertheless contains areas of interest which deserve closer examination. In the first place, the Leeds Chartists managed to stimulate organisation in many locales which previous radical campaigns had failed to proselytize. 'Master ridden' and 'Whig-ridden' places like Armley and Wortley both had their NU branches in 1838 and 1839, and within Leeds itself local NU branches temporarily flourished. The idea of sending missionaries to the out-townships to establish NU branches was first raised in early September 1838, as part of the Leeds NU's preparations for the Peep Green meeting. But, although O'Connor helped to set up branches in Armley and 'flat and inactive' Morley in the week before Peep Green, a concerted missionary campaign was beyond the resources of a small Leeds NU branch whose other priority was raising sufficient money to buy a green flag.[118] In the aftermath of Peep Green George White led a small Leeds delegation, which despite the same vociferous opposition and taunts about Chartist 'failures' and 'revolutionary' intentions, managed to get a small NU branch off the ground at Wortley.[119] In January White was again involved (with Mr. Chester) in setting up the West End NU branch in Gott Lane; and a month later, with National Convention proceedings infusing 'new life into the inhabitants of Leeds', the central NU branch decided to meet monthly for the purpose of 'more effectually agitating the borough'. This was eventually formalised as the 'Leeds Agitation Committee'.[120]

With a Peep Green meeting again providing a stimulus and a focus, in Leeds terms, progress was spectacular. Ten unions were formed in late March and April 1839. The *Star* proclaimed 'Leeds is alive', 'this town does really progress with railway speed'.[121] Some of these NU branches had short and precarious lives. At Bramley, a

---

115 *NS* 6 July 1839.
116 On the build-up to the sacred month and talk of 'ulterior measures' see *NS* 29 June, 3, 17 Aug. 1839 and Harrison, 'Chartism in Leeds', p. 78.
117 *NS* 7 Dec. 1839.
118 *NS* 8 Sept. 1838.
119 *NS, LM* 27 Oct. 1838.
120 *NS* 15 Jan.; 16 Feb.; 27 Apr. and 4 May 1839.
121 These comprised a revived branch at Armley, and new branches at Kirkstall, East End, South

'hot-bed of Whiggery', the Chartists faced opposition from Whig and Tory 'respectables' who, after failing to adjourn the inaugural meeting, threatened the licensee of the proposed meeting place. After the local bell-man had refused to call an open-air meeting, NU members finally raised an audience for George White's talk by parading the village. Accommodation also caused problems at Hunslet and may have lain behind the Armley Chartists decision to meet outdoors on Armley Moor in mid-May. Unfortunately, it snowed! Their accommodation problem was finally solved by setting up one of their members as beershop keeper.[122]

Many of these branches continued to meet after the Peep Green meeting, but there are few reports of meetings after the end of June. This does not necessarily mean that all branches folded after the rejection of the National Petition and the indecision about ulterior measures. Bronterre O'Brien lectured to the Bramley men in July, and when Charles Connor of Leeds spoke at Armley in August the NU branch was reported to have nearly a hundred members. The Woodhouse RA, of which there had been no printed reports since early May, sent subscriptions for Frost in December 1839.[123] Many of these local branches were certainly small in size and short-lived; but their very existence and survival in acknowledged bastions of 'Whiggery' indicates that Chartist penetration, though never deep, was at least broad in the Leeds area.

One of the most flourishing off-shoots was the East End NU formed in early March 1839. The story of this branch highlights a second aspect of Leeds Chartism which merits closer investigation – the splits within the local Chartist body occasioned by William Rider's seemingly erratic actions as one of the West Riding's National Convention delegates. Rider's resignation from the National Convention, due to his frustration with its lack of principles and action, and his subsequent immediate rethink, gave rise to machinations by fellow delegates to have him removed as a member. Only O'Connor's intervention saved him. As J. F. C. Harrison has emphasised, this episode undermined the assembly's reputation and gave the *Leeds Mercury* free rein to mock 'the refactory conduct of the illustrious member for the West Riding – William Rider, Esq., heretofore stuff-weaver, afterwards printer's runner, and now stipendiary Senator, and colleague of Feargus O'Connor Esq., and that "decent fellow", Peter Bussey Esq.'[124] The wider, local ramifications of this affair, however, have been overlooked.

Rider's outburst that he had lost all confidence in the Convention can be seen as part of a wider and growing frustration with the direction of the local and national movement. After years trying to rouse docile Leeds, his contact with the like-minded London Democrats, such as George Julian Harney and Charles Neesom, must have been like a breath of fresh air. It certainly stimulated him into sharp criticisms of the prevarication of the Convention and some of its delegates:

> However other men may act, I will not preach one doctrine in the North, and another here: neither will I spend my strength in talking for

---

End, York Road (all Leeds), Woodhouse, Hunslet, Holbeck, Bramley and Horsforth; *NS* 18 May 1839.

122 *NS*, 4, 11, 18 May, 15 June (Bramley); 18 May (Hunslet); 18 May, 22 June 1839 (Armley).

123 *NS* 13 July; 3 Aug.; 14 Dec. 1839.

124 Harrison, 'Chartism in Leeds', p. 77, fn. 2, quoting *LM* 27 Apr. 1839,

weeks about rules and regulations, as though we were sent here for life; nor will I waste time by exposing the evils of the factory system, as though we were sent as a Short Time Committee.[125]

And it confirmed his uncompromising, aggressive physical-force stance.[126]

Rider's conduct at the Convention clearly embarrassed other Leeds Chartists and his only pocket of consistent support was in his native East End where the NU, formed in early March, came out strongly in his favour in May and censured the other West Riding delegates for having accepted his resignation. The following week Rider and another prominent local Chartist 'operative', David Black, spoke to an East End resolution, condemning petitioning as 'an expensive farce'. At their meeting in early June the East End men stated their position unequivocally:

> ... this meeting is of the opinion that the present movement will not terminate successfully, or our cause be triumphant, without the exercise of the physical energies of the oppressed working men. And we who are now assembled cannot recognise the Quixotic heroes who battle with the teapot, or the vociferators of 'peace, law and order', as being sincere friends of liberty; but on the contrary, we consider them to be the worst enemies of the people's cause.[127]

With the main NU branch moving towards a more conciliatory stance the divisions within local Chartism spilt over into public acrimony and secession.[128] The East End NU reformed itself into the Leeds Democratic Association.[129] Meanwhile, Rider continued to condemn 'sham-Radicals' and the 'timidity' of the Convention, and to complain of the 'empty talkers' who were guiding the movement.[130] Little is known about the Leeds DA. It is likely that it soon folded or went underground after the calling off of the sacred month.[131] The split was not irreconcilable. Leading figures, such as David Black and Thomas Bottomley, who had been involved in the LDA breakaway, were apparently welcome on other Chartist platforms; and Rider himself, after a brief exile, returned to the mainstream of activity.[132]

---

125 *NS* 30 Mar. 1839.

126 See, for example, his letter and speech in *NS* 30 Mar., 6 Apr .1839. Opposition to 'moral-force humbug' is in *NS* 11 May 1839.

127 *NS* 11, 18 May; 8 June 1839. The East End included a community of stuff-weavers, Rider's former trade. David Black was prominent locally in 1839-40, but there is no evidence for Chartist activity thereafter.

128 *NS* 22 June, 6 July 1839.

129 The model was the London Democratic Association, and 'Citizens' Harney, Marsden, Coombe and Major Beniowski were elected honorary members of the Leeds DA, *NS* 22 June 1838. On the LDA see, J. Bennett, 'The London Democratic Association 1837-41: a study in London Radicalism', in Epstein and D. Thompson, *Chartist Experience*, pp. 87-119. The Leeds DA is not mentioned in Harrison's study.

130 *NS* 6 July 1839.

131 The *Star* did not report its activities and proposed to charge for a notice of an August meeting, *NS* 3 Aug. 1839.

132 For example, Black spoke at the 'National Holiday' meeting, *NS* 17 Aug. 1839. On Rider after 1839, see Harrison, 'Chartism in Leeds', p. 81, fn. 6 and 7.

The split between the East End democrats and the main Chartist body in Leeds, though relatively minor, underlines the need for careful scrutiny of local Chartist divisions. These rarely revolved around the simplistic moral-force/physical-force, O'Connorite/Lovettite divisions which coloured so much of early Chartist historiography. Whilst Rider condemned his opponents as 'sham-Radicals' and moral-force men, many like George White, whom Rider attacked in July for his 'incoherent tirade of abuse' against the democrats, were equally vociferous advocates of arming and physical force.[133] The source of tensions frequently lay in their diverging assessments of the political realities facing proponents of ulterior measures. The temporary secession in Leeds can best be explained by reference to the subtle differences of emphasis within the 'physical-force' camp, alongside issues of loyalty to the Convention and to the NU structure which O'Connor helped to set up. Questions of personality, particularly Rider's consistently cantankerous nature, were also a significant factor.[134]

A third aspect of early Chartism in Leeds which merits further scrutiny, and which may have impacted on the formation of the Leeds DA, is the timing and extent of the change in the emphasis of local activity. J. F. C. Harrison sees the major watershed as the failure of the Risings and the arrests of winter 1839-40.[135] The detailed evidence from the *Northern Star* points to a rather different conclusion: that although some new leaders emerged in Leeds Radical Universal Suffrage Association of early 1840, a major change of direction occurred much earlier, certainly after the sacred month fiasco, and possibly before. This re-set was overseen by the existing 'physical-force', 'O'Connorite' leadership including people such as George White, Joseph Jones and the self-declared 'revolutionist' Charles Connor. The realisation that the Charter would only be won after a long hard slog, and the organisational changes this required, were possibly appreciated even before the National Petition had been formally rejected.

In Leeds, for example, the quarterly NU meeting of early June 1839 not only elected branch officials (as usual) and stressed the necessity of a well-organised agitational system in the West Riding; it also recommended improvements in the Union room, including a thorough cleansing, the erection of a platform and a pulpit (for Sunday preaching), and the establishment of a library and reading room. Members also 'requested the secretary George White to solicit the aid of those gentlemen who take an interest in the advancement of the industrious classes'.[136]

The sermons started right away, and other aspects of what might be termed a more sober gradualist approach emerged more clearly in the weeks after the sacred month debacle. The *Star* reported in early September that 'real radicalism' was 'flourishing' and that NU numbers had doubled since the White/Wilson affair (their prosecution for National Rent extortion). The determination was 'no longer to be a party in name

---

133 *NS* 6 July 1839. For a sample of the views of White, a self-declared 'Revolutionist', see *NS* 6 Apr. 1839.

134 Rider had an abrasive tongue and pen and he also hints at domestic difficulties at this time, *NS* 6 July 1839. The dispute did not focus around O'Connor's leadership; see, for example, *NS* 11 Apr. 1839, in which Rider places O'Connor alongside Harney, Marsden and Neesom as 'honest men'.

135 Harrison, 'Chartism in Leeds', pp. 79-81.

136 *NS* 8 June 1839.

but one in fact'. Other plans included 'a committee to superintend the municipal elections', and a Chartist co-operative store. Two weeks later the Chartists were reported to have taken over a 'commodious and well-fitted' Hall, which doubled as NU meeting place and Christian Chartist Chapel.[137]

The tone of local Chartism took on more gravity. At the inaugural meeting in the new premises George White and a Wesleyan shopkeeper discussed the applicability of Chartism to Christianity. Two weeks later Peter Bussey delivered two lectures on the origins and history of governments – the first of them to the newly-formed Leeds Female Radical Association. With the advantages of temperance being promulgated from the platform and with George White advocating the creation of ward committees to press for 'Radical' town-councillors and extolling the virtues of co-operation, the focus and horizons of Chartism had clearly shifted.[138] This did not prevent the Chartists seeking to capture local meetings whether on the Corn Laws or on national education.[139] However, such occasions probably only highlighted the Chartists' relative weakness and the need to create a broader base of support.

This strategy appeared to be working. The *Star* commented in early October that 'never was there better feeling or more unanimity amongst the Radicals of this town ... [they] are weekly adding to their number the intelligent and steady working men'.[140] The use of the term 'Radical' instead of 'Chartist' is significant and indicates renewed attempts to secure a broad radical alliance. However, the attempt to forge links with local radical-liberals, which had found formal expression in the Leeds Radical Central Municipal Election Committee, did not long survive the municipal elections.[141] At a North East Ward dinner in November to mark the recent struggle to elect Gregory (a radical councillor), Chartists such as O'Connor, David Black, Atkinson and Joseph Jones sat round the table with Christopher Heaps (a prominent 'Liberal'), Samuel Smiles (editor of the *Leeds Times*) and George Greig (secretary of the Anti-Corn Law Association). Harmony prevailed until, at the end of a toast to 'the immortal memories and political writings of [deceased radicals such as] Paine, Cartwright, Franklin, Washington, Cobbett, Hunt, Beaumont, Detroisier, and others', the *Mercury*'s reporter maliciously added 'Frost'. O'Connor promptly stood up, grabbed him by the collar and demanded an apology.[142] In the following week's *Star*, O'Connor repudiated the 'Whig and Radical Coalition' and reported that 'the Radicals of Leeds' would in future 'never ... in principle, or upon any question of local policy, direct or indirectly countenance or support the Whig faction'.[143]

The clash with the radical wing of local Whig-liberalism does not appear to have frightened off new adherents or diminished the stress on wider radical concerns. In early December William Parker, 'an operative blacksmith', lectured the NU branch on the social, physical and moral evils of intoxicating drinks; and George White urged

---

137 *NS* 15 June; 7 Sept; 15 Sept. (letter of James Atkinson); 7 Sept.; 21 Sept. 1839.

138 *NS* 28 Sept., 5 Oct.; 12 Oct. 1839.

139 *NS* 31 Aug.; 7 Sept. 1839.

140 *NS* 5 Oct. 1839.

141 *NS* 19 Oct. 1839.

142 *LT* 23 Nov. 1839. John Frost, the leader of the Newport Rising, was under arrest and shortly to be tried for high treason.

143 *NS* 30 Nov. 1839.

formation of a committee to collect funds to defend arrested Chartists. His supporters included Andrew Gardner, later Secretary of the 'moderate' Leeds Radical Universal Suffrage Association; and the committee's officers were Alfred Mann, a moderate radical, and Mr Standing, whose Temperance Coffee House had served as a meeting place for the early Leeds NU.[144] The emergence of one or two new leaders and the re-adherence of some former allies and supporters did not mean the class-conscious and aggressive bite had totally gone out of Leeds Chartism. O'Connor and the local leaders may have been looking to a longer-term victory but they still knew how to use potent and immediate issues like unemployment. Thomas Bottomley, Charles Connor and George White were all prominent in the meetings on local distress in December 1839 and in moves to arouse the consciences of local 'respectables'.[145]

Their efforts ended in a bitter, recriminatory meeting at the Leeds Court House which exposed the stark social divisions which existed in the town.[146] The close analysis of events in Leeds in the second half of 1839 points to the need for a more subtle interpretation of early Chartist activity. 'Physical-force', confrontational attitudes and tactics, and moderate, gradualist sect-like approaches were not necessarily mutually exclusive. The ascendancy of one or the other was not due to the primacy of one group of leaders over another, but owed more to local conditions and to perceptions of what was possible both locally and nationally. When it became clear that the Charter would not be won overnight – and even the sanguine O'Connor was talking in November of 'the present system' lasting half a year or even a year – all local leaders, except the Democrats, appear to have supported new policies and new methods.[147] The early revival of Leeds Chartism in 1840 was not then as remarkable as it first appears. All its chief aspects had been prefigured in the previous year. Nor was the form it took partly due to the removal of O'Connor's influence. He and his supporters had already laid the foundations for new lines of Chartist organisation and activity in the second half of 1839.[148]

b) Bradford

A. J. Peacock's extensive study of early Chartism in Bradford precludes the need for a detailed narrative account.[149] This section therefore concentrates on aspects of Chartist activity in the wider district, focusing particularly on the identification of local leaders,

---

144 *NS* 7 Dec. 1839. The shop of David Green, Owenite bookseller and committee member of the Leeds WMA in 1837, was a collecting point for subscriptions for Frost. Contributions from Leeds included 23*s* from the Leeds Universal Suffrage Teetotal Association, *NS* 28 Dec. 1839.

145 *NS* 14, 21, 28 Dec. 1839.

146 *NS* 28 Dec. 1839. On the class divisions, see the letter from an 'Ultra Radical', *NS* 9 Nov. 1839, quoted on p. 485 below.

147 *NS* 30 Nov. 1839.

148 This interpretation differs from that given in Harrison, 'Chartism in Leeds', p. 80, which talks of local Chartists reverting 'to their own indigenous brand of radicalism', 'once the pressure of O'Connorism was removed'.

149 Peacock, *Bradford Chartism, 1838-40*.

the relationship between the centre and outlying Chartist branches, and the distinctive features the local movement.

The ample coverage of radical activities in the local and Chartist press makes it possible to isolate a cadre of leaders and activists who were prominent during the period between the formation of a NU branch (September 1838) and the ill-fated Bradford Rising (January 1840). The most recognisable and famous was Peter Bussey, the woolcomber turned beershop-keeper and merchant who, as one of the West Riding's five delegates to the first National Convention, was the pre-eminent figure of early Chartism in the area. Yet the district also possessed other Chartist leaders of considerable stature and experience: men such as Joseph Brook, a handloom weaver from Little Horton; James Clarkson, a solicitor who frequently acted on behalf of prosecuted Chartists and Socialists; John Jackson, the veteran radical woolcomber from Great Horton; and William Thornton, 'a staunch Radical and Primitive Methodist Local Preacher', who frequently participated in Bradford meetings during this period.[150]

This group of established radical figures, together with a number of newer leaders, who came to play an increasingly important role in the local movement, carried out the systematic agitation (later formalised as the Bradford Northern Union Plan) of the out-townships and villages of the district. Their names (but rarely their speeches) recur constantly in local columns of the *Northern Star*: addressing small gatherings in schoolrooms, pubs or the houses of local radicals, spreading the message and establishing or rejuvenating branches of the NU. The 'speakers', then, formed one key element in the local Chartist leadership. The 'new' leaders included John Arran, (former blacksmith and schoolmaster, and now fiery Methodist preacher, Chartist lecturer, local treasurer and delegate to West Riding meetings); Henry Hodgson, (woolcomber, delegate and chair of the NU); George Flinn, (woolcomber, formerly of Kidderminster, who with Hodgson was heavily involved in the insurrectionary activities of late 1839); and Edmund Whitney ('operative'). Other contributors included Henry Burnett, A. Heyworth and John Bowden.[151] A group of more shadowy, background organisers and officials may also have been important, though less publicly prominent. These include James Ibbetson (former 'operative', bookseller and unstamped victim and now chief agent for the *Star*, whose bookshop was an important part of the local Chartist network); John Binns (Chair of the Bradford District general committee meeting, delegate and treasurer of the National Rent); John

---

150 *NS* 16 Feb. 1839. 27 Apr., 4 May 1839. (Thornton). Thomas Cliffe of Halifax (possibly in his role as an itinerant bookseller) also appeared regularly on the platform and in the local press in Bradford.

151 John Arran (1803-1878) was described in the 1841 Census as a 'News Agent' and remained very active in the early 1840s. He was tried along with O'Connor and other leading Chartists at Lancaster Assizes in 1843 and was less prominent thereafter. Henry Hodgson (1814-1882) was born in Carrickfergus, Ireland and came to Bradford from Haworth in 1839. Originally a woolcomber, he became a 'warp dresser' and remained active in Chartist and later Liberal politics throughout his life (*BO* 8 Mar. 1882). Edmund Whitney (1811?-1855?) was in all likelihood a Horton-based woolcomber. John Bowden (1806?-?) was another 'incomer' woolcomber. There was a trade union leader of the same name in the early 1830s.

S. Shackleton (newsagent, delegate and treasurer of the Stephens Fund) and S. Emmett (secretary of the latter fund). All four appear but rarely on the local platform.[152]

Chartism in the Bradford area was highly organised with a close symbiotic relationship between centre and localities. Once the NU title had been formally adopted in September 1838, branches were quickly formed at Pitt Lane, White Abbey, Wapping, Bowling Lane, and Great Horton.[153] The impetus came initially from the centre. 'T W' of Bradford had written to the *Star* in late September 1838, advocating the establishment of political missionaries, in the belief that 'there are many small towns and populous villages ... the inhabitants of which long to join in the universal demand of the people's rights, but through timidity, or something else, do not like to be the first to move in the good work'.[154] However some of those involved in this process themselves originated, or were still based in the out-townships.[155]

The close, two-way relationship between central and branch unions was soon formalised in the Great Northern Union District Committee, comprising of delegates from each of the local RA or NU branches, which met regularly in Bradford (usually at Bussey's beershop) and came to act as the chief co-ordinating body for Chartism in the district.[156] Although there were undoubtedly areas of hardcore Chartist support in the centre of Bradford itself, for example amongst the predominantly Irish combers (and their wives) of the Nelson Court area, the real strength of Chartism in the wider area lay in the support it enjoyed amongst the proverbially taciturn handloom-weavers (and also the outworking combers) of the surrounding villages.[157]

Some of these villages, particularly those on the Bradford-Halifax axis, quickly became Chartist strongholds. At Horton, which had long been recognised as a democratic centre, 150 people were reported to have enrolled in the local NU branch, and regular monthly meetings, often chaired by local radical 'veterans', were held throughout the winter of 1838-9.[158] At Clayton, where a NU branch was formed in November 1838, the leading figures were Michael Scholefield, William Fox, 'a labouring man' and Benjamin Sowden, a stuff weaver who gave evidence to the 1838 Handloom-Weaving Commission. In spite of typical difficulties with the trustees of the Baptist School Room (their meeting place), local Chartists here remained strong and fairly active. Indeed, the *Northern Star* boasted that out of the 109 special constables sworn in at Clayton, due to public order concerns about the May 1839 Peep Green meeting, '93 are Chartists'.[159]

---

152 Ibbetson faced complaints about his distribution of *Star* portraits and in April 1839 tendered his resignation to the local NU for undisclosed personal reasons, (*NS* 19 Oct. 1838, 27 Apr., 4 May 1839). Other interesting, if hazy, figures are George Hopkins (local *NS* agent) and John Peacock, a draper, (see Peacock, *Bradford Chartism*, p. 21).

153 *NS* 15, 29 Sept., 13 Oct. 1838.

154 *NS* 6 Oct. 1838.

155 For example, Joseph Brook lived in Little Horton, John Jackson in Great Horton, and Peter Bussey had previously resided in Bradford Moor.

156 *NS* 20 Oct. 1838, 23 Mar., 27 Apr. 1839; Peacock, *Bradford Chartism*, p. 18.

157 *NS* 30 Mar. 1839; D. Thompson, *Early Chartists*, p. 284. George Flinn lived in Nelson Court. See also, Peacock, *Bradford Chartism*, pp. 48 and 18-19.

158 *NS* 29 Sept., 27 Oct., 17 Nov., 8, 15 Dec. 1838, 19 Jan., 16 Mar. 1839.

159 *NS* 24 Nov., 22 Dec. 1838; 15 June; 11 May 1839.

Along the road from Clayton, at Queenshead, the Chartist presence was equally strong. The Northern Union branch which had been established in November 1838 remained publicly active throughout the next nine months, and when the movement went underground in the winter of 1839, Queenshead was certainly involved in insurrectionary preparations.[160] As elsewhere, public meetings in the township relied heavily on outside speakers from Bradford and further afield, though the meetings were usually chaired by a local man – usually Joseph Crossland or Christopher Shackleton. However, one local Chartist figure initially stood out above all others: Jonathan Bairstow, a tall, young nonconformist minister with a musical voice. Bairstow, who had lectured in favour of radicalism at the inaugural RA meeting in January 1838, achieved local fame as a formidable physical-force preacher, and in summer 1839 he became the official West Riding missionary.[161]

His popularity indicates something of the religious fervour and overtones which distinguished Chartism in the weaving villages of the Halifax-Bradford hinterland. The local Chartists here came to rely upon the more democratic nonconformist sects for meeting places. The lectures and sermons of preachers like Bairstow, Barker of Shelf, John Arran, William Thornton and Benjamin Rushton of Ovenden also became a major expression of local Chartist solidarity and endeavour.[162] Chartist sermons were popular elsewhere in the Bradford district, but the most usual mode of proceeding in these communities tended to be the small, informal NU branch meeting held in the home of a local member or the house of a local publican or beerseller.

It is difficult to gauge how active local NU branches actually were. Meetings may only have been reported when Bradford delegates attended or important issues were discussed. Some may have been short-lived, whilst others possibly languished in the hiatus between West Riding meetings. The Thornton branch, for example, reported an influx of new members following a public meeting addressed by Edmund Whitney of Bradford in March 1839.[163] Yet the constant trickle of subscriptions to the various funds, which gave the early Chartist movement a thread of continuity and its sense of purpose, would indicate that much local activity and enthusiasm went unnoticed.

The western out-townships formed the real Chartist heartland, but there was also strong support in the villages to the south and east of the town. Bowling, Bowling Lane, North Bierley and West Bowling were amongst the districts which made up the strong Bradford contingent to the October 1838 Peep Green meeting. Local leaders in

---

160 *NS* 10 Nov., 8, 29 Dec. 1838, 19 Jan., 30 Mar., 4 May, 15 June, 20 July 1839. On Queenshead as a Chartist centre see, D. Thompson, *The Chartists*, pp. 245-6. For its involvement in underground activity see D. Thompson, *Early Chartists*, p. 280, and p. 465 below.

161 *NS* 20 Jan., 29 Dec. 1838; *BO* 15 Nov., 6 Dec. 1838. Crossland, 'a Radical', chaired most of the 1838 meetings. Shackleton, a handloom weaver (1808-1853), was 'one of the finest speakers in the district' and went on to become a leading West Riding Chartist in the 1840s. On Bairstow, another former weaver/orator (1822?-1853?), who relocated to Leicester in 1841, see R. G. Gammage, *History of the Chartist Movement, 1837-53* (London: Merlin Press, 1969 edn.), pp. 210-11; *NS* 15 June 1839.

162 For a vivid description of a Chartist sermon preached by Rushton, see F. Peel, *Spen Valley: Past and Present* (Heckmondwike: Senior and Co., 1893), pp. 318-19.

163 *NS* 9 Mar. 1839.

these villages are less easy to identify. The name which recurs most frequently in this area is William Rouse, a stuff-weaver from Bowling, but other figureheads are rarely identified in the occasional reports from these branches, possibly because of fears of victimisation.[164]

Bradford missionaries also tried their luck in some of the villages and townships on the fringes of the district. To the south, at Oakenshaw (a hamlet of about twenty-five houses dependent on agriculture and the manufacture of blankets), and Birkenshaw (on the border with the Dewsbury district) delegates from Bradford (and Dewsbury) met with some opposition from local Whigs in November and December 1838, but still managed to set up NU branches.[165] To the north, attempts were made to stir up other traditionally Whig strongholds. The mixed woollen-worsted weaving area around Idle boasted an active NU branch during the winter months 1838-9, and nearby Shipley pointed to about thirty members in the local RA as evidence that it was awakening from 'the torpor of Whiggery'. The following year the National Petition had been adopted and (despite fears of victimisation) local committees formed at both Baildon and Guiseley. The culmination of agitation in this area came in the form of a sizeable public meeting on Baildon Green in April 1839 addressed by Bradford speakers.[166]

It is an indication of the strength of Chartism in the district that Pudsey, the fiercely independent centre of the domestic (woollen weaving) system, did not remain untouched. Bussey had spoken to a local Working Man's Association (a mutual instruction society which grew more political) as early as September 1838, though the Charter and Petition were not formally adopted until April 1839. The *Northern Star*'s optimistic belief that 'this town, if properly agitated, will no doubt become one of great importance in the ranks of Radicalism', was not fulfilled here or in many of the other outlying towns and villages.[167] Yet the very establishment of a Chartist presence in these traditionally apathetic or 'cowed' villages was no mean achievement.

The sheer volume of activity would indicate that Bradford was perhaps the strongest and liveliest of the early Chartist districts in the West Riding. This is confirmed by the size of Bradford contingents to the major West Riding meetings and the constant flow of subscriptions to the various Chartist funds.[168] Bradford was always quick to react to outside stimuli. It readily adopted the torchlight format for its winter meetings in 1838, and when the news of Stephens' arrest reached the town, Bussey was to be found at a hastily convened public meeting recommending every man to 'provide himself with a rifle and practice shooting at a mark'.[169]

Such sentiments were commonplace at meetings throughout the 1838-9 period. From the start Chartism in the area had a stridently militant tone which virtually all

---

164 *NS* 20 Oct. 1838. Rouse (1797-1861?) gave evidence to the Handloom-weavers Commission in 1838 and was an established local leader.

165 *NS* 17 Nov., 1, 15, 29 Dec. 1839. Peel, *Spen Valley*, p. 291.

166 *NS* 13 Oct., 1 Dec. 1838, 26 Jan., 11 Feb. 1839 (Idle); 29 Dec. 1838 (Shipley); 16 Mar. (Baildon), 30 Mar. 1839 (Guiseley); 6 Apr. 1839 (Baildon Green meeting).

167 *NS* 15 Sept. 1838; 20 Apr. 1839.

168 Peacock, *Bradford Chartism*, p. 18. For Col. Angelo's assessment in 1839, see TNA: HO 40/51 f. 437, 'Memorandum relative to Bradford'.

169 *NS* 5 Jan. 1839.

local leaders endorsed. For example, Joseph Brook proudly proclaimed that he 'had been trained in the use of arms' and was well 'acquainted with the use of the firelock', whilst a moderate 'brother Radical' berated Bussey for his 'eloquent appeals to the power of dry gunpowder and cold steel'.[170] By 1839 the first reports of drilling and arming in the district were filtering through.[171] The customary lull following the Whit Monday Peep Green meeting was not the end of the Chartist 'fever' in Bradford as the *Leeds Mercury* optimistically believed.[172] The arrests following the Bull Ring Riots and the rejection of the National Petition injected new life into the local movement. Open-air meetings proliferated, a system of classes was adopted, and exclusive dealing set in motion. By the end of the month there was reported to be 'great excitement' throughout the district, and between 10,000 and 12,000 people reputedly gathered to hear the results of the district committee's deliberations upon the national holiday.[173] Bradford was one of the few areas which remained solidly in favour of the sacred month and the cancellation was taken very badly indeed.[174]

After the sacred month Chartism in the town adopted some of the more sober, respectable forms of activity so common elsewhere in the Riding. Some of this may, as A. J. Peacock speculates, have been a front to hide other activities.[175] Certainly the local movement re-organised itself and elements went underground after the disappointing failure of ulterior measures. Local magistrates found it increasingly difficult to permeate Chartist cells, and without doubt there was serious insurrectionary planning in Bradford and the western out-townships both before and after the Newport Rising.[176] According to the obituary of John Jackson, Bradford moral-force advocate and 'old school' Reformer, it was through 'him more than by any other man amongst them in the town [that] the Chartists were saved from the folly and mistake of turning out in arms to meet the South Wales men under "Frost, Williams and Jones"'.[177]

'Generalissimo of the forces', Bussey was at the heart of these plans, and his well-documented loss of nerve and disappearance after the Newport debacle should, in theory, have been a major setback.[178] In reality insurrectionary plotting continued apace, indicating both the resilience of local networks and the uncompromising nature of Bradford Chartism. Local Chartists considered, and magistrates feared, a rising the

---

170 *LT* 15 Sept., *BO* 13 Sept., 29 Nov.; *NS* 22 Dec. 1838.

171 *NS* 20 Apr., *LM* 13 Apr. 1839. See also TNA: HO 40/51, f. 61, 63, 65, 67, 69, 83, depositions about drilling.

172 *LM* 8 June 1839.

173 *NS* 20, 27 July 1839.

174 See Peacock, *Bradford Chartism*, p. 22; and James Epstein, *The Lion of Freedom: Feargus O'Connor and the Chartist Movement, 1832-42* (London: Breviary Stuff, 2015 edn.), p. 157.

175 Peacock, *Bradford Chartism*, pp. 23, 28 and 32.

176 See, for example, HO 40/51 f. 177, Thompson, Hird and Hardy to Lord Normanby, 17 Nov. 1839.

177 *BO* 17 Mar. 1875.

178 The sarcastic label was used in a prescient letter warning operatives about Bussey's 'duplicity and delusion' (*BO* 31 Jan. 1839). For the widespread recognition of Bussey's projected role, see the note signed by James Rawson and Thomas Aked (Halifax) reprinted in Dalby, 'The Chartist Movement in Halifax', p. 108.

following weekend. This did not materialize, but Bradford remained on edge with regional delegates reiterating the people's determination 'that Frost should not be sacrificed'.[179] Henry Hodgson attended shadowy delegate meetings in Manchester and Dewsbury in early December and represented Bradford at the second National Convention in London, which commenced on 19 December 1839. All of these meetings discussed plans for a rising, eventually settling on 12 January as the starting date.[180] Accordingly, ignoring injunctions in the *Star* to refrain from 'damaging the cause of Frost and his associates ... by any outbreak of physical violence', significant numbers of Bradford Chartists assembled on the night of 11-12 January. Queenshead, Clayton and Horton insurgents allegedly fired guns in the air, and the road between Bradford and Halifax was reportedly 'completely filled with men bearing torches and spears with them'.[181] However, they failed to link up with other pockets of rebellion, possibly because, as A. J. Peacock suggests, Hodgson pulled local Chartists back from full participation in what became known as the 'Dewsbury Rising'.[182]

Undeterred by this damp squib, 'one last insurrectionary flicker' briefly illuminated Bradford two weeks later, when sizeable numbers of Chartists gathered with hopes of carrying out plans to take a local market, purloin equipment for a potential Chartist army and seize cannon from a local ironworks, before heading to London via Dewsbury. The ambitious scheme never really got off the ground and the rising petered out when expected rebel reinforcements from Halifax and Leeds never arrived.[183] As A. J. Peacock argues, this last attempt to help Frost was a serious endeavour involving hundreds rather than scores of participants. It was, however, fatally compromised by the increasingly extravagant rhetoric of itinerant Scottish insurrectionist Robert Peddie and infiltration by spies, notably the notorious James Harrison.[184] Arrests ensued and the records of the subsequent trials provide a rich source of insights into the operation of clandestine networks, the seriousness of local insurrectionary intent and the challenges faced by Chartist leaders. By late autumn 1839, some of these had already withdrawn or, like John Jackson, opposed plans for insurgency; but it is clear that many established figures, as well new leaders who emerged from the Chartist classes, were deeply involved in the events that marked the end of the first phase of Chartism.

c) Huddersfield

In spite of a reasonably 'early start', impressive initial enrolment into the local NU branch and vigorous preparations for the October 1838 Peep Green Meeting, 'Huddersfield, brave Huddersfield' never became a stronghold of early Chartism in the West Riding.[185] It is possible that the lack of activity after the autumnal rally is a

---

179 *NS* 7 Dec. 1839 (Joseph Jones of Leeds at the Newcastle delegate meeting).
180 Peacock, *Bradford Chartism*, pp. 35-7.
181 *NS* 11 Jan. 1840; local press reports for 18 Jan. 1840, cited in Peacock, *Bradford Chartism*, p. 38 and Chase, *Chartism*, p. 135.
182 Peacock, *Bradford Chartism*, p. 38.
183 Chase, *Chartism*, pp. 137-8; Peacock, *Bradford Chartism*, pp. 39-46.
184 Ibid., pp. 44,; pp. 39-53 (Peddie); pp. 40-48 (Harrison).
185 *NS* 29 Sept., 6 Oct. 1838.

deception of the sources. There were constant complaints from the *Star* office that Huddersfield was sending in its parcel too late, though the paltry £7 collected for the National Rent by the beginning of January 1839 would indicate that this dilatoriness was a symptom and perhaps a contributory cause of local apathy.[186] Huddersfield's relative backwardness was noticed by others. The Barnsley Radicals, for example, asked, 'where is Huddersfield? what has that mighty town been doing? surely after thou hast been the rallying point for the Radicals of England all these years, £7 is not all that can be found within thy walls?'[187] Although they successfully captured a Whig-sponsored Corn Law repeal meeting in February, local Chartists generally remained subdued in the early months of 1839. Activity at this time mainly focused on the organising of collections for the Stephens Fund.[188] Huddersfield speakers figured prominently at the May Peep Green meeting, but a local magistrate reported that Huddersfield did not furnish its 'usual quota', and the local procession was described as being 'poor and insignificant'.[189]

In early July the *Northern Star* proclaimed that 'Huddersfield is again beginning to stir itself', but in August the official view (from the same magistrate) was that 'since the meeting at Peep Green in May last, there has never been the slightest public demonstration of the working classes in this Town'.[190] The surprise arrival and enrolment of forty cordwainers at a regular Monday evening NU branch meeting in late July gave the branch a boost, but the lack of response from other trades, and in particular 'the improbability of getting the factory hands in this district to make a general stand' made the sacred month a non-starter in the area. Indeed, the town's only gesture, a rain-swept meeting on Saturday 10 August, attracted a disappointingly small audience.[191] The national holiday fiasco was clearly a blow to the credibility of local Chartists, and ten days later local magistrates reported that 'many are giving up following the delusion altogether'.[192] Although the *Northern Star* talked of 'the spirit of good feeling amongst the Radicals in the district' and reported attempts to re-organise the local movement, in reality activity was at a very low level – a fact which the *Star* admitted in late November.[193]

The 'late events in Wales' [Newport] re-awakened local radicals in November and December. Huddersfield had always been a strong supporter of 'victims'. It is possible, indeed highly probable, that the town's well-connected leaders knew something of the insurrectionary plots of late 1839. A Huddersfield Chartist defending one of the new, more sober, leaders who emerged in the early 1840s recalled the 'unprincipled leaders of former times', 'the leaders of the old Northern Union in Huddersfield' who had

---

186 For example, *NS* 13 Oct., 10, 17 Nov. 1838, 18 May 1839.
187 *NS* 16 Feb. 1839.
188 *NS* 26 Jan., 9 Feb., 23, 30 Mar. 1839.
189 TNA: HO 40/51 f. 167, Laycock to Harewood, 22 May 1839.
190 *NS* 6 July 1839; TNA: HO 40/51 f. 367, Laycock to Russell, 8 Aug. 1839.
191 *NS* 3 Aug.; 17 Aug. 1839. This was despite earlier local protests about the abandonment of the sacred month, Hovell, *Chartist Movement*, p. 169.
192 TNA: HO 40/51 f. 449, Laycock to Russell, 22 Aug. 1839. This contains a full report of the 10 Aug. meeting.
193 *NS* 21, 28 Sept.; 19 Oct.; 30 Nov. 1839.

been concerned in 'circumstances that would make us startle if related'.[194] However, though some local Chartists may well have taken up Oastler's earlier advice to arm or bought one of Tinker's daggers, there is no evidence to connect Huddersfield directly with the risings.[195] Despite the town being identified by the Home Office in May 1839 as a potential trouble spot and thereby the recipient of a royal proclamation prohibiting arming and drilling, there were few alarmist reports of weapons being acquired or outdoor manoeuvres.

The circumspection which Malcolm Chase identifies as a distinctive feature of the district's approach to the potential use of violence may indeed, as he suggests, have owed much to the 'collective memory' of Huddersfield's involvement in the Yorkshire Rising of Easter 1820. Whatever its precise origin, the wariness of this generation of leaders is much in evidence.[196] Thomas Vevers, the Huddersfield delegate to a Stephens Defence Fund meeting at Ashton-under-Lyne in April 1839, 'was authorised to say that when the proper time arrived, they were as well prepared as any town in the country, but would be very carefully guided in their course to physical-force'. At the time of the sacred month most local leaders appear to have adopted the same cautious stance.[197] The year ended on a traditional note, with local radicals raising money for the Frost Defence Fund, attacking the local Whigs, and involving themselves in a local meeting on unemployment and distress.[198]

An examination of the main people involved in these activities reveals a marked degree of continuity in the local leadership. A number of familiar names recur during the early Chartist period. The pre-eminent local figure was Lawrence Pitkethly, linen draper, West Riding delegate to the Convention and undoubted leader of the Huddersfield radicals.[199] Beyond 'Old Pitt' the most active leaders were Samuel Binns (local secretary, a woolsorter, whose newsroom in Pack Horse Yard was an early meeting place); George Barker (leading co-operator and prominent local speaker); Stephen Dickinson (another *Star* agent and local official whose clothes warehouse became the NU's regular venue); John Leech (Pitkethly's business and political right-hand man); and James Matthewman (co-operator and early delegate to West Riding meetings).[200] Beyond these come a number of people whose depth of involvement or level of activity is more open to doubt. They possibly remained key elements in the local radical network – as mentors, advisers or officials – without participating in the day-to-day aspects of the local movement and included established radical figures such as William Stocks jnr. (a small manufacturer, who acted as District Treasurer for the

194 *NS* 1 Jan. 1842.

195 See, for example, the audience's assertion 'we have armed', TNA: HO 40/51 ff. 435-525, Report of a Chartist Meeting at Huddersfield, 10 Aug. 1839; Chase, 'Chartism in Huddersfield', p. 72.

196 Chase, 'Chartism in Huddersfield', p. 69.

197 *NS* 27 Apr. 1839; TNA: HO 40/51 f. 449, Laycock to Russell, 22 Aug. 1839.

198 *NS* 21 Dec. 1839.

199 Felix Driver, 'Tory Radicalism? Ideology, Strategy and Locality in Popular Politics during the Eighteen-Thirties', *Northern History*, 27 (1991), pp. 124-7.

200 Samuel Binns (1801-?), the 'keeper of the Radical and Chartist Newsroom', was allegedly deprived of work because of his radical views and eventually filed for bankruptcy (*LM* 2 Feb, *LT* 9 Feb, 1839; *LM* 22 Apr. 1843).

Stephen's Fund and was involved in major public meetings); John Hanson (operative woollen spinner and an experienced radical, ten hours and anti-poor law activist whose involvement became increasingly sporadic); the respectable William Cook (treasurer of the NU branch); and Christopher Tinker (the leading radical bookseller in the town).

Outside the town itself, the out-townships and outlying villages boasted a number of prominent and experienced local leaders. Huddersfield radicalism had always been heavily dependent on these communities to supply it with both muscle power and bursts of agitational energy. And, although there is some evidence of the localities pursuing a more independent line of action, district co-operation and organisation was still a feature of the Huddersfield area. A local delegate committee had met as early as September 1838 and meetings of the 'district central committee' continued to be held at fairly regular intervals during the next year and beyond.[201] In this sense, Huddersfield was one of the more organised Chartist localities. There was also some multiple representation by delegates at the West Riding meetings, though the chief centres in the district (Huddersfield, Almondbury, Honley and Lepton/Kirkheaton) usually sent their own representative.

Even in these predominantly fancy-weaving villages to the south and east of the town, the locus of the movement's most tenacious and consistent support, there were significant variations in levels of activity and involvement. Although slow in formally adopting in the National Petition and Charter, Almondbury retained its radical reputation and the district furnished its usual quota of support for the October 1838 Peep Green meeting, where Samuel Dickenson, its most prominent radical orator, made a forceful speech.[202] The public face of the Almondbury Chartists is less evident in 1839. However, the subscription lists for the National Rent and J. R. Stephens, the spread of organisation to neighbouring hamlets, plus regular involvement at the West Riding delegate meetings and occasional public meetings all indicate a consistently strong Chartist presence. This is confirmed by the choice of Samuel Dickenson to chair the May 1839 Peep Green meeting and the solid observance of the three-day national holiday in the village.[203]

The mellowing of local radicalism, belying its reputation as a supplier of 'bludgeon men', is indicated by the moderate tone of the resolutions passed at the public meeting to launch the holiday. These stressed peaceful methods, particularly the withdrawal of deposits from banks and abstention from excisable articles. The area's residual caution may have been the result of a realistic appraisal of the tactical options available or the legacy of 1820, but it may also have been a product of the campaigning fatigue that impacted Huddersfield. Like its urban neighbour, Almondbury contained several highly experienced and well-established figures who had been active since the early

---

201 *NS* 22 Sept. 1838. For district delegate meetings, see NS 24 Nov. 1838, 4 May 1839, 22 June, 7, 28 Sept., 2 Nov., 21 Dec. 1839.

202 *NS* 8 Dec.; 16 Oct. 1838. The township of Almondbury included Chartist branches at the hamlets of Newsome, Berry Brow and Lowerhouses as well as the Almondbury RA/WMA, *NS* 30 Mar. 1839.

203 *NS* 25 Mar. (Peep Green); *NS* and *LT* 17 Aug. 1839 (national holiday).

1830s. Although a few new leaders emerged, the degree of continuity with previous radical agitations is striking.[204]

Elsewhere in the fancy-weaving district the Chartist presence is more difficult to discern, but subscription lists in particular reveal Chartist organisations and support in many of the small settlements and hamlets which dotted the area. Two of the bigger centres, Lepton and Kirkheaton, regularly delegated Thomas Vevers to attend West Riding meetings and local NU branches organised collections for the various Chartist funds.[205] Vevers, who also on occasions represented Huddersfield at West Riding meetings, hailed from Dalton, a village just outside Huddersfield, and acted as a link between the villages and the centre. A highly respected radical veteran and major district figure, he spoke at the May 1839 Peep Green meeting and confirmed his regional stature by being elected as one of the supplementary (Convention) delegates in July 1839.[206] The identification of less prominent village leaders is more difficult, but names like John Smith jnr. of Lepton, John Broadbent (a weaver) and James Dronsfield of Kirkheaton, and J. Ratcliffe of Berry Brow fall into this category.

The same problems of identification recur when we turn to other groups of villages in the Huddersfield hinterland. A number of the out-townships in the immediate vicinity of Huddersfield had Chartist organisations or took part in Chartist activities (for example, sermons for Stephens, collections for National Rent), but often only the name of the local *Northern Star* agent survives.[207] Further afield in the predominantly woollen weaving villages along the Colne and Holme valleys, where, as Alan Brooke notes, radicalism was less strongly embedded, information is scarce.[208] Linthwaite certainly boasted a flourishing NU branch, and Chartist organisations were also established at Holmfirth, Slaithwaite and possibly Armitage Bridge and South Crossland.[209]

In the mixed woollen/fancy township of Honley, four miles south of Huddersfield, a NU branch, based on a pre-existing WMA, had a vigorous early life.[210] When O'Connor visited the village in November 1838 an estimated two to three thousand people escorted him in pouring rain to the house of 'a patriotic joiner, Mr Kay', who removed a window to allow O'Connor to speak to the crowd outside. His carriage

---

204 For example, the Chartist speakers or delegates who had also been active in 1829-30 include Samuel Dickenson, George Beaumont, Abraham Donkersley, John Eckersley, T. Haner, Samuel Midgeley, Solomon Thwaite, William Sykes and possibly John Heaton and George Beaumont. The majority were fancy weavers.

205 For example, Lepton, *NS* 22 June, 21 Dec. 1839. The Kirkheaton branch of the Fancy Weavers' Union also contributed to the National Rent, *NS* 9 Mar. 1839.

206 *NS* 9 Feb. (Huddersfield meeting); 25 May (Peep Green); 27 July 1839 (supplementary delegate). Also, *NS* 27 May 1843 (for his obituary).

207 For example, Dalton, Yew Green/Lockwood, Lindley, Paddock come into this category. The *NS* Agent at Lindley was Edward Shaw, who in 1832 had been secretary of the local co-operative society, *LYC* Oct. 1832.

208 Brooke, 'The Roots of Chartism', p. 19. Brooke notes that the Colne valley, for example, housed 'a higher proportion of independent clothiers and relatively well-off mill workers'.

209 *NS* 10 Oct., 1 Dec. 1838, 9 Feb., 4 May 1839 (Linthwaite and Slaithwaite); 1 Dec. 1838 (Holmfirth).

210 *LT* 1, 15 July 1837; *NS* 3 Feb., 16 June, 1 Sept., 13, 16 Oct. 1838.

then went on to Holmfirth where O'Connor, Dr. Taylor, Pitkethly, William Cunningham and Mark Crabtree addressed the rain-soaked crowd. The *Star* rejoiced that 'Holmfirth, long slumbering and Whig-ridden Holmfirth, broke the bonds of union on Saturday inst. and bid adieu to Whiggery for ever'. On their way back to Huddersfield O'Connor was cheered along the torchlined route and virtually dragged from his carriage and forced to speak at Armitage Bridge.[211] Such enthusiasm was impossible to maintain, particularly in places like Holmfirth where the radical base was weak. At Honley, however, the Chartist presence under an identifiable group of established leaders, was clearly more substantial and long-lasting.[212]

Resistance to the new poor law remained a preoccupation of radicals throughout the district. At Lepton, a fancy-weaving centre four miles south east of Huddersfield, popular opposition took the form of overseers initially refusing to 'give up' their ratebooks to the pro-poor law Huddersfield Guardians. Under threat of prosecution they retrieved them, only for a large crowd to purloin them and bury them in a wood.[213] Support for Stephens was also strong, with large sums being collected through numerous local sermons and meetings. As in the villages around Bradford and Halifax, village Chartism had close links with 'democratic' religious bodies. Connections with the Primitive Methodists, the labourers' denomination, were particularly strong. Meetings were occasionally held in Primitive Methodist rooms, and after Stephens' arrest local preachers such as William Cliffe, Joseph Newsome and Samuel Crossland of Paddock delivered scores of sermons to raise money for his defence fund. Indeed, the 'Primitive Methodists of Huddersfield' were singled out for praise for their 'exertions' on behalf of Stephens. Their attitude contrasted neatly with Wesleyan Methodists who closed their chapels and expelled a local preacher who attended the May 1839 Peep Green meeting.[214]

Such persecutions helped the cause but, particularly in Huddersfield itself, the impression of lethargy is inescapable and, in view of the town's previous record, all the more surprising. No single reason can explain this muted response to early Chartism. The election campaigns of 1834 and 1837 had caused internal divisions and recriminations. Relationships between the radicals of the town and the outlying villages were never again as close as they had been in the early 1830s.[215] After a decade of relentless campaigning on a host of issues, agitational fatigue may also have been a factor. It may not be coincidental that a number of the town's main leaders emigrated, moved or pursued other interests in the 1840s.[216] More immediately, the loss, low

---

211 *NS* 10 Nov. 1838.

212 On Holmfirth and its 'tailor' leader see *LM* 25 May 1839. For Honley meetings see *NS* 15 Dec. 1838, 2 Mar., 4 May, 29 June, 16 Nov. 1839. Leaders included Joseph Whitehead, Walker Green, Joseph Eastwood (greengrocer), Matthew Buckley (weaver), and Edward Haigh (Huddersfield area delegate at the 28 October West Riding delegate meeting).

213 *NS* 4 May 1839; John Knott, *Popular Opposition to the 1834 Poor Law* (Beckenham: Croom Helm, 1986), pp. 192-3. See also *LM* 15 May 1839 – for an assault on an overseer, and the continued resistance of Lepton and Kirkheaton.

214 On sermons and praise for the Primitive Methodists, see *NS* 30 Mar. 1839; on the case of Benjamin Haigh, see *NS* 6 July 1839.

215 See above, pp. 313-5 and pp. 345-8.

216 For example, Tinker emigrated to the United States in 1842. Pitkethly may have visited him

profile or other pre-occupations of a number of experienced leaders who had directed the campaigns of the early and mid-1830s did not help matters.[217] The competing attractions of the Owenite socialists may also have drawn away some potential support and energies.[218]

Huddersfield had a strong co-operative base and its socialist branch was one of the largest in the country. The town proportionally was the biggest contributor to the Owenite community fund.[219] Although Chartists and Owenites often shared aims, venues and leaders, they nevertheless competed for the attention and penny subscriptions of local working people. Indeed, as Malcolm Chase surmises, the very vitality and diversity of the working-class associational culture – with its educational, temperance, co-operative and friendly society arms – may inadvertently have undermined a sole focus on the suffrage question.[220]

However, the chief drain on energies and the main distraction (and possibly source of divisions) appears to have been the town's close involvement with Oastler and the anti-poor law cause. The organisation of tributes to mark Oastler's departure from Fixby Hall, the 'Acland' riots of November 1838, and the prosecution of leading anti-poor law Guardians all commanded local attention and money at times when other areas were concentrating solely on the Charter and Petition.[221] Small wonder that Pitkethly, speaking at a Dewsbury RA dinner in November 1838, had felt the need to defend 'the Huddersfield men from allusions made because of their determined opposition to the Poor Law and to stress that they were as keen as any Radicals to gain Universal Suffrage'.[222] The final blow came in early 1839 with the revelation of James Brook's secret correspondence with the Poor Law Commission.[223] Like Abraham Wildman's defection in Keighley, this damaged the radical cause greatly and eroded

---

when he travelled to the country in 1842-3 'to scout out communities for emigration'. 'Pit' probably left Huddersfield for Manchester in the late 1840s; see John Halstead, 'The Huddersfield Short Time Committee and its radical associations, c.1820-1876', in John A. Hargreaves and E. A. Hilary Haigh (eds.), *Slavery in Yorkshire: Richard Oastler and the Campaign against Child Labour in the Industrial Revolution* (Huddersfield: University of Huddersfield Press, 2012), p. 142. John Hanson was most active as an Owenite socialist and in all likelihood suffered a stroke in the 1843-4 period.

217 Robert Buchanan had left the town, John Hanson and William Stocks jnr. do not appear to have been as prominent as formerly, Pitkethly was in London as a Convention delegate, and both James Brook and Stephen Dickinson were under threat of prosecution for anti-poor law activities.

218 See, for example, *NS* 23 Feb., 16 Mar. 1839.

219 Chase, 'Chartism in Huddersfield', p. 79, fn. 21.

220 Ibid., pp. 67-8.

221 See Cecil Driver, *Tory Radical, The Life of Richard Oastler* (New York: Oxford University Press, 1946), pp. 384-7 and 406; *NS* 17, 24 Nov., *LM* 24 Nov. 1838; *NS* 8 Dec. 1838, 9, 16 Mar. 1839. An opportunistic lecture by James Acland, an advocate of the new poor law, in the Huddersfield Philosophical Hall was violently disrupted by a hostile crowd, see Knott, *Popular Opposition*, pp. 190-1.

222 *NS* 17 Nov. 1838.

223 *NS* 12, 19, 26 Jan.; 2 Feb. 1839. Brook, a leading figure in the ten hours and anti-poor law campaigns, applied for the much sought-after post of poor-rate collector. He claimed he did so for the best of reasons – to acquire better electoral information for the radicals.

the credibility of the established radical leadership in the town.[224] Neither new leaders nor radical stalwarts were ever really able to overcome these diversionary pressures and fully re-energize the local movement.

d) Halifax

The early strength of Chartism in the Halifax district was founded on a firm, pre-existing radical base. This extended beyond the confines of the town itself. Indeed, the many small but flourishing associations in the outlying villages gave Halifax Chartism a strong backbone of support and also many of its distinctive features. This section, whilst providing a brief account of the general development of Chartism in the area, also seeks to highlight a few of these characteristics.

The picture of the early Chartist take-off in Halifax is by no means complete. The NU was formally established in the town at a joint Radical and anti-poor law public meeting, which also formally adopted the Birmingham petition.[225] In general, though, much local activity went unnoticed. The dispersed nature of settlement in the parish, the largest in England, made it impractical to hold such large-scale meetings regularly, and full reports of the smaller gatherings, lectures, sermons and discussions which made up the normal pattern of local activity were rarely furnished to the *Northern Star*. A large Halifax contingent marched behind two bands to the October 1838 Peep Green meeting and a local leader, Robert Wilkinson, chaired the proceedings.[226] By early in the new year, with branches in many of the districts' villages and hamlets and with £39 contributed to the National Rent, Halifax was firmly established as a major early Chartist centre.[227]

There is plenty of evidence of a close and continuing relationship between the central and outlying associations. For example, William Thornton and Robert Sutcliffe from Halifax attended the inaugural meeting of the Mytholmroyd RA, and Halifax supplied speakers for radical meetings at outposts such as Luddenden and Wadsworth.[228] However, unlike in other areas, this 'missionary' activity was never formalised into an 'Agitation Council' or 'Plan'.

The traffic was not all one way. A number of important district leaders hailing from the out-townships and villages regularly took part in Halifax meetings. Also, delegates from the outlying associations met at the Labour and Health Inn in June 1838, and district delegate meetings supervised local preparations for the big West Riding demonstrations of October 1838 and May 1839.[229] These never became the routine area meetings attempted at Huddersfield and achieved at Bradford, and it is

---

224 See p. 426 below.

225 *NS* 28 July, 4 Aug. 1838.

226 *HG* 20 Oct., *NS* 16 Oct. 1838.

227 See *NS* 3 Feb. 1839. For Halifax's emergence as an anti-poor law and early Chartist stronghold, see Dorothy and E. P. Thompson, '"The Dignity of Chartism": Halifax as a Chartist Centre', in Roberts (ed.), *The Dignity of Chartism*; and Catherine Howe, *Halifax 1842: A Year in Crisis* (London: Breviary Stuff, 2014).

228 *NS* 3 Nov. 1838, 5 Jan., 11 May 1839. This was merely continuing a well-established process, see *NS* 3 Feb., 21 Apr. 1838.

229 See below, p. 419. On delegate meetings, see *NS* 9 June, 6 Oct. 1838, 20 Apr. 1839.

doubtful if Halifax was ever formally organised as a district. However, the fact that the Halifax area only sent one representative to West Riding delegate meetings indicates that, whilst local associations retained a good deal of autonomy, the regular Saturday evening meetings of the Halifax RA in practice acted as a central focus and reference point for the district.

Fortunately, it is reasonably easy to identify many of the main local leaders. This 'inner circle' was comprised of people such as Benjamin Rushton (weaver); Robert Wilkinson (shoemaker); Robert Sutcliffe (shoemaker); Thomas Cliffe (shoemaker? and later bookseller); Robert Tetley (book-hawker); William Thornton (woolcomber); Henry Rawson (a respectable elector); William Kidson Thorburn (grocer); and Abram Hanson (shoemaker).[230] Most were town based, but a few like Rushton, Thornton and Hanson hailed from the neighbouring villages and townships.

The names of other village leaders are more difficult to discover. The typical village gathering tended to be small in scale and convivial, educational or quasi-religious in emphasis. Occasionally the name of a local speaker is revealed in press reports, or it is possible to identify the name of the *Star*'s local agent or the keeper of the local meeting place, but there is no way of knowing how important or representative such figures were. In Elland, a flourishing and diligently reported radical centre in 1838, the most prominent local leaders were Abram Hanson; Richard Grassby (basket maker and local agent for the *Northern Star*); Francis Popplewell (veteran radical shoemaker); Daniel Marsden (beerseller?); and Thomas Stewart (Unitarian minister), but for other townships the chief sources provide insufficient information.[231]

The prominence of figures such as Rushton, Thornton and Hanson, both locally and regionally, illustrates one of the distinctive features of the local movement: its religious aspect. Many of the local associations held their meetings in nonconformist chapels and school-rooms, and prayers, hymns and sermons were commonplace at such gatherings. The Halifax RA's annual dinner in January 1839 had recommended radical prayer-meetings to petition 'the king of kings and lord of lords' to grant them universal suffrage'.[232] After Stephens' arrest, protest meetings were held throughout the parish and considerable sums were raised by the series of sermons preached throughout the district in the first half of the year.[233]

---

230 Elijah Crabtree, a wholesale beer-seller and Hon. Sec. of the RA in early 1838, does not appear on the public platform in this period and has not been included in this list. Dorothy Thompson in *The Chartists*, p. 24, designates Robert Sutcliffe (1808-?), a *Star* agent, as a weaver. My research indicates that he was cordwainer, though it is possible that he was both. He remained politically active in Chartist and ten hours campaigns into the 1840s.

231 Richard Grassby (1802-?) was a Hull-born basket maker. He later re-appears in the Chartist press writing from Leith on behalf of the Society of Journeymen Basket Makers (*NS* 12 Dec. 1846). Daniel Marsden (1803-62) a beershop keeper and woollen spinner remained actively involved in Chartism into the 1850s. It would be intriguing to know if he was the local coal-miner of the same name who was badly injured in a fire-damp explosion in 1831 and was convicted for sending a threatening letter to coal masters (about wages) a couple of years later (*People's Paper* 7 Apr. 1855; *HE* 22 Oct. 1831; *LI* 18 Nov. 1833).

232 *NS* 5 Jan. 1839.

233 *NS* 5, 12 Jan. 1839; for example, the Stephens Committee, which met regularly on Tuesday

Rushton and Hanson figured prominently in this programme of activity, but Chartist preachers from the Halifax-Bradford fringes, such as Jonathan Bairstow and Benjamin Brearley of Queenshead and Barker of Shelf, were also popular visitors to the area. William Thornton who hailed from Skircoat Green, also worked tirelessly to raise money and attained a regional reputation. It was Thornton, Feargus O'Connor's Archbishop of York in waiting, who opened the May 1839 Peep Green meeting with a prayer.[234] At this meeting Ben Rushton, who 'had given nothing to the parsons since 1821', seconded a resolution proposed by John Arran (a Methodist local preacher from Bradford) 'not to attend any place of worship where the administration of services is inimical to civil liberty', and Abram Hanson expounded an aggressive democratic brand of Christianity. He attacked the present sectarian preachers:

> They preached Christ and a crust, passive obedience and non-resistance. Let the people keep from those churches and chapels ('we will!'). Let them go to those men who preached Christ and a full belly, Christ and a well-clothed back – Christ and a good house to live in – Christ and Universal Suffrage.[235]

Often this religious backcloth was overlain with educational aspirations. In April 1838, for example, the biblical-sounding Mount Pellon RA devoted a collection taken during sermons preached by Rushton, Bairstow and Thornton to the adult school with which it was connected. The Elland RA ran a flourishing 'Radical School' around the same time, and the following spring (1839) a similar project was floated at Northowram.[236]

The intertwining of the political-religious-educational strands which made up the fabric of local Chartist life is further shown in the lectures with which the New Pellon RA (which was soon to have its own Radical Sunday School) choose to celebrate its first anniversary: Brearley of Queenshead on 'The five points of Radicalism and the Consistency of a Member of a Religious Community advocating them' and Rushton of Ovenden on 'The Connection of Church and State and the System of Finance'.[237]

The Halifax Chartists began 1839 in a buoyant mood. The area had made substantial contributions to the regional effort to collect signatures for the Petition and money for the National Rent, and the town itself boasted six *Northern Star* agents. In February local Chartists confirmed their local ascendency by successfully capturing a Corn Law Repeal meeting convened by their former radical-liberal allies.[238] Beyond the town, a number of new localities were brought into the Chartist fold. In May the district again made a colourful and significant contribution to the West Riding Peep

---

evening, was ready to send off (another) £20 to the Manchester committee, *NS* 30 Mar. 1839.

234 Benjamin Wilson, *The Struggles of an Old Chartist* (Halifax: John Nicholson, 1887), p. 3. O'Connor allegedly put his hands on Thornton's shoulder and said 'Well done, Thornton, when we get the People's Charter I will see that you are made the Archbishop of York'.

235 *NS, HG* 25 May 1839.

236 *NS* 21 Apr.; 14 Apr. 1838; 29 June 1839.

237 *NS* 5 Jan., 30 Mar. 1839.

238 *HG* 16 Feb. 1839.

Green meeting. Benjamin Wilson, then not yet fifteen-years old, later recalled his first Chartist event:

> ... we joined the procession in Halifax, which was a very large one headed by a band of music and marched by Godley Lane and Hipperholme, at which place the Queensbury [Queenshead] procession joined us; on reaching the top of the hill above Bailiffe Bridge we met the Bradford procession, headed by Peter Bussey, on horseback, and wearing a green sash.[239]

Local enthusiasm and optimism appear to have declined significantly in the following months, however. The Labour and Health caucus continued to meet regularly, but rarely sent in reports of their deliberations to the *Northern Star*. Possibly because of fears of arrest, their statements became more guarded and the tone of their activity more temperate.[240] In early May 1839 the RA had disowned advocates of physical force and condemned arming and drilling. In a more ironic vein, the association later in the month resolved to apply to the Lord Lieutenant of the West Riding for a supply of arms to protect life and property – in the spirit of the Home Secretary, Lord John Russell's letter to lord lieutenants recommending the formation of armed militia.[241] The Mixenden RA, which had earlier sent a vote of thanks to West Riding magistrates for preventing the sale of spirits at Peep Green, resolved in early June to abstain from all intoxicating drinks and abstain from other excisable articles until the Charter became the law of the land.[242] Other 'ulterior measures' were also canvassed and tried. The Vicar of Sowerby, for example, complained of threats and vigorous exclusive dealing against respectable shopkeepers who refused to contribute to the Chartist cause.[243]

The sacred month was never a popular local option. The Halifax RA had expressed its reservations as early as the end of June, and although the Birmingham outrages and the launching of the National Defence fund gave rise to new bursts of public activity, unsurprisingly the Halifax response to the three-day national holiday was lukewarm.[244] Thomas Cliffe admitted to an impromptu outdoor gathering in Bradford on 7 August that they were 'not so well prepared at Halifax', and local leaders who gathered the next day to consult with their followers on how to act, displayed caution and pragmatism. Robert Tetley 'advised the working men to keep in their situations, and not, by foolishly leaving them, let others "pop into their shoes," and thus deprive themselves of bread'. An 'operative named Gibson' similarly judged the sacred month 'inapplicable' in their present circumstances, whilst nevertheless urging people to arm and abstain from excisable articles. Eventually when the vote for having a 'holiday' was taken only half were in favour – a large number being undecided. On the day itself

---

239 Wilson, *Struggles*, p. 3.
240 Troops were also now stationed in the town, and local Chartists were worried about spies and *provocateurs* within the movement.
241 *NS* 1 June, 18 May 1839.
242 *NS* 1, 15 June 1839.
243 TNA: HO 40/51, f. 257, Rev. W. H. Bull to Russell, 26 July 1839.
244 *NS* 6, 20, 27 July 1839.

only 300 or 400 people (the *Star*'s estimate) assembled at the RA Room in Jail Lane to hear speeches from familiar radical stalwarts and to pass an address to the Queen.[245]

After this dampener the local movement in Halifax went into further decline – at least in its public manifestations. In October, for example, it was hoped that a public dinner for the West Riding's Convention delegates would 'infuse fresh spirit or life into the Radical ranks by pointing out the cause of recent failures'. It is doubtful whether it succeeded, for a month later a local witness reported to local magistrates that he had been 'a few nights in company with one of the Chartist leaders named Thornburn [Thorburn?] who was at the time a little intoxicated, and talking of the state of the people, Thornburn said, 'that Chartism was now at a very low ebb, that on last Wednesday night all their books and papers were burnt".[246]

Below the surface, particularly in the villages which touched upon the environs of Bradford, the picture may have been very different. Some energies went underground in the autumn and winter of 1839-40. Insurrectionary preparations and planning took place in a number of the outlying villages and it is likely that local leaders knew of, or were involved in, conspiratorial activity.[247] Much may have centred around the mysterious personage of Thomas Kitchenman who was the Halifax delegate at all the West Riding delegate meetings at this time.[248] Certainly there is evidence to link Halifax (albeit in some cases tenuously) with all the major instances when risings were expected or actually occurred. Two informants told local magistrates in November that 'from the information we have received had not Peter Bussey taken badly they would have commenced the same day that Frost did'.[249] Although the public voice of Halifax Chartism was muted, the area remained a Chartist stronghold – a fact recognised by the local magistracy who remained extremely worried right into January 1840 and pressed for military protection.[250]

---

245 *BO* 8 Aug. 1839; *HHE* 10 Aug. 1839; *NS*, *HG* 17 Aug. 1839.

246 *NS* 17 Oct. 1839; Dorothy and E. P. Thompson, 'Halifax as a Chartist Centre', p. 3 [Original MS]. William Thorburn, a radical, had chaired the January 1838 Halifax RA meeting that had advocated the five points of the radical reform programme, *HG* 23 Jan. 1838.

247 See Dalby, 'The Chartist Movement in Halifax', pp. 109-10, for references to Ovenden and Queenshead. Dorothy and E. P. Thompson 'Halifax as a Chartist Centre', p. 92, mentions Thornton and William Cockcroft (a Halifax weaver) as local leaders.

248 Kitchenman has no previous recorded public appearances before this time. A 'Thomas Kitchenman', in his early twenties was a Barnsley insurgent in 1820 (a relation of his, Stephen, was a local Luddite delegate and very active in Union Society politics and the rising between 1816-20). A 'Thomas Kitchenman' was arrested for drilling men in Halifax in 1848. The 1851 census records a 58 year-old Thomas Kitchenman, a woolcomber, living in the same area of Halifax from where the driller came. The name is not a common one, and although the different scenes-of-action weighs against the Barnsley and Halifax man being the same, a connection cannot be ruled out. I am grateful to John Baxter and Dorothy Thompson for giving me access to this information. *NS* 5 Oct., 2 Nov., 21 Dec. 1839.

249 Note signed by James Rawson and Thomas Aked, n.d. (but probably late November 1839) reprinted in Dalby, 'The Chartist Movement in Halifax', p. 109. Dorothy and E. P. Thompson, 'Halifax as a Chartist Centre', p. 93, fn. 44 note that a 'James Rawson' was an active Chartist and float the possibility that he was an informer.

250 Draft letter from J. R. Ralph to Col. Wemyss, 28 Jan. 1840, reprinted in Dalby, 'The Chartist Movement in Halifax' p. 111.

e) Keighley

A true estimate of the strength and pervasiveness of early Chartism in Keighley is hampered by a paucity of information. Whether because of the town's relative isolation, the local correspondents' lethargy, or a lack of activity to report, the *Northern Star* and other West Riding papers include only sparse coverage of Chartist endeavours. There are always dangers in interpreting relative silence as inertia, but in the case of Keighley this conclusion appears inescapable. Given the town's traditions of radical, short time and trade union activity, the early Chartist response in Keighley is all the more surprising.

In spite of radical involvement in meetings on the factory question and the Bridget Cone case, local radicalism was acknowledged to be in a state of 'lethargy' in early June 1838.[251] A major public meeting and a dinner to O'Connor formally introduced the Northern Union idea to Keighley in late July, giving radicals a much-needed fillip. However, though the RA continued to hold occasional meetings and debates, there is no evidence to indicate a quickening of pace in the weeks before the October Peep Green meeting.[252] The Keighley radicals certainly took part in preparations, but no local speakers addressed the assembly and the Keighley presence did not merit a mention in any of the reports.[253] Momentum picked up in the winter of 1838-9. The RA met in late November to organise the systematic collection of National Rent and by the middle of January, when a very respectable £25 had been collected, radical spirits were said to be high.[254] Sermons in the local Primitive Methodist Chapel to raise subscriptions for the popular J. R. Stephens provided another focus for activity in early 1839, but hereafter the local movement went into something of a decline.[255] In April 1839 the *Leeds Mercury* reported that, 'At Huddersfield and Keighley the Chartists have suffered complete defeats; and in short the silly clamour for 'Universal Suffrage', and the ineffably absurd 'Peoples' Charter' is dying away'.[256]

The Peep Green meeting in May caused a brief stir. About a hundred Keighley men attended, but a Bingley magistrate writing to Lord Harewood, the Lord Lieutenant, at the time of the rally believed there to be 'very few chartists ... in either this parish or at Keighley'.[257] The town's sole response to the sacred month was an unspectacular public meeting on a Tuesday evening, 12 August, which followed the Convention's advice and passed an address to the Queen.[258] The town continued to send a steady trickle of money to the various Chartist funds, but never contributed significantly to the wider missionary effort. Bradford speakers had provided an 'outside' input for radical meetings in Bingley in April 1839; and in late August when the Chartists of Cross Hills (a small outlying worsted manufacturing village) turned to

---

251 *NS* 5 May, 9 June 1838.
252 *NS* 4 Aug.; for example, 8 Sept. 1838 (Vincent spoke, along with delegates from the Stalybridge cotton spinners).
253 *NS* 13, 16 Oct. 1838.
254 *NS* 24 Nov., 1 Dec. 1838; 26 Jan. 1839.
255 *NS* 16, 23 Feb. 1839; also, resolutions at public meeting, *NS* 29 Dec. 1838.
256 *LM* 6 Apr. 1839.
257 *LM* 25 May 1839; WYAS: HP, Box 2, W. Ellis to Harewood, 25 May 1839.
258 *NS* 17 Aug, 1839.

the Keighley radicals to help them form a RA, the Keighley men could only muster a small contingent to march the five miles to the village. Their middle-class opponents had a field day, announcing that Chartism was dead and that there were only thirty-two Chartists in Keighley.[259]

The range of Chartist activity which continued into autumn and early winter followed a familiar pattern: temperance and radical lectures, the formation of a female RA, and debates with Owenite socialists on the respective merits of their two systems.[260] Frost's arrest and prosecution re-activated radical instincts and tapped into the residual store of popular support. A well-attended Keighley meeting raised nearly £5, and the neighbouring villages also sent in contributions.[261] There were apparently some fears about secret Chartist activity around the time of the Bradford rising. However, although local Chartists may have been more circumspect in their operations and may have adopted the class meetings form of organisation, there is no evidence to link the town with insurrectionary activity elsewhere in the Riding. The Home Office was certainly not worried and the request for a small military force was rejected.[262]

A number of reasons can be put forward to explain why Chartist organisation and support in Keighley never really flourished in the early period. In the first place, the town laboured under geographical disadvantages. The majority of the hundred or more stalwarts who attended the May 1839 Peep Green rally did the thirty-six mile round trip on foot.[263] Cost as well as distance may also have been a factor in the fact that Keighley only twice sent delegates to the regular West Riding delegate meetings (usually held in the Dewsbury area) which co-ordinated regional activity. This can only have increased the town's sense of relative isolation.

Secondly, the strength and persistence of local opposition may have inhibited the public expression of Chartist sympathies and possibly also diverted energies. The *Northern Star* in February 1839 noted one employer's fury at finding a pro-Stephens placard hung in his factory, and a number of prominent Whig and Tory 'millocrats' were amongst the Chartists' main opponents. When Chartist leader Thomas Knowles engaged the local bellman to announce a Female Radicals' meeting in October 1839 two local Whig magistrates (and major worsted manufacturers) threatened the bellman's job, and the RA was forced into using a large rattle.[264]

The Keighley Chartists' local difficulties were epitomised by their problems in securing a meeting place. Initially all suitable options, including the chapels 'with which the town abounds' and the Mechanics Institute, had been closed off, leaving local leaders to risk the vagaries of the weather. David Weatherhead's purchase of the old Primitive Methodist Chapel as a Working Men's Hall in late spring 1839 solved

---

259 NS 13,27 Apr. 1839 (Bingley); 7 Sept. 1839 (Cross Hills). The *Star* gave the figure as a hundred Chartists and pointed to the rival attraction of the 'Bingley Tide' an anniversary day for Sick and Friendly Societies.

260 NS 28 Sept., 12, 19, 26 Oct. 1839.

261 NS 21 Dec. 1839.

262 TNA: HO 40/57 f. 291, Information of Edmund Laycock and Thomas Wall, 28 Jan 1840; Briggs, 'Keighley', pp. 312-3.

263 LM 25 May 1839.

264 NS 23 Feb.; 27 Apr.; 12 Oct. 1839. This continued to be a problem, see NS 3 Apr. 1841.

this particular problem; and local Chartists sarcastically celebrated the acquisition of a venue where 'the labouring class ... can meet without having to wound the feelings of the saints, or retard the progress of scientific discovery'.[265]

The politics of parochial administration formed another setting for conflict with local adversaries. Chartist defeats here were both a source and a symptom of their relative weakness. In October 1838, for example, when other areas were rousing their neighbourhoods for the Peep Green meeting, Keighley radicals were locked-in conflict with the local 'Church party' over the ever-contentious issue of church rates. Allegations of vote-rigging, employers' intimidation of their workmen, anti-radical exclusive dealing, and magisterial bias followed a narrow radical defeat and the prosecution of a leading radical for assaulting the (former radical) chairman of the vestry meeting.[266] The following April Chartists once again cried foul and railed against the sharp practices of local factory lords and respectables after further defeats at Poor Law Guardian and parish elections. Radical morale was at a low ebb. They did not even bother to attend the Court Leet where in recent years their popularly elected candidate had been rejected at the instigation of 'our, Whig and Tory opponents'. The *Star's* local correspondent commented tellingly on radical exhaustion:

> the Radicals are getting tired of this desultory kind of warfare against opponents, who, however despicable in number and argument themselves, are rendered all powerful by the assistance they receive from corrupt Government.

Local events confirmed 'the Radicals in their worst opinion of a middle as well as upper-class, legislation'.[267]

The depth and persistence of local distress further fuelled this antagonism to local employers and respectables, but, equally, made the task of formal organisation, fund-raising and generally enthusing more difficult for local leaders. The *Leeds Times* had reported severe distress amongst the combers and weavers, the bulk of the local working population, in June 1837 and prospects remained grim throughout the winter and early part of 1838. The RA's address to launch the National Rent appeal on late November 1838 informed local inhabitants, 'we seek not to injure the wealth of the rich, however, acquired; we want not to shed blood, but we do want a fair day's wage for a fair day's work; it is our right and we are determined to have it'.[268] Even when trade improved, as it did in early 1839, combing wages remained under pressure and never recovered their former level. The local villages' contributions for Frost in late 1839 were valued all the more for being raised 'by poor weavers and woolcombers, either entirely out of work, or only partially employed'.[269]

Other pre-occupations or counter-attractions supplied an additional factor in early Chartism's low profile in Keighley. As well as a variety of minor nonconformist sects, Keighley also possessed a small but lively Owenite socialist group which periodically

265 *NS* 27 Apr.; 6 July 1839.
266 *NS* 6, 13 Oct., 3 Nov. 1839.
267 *LM* 13 Apr., *NS* 27 Apr. 1839.
268 *LT* 17 June 1837; *NS* 1 Dec. 1838.
269 *NS* 16 Feb.; 21 Dec. 1839.

tested itself in open debate with the Chartists and may well have drawn on similar groups for its main support.[270] As at Huddersfield, the radicals' earlier vigorous commitment to the anti-poor law cause in 1837 and early 1838 may have drained energies and become something of a diversion. Although a local worthy, writing to Lord Harewood in May 1839, noted with satisfaction the relatively smooth implementation of the new poor law, popular opposition took a long time to die away.[271] When the poor-rate collector visited the near-by village of Thwaites in late 1838 he invariably wore old clothes, in the knowledge that he would be pelted with dirt; and the first meeting of the Board of Guardians in August 1838 had to be held behind closed doors, guarded by constables. Abraham Wildman, one of the local radicals who had helped to induce this siege mentality by 'breathing death and destruction' to the new Poor Law the previous year, possibly inflicted grave damage on radical credibility by becoming the Board's new relieving officer.[272]

The defection of Wildman, a leading radical and ten hours' advocate, and the political shape-shifting of another prominent factory reformer, J. B. Aked, both point to a final factor in Chartism's slow early development in Keighley – the exhaustion and perhaps ossification of the local leadership.[273] The most prominent of the front-line leaders of early Chartism in Keighley had all been active in radical and factory reform politics since the early 1830s, and other local leaders – Thomas Knowles, John Garnett, John Smith – also belonged to the same generation of radicalism.[274] Although a few new names emerge in the early Chartist period, such as John Waterhouse, a young woolcomber/barber 'of the Ranter persuasion', there does not appear to have been a major infusion of fresh blood. A few stalwarts like Joseph Firth and the Constantine family, comprising Isaac, a woolcomber and his two sons, Thomas and John, both combers and Chartist preachers active from the late 1830s to 1842, ensured a degree of continuity.[275] However, the existing leadership struggled to revitalise grassroots organisations and re-define local tactics. The interplay between established and new radical leaders, and between the town centre and the out-townships, which is a characteristic of the stronger Chartist districts such as Bradford and Dewsbury does not appear to have occurred in Keighley.

---

270 See, for example, NS 29 Sept. 1838; 26 Oct. 1839.

271 WYAS: HP, Box 2, W. Ellis to Harewood, 25 May 1839.

272 NS 27 Oct.; 25 Aug. 1838.

273 The *Northern Star*'s account of a Keighley Church Rate meeting commented that Aked's 'innumerable conversions to all kinds of creeds and political opinions have rendered him notorious', NS 6 Oct. 1838

274 Thomas Knowles (1813-1843?), keeper of Knowles' Temperance Hotel and a 'celebrated Chartist lecturer', was active in the 1838-42 period. John Garnett, (1802-1852+), a Scottish born worsted weaver, and later a schoolmaster and news vendor, remained an important local Chartist until at least the late 1840s.

275 On John Waterhouse (1814-1851+) see, LT 10 Mar. 1838; NS 3 Apr. 1841. Isaac Constantine (1791?-?) 'an intelligent working man' spoke at the inauguration of the Keighley Working Men's Hall (NS 6 July 1839). His sons Thomas (b. 1816?) and John (b. 1821) were both Chartist missionaries.

f) Dewsbury

The Dewsbury district was an area of keen Chartist activity and support throughout the 1838-40 period. Dewsbury itself had possessed an active RA since September 1837, and even in previously quiescent places, like Birstall and Mirfield, RAs were flourishing by early spring 1838. Although the district was preoccupied with vigorous anti-poor law activities during the summer months, by the beginning of September regular meetings were being held by local associations at Heckmondwike, Liversedge, Gomersal and Ossett. Unsurprisingly, the district mustered a strong turnout at the October Peep Green meeting (held on its doorstep), but, more impressively, had contributed over £46 to the National Rent by early February 1839, a figure which compares favourably with that raised in other early Chartist strongholds.[276]

Chartism continued to flourish during the first half of 1839. In June local Chartists were planning to build a 'People's Hall' in Heckmondwike, and a few weeks later Dewsbury radicals, who gathered in their thousands to hear Bronterre O'Brien, met nightly in the open-air to read papers and discuss grievances, and began a system of 'exclusive dealing'. Although the state of trade prevented the local workers from being able 'to stand the sacred holiday' in August, the three-day national holiday met with an impressive response.[277] This was certainly the view of local magistrates, who recalled five months later that, in contrast to the 'feeble' or 'contemptibly feeble' displays in neighbouring Leeds, Huddersfield and Barnsley, the 'Three glorious days' of August were vigorously supported:

> No one who saw the thousands that were beat up by the sound of drum and marched into the Town from all the villages marshalled in regular array and many of them carrying many bludgeons could dispute the truth of the boast made by their leaders as they addressed them from the Market Cross that the place was in their power and that if they pleased they could lay it [to] ashes.[278]

After this, information about local Chartism becomes scarce and it is likely that, as at Bradford, part of the movement went underground. Local industrial conflict and increasing distress probably heightened tensions, and in early October a 'strong muster' gathered to hear Charles Neesom of the London DA 'and several other friends of freedom' deliver a series of animating and 'heart-stirring' speeches. Afterwards 'many persons enrolled themselves as member of a joint stock company for establishing for themselves a commercial independence of the middle-men.'[279] Unless this was merely a smokescreen for insurrectionary plotting, it provides another indication that at the grass-roots level moral- and physical-force aspirations were inter-mixed and not necessarily mutually exclusive. That said, some disguise would have been useful since a few tantalising inadequate scraps of evidence indicate

---

276 NS 13, 16 Oct. 1838; 2 Feb. 1839. The nearest comparable figure was £41 from Bradford.
277 NS 26 June; 20 July; 17 Aug., 28 Sept. 1839.
278 TNA: HO 40/57 f. 235, Hall, Clay and Watts to Greenwood, 16 Jan. 1840.
279 NS 28 Sept., 26 Oct. (Carpet weavers' strike); 12 Oct. 1839 (Neesom). On Neesom, see D. Thompson, The Chartists, p. 137.

considerable local involvement in the arming and plotting which culminated in the still rather murky Dewsbury Rising of January 1840.[280]

The make-up of the local Chartist movement reflected a diverse, decentralised industrial structure. The contrasts between places only a few miles apart could be striking. So whilst Cleckheaton supported Chartism in only a 'half-hearted way', contiguous settlements like Heckmondwike and Liversedge were strong physical-force centres.[281] Equally, whilst Ossett responded quickly to the publication of the People's Charter, the Batley area was not roused until the following spring.[282] As the focal point of the district, Dewsbury undoubtedly had a special place in the local movement. It was the venue for a number of major public meetings and dinners attended by figures of regional and national repute. The Dewsbury association also played a role in rousing the surrounding area. A deputation of Dewsbury radicals, for example, gave advice on conduct and procedure to the nascent Ossett RA in September 1838, and speakers from Dewsbury frequently visited neighbouring associations.[283] In line with other Chartist strongholds, the Dewsbury RA formally established an 'agitational council' for 'Dewsbury and its neighbourhood' in June 1839.[284]

Local associations, however, retained a good deal of autonomy. Each normally sent their own representative to the West Riding delegate meetings, which in the absence of formal District Committee meetings on the Bradford model, probably provided the main meeting place for local leaders. The regional context was particularly important for the Dewsbury district. All West Riding delegate meetings of the period were held in the Heckmondwike/Liversedge area and, partly through ease of attendance, the Dewsbury district exerted a strong influence on regional policy. Up to half or more of West Riding delegates normally came from the immediate vicinity, and a number of local men held prominent positions in the regional organisation of the early movement.[285]

The identification of the main local leaders is not always easy. The area did not possess a great number of accomplished speakers. The normal pattern of activity for the area tended to be one of routine weekly or fortnightly meetings, (usually low-key, small-scale and under-reported), interspersed with occasional, larger formal gatherings bolstered by the presence of guest speakers from the surrounding districts. For example, the Liversedge RA held its anniversary dinner on Christmas Day 1838, in a room adjoining a meeting of West Riding delegates, 'several of whom took the

---

280 For Neesom's presence see *NS* 12 Oct., 2 Nov., 14 Dec. 1839, and below, pp. 472-3.

281 Peel, *Spen Valley*, pp. 315-19, 349-52. See also *NS* 23 Feb. 1839 (Liversedge).

282 *NS* 15, 22 Sept. 1838; 9, 30 Mar. 1839.

283 *NS* 22 Sept.; 6 Oct., 15 Dec. 1838.

284 *NS* 8, 15, 22 June 1839.

285 For example, Samuel Healey (printer, 1818?-1846?), the first permanent West Riding secretary, was replaced by Abel Goodall in August 1839, when he moved away from 'the central part of the district' (*NS* 17 Aug. 1839). It is possible that he moved to Skipton where a printing partnership with John Garnett was dissolved in early 1840. He reappears in Chartist and radical campaigns in Leeds in the early 1840s.

opportunity of addressing their brother radicals'.[286] Metropolitan figures like O'Connor, O'Brien and Neesom were also popular visitors to the area.

The district's native leaders fall into two main categories. The first group – the chief district leaders – comprised a band of local men who achieved some standing and importance outside their immediate locality, as notable public speakers, key organisers or diligent West-Riding officials. The most prominent were Samuel Healey (printer?) of Dewsbury; John Haigh snr. (tailor) of Ossett Street Side; Abel Goodall (shoemaker) of Heckmondwike; Morritt Mathews (Quaker 'currier') of Liversedge; and, later, Francis Law (hatter) and William Wilby (a working man) of Dewsbury.[287] Other possible additions to this group include a handful of respectable lower middle-class figures who held important positions of respect and trust in the local movement. James Penny, a Liversedge grocer, for example, became West Riding Treasurer in 1839, and, though not a prominent platform speaker, was a key network figure.[288] Luke Firth, a woolstapler, though well-connected with leading Chartists, was apparently a strong opponent of physical-force, sentiments which are unlikely to have endeared him to the local adherents.[289] The pre-eminent figure, however, was Titus Senior Brooke, Dewsbury druggist and newsagent, and radical stalwart of more than local repute. Active on a variety of platforms throughout the 1830s, the Dewsbury RA held a dinner in his honour in November 1838. The following year he stood bail for Joseph Crabtree, a Barnsley Chartist charged with sedition and was praised in the *Star* as 'the only one of the middle classes, who has remained firm to the cause of the people'. A classic town-radical he provided a bridge to the wider body of reformers. So, when in June 1839 local Chartists refused on principle to support Whig-liberal opposition to church rates until 'they help us to get Universal Suffrage', Brooke endorsed the radicals' appraisal of the Whigs but unsuccessfully sought to persuade them to drop their controversial amendment.[290]

The second level of leadership comprised the leaders who chaired or regularly participated in local RA or NU meetings or who served as delegates to the West Riding meetings. In Dewsbury itself, additional names include Samuel Allatt, 'hatter' and 'working man', who became Chair of the local RA; George Hall, who was often the association's delegate; and possibly John Dibb (an established town radical) and Thomas Field.[291] In the Heckmondwike/Liversedge area local leadership was provided

---

286 *NS* 29 Dec. 1838.

287 John Haigh (1792?-1861+); Abel Goodall (1799?-1877?); Morritt Matthews (1771?-1850?); Francis Law (1805?-1886?); William Wilby (1812?-1877).

288 James Penny (1799-1861), a grocer and later a corn miller employing ten people, remained active into the 1840s. He was recognised as a 'true friend of the people' (*NS* 11 Dec. 1841).

289 On Firth, see Peel, *Spen Valley*, pp. 351-2; for Penny becoming treasurer, see *NS* 13 July 1839.

290 *NS* 17 Nov. 1838, *LI* 28 Sept. 1839; *NS* 28 Sept. 1839; 8 June 1839. Brooke was married to one of Charlotte Brontë's best friends and was acquainted with Patrick Brontë. According to D. Thompson, *The Chartists*, p. 28, he had been imprisoned during the War of the Unstamped.

291 Samuel Allatt (1806-1877) was described as a 'hat maker' in the 1851 Census. John Dibb, a clog and pattern maker, was secretary of the Dewsbury RA in 1838, but has no recorded public appearances in 1839. 'Thomas Holt, alias Field' of Chickenley was one of the people

by people such as Joseph Atkinson (blanket weaver), Thomas Wass (grocer) and Joseph Hatfield, (New Connexion local preacher and former carpet weaver who also acted as the *Star*'s local agent).[292] In the Ossett/Gawthorpe/Chickenley district, John Moorhouse, Abraham Hollingsworth and William Moseley Stott, a hairdresser who later became a prominent West Riding figure, stood second in line to John Haigh, the area's pre-eminent Chartist.[293] In the vicinity of Birstall/Gomersal the key leaders appear to have been William Fox, who chaired a West Riding delegate meeting in May 1839, and George Crowther (operative blanket manufacturer). Similar roles in the Batley/Batley Carr area were performed by Benjamin Bromley and John Porritt, in Mirfield by Benjamin Pearson (tailor), in Earlsheaton by Jeremiah Marsden (blanket weaver), and in Hanging Heaton by Edward Newsome (shoemaker).[294]

Such a cursory summary probably does scant justice to the memory and efforts of some dedicated and important local leaders. Others may have been omitted altogether, because their names or activities simply did not reach the columns of the *Northern Star* or attract the notice of local magistrates. Frank Peel's account of Chartist period in the Spen Valley refers to figures such as Daniel Hinchcliffe, whose house was the rendezvous for Heckmondwike's physical-force Chartists; Gabriel Redfearn, a blanket weaver who was apparently the oracle of the Chartist movement in Littletown (near Liversedge); and Benny Beaumont, who performed the same function in Millbridge.[295] These may have belonged to an underground side of the movement which it is impossible, at this distance, to penetrate. Equally, it is likely that many 'overground' leaders have simply been lost to posterity.

The religious component of early Chartism in the Dewsbury district was not as pronounced as in the Bradford-Halifax area. Local Chartist unions tended to meet in pubs or beershops rather than chapels or school rooms, and, with the notable exception of Joseph Hatfield (of Heckmondwike) and possibly John Bedford, few Methodist or other local preachers were prominent in the local movement. That is not to say that the religious side was absent. The intriguingly named Doghouse Female Radical Association closed the meeting, (at which it had raised £1.5s.3d for the Stephens Defence Fund), with 'the first of Wesley's hymns 'O for a thousand tongues to sing".[296] Two months later a sermon by William Hill before a huge gathering in Dewsbury raised a further £10 for the Fund, and Rushton, Bairstow, Thornton and Arran were

---

arrested during the anti-poor law disturbances in 1838, *NS* 25 Aug. 1838.

292 For Wass, see Peel, *Spen Valley*, p. 316; for Hatfield (1794?-1869?), ibid., pp. 349-50.

293 John Moorhouse (1802-1875), the son of a clothier, was an 'Engine and Machine Smith', who spent part of the 1840s in Denmark, where he met his second wife, before returning to work in Leeds. W. M. Stott (1816-?) a radical stalwart, named one of his sons after the United Irishman Robert Emmett and served as West Riding secretary in 1840.

294 *NS* 4 May 1939 (Fox chaired a similar gathering in 1848). Benjamin Bromley (1806-1868?), a clothier and 'working man', remained a Chartist and factory reform stalwart into his fifties (*NS* 4 July 1846; *LI* 21 Nov. 1857). Benjamin Pearson (1789-1855) often acted as treasurer of local Chartist funds. Jeremiah Marsden (1789-1855) was variously described as 'an operative', a 'cloth weaver' and a 'blanket weaver'. Edward Newsome (1796?-1871) was a 'cordwainer'.

295 Peel, *Spen Valley*, pp. 315-9.

296 *NS* 30 Mar. 1839.

all frequent and popular visitors to the area.[297] Yet, in general, the Chartist sermon was not a distinctive feature of the local movement.

A more characteristic and perhaps underestimated feature of the local scene was the musical tradition, which showed itself in the participation of many local bands at Chartist meetings. The use of bands to literally drum up support and publicise radical meetings was a time-honoured tactic. The report of the Oct 1838 Peep Green meeting cites the involvement of numerous bands – all adding colour, excitement and (with luck) harmony to the occasion. Interestingly, Frank Peel's account of early Chartism in Littletown mentions the formation of a small Chartist band which soon became popular and helped to keep up local enthusiasm. 'Bands of Music' apparently signalled the start of the three-day 'National Holiday' by parading the streets of the different villages of the district, before eventually leading processions to a mass meeting in Dewsbury.[298] It appears that at the height of Chartist expectation and excitement, all the local communities' indigenous cultural resources were put at the disposal of the Chartists.

Even allowing for local variations and the hyperbole of both Chartist leaders and opponents alike, the tone of the early Chartist movement in the Dewsbury area was uncompromisingly militant. Advocates of Corn Law repeal dared not hold a public meeting on the issue in Heckmondwike, whilst in Ossett the *Mercury* alleged that physical-force Chartists had influenced people not to sign an anti-Corn Law petition.[299] In April 1839 Abel Goodall of Heckmondwike calculated that twenty of the local Association were armed and that 'in two or three weeks they would have twenty more'. The radicals of neighbouring Liversedge, another physical-force stronghold, had issued a militant Address two months earlier and in July the hostile *Mercury* reported growing Chartist threats and intimidation in Dewsbury.[300]

The ideas of the more forceful members of the Convention also evoked a sympathetic response in the Dewsbury area. The Heckmondwike RA had for a time in early 1839 styled itself the Heckmondwike Democratic Association. Harney and Neesom of the London DA were popular visitors to the area and in late May 1839 a crowded meeting of the United Association of Ossett, Gawthorpe and Chickenley had declared itself satisfied with William Rider's conduct at the Convention.[301] Neesom stayed in Liversedge in November 1839 and had earlier addressed the anniversary dinner of the Chickenley RA.[302] By this time, however, the local movement had largely gone underground and information about local organisations and leaders becomes scarce.

Exactly where Dewsbury fitted into the complex mix of rumours and verified events which preceded and followed the Newport Rising may never be fully known. As A. J. Peacock speculates, 'momentous, decisions' may have been reached at the

---

297 *NS* 11 May 1839; for a vivid description of a Chartist sermon at Littletown, by Rushton see, Peel, *Spen Valley*, pp. 318-19.

298 *NS* 16 Oct. 1838; Peel, *Spen Valley*, p. 316; *NS* 17 Aug. 1839. Bands were also prominent on other days of the holiday.

299 *NS* 2 Mar. 1839; *LM* 9 Feb. 1839.

300 *NS* 27 Apr.; 23 Feb.; *LM* 27 July 1839.

301 *NS* 19 Jan.; 1 June 1839.

302 *NS* 2 Nov. 1839.

West Riding delegate meeting held at Heckmondwike in late September, and it is likely that Dewsbury was one of the places that George White visited (at Peter Bussey's instigation) to call off the Yorkshire part of the rising. Certainly, the Dewsbury Chartists were sufficiently bemused by the sudden turn of events to seek clarification from O'Connor about his part in proceedings.[303] Undaunted after the bloody failure at Newport, however, Dewsbury continued to play its part in deliberations about ways of saving Frost and obtaining the Charter. The town was the location of an under-reported West Riding delegate Meeting on 12 December and one of the three places chosen to send representatives to a second Convention in London. Delegate meetings continued to be held in Dewsbury in late December and early January and these decided on 12 January as the date for a rising. In spite of the fact that O'Connor, doyen of the Dewsbury Chartists, apparently 'lost his nerve' and came out against the scheme, some local Chartists carried on with the plan.[304]

Few concrete facts are known about the Dewsbury Rising of Saturday evening and Sunday morning (11-12 January 1840), largely because only two people were ever arrested for their part in the events. Nevertheless, what emerges from Home Office accounts is a picture of a fairly extensive, well-planned and disciplined rising. Sizeable numbers of people were involved (particularly from the blanket-weaving townships on the outskirts of Dewsbury, such as Earlsheaton) and although guns were allegedly fired indiscriminately, there was no bodily violence or looting. All the street lights were put out, but ironically (or perhaps deliberately) the only window broken was in a wine and spirit shop owned by Thomas Todd, a former ally and prominent 'town-radical'. In spite of the fact that the plot was apparently forestalled by mishaps and 'absent friends', for a few hours the insurgents to all extents and purposes held Dewsbury.[305] The main leaders escaped detection and lived to fight another day.

3: Leadership and Support

Introduction

Contemporaries tended to recognize just two categories of Chartists: 'stalwarts' and 'fairweather birds'.[306] Some later commentators have also used simple bipartite divisions – between leadership and rank and file, platform and crowd, party and mass or those above and below the platform – when analysing the personnel of the Chartist movement.[307] Other writers have attempted more sophisticated analyses. James Epstein, writing about Nottingham, breaks down Chartist adherence into two distinct but necessarily fluid 'levels of support' – the 'soft core' of local supporters and sympathisers and a smaller 'hard-core' who made up the membership of the local

---

303 Peacock, *Bradford Chartism*, pp. 31-9; *NS* 23 Nov. 1839.

304 *NS* 14 Dec. 1839; Peacock, *Bradford Chartism*, pp. 35-37.

305 This paragraph particularly draws on Peacock, *Bradford Chartism*, pp. 37-38 and TNA: HO 40/57 ff.141, 145, 149, 165, 181, 217, 235, 327.

306 Jones, *Chartism and the Chartists*, p. 23.

307 See, for example, F. J. Kaijage, 'Labouring Barnsley, 1816-1856: A Social and Economic History', Unpub. PhD thesis, University of Warwick, 1975, p. 445; D. Thompson, 'Chartism as a Historical Subject', *Bulletin of the Society for the study of Labour History*, 20 (1970), p. 11.

Chartist 'party'. It was from this latter group of 'activists' that the town's leaders were drawn.[308] Taking a broad look at the whole movement, Edward Royle delineates six categories of support and involvement: 'the national leadership'; 'the lesser (regional) leaders'; 'the truly local leaders'; 'the loyal followers' in the localities; 'the followers who drifted in and out of the Chartist societies and meetings with the ebb and flow of popular enthusiasm', and, lastly, 'the most numerous band of all, working men and women, hardly touched, or touched not at all by Chartism.'[309]

An alternative way of conceptualising the movement is to see it as comprising four fluctuating but concentric spheres of activity and involvement, each diminishing greatly in numerical size but increasing in terms of concentration. The large, all-embracing, outer ring encompasses the vast and largely anonymous mass of Chartist supporters and sympathisers who drifted in and out of the movement according to the immediacy of specific issues or circumstances. Just occasionally we get to hear their voices; like that of G. Kirman, a starving tailor and veteran of Trafalgar, who moved a resolution at a meeting of unemployed operatives on Hunslet Moor in Leeds in December 1839. The 'old tar' professed simply that, 'He wanted peace and plenty of work, so that they could keep their families, and go to a place of worship'.[310]

The occasionally patronising accounts of such contributions cannot disguise the broad attraction of Chartist principles and ideas in the West Riding textile district. The impression provided by visiting radical missionary, Henry Vincent, of 'a general and almost universal radical opinion' in every town, is broadly corroborated by concerned local magistrates in correspondence to the Home Office.[311] Hundreds of thousands of people associated themselves with the movement's fortunes and made up the massive Chartist crowds which attended the Peep Green meetings, read or listened to the *Northern Star*, and signed the National Petition. These acts were the badges of their allegiance. A Prison Inspector who interviewed the Bradford prisoners who had become involved in the 'direct action' side of the movement in the winter of 1839-40, noted that one, Hutton, was a 'Chartist only by reading the Star newspaper', whilst William Brook, 'Is a Chartist in opinion but has only attended one meeting'. The last point is important since it is clear that the vast reservoir of goodwill and support which Chartism enjoyed was not always translated into paid-up party members. Benjamin Wilson, for example, recalls that even 'when the agitation was at its height, very few of those attending its meetings joined the Association or subscribed to its funds'.[312]

---

308 Epstein, 'Chartist Movement in Nottingham', p. 229.

309 Royle, *Chartism*, pp. 75-6. The useful analogy of a modern football club's supporters, which he introduces, can possibly be extended to illustrate the variable size of his last category, at least in the West Riding. The support enjoyed by a club extends beyond paid-up members of an 'official' supporters' club or even those who regularly attend matches, to the tens of thousands of people (or more) who loosely identify with a club and follow its fortunes on social or local media, and who at times of particular excitement (e.g. a successful league or cup run) become more intimately involved in their team's fortunes.

310 *LM* 21 Dec. 1839.

311 Labour History Archive and Study Centre (LHASC), Manchester, Vincent MSS 1/1/10, Vincent to Miniken, 26 Aug. 1838.

312 TNA: HO 20/10, Prisons. For a full interpretation of this and other evidence about Chartist prisoners see, C. Godfrey, 'The Chartist Prisoners, 1839-41', *International Review of Social*

This should not be attributed to a lack of interest or commitment, rather it stemmed from the fact that times were hard and permanent formal political or trade societies (with regular meetings and subscriptions) were far from being the norm for most working people.

The next, more concentrated ring of Chartists included the movement's staunch adherents and hardcore supporters. These were the paid-up party members who formally joined the local RA or NU branch, who clubbed together to buy a regular *Northern Star*, and whose pennies swelled the coffers of the Stephens Fund or National Rent and, for a time in 1838-9, the profits of local blacksmiths and gun-makers. They also participated fully in the cultural educational side of local branch life and could be relied upon to turn out for small local meetings or events whatever the extremes of climate or interest. Who they were and how many they were is difficult to say. Sources like the record books of the Great Horton National Charter Association (NCA) and membership lists of the NCA make identification easier after 1840. In the earlier period, however, we have to rely on names or initials on subscription lists and on indications like the 256 members who had enrolled in Huddersfield Northern Union by October 1838 or the 112 stalwarts who walked the seventeen miles from Keighley to attend the May 1839 Peep Green meeting.[313]

No hard and fast division is possible between this group and the next inner ring, the Chartist activists, and clearly any dividing line is fairly arbitrary. The activists were the 'party workers', often shadowy background figures whose names crop up occasionally in the Chartist or local press seconding a resolution at a small local meeting or dinner. They were the messengers and marshals, the canvassers and collectors, the minor committee-men who saw to the printing and posting of bill-stickers, who contacted the local band or bellman, and who acquired a suitable venue or hustings-wagon for meetings. All were thorough-going radicals without whom the rough early prototype of the Chartist party machine would have quickly ground to a halt.[314]

An insight into the workings of this group is provided by a retrospective account of the 'Radical Life' of William Armitage, hailing from South Crosland, near Huddersfield. A slubber at a local factory, his 'first political action' came at an STC meeting in 1835 when Lawrence Pitkethly gave him a book 'to collect moneys for the families of the Dorsetshire [Tolpuddle] labourers', He accordingly 'went from mill to mill and to factory and workshop in the prosecution of that good work'. He was familiar with all the leading factory reformers and, though not a platform speaker, 'engaged in work quite as useful ... and after working from five in the morning to nine at night without intermission at W. W. and H. Stables, at Crosland Factory ... was often engaged to procuring signatures to petitions and collecting subscriptions'.

History, 24 (1979), pp. 189-210. Wilson, *Struggles*, p. 10. Jones, *Chartism and the Chartists*, p. 83, talks of an army of non-enrolled adherents.

313 Peacock, *Bradford Chartism*, p. 19. Lists of local people nominated to the General Council of the NCA are given in the *Northern Star*, 1841-3; *NS* 6 Oct. 1838, 25 May 1839.

314 Included in this category might be some of the Huddersfield NU committee listed in *NS* 29 Sept. 1839, or John Wilson, the Leeds National Rent 'collector' arrested with George White in July 1839, see *NS* 27 July, 3, 10 Aug., 21 Sept. 1839.

Under the guidance of Pitkethly, his political commitment was equally strong. He 'canvassed for subscribers' for the *Northern Star*, 'ordered ten copies of the first number' and later attended the Peep Green Chartist rallies. He subsequently resolved to abstain from 'intoxicating liquors and tobacco' as part of his commitment to 'ulterior measures'. He also recalled the 'great excitement' and volatile atmosphere surrounding the trials of Frost, Williams and Jones in the winter of 1839-40 and collected subscriptions for the Chartist Defence Fund.[315]

The final core of the movement comprised the actual leaders. These were the hyper-activists, the 'agitators', organisers and major officials who regularly convened and spoke at important public meetings and dinners, developed policy and tactics, travelled as missionaries, lecturers or delegates, and acted as the *Northern Star*'s chief agents, reporters and correspondents. Many were also intimately involved in the minutiae of branch life, but what distinguishes them from other local activists and supporters is the level (both in terms of amount and importance) and the type of their involvement. Put simply, they were involved often, in varying capacities, and at a high level in local Chartist affairs. However, they were more than mere willing workhorses, they also exercised certain important leadership or supervisory functions – as mediators of ideas, managers of discontent and organisers of action. Most importantly of all, they were accepted in these roles by their contemporaries.

Leadership

a) Levels

In spite of some of the difficulties of identification outlined earlier, and in some of the local studies, it is nevertheless possible to compile lists of early Chartist leaders in most West Riding localities.[316] From these it is possible to identify and examine a number of different leadership levels and sub-strata within the West Riding region.

The top level comprises a small group of important local leaders who attained regional standing as actual or supplementary delegates to the Convention, key West Riding officials and organisers, prominent platform personalities or Chartist lecturer-preachers. Often acting in more than one of these capacities, they functioned as a 'middle band', bridging the gap between national leadership and the localities, and became pivotal figures in early Chartism. They included people such as Lawrence Pitkethly, 'There was no man better known in the West Riding than "Old Pitt"' according to Lloyd Jones; Peter Bussey, whose stout profile adorned one of *The Charter*'s woodcut portraits of Convention delegates; the tirelessly combative William Rider; Joshua Hobson, publisher and printer of the *Star*; and William Hill, its editor.[317] George White of Leeds and Jonathon Bairstow of Queenshead also took on important regional organising and speaking roles in this period.

---

315 On William Armitage (1815-1893) see *HDE* 26 Dec. 1885 and 16 Feb. 1886. These accounts are broadly accurate, though some names have been misremembered or events telescoped.
316 See above, p. 415.
317 *NWC* 16 Aug. 1879; *The Charter* 5 May 1839; *NS* 27 Apr. 1839.

The second major level of leadership is made up of the prominent local Chartist leaders in each of the main centres of the textile district. Our knowledge of the size and composition of these groups naturally varies according to the vigour of local activity and the rigour with which it was reported. However, in most places it is possible to identify an 'inner circle' of between half a dozen and a dozen key figures whose names recur in the sources.[318] A few of these leaders, for example, 'Radical Bob' Wilkinson in Halifax, fulfilled a number of representative and public facing roles in local agitations. Others, such as Stephen Dickinson or Christopher Tinker in Huddersfield, rarely addressed public meetings but acted as versatile network figures. Tinker, a committee member of the Huddersfield NU, signed requisitions for meetings, sold tickets for Chartist events, acted as a collection point for victim funds and famously displayed a dagger in the window of his bookshop in Market Walk.[319] Often such figures also sold the *Northern Star*, a function which reinforced their pivotal role in the local movement.

Many town leaders, however, are chiefly recognisable by virtue of a particular type of involvement; such as the Bradford 'speakers', who systematically agitated the out-townships and villages of the district; or John Leech of Huddersfield, a diligent organiser and official. A few established, respected town figures, such as John Hanson in Huddersfield or T. S. Brooke in Dewsbury, served in a variety of capacities but increasingly acted more as advisers and mentors than as active leaders. Beyond them lay countless fringe figures – relative newcomers, occasional delegates or lesser officials whose names crop up just once or twice, and whose true position in the emerging movement will only be revealed through more intensive local research.

Much also remains to be discovered about the variety and intensity of Chartism in the smaller manufacturing communities of the West Riding, in which a third band of leaders – the village or small-town radicals – operated. This is the one about which we know the least and is perhaps the most intriguing level of leadership. Occasionally, as we have seen, village-based radicals became important figures within their district or the region as a whole. However, functioning chiefly as 'parish pump' leaders, most remained known primarily within their own immediate locality. Here they operated as community spokespeople and performed a wide range of leadership functions. John Smith jnr. of Lepton near Huddersfield, for example, chaired the local WMA, spoke at anti-poor law meetings, collated evidence for the Handloom Weavers' Commission, and supported the Glasgow cotton spinners. In 1842 he served as secretary of the Handloom Fancy Weavers' Committee, a revival of local trade unionism.[320] He serves as an archetypal community leader, but similar figures can be located in contiguous radical strongholds such as Elland, Almondbury and the manufacturing townships of the Dewsbury area, or in the heartland of village Chartism, the handloom-weaving

---

318 See, for example, John Bates' recollections in *Halifax Courier* 7 Mar. 1895, or the reference in NS 22 Dec. 1838 to the exertions of a 'few good men and true' in Leeds.

319 John Halstead, 'The Voice of the West Riding: promoters and supporters of a provincial unstamped newspaper', in C. Wrigley (ed.), *On the Move: Essays in Labour and Transport History Presented to Philip Bagwell* (London: Hambleton Press, 2003), p. 39.

320 On Smith, see *LT* 27 July, 28 Oct., 9 Dec. 1837; *NS* 1 Sept. 1838; and Webb Coll., A, XXXVIII, ff. 151-6. See also *LT* 16 Apr. 1842 for his response to a former fancy weavers' leader's (George Beaumont) scepticism about the efficacy of strikes.

settlements around Bradford and Halifax. Here it is possible to identify similar figures who, by attending 'main town' dinners and meetings, addressing or hosting village gatherings, collecting National Rent and Petition signatures, and serving as local officials and *Star* correspondents or agents, provided the backbone of Chartism in the localities.[321]

The different levels of leadership outlined above – regional, district and township/village – overlapped and interacted at a number of points. In the first place, a few key figures operated at more than one level and thereby helped to minimise any gaps or friction between the regional leadership and the independent, proudly democratic localities. Equally, contact between centre and out-townships was facilitated by the practice of the main town association exporting speakers and organisational 'know-how' to neighbouring villages. Yet the traffic in radical enthusiasm and leadership was far from being all one-way. In areas like Huddersfield, Halifax, and Bradford, many of the key district leaders, as well as much of the more vociferous radical support, traditionally came from the outlying townships, and in both Bradford and Huddersfield this strong reciprocal relationship became formalised in the early Chartist period with the inauguration of regular district delegate meetings.

b) Occupational analysis

Bearing in mind the caveats already outlined in the initial chapter and the overview of regional activity sketched above, it is clear that the early Chartist leadership in the West Riding textile district was provided by three main occupational groupings, each successively diminishing in size and importance: firstly, a large group of skilled workers from the domestic/workshop-based textile trades (especially handloom weaving and woolcombing) and the 'lower' artisan trades such as tailoring and shoemaking; secondly, a varied cohort of shopkeepers and tradesmen, including booksellers, publicans and beershop keepers; and, thirdly, a small group of small manufacturers and lower professional people. These categories are far from being self-contained and necessarily include important areas of overlap and ambiguity. However, they provide a rough and ready framework for discussing the make-up of the movement's leadership and the processes by which 'working men' assumed a greater prominence as leaders and leadership simultaneously became more professionalised.

An overview of Chartist leaders in the West Riding localities indicates that they generally came from within occupations which satisfied one or more of the following inter-related criteria. Firstly, jobs which allowed them sufficient time, money or control over their labour process to give them the opportunity and independence to take a leading part in the movement. Secondly, occupations with strong traditions of radical, trade or community leadership and involvement. Thirdly, jobs which by their very nature brought them into close, daily contact with the local working population and led them to develop and offer particularly valuable skills and resources.

Amongst the working men who led the early Chartist movement the textile influence was predominant. This is not surprising since, as Dorothy Thompson

---

321 Examples of other village leaders include Samuel Midgley and John Eckersley (Almondbury), Archibald Leighton (Haworth), William Fox (Birstall), Benjamin Bromley (Batley).

emphasised, the textile trades were 'Britain's main productive industries, both in the home and export markets'.[322] Numerous domestic handloom weavers and woolcombers acted as important local leaders in the manufacturing towns and villages of the West Riding. In Bradford, for example, woolcombing provided the main single source of leaders – a fact which not only reflected the trade's prime position in the town's adult male labour market, but also local traditions of leadership. The trade had provided key figures in both the trades' unions and radical organisations of the early 1830s. Combers, sitting in groups around a comb pot, were renowned for their political discussions. At Keighley, where they formed an important segment of the working population, woolcombers had a reputation for being 'advanced politicians, chartists and the like' and were consistently at the forefront of working-class movements.[323]

Outside the main centres, particularly in the industrial out-townships and villages around Huddersfield and Dewsbury and in the Halifax-Bradford hinterland, the vast majority of prominent leaders can be identified as handloom weavers. At Almondbury, outside Huddersfield, all but a few of the early Chartist leaders were weavers in the local 'fancy' trade. The major towns contained a sprinkling of leaders who eventually forsook the combing pot or loom to become full-time radicals – people such as Joshua Hobson (ex-weaver and joiner), George White (ex-comber) and William Rider, who as late as 1835 still signed himself 'In the rank of the 800,000 [handloom weavers]'. In the outlying communities, however, leaders such as Benjamin Rushton, Joseph Brook, Christopher Shackleton and John Smith jnr. continued to work to the repetitive *lattitat* rhythm of the loom. This predominance reflected not just the numbers of weavers working in the West Riding textile villages, or their vigorous support for Chartism, but also the rich traditions of education, organisation and leadership on which they were able to draw.[324]

Shoemakers provided the most important non-textile group. The trade, though a numerically large one, had particularly strong traditions of radicalism and leadership. As the author of an appreciation of Abram Hanson noted, 'Go into any village in England, and you may safely take long odds that the shoemakers will be found the most prominent member of the little community'. He was often also the most highly politicised. 'Our friend', Hanson, 'like most intelligent shoemakers ... was an ultra-democrat'; so were Abel Goodall, the Heckmondwike Chartist, the Irish-born Michael Scholefield in Bradford and 'Radical Bob' Wilkinson of Halifax.[325] Tailoring, another

---

322 D. Thompson, *The Chartists*, p. 63.

323 Woolcomber-leaders at Bradford in 1839 included George Flinn, Henry Hodgson and William Thornton. Peter Bussey was a former woolcomber; W. Cudworth, *Rambles round Horton* (Bradford, 1886) p. 27, quoted in Peacock, *Bradford Chartism*, p. 3 (for the reminiscence about combing-shops). See *Goodfellowship in Keighley: Eboracum Lodge, Independent Order of Oddfellows, 1823-1923* (Keighley, 1923), p. 16 (for Keighley combers).

324 At Almondbury prominent leaders such as Samuel Dickenson, Abraham Donkersley, William Sykes, Solomon Thwaite were all fancy weavers. For Rider see *LT* 9, 30 May, 13, 20 June 1835. On the rich cultural traditions of the handloom weavers, see E. P. Thompson, *The Making of the English Working Class* (Harmondsworth: Penguin, 1968 edn.), pp. 322-6.

325 *BS* 8 Feb. 1879; on Goodall see Peel, *Spen Valley*, pp. 315-6. For a general discussion of 'political shoemakers', see E. J. Hobsbawm and Joan Wallach Scott, 'Political Shoemakers',

trade where the very nature and traditions of the job encouraged political discussion and involvement in working-class movements, also supplied a number of important local figures.[326]

A few other individual trades stand out. The local Chartist leadership included hatters, joiners, printers, blacksmiths, metal-workers, woolsorters, as well as many plain 'operatives' and 'working men'.[327] The variety of occupations indicates something of the breadth of Chartist involvement and appeal. The apparent absence of leaders from newer, factory occupations is noticeable but by no means decisive, since adult male factory work was confined to limited branches and processes within the textile trades, and the rigid separation of 'factory' and 'domestic' systems never existed in reality. Equally, factory-based workers faced greater risks of victimisation and had fewer opportunities for participation in radical movements.[328]

The large minority of shopkeepers and retailers who figured amongst the West Riding movement's key leaders included numerous grocers, booksellers, publicans and beershop keepers, plus a sprinkling of drapers, clothes sellers, hairdressers and assorted hawkers. Such people were in daily face-to-face contact with working people and naturally moved on from providing their customers' everyday requirements to supporting and servicing their political and industrial movements. Local shopkeeper-leaders rarely displayed the characteristics of a separate interest-group within early Chartism. The majority existed on the class borderline and remained very much part of the local working community. Many took their social and political allegiances from their customers rather than from any relationship with capital and property.[329]

Part of the reason for this was that a number were formerly 'working-men' themselves. However, there were also other very practical reasons why working-class movements included a disproportionate number of shopkeeper-leaders. In the first place, the very nature of their work required literacy and numeracy, plus basic organisational or 'public relations' skills. Secondly, they often had the flexibility and opportunity to participate in radical agitations. Lawrence Pitkethly, who travelled extensively for commercial and agitational reasons, could always leave John Leech in charge of his business. Thirdly, from the movement's point of view they had the considerable advantage of being able to invest money as well as time in local agitations. Thus, Keighley Chartist's difficulties in finding suitable premises for their meetings ended when D. W. Weatherhead, a prosperous Chartist grocer, bought an

---

Past and Present, 89 (1980), pp. 86–114.

326 For example, Charles Connor (Leeds), John Haigh (Ossett Street Side), and Robert Buchanan (Huddersfield).

327 In the West Riding these latter designations usually denoted textile workers.

328 See below, pp. 445–7.

329 The question of the role of 'small employers, shopkeepers and independent professional men' in local leadership is posed in D. Thompson, 'Notes on Aspects of Chartist Leadership', p. 30. For a different assessment of shopkeeper radicalism in North-East England over a longer period, see T J Nossiter, 'Shopkeeper Radicalism in the Nineteenth Century' in T. J. Nossiter, A. H. Hanson and S. Rokkan (eds.), *Imagination and Precision in the Social Sciences: Essays in Memory of Peter Nettl* (London: Faber, 1972), pp. 407–31. Also see R. J. Morris, 'The Rise of James Kitson: Trades Union and Mechanics Institution, Leeds 1826–51', *Publications of the Thoresby Society*, 53 (1973), p. 187.

old Primitive Methodist Chapel 'on behalf of the Radical Association for £300, nearly the whole of which he had advanced himself, through his ardent wishes for the good of the labouring class'.[330]

Elsewhere the constant problem of finding, cheap, safe and independent meeting places was often solved by using the houses and rooms of shopkeeper-leaders. Huddersfield Chartists met at Stephen Dickinson's shop or at Samuel Binns' Newsroom; delegates from the Bradford district convened at Peter Bussey's pub; and, after pressure from the local magistrates had prevented the use of the Black Bull, Liversedge, West Riding delegate meetings came to be held at the Heckmondwike shop of Thomas Wass, 'a fire-eating grocer'.[331] Finally, as ratepayers and possessors of the vote, shopkeepers formed an obvious link between the local community and the formal political system. As the spread of exclusive dealing campaigns from 1831-2 onwards bears testimony, shopkeepers were an obvious stress point where the pressure of the unenfranchised masses could be exerted. As Joshua Hobson put it in 1837: 'The way to their brains is through their pockets – FIND IT'.[332]

In addition to the politicised shopkeeper element in the leadership, each locality usually had one or two respectable middle-class leaders, whether small manufacturers, merchants or lower professional people. Some (for example, quack doctors or schoolmasters) were clearly close to the working community in terms of income, contact and outlook. A few, such as William Hill or Joseph Hatfield, were former weavers or came from weaving stock.[333] Others, however, were quite 'well-off'. Morritt Matthews, a master currier, owned a dozen properties (possibly including the local Radical Association's meeting place) on Church Street, Dewsbury in 1837.[334] Although few in number, figures such as James Clarkson, a Bradford solicitor who operated as West Riding Chartism's lawyer, Luke Firth, a woolstapler who was 'intimate with most of the leading politicians in the Chartist era', and Morrit Matthews, who became West Riding Treasurer in 1839, were often influential leaders who supplied useful talents and services to the local movement.[335]

The important servicing functions performed by members of this group brings us back to the question of the increasing 'professionalisation' of local leadership during the pre- and early Chartist period. The West Riding movement did not become more professional in the sense of being increasingly dominated by shopkeepers and lower

---

330 *NS* 6 July 1839.

331 *NS* 27 Apr. 1839; for Wass, see Peel, *Spen Valley*, p. 316.

332 Joshua Hobson, *Now then – heads of families … etc.* (Leeds, 1837), quoted in Chase, 'Chartism in Huddersfield', p. 66.

333 Knott, *Popular Opposition*, p. 104; Peel, *Spen Valley*, pp. 349-51.

334 Morritt Matthews (1771?-1850?), a prominent Quaker, was apprenticed as a shoemaker and became a currier and later a 'dyer, dealer and chapman'. 'A public-spirited man' he was instrumental in setting up the Dewsbury Mechanics Institute in 1826. His youngest son, born to his second wife, was christened 'Feargus' in 1841, the year in which he was also declared bankrupt and forced to sell his properties (*Batley News* 14 Feb. 1885; *LM* 9 Jan, *LI* 1 May 1841).

335 Peacock, *Bradford Chartism*, p. 23; Peel, *Spen Valley*, p. 351; for Morritt Matthews see H. M. Docton, 'Chartism in Dewsbury' (unpublished typescript in Dewsbury Public Library) and Peel, *Spen Valley*, p. 316.

middle-class leaders. Rather, the growing presence of individuals within the leadership cohort who followed 'the trade of agitation' indicates that many working-class radicals found their way into occupations which allowed them the independence and leisure to participate more fully in local campaigns.[336] For example, leaders such as Peter Bussey in Bradford or William Vevers in Huddersfield used the opportunity presented by the Beer Act of 1830 to establish beershops and radical bases, while other leading figures found themselves increasingly able to make all or part of their living out of their radical involvement – as booksellers, printers, newspaper agents, reporters, lecturers or delegates; or through keeping a radical meeting place or newsroom. In doing this they enabled the movement to become more rigorously and permanently organised.

They also added greatly to local radical facilities. The Freeman's Inn, which Joseph Crabtree opened in Barnsley specifically to accommodate radical meetings, included a large reading room. When Christopher Tinker took over the Albion Inn in Huddersfield in 1833 he used part of the premises as a newsroom and laid the foundations of his bookselling business. In February 1838, for example, we find the Socialist and Chartist Robert Buchanan announcing the establishment of a newsroom at his new tailoring premises in Huddersfield. Interestingly, when he left the area the newsroom was taken over by Samuel Binns, a radical colleague. A year later George White, the woolcomber, began his transition to becoming a full-time agitator by being appointed as 'newsagent to the Leeds Northern Union'. Shortly afterwards Jonathan Bairstow of Queenshead became the West Riding's first paid missionary.[337] It is clear that, indirectly as shopkeepers, or directly as full-time organisers, many key local figures relied on the early Chartist movement for all or part of their income. The professionalisation of some levels of local leadership was well underway before 1840 and the foundation of the National Charter Association.

c) Local variation and change

The winter of 1839-40 has widely been considered a decisive watershed in the history of the Chartist movement, when a number of key local and regional leaders dropped out and were replaced by a new generation of younger men, 'determinedly working-class in their allegiances, who reorganised the movement, and developed a variety of forms of activity and organisation'.[338] A definitive assessment of how the West Riding evidence fits this overall national picture must await more intensive local work on the post-1840 period. However, a broad overview of existing primary and secondary material indicates some support for this view, as well as considerable local fluctuations in the extent and timing of any discontinuity.

---

336 On this process, see Paul Pickering, 'Chartism and the "Trade of Agitation" in Early Victorian Britain', *History* 76, 247 (1991), pp. 221-37

337 Kaijage, 'Labouring Barnsley', p. 479. *VWR* 6 July 1833; *NS* 24 Feb. 1838; for Lloyd Jones' assessment of Buchanan see *NWC* 4 June 1879; *NS* 20 July; 4 May 1839. George White was the original first-choice to be a missionary (along with Benjamin Rushton), but had to pull out 'on account of his employment', *NS* 15 June 1839. He was still categorised as a 'woolcomber' in *LI* 14 Dec. 1839.

338 D. Thompson, 'Chartism as a Historical Subject', p. 11. The question of drop-out is also posed in D. Thompson, *Early Chartists*, pp. 21 and 27.

It is perhaps worth stressing some of continuities first. Many of the activities and institutions of the early Chartist period – local and regional delegate bodies, paid missionaries, Chartist schools, co-operative societies and other cultural manifestations of a vigorous branch life – prefigured post-1840 developments. Indeed, many of the key local figures who set up this framework remained active and important leaders in the middle Chartist period. There was, for example, much continuity in local leadership at both Halifax and Keighley. After the decisive break from the 'Liberals' in 1836 the occupational profile of leadership at Halifax remained diverse but always included a significant number of working men, many of whom survived the dislocation of 1839-40.[339]

In Huddersfield, the local leadership was supplied mainly by shopkeepers and skilled artisans, reinforced on public occasions by handloom-weavers from the outlying townships. The absence of a substantial working-class presence in the town itself clearly contributed to early Chartist 'lethargy' there. Yet, more importantly, the area's anti-poor law pre-occupations and the appeal of Owenite socialism amongst the small tradesmen and artisans meant that a number of long-established town leaders, such as William Stocks jnr., John Hanson and Christopher Tinker, were unable to devote their full attention to the nascent Chartist movement. From the start local leadership was vested in a handful of continuing radical stalwarts, aided by a number of relatively new leaders. It was the latter who became the backbone of middle Chartism in Huddersfield.[340]

Leeds, with its diverse occupational structure, was another relatively backward early Chartist centre. Unlike Bradford with its woolcombers, it it lacked a single predominant trade group to provide leadership and support. As J. F. C. Harrison has noted, 'In Leeds, Chartism had to strike roots in ... the soil of factory operatives, shopkeepers and small tradesmen'. The flowering was never that spectacular. By the time of the formation of the first NU branch in June 1838, a number of respectable shopkeepers and skilled artisans (mainly the 'radical-liberal' and Owenite socialist elements in the original WMA) had dropped out, leaving the main burden of leadership to a varied group of old and new leaders, including shopkeepers and workers from the 'lower' skilled trades, from what Harrison termed 'the physical force

---

339 At Keighley familiar names such as David Weatherhead, Joseph Firth, Thomas Constantine, Thomas Knowles and Joseph Vickers, a shoemaker, (1810-1852) recur in the post-1840 period. In the Halifax area, Ben Rushton, Robert Wilkinson, Robert Sutcliffe and Thomas Cliffe remained active after the winter of 1839-40. According to Dorothy and E. P. Thompson, 'Halifax as a Chartist Centre', pp. 102-3, the major change in local leadership occurred in the two or three years after 1842, when younger men like Ben Wilson, Isaac Clisset, John Snowden, George Webber, John Culpan and Christopher ('Kit') Shackleton came to the forefront of the local movement.

340 These radical stalwarts were people like Lawrence Pitkethly, John Leech, Stephen Dickinson, and Thomas Vevers. The 'new' leaders included Samuel Binns, George Barker, James Matthewman (1803?-1870?), a woollen weaver, and William Cunningham (1815?-?) an Irish-born woollen weaver/clothier who settled in Holmfirth. New blood came into the local leadership in the 1841-2 period when names like Edward Clayton (tailor/bookseller) and John Kelso (printer) became more prominent.

wing of Leeds Chartism'.[341] This often fractious cohort were strong supporters of arming and ulterior measures but also, as realities and arrests impinged, oversaw the establishment of a broader cultural base during the autumn and early winter of 1839 and engaged in tactical alliances to secure municipal representation. Nevertheless, as shown around the turn of the year, it was still capable of promoting what the *Leeds Mercury* termed 'revolutionary doctrines' and organising a temporary challenge to the dominant Whig-liberal elite.[342]

In more advanced Chartist areas like Bradford and Dewsbury, a break in the pattern of leadership appears to have taken place in the winter of 1838-9. With the exception of T. S. Brook, a number of respectable Dewsbury leaders, often with long radical pedigrees, seemingly dropped out of conspicuous involvement as priorities turned from local poor law opposition to a wider, uncompromising radical programme. Their place was taken by a pre-existing, but now increasingly prominent, group of working-class radicals leading what the Tory *Leeds Intelligencer* called the 'shoeless, shirtless and shameless persons' who attended local meetings.[343]

In Bradford an analysis of seventeen radicals and Chartists active between the establishment of the *Northern Star* in November 1837 and the Bradford Rising of January 1840 reveals a varied social and occupational profile. However, it is noticeable that by the winter of 1838-9, with its torchlight processions and 'eloquent appeals to the power of dry gunpowder and cold steel', a number of established town leaders had withdrawn and a group of more forceful leaders had replaced them. On the whole these were working men, including a tranche of active or former woolcombers.[344] A number of these, as well as some of the established leaders, were actively involved in the insurrectionary plotting of winter 1839-40. The failure of the risings forced a few of the most prominent local leaders to flee. Peter Bussey, in all likelihood the person who sent George White round the region to cancel the Yorkshire part of the

---

341 Harrison, 'Chartism in Leeds', p. 72 and 75-81. The early Chartist leadership in the town comprised people such as David Black ('operative'), Thomas Bottomley, Charles Connor (tailor), Joseph Jones (shoemaker), James Illingworth (innkeeper), Francis Phillips (barber), William Rider (former stuff-weaver), and George White (woolcomber).

342 *LM, LT* 28 Dec. 1839. It is possible that Harrison overestimates the extent of a swing back to moderation signified in the emergence of 'new' leaders and the re-emergence of officers such as Benjamin Knowles, Joseph Wilkinson, Andrew Gardner and James Illingworth, Harrison, 'Chartism in Leeds', pp. 80-1.

343 *NS* 28 Sept. 1839. The *Leeds Intelligencer*'s insinuations were condemned in *NS* 6 Oct 1838. The 'town radicals' who largely withdrew include William Rhodes (gentleman and maltster), Thomas Todd (wine and spirit merchant), Matthew Healey (a respectable elector) and William Newsome (oil merchant and Chief Constable of the town). The new leaders were Samuel Allatt ('hatter and working man'), Samuel Healey (printer?), Francis Law (hatter) and William Wilby (working man). In the townships outside Dewsbury their equivalents were people such as Abel Goodall (shoemaker, Heckmondwike), William Fox (blanket weaver?, Birstall), John Haigh, snr. and jnr. (both tailors, Ossett Street Side) and Abraham Hollingsworth (weaver?, Gawthorpe).

344 This paragraph draws extensively on Peacock, *Bradford Chartism*, and on my own listings. The people who gradually left the frontline of local radicalism include Samuel Bower jnr. (bookseller), William Carlisle (tailor), Squire Farrar (attorney's clerk), John Douthwaite ('operative') and Christopher Wilkinson (bookseller).

November rising, 'lost his nerve' and decamped to America, prompting a satirical Bradford street-ballad alleging that 'Equality Peter' had also run off with Chartist funds.[345] Fearing arrest, William Thornton similarly left for America; whilst George Flinn went on the run and was not captured until a year later.[346] Notwithstanding this forced exodus, a number of familiar names still recur in the early 1840s alongside some new leaders.[347]

The West Riding does not fit neatly into a ready-made pattern. Some places undoubtedly witnessed the disproportionate drop out of long-established town leaders and the emergence of newer, more militant leaders. However, the timing of the trend varied considerably. Often it was the sacred month rather than the failure of the risings which was the decisive turning point; whilst in the stronger Chartist centres a shift in the local balance can be detected in winter 1838-9. Whatever the precise timing, it is clear that the very weight of Chartist support and the momentum of events generally prevented the local leadership from becoming fossilised, regressive and interested only in self-perpetuation. As befits an advanced Chartist region, innovation and change came early. In this way the danger of the ossification of local leadership was largely avoided.

Support

a) Factory and non-factory

It is a mistake to see adherence to the early Chartist cause in the textile district as being solely concentrated amongst the declining, outworking textile trades, particularly handloom weaving and woolcombing.[348] These groups certainly made up a significant element since in some localities they comprised a large part of the local workforce. Chartism's real strength and coherence, however, stemmed from the fact that it enjoyed a broad base of support from all the main trades and the majority of the working population, particularly in the smaller industrial townships and villages. In analysing the make-up of Chartist adherence in any given locality simple distinctions between skilled and unskilled, factory and home-based workers are less useful than they first appear. As Robert Sykes has written of Lancashire, 'Chartist attachment cut across the divisions between factory and domestic, or workshop, employment'.[349] The same was true of the West Riding, where the factory sector was less well developed

---

345 Peacock, *Bradford Chartism*, pp. 48-9; Chase, *Chartism*, p. 132, dismisses the allegation.

346 Ray Boston, *British Chartists in America, 1839-1900* (Manchester: Manchester University Press, 1971), p. 95. Peacock, *Bradford Chartism*, p. 48.

347 Familiar speakers include James Clarkson, Henry Hodgson, Joseph Brook, Joshua Rawnsley and John Arran (who also went to America in 1842). 'New' names in the early 1840s include James Dewhirst (painter), R. Ross (woolcomber) and John W. Smyth (shoemaker).

348 This view pervades Mark Hovell's pioneering study of *The Chartist Movement*, see, for example, pp. 169-70, and is reiterated by W. H. Chaloner in his bibliographical introduction, p. iv.

349 Robert Sykes, 'Early Chartism and Trade Unionism in South-East Lancashire', in Epstein and D. Thompson (eds.), *The Chartist Experience*, p. 153.

and where differences in the type and nature of factory employment, as well as distinctions between 'upper' and 'lower' skilled trades, were also significant.

It is difficult to talk of 'factory workers' with any clear meaning in the late 1830s. In flax and worsted spinning centres such as Leeds and Bradford the majority of 'factory workers' were women and children. Adult males comprised a mere 6% of the factory workforce in Bradford in 1833.[350] Such workers usually held supervisory roles or comprised skilled craftsmen in ancillary processes. They were well-paid and shared much in common, in terms of attitudes, outlook and status, with non-factory-based, 'upper' skilled artisans. The adult male mill workers who worked in the preparatory and finishing mills in the woollen sector similarly relied on and had a pride in their manual skill and oversaw the work of juvenile labour. Like their equivalents in the worsted and linen industries they were relatively well remunerated and held key roles in the productive process; but, numerically at least, they were not a highly significant sector of the local workforce.

Indeed, in the early Chartist period it is extremely difficult to draw rigid demarcation lines between factory, workshop and domestic employment. A number of important branches of the textile trades were performed in all three settings and workers might move from one to another and back again. Some departments in factories such as woolcombing shops or finishing departments had the size, shape and feel of a small workshop, whilst successful domestic arrangements for combing, weaving or finishing might easily develop into a small workshop. Equally, if the majority of handloom weavers or woolcombers were not physically located in factories and had a superficial independence, they were often employed directly by, and dependent on factory-owning or renting master-manufacturers for materials and equipment. They might operate outside the scope and supervision of day-to-day factory discipline, but they were nevertheless adjuncts of the factory system.

In examining the composition of early Chartist support in the West Riding, the distinction between the better-paid and more secure 'upper' skilled trades and the less well remunerated and often threatened 'lower' skilled trades is perhaps most useful.[351]

The little evidence that exists about early Chartist allegiances tends to confirm the contention that the bulk of support particularly in the larger centres, was derived from the 'lower' skilled trades; from the depressed and increasingly dispensable textile outworkers and from the major artisan trades, particularly in the clothing and building sectors. Beyond the main towns, with their greater potential for sectionalism, it is likely that Chartist support cut across simple factory/non-factory divides. The subscription lists for Chartist funds include contributions from workers who can definitely be identified as factory-based. Ossett's £4 contribution to the Stephens Defence Fund in early March 1839 was collected in 'factories, Houses and Associations'. 'Workpeople' at Clough Hill, S. Cook's Mill, Lawford's factory and

---

350 Theodore Koditschek, *Class Formation and Urban-Industrial Society: Bradford, 1750-1850* (Cambridge: Cambridge University Press, 1990), p. 360.

351 This distinction is mapped out in Iorwerth Prothero, 'London Chartism and the Trades', *Economic History Review*, 24, 2 (1971), pp. 209-12.

Messr's Starkey's Mill similarly contributed to the Liversedge effort, and 5*s* for the National Rent came from 'Kay's Factory'.[352]

The *Northern Star* and Chartist ideas both circulated in the factories. The case of Robert Winterburn, an outworking woolcomber who was sacked for selling the *Star* in Wood and Walker's worsted-spinning factory in Bradford, provides evidence for Chartist support in the factories and for the close interplay between 'factory' and 'non-factory' workers. It also illustrates the very real and practical barriers which prevented factory workers from demonstrating their support for the Chartist cause. Long working hours and the actions of certain 'millocrats', for example, caused 'workpeople' from local factories who had bought tickets for a dinner to honour Peter Bussey in January 1839 to miss their meal.[353]

Such workers were under far closer, more direct employer supervision than the outworkers or the traditional craftsmen who worked in a factory setting. A bitter letter from 'the operatives employed in several factories near Huddersfield' was read by Pitkethly to the West Riding Peep Green meeting held on Monday 15 October 1838. Signed 'for and on behalf of the Prisoners', it complained of their employers' ('our tyrannical oppressors') refusal to grant a day's holiday and of threats of dismissal. Unlike their counterparts working at home or in small workshops, they did not have the option of taking 'Saint Monday' and joining their 'brethren' in 'the great and glorious demonstration'. Their contribution to Chartism would necessarily have to take a different form:

> We are very poor, but our last penny will be paid in support of the expense (of the meeting), and our only consolation is that we can ... attach our names to the National Petition.[354]

The factory workers of Dewsbury were no less enthusiastic, but perhaps more audacious and better organised. Writing of preparations for the Peep Green meeting, the *Star*'s local correspondent reported that,

> Several of the mills have agreed to stop work on that day; and the workpeople of those mills that the masters will not stop on that day, have determined that as they have had holidays on purpose to please their masters [i.e. lay-offs] they will have a holiday on this occasion to please themselves.[355]

Progress was even being made in Leeds before the May 1839 Peep Green meeting. A report on the state of the district in late April reported that 'subscriptions are going

---

352 *NS* 9, 30 Mar. 1839; see also *NS* 6, 20 Apr. (Lee Bridge spinners and Row Royd's Mill), and 13 July 1839 (for contributions from female power-loom weavers at Bradford). In 1839 factory wages were being squeezed as well as outworking wages.

353 *NS* 16 July 1839 (for subscriptions from Wood and Walker's mechanics, see *NS* 30 Mar. 1839); *BO* 17 Jan. 1839.

354 *NS* 16 Oct. 1838.

355 *NS* 13 Oct. 1838.

forwards at all the Unions [Northern Union], and through the several workshops and factories, towards effectively agitating the town and neighbourhood'.[356]

In general, though, the weight of evidence from the larger manufacturing centres indicates that the new and 'upper' skilled groups of factory-based adult male textile workers, such as the spinning overlookers in worsted and flax or the slubbers and spinners in woollen, were not particularly strong supporters of the Chartist brand of radicalism. In Leeds, for example, the operatives of Holbeck and Hunslet, where the larger factories were concentrated, had traditionally espoused a more circumscribed version of radicalism which it shared with others in the upper trades of the town and with local tradesmen and small manufacturers. Formalised in the Holbeck Operative Reform Association, this strand of radicalism only occasionally and temporarily became intertwined with popular Chartism. Its closest ties remained with the 'mainstream' Whig-liberalism of Baines and Marshall. When a strong *Star* editorial on a Leeds meeting for a new (limited) Factory Bill in April 1839 condemned local slubbers, 'whose immediate gains are derived from the toil of poor children', it could presumably do so without alienating a lot of existing support.[357]

However, it should not be assumed that all of the 'upper' skilled trades, whether factory-based or not, were hostile or indifferent to Chartism. Evidence is not abundant but, as in Lancashire, there are indications that the engineering and metal working trades were on occasions sympathetic to the Chartist cause. The *Northern Star* of 10 August 1839 records a donation of £1.10*s* for the National Defence fund from 'a few friends' at Wellington Foundry, Leeds. Subscriptions for J. R. Stephens from Bradford in March 1839 included £1.1*s*.8*d* from Wood and Walker's 'mechanics' and 6*s*.9*d* from Messrs Matthew and W. Allen's 'machine shop'. Equally, the *Star*'s sympathetic coverage of the Bradford iron moulders' dispute in October 1838 may have built bridges with this trade.[358] A Bradford correspondent reporting on short time working in local factories in early November 1839 believed that the 'large numbers of mechanics out of employment, and others working up their notice ... will strengthen the Radical ranks'. Even the better-paid and traditionally more exclusive textile branches included Chartists among them. The Huddersfield woolsorters had lasting Chartist connections and Bradford subscriptions for Stephens in March 1839 included 3*s*.6*d* from 'a few woolsorters'. Finally, common sense suggests that workers in the 'upper' trades were one of the few groups capable of paying regular subscriptions or making significant donations to Chartist funds.[359]

Chartist support, then, was not solely confined to the most deprived and depressed outworking or domestic trades. However, the problems of effectively and assertively harnessing this mass broad-based support – particularly the latent support for Chartism in the factories – were highlighted during discussions of and responses to the sacred

---

356 *NS* 4 May 1839.

357 *NS* 20 Apr. 1839.

358 Sykes, 'Early Chartism and Trade Unionism', pp. 180-1; *NS* 10 Aug.; 30 Mar. 1839; 27 Oct. 1838. See also *NS* 14 July 1838.

359 *NS* 2 Nov.; 30 Mar. 1839. On the Huddersfield woolsorters and later Chartist ventures , see above, p. 90. Sykes, 'Early Chartism and Trade Unionism', p. 154, makes the point that there were very few aloof, truly aristocratic trades in Lancashire.

month. The challenges of organising an effective stoppage at a time of distress, low wages and high unemployment were universally recognised. This, together with the unevenness of preparation nationally, was one of the chief reasons for dropping the idea of a general strike and replacing it with the largely symbolic national holiday. As Peter Bussey reported to the Convention in late July, after his travels in the north, 'in one of the densest manufacturing districts, the masters had given notice that if the Convention did not now make the men cease work on the 12th of August, the masters would, as it would be to them a great kindness'. In Leeds the NU had decided early on that 'the majority of the working classes of this town could, or would not act up to it [the sacred month]' and 'would entail misery upon themselves and their families, while there would be found plenty of working men who would fill up their places'. In Huddersfield the NU made belated attempts to involve the local trades, but soon realised that the sacred month was a non-starter owing to 'improbability of getting the factory hands in this district to make a general stand'.[360]

The largely symbolic gesture of a cessation of labour, a 'holiday' lasting one, two or three days, met with a variable response in the West Riding. Support was most solid and widespread in areas where the majority of the adult male labour force were not based in factories or were only indirectly under the control of master-manufacturers, or in areas where feelings and support were running high enough to risk a token stoppage. In the predominantly home-based fancy-weaving area of Almondbury, outside Huddersfield, only one loom in ten was reported to be working. In the Dewsbury area, (a stronghold of the domestic system, but which also contained a number of mills and factories), shops and pubs were closed and large meetings gathered on all three days (Monday to Wednesday). In Bradford, where Bussey's constituents were greatly disappointed by the decision to postpone the sacred month, mill owners were threatened with violence if their establishments were kept open on Monday 12th and large numbers stayed away from work. Significantly, though, the Bradford men and women chose Saturday, Sunday and Monday (the latter two traditionally viewed as potential days of rest) as their three days. It is doubtful whether the distressed weavers or combers, or the parts of their families who worked in the mills, could in reality have afforded even a short 'holiday'.[361]

This may also account for the lack of response from the factories of Huddersfield or the stuff-weavers of the Halifax area. For closely supervised factory hands, as for dependent and poorly-paid outworkers, even a token strike was costly and highly dangerous. At the Halifax meeting on Thursday 8th August to consider what 'Holiday' action to take, Benjamin Rushton spoke of 'the seriousness of refraining from work in small numbers, as it might be not for three days only, but for a much longer period' and some members 'enquired what they were to do for the three days, for when they worked one day it was to earn victuals for the next'. Not surprisingly only a few hundred local men struck and met to hear speeches on the following Monday. The few that could afford or risk the luxury of an extended 'Saint Monday' merely to demonstrate their 'union and determination' probably did so in the

---

360 *NS* 3, 17 Aug. 1839.
361 *NS* 17 Aug. 1839; Peacock, *Bradford Chartism*, p. 23.

knowledge that they could make up lost time later in the week.[362] For the majority of the labour force this option was simply not open to them.

b) Chartism and Trade Unions

Robert Sykes' examination of the links between trade unionism and early Chartism in Lancashire revealed an extensive overlap.[363] Formal connections were clearly weaker in the West Riding, where unions in the major textile branches had suffered major defeats only four years earlier. For example, there do not appear to have been any organised boycotts of the Coronation celebration by the trades in mid-summer 1838, nor did the West Riding trades play a large part in organising political meetings or collecting signatures for Chartist Petitions in 1838-9. Like friendly societies, many trade unions had strict 'no politics' rules and, as Sykes has stressed, trade societies took on board extra risks when they publicly supported radical causes.[364] Reciprocally, a number of Chartist leaders had reservations about the value of trade unions and strikes in permanently ameliorating the economic situation of the working class.[365] However, as the subscription lists occasionally reveal, individual trade societies and organised groups of workers gave some support to various Chartist funds.

Trade unions at this period were strongest and most highly developed in the more exclusive 'upper' skilled trades where Chartism found less consistent support. Most unions tended to be small-scale, localised and insular in outlook. A number of local trades fought defensive or aggressive actions to protect or improve wages and conditions in the early Chartist period, but, in general, the low level of economic activity acted as a drag on the development of formal organisations.[366] There were few large-scale strikes to stimulate such bodies or to foster links with radicalism, and a number of trades probably had no permanent trade organisation.[367]

United trades' action and organisation was also rare. The establishment of the Dewsbury United Trades' Society in March 1838 signalled the re-emergence of notions of mutual support, but it is likely that this was short-lived.[368] Equally, it seems that the Bury model of a politically-orientated Trades' Council was never taken up in Yorkshire. As feelings on the Glasgow issue and fears about the outcome of the 1838 Select Committee died down, the motivation for formal inter-trade co-operation also diminished.[369] However, the 'politicising' effect of the Glasgow agitation on the trades was not completely lost. The interconnection between the Dewsbury Society,

---

362 NS 17, 10 Aug. 1839.

363 Sykes, 'Early Chartism and Trade Unionism', p. 152 ff. See also Jones, *Chartism and the Chartists*, p. 139.

364 Sykes, 'Early Chartism and Trade Unionism', p. 153.

365 See, for example, NS 30 June 1838 on the Oldham hatters' strike; and NS 31 Mar. 1838, editorial by O'Brien.

366 For example, NS 19, 25 May (Leeds bricklayers); 9 June (Bradford carpenters and Joiners); 27 Oct. 1838 (Bradford iron moulders).

367 For example, apart from the blanket weavers and fancy weavers, none of the handloom-weaving branches were 'organised', nor had they been since 1834.

368 NS 17, 24, 31 Mar. 1838.

369 NS 31 Mar., 14 Apr. 1838; Sykes, 'Early Chartism and Trade Unionism', p. 163.

radicalism and the handloom weavers' agitation has already been noted, and a number of the traditionally radical trades (and some without this heritage) contributed to the early Chartist effort.[370]

The woolcombers, for example, remained inveterate trade unionists and radicals. The Bradford instructions for the October 1838 Peep Green meeting requested members of the NU to head the procession, followed by 'the members of the United Trades who may think proper to form part of the procession amongst whom will be the Woolcombers' Society.' The Huddersfield factory operatives, whose letter about their 'imprisonment' was read to the rally, spoke of their 'committee' unsuccessfully seeking to negotiate a 'general holiday' and pledged that, despite being 'very poor ... our last penny will be paid in support of the expence [of the meeting]'. They poignantly signed their letter 'John Powlett' – the *nom de guerre* of the secretary of the Clothiers' Union in the early 1830s.[371]

In the non-textile artisan sector it was more common for individual workshops rather than formal trade bodies to make contributions. Nevertheless, a few radical Leeds brushmakers (a traditionally non-political craft) collected and sent £1.14*s* for the National Rent from their club-house in February 1839, and forty cordwainers who came as a body to enrol themselves in the Huddersfield NU in late July 1839, possibly following a national or at least a northern trend.[372] Later in the year 'a few stonemasons in Leeds, who are resolved to do more in future' subscribed 5*s*.8*d* to the Frost defence fund, and a large body of masons working on the Manchester and Leeds Railway at Mirfield, 'a great number' of whom were *Star* subscribers, raised £1.18*s*.6*d* for Frost.[373]

'Political' language and concerns – evident in the conclusion of a London stonemason's letter reminding his 'fellow-workmen that they will never have any real protection for their labour until they have a fair and free representation in Parliament' – are also noticeable in the bitter and class-conscious Address of the Heckmondwike carpet weavers, written during a long and bitter dispute with local manufacturers. It speaks of a 'mighty revolution' being at hand which, 'provided the labouring classes be firmly united', will 'be a revolution from degradation and misery, to comparative prosperity, through the proper direction of our skill and industry'.[374] Heckmondwike, a seat of physical-force sentiments, was implicated in the insurrectionary planning of this period. As distress deepened, throwing large numbers out of work or onto shorter hours and reduced wages, the message that only real radical reform would permanently alleviate the working class from economic distress took on greater meaning and force.[375]

---

370 See above, pp. 389-90.

371 *NS* 13; 16, 27 Oct. 1838. See John Sanders, 'John Douthwaite and "John Powlett": Trades' Unionism and Conflict in Early 1830s Yorkshire', *Labour History Review*, 86, 1 (2022), pp. 8-17.

372 *NS* 9 Feb.; 3 Aug. 1839; Sykes, 'Early Chartism and Trade Unionism', p. 163.

373 *NS* 14; 28 Dec. 1839.

374 *NS* 26 Oct. 1839. The stonemason was using the *Star* to warn Yorkshire masons not to apply for 'blacked' work on the London and Blackwall railway. The carpet weavers' strike was one of the few major local disputes.

375 For example, in Bradford, *NS* 2 Nov. 1839.

Whilst formal links between trade unions and Chartism were relatively rare, membership of or support for both trade and political organisations should not be seen as mutually exclusive for the majority of workers. There were few major industrial conflicts in 1838-9, political radicalism was clearly in the ascendency and there were obvious risks on both sides of any connection becoming explicit. Nevertheless, it is clear that trade unionism and political radicalism shared ideas, leaders, meeting places, organisational forms and personnel. Many Chartists had been, were or would again become active supporters of trade unions. The Chartist leadership clearly understood that their lack of consultation with the trade societies had contributed to the sacred month debacle and subsequently became far more conscious of the need to develop closer links with trade unions.[376]

c) Chartism and Friendly Societies

The 1830s saw a vast expansion of friendly and benefit societies in the West Riding, particularly amongst the affiliated 'secret orders' with regional or national links such as the Oddfellows, the Ancient Foresters and the Druids.[377] On the surface there would appear to be few direct connections with Chartism. The societies were secretive, fairly insular bodies with strict 'no politics' rules. Equally, some Chartists deprecated the societies' love of ritual and quasi-religious ceremony. However, with their stress on working-class independence, dignity and self-management, the secret orders' underpinning values intersected with many of the ideas expressed on the Chartist platform. They also shared much support and membership. For example, Dorothy Thompson's research indicated that most of the male Chartists in Halifax were Oddfellows.[378]

The new Poor Law Act impinged directly on the friendly societies' concerns and may have stimulated an influx of new members. As Jeremiah Marsden, chairman of a meeting of Dewsbury friendly societies in January 1838 stressed, 'the lower orders of the community' through regular contributions helped to prevent a heavy burden on the poor rates, 'and so detestable to them is the idea of becoming pauperised themselves, that their endeavours to prevent it are incessant'.[379] This picture is supported by evidence given to the Handloom Weavers' Assistant Commissioner, H. S. Chapman, in 1838. William Kershawe of Birstall spoke of twenty to thirty societies,

---

376 This widespread neglect, a major organisational weakness of early Chartism, resulted partly from sanguine expectations that the struggle would be won by massive popular displays in 1839. The 'capturing' or building of links with other working-class organisations was therefore felt to be unnecessary.

377 See, for example, *LM* 7 May, 4 June 1836; *BO* 18 Jan., 7 June, 9 Aug. 1838 (for information about lodges in Bradford, particularly the Ancient Foresters); *NS* 3 Mar. 1838 (on the Foresters); 23 Feb 1839 (on the Oddfellows); 13 Apr 1839 (on Keighley societies). The frequent newspaper reports of anniversaries reveal how frequently local lodges had started in the 1830s. See also, BPP. Reports from Assistant Handloom Weavers' Commissioners, 1840, XXIII, p. 539.

378 Dorothy Thompson, *The Chartists*, p. 112, cited in Simon Cordery, 'Friendly Societies and the Discourse of Respectability in Britain, 1825-1875', *Journal of British Studies*, 34, 1 (1995), p. 47.

379 *NS* 27 Jan. 1838. Marsden became a Chartist leader.

'free gifts, secret orders, sick clubs and funeral briefs', in his area and of weavers on just 7s or 8s a week contriving 'to spare enough to keep up subscriptions to one or more society'.[380] This sobriety and striving for independence found an echo in Chartism and the *Northern Star*, for ideological as well as commercial reasons, regularly recorded friendly societies' activities, particularly their annual festivities.[381]

A number of important local Chartist leaders, such as Jeremiah Marsden of Dewsbury, Michael Scholefield of Clayton, Joseph Firth and James Bedford of Keighley and possibly Richard Grassby of Elland, were prominent in friendly society affairs and other Chartist leaders were certainly members.[382] It is likely that, particularly in the close-knit weaving and textile outworking communities, the same skills and standing which made certain key figures the natural spokesmen on trade or political issues also meant that they took on leading roles in local friendly societies.

Despite having active Chartists amongst their leaders and supporters, the non-political stance of the societies was zealously guarded. The sixth anniversary dinner of No. 116 lodge of the Free and Ancient Gardeners in Bradford included a toast to Feargus O'Connor but also, for good measure, to the Queen and the Duke of Wellington. After Michael Scholefield, representing the Clayton Ancient Foresters, had allegedly introduced 'republican sentiments' at a Bradford delegate meeting of 'Trades, Orders and Societies' to plan a Coronation procession in June 1838, he was disowned by the order's Executive Council (then based in Bradford) who stressed the 'purely philanthropic' and non-political nature of the order. However, amongst the distressed weavers of Clayton, who in all probability made up the majority of the local Foresters' court, it is less likely that such sentiments would have earned disapproval.[383]

In a district of instinctively radical communities it was almost inevitable that democratic politics and religion would impinge upon local friendly societies' activities. Thus the Order of the Golden Fleece in Queenshead celebrated its anniversary in October 1838 by hearing William Thornton deliver a sermon in a Primitive Methodist chapel. His fellow preacher, John Arran of Bradford, raised £2.8s for 'the West-Riding [Chartist Defence] Fund' by delivering 'two very impressive sermons' to 'the Foresters' Court' in Barnsley in August the following year.[384] In the Huddersfield area the 'Secret Orders' held two important district delegate meetings (both in 'radical' pubs) in the weeks preceding the October 1838 Peep Green rally. A further meeting after the monster demonstration, anticipating later discussions of ulterior measures, considered withdrawing money from the banks and 'placing it to be of more advantage to the labouring classes'. The intention was not simply to destabilise the financial system, but to invest in plans to benefit the working class, for example by establishing 'a London daily paper, exclusively to watch the people's interest'.[385] Setting

---

380 See also, BPP Reports from Assistant Handloom Weavers' Commissioners, 1840, XXIII, p. 539.

381 See, for example, report of convivial and ceremonial activities at a Clayton Ancient Foresters' lodge, *NS* 2 Mar. 1839.

382 For example, *NS* 26 Oct. 1839 (James Bedford); *BO* 27 Sept. 1838 (Joseph Brook).

383 *BO* 7 June; 21 June, 9 Aug. 1838; *NS* 20 Oct. 1838. Clayton was a strong Chartist centre.

384 *NS* 6 Oct. See also *NS* 3 Aug. 1839 (Great Horton); 17 Aug. 1839 (John Arran at Barnsley Foresters' court).

385 *NS* 22 Sept.; 20, 27 Oct., 3 Nov. 1838. The failure of sufficient delegates to turn up suggests

a 'noble example', 'Independent Odd Fellows' in Almondbury went one step further 'by establishing a co-operative provision warehouse instead of lodging their surplus money in the banks'.[386] Two months later Bradford Chartists marched behind the Ancient Foresters' Band to the May 1839 Peep Green gathering and used the Oddfellows Hall as their main public meeting place until pressure was applied on the landlord in May 1839.[387]

Societies, as opposed to individual members, made occasional contributions to Chartist Funds. The Honley 'secret orders' collected 10s.9d for J. R. Stephens at their Easter anniversaries in 1839, and the West Riding delegate meeting in late January singled out the Ossett Street Side Druidesses for their generous contribution to the National Rent.[388] Such gestures are only rarely recorded. Those that were noted are significant because they demonstrated the unanimity and sense of urgency needed to override the block imposed by the 'no politics' rule. They indicate that far from being a peripheral aspect of working-class life, Chartism enjoyed support within, or in some cases penetrated, one of the key institutions of independent working-class endeavour.

4: Regional and National Perspectives

Relations between local Chartist districts and with the national movement's main leadership were mediated through a number of interlinked means: the formal coming together of individual leaders at public meetings and dinners, delegate meetings, informal contact, and the columns of the *Northern Star*. The Leeds-based paper was particularly important in drawing together the regional agitation and linking it to the wider national movement. In James Epstein's words, it gave 'local working-class protest a national focus and gave local radicalism national coverage'.[389] Through its agents, correspondents, shareholders and reporters it extended a pre-existing radical network and aided the emergence of part-time, and occasionally full-time, 'professional' organisers and agitators. Epstein has outlined the crucial role that the *Star* played in nationalising the Chartist movement; yet it also had important regional dimensions and a strong provincial impact.

In its origins and birth the *Star* was closely connected with previous radical publishing initiatives in the region, ranging from Hobson's *Voice of the West-Riding* in 1833-4 to William Hill's proposed *Yorkshire Liberator* in 1837 and Hobson's *Justifier* project later the same year. Also, the same groups of established 'town radicals' who had organised and spoken at O'Connor's tours of 1835-7 were active in promoting the *Star* in the West Riding localities in the second half of 1837. As Malcolm Chase notes, the bulk of the share capital that O'Connor had to raise to get the project off the ground came from the textile district.[390]

---

that cautious local 'secret orders' gave the idea a wide berth.

386 *NS* 30 Mar. 1839.

387 *NS* 11, 18 May 1839.

388 *NS* 13 Apr.; 2 Feb. 1839. See also *NS* 1 June 1839 (Almondbury Shepherdesses).

389 James Epstein, 'Feargus O'Connor and the Northern Star', *International Review of Social History*, 21 (1976), p. 51. The discussion below draws heavily on this study.

390 *BO* 12, 19 Jan. (*Liberator*); 11 May, 16 June 1837 (*Justifier*); Epstein, 'Feargus O'Connor and the Northern Star', pp. 63-4; Chase, *Chartism*, p. 16.

Radical readers and agents in these same localities provided a firm foundation from which the *Star*, never 'a mere Leeds paper', was able to develop a wider national readership and distribution; Epstein has calculated that 'almost half the *Star*'s early circulation of over 10,000 copies a week came from Leeds, Bradford, Halifax and Huddersfield'.[391] Although local correspondents varied in their efficiency and enthusiasm, the *Star* nevertheless gave extensive coverage to a wide range of local activity.[392] By means of these local reports, the letters it printed, the messages in the 'To Correspondents' column, and the accounts of West Riding demonstrations and delegate meetings, it served as a vital channel of communication and source of information within the region and beyond. As O'Connor told the anniversary dinner of the Dewsbury RA in September 1838:

> Formerly all their meetings were confined to the walls, or to a finger's length of ridicule in some factious journal. Huddersfield did not even know what the men of Dewsbury were about, while now on Saturday morning, their glorious sentiments and determination would be carried on the wings of the press to all corners of the land.[393]

The importance which local leaders attached to the *Star*'s coverage of local affairs can be seen from a critical resolution passed by the March 1839 West Riding delegate meeting, which censured 'the managers of the Northern Star … for their neglect of local matter connected with the present movement, especially as to the reports of public meetings, and the formation of associations in new places, at the same time useless and foolish matter is being continually inserted which ought to be dispensed with'. The *Star*'s very success (and profits) also made it a target for sniping. Joshua Hobson, replying to Dr Fletcher's insinuations against O'Connor in October 1839, expressed his 'astonishment that the only Radical paper which has succeeded should be charged with success as a crime! While the failure of others should be rewarded with sympathy'.[394]

Yet, despite such manifestations of jealousy and occasional eruptions of local dissatisfaction, the *Star* remained hugely popular. Reading it (or listening to it being read) became a badge of allegiance, toasts were regularly drunk in its honour, and meetings frequently began with readings from the paper. Local leaders recognised its invaluable role and it became an inseparable adjunct to the movement's local and regional leadership and organisation. Moreover, through its editorials, its wide-ranging accounts of meetings throughout the country, and its reports on the proceedings of the Convention, it helped to overcome local and regional barriers and made explicit the national dimensions of the movement.[395]

---

391 *NS* 26 May 1838; Epstein, 'Feargus O'Connor and the Northern Star', p. 65.

392 There were regular complaints in the 'To Correspondents' section of the *Star* about the lateness of forwarding copy and missed deadlines; for example, see *NS* 30 Mar., 13 July, 17 Aug. 1839.

393 *NS* 28 Sept. 1839.

394 *NS* 30 Mar.; 5 Oct. 1839. See also the malicious report about Bussey, Ibbetson and Heywood of Manchester setting up a rival to the *Star*, *NS* 16 Nov. 1839.

395 Epstein, 'Feargus O'Connor and the Northern Star', pp. 61, 71-3, 76.

The *Star* provides occasional evidence of a second element of the regional movement: the importance of interpersonal ties and informal contact in building up and sustaining networks of leadership and organisation. Many of the main West Riding leaders were long-standing friends and acquaintances and much of the co-ordination of the regional movement must have been achieved through private correspondence and informal contact.[396] The major West Riding gatherings, smaller local dinners and assemblies, as well as private, convivial or business meetings, all provided occasions for leaders to meet together, seal or renew friendships, exchange experiences and indulge in much unseen bridge-building, planning and co-ordination. Local leaders often 'guested' at each other's major rallies or public dinners and helped out in times of need. So, when the victimised Barnsley Chartist leader Joseph Crabtree was struggling to make a living in the winter of 1838-9, he used Peter Bussey's house in Bradford as a base from which to sell clothes.[397]

A third key feature of the regional movement was the organisation and realization of major public gatherings. The two Peep Green meetings of October 1838 and May 1839, were particularly important for stimulating Chartist interest, organisation and recruitment. In the weeks preceding them the *Star* was full of reports of local meetings, new NU branches, and details of marching arrangements. With their bands, banners, and processions they provided living proof of the rich traditions of radical protest and culture and a vivid demonstration of the depth of popular support for the cause. The *Northern Star* asserted in October 1838 that 'one would have supposed that all Yorkshire was literally on foot', and Benjamin Wilson recalled witnessing 'for almost an hour … the continuous arrival of processions from different directions, with bands playing and banners flying' at the Whit Monday meeting the following year.[398]

Opponents were quick to puncture the *Star*'s habitual overestimates of the size of the Chartist crowd and to denigrate its motivations. In October 1838 the *Mercury* alleged that 'on the outskirts of those who listened to the speakers', the event had 'the appearance of an ordinary fair, – eating, drinking and gambling in booths being freely indulged in' and that 'the great bulk of the parties present manifested the utmost indifference to the spouting'. Even the *Star* itself admitted that less than ten per cent of people who attended the vast May 1839 gathering were actually able to hear the speakers.[399] However, like the worldwide anti-Iraq War demonstrations in 2003, the key thing was not that protesters listened to all the speeches, but that they were there. Try as the respectable press might to play-down the turnout and denigrate the participants, the West Riding meetings of 1838-9 provided a morale booster for participants, a source of legitimation for the local and regional leadership and a cause of anxiety for the authorities.[400]

---

396 For wider inter-regional contacts see TNA: HO 40/47 f. 529 ff. Pitkethly's intercepted letters to Joseph Broyen of Sutton in Ashfield (near Mansfield).

397 *NS* 21 Apr. (Bussey and Thornton at Dewsbury); 22 Sept. 1838, 26 Jan. 1839 (Crabtree), also *LM* 26 Jan. 1839.

398 *NS* 16 Oct. 1838; Wilson, *Struggles*, p. 3.

399 *LM* 20 Oct. 1838; *NS* 25 May 1839. Paul Pickering, 'Class Without Words: Symbolic Communication in the Chartist Movement', *Past and Present*, 112 (1986), pp. 153-54 discusses the acoustic challenges of radical meetings.

400 See, for example, *LM* 20 Oct. 1838; 25 May 1839.

Yet, the very size and transient nature of these set-piece demonstrations, modelled on the regional gatherings earlier in the decade and drawing on a long radical tradition, also serve to highlight the limits of this form of activity. They were hard to follow up and left something of a vacuum in their wake. Equally, it is evident that some of the NU branches hurriedly established in preparation for such meetings were short-lived or never achieved any formal existence. Apart from fostering a sense of strength, solidarity and identity, the mass rallies could be seen and felt to have achieved little. The vast marshalling of working-class opinion, in the form of petition signatures and attendance at public meetings, seemingly counted for nothing. The model of mass public meetings deployed successfully during the Catholic emancipation and reform crises was increasingly seen to be deficient and the mass public meeting a limited and ineffective weapon in the fight for working-class rights. Some of the bitterness (particularly towards the local Whig-liberal middle class) can be attributed to working-class frustration that, while the game appeared to be the same, the rules had changed. Instead of being loyal supporters of a popular cause, they were now demonized as dangerous insurrectionists by the very people who had previously been very happy to draw on and mobilize their support.

A fourth component of the organisation of the early Chartist movement in the region, the West Riding delegate meetings, played a pivotal role not only in planning major events like the Peep Green meetings, but also in developing inter-district links and a sense of regional identity and direction. The meetings owed much to the past experience and organisational models of factory reform, trade union and anti-poor law agitations. But in the early Chartist period the West Riding delegate meeting became a more permanent and central feature of the regional movement.

Delegates included many familiar local leaders, but also some lesser-known names who may have been respected and reliable sympathisers with the time and experience to attend such gatherings, and be entrusted with the contributions of their local associations. However, the Chartist vision and practice of democracy meant that such delegates had little scope for independent action. As Peter Gurney notes, Chartists 'believed in the idea of delegation rather than representation, and this was a major distinguishing feature between them and many of their middle-class sympathisers from the start'.[401] Delegates were held directly accountable to the local associations they represented. In theory, all local RAs were entitled to attend the meetings. In practice delegates from all the major towns except Keighley attended regularly (sometimes representing the whole district), with the remaining delegates coming mainly from the numerous small RA and NU branches of the Dewsbury area.[402]

The meetings which began in September 1838 continued at monthly or shorter intervals (according to pressure of events) right through 1839. They were invariably held in the Dewsbury area; initially at one of the large coaching and carrying inns but later, as the authorities' surveillance increased, at the pub or house of a radical

---

401 Peter Gurney, *Wanting and Having: Popular politics and liberal consumerism in England, 1830-70* (Manchester: Manchester University Press, 2015), p. 117.

402 This and the following paragraphs are based on a detailed analysis of all the West Riding meetings in 1838-9. See also *NS* 30 Mar. 1839 (invitations to RAs); 27 Apr. 1839 (T. Vevers at Manchester).

supporter or leader.[403] Their purposes were primarily functional, the first three meetings oversaw the preparations and defraying of expenses for the West Riding meeting. Then, after a break of two months, the meetings re-started as a regional gathering of NU delegates and supervised the collection of the National Rent and the region's support for and liaison with its National Convention delegates.[404] These functions remained the staple fare of the gatherings during spring and early summer 1839, however, after the May Peep Green meeting the delegates took on a more proactive role. The June meetings appointed Samuel Healey of Dewsbury as West Riding Secretary and William Ashton of Barnsley and Jonathan Bairstow of Queenshead as paid West Riding missionaries. In late July a well-attended meeting resolved to put all suggestions for ulterior measures from the Convention 'into full operation' and authorised Bussey to tell the Convention of the state of readiness of the West Riding district.[405]

Around this time, with details of Chartist arrests featuring regularly in the *Star*, the reports of the meetings become more circumspect. Delegates had been asked to bring proper credentials to the late July gathering; and at this meeting the result of the election of supplementary delegates – to replace the existing National Convention delegates (in the event of arrest) – were announced. In September the collection of the National Rent was temporarily discontinued and efforts shifted to the support of victims.[406]

Hereafter the proceedings of the delegate meetings become more difficult to interpret. The meeting of late September was a small-scale but high-powered affair with delegates representing a district rather than a single branch. Ostensibly (and probably in reality) the meeting talked about the Defence Fund, Chartist prisoners, new agitational initiatives and plans for Chartist hustings candidates. However, as A. J. Peacock speculates, there is circumstantial evidence that 'momentous decisions' relating to possible risings were taken here. Certainly, the following meeting on 21, or more probably 28, October was a curious affair. The *Star*'s report was unusually brief and the meeting (which again comprised representatives from all the major centres, including Barnsley) passed a couple of cryptic resolutions.[407] What seems certain is that the delegate framework was as serviceable for insurrectionary planning as for arranging demonstrations or collecting funds. Delegate meetings were not fully reported hereafter. For example, the *Star*'s report of the 12 December meeting gives no location or speakers and only brief resolutions are given. These included the decision that 'the districts of Dewsbury, Bradford, and Sheffield be appointed to elect the delegates' to be sent from the West Riding to a second 'General Convention' in London. This Convention planned a rising for early January and all three of the West Riding centres represented were the locations of risings later in the month.[408]

403 Locations were the Yew Tree Inn, Roberttown; Globe Inn, Millbridge; S. Middlebrook's Black Bull Inn, Liversedge; T. Wass' house, Heckmondwike. See also Peel, *Spen Valley*, pp. 280-1.

404 *NS* 29 Dec. 1838; 2 Feb. 1839.

405 *NS* 15 June; 3 Aug. 1839.

406 *NS* 13 July; 7 Sept. 1839.

407 *NS* 5 Oct.; 2 Nov. 1839; Peacock, *Bradford Chartism*, pp. 31-2.

408 A report from Bradford in *NS* 7 Dec. 1839 indicates that the 25 November delegate meeting

However, further speculation about these still murky episodes must await the discussion below on some early Chartist themes.

5: Early Chartist Themes

a) Physical Force, the Rhetoric of Resistance and Chartist Arming

The presumed simple dichotomy between 'moral force' and 'physical force' Chartism, and its supposed advocates, has distorted much of the historical writing on the early Chartist period.[409] Although the subject of constant discussion and debate, the moral force/physical force divide was only briefly the cause of major internal controversy in late 1838 when a number of established radical leaders in Birmingham, London and Scotland clashed with O'Connor over the latter's support for J. R. Stephens. For most of the time it was, as James Epstein has stressed, 'an issue of relatively little concern or disagreement among either rank and file Chartists or the majority of Chartist leaders.'[410] One would be hard pressed to find a West Riding leader of any description who had not at one time uttered what might be termed 'physical force' sentiments. For example, the former trade union leader and respected radical and Owenite socialist, John Douthwaite, who clashed with Bussey in Bradford and never took a leading role in Bradford Chartism, expressed a commonly held view in condoning the actions of the Canadian rebels in early 1838: 'I do not like resorting to physical force. I am for peace wherever it can be consistently maintained, but I cannot blame the Canadians for the part they have taken'.[411]

'Moral force' and 'physical force' were not two mutually exclusive options, but part of an interrelated whole.[412] National and local leaders constantly referred back to the models of the Catholic emancipation agitation of 1828-9 and the reform crisis of 1831-2. In both cases the effective harnessing of 'moral' power allied to the threat or reality of 'physical' action had seemingly forced reforms from a reluctant government. In the early Chartist period the accepted common view and the political conditioning of the vast majority of local leaders told them that a display of moral force alone, without the backing or implied threat of physical force to give it weight and substance, would be insufficient: 'Like trying to drive in a nail with a feather' according to one radical veteran speaking at Leeds. As Epstein notes, 'even moderate radicals were unwilling categorically to dismiss the possibility of a resort to 'physical force".[413]

That is not to say that leaders did not identify themselves occasionally as 'moral force' men or as advocates of 'physical force'. But the two positions were not

---

was held but not reported; *NS* 14 Dec. 1839; Peacock, *Bradford Chartism*, p. 35.

409 For example, this division is at the heart of J. T. Ward's discussion of 1838-9 in *Chartism*, Chapter 5, p.111 ff.

410 Epstein, 'Feargus O'Connor', p. 227.

411 D. Thompson (ed.), *Early Chartists*, pp. 20-1; Jones, *Chartism and the Chartists*, p. 149; *BO* 18 Jan. 1838 (Douthwaite had espoused similar views during the previous year's Bradford anti-poor law riots)

412 Thompson, *Making*, pp. 683-4.

413 *NS* 13 Oct. 1838; Epstein, 'Feargus O'Connor', p. 228.

necessarily diametrically opposed. Definitions of moral force and physical force measures were frequently hazy and uncertain, and the boundary between the two was often blurred. Furthermore, thresholds and definitions were not necessarily constant and could vary according to the local and national circumstances. For one of the few local leaders who attempted to define it, James Bedford of Keighley, 'Moral Force', included 'all the means of resistance possessed by people of a legal nature, and over which the Government could have no control, such for instance, as exclusive dealing, refraining from all excisable articles, with a variety of others, which in his opinion, were sufficient in themselves to procure the suffrage any time when the people could be persuaded to act upon them'.[414] However, he was writing at a time when the local movement was in decline and could hardly muster a physical presence. Equally, even fairly innocuous tactics like exclusive dealing could have an aggressive intimidatory aspect. As with the sacred month itself, the question of whether it was judged a 'moral' or 'physical' action depended largely on how it was carried out and how the authorities responded.

Fears of premature steps and expectation of government repression were constant themes in Chartist speeches in 1839. They lay behind the caution that Pitkethly's expressed in his letters to Joseph Broyen in Nottinghamshire, as, for example, in March 1839:

> I intend to advise a run upon the Savings Banks if the petition is rejected I have other moral means which will be more safe and also more speedy than reasonably could be expected by physical force.[415]

Six months later when all moral means had palpably failed, and insurrectionary planning (of which Pitkethly certainly knew something) was in full swing, he is to be found stressing his belief 'that unless the people had something beyond moral force to strengthen them in their demand for justice, they had a very bad chance of ever obtaining it.'[416] However, whilst such leaders advocated arming, indulged in grand rhetorical gestures and liked to have, or pretend to have, a physical force card in their hand, they also showed a marked reluctance to ever play it. Consequently, a number of major leaders, none more so than O'Connor himself, performed amazing feats on the 'verbal highwire', balancing loyal constitutionalism and insurrectionary exhortation.[417] The imprisonment of colleagues, the fear of spies, the realistic appraisal of possibilities, and the approach of the time when rhetoric had to be converted into action all tended to focus people's minds in the summer of 1839 and induce caution or at least a re-think. Even though the NU and LDA shared the same motto – 'peaceably if we may; forcibly if we must', relatively few major West Riding leaders echoed the language and endorsed the Jacobin beliefs of Harney and the London Democrats with their emphasis on the forcible, insurrectionary overthrow of the government.[418] Many,

---

414 *NS* 26 Oct. 1839.

415 TNA: HO 40/47 f. 530 ff, Pitkethly to Broyen 4 Mar 1839. Pitkethly was a strong advocate of arming and an opponent of 'moral force ruin'.

416 *NS* 26 Oct. 1839.

417 Jones, *Chartism and the Chartists*, p. 150.

418 D. Thompson (ed.), *Early Chartists*, p. 19; see Rider's letter, *NS* 11 May 1839 for an example

though, expected repression (another Peterloo) favoured defensive arming and believed in physical force as a last resort in the event of outside attack.

Some extremely violent language issued forth from the early Chartist platform and press but, as Dorothy Thompson has pointed out, much of this was 'a style of speech – a rhetorical device which both their followers and the authorities recognised to be a form of bluff'.[419] This lexical mode was very much part of the radical tradition. An early pamphlet about the 1833 Huddersfield election emanating from Joshua Hobson's Union Free Press memorably asterisks an account of the arrival of the military, 'those antiquated sons of carnage, (the man-butchers) whose use is all but obsolete, and whose TERRORS, like those of Ghosts, have vanished away before knowledge and moral power ... these relics of Vandalism'. The codicil at the foot of the page, however, explains, 'These observations are to be viewed abstractedly, for as regards the troop in question, they behaved well, and their Commander, (Capt. Evans) acted in the most praiseworthy manner'.[420]

In the early Chartist period the right to arm and to resort to physical force was justified by a battery of constitutional, moral and historical arguments and appeals to 'natural rights'.[421] As John Baxter has argued, 'The Chartist invocation to arm and if necessary fight was confidently thundered from the movement's newspapers and pamphlet presses, defiantly proclaimed from hundreds of market place and street corner tribunes and was discussed at all levels of organisation from the national conventions held in 1839 and 1840 down to the smallest "section" and "class meeting"'.[422] A number of key motifs recur in the speeches of local and national leaders. Firstly, the disclaiming of violence coupled with the willingness to die for the cause rather than endure tyranny. Pitkethly, at a meeting on the Glasgow spinners' case in early 1838, declared 'that he objected to revolution, but rather than submit to live like a slave, he would die'. William Rider at Leeds in October 1838, reminded his audience how

> Some of their opponents had charged them with using violent language. Why they had petitioned and humbug petitioned, long enough, but their petitions had been scornfully rejected, and was it right that they should tamely sit down to be insulted? No, they were determined to demand their rights, and if they were still refused, they were determined to die by the edge of the sword rather than continue to live in bondage.[423]

The second motif stressed the essentially defensive nature of arming, and sought to shift any blame for the Chartists' recourse to physical force onto the authorities, for

---

of a local supporter.

419 D. Thompson (ed.), *Early Chartists*, pp. 18-9.

420 *The Woodites' "forget me not!" being a Sketch of a New Political Farce called the Whig Tomfoolery Election...etc* (Huddersfield: Union Free Press, 1833), p. 14.

421 Epstein, 'Feargus O'Connor', p. 216. For example, see George White, *NS* 15 Dec. 1838.

422 John Baxter, 'Armed Resistance and Insurrection: The Early Chartist Experience', *Our History*, 76 (1984), p. 4.

423 *NS* 27 Jan.; 13 Oct. 1838.

either directly provoking an outbreak or refusing to grant necessary reform. William Rider told the inaugural meeting of the GNU in June 1838 how 'he had taken the liberty of providing himself with a good brown musket, lest the Government of the Whigs might cause the lot of militiamen to fall upon him. (Immense cheers, and well done Rider.) The resolution which he was about to move was to prevent physical force – it was a better kind of arms – it was Universal Suffrage. (Great cheering.)'[424] In a particularly evocative passage of their Address to 'Brother Radicals and Fellow Countrymen of the United Kingdom', the Liversedge Radicals declared,

> the Government is determined to crush us. You must be prepared to meet the event. With all their cant about moral force, they are evidently preparing to use physical force, and we have therefore no alternative but to sink quietly into abject slaves, or shew that determined front of men who are conscious of their rights, and are determined to obtain them, or perish with arms in their hands in making the attempt. Away with all sickly stuff about patience and petitions, have they not arrested Stephens? Are we to stand idly by and be patient while they crush out best men? Or are we to remain unmoved until they glut in his streaming blood and not make a determined effort to prevent it?[425]

The sense of frustration and class bitterness which marked so many early Chartist declarations in the West Riding was heightened all the more by constant references to 1832 and the moral force hypocrisy of Baines and his Whig-liberal middle-class allies. Feargus O'Connor encapsulated this more recent motif at a Leeds preparatory meeting for the October 1838 Peep Green meeting. Referring specifically to Baines' words and stance in 1832, he told his audience that 'They could say, that thus far their agitation had been peaceful, and, while they had been talking of physical force, they had been working morally; whereas the agitators of 1832, while they talked of moral force, were working physically.'[426]

Peter Bussey's speech at a Queenshead torchlit gathering in October 1838 brings together a number of these themes and illustrates the quasi-theatrical nature of much of the Chartist rhetoric of resistance. He declared that the present movement

> was not an agitation like that of 1832, on the Reform Bill, when the manufacturers locked up their factories, and ordered their slaves to attend the meeting at Wakefield, to secure their enfranchisement. No, it was an agitation arising out of empty stomachs – of hungry bellies and starved backs – an agitation of principle, which was steadily working its way through the entire community, and should the governing powers raise up a Caesar, to stand betwixt the people and

---

424 *NS* 9 June 1838.
425 *NS* 23 Feb. 1839.
426 *NS* 13 Oct. 1838. See also engraving, *NS* 5 Jan. 1839.

liberty, he had not the least doubt, but the people would produce a Brutus.[427]

The emphasis on physical force was a particular feature of early Chartism in the late autumn and early winter of 1838. Following on from a series of torchlight meetings (mainly in Lancashire, but a few in the West Riding) and mass demonstrations at Kersal Moor (Salford) and Peep Green, the movement was briefly characterised by a sense of imminent confrontation and a feeling that events must soon come to a head. The moral force/physical force debate became a major preoccupation, so much so that the *Star* in late December feared that it was becoming hackneyed.[428]

Questions of arming and the legality of physical force were openly debated. At a rowdy Bradford radical meeting in late November 1838, which the *Bradford Observer* sarcastically characterised as 'an admirable display of a house divided against itself', Peter Bussey, Joseph Brook and James Clarkson spoke in favour of arming, with the latter reading extracts 'to shew the legality of possessing and using arms'. Christopher Wilkinson and Squire Farrar spoke equally passionately against. It was left to William Sharman, woolcomber radical, trade unionist, ten hours advocate and Waterloo veteran to add a dose of realism to the proceedings, asking, 'are you prepared for the sweeping effects of a cannon ball; he has seen one open a street in an army... He had no wish to throw a damp on their spirits, but he wished them to consider all the consequences which a resort to physical force would draw on them.'[429]

In Leeds William Rider defended the right not only to possess arms but also 'to use them (when all other means have failed) in defence of his liberty, his life and his property'; and a *Star* editorial in November 1838 sought to separate the right to possess arms from the threat to use them in an uprising against the government, 'we believe the people know better than to attempt any insurrection.'[430] Such equivocal sentiments can be interpreted part of an elaborate game of bluff, but it is also true that the West Riding movement included leaders with military experience and, as John Baxter notes, 'contained men who had before used or been prepared to use arms for the democratic cause'.[431] The ensuing tensions and ambiguities were sufficient to frighten off some potential support. In Bradford a number of established radical leaders on the moderate wing of the local leadership withdrew at this time. Meanwhile in Horsforth, near Leeds, in May 1839, George White encountered local opposition to the NU plan because of its perceived commitment to physical force, and only won the day and established a local branch after stressing that the NU was pledged to use all moral means before the last resort.[432]

One of the more intractable problems of the early Chartist period is in deciding how far the violent rhetoric and call to arms was actually converted into the possession

---

427 *NS* 10 Nov. 1838.

428 *NS* 29 Dec. 1838.

429 *BO* 29 Nov. 1838; *LT* 1 Dec. 1838. Sharman recommended abstinence from all excisable articles as his preferred mode of securing their objectives.

430 *NS* 1 Dec. 1838; *NS* 24 Nov. 1838.

431 For example see Joseph Brook, above p. 410 ; Baxter 'Armed Resistance and Insurrection', p. 15.

432 *NS* 18 May 1839.

of arms and a readiness to use them. Evidence from the West Riding, as elsewhere, is either unreliable or ambiguous. Local magistrates, made edgy by their isolation, their incomprehension and sometimes by the Chartists' very discipline and organisation, occasionally indulged in a game of bluff and counter-bluff with the regional military commanders over the question of military protection. Their reports are clearly sometimes exaggerated. However, at other times, particularly during the second half of 1839, their widely acknowledged inability to penetrate the re-organised Chartist classes meant that they often had little idea of precisely what was going on.[433]

Neither can the utterances of the Chartist leadership and press always be taken at face value. At times when they still felt that the threat of violence might carry the day, local and national leaders had an interest in highlighting and perhaps exaggerating the extent of arming and drilling. The *Star* itself reported manoeuvres on Lidget Green, outside Bradford, in April 1839, and a week later it readily quoted Abel Goddall's estimate of armed Heckmondwike Chartists.[434] Conversely, at other times, in the wake of arrests or in anticipation of imminent repression, *Star* editorials and speeches of local leaders, though still defiant, are notable for their stress on constitutionalism, non-provocation and peacefulness. The two stances are not in fact opposite extremes, merely two tactical sides of the same coin. It is particularly difficult to get behind the public caution expressed by so many Chartist leaders at times of particular tension. What they were saying privately (or publicly, but which was not reported) may well have been different. In contrast to a local informer's report, the *Star*'s official rendering of speeches at the May 1839 Peep Green meeting makes few direct references to arming. Also, as shown later in the year, in some places the public face of the movement might camouflage more covert activities.[435]

Given the inadequacy of the evidence, an estimation of the extent of both arming and insurrectionary planning will always be lodged in the realms of guesswork. In the case of arming J. T. Ward has written that, 'after making all allowance for the exaggeration of 'physical force' propagandists and timid authorities alike, it is certain that considerable numbers of men had taken anti-Poor Law and Chartist militants at their word and had stored assorted arms'. Pitkethly, writing privately to a Nottinghamshire leader in August 1838, reported that 'The people are vowing vengeance they are arming and preparing to arm in many districts'. Oastler himself was pleased to inform the government in February 1839 that arming 'is carried on to a very considerable extent. It is my opinion that at this moment many thousands of persons are armed'. These he stressed were all 'sober, thoughtful, industrious, moral men, who have no wish to injure anybody either in their persons or their property'.[436]

The notion of 'arming' covered a wide range of options and generally involved making a symbolic gesture rather than a serious threat to the local balance of firepower. A variety of weapons were on offer, from cutlasses and caltrops to pikes and

---

433 See, for example, WYAS: HP, Box 2, Thompson to Harewood, 8 July and 2 Aug. 1839.
434 *NS* 20; 27 Apr. 1839.
435 TNA: HO 40/51 ff. 153-9, Deposition of John Brown, 22 May 1839; *NS* 25 May 1839; Peacock, *Bradford Chartism*, p. 32.
436 Ward, *Chartism*, p. 119; TNA: HO 40/47, Pitkethly to Broyen, 8 Aug. 1838; HO 40/40 ff. 374-411, Examination of Richard Oastler, 7 Feb. 1839.

pistols.[437] William Armitage of South Crossland recalled being shown 'samples of hand grenades and street bombs' by 'a perfect stranger', who he took to be a spy, in early 1840.[438] Leaving aside the possible pitfalls of entrapment, it is likely that few working men, no matter how 'sober' or 'industrious', could have afforded outright the 17s and 25s needed to buy a pistol. Even with the penny or six-pence clubs and their raffles, which Oastler cited as one way in which the poor workers might procure hardware, the arming of a substantial body of men would have taken inordinately long. Pikes were cheaper and more popular, whilst the 'dirk, or dagger or clasp knife' which might cost between 1s and 11s and which Oastler wished to be sent on to the Home Secretary, to assure him that he was not 'joking', was allegedly in great demand in Lancashire and Yorkshire. Christopher Tinker of Huddersfield, who attracted much magisterial attention when he displayed a foot-long dagger in his shop window in February 1839, had certainly been in Sheffield earlier in the month to order a supply of 'these very powerful weapons'.[439]

Oastler, aware of the financial realities faced by his supporters, advised 'those persons who are too poor to provide themselves with more costly weapons of defence, to have a rough club with an iron spike at the end of it'. Other cheap additions to the poor man's arsenal included 'a sort of hand grenade', which the mayor of Leeds sketched for the benefit of the Home Office, and 'sizing sticks' (five or six feet long) which Bradford Chartists drilling on Fairweather Green used as substitute muskets.[440] For many people it is likely that 'being armed' involved adapting some existing item of domestic hardware or sharpening up an old knife, or possibly just a state of mind.

Whatever its precise form or nature, the extent of arming and related activities varied within the West Riding. In Leeds there is no evidence of arming, whilst in the Keighley area there is but one unsubstantiated report of regular drilling.[441] In Huddersfield, where Tinker displayed his dagger, the magistrates do not appear to have been unduly worried and there are no reports of drilling. Local adherents who had taken Oastler's advice kept their weapons to themselves. Most of the evidence for arming comes from the three leading early Chartist centres: Halifax, Bradford and Dewsbury.

In the Halifax area there was a contrast between the town itself and the outlying villages. At the Halifax RA's annual dinner in January 1839, Thomas Cliffe had welcomed the improvement in trade (particularly the 'gun trade'), but Robert Tetley had stressed that 'the political Union of Halifax have not provided themselves with arms'. In May, the RA unanimously resolved 'to apprehend or cause to be apprehended' any person or persons who may be found recommending an

---

437 See Chase, *Chartism*, p. 62. Caltrops, spiked iron balls, were an anti-cavalry device.
438 *HDE* 26 Dec. 1885.
439 TNA: HO 40/40 f. 374 ff, Examination of Richard Oastler, 7 Feb. 1839.; HO 40/51 ff. 25-29, Laycock to Russell, 5 Mar. 1839 (deposition of William Duke). See also, WYAS: HP, Box 1, Walker to Harewood, 10 Feb. 1839 and HO 40/40 f. 295, W. Emery to Russell, 25 Nov. 1838.
440 TNA: HO 40/40 f. 374 ff, Examination of Richard Oastler, 7 Feb. 1839; HO 40/51 f. 75, Holdforth to Phillips, 6 May 1839; f. 83, Deposition of John Rhodes, 6 May 1839.
441 HO 40/51 f. 75, Holdforth to Phillips, 6 May 1839; WYAS: HP, Box 2, C. L. Brandling to Harewood 17 May 1839.

organisation of physical violence, or any kind of training or drilling to the unlawful use of arms'.[442] In the worsted weaving hamlets outside Halifax, however, 700 men were reported to be armed with muskets in late March and a Halifax magistrate shortly afterwards wrote of arming and drilling, mainly by handloom weavers. Sir Charles Napier, the new Northern Commander, voiced constant warnings about the unsatisfactory billeting arrangements for the troops in the town.[443] Even after public drilling ceased, arming may well have continued and gathered pace with the onset of winter and the development of insurrectionary plans. The out-townships and villages between Halifax and Bradford were clearly heavily involved in both aspects. A local magistrate, writing on 12 November, reported that in the out-townships Chartists were 'busy grinding their pikes and casting balls'. Queenshead, almost equidistant between the two main towns, was a focal point for the preparations. An undated letter (probably late 1839) from two Halifax informers reported that in Queenshead, 'they was casting Bullets from Saturday Night until Sunday Night' and one of the speakers at a Queenshead meeting attended by Harrison, the Bradford spy, in early December reported '260 or 270' well armed men at the ready.[444]

The evidence for arming in the Bradford area itself is even more convincing. A. J. Peacock has outlined how the exhortation to arm and its practical implementation permeated all levels of the local movement.[445] In January 1839 Peter Bussey is to be found urging the purchase of firearms and the formation of 'target societies':

> Arm yourselves. Let all who can, purchase a rifle. Let those who cannot purchase a rifle get a musket. Those who cannot get a musket, let them buy a brace of pistols, and those who cannot get pistols must get a pike, aye, a pike, with a shaft eight feet in length, and a spear fourteen inches long at the end of it (tremendous cheers).[446]

Seven months later, a Bradford gunsmith spoke of 'almost daily applications for Soldiery Guns', whilst in nearby Shipley a local smithy was 'Manufacturing Spears for the use of Charterists'.[447] Thomas Cliffe of Halifax, pondering the likely postponement of the sacred month, found a receptive audience for his belief that the time for talking about physical force was over: 'They knew what to do; they must talk it over in their houses and reflect upon it … and prepare those beautiful fire-place ornaments which the Bill of Rights told them they had a right to be possessed of'.[448] The deposition of

---

442 *HG, NS* 5 Jan.; *NS* 18 May 1839.
443 *HG* 30 Mar. 1839; TNA: HO 40/43, J. R. Ralph to Col. Wemyss 20 Apr. 1839 quoted in D. and E. P. Thompson, 'Halifax as a Chartist Centre', pp. 90-1; Dalby, 'The Chartist Movement in Halifax', pp. 108-9.
444 Ibid., pp. 109-10; D. and E. P. Thompson, 'Halifax as a Chartist Centre', p. 94; D. Thompson (ed.), *Early Chartists*, pp. 280-2.
445 Peacock, *Bradford Chartism*, pp. 28-9. See also, D. Thompson (ed.), *Early Chartists*, p. 208, and WYAS: HP, Box 1, Horsfall to Harewood, 13 Apr. 1839.
446 *BO* 31 Jan. 1839.
447 *NS* 5 Jan 1839; WYAS: HP, Box 2, depositions of W. Egan and J. Glover, 26 July 1839, quoted in Chase, *Chartism*, p. 96.
448 *BO* 8 Aug. 1839.

WORKERS OF THEIR OWN EMANCIPATION

the disgruntled wife of a Windhill Chartist in late November gives a feel of the domestic reality of Chartist arming:

> I left him a fortnight since today. Before I left him I became very much alarmed, in consequence of my husband having become a Chartist and having bought five arms into the house – he had a double barreled pistol, and a single barreled one, and a day or two before the third of November, he brought a gun into the house, and I found a quantity of gunpowder in a chest of drawers – about the size of a half-pound of tea – he had a pot full of leaden Bullets which would hold about half a pint, I took away those of them which I now have at home at Eccleshill.[449]

The evidence from Dewsbury is more patchy. Arming was not new; one of the people arrested for taking part in the Dewsbury anti-poor law disturbances of August 1838 had a loaded pistol in his possession and several 'labouring people' had allegedly recently bought gunpowder from the local ironmonger. As we have seen, Heckmondwike Chartists openly boasted about their preparations in April 1839 and three months later a meeting of West Riding magistrates received reports of drilling in the Morley (and Birstall Hill field) area and of secret caches of arms.[450] This might easily be dismissed as scaremongering were it not for the corroborating evidence supplied by both Frank Peel's local histories and the contemporary accounts of gunfire during the Dewsbury Rising of January 1840. Whilst Peel may occasionally have telescoped events, he is generally reckoned to be an accurate source. His anecdotes and background information about local Chartists – like Dan Hinchcliffe of Walkey Lane, Heckmondwike, whose house served a 'general rendezvous', or Thomas Wass who helped to provide pikes and spears and to hide these in a dung-heap in Walkey Lane when Hinchcliffe was expecting a search, may owe something to later romanticisation, but they often have an authentic ring and add a vital extra dimension to our knowledge of the unseen side of local Chartism.[451]

The leaders' rhetoric and the traditional radical scenario on which it was based had, however, stored up some problems for the future. It was relatively easy to talk about the ultimate weapon of physical force and a 'death or glory' willingness to fight for liberty when there were plenty of moral force options to try out and, in any case, the main protagonists recognised and allowed for the fact that they were indulging in shadow-boxing. The difficulty came when, in the summer, it became necessary to take off the kid gloves and convert words into action. Particularly in strongly radical enclaves within some of the main towns and in the surrounding industrial villages, the constantly restated maxim that 'a musket was an essential article of furniture in every Englishmen's home'[452] had induced a number of people to arm themselves or think of arming. They and others no doubt felt let down and confused when, after the failure of the Petition, the cancellation of the sacred month, the damp squib of the national

---

449 TNA: HO 40/51 f. 685, Deposition of Sarah Ward, 29 Nov. 1839.
450 WYAS: HP, Box 1, Depositions relating to the Dewsbury Riots, dated 20 Aug. 1838; *NS* 27 Apr. 1839; WYAS: HP, Box 2, C. L. Brandling to Harewood, 17 May 1839.
451 Peel, *Spen Valley*, p. 316.
452 D. Thompson (ed.), *Early Chartists*, p. 19.

holiday and the disbanding of the Convention, the main national and regional leaders' enthusiasm for 'physical' action did not match their former utterances.

b) Intimidation, Restraint and Reaction

For all the evidence of the movement's proverbial self-discipline, early Chartists undoubtedly participated in a range of violent or intimidatory activities. For example, many areas adopted an aggressive variant of exclusive dealing in the summer of 1839. Activists went round shopkeepers and publicans soliciting donations for the National Rent and ascertaining who were the friends of the Convention. In late July two of the Leeds collectors, George White and John White, allegedly overstepped the fine line between encouragement and extortion and found themselves answering charges of intimidation. Chartists at Sowerby Bridge reportedly told a local grocer who refused to support them that they would 'put down his name in Red Ink as one of the first to be attacked, when they rise, and they told his wife that she would be taken off before the end of this month.' Meanwhile, shopkeepers in Bradford feared for their lives and property after refusing to give money to the local Chartists. The Leeds prosecution, however, curbed local enthusiasm for this ulterior measure.[453]

The line between offensive and defensive ideas and intentions cannot be drawn too sharply. Chartist talk of violence was almost exclusively based on the notion that agitational pressure would inevitably provoke a violent response from the authorities, such as arrests, forcible break-up of meetings, draconian measures.[454] An appreciation of the monopoly of power which the government enjoyed and a fear of permeation by spies ensured that relatively few people actually crossed the threshold of violence. Had a provocative Peterloo-style action actually occurred then the position and the numbers might have been very different. However, in reality the Chartists' sense of discipline and restraint and their very understandable fears prevailed and most Chartists confined themselves to violent language or postures.[455]

In her overview of the early years of the movement Dorothy Thompson posed the question of how far Chartism, by channelling popular energies into quasi-constitutional channels, reduced violence in the community. Using Huddersfield as an example she noted that 'the folk violence of effigy-burning [in 1831] and the direct action of the anti-Poor Law campaign gave way to the disciplined organisation of the Chartists in which thousands could gather, often with arms, often in conditions of great political tension or economic distress, and yet remain completely peaceful'.[456] The point is well made but perhaps overstated. In the first place, the early Chartist

---

453 Harrison, 'Chartism in Leeds', pp. 78-9; TNA: HO 40/51 f. 257, Rev. W. H. Bull to Russell 26 July 1839; f. 273, Memorial of Bradford shopkeepers 24 July 1839; f. 453 ff, report on James Matthewman's speech at Huddersfield public meeting, 10 Aug. 1839.

454 See D. Thompson (ed.), *Early Chartists*, p. 21. See also the *Star*'s stress on the need for 'universal arming' for 'self-defence' before starting the sacred month, *NS* 3 Aug. 1839.

455 TNA: HO 40/51 f.453 ff, report on James Matthewman's speech. Even the floridly violent speech of William Martin who recommended proceeding 'on a given day' is couched in traditional, ambiguous rhetoric.

456 D. Thompson, 'Chartism as a Historical Subject', p. 11.; also, *Early Chartists*, p. 16.

years were not without instances of popular violence.[457] Secondly, their relative dearth can generally be attributed to other factors. The usual triggers of most incidents of collective violence during this period were noticeably absent. There were no parliamentary elections or major strikes in the area, and easily identifiable and attackable targets like the Poor Law Commissioners or the Metropolitan Police rarely presented themselves. It should also be noted that the anti-poor law and factory campaigns, which at times condoned and encouraged manifestations of popular 'folk' violence, were orchestrated by some of the same radical leaders who became Chartists.[458] As Katrina Navickas has argued, violence was not necessarily backward-looking, 'but rather a carefully chosen tool in the repertoire of protest'.[459] Early Chartist leaders, temporarily at least, saw the virtues of other options.

Nevertheless, it is undeniable that the early Chartist movement in the West Riding possessed a high degree of organisation and self-restraint. This was particularly noticeable at the large public gatherings which the local leadership managed with great precision and sense of discipline. An Almondbury informant, reporting to local magistrates on the May 1839 Chartist meeting, recalled how many in the local procession had wanted to take the quicker (footway) route to Peep Green but that Pitkethly stopped them and 'desired them to follow the procession'. They fell into line and soon joined the growing Huddersfield contingent.[460]

The same sense of discipline, organisation and obedience was also noted by Bradford magistrates during the Chartist occupation of the Parish Church in early August: 'so well did they obey the instructions of their leaders that not any interruption took place to the performance of the service.'[461] Such control and restraint could in itself be intimidating and was intended to be such. It was nevertheless remarkable. Indeed, one of the more striking characteristics of the early Chartist movement is the gap between violent or provocative rhetoric and actual cases of large-scale violence. This was due in part to the models of protest which dominated Chartist thinking. The problem came when these templates were found to be inoperative, when the marshalling of a large body of opinion backed up by more violent posturing counted for nothing and when the government and the local authorities did not impose blanket repression as in the post-war years. This left both the national and local leadership in a cleft-stick: whether to follow the logic of their rhetoric and cross the threshold of violence or to lose face, reassess and plan a longer-term strategy. Some leaders chose a single path (or dropped out of the movement), others wavered. The result was confusion and the abortive insurrectionary activity of winter 1839-40.

Reactions of the local authorities and their allies to the Chartist rhetoric of resistance and its physical force assumptions are therefore also worth studying. There is no doubt that, at times, the largely hidden menace of Chartism scared the living

---

457 For example, the Todmorden anti-poor law disturbances of November 1838, see Navickas, *Protest*, pp. 139-40.

458 See, for example, TNA: HO 40/41 f. 239-43, Moore to Col. Maberley, 12 Nov. 1838, for an account of the 'Acland' riot in Nov 1838.

459 Navickas, *Protest*, pp. 131-2.

460 TNA: HO 40/51 f. 153-9, deposition of John Brown, 22 May 1839.

461 TNA: HO 40/51 f. 347, Lister, Thompson, Busfeild and Hird to Harewood, 6 Aug. 1839.

daylights out of many respectable inhabitants of the more isolated West Riding towns. In Bradford, where the nearest magistrate lived over two miles from the centre of the town, residents were said to be in a state of high excitement in early August 1839 and their fears prompted substantial withdrawals from the savings bank, inadvertently initiating a Chartist ulterior measure. The arrival of an additional troop of cavalry in Halifax in December 1838 had been 'a source of great satisfaction to all the respectable inhabitants' of the town.[462] An anonymous correspondent writing to Lord John Russell in late July 1839 spoke of the Chartist intention to cause a famine by destroying all cattle and corn and urged the government to declare a solemn fast and the nation to humble itself in sackcloth and ashes 'to implore the Almighty to avert the threatened Rebellion.' The Chartists were more than aware of the fearsome reputation they had attained by autumn 1839. Referring to the hysterical press coverage of the movement at this time, the *Star* observed sarcastically that 'not a pig could be stolen, a horse throw its rider, or a child wet the bed for the last six months, in which the Chartists have not been concerned.'[463]

In general, the local press sought to ridicule or play down the importance of Chartism, and local magistrates tried to present a picture of steadiness and control. However, at times of particular crisis or local excitement, both the local newspapers and magistracy dropped the mask to reveal their extreme nervousness, uncertainty and fear. Two weeks after the *Star* had sought to exonerate the Chartists from complicity in bed-wetting, the paper reported how Bradford magistrates on receiving information of a large Chartist meeting on Fairweather Green went scurrying to the local military commander, only to find that the 'meeting' was a number of people engaged in a footrace.[464]

In such circumstances one of the main concerns of the Home Office and the northern military commander, General Napier, was to prevent frightened or particularly zealous local magistrates and special constables from over-stepping the mark and provoking a confrontation.[465] The government increasingly flexed its muscles, with its ban on torchlight meetings, the arrest of Stephens in December 1838, followed by further arrests in Lancashire and Birmingham in summer 1839. It also occasionally made intimidating noises itself and encouraged the harassment of local Chartist activity. In general, however, there was a genuine reluctance to create martyrs or to attack Chartism directly in the areas in which it was strong.[466] This policy can be seen in action early on when Home Secretary Lord John Russell wrote privately to Lord Harewood (West Riding Lord Lieutenant) in September 1838 stating his reasons for not prosecuting Oastler after one of his more violent rhetorical flourishes:

---

462 TNA: HO 40/51 f. 437, Memorandum of Col. Angelo, 19 Aug. 1839; draft letter from J. R. Ralph to Col. Wemyss, 28 Dec. 1838, reprinted in Dalby, 'The Chartist Movement in Halifax', p. 106.

463 WYAS: HP, Box 2, Anonymous letter sent to Lord John Russell, 26 July 1839; *NS* 12 Oct. 1839.

464 *NS* 26 Oct. 1839.

465 See, for example, the keenness of Huddersfield magistrates to prosecute speakers after the 10 Aug. meeting, TNA: HO 40/51 f. 375, Brook, Starkey and Sutcliffe to Russell, 10 Aug. 1839.

466 This, together with local leaders' circumspection, may explain why there was no round of arrests in the West Riding in the summer of 1839.

As far as I can perceive, this gentleman's exhortation to the people to arm is not likely to induce them to lay out their money on muskets or pistols – so long as mere violence of language is employed without effect, it is better I believe not to add to the importance of the mob-leader by prosecution – I should for the same reason wish the great meetings for universal suffrage and the like to be uninterrupted, care being taken to guard against a breach of the peace by civil force – or if necessary by military aid.' However, he added: 'The matter would assume a different complexion if from discontent at the Poor Law, the high price of bread or any other cause, combinations formed for the purpose of intimidating by physical force should be organised.[467]

After reports of arming and drilling filtered through to the Home Office in Spring 1839, the government took the precaution of swearing in special constables. Over 1,800 special constables were enrolled in the Bradford area alone. In addition, the government acceded to the request of the West Riding magistrates in mid-May to support the establishment of local volunteer armed associations in the manufacturing districts.[468] By the summer of 1839 middle-class arming was probably outstripping that by Chartists in many areas. In late July Leeds Magistrates requested a hundred cutlasses for the local volunteers for an armed association and requested that three hundred cutlasses, pistols and ammunition to be kept for them at Leeds Barracks (until the force was properly organised in Bradford). The Bradford magistrates trusted their special constables with cutlasses but felt 'great reluctance in giving pistols etc to the inhabitants without... their at all understanding the use of them... and would if brought into activity be under little or no control.' For this reason Colonel Angelo recommended sending an experienced Metropolitan Police Officer to organise Pensioners as a supplementary armed force and urged the immediate quartering of regular troops in Bradford.[469]

Chartists were quite aware of the advantage which regular troops gave to their adversaries. The response of both local and national authorities, however, was more subtle than merely relying on the presence of troops or the creation of local militia to subdue radical spirits and aspirations. They played the situation coolly, and by generally avoiding provocative action failed to fulfil the Chartist prophecy of an imminent violent attack on the movement. Although clashes such as those at Birmingham in July gave fresh credibility to the Chartist vision of violent confrontation, large-scale repression never happened, at least not in the West Riding.

---

467 WYAS: HP, Box 1, Russell to Harewood, 18 Sept. 1838.
468 TNA: HO 40/51 f. 111, Paley and Hird to Russell, 13 May 1839; WYAS: HP, Box 2, Meeting of West Riding Magistrates, 18 May 1839.
469 TNA: HO 40/51 f. 253, Holdforth to Russell, 25 July 1839; f. 291 and 309, Harewood to Russell, 27 July and 2 Aug. 1839; f. 363, Lister to Harewood, 7 Aug, 1839; f. 347, Lister, Thompson, Busfeild and Hird to Harewood, 6 Aug. 1839; f. 437, Col. Angelo Memorandum relative to Bradford, 19 Aug. 1839.

c) Conspiracy and Insurrection

The account of the West Riding textile district's participation in Chartist insurrectionary planning and action in late 1839 and early 1840, painstakingly put together by A. J. Peacock over half a century ago, has been usefully supplemented by valuable additions and overviews. Malcolm Chase, for example, rightly pays detailed attention to the Newport Rising and the subsequent insurrectionary after-shocks, including those in the textile district.[470] A number of aspects of the resulting composite narrative, however, deserve some emphasis. In the first place, it is clear that plans had been in the offing for some time. Possibly as early as the summer of 1839, a number of Convention members, including Peter Bussey, were meeting privately to lay plans which culminated in the Newport Rising.[471] With Bussey at the helm, the West Riding was pencilled in to act alongside South Wales and possibly North East England as one of the focal points for the insurrection.[472] Secondly, there were strong connections between the region and the Newport affair. John Frost was well-known in the West Riding and, for example, had led the Bradford procession to the May 1839 Peep Green meeting.[473] He was scheduled to speak in Halifax (alongside Bussey, O'Connor, Pitkethly and Dr. John Taylor) on 21 October 1839; an engagement, A. J. Peacock suggests, was carefully crafted to confuse the authorities about key Chartist leaders' whereabouts.[474] Thirdly, and perhaps most interestingly, even after the failure at Newport and the desertion of a key West Riding leader (Bussey), Chartists in the more militant districts continued with their plans and plotting.[475] For example, a covert meeting in the home of a Halifax Chartist in the week after Newport delegated one of their number to liaise with other localities with a view to 'going to work, and to do it in a better fashion than it had been done in Wales'. The West Riding was well represented at delegate conferences in December in Newcastle and Manchester, at which tactics for saving Frost and carrying the Charter by force were in all probability discussed. Bradford, Dewsbury and Sheffield all sent delegates to the second

---

470 Peacock, *Bradford Chartism*, pp. 24-53; John Baxter, 'Armed Resistance and Insurrection', pp. 1-38; David J. V. Jones, *The Last Rising: The Newport Chartist Insurrection of 1839* (Cardiff: University of Wales Press, 2014); Chase, *Chartism*, pp. 106-110, 128-39.

471 Epstein, 'Feargus O'Connor', pp. 338-9; Peacock, *Bradford Chartism*, p. 28.

472 Chase, *Chartism*, pp. 107-9.

473 *NS* 18 May 1839.

474 *NS* 19 Oct. 1839; Peacock, *Bradford Chartism*, p. 32. For a full discussion of the connections see Peacock, *Bradford Chartism*, p. 33 ff; see also TNA: HO 40/51 f. 685, Deposition of Sarah Ward, 29 Nov. 1839; and note signed by James Rawson and Thomas Aked (Halifax) reprinted in Dalby, 'The Chartist Movement in Halifax', p. 108.

475 On Bussey's loss of nerve and subsequent emigration; and on plans for a rising on 9 Nov. see, Peacock, *Bradford Chartism*, pp. 32-4. The West Riding was well represented at delegate conferences in December in Newcastle and Manchester at which tactics for saving Frost and carrying the Charter by force were in all probability discussed. Bradford, Dewsbury and Sheffield all sent delegates to the second Convention which made definite insurrectionary plans. On the mysterious Dewsbury delegate meetings in late December and early January see Peacock, *Bradford Chartism*, p. 36; and on the 12 and 26 January risings and their background, ibid., pp. 38 and 39-46.

Convention at which insurrectionary plans were definitely drawn up.[476] Peacock's detailed reconstruction of this clandestine Chartist activity in the winter months of 1839-40 provides a detailed examination of the Chartist underground, but a number of aspects still require explanation or further investigation.

Uncertainties still exist about the precise role of West Riding delegate meetings in the autumn and winter of 1839. Reports on them become increasingly brief and circumspect. It is unclear, for example, why the *Star* report on the October meeting was dated 'Monday 21 October' when the meeting was due to take place on 28 October. The likelihood is that the meeting did in fact take place on the 28th and that messages were hurriedly sent to Newcastle, Huddersfield and possibly Newport. However, it is puzzling why delegates decided to wait upon Mr O'Connor at Huddersfield to 'inform him of the decision of this meeting', when O'Connor was reported to be out of the country – a fact which delegates would surely have known.[477] The identity of some of the delegates at the September and October meetings is also suggestive of the nature of the discussions taking place. Two delegates (Thomas Kitchenman and William Vallance) had possible links with the Grange Moor insurrection of 1820, and Peter Bussey, George White, Henry Hodgson and Francis Law were all deeply implicated in the events of November 1839 or January 1840. The fact that the 25 November delegate meeting was not reported in the *Star* also speaks volumes for Chartist fears of arrests or for insurrectionary planning or both.[478]

Secondly, the presence in the West Riding and the role, if any, of Charles Neesom (Chartist tailor and former London Democratic Association ally of William Rider) at this time has never been adequately explained. He spoke at the anniversary dinner of the Chickenley RA on 26 October and was therefore in the area when the late October West Riding delegate meeting took place. The *Star* of 7 December replied to an enquiry from 'A sufferer in 1819' that 'Mr O'Connor knows nothing of Mr Neesom's movements. There is not a warrant against Mr Neesom; he has not been delegated by the trades of London'. The following week Neesom, writing from Mill Bridge, near Liversedge replied to O'Connor's insinuations and outlined his credentials; but it is likely that he, like George Julian Harney in the north-east, was deeply involved in insurrectionary preparations.[479]

---

476 Chase, *Chartism*, p. 131, citing TNA: HO 40/43, Wemyss to Home Office, 12 Nov. 1839 ???
On the mysterious Dewsbury delegate meetings in late December and early January, see Peacock, *Bradford Chartism*, p. 36; and on the 12 and 26 January risings and their background, ibid., pp. 38 and 39-46.

477 *NS* 5 Oct.; 2 Nov. 1839; see also message in *NS* 26 Oct. 1839 that William Vallance will attend the delegate meeting on 'Mon next' (i.e. 28 Oct.) as Barnsley's representative. Epstein, 'Feargus O'Connor', p. 338, says O'Connor left for Ireland on 5 Oct and did not return until 2 Nov.

478 On the 1820 rising at Grange Moor (eight miles east of Huddersfield) see Malcolm Chase, *1820: Disorder and Stability in the United Kingdom* (Manchester: Manchester University Press, 2013), pp. 122-9. For Kitchenman, see above, p. 422, fn. 248. William Vallance, the Barnsley delegate, was a relation of John Vallance, whose transportation for his part in Grange Moor was cancelled in 1821. The 25 November meeting was referred to in a report from Bradford *NS* 7 Dec. 1839.

479 *NS* 2 Nov.; 7, 14 Dec. 1839. Neesom, a native of Yorkshire, had been in the same

In the jigsaw puzzle of late 1839-40 insurrectionary activity, Dewsbury remains the missing piece. There is no doubt that the Dewsbury area (with or without Neesom's advice) played a central role in the planning of the West Riding risings. Evidence from Birmingham in November reveals that delegates (Senior and Whittaker) from a committee sitting at Dewsbury had been to the town in the middle of the month, gathering information about the readiness of local groups.[480] Towards the end of the month the Dewsbury Chartists sought clarification from O'Connor about his part in calling off the 4 November Yorkshire rising. His cryptic reply denied any 'part in the foul trick played upon the people' and implicated the already absconded Bussey.[481] Tellingly, when fresh plans were afoot in December they sought to tie O'Connor to insurrection by electing him as their delegate to the second Convention. Dewsbury hosted the West Riding meeting which delegated three representatives to attend the Convention and the regular delegate meetings (perhaps of a West Riding or a Northern committee) held in the town in late December and early January, were in regular communication with the Convention.[482] When the *Star* of 4 and 11 January 1840 came out with warnings against taking vengeance and recommendations for peaceful constitutional action in successive editorials, the Dewsbury Chartists were alleged to be extremely angry and even threatened editor William Hill's life. According to William Ashton of Barnsley, the editorial of 11 January in particular 'struck dismay in tens of thousands' and 'the whole affair was blown to atoms by that accursed paper'.[483] The attempt at a 'second Newport' in Dewsbury on the night of 11-12 January fizzled out when promised support from other areas failed to materialize. The final throw of the dice in Bradford on 26 January was similarly undermined by over-optimistic calculations about the extent of support, the practical difficulties of communication and infiltration by spies.[484]

The precise role of the national and local leadership in the events of late 1839-40 can only be a matter of speculation. Conspiracy, as Malcolm Chase notes, generally leaves limited evidence.[485] Feargus O'Connor certainly knew much about the

---

(Dewsbury) area in early October, and in late November he spoke at Halifax, *NS* 30 Nov. 1839. Millbridge, situated on a major crossroads, is in the Heckmondwike/Liversedge area – the location of the West Riding delegate meetings and a physical-force centre. Neesom claimed to be the delegate of a committee 'composed of one member from each political association in London'.

480 TNA: HO 40/50, Francis Burgess to Phillips, (enclosing Wilson's report of 19 Nov and Tongue's report of 18 Nov. 1839), I am grateful to John Baxter for this reference. 'Whittaker' was possibly William Whittaker 'cloth manufacturer' (probably handloom-weaver) of Ossett who chaired the first anniversary dinner of the Ossett and Gawthorpe RA, *NS* 12 Oct. 1839. 'Senior' may possibly be Robert Senior who spoke at a meeting of the Chickenley RA, *NS* 29 June 1839. The Ossett, Gawthorpe and Chickenley Associations were closely linked. Interestingly, Neesom spoke at the Chickenley anniversary dinner, *NS* 2 Nov. 1839.

481 *NS* 23 Nov 1839; Chase, *Chartism*, p. 132.

482 *NS* 23 Nov.; 21 Dec. 1839; TNA: HO 40/51 f. 657, Paley, Thompson and Hird to Normanby, 17 Dec. 1839; Peacock, *Bradford Chartism*, p. 36.

483 *NS* 3 May 1845.

484 *LM* 18 Jan. 1840; Also see above, pp. 431-2 and 410-11, for discussion of the Dewsbury and Bradford Risings.

485 Chase, *Chartism*, p. 106.

insurrectionary intentions of the second Convention and may have been more intimate with the precise details of the initial plans for simultaneous risings on 4 November than James Epstein acknowledges. O'Connor's intimate connections with the West Riding make it difficult to believe that he was not at least partly conversant with the plans that were afoot. [486] The local leaders appear to have fallen into three main categories: those who stayed well away or, like John Jackson in Bradford, actively discouraged any insurrectionary activity; those who knew of the plans and possibly dabbled in them; and those who were in it up to their necks. The precise threshold between the second and third categories is difficult to establish, but together they include many of the chief local leaders. Peter Bussey was due to lead the Bradford rising of 4 November and one of Henry Hetherington's shop assistants apparently wrote to the Home Office after Newport suggesting that 'the Government have an eye on Mr Pitkeithley of Huddersfield' and noting that, 'it seems generally known among the Chartist leaders that an outbreak would take place from what I could understand'.[487]

In Bradford the two most prominent Chartists of the late 1839 period, Henry Hodgson and George Flinn, were heavily involved in the plans for the January rising, as was William Brook, fiery joiner and brother of former soldier and physical-force advocate Joseph Brook, one of the key local figures of the decade. In Leeds William Rider was present at or knew of a meeting which put Robert Peddie in touch with the Bradford militants, and leaders such as Joseph Jones and David Black were involved in the preliminary meetings which led to the second Convention.[488]

In the Dewsbury area it is probable that many of the local delegates who attended the West Riding and other delegate meetings of late 1839 knew of and took the lead in insurrectionary plans. These included people such as John Haigh and his son of the same name in the Ossett, Gawthorpe and Chickenley localities, Francis Law of Spinkwell, Thomas Field and Samuel Allat of Dewsbury, and Thomas Wass of Heckmondwike. In all cases it is likely that far from being hot-headed fanatics who deluded and 'led on' their constituents, these local figures were responding to a groundswell of local opinion and following through the logic of an earlier declared position. In Bradford in late November, for example, it is interesting to note that an

---

486 See Epstein, 'Feargus O'Connor', p. 340 ff.

487 Bussey was also implicated in the Bradford arming. The arrest of John Livesey in Lancashire revealed letters from Bussey ordering guns, *Manchester Guardian* 17 Aug. 1839, (reference from Sykes, 'Popular Politics', p. 579). For Pitkethly see, TNA: HO 40/44, ff. 958-9, R. T. Edwards to HO, 6 Nov. 1839, quoted in Epstein, 'Feargus O'Connor', p. 339. This is the only evidence suggesting Pitkethly's involvement. His writings reveal him to be a cautious advocate of any 'move' arguing for the need to seize the right moment. He particularly feared 'any premature step' which would ruin the cause, *NS* 6 July 1839 and letters to Joseph Broyen, In TNA: HO 40/57. He also knew that his letters were amongst those seized by Mansfield magistrates.

488 Peacock, *Bradford Chartism*, pp. 35 ff; p.39 ff. (on Peddie); p. 42 (Rider); pp. 42-3 (William Brook); *NS* 7, 21 Dec. 1839. For further information on William Brook, see HO 20/10 Prisons and *NS* 8 Jan., 28 May, 16 July 1842. It is not possible to name any established town leaders in Halifax or Huddersfield who were involved, but for insinuations about Huddersfield leaders, see pp. 412-3 below.

address urging the government to inquire into the causes of insurrection was rejected by a majority at a public meeting and a stronger resolution supporting Frost substituted in its place.[489]

The insurrectionary activity of late 1839-40 was not the product of an ignorant or desperate rank and file being duped and led on by headstrong leaders. Rather it reflected the collective experience and will of a few geographically and numerically small but well-integrated communities, such as the Nelson Court area of Bradford, Queenshead, Clayton and some of the villages and hamlets around Dewsbury (Heckmondwike, Earlsheaton, Chickenley, Gawthorpe). The numbers involved in serious preparations and activity were never large, but neither were they negligible.[490] Equally it is clear that the network within which this activity took place was a very wide one, and included many prominent local leaders.

The regional movement can be seen to be operating on two levels at this time. At one level was the development of a wider Chartist culture, involving prayer-meetings, discussions, lectures, various strands of educational, religious, co-operative and temperance activity, collections for Frost and addresses to the Queen. At the other, underground, level there was insurrectionary planning, secret meetings, cryptic messages and shadowy delegates travelling between the main conspiratorial centres. Although some of the mainstream activities can be shown to be 'fronts' and leaders occasionally talked an ambiguous and euphemistic language,[491] the 'clandestine' and 'cultural' manifestations of Chartist endeavour were not necessarily incompatible. They were linked through activities such as the attempts to re-organise all localities on the 'class' basis using the 'silent system', like the securing of safe meeting places and the collection of money to 'defend' Frost.

The latter verb can be interpreted in two ways. William Armitage, one of the collectors for Chartist defence funds, revealed in his memoirs just how keenly the fate of Frost, Williams and Jones was followed in the Huddersfield area. In Bradford, also, the news that they were to be 'hung, drawn and quartered' created 'a sensation', with 'nearly everyone' judging it 'as cruel in the extreme, and breathing vindictiveness rather than justice'.[492] As the recollections of a sober young Queenshead Chartist, John

---

489 For example, on Francis Law's involvement with the Sheffield plotters, see John Baxter, 'The Life and Struggle of Samuel Holberry, physical force Chartist', in B. Moore, S. Holmes and J. L. Baxter (eds.), *Samuel Holberry: Sheffield's Revolutionary Democrat* (Sheffield: Holberry Society, 1978) p. 14; *NS* 30 Nov. 1839 (Bradford meeting).

490 Dr John Baxter in his work on the insurrectionary underground has estimated a possible thousand people being under arms on the night of the Dewsbury Rising.

491 For example, the itinerant Chartist preacher William Martin, raised a cheer in Bradford in advance of the 'Sacred Holiday' when he spoke of the need to 'provide plenty of butter [knives?]' (*BO* 8 Aug. 1839). Other euphemisms include 'biscuits' (muskets), 'flitches of bacon' (arms generally) and 'flour' (gunpowder). The latter adds poignancy to reports of Bussey being found, on the night of the intended West Riding rising, 'behind the flour sacks!' I am grateful to Dr Baxter for drawing my attention to Chartist euphemisms.

492 *HDE* 26 Dec. 1885; *Northern Liberator* 25 Jan. 1840, quoted in Peacock, *Bradford Chartism*, p. 42. The prisoners' appeals were rejected and their executions planned for 6 February. This was eventually commuted to transportation for life following an extensive campaign inside and outside Parliament.

Bates, make clear, the insurrectionary talk and preparations of late 1839 were not the preserve of a few 'deviants' and fanatics:

> A large number of plots were arranged in secret... I have attended several secret meetings at which we have planned revolution... But I never had anything to do with the riots, and after the first riot, I became more discreet and did not attend secret meetings. I never did anything illegal except to attend meetings and if I had to live over again, I should not want to alter what I did.[493]

d) Culture, Class and Conflict

James Epstein's pioneering study of Chartist culture and organisation in Nottingham emphasised the importance of the 'cultural manifestations of Chartism'. He argued that 'the cultural sphere was one of vital class self-definition and continual conflict' and that this aspect complemented the more formal side of the movement (with its public meetings and petitions), and also its direct-action element.[494] Subsequent writers have explored some of the different manifestations of the vibrant Chartist culture that emerged in these years.[495] A number have noted a shift, from outdoors to indoors, from exhortation to education, from the spoken to the written word. There were also changes in form and tone, like the replacement of political dinners by tea parties and evening soirées that Peter Brett detects from the mid-1839 onwards.[496] The new emphasis on cultural activities is often interpreted as part of Chartists' recognition of the need to create a more sustainable movement after the failure of the mass meetings, petitioning and 'ulterior measures' of 1838-9.

Epstein's Nottingham case study focuses on the 1840s when, in the wake of the defeats and disappointments of the early Chartist period, 'local chartists gave increased expression to the cultural side of their radical commitment.'[497] Writing of Huddersfield in the early 1840s, Matthew Roberts also notes that 'the movement evolved into something different ... organisation, lectures, committees, education were the order of the day; not the boisterous but all too fleeting atmosphere of the mass platform'.[498] However, it is clear from a number of the early Chartist district profiles outlined above

---

493 *Bradford Daily Telegraph*, 7 Mar. 1895. Bates had only recently taken the total abstinence pledge, Carter, *John Bates*, p. 3. For Queenshead as an insurrectionary centre, see Peacock, *Bradford Chartism*, pp. 38 and 43; Dalby, 'The Chartist Movement in Halifax', p. 109 and *LI* 19 Nov. 1839.

494 Epstein, 'Chartist Movement in Nottingham', p. 222. This builds on the pioneering discussion of Chartist cultural activity in Eileen Yeo, 'Robert Owen and Radical Culture' in S. Polland and J. Salt (eds.), *Robert Owen: Prophet of the Poor* (London: Macmillan, 1971), pp. 104-8.

495 For example, Timothy Randall, 'Chartist poetry and song', in Ashton, Fyson and Roberts (eds.), *The Chartist Legacy*, pp. 171-95; Matthew Roberts, '"God Save the Paddock Flag": Anti-Poor Law and Chartist Banners, 1837-1844', in Hargreaves (ed.), *The Charter our Right!*, pp. 39-61.

496 Brett, 'Political Dinners', p. 550.

497 Epstein, 'Chartist Movement in Nottingham', p. 221.

498 Roberts, '"God Save the Paddock Flag"', p. 54.

that many aspects of what Epstein terms the 'cultural manifestations of Chartism' – tea parties, prayer meetings, Chartist chapels and schools, lectures and discussion groups, temperance and co-operative activity – were already present and well-established in the late 1830s; indeed, some were also features of the pre-Chartist phase.

The cultural side of the movement became more prominent and more diverse in the aftermath of the first Convention and the failure of ulterior measures. Apart from insurrectionists committed to seeing things through in 1839-40, leaders and supporters alike increasingly realised that the attainment of working-class political rights would only result from a sustained, long-term campaign. But the switch in the emphasis of local activity revealed in many sources is partly a deception. By the summer of 1839 traditional forms of open constitutional agitation, the public meetings and rallies with their petitions and addresses, had become more difficult (partly as a result of middle-class harassment) and more dangerous. Moreover, they were now judged to be less appropriate: the Petition had failed, ulterior measures had been found wanting and there were no obvious causes or major issues to agitate.

Whilst it diversified and took on new importance in the second half of 1839, the cultural side of Chartism, and before it radicalism, had always been there. In the hyperactive months of late 1838 and early 1839 this cultural/convivial base had been overlain with more immediate pre-occupations – preparations for the Peep Green meetings, missionary activity to set up NU branches, collections of money for the National Rent and for the Stephens Fund, and collections of signatures for the Petition, electing delegates for the National Convention, and countless local meetings and initiatives. When the pressure eased and the movement had time for reflection and re-assessment, the ever-present backdrop of small convivial gatherings meetings, educational and religious activities, comes more sharply into focus. Although this backcloth occasionally hid covert activities, it is misleading and fanciful to suppose that the Chartists were conducting an elaborate charade. The essential point is that, whether sober and serious or convivial and humorous, the cultural forms complemented rather than replaced other modes of activity.

Similarly it could be argued that many of what some might term 'moral' or moderate activities, prayer meetings, 'Churchgoings' or co-operative plans, had confrontational aspects. A Bradford magistrate, noting the difficulties of obtaining information about local activity in late 1839, 'as the Chartists now meet in sections at each other's houses under the pretence of prayer Meetings and commence by Singing Hymns and prayers', was mistaken in seeing these gatherings as cynical parts of a wider pretence.[499] Although such meetings might be, and often were, used for insurrectionary planning, the likelihood is that the religious observances were genuine and formed an integral part of an organic cultural experience which instilled bonds of allegiance and solidarity. It was not incongruous for Thomas Bottomley, uncompromising Leeds East End operative and Chartist, to open a meeting of unemployed workers in December 1839 'by reading a hymn, which had been composed specially for the occasion, and which was afterwards sung by the assembly',

---

499 TNA: HO 40/51 f. 687, Thompson to Lord Normanby, 2 Dec. 1839.

and then go onto to proclaim that, 'Nothing would be done till they declared at once that they would have bread or blood'.[500]

The wide range of convivial or cultural events and facilities provided by local NU branches – political lectures, Sunday sermons, anniversary dinners, family tea-parties, newsrooms, temperance societies, libraries, adult schools – dovetailed neatly with local branch and public meetings and with other aspects of Chartist endeavour, like the organisation of exclusive dealing, the occupation of church pews, or the collection of petition signatures. This range of cultural pursuits was generated spontaneously and indigenously and satisfied a desire for participation in independent, alternative forms of education or entertainment. Such activities, like the Chartist band at Heckmondwike, also helped to keep up and maintain interest and enthusiasm.[501] Finally, on the purely practical level, it is clear that part of the rationale for permanent organisation and a vigorous branch life stemmed from the need to collect money regularly in order to support victims and pay for the wider agitation.

The cultural institutions and convivial activities which West Riding Chartists established do not demonstrate 'moral force' predilections or an accommodation to middle-class 'respectable' culture and values. They arose out of fiercely independent and class-conscious communities who, as we have seen from the local studies, often inclined towards 'physical force' rhetoric and, sometimes, activity. Although less obvious or public, their rejection of middle-class ideas and cultural institutions through these activities was just as real as their challenge to middle-class public meetings or religious observances.

The Chartist concern for education took many forms; for example, mutual discussion groups, informal *Northern Star* readings, adult reading and writing classes, libraries and newsrooms, even William Hill's schoolmasterly reprimands to ungrammatical *Star* correspondents.[502] Much Chartist activity was in a broad sense educative; and virtually all Chartist leaders accepted instruction as a vital weapon in the fight for political emancipation. The Chartist conception of education, not surprisingly, was highly political. It is revealed in the 1837 definition of Bradford radical and later Chartist John Jackson: 'we want education – I use the term in its most comprehensive sense, not as the mere acquisition of reading and writing, and accounts, but of sound political knowledge, so that we should know our social and political rights and be able to use our moral force to the best advantage.' Two years later Chartist speakers addressed a public meeting in June 1839 at Northowram, near Halifax, to set up a school to teach the science of 'Social and Political Economy' and explain the 'Science of Government', and afterwards were engaged to give lectures.[503]

---

500 *LM* 21, 28 Dec. 1839.

501 Peel, *Spen Valley*, p. 316.

502 On the informality of working-class radical educational experience see, R. Johnson, '"Really Useful Knowledge": Radical Education and Working-Class Culture', in J. Clarke, C. Critcher, R. Johnson (eds.) *Working-Class Culture: Studies in History and Theory* (London: Hutchinson, 1979); for an adult school see the Elland RA school teaching reading, writing and politics, *NS* 14 Apr. 1838; on William Hill (whose lectures on grammar and the English language were always in demand), see Epstein, 'Feargus O'Connor and the Northern Star', p. 76.

503 *LT* 21 Aug. 1837; *NS* 29 June 1839. The lecturers were Cliffe and North (probably William

Lectures, whether formalised in a radical school or as an occasional input into branch life, together with the informal discussion of the *Star*'s content, comprised the staple educative fare of many local Chartists. Like Bussey's lectures to the Leeds female radicals in October 1839, they normally and explicitly tackled questions on politics, history and religion which were excluded from the curriculum of institutions under middle-class, often local Whig patronage, such as the Mechanics Institutes. The Whig government's record on education was sarcastically referred to by Pitkethly in October 1839:

> Yet with all their boasted schooling and plans for education, more than double of the people's money could be expended in building houses for horses than was given for educational purposes.[504]

While formal connections between Chartism and temperance were not particularly strong in the West Riding in the early period, the relationship between intemperance and the working class's political exclusion was commonly drawn. John Bates, writing of Queenshead in 1839, recalled how he and some of his Chartist companions 'were soon convinced that no Charter could bring much happiness while the people were so demoralised with strong drink. Many of the Chartists would be drunk while attending their meetings; and much of the misery could be directly traced to drunkenness'.[505] A number of actual or prototype Chartist organisations, such as the Almondbury WMA, resolved not to meet in pubs; and when the New Pellon WMA held its first anniversary (at a school room) in June 1839, only tea and temperance beverages were consumed. John Bates and some of his fellow Chartists joined the Queenshead Temperance Society after hearing Christopher Shackleton engage with the local Temperance Society on the question of 'the relative merits of Chartism and Teetotalism in the elevating of the country'.[506] Significantly, the Queenshead Chartists, including Bates, were heavily implicated in insurrectionary preparations taking place in the area in the autumn and winter of 1839. There are clearly major difficulties in ascribing or attaching a 'middle-class' label to their temperance activities. As Bates, who later became Secretary of the Queensbury Temperance Society, recalled on his eightieth birthday in 1895, 'my politics, like my Teetotalism sprang from a desire that was early kindled in me to do something to right the wrongs of the working classes'.[507]

The connections between early Chartism and the more democratic religious denominations has been noted in several of the local studies. The West Riding movement, as befitting its age, was imbued with religious language and forms and included a number of prominent local preachers in its first line of leadership.[508] The

---

North of Clayton).

504 *NS* 12 Oct. (Bussey); 26 Oct. 1839 (Pitkethly).

505 Carter, *John Bates*, p. 3.

506 *LT* 23 Dec. 1837; *NS* 29 June 1839; Carter, *John Bates*, p. 3.

507 Carter, *John Bates*, p. 2.

508 For example, Benjamin Rushton, William Thornton, John Arran, Jonathon Bairstow, Abram Hanson. For Chartist connections with 'democratic' religion in other areas see, Epstein, 'Chartist Movement in Nottingham', p. 249 ff.; J. F. C. Harrison, 'Chartism in Leicester', in Briggs (ed.), *Chartist Studies*, p. 129 ff. For an introduction to the religious aspects of

religion these leaders espoused was uncompromisingly militant and egalitarian. John Arran of Bradford, moving a resolution at the May 1839 Peep Green meeting, uttered, in the words of the Tory *Halifax Guardian*,

> the most rank blasphemy, (he) said that Christ was the greatest democrat that ever lived, that there should be no such thing as superiority, or inferiority in the world, that they should cast the hypocrites (i.e. the Ministers of God who did not support Universal Suffrage) on their own resources, and they would then begin to bring forth the fruits of repentance.

The resolution which Arran moved urged the Chartists 'not to attend any places of worship where the administration of services is inimical to civil liberty… but to meet in such a way and manner in our separate localities in future as the circumstances of the case require'.[509]

A number of Chartist localities did indeed set up their own Chartist chapels and conduct their own sermons and services. But the Chartist assertion of independence went deeper and further. As well as participating in the continuing battle against the established Church over the issue of church rates, Chartists also made more direct and public demonstrations of their distaste for the hypocrisy of canting middle-class Christians. In March 1839 the *Star* reported a pre-planned mass walk-out from the Ambler Thorn Methodist New Connexion chapel in the middle of a service preached by the Rev. G. Beaumont a pro-Poor Law Guardian.[510] More spectacular were the 'walk-ins' staged by local Chartists in late summer 1839. The Bradford Chartists took up Richard Carlile's idea of reviving the use of the parish church as a popular meeting place and, beginning on Sunday 4 August, took possession of Bradford Parish Church in a well-planned and disciplined operation. The following week as part of their 'National Holiday' sequence of demonstrations they again served notice of their intention to occupy the Church and sent a recommended text to the clergyman. Dewsbury Chartists also adopted the tactic and attended Church in great numbers on the Sunday preceding their three days of meetings, and Halifax followed suit on the two following Sundays.[511]

The 'churchgoings' of early August epitomise the prevailing tone of class hostility and a willingness to confront their middle-class 'respectable' opponents directly and publicly. The occupations can also be seen as a clever riposte to middle-class inspired harassment of the Chartists' public spaces. The same issue of the *Star* in which Carlile

---

Chartism, see Eileen Yeo, 'Christianity in Chartist Struggle, 1838-42', *Past and Present*, 91 (1981), pp. 109-39.

509 *HG, NS* 25 May 1839.

510 *NS* 30 Mar. 1839.

511 *NS* 13 July 1839 (Carlile's letter); TNA: HO 40/51 ff. 347, Lister, Thompson, Busfeild and Hird to Harewood, 6 Aug. 1839; and f. 387 Harewood to Russell, 11 Aug. 1839; also WYAS: HP, Box 2, Thompson to Harewood, 2 Aug. 1839, and *BO* 15 Aug. 1839 (for Bradford); *NS* 17 Aug. 1839 (for Dewsbury); Yeo, 'Christianity in Chartist Struggle', p. 123, fn. 41 (for Halifax). For a detailed discussion of the occupation of churches, see Yeo, 'Christianity in Chartist Struggle', pp. 123-37.

suggested the Church meetings idea also contains the news that after finding all places shut to them, often as a result of magisterial threats against licensees, the 'Radicals of Bradford' had at last found a large room 'in which they can assemble without being compelled to meet under the broad canopy of Heaven'.[512]

The problem was not new. However, it tended to become more prevalent and pressing throughout the textile district as middle-class fears and hostility reached fresh peaks in the winter of 1838-9 and the summer of 1839. Trustees of the Baptist School Room in Clayton, for example, objected to the local RA using it for meetings in December 1838. Two weeks later the Dewsbury RA was temporarily made homeless after pressure on a local landlady. In March the West Riding delegate meeting passed a vote of censure on trustees of the Mold-Green School, Dalton, for refusing 'an honest member of their own body' the use of the school for a Chartist lecture. Chartist condemnations however counted for little and similar instances of petty local harassment and cussedness occurred throughout the early Chartist period.[513]

The way in which such obstruction and hostility handicapped local agitational efforts is illustrated by a *Star* report of a Chartist public meeting at Middlestown, near Horbury, in Spring 1839. The visiting Dewsbury speakers had to hold the meeting outdoors and used a stone wall as hustings. One speaker (William Wilby) had spoken for just fifteen minutes when he was pushed from the wall by employees of Lord Wharncliffe's (the local landowner) tenants. A slightly more subtle but no less effective form of aristocratic-inspired harassment came in summer 1839 with Lord John Russell's encouragement to local magistrates to use their powers to withdraw publicans' licences. This met with a characteristically positive and optimistic response from 'WP' who urged the creation of a common West Riding fund to finance the erection of public buildings to house working-class public meetings and a wide range of other 'cultural' activities.[514] The scheme itself was never taken up but a number of areas, following the example of Keighley, set about creating independent Working Men's Halls. The Liversedge and Heckmondwike radicals exasperated at Whig-inspired ejection from pubs and schools, planned the creation of a 'People's Hall' on the basis of £1 shares. The Bradford Radicals followed suit with similar plans for a 'Working Men's Hall' in October; whilst in Leeds substantial improvements were made to the Radical room.[515]

Some of the problems of safely accommodating smaller, village or local branch meetings were partially solved by adopting the 'class system' and meeting in private houses or by encouraging a Chartist member to set himself up as a beershop keeper. However, the Chartist 'accommodation problem' remained a perennial one and one which illustrates that, like their acquisition of arms, Chartists' development of alternative 'cultural' institutions had a defensive aspect based on notions and experience of an aggressive, antagonistic and oppressive local middle class.

---

512 *NS* 13 July 1839.

513 *NS* 22 Dec. 1838; 5 Jan.; 30 Mar. 1839. See also *NS* 11 May (Hunslet), 16 Nov. 1839 (Almondbury).

514 *NS* 4 May; 8 June 1839.

515 *NS* 29 June; 26 Oct.; 8 June 1839. The long-standing project for a 'People's Hall' in Halifax, however, had been abandoned in January 1839, *LM* 26 Jan. 1839.

Chartist involvement in exclusive dealing and its natural extension, consumer co-operation, was based on similar ideas and could also have a sharp, class-conscious cutting edge. In late April, the Bradford NU had pledged 'not to deal with any shopkeepers of others, whether they sell meat or drink, if they are our known enemies'.[516] The tactic of canvassing shopkeeper support, which a number of local Chartist branches adopted during July and August 1839, had a strong confrontational aspect, as we have seen. The *Star* in September also records a consumer boycott of Bradford milksellers who had tried to impose their winter prices early.[517] Women were heavily involved in this and Chartist strictures on exclusive dealing constantly stressed the need to mobilise female Chartist supporters. It is possible that this provided one of the spurs towards the establishment of separate female Radical Associations in the summer and autumn of 1839. However, although consumer boycotts of various sorts might work in smaller communities or might successfully influence the price of individual products or the actions of isolated shop-keepers, they were far more difficult to organise and sustain in the larger urban centres.

One response to this inability to mount effective exclusive dealing campaigns was to turn to consumer or producer co-operatives. Pitkethly, himself a retailer, suggested to Glasgow meeting that, 'were the people to set up for themselves, the shopkeeper would soon find that their services could be dispensed with'. Radicals had long admired the independence and perseverance of the surviving co-operative societies and respected their attainment in limited numbers of the franchise. Similarly, the co-operators included in their midst many radical supporters and sympathisers. The Huddersfield Co-operative Society, for example, generously contributed towards defraying the general expenses of the October 1838 Peep Green meeting and made other subscriptions to Chartist funds, and the 'Co-operative Committee Room' housed the meeting to launch the National Petition in Ripponden.[518]

The involvement of Chartists in Leeds, Dewsbury and, possibly, Huddersfield in new co-operative ventures was not part of a 'toning down' of their activity. George White, a strident physical force advocate, was involved in Leeds and the proposed Dewsbury 'joint-stock company' was floated after hearing several animated and 'heart-stirring speeches', including one from Charles Neesom. At the Huddersfield national holiday meeting two months earlier, George Barker, 'a moral force man', had advocated setting up independent shops and workshops after a strong attack on 'the shopocracy', and money-mongers and 'the wholesale and retail dealers'. When a scheme finally got off the ground, the Primitive Methodists, through a 'Philanthropic Society', took the lead in forming a society to open a general store warehouse 'so as to let the labourers have all necessary articles at a reasonable price, finding the

516 *NS* 4 May 1839.

517 *NS* 14 Sept. 1839. There was a similar boycott the previous year, *NS* 18 Aug. 1838. Both are interesting echoes of the 'milk and butter boycotts' of 1829.

518 *NS* 26 Oct. 1839; 20 Oct. 1838 (resolution of thanks from Huddersfield NU); 5 Jan. 1839 (Ripponden: on this society, see Thompson, *Making*, p. 873). See also *NS* 11 May 1839 (advert for co-operative delegate meeting in Huddersfield).

shopkeepers will not sympathise with the working man, until he is finding his trade and money loss'.[519]

Co-operation, like other elements of the developing Chartist culture, was not a late addition to the radical repertoire. Commenting on the Oldham Hatter's strike in July 1838, William Hill had stated a widely held radical and socialist standpoint:

> The fact is, as we have told the working men of Yorkshire and Lancashire, hundreds of times, that so long as they will hire themselves to the distributors of wealth, instead of producing for themselves and hiring the distributors, it will ever be thus.[520]

The renewed stress given to co-operative schemes in late 1839, though signifying a longer-term perspective for emancipation, was merely the re-stating of a long-held belief in the desirability of developing institutions and activities which would foster working-class independence and self-sufficiency in a hostile political and economic atmosphere.

The strong sense of class that permeated the early Chartist movement underpinned many of these activities. It arose out of both a bond of common experience and identity amongst large sections of the working population and a shared distrust or hostility (often reciprocated) to the middle and upper classes. This sense of class identity comes across in the speeches of Chartist leaders, in the issues they took up, in the way they consistently opposed the perceived or real machinations of their upper or middle-class opponents, as well as in the cultural activities they engaged in.

The Chartist conception of class, however, was not particularly sophisticated. It owed much to the traditional radical analysis of 'Old Corruption' and to ingrained notions of rich and poor, tyrants and slaves, drones and bees, might and right, productive and non-productive classes. Onto this, though, had been fused newer elements, engendered partly by the property divisions established in the 1832 Reform Act, partly by the harsh economic realities experienced by many industrial communities, and partly through the development of ideas of an alternative political economy formulated during the 1820s and 1830s. These diverse strands did not always knit neatly together and at times the joins between them showed. In addition, the tendency to attribute all ills ultimately to political causes meant that the nature of economic relationships were rarely analysed in any great depth and that undue emphasis was placed on the role of parasitic financial middlemen of different sorts.[521] There is a sense that the language of class was vainly seeking to catch up with contemporary changes and struggling to describe the reality which working people were perceiving and experiencing. Whilst leaders might still talk in terms of 'tax eaters'

---

519 *NS* 28 Sept. (Leeds); 12 Oct. (Dewsbury); 19 Oct. (Huddersfield). For Barker see, TNA: HO 40/51 f. 453 ff, Report of Chartist Meeting at Huddersfield, 10 Aug. 1839.

520 *NS* 14 July 1838.

521 The groups identified included 'money-mongers', 'capitalists', and 'Jews' and serves as a reminder of 'the broad mood of anti-Semitism that manifestly disfigured English nineteenth century radicalism'. Although 'casual and economic rather than racialist or systemic', this trope – a legacy of the Cobbettite 'Old Corruption' analysis – lingered well into the Chartist years. See, Chase, *Chartism*, p. 288.

and 'monopolists', or might see the fundamental division as being between the productive and non-productive classes, it is clear that what they meant by these terms or who they included in these groups was changing and becoming more sharply defined. This can be seen in a brief consideration of how a few local Chartists articulated their understandings of class relations.

Peter Bussey's picture of the class structure comprised a pyramid with working men at the bottom, then progressive layers comprising the 'shop-keeper or middle-class man', the manufacturer, the merchant, the landed man, right up to the Queen. J. Ambler, a *Star* subscriber from Ambler Thorn, near Halifax, wrote of three classes: the aristocracy and nobility; the middle-classes comprising traders, merchants and manufacturers; and the working-classes ('the most useful'). In his view, class distance and distrust had increased over the last fifty years, leading to a 'silent enmity'. And there is plenty of evidence to support the notion of growing mutual distrust and hostility within hitherto well-integrated working communities in the early Chartist period.[522]

The mainspring in any exploitative system which produced and perpetuated a structure of class differentiation, however, was ultimately seen as being political. For Bussey, extortion started at the top of the pyramid and went down progressively, each level extracting from the one below through the exercise of its political and legislative power. Thus, the middle class were attacked and opposed primarily and ultimately on the grounds of being willing political oppressors who had joined the working-classes 'natural enemies', the aristocracy.[523] They were vilified for being corrupt politically rather than because they were employers. However, it was recognised that their political power enhanced the economic power that they already enjoyed over the operatives.

Whilst the political relationship was seen as the prime mover of relationships between classes, in the West Riding, with its recent legacy of trade union, factory reform and anti-poor law struggles, the lines between their oppressors' 'political' and 'economic' roles were often blurred and seen to be inseparable. If the Chartist theory of class was often limited and unsophisticated, it was increasingly expressed in uncompromising language which had a direct and strong practical impact.

Antagonism to the middle class, particularly the 'householder Whigs' in both their political and employing roles, is a constant theme of the speeches of countless local leaders, speakers and writers. Pitkethly, in March 1839, talked of 'the coercion of your employers, and of the middle men in general' and warned that 'while they are rolling in luxury, they will look down from their false eminence with distain ... [and] they will treat you with the most inordinate contempt.' In an earlier grisly metaphor he argued that 'the Whigs have come in for the purpose of reducing your bodies to perfect skeletons, and grinding your bones into gold dust, which is easily convertible into sovereigns, which are employed to purchase steam-looms, bugbears, devils, and all sorts of internal instruments with which to work you to death, or keep you starving

---

522 *NS* 17 Aug. 1839 (Bussey); 19 Oct. 1839 (Ambler); see, for example, Guiseley operatives and manufacturers, *NS* 30 Mar. 1839.

523 See, for example, Barker's speech, TNA: HO 40/51 f. 453 ff, Report of Chartist Meeting at Huddersfield, 10 Aug. 1839.

in rags and tatters.'[524] In early 1839 the Liversedge radicals, after first attacking aristocratic wealth, condemned the 'factory lords' as 'more vain, more insolent, more tyrannical, and in some instances almost as wealthy as the Aristocracy.' The same edition of the *Star* which reports the early finish of a Leeds NU branch to 'allow members to prepare for that small portion of employment now left us by our natural protectors, the money-mongers', also contains a poignant and extremely bitter account of an accident to a woolcomber attending combing machines at a Bradford factory. The man fractured his skull, but as no one could be spared to carry him home, he was laid down on wool to the end of the day and given wages for only three-quarters of a day. The paragraph concludes by informing readers that 'the slave died on Wednesday morning five o'clock. This is free and happy England.'[525]

The Chartists publicly confronted their middle-class opponents wherever possible. Meetings on the Corn Laws, factory reform, national education and distress were all taken over by local Chartist groups. In February 1839, for example, Chartists successfully swamped Corn Laws repeal meetings in Huddersfield, Halifax and Bradford. At the latter a local manufacturer's attempt to relate the Corn Law issue to the predicament of handloom weavers was met by indignant shouts of 'why you do it all by steam now; you care nothing about us'.[526] Local bitterness and class hostility also emerged openly at the end of 1839 when extreme distress hit all areas. Huddersfield magistrates solicited military aid on account of 'the threatening tone and aspect of the working class'; and the *Star* reported that in Bradford 'stout, healthy young men may be seen standing in groups in the streets, having little or no work either in their hands or their jaws.'[527]

Around the same time a Leeds 'Ultra-Radical' painted a similar picture with a familiar contrast:

> See there, as you walk along, a person indifferently clad, lean and lanky, pale-visaged, cheeks collapsed, and awkward gait – that is the labourer coming from the mill or the loom; but there, on the other hand, is a fat portly individual, firm, erect and richly apparelled – he labours not, but whence comes his food? Why it is filched from the produce of that poor labourer.[528]

It is clear that the non-labouring exploiter outlined here could equally be a factory-owning manufacturer as a financial or mercantile middle-man. Similarly, although the second address of the Heckmondwike Carpet Weavers in the middle of a fight against 'the Bond' is replete with general references to 'Mammon-worshippers', 'the money-profit of a capricious few', and 'the domineering influence of money', the specific

---

524 *NS* 3 Apr. 1839; 10 Nov. 1838.

525 *NS* 23 Feb. 1839; 29 Dec. 1838.

526 *NS, LM* 9, 16 Feb. 1839 (Corn Law meetings).

527 TNA: HO 40/57 f. 197, Walker, Battye and Brook to Napier, 14 Jan. 1840; *NS* 14 Dec. 1839.

528 *NS* 9 Nov. 1839.

target of its attack is the group of local master-manufacturers, many of them allegedly 'upstarts' from the ranks of the labourers.[529]

This sense of class also had a positive, assertive aspect. As well as misfortune, the columns of the *Star*, with its accounts of friendly society festivities, local trades disputes and self-help institutions, celebrated the strength and vitality of independent working-class culture and activity. A proud belief in the value and worth of working people acting independently is also evident in the paper and in the resolutions and democratic proclivities of local NU branches.[530] The practice of active 'working men' chairing public meetings became widespread in the early Chartist period.[531] In April 1839, after the resignation of the Birmingham delegates to the Convention, the Leeds NU branch implored the men of Birmingham 'to put good working men in the place of those middle-class men who have seceded from the convention'; and Bussey agreed with O'Connor that the 'sham-radical' leaders' places should be filled up with 'the blistered hands and the fustian jackets.'[532]

The mutual hostility generated in 'apathetic' Leeds, through attempts to secure aid for distressed workers in December 1839, illustrates the potential volatility of local class relationships. The reluctance of the town's 'leading and influential gentlemen' to provide anything more substantial than sympathy, following two meetings of unemployed operatives on Hunslet Moor, led to a bitter confrontation in the Leeds Court House. The public meeting to discuss a public subscription for aid, featured a controversial cameo appearance from Robert Owen and fully exploded when Thomas Bottomley, chair of 'the unemployed operatives' committee', Leeds East End Chartist leader and ally of William Rider, justified starving workers taking food 'from the common stock' and proposed that the Relief Committee should be formed entirely of working men. Chaos ensued. Some middle-class attendees walked out, voicing the belief that '*Beggars* should not be choosers' and alleging that 'his Chartist and Socialist supporters' had backed Bottomley's 'bread or blood' stance.[533] The *Mercury* and its allies revelled in condemning the 'revolutionists' and their 'help-yourself system'. The *Star*, for its part, made the most of the confrontation, commenting:, 'Truly, it was the starving, industrious class, against the pampered idlers who fatten upon the produce.'[534]

This episode provides a striking contrast to a similar series of meetings held two years earlier in 1837 when, after passing determinedly non-political resolutions, the unemployed workers' discontent had been assuaged by the platitudes of local 'respectables' and a plan to level and drain Woodhouse Moor, ironically one of the Leeds operatives' traditional meeting places. Two years later George White, leading Chartist and self-declared 'revolutionist', speaking to a packed radical meeting in December 1839, a few hours after the second meeting of unemployed workers, denounced their opponents' slanders that they were levellers (of historical notoriety)

---

529 *NS* 26 Oct. 1839.
530 On how Chartists practised democracy, see Gurney, 'The Democratic Idiom', pp. 581-2.
531 For example, Joseph Jones, shoemaker, chairing a Leeds NU meeting, *LT* 21 Dec. 1839.
532 *NS* 6 Apr. 1839.
533 *NS*, *LT*, *LM* 14, 21 and 28 Dec. 1839.
534 *LM* 28 Dec. 1839; *LI* 4 Jan. 1840; *NS* 28 Dec. 1839 (for *Star* comment).

who 'wanted 'to rob and plunder'. They merely desired 'to keep the money-grubbers' hands out of their pockets'. He continued,

> Both factions alike [Tories and Whigs] robbed the working man of £100, and then charitably gave him half-a-crown to alleviate his distress. (Cheers.) The Radicals alone were the men for the operatives; and they only wanted that, by the exercise of his own abilities, every man should be enabled to earn enough for his wife and family, without begging of any body. And what was the remedy for this begging system? Universal Suffrage. (Cheers.)[535]

Even in hard to rouse Leeds the operatives and their leaders had come a long way in just a couple of years.

The 1839 gatherings of unemployed workers also harked back to the distress meetings which had first stimulated working-class political activity in the textile district a decade earlier. Yet the main protagonists were far from being back where they started. In terms of agency and analysis, leadership and organisation they had travelled far. Supported by a mass-circulation newspaper and underpinned by a dense network of local leaders, the newly coined 'Chartist' movement built on the common experiences and voiced the grievances of an increasingly class-conscious body of workers.[536] By late 1839 the groundwork had been laid for what Malcolm Chase rightly calls 'the first (and arguably still the greatest) mass political movement in industrialised Britain'.[537]

---

535 *LM* 1, 8 July, 5 Aug. 1837; *NS* 21 Dec. 1839.

536 The term 'Chartism' started to be adopted in early 1839 and 'Chartist' or 'Charterist' became descriptors of adherents of the movement.

537 Chase, *Chartism*, p. 7.

Epilogue

This book marks the end of a long authorial journey, but in many ways is only the beginning. Despite its veneer of completeness, the account only scratches the surface. Much still remains to learnt about the popular radical leaders, organisations and communities of the West Riding textile district during the reform and early Chartist era. The original research was based on a particular range of primary sources. The interrogation of additional sources (parish and chapel records, benefit and friendly society minutes, business records), and further studies of material culture, may provide valuable infilling and add texture to the lives and interpretations sketched here. Second, the ongoing digitalisation of key sources and the development of more sophisticated analytical tools provide opportunities for identifying more leaders and mapping their activities more accurately. New technologies enable existing data and assumptions to be revisited and tested. Third, collaboration between tenured and lay researchers offers many opportunities to broaden and deepen our knowledge. Whether as individuals or as members of local heritage organisations or U3A groups, analog antiquarians and digital detectorists both have much to contribute to a richer understanding of the histories of industrial towns and villages of the textile district. Equally, linking with the findings from thousands of family history investigations provides another potential means of throwing light on the lives of local leaders and their communities. Such a new synthesis offers the opportunity to place key individuals and the organisations they serviced more securely within the collective biographies of the radical communities in which they lived.

Early Chartism was the culmination of the series of overlapping and mutually reinforcing working-class agitations which flourished in the 1829 to 1839 period. Although there were considerable variations in the level and intensity of activity and support, the early Chartist movement displayed a high degree of organisation and achieved an unprecedented depth of penetration within the industrial communities of the textile district. 'I had always been a Chartist since I knew what politics meant' recalled a veteran Pudsey worker in the late Victorian era.[1] These communities, with their strong oppositional traditions and nonconformist inclinations, spawned a cadre of highly capable and experienced leaders. The development of this leadership cohort was not coincidental. It was a by-product of the process of class formation that E. P. Thompson outlined in his seminal work. A shared awareness among working people of their common values, interests and experiences, bred a tangible sense of class which informed their understanding of their situation and their actions. Bolstered by the ties of occupation and community, this sense of a distinct identity was particularly strong in the small manufacturing towns and villages that dotted the textile district.

Yet despite its depth of support, robustness of organisation and experienced leadership cohort, the early Chartist movement failed to achieve its aim – the six points – and the consequent, much-hoped for 'amelioration'. A key source of weakness was not so much the calibre of individual leaders or the efficiency of the networks and organisations within which they operated; as the tactical framework they inherited and adopted. The lessons of previous agitations, particularly the reform crises of 1831-2 and what Malcolm Chase termed 'the fevered but fertile post-Waterloo years', remained fresh in the minds of the dominant generation of West Riding early Chartist leaders.[2] In 1838-9, however, they found that the mobilisation of a large body of popular support and the adoption of threatening language and postures did not scare the government into concession (rather it tied the middle class more closely to the authorities); nor did it provoke crude counter measures or the blanket repression that they anticipated. In the face of a more measured governmental approach the limits of the mass popular platform as a radical tactic began to become apparent. Equally the fact that few other areas of the country were at similar stages of radical development and the abdication of 'central', national leadership (of the Convention) in the summer of 1839 dampened West Riding hopes. Frustration and resignation alike conditioned the attitudes of many local leaders in the autumn and early winter of 1839 and led them to join with their constituents in both 'cultural' and 'confrontational' activities. The latter mode found its most obvious expression in the Risings of January 1840.

In spite of apparent failure in both constitutional and insurrectional activities, the creative energies and communal enthusiasms which were channelled into the early Chartist movement, and the agitations which preceded it, were not all lost. Indeed, the gains were immense. The movement was able to re-organise and recalibrate its timescales and ambitions. West Riding Chartism's ability to survive the leadership losses of 1839-40, despite the impact of arrests, imprisonments, and 'political emigrations', and the enervating effect of campaign fatigue and disillusionment, was impressive. This resilience was a product of the robustness of the leadership group that emerged in the preceding years, the strength of the organisational infrastructure they created and serviced, and particularly their strong roots in a shared radical culture.

---

1 Joseph Lawson, *Letters to the Young on Progress in Pudsey during the last Sixty Years* (Stanningley: J.W. Birdsall, 1887), p. 132, quoted in Malcolm Chase, *Early Trade Unionism: Fraternity, Skill and the Politics of Labour* (London: Breviary Stuff, 2010 edn.), p. 144.
2 Chase, *Early Trade Unionism*, p. 112.

The multi-faceted campaigns of these years made an immense contribution to the development of an articulate, independent-minded and self-aware working class whose insistent political and social demands were to echo down the century and beyond.

These echoes are worth noting, since as Malcolm Chase has argued, 'the history of social movements of the 1830s and 1840s is extraordinary compared to anything that had gone before (or arguably went after) for reasons of their national scope, political ambitions and intellectual reach'.[3] The era was one of profound political change and sporadically severe economic dislocation, with the ever-present threat of technological innovation and an exponential increase in the speed and reach of mass communication. The working population faced significant adjustments and challenges whose effects they did not know the outcome. The 'distress' they experienced was consequently as much psychological as material. Their response found expression in a range of different forms: in radical political programmes, oppositional campaigns and assertive trade unionism; in co-operative stores, friendly societies, and different manifestations of mutuality; in educational endeavours, journalistic ventures and temperance pledges; in millennial religion, anti-clericalism and Owenite socialism; and in incendiary rhetoric, performative violence and insurrectionary preparations.

Just as scholars are seeking to re-evaluate the environmental cost of industrialisation, it is perhaps fitting to reassess the responses of some of the people who were first confronted with the impacts of cyclical economic uncertainties and emerging structural changes. If the analysis that local leaders articulated was often a hybrid (fusing elements of the critique of 'Old Corruption', traditional 'moral economy' and Owenite-inflected newer emphases of the labour theory of value) it is because the territory in which they operated was complex, transitional and indeterminate.

It is no longer adequate to arraign early Chartist leaders for being backward looking in their continued adherence to the rhetoric of 'Old Corruption' and for being insufficiently bold in their critique of industrial capitalism.[4] They could only deal with what was in front of them. For all the anachronistic language associated with attacks on the system of placeholders and sinecures operating around government and the royal court, the last vestiges of 'Old Corruption' remained a real and not inconsequential drain on public resources; and, then as now, indirect taxes fell disproportionately hard on the poor. In its heyday, as Roderick Floud shows, 'it provided extraordinary sums – in modern terms – to those who profited from it'.[5] Equally, as Chapter 2 indicates, industrialisation was a gradual, uneven, non-linear process, which impacted on various groups of workers differentially. It is harsh to condemn leaders for not being clairvoyants able to foresee the eventual consequences of full industrialisation or for entertaining hopes that workers might exert political and industrial pressure to influence the pace and direction of economic change. That their

3   Chase, *Early Trade Unionism*, p. 114.
4   Gareth Stedman Jones, 'The Language of Chartism', in J. Epstein and D. Thompson (eds.), *The Chartist Experience: Studies in Working-Class Radicalism and Culture, 1830-1860* (London: Macmillan, 1982), pp. 3-58.
5   Roderick Floud, *An Economic History of the English Garden* (London: Penguin, 2020), p. 70.

response was primarily political should come as no surprise in an era when the levers of power, though wielded by a narrow elite, were more accessible. Their recourse to constitutionalism and the language of 'Old Corruption' was a natural corollary of this. However, this language was often re-fashioned through its convergence with an emerging awareness of class identity.

This sense of class was based on common experiences of precarious employment, uncertain income and fears about the de-skilling and the potentially socially and economically degrading impact of new technology. Operatives working independently increasingly bore the costs and risks of their employment or were forced to submit to the disciplines of the factory. The ferocity of the response in the West Riding to the continued use of child labour in factories or the implementation of the new poor law can, in part, be explained in part by the aggregated fears and resentments built up in communities rocked by the instabilities of new economic relationships, and appalled by what were perceived as the immoral Malthusian acts of an ideologically constrained, uncaring government. They were perhaps the first outpourings of a proto-precariat.[6]

As the post-industrial era plays out in western democracies and (as some writers have argued) economies revert to a rentier mode, and as global evidence mounts of the appropriation of political power by narrow elites to further their economic and sectional interests, the language of 'Old Corruption' perhaps begins to regain some traction.[7] Stripped of its hyperbolic and sometimes unsavoury elements, at its heart lay a critique of fundamental inequalities of wealth and political power: topics which have increasingly engaged modern-day economists and social scientists.[8]

The immorality of imbalances of wealth and unequal power relations similarly exercised local leaders of working-class movements in the 1830s. In order to counteract 'the universal oppression, hunger, misery and degradation, of the great body of the working people, throughout the nation', a local correspondent to the *Voice of The West-Riding* urged every worker to join the Trades' Union: 'The working man fills the Cup of Plenty to the Brim, but it is snatched from his lips to have its contents poured into the reservoir of the Men of Wealth, leaving to the industrious man who filled the Cup, only a meagre and scanty portion of the Dregs!!'[9] Thomas Hirst's conclusions, though more considered, were no less stark. Brandishing an array of co-operatively produced goods from northern England, at the London Co-operative Congress in April 1832, he assigned 'the cause of distress' not to the use of machinery itself but the 'ill-directed production of that machinery' and the concomitant system of

6 For the notion of a 'precariat', a class defined by insecure income and employment, see Guy Standing, *The Precariat: The New Dangerous Class* (London: Bloomsbury, 2011).

7 For example, see Brett Christophers, Rentier, *Capitalism: Who Owns the Economy, and Who Pays for It?* (London: Verso, 2020).

8 For example, Thomas Piketty, *Capital in the Twenty-First Century* (Cambridge, Mass: Harvard University Press, 2013); *Capital and Ideology* (Cambridge, Mass: Harvard University Press, 2020); Richard Wilkinson and Kate Pickett, *The Spirit Level: Why More Equal Societies Almost Always Do Better* (London, Penguin Books, 2009); Sam Friedman and Daniel Laurison, *The Class Ceiling: Why it Pays to be Privileged* (Bristol: Policy Press, 2020).

9 *VWR* 12 Apr. 1834, letter from "An Advocate of the Rights of Industry", describing the funeral of a member of the Huddersfield Trades' Union at Lindley.

'competition and monopoly'. He further reflected: 'Strange that riches should lead to poverty – abundance to want – and plenty to starvation. He trusted this would not be put in printed history, for generations unborn would think those who lived in the present day not right in their heads'.[10]

The paradox that Hirst identified remains with us and has continued to engage historians and economists during the two succeeding centuries. All the evidence suggests that current generations are equally embarrassed by the persistence of the drivers of inequality. The past may be a foreign country but we regularly journey close to its borders. It is easy to transpose George Beaumont's condemnation of soup kitchens in 1829 to contemporary critiques of food banks; or to find modern-day subscribers to the essence of Thomas Hirst's contention that 'the newspapers – at least the generality of them – are bribed by the rich to advocate their cause against the cause of the poor'; or to locate the 'want of humanity' and morality that factory and anti-poor law activists condemned, in current policy discourse and action.[11] It is also notable that many of the progressive solutions to current economic and environmental challenges are often couched in terms of the need for the sort of fundamental political change and democratic renewal that the Chartists urged.

The story of how early working-class leaders and organisations responded to their volatile political and economic environment is not just of historical interest. It is also instructive. In addition to rescuing these leaders from 'the enormous condescension of posterity',[12] and reclaiming them from the indifference or relativism of post-modernity, it is also appropriate to celebrate their persistence and resilience and re-appraise their ideas and actions.

---

10 Proc. (London) C.C. April 1832; and *PMG* 5 May 1832, cited in Alan J. Brooke, 'Thomas Hirst – Huddersfield's pioneer co-operator', available at https://undergroundhistories.wordpress.com/2013/06/09/thomas-hirst#huddersfields-pioneer-co-operator/ (accessed 2 Aug. 2022)

11 See above, p. 142 (Beaumont); *PMG* 5 May 1832 (Hirst).

12 E. P. Thompson, *The Making of the English Working Class* (Harmondsworth: Penguin, 1968 edn.), p. 13.

Bibliography

ADDY, J. (ed.), *A History of the Denby Dale Urban District* (Huddersfield: E.M. Walker, 1974)

"ALFRED" (SAMUEL KYDD), *History of the Factory Movement* (London: Simpkin, Marshall and Co., 1857)

AIKIN, J., *A Description of the Country from Thirty to Forty Miles Round Manchester* (London: J. Stockdale, 1795)

ANON., *An Address to the Members of the Trades Union* (Huddersfield, 1833)

ANON., *Last Days of Christopher Shackleton, Advocate of Free Thought* (Halifax: John Spencer, 1855)

ANON., *The Woodites' "forget me not!": being a sketch of a new political farce called the Whig Tomfoolery Election, … etc.* (Huddersfield, 1833)

ANON., *Death of Mr Joshua Hobson* (Huddersfield, 1876)

ANON., *Goodfellowship in Keighley: Eboracum Lodge, Independent Order of Oddfellows, 1823-1923* (Keighley, Feather Brothers, 1925)

ARMSTRONG, A., *Stability and Change in an English County Town: A Social Study of York, 1801-51* (Cambridge: Cambridge University Press, 1974)

ARMYTAGE, W. H. G., *Heavens Below: Utopian Experiments in England, 1560-1960* (London: Routledge, 1961)

ASPINALL, A. (ed.), *Early English Trade Unions: Documents from the Home Office Papers in the Public Record Office* (London: Batchworth Press, 1949)

ASHTON, O., 'Orators and Oratory in the Chartist Movement, 1840-1848', in O. Ashton, R. Fyson and S. Roberts (eds.), *The Chartist Legacy* (Woodbridge: Merlin Press, 1999), pp. 48-79

ASHTON, O., FYSON, R., AND ROBERTS, S. (eds.), *The Duty of Discontent: Essays for Dorothy Thompson* (London: Cassell, 1995)

———— (eds.), *The Chartist Legacy* (Woodbridge, Merlin Press, 1999)

ASHWORTH, D., 'The Treatment of Poverty', in D. G. Wright and J. A. Jowitt (eds.), *Victorian Bradford. Essays in Honour of Jack Reynolds* (Bradford: City of Bradford Metropolitan Council, 1981), pp. 81-100

BAINES, E., *History, Directory and Gazetteer of the County of York* (Leeds: Edward Baines, 1822)

BAINES, E. JNR., *Life of Edward Baines* (London: Longman et al, 1859 edn.)

BALMFORTH, O., *Handbook of the 27th Co-operative Congress, Huddersfield 1895* (Huddersfield, 1895)

————, *A History of Fifty Years' Progress, 1860-1910, of the Huddersfield Industrial Society Ltd.* (Manchester, Co-operative Wholesale Society, 1910)

BAXTER, J. L., 'Early Chartism and Labour Class Struggles: South Yorkshire, 1834-40', in S. Pollard and C. Holmes (ed.), *Essays in the Economic and Social History of South Yorkshire* (Sheffield: South Yorkshire County Council, 1976), pp. 135-58

————, 'The Life and Struggle of Samuel Holberry, physical force Chartist', in B. Moore, S. Holmes and J.L. Baxter (eds.), *Samuel Holberry: Sheffield's Revolutionary Democrat* (Sheffield: Holberry Society, 1978)

————, 'Armed Resistance and Insurrection: The Early Chartist Experience', *Our History*, 76 (1984), pp. 1-38

BAXTER, J. L. AND DONNELLY, F. K., 'The Revolutionary 'Underground' in the West Riding: Myth or Reality?', *Past and Present*, 64 (1974), pp. 124-32, and rejoinder by J. R. Dinwiddy, pp. 133-5

BAXTER, J. L. AND STANLEY, J., *The Road to Insurrection in the Industrial West Riding 1819-20* (York: Borthwick Institute for Archives, 2022)

BECKWITH, F., 'The Population of Leeds during the Industrial Revolution', *Publications of the Thoresby Society*, 41 (1954), pp. 118-196

BELCHEM, J., 'Radicalism as 'Platform' Agitation in the periods of 1816-21 and 1848-51: with special reference to the leadership of Henry Hunt and Feargus O'Connor', Unpublished DPhil thesis, University of Sussex, 1974

_____, *'Orator' Hunt: Henry Hunt and English Working Class Radicalism* (London: Breviary Stuff, 2012)

_____ and EPSTEIN, J., 'The nineteenth-century gentleman leader revisited', *Social History*, 22, 2 (1997), pp. 174-93

BELLAMY, J. M. AND SAVILLE, J. (eds.), *Dictionary of Labour Biography, Volumes 1-10*, (London: Macmillan, 1972-1999)

BENBOW, W., *Grand National Holiday, and Congress of the Productive Classes* (London, 1832)

BENNETT, J., 'The London Democratic Association 1837-41: a study in London Radicalism', in J. Epstein and D. Thompson (eds.), *The Chartist Experience: Studies in Working-Class Radicalism and Culture, 1830-1860* (London: Macmillan, 1982), pp. 87-119

BERESFORD, M. W, 'The face of Leeds, 1780-1914', in D. Fraser (ed.), *A History of Modern Leeds* (Manchester: Manchester University Press, 1980) pp. 72-112

BERESFORD, M. W. AND JONES, G. R. J. (eds.), *Leeds and Its Region* (Leeds: British Association for The Advancement of Science, 1967)

BEZUCHA, R. J., *The Lyon Uprising of 1834: Social and Political Conflict in the Early July Monarchy* (Cambridge, Mass.: Harvard University Press, 1974)

BLACK, L. AND ROBERTSON, N. (eds,), *Consumerism and the Co-operative Movement in Modern British History: Taking Stock* (Manchester: Manchester University Press, 2009)

BONWICK, J., *The Romance of the Wool Trade* (London: Griffin, Farran and Co, 1887)

BOSTON, R., *British Chartists in America* (Manchester: Manchester University Press, 1971)

BOWLEY, A. L., 'Wages in the Worsted and Woollen Manufactures of the West Riding of Yorkshire', *Journal of the Royal Statistical Society*, 45 (1902), pp. 102-26

BOWER, S., *The Peopling of Utopia* (Bradford, 1838)

BRENTANO, L., 'Growth of a Trade Union', *North British Review*, 53 (1870-1), pp. 59-114

BRETT, P., 'Political dinners in Early Nineteenth Century Britain: Platform, Meeting Place and Battleground', *History* 81, 264 (1996), pp. 527-52.

BRIGGS, A., 'Industry and Politics in Early Nineteenth-century Keighley', *Bradford Antiquary*, ns. 35 (1950), pp. 305-17

_____, 'The Background of the Parliamentary Reform Movement in Three English Cities, 1830-2', *Cambridge Historical Journal*, 10 (1952), pp. 293-317

_____ (ed.), *Chartist Studies* (London: Macmillan, 1959)

_____, 'The Language of "class" in Early Nineteenth Century England' in, A. Briggs and J. Saville, (eds.), *Essays in Labour History* (London: Macmillan, 1960), pp. 43-73

BROCK, M., *The Great Reform Act* (London: Hutchinson, 1973)

BROOKE, A. J., *The Handloom Fancy Weavers c.1820-1914* (Honley: Workers' History Publications, 1993)

_____, 'Labour disputes and Trade Unions in the Industrial Revolution', in Hilary Haigh (ed.), *A Most Handsome Town: Aspects of the history and culture of a West Yorkshire Town* (Huddersfield: Kirklees Cultural Services, 1992), pp. 221-40

_____, 'The Roots of Chartism in the Huddersfield Area c1826 to c1838', in J. A. Hargreaves (ed.), *The Charter Our Right! Huddersfield Chartism Re-considered* (Huddersfield: Huddersfield Local History Society, 2018), pp. 19-38

_____, 'Economic Distress and the Revival of Radicalism in the Huddersfield Area 1826-1830' in 'We are Weary of Slavery', available at https://undergroundhistories.wordpress.com/we-are-weary-of-slavery/ (accessed 14 May 2022)

_____., 'Radicalism, Reform and Class Conflict in Huddersfield 1831-1834', in 'Dangerous Societies' available at https://undergroundhistories.wordpress.com/dangerous-societies/ (accessed 14 May 2022)

_____, 'Thomas Hirst – Huddersfield's pioneer co-operator' available at https://undergroundhistories.wordpress.com/2013/06/09/thomas-hirst-huddersfields-pioneer-co-operator/ (accessed 2 Aug. 2022)

BROOK, R., *The Story of Huddersfield* (London: MacGibbon and Key, 1968)

BURNLEY, J., *The History of Wool and Wool Combing* (London: Sampson Low, Marston, Searle and Rivington, 1889)

BUTLER, J. H., 'The Origins and Development of Retail Co-operative Movement in Yorkshire during the Nineteenth Century', Unpublished. PhD thesis, University of York, 1986

BUTLER, J. R. M., *The Passing of the Great Reform Bill* (London: Longmans, Green and Co, 1914)

BUTT, J. AND WARD, J. T. (eds.), *Scottish Themes: Essays in Honour of Professor S.G.E. Lythe* (Edinburgh: Scottish Academic Press, 1976)

BYTHELL, D., *The Handloom Weavers: A Study in the English Cotton Industry during the Industrial Revolution* (Cambridge: Cambridge University Press, 1969)

CALHOUN, C., *The Roots of Radicalism: Tradition, The Public Sphere and Early Nineteenth-Century Social Movements* (Chicago: Chicago University Press, 2012)

CAMM, J. C. R., 'Industrial Settlement in the Colne and Holme Valleys, 1750-1960', Unpublished MSc thesis, University of Hull, 1963

CARR, H. J., 'John Francis Bray', *Economica*, 7, 28 (1940) pp. 397-415

CARTER, A. C., *John Bates of Queensbury, the Veteran Reformer* (Queensbury, 1895)

CHADWICK, S., *'A Bold and Faithful Journalist': Joshua Hobson 1810-1876* (Huddersfield: Kirklees Libraries and Museums Service, 1976)

CHALONER, W. H. (ed.), 'The Reminiscences of Thomas Dunning, 1813-94',

Transactions of the Lancashire and Cheshire Antiquarian Society, 59 (1947), pp. 111-22

CHASE, M., 'Building identity, building circulation: engraved portraiture and the Northern Star', in J. Allen and O. Ashton (eds.), *Papers for the People: A study of the Chartist Press* (London: Merlin Press, 2005), pp. 3–24

_____, *Chartism: A New History* (Manchester: Manchester University Press, 2007)

_____, *Early Trade Unionism: Fraternity, Skill and the Politics of Labour* (London: Breviary Stuff, 2010 edn.)

_____, *The People's Farm: English Radical Agrarianism 1775-1840* (London: Breviary Stuff, 2010 edn.)

_____, *1820: Disorder and Stability in the United Kingdom* (Manchester: Manchester University Press, 2013)

_____., 'The "local state" in Regency Britain', *Local Historian*, 43 (2013), pp. 266-78

_____, *The Chartists: Perspectives and Legacies* (London: Merlin Press, 2015)

_____, 'Chartism', in M, Childs *et al.*, *Campaigning for Change: Lessons from History* (London: Friends of the Earth, 2017), pp. 41-52

_____, 'Chartism in Huddersfield and its vicinity: the cultural dimension', in J. A. Hargreaves (ed.), *The Charter our Right! Huddersfield Chartism Re-considered* (Huddersfield: Huddersfield Local History Society, 2018), pp. 63-81

_____, 'Labour History's Biographical Turn', *History Workshop Journal*, (Autumn 2021), pp. 194-207

_____, 'Alice Mann [née Burnett] 1791-1865', *Oxford Dictionary of National Biography*, available at https://doi.org/10.1093/odnb/9780198614128.013.369115, accessed 4 May 2021

_____, 'Elizabeth Hanson [née Fell] 1797/8-1886', *Oxford Dictionary of National Biography*, available at https://doi.org/10.1093/odnb/9780198614128.013.369109, accessed 4 May 2021

CHRISTOPHERS, B., *Rentier Capitalism: Who Owns the Economy, and Who Pays for It?* (London: Verso, 2020)

CHURCH, R. A., 'Labour Supply and Innovation, 1800-60: The Boot and Shoe Industry', *Business History*, 12, 1 (1970), pp. 25-45

CLAEYS, G., *Citizens and Saints: Politics and Anti-Politics in Early British Socialism* (Cambridge: Cambridge University Press, 1989)

_____, *Owenite Socialism: Pamphlets and Correspondence, Vol. IV, 1832-1837* (Abingdon and New York: Routledge, 2005)

CLAPHAM, J. H., *An Economic History of Modern Britain. Vol. I: The Early Railway Age* (Cambridge, Cambridge University Press, 1926)

COLE, G. D. H., *A Century of Cooperation* (Manchester: Co-operative Union, 1944)

_____, *Attempts at General Union: A Study in British Trade Union History 1818-34* (London: Macmillan, 1953)

_____, *Chartist Portraits* (London: Macmillan, 1965 edn.)

_____, *The Life of Robert Owen* (London: Frank Cass and Co., 1965 edn.)

COLLET, C. D., *History of the Taxes on Knowledge* (2 Vols) (London: T. Fisher Unwin, 1899)

COLLINSON, E., *The History of the Worsted Trade and Historic Sketch of Bradford*

(Bradford: C. Stanfield, 1854)

CONNELL, E. J. AND WARD, M., 'Industrial Development, 1780-1914', in D. Fraser (ed.), *A History of Modern Leeds* (Manchester: Manchester University Press, 1980), pp. 142-76

CORDERY, S., 'Joshua Hobson, 1810-1876', in J. M. Bellamy and J. Saville (eds.), *Dictionary of Labour Biography*, VIII (London: Macmillan, 1987)

———, 'Joshua Hobson and the Business of Radicalism', *Biography*, 11, 2 (1988), pp. 108-123

———, 'Friendly Societies and the Discourse of Respectability in Britain, 1825-1875', *Journal of British Studies*, 34, 1 (1995), 35-58

———, *British Friendly Societies, 1750-1914* (Basingstoke and New York: Palgrave Macmillan, 2003)

CRABTREE, G., *A Brief Description of a Tour through Calder Dale* (Huddersfield: J. Hobson, 1833)

CRABTREE, J., *A Concise History of the Vicarage and Parish of Halifax* (Halifax: Hartley and Walker, 1836)

CREIGHTON, C., 'Collective Action and Domestic Practices: England in the 1830s and 1840s', in Y. Taylor and E. Casey (eds.), *Intimacies, Critical Consumption and Diverse Economies* (London: Palgrave Macmillan, 2015), pp. 13-35

CROFT, W. R., *The History of the Factory Movement : or Oastler and His Times* (Huddersfield: George Whitehead and Sons, 1888)

CROSS, S. J., 'The Experience of Owenite Socialism and Anti-Socialism in Halifax, 1829-1845', *Transactions of the Halifax Antiquarian Society*, 15 (2007), pp. 91-111

CRUMP, W. B. (ed.), *The Leeds Woollen Industry, 1780-1820* (Leeds: Thoresby Society, 1931)

CRUMP, W. B. AND GHORBAL, G., *History of the Huddersfield Woollen Industry* (Huddersfield: County Borough of Huddersfield, 1935)

CUDWORTH, W., *Round about Bradford* (Bradford: Thomas Brear, 1876)

———, *Rambles around Horton* (Bradford: Thomas Brear, 1886)

———, *Condition of the Industrial Classes of Bradford and District* (Bradford: William Byles and Son, 1887)

———, *Histories of Bolton and Bowling* (Bradford: Thomas Brear, 1891)

———, *Manningham, Heaton and Allerton* (Bradford: W. Cudworth, 1896)

DALBY, G. R., 'The Chartist Movement in Halifax and District', *Transactions of the Halifax Antiquarian Society* (1956), pp. 92-111

DANIELS, G. W., 'The Organisation of a "Turn Out" of Bolton Machine-Makers in 1831', *Economic History*, 2 (1930-3), pp. 111-6

———, 'A "Turn Out" of Bolton Machine-Makers in 1831', *Economic History*, 1 (1926-9), pp. 591-602

DEAN, D. A., 'The Economic and Social Development of Dewsbury in the 19th Century', Unpublished MA thesis, University of Sheffield, 1963

DEWHIRST, I., *A History of Keighley* (Keighley: Keighley Corporation, 1974)

———, *Victorian Keighley Characters* (Nelson: Hendon Publishing Co, 1990)

DINGSDALE, A., 'A Yorkshire Mill Town: A Study of the Spatial patterns and processes, processes of urban-industrial growth and the evolution of the spatial structure of

Halifax, 1801-1901', Unpublished PhD thesis, University of Leeds, 1974

DODD, G., *The Textile Manufactures of Great Britain* (London: Charles Knight and Co., 1844)

DONNELLY, F. K., 'Ideology and Early Working-Class History: Edward Thompson and His Critics', *Social History*, I (1976), pp. 219-38

DRIVER, C., *Tory Radical: The Life of Richard Oastler* (New York: Oxford University Press, 1946)

DRIVER, F., 'Tory Radicalism? Ideology, Strategy and Locality in Popular Politics during the Eighteen-Thirties', *Northern History*, 27 (1991), pp. 120-38

————, *Power and Pauperism: The Workhouse System, 1834-1884* (Cambridge: Cambridge University Press, 1993)

DURR, A., 'William King of Brighton: Co-operation's prophet?', in S. Yeo (ed.) *New Views of Co-operation* (London: Routledge, 1988), pp. 10-26.

DYOS, H. J. & WOLFF, M. (eds.), *The Victorian City: Images and Realities* (London: Routledge and Kagan Paul, 1973)

EDSALL, N. C., *The Anti-Poor Law Movement* (Manchester: Manchester University Press, 1971)

EPSTEIN, J. AND THOMPSON, D. (eds.), *The Chartist Experience: Studies in Working-Class Radicalism and Culture, 1830-1860* (London: Macmillan, 1982)

EPSTEIN, J., 'Feargus O'Connor and the Northern Star', *International Review of Social History*, 21 (1976), pp. 51-97

————, 'Feargus O'Connor and the English Working-class Movement, 1832-41: A study in national Chartist leadership', Unpublished PhD Thesis, University of Birmingham, 1977

————, 'Some Organisational and Cultural Aspects of the Chartist Movement in Nottingham', in J. Epstein and D. Thompson (eds.), *The Chartist Experience: Studies in Working-Class Radicalism and Culture, 1830-1860* (London: Macmillan, 1982) pp. 221-68

————, 'Radical Dining, Toasting and Symbolic Expression in Early Nineteenth-Century Lancashire: Rituals of Solidarity', *Albion*, 20, 2 (1988), pp. 271-91

————, *Radical Expression: Political Language, Ritual and Symbol in England, 1790-1850* (London: Breviary Stuff, 2014 edn.)

————, *The Lion of Freedom: Feargus O'Connor and the Chartist Movement, 1832-42* (London: Breviary Stuff, 2015 edn.)

FEATHER, G. A., 'A Pennine Worsted Community in the Mid-19th Century', *Textile History*, 3 (1972), pp. 64-91

FIRTH, G., 'The Bradford Trade in the Nineteenth Century', in D. G. Wright and J. A. Jowitt (eds.), *Victorian Bradford. Essays in Honour of Jack Reynolds* (Bradford: City of Bradford Metropolitan Council, 1981), pp. 7-36

FLOUD, R., *An Economic History of the English Garden* (London: Penguin Books, 2020)

FOSTER, J., 'Nineteenth Century Towns – A Class Dimension', in H. J. Dyos (ed.), *The Study of Urban History* (London: Edward Arnold, 1970), pp. 281-90

————, *Class Struggle and the Industrial Revolution: Early Industrial Capitalism in Three English Towns* (London: Weidenfeld and Nicholson, 1974)

FRASER, D., 'Politics in Leeds, 1830-52' Unpublished PhD Thesis, University of Leeds,

1969

————, Series of articles on Churchwardens, Poor Law, Water Supply and Improvement, *Publications of the Thoresby Society*, 53 (1970), pp. 1-81

————, 'Poor Law Politics in Leeds, 1833-1855', *Publications of the Thoresby Society*, 53 (1970), pp. 23-49;

————, 'The Leeds Churchwardens, 1828-50', *Publications of the Thoresby Society*, 53 (1971).

————, 'The Fruits of Reform: Leeds Politics in the 1830s', *Northern History*, 7 (1972), pp. 89-111

————, 'The Agitation for Parliamentary Reform', in J. T. Ward (ed.), *Popular Movements c.1830-1850* (London: Macmillan, 1970), pp. 54-77

————, *Urban Politics in Victorian England: The Structure of Politics in Victorian Cities* (Leicester: Leicester University, 1976)

———— (ed.), *A History of Modern Leeds* (Manchester: Manchester University Press, 1980)

————, 'Politics and Society in the Nineteenth Century' in D. Fraser (ed.), *A History of Modern Leeds* (Manchester: Manchester University Press, 1980), pp. 270-300

FRASER, W. H., 'Trade Unionism', in J. T. Ward (ed.), *Popular Movements c. 1830-1850* (London: Macmillan, 1970), pp. 95-110

————, 'The Glasgow Cotton Spinners, 1837', in J. Butt and J.T. Ward (eds.), *Scottish Themes: Essays in Honour of Professor S. G. E. Lythe* (Edinburgh: Scottish Academic Press, 1976), pp. 80-97.

FRIEDMAN, S. AND LAURISON, D., *The Class Ceiling: Why it Pays to be Privileged* (Bristol, Policy Press, 2020)

FURLOUGH, E. AND STRIKWERDA, C. (eds.), *Consumers against Capitalism? Consumer Co-operation in Europe, North America and Japan, 1840-1990* (Lanham: Rowman and Littlefield, 1999)

GAMMAGE, R. G., *History of the Chartist Movement, 1837-54* (London: Merlin Press, 1969 edn.)

GARNETT, R. G., *Co-operation and the Owenite Social Communities in Britain 1825-45* (Manchester: Manchester University Press, 1972)

GASH, N., *Politics in the Age of Peel* (London: Longmans, Green and Co, 1953)

————, 'English Reform and French Revolution in the General Election of 1830', in R. Pares and A.J.P. Taylor (eds.), *Essays Presented to Sir Lewis Namier* (London: Macmillan, 1956), pp. 258-88

————, 'Brougham and the Yorkshire Election of 1830', *Proceedings of the Leeds Literary and Philosophical Society*, 8 (1956), pp. 19-35

————, *Mr Secretary Peel: the Life of Sir Robert Peel to 1830* (London: Longman, 1961)

GENT, D., 'The Politics of Disinterest: The Whigs and The Liberal Party in the West Riding of Yorkshire, 1830-1850', *Northern History*, 49 (2012), pp. 303-22.

GILDART, K., HOWELL, K. AND KIRK, N. (eds.), *Dictionary of Labour Biography, Vol. 11* (Basingstoke: Palgrave Macmillan, 2003)

GILDART, K. AND HOWELL, K. (eds.), *Dictionary of Labour Biography, Vols. 12-15*

(Basingstoke: Palgrave Macmillan, 2004-2020)

GILES, C., 'The Huddersfield Woollen Industry and its Architecture', in E.A. Hilary Haigh (ed.), *A Most Handsome Town: Aspects of the history and culture of a West Yorkshire Town* (Huddersfield: Kirklees Cultural Services, 1992), pp. 275-302

GILL, J. C., *The Ten Hours Parson: Christian Social Action in the Eighteen-thirties* (London: SPCK, 1959)

_____, *Parson Bull of Byerley* (London: SPCK, 1963)

GLOVER, F. J., 'The Rise of the Heavy Woollen Trade of the West Riding of Yorkshire in the 19th Century', *Business History*, 4 (1962), pp. 1-21

_____, 'A Yorkshire Blanketmaker's Diary', *Bradford Textile Society Journal*, (1962-3), pp. 84-109

GODECHOT, J., *La Presse Ouvriere, 1819-1850* (Paris: Societe d'Histoire de la Revolution de 1848, 1966)

GODFREY, C., 'The Chartist Prisoners, 1839-41', *International Review of Social History*, 24 (1979), pp. 189-210

GOSDEN, P. H. J. H., *The Friendly Societies in England, 1815-75* (Manchester: Manchester University Press, 1961)

_____, *Self-Help: Voluntary Associations in the 19th Century* (London: Batsford, 1973)

GRAY, R. Q., 'The Languages of Factory Reform in Britain, c. 1830–1860', in P. Joyce (ed.), *The Historical Meanings of Work* (Cambridge: Cambridge University Press, 1987), pp. 143-79

_____, *The Factory Question and Industrial England, 1830-1860* (Cambridge: Cambridge University Press, 1996)

GREGORY, D., *Regional Transformation and Industrial Revolution: A Geography of the Yorkshire Woollen Industry* (London: Palgrave Macmillan, 1982)

GRIFFIN, E., 'The Making of the Chartists: Popular Politics and Working-Class Autobiography in Early Victorian Britain', *English Historical Review*, 129, 538 (2014), pp. 578–605

GRIFFITHS, D., 'Huddersfield in Turbulent Times, 1815-1850: Who Ruled and How?', *Northern History*, 52 (2015) , pp. 101-124

_____, *Pioneers or Partisans? Governing Huddersfield 1820-1848* (Huddersfield: Huddersfield Local History Society, 2008)

GURNEY, P, 'George Jacob Holyoake: Socialism, Association and Co-operation in Nineteenth-Century England', in S. Yeo (ed.) *New Views of Co-operation* (London: Routledge, 1988), pp. 52-72

_____, *Co-operative Culture and the Politics of Consumption in England 1870-1930* (Manchester: Manchester University Press, 1996)

_____, *Wanting and Having: Popular Politics and Liberal Consumerism in England, 1830-70* (Manchester: Manchester University Press, 2015)

_____, 'The Democratic Idiom: Languages of Democracy in the Chartist Movement', *The Journal of Modern History*, 86 (2014), pp. 566-602

HALL, F. AND WATKINS, W. P., *Co-operation - A Survey of the History, Principles and Organisation of the Co-operative Movement in Great Britain and Ireland* (Manchester, The Co-operative Union Ltd., 1934)

HALL, R. G., 'A United People? Leaders and Followers in a Chartist Locality, 1838-1848', *Journal of Social History*, 38 (2004), pp. 179-203

———, *Voice of the People: Democracy and Chartist Political Identity, 1830-1870* (Monmouth, Merlin Press, 2007)

———, 'At the Dawn of the Information Age: Reading and the Working Classes in Ashton-under-Lyne, 1830–1850', in J. J. Connolly *et al.*, (eds.), *Print Culture Histories Beyond the Metropolis* (Toronto: University of Toronto Press, 2016), pp. 243-67

———, 'A Bookshop of their Own': reading and Print in Chartism, 1838-1850', *English Historical Review*, 136, 581 (2021), pp. 894-917

HALSTEAD, J., 'The Voice of the West Riding: promoters and supporters of a provincial unstamped newspaper', in C. Wrigley (ed.), *On the Move: Essays in Labour and Transport History Presented to Philip Bagwell* (London: Hambleton Press, 2003), pp. 22-57

———, 'The Huddersfield Short Time Committee and its radical associations, c.1820-1876', in J. A. Hargreaves and E. A. Hilary Haigh (eds.) *Slavery in Yorkshire: Richard Oastler and the Campaign against Child Labour in the Industrial Revolution* (Huddersfield: University of Huddersfield Press, 2012), pp. 91-144

———, 'The Charter and something more! The politics of Joshua Hobson', in J. A. Hargreaves (ed.), *The Charter Our Right! Huddersfield Chartism Re-considered* (Huddersfield: Huddersfield Local History Society, 2018), pp. 83–122.

———, 'Notable Co-operator – Thomas Hirst 1792-1833', *Huddersfield Local History Society Journal*, 30 (2020), pp. 61-7

HANLEY, R., 'Slavery and the Birth of Working-Class Racism in England, 1814-1833', *Transactions of the Royal Historical Society*, 26 (2016) pp. 103-24.

HANSON, J., *Humanity against Tyranny* (Leeds, 1831)

HANSON, T. W., *The Story of Old Halifax* (Halifax, F. King and Sons, 1920)

HARGREAVES, J. A. AND HILARY HAIGH, E. A. (eds.), *Slavery in Yorkshire: Richard Oastler and the Campaign against Child Labour in the Industrial Revolution* (Huddersfield: Huddersfield University Press, 2012).

HARGREAVES, J. A., 'A Metropolis of Discontent' in E. A. Hilary Haigh (ed.), *Huddersfield, A Most Handsome Town: Aspects of the History and Culture of a West Riding Town* (Huddersfield: Kirklees Cultural Services, 1992), pp. 189-220

———, '"Evangelical Piety and Gallic Flippancy": Religion and Popular Protest in Halifax Parish in the Age of Revolution', in K. Dockray and K. Laybourn (eds.), *The Representation and Reality of War. The British Experience* (Stroud: Sutton Publishing, 1999), pp. 61-82

———, 'Mathew Balme (1813-1884), factory reformer', *Oxford Dictionary of National Biography* (Oxford: Oxford University Press, 2004).

———, 'Introduction: "Victims of slavery even on the threshold of our homes": Richard Oastler and Yorkshire Slavery', in J. A. Hargreaves and E. A. Hilary Haigh, *Slavery in Yorkshire: Richard Oastler and the Campaign against Child Labour in the Industrial Revolution* (Huddersfield: Huddersfield University Press, 2012), pp. 1-11

———, '"Treading on the edge of revolution?" Richard Oastler (1789-1861)', in J.

A. Hargreaves and E. A. Hilary Haigh (eds.), *Slavery in Yorkshire: Richard Oastler and the Campaign against Child Labour in the Industrial Revolution* (Huddersfield: Huddersfield University Press, 2012), pp. 201-28

_____, (ed.) *The Charter Our Right! Huddersfield Chartism Re-considered* (Huddersfield: Huddersfield Local History Society, 2018)

_____, '"Hats Off": Methodism and Popular Protest in the West Riding of Yorkshire in the Chartist Era: A Case Study of Benjamin Rushton (1785-1853) of Halifax', *Proceedings of the Wesley Historical Association*, 57 (2010), pp. 161-177

_____, 'Benjamin Rushton 1785–1853', *Oxford Dictionary of National Biography*, available at https://doi.org/10.1093/ref:odnb/54102, accessed 16 July 2022

HARRISON, J. F. C. AND THOMPSON, D., *Bibliography of the Chartist Movement, 1837-1976* (Sussex, Harvester Press, 1978)

HARRISON, J. F. C., 'Chartism in Leeds', in A. Briggs (ed.), *Chartist Studies* (London: Macmillan, 1959), pp. 65-98

_____, 'Chartism in Leicester', in A. Briggs (ed.), *Chartist Studies* (London: Macmillan, 1959), pp. 99-146

_____, *Living and Learning, 1790-1960: A Study in the History of the English Adult Education Movement* (London: Routledge, 1961)

_____, *Robert Owen and the Owenites in Britain and America: The Quest for the New Moral World* (London: Routledge and Kegan Paul, 1969)

HARTE, N. B. AND PONTING K. G. (eds.), *Textile History and Economic History: Essays in Honour of Miss Julia de Lacy Mann* (Manchester: Manchester University Press, 1973)

HARTWELL, R. M., 'The Yorkshire Woollen and Worsted Industry, 1800-50', Unpublished DPhil thesis, University of Oxford, 1955

HEAD, Sir G., *A Home Tour throughout the Manufacturing Districts of England in the Summer of 1835* (London: Cass, 1968, 2nd edn.)

HEATON, H., 'An Early Victorian Business Forecaster in the Woollen Industry', *Economic Journal (Economic History)*, (1933), pp. 553-74

_____, *The Yorkshire Woollen and Worsted Industry from the Earliest Times up to the Industrial Revolution* (Oxford: Clarendon Press, 1965, 2nd edn.)

HEMINGWAY, V. W., 'Parliamentary Politics in Huddersfield, c.1832-53', in E. A. Hilary Haigh (ed.), *Huddersfield, A Most Handsome Town: Aspects of the History and Culture of a West Riding Town* (Huddersfield: Kirklees Cultural Services, 1992), pp. 481-500

HILARY HAIGH, E. A. (ed.), *A Most Handsome Town: Aspects of the history and culture of a West Yorkshire Town* (Huddersfield: Kirklees Cultural Services, 1992)

HIRST, W., *History of the Woollen Trade for the Last Sixty Years* (Leeds: Moody, 1844)

HOBSBAWM, E. J. AND SCOTT, J. W., 'Political Shoemakers', *Past and Present*, 89 (1980), pp. 86-114

HOBSBAWM, E. J., 'Friendly Societies', *Amateur Historian*, 3 (1957), pp. 95-101

_____, *Labouring Men: Studies in the History of Labour* (London: Weidenfeld and Nicolson, 1964)

_____, *Industry and Empire: An Economic History of Britain Since 1750* (London: Weidenfeld and Nicolson, 1968)

HODGSON, J., *Textile Manufacture and Other Industries, in Keighley* (Keighley: A. Hey, 1879)

HOLLIS, P., *The Pauper Press: A Study in Working-Class Radicalism of the 1830s* (Oxford: Oxford University Press, 1970)

———, *Class and Class-Conflict in Nineteenth-Century England, 1815-50* (London: Routledge and Kegan Paul, 1973)

HOLMES, R., *Keighley, Past and Present: ... etc.* (Keighley, 1858)

HOLYOAKE, G. J., *The History of Cooperation in England* (2 Vols) (London: London, Trübner and Co., 1875-9)

HONEYMAN, K., *Women, Gender, and Industrialisation in England, 1700-1870* (Basingstoke: Macmillan, 2000)

HOVELL, M., *The Chartist Movement* (Manchester: Manchester University Press, 1966 edn.)

HOWE, C., *Halifax 1842: A Year in Crisis* (London: Breviary Stuff, 2014)

HOWELL, P., 'The local background of Chartism revisited: a note on the geography of popular politics in early Victorian Britain', *Area* 28, 2 (1996), pp. 150-9

HUDSON, P., 'Proto-industrialisation: The Case of the West Riding Wool Textile Industry in the 18th and 19th Centuries', *History Workshop Journal*, 12 (1981), pp. 34-61

———, *The Genesis of Industrial Capital: a study of the West Riding wool textile industry, c. 1750-1850* (Cambridge: Cambridge University Press, 1986)

HUMPHRIES, J., *Childhood and Child Labour in the British Industrial Revolution* (Cambridge: Cambridge University Press, 2010)

INGLE, G., 'The Bradford Hand-Loom Weavers' Riots of 1826', *Bradford Antiquary*, 3, 17 (1994), pp. 3-16

JACKSON, J., *The Demagogue Done Up: An Exposure of the Extreme Inconsistencies of Mr. Feargus O'Connor* (Bradford: Wilkinson, 1844)

JAGGER, M. A., *History of Honley and Its Hamlets* (Huddersfield: Alfred Jubb and Co, 1914)

JAMES, J., *The History and Topography of Bradford* (London: Longman, Green, Brown and Longman, 1841)

———, *A History of the Worsted Manufacture in England ... etc* (Bradford: Stanfield, 1857)

JANSE, M., '"Association is a Mighty Engine": Mass Organization and the Machine Metaphor, 1825–1840', in H. te Velde and M. Janse (eds.), *Organizing Democracy: Reflections on the Rise of Political Organizations in the Nineteenth Century* (Basingstoke: Palgrave Macmillan, 2017), pp. 19-42.

JEFFREYS, J. B., *The Story of the Engineers, 1800-1945* (London: Lawrence and Wishart, 1945)

JENKINS, D. T. AND PONTING, K. G. *The British Wool Textile Industry, 1770-1914* (London: Pearson Education, 1982)

JENKINS, D. T., *The West Riding Wool Textile Industry 1770-1835: A Study in Fixed Capital Formation* (Edington, Wiltshire: Pasold Research Fund Limited, 1975)

JENKINS, J. G. (ed,), *The Wool Textile Industry in Great Britain* (London: Routledge and Kegan Paul, 1972)

JOHNSON, R., "'Really Useful Knowledge": Radical Education and Working-Class Culture', in J. Clarke, C. Critcher, R. Johnson (eds.), *Working-Class Culture: Studies in History and Theory* (London: Hutchinson, 1979), pp. 75-102

JONES, D. J. V., 'Chartism in Three Welsh Communities', *Welsh History Review*, 6 (1972-3), pp. 243-61

_____, *Chartism and the Chartists* (London: Allen Lane, 1975)

_____, *The Last Rising: The Newport Chartist Insurrection of 1839* (Cardiff: University of Wales Press, 2014)

JOWITT, J. A., 'Parliamentary Politics in Halifax, 1832-1847', *Northern History*, 12 (1976). pp. 172-201

_____, 'The Pattern of Religion in Victorian Bradford', in D. G. Wright, and J. A. Jowitt (eds.), *Victorian Bradford: Essays in Honour of Jack Reynolds* (Bradford: City of Bradford MDC, 1982), pp. 37-62

JUDGE, K., 'Early Chartist Organisation and the Convention of 1839', *International Review of Social History*, 20 (1975), pp. 370-97

KAIJAGE, F. J., 'Labouring Barnsley, 1816-1856: A Social and Economic History', Unpublished PhD thesis, University of Warwick, 1975

KIDDIER, W., *The Old Trade Societies* (London: George Allen and Unwin, 1930)

KIRBY, P., *Child Labour in Britain, 1750-1870* (Basingstoke: Palgrave Macmillan, 2003)

KIRBY, R. G. AND MUSSON, A. E., *The Voice of the People, John Doherty 1798-1854: Trade Unionist, Radical and Factory Reformer* (Manchester: Manchester University Press, 1975)

KIRK, N., 'In defence of class: a critique of recent revisionist writing upon the nineteenth-century English working class', *International Review of Social History*, 32, 1 (1987), pp. 2-47

KNOTT, J., *Popular Opposition to the 1834 Poor Law* (Beckenham: Croom Helm, 1986)

KODITSCHEK, T., *Class Formation and Urban-Industrial Society: Bradford, 1750-1850* (Cambridge: Cambridge University Press, 1990)

LAWSON, J., *Letters to the Young on Progress in Pudsey during the Last Sixty Years* (Stanningley: J. W. Birdsall, 1887)

LENTON, J. H., 'Wages in the Leeds Area, 1770-1850', Unpublished MPhil thesis, University of Leeds, 1969

LEWIS, B., *The Middlemost and the Milltowns: Bourgeois Culture and Politics in Early Industrial England* (Stanford, CA: Stanford University Press, 2001)

LINTON, W. J., *James Watson, A Memoir … etc.* (Manchester: Abel Heywood and Son, 1880)

LOCKLEY, P., *Visionary Religion and Radicalism in Early Industrial England: From Southcott to Socialism* (Oxford: Oxford University Press, 2012)

LOPATIN-LUMMIS, N., *Political Unions, Popular Politics and the Great Reform Act of 1832* (Basingstoke: Palgrave Macmillan, 1999).

MACHIN, F., *The Yorkshire Miners: A History* (Barnsley: National Union of Mineworkers, 1958)

MAEHL, W. H., *The Reform Bill of 1832: Why Not Revolution?* (New York: Holt, Rinehart and Winston, 1967)

MARTIN, J., 'Popular political oratory and itinerant lecturing in Yorkshire and the

North East in the age of Chartism, 1837-60', Unpublished PhD thesis, University of York, 2010

———, '"Oastler is welcome": Richard Oastler's triumphant return to Huddersfield, 1844', in J. A. Hargreaves and E. A. Hilary Haigh (eds.), *Slavery in Yorkshire: Richard Oastler and the Campaign against Child Labour in the Industrial Revolution* (Huddersfield: University of Huddersfield Press, 2012), pp. 173-200

MATHER, F. C., *Public Order in the Age of the Chartists* (Manchester: Manchester University Press, 1959)

———, *Chartism* (London: The Historical Association, 1965)

———, 'The General Strike of 1842: A Study in Leadership, Organisation and the Threat of Revolution during the Plug Plot Disturbances', in R. Quinault and J. Stevenson (eds.), *Popular Protest and Public Order* (1974), pp. 115-40

MATTHEWS, R. C. O., *A Study in Trade-Cycle History. Economic Fluctuations in Great Britain 1833-42* (Cambridge: Cambridge University Press, 1954)

MAW, B., 'Robert Owen's Unintended Legacy: Class Conflict', in C. Williams and N. Thompson (eds.) *Robert Owen and his Legacy* (Cardiff: University of Wales Press, 2011), pp. 155-173

MAYHALL, J., *The Annals of Yorkshire* (London, Simpkin, Marshall and Co., 1878)

McLAINE, W., 'The Engineers' Union', Unpublished PhD thesis, University of London, 1939

MESSNER, A., 'Land, Leadership, Culture, and Emigration: Some Problems in Chartist Historiography', *Historical Journal*, 42, 2 (1999), pp. 1093-1109

MONTGOMERY, F. A., 'Glasgow Radicalism, 1830-48' Unpublished PhD Thesis, University of Glasgow, 1974

MORGAN, C. J., 'Demographic Change, 1771-1911', in D. Fraser (ed.) *A History of Modern Leeds* (Manchester: Manchester University Press, 1980), pp. 46-71.

MORGAN, S., *Celebrities, Heroes and Champions: Popular Politicians in the Age of Reform, 1810-67* (Manchester: Manchester University Press, 2021)

MORRIS, R. J., 'The First Urban Immigrant: The Irish in England, 1830-1850', *The Institute of Race Relations Newsletter*, 3 (1969)

———, 'The Rise of James Kitson: Trades Union and Mechanics Institution, Leeds, 1826-1851', *Publications of the Thoresby Society*, 53 (1973), pp. 179-200

———, *Cholera, 1832: The Social Response to an Epidemic* (London: Croom Helm, 1976)

———, *Class and Class-Consciousness in the Industrial Revolution 1780-1850* (London: Palgrave, 1979)

———, *Class, Sect and Party: The Making of the British Middle Class, Leeds 1820-1850* (Manchester: Manchester University Press, 1990)

MUSSON, A. E., 'The Ideology of Early Co-operation in Lancashire and Cheshire', *Transactions of the Lancashire and Cheshire Antiquarian Society*, 68 (1958), pp. 117-38

———, *Trade Union and Social History* (London: Routledge, 1974)

NAPIER, W. F. P., *The Life and Opinions of Gen. Sir Charles James Napier* (London: John Murray, 1857)

NAVICKAS, K., 'What happened to class? New histories of labour and collective action in Britain', *Social History*, 36, 2 (2011), pp. 192-204

_____, *Protest and the Politics of Space and Place, 1789-1848* (Manchester: Manchester University Press, 2016)

NEUHEISSER, J., 'Forgotten Gentleman Leaders: Local Elites, Conservative Constitutionalism and the Public Sphere in England, c. 1820-1860', *Journal of Modern European History*, 11 (2013), pp. 474-494

_____, *Crown, Church and Constitution: Popular Conservatism in England, 1815-1867* (New York and Oxford: Berghahn, 2016)

NOSSITER, T. J., 'Shopkeeper Radicalism in the Nineteenth Century', in T. J. Nossiter, A. H. Hanson and S. Rokkan (eds.), *Imagination and precision in the Social Sciences: Essays in memory of Peter Nettl* (London: Faber and Faber, 1972), pp. 407-31

OASTLER, R., *Facts and Plain Words on Everyday Subjects* (Leeds, 1832)

_____, *Huddersfield Election. The Pearking or (If you will have it so) The Biter Bit in answer to the Question who is to Blame?* (Huddersfield, 1834)

_____, *A letter to the Editor of the 'Argus and Demagogue'* (Huddersfield, 1834)

O'GORMAN, F., 'Campaign Rituals and Ceremonies: The Social Meaning of Elections in England, 1780-1860', *Past and Present*, 135 (1992), pp. 79-115

OLIVER, W. H., 'Organisations and Ideas behind the Efforts to Achieve a General Union of the Working Classes in England in the early 1830s', Unpublished PhD thesis, University of Oxford, 1954

_____, 'The Labour Exchange phase of the Co-operative Movement', *Oxford Economic Papers* ns.10 (1958), pp.355-67

_____, 'The Consolidated Trades' Union of 1834', *Economic History Review*, 2nd. ser., 18 (1964), pp. 77-95

PAHLMAN, A., 'Rise and Fall of the North-West of England Co-operative Company', *Co-operative Review*, 9 (July 1935), pp. 206-12

PARSONS, E., *The Civil, Ecclesiastical, Literary, Commercial, and Miscellaneous History of Leeds, Halifax, Huddersfield, Bradford, Wakefield, Dewsbury, Otley, and the Manufacturing Districts of Yorkshire* (Leeds: F. Hobson, 1834)

PARSSINEN, T. M., 'Association, Convention and Anti-Parliament in British Radical Politics, 1771-1848', *English Historical Review*, 88 (1973), pp. 504-33

PATTERSON, A. T., *Radical Leicester: A History of Leicester 1780-1850* (Leicester: Leicester University College, 1954)

PAUL, W., *A History of the Origins and Progress of Operative Conservative Societies* (Leeds, 1838)

PEACOCK, A. J., *Bradford Chartism, 1838-40* (York: Borthwick Institute of Historical Research, 1969)

PEEL, F., *Spen Valley: Past and Present* (Heckmondwike: Senior and Co, 1893)

_____, *The Risings of the Luddites, Chartists and Plug-drawers* (London: Routledge, 1968 edn.)

PICKERING, P. A., 'Class Without Words: Symbolic Communication in the Chartist Movement', *Past and Present*, 112 (1986), pp. 144-62

_____, 'Chartism and the "Trade of Agitation" in Early Victorian Britain', *History* 76, 247 (1991), pp.221-37

PITKETTY, T., *Capital in the Twenty-First Century* (Cambridge, Mass: Harvard University Press, 2013)

_____, *Capital and Ideology* (Cambridge, Mass: Harvard University Press, 2020)

POLLARD, S. AND SALT, J. (eds.), *Robert Owen: Prophet of the Poor* (London, Macmillan, 1971)

POLLARD, S., 'Nineteenth-Century Co-operation: From Community Building to Shopkeeping', in A. Briggs and J. Saville (eds.), *Essays in Labour History* (London: Macmillan, 1960), pp. 74-112

PORTER, J. H. (ed.), *Provincial Labour History (Exeter Papers in Economic History No. 6)* (Exeter: University of Exeter, 1972)

POSTGATE, R. W., *The Builders' History* (London: The Labour Publishing Company, 1923)

PRIESTLEY, J. H., *The History of the Ripponden Co-operative Society* (Halifax: F. King, 1932)

PROTHERO, I. J. AND PARSSINEN, T. M., 'The Tailors' Strike of 1834 and the Collapse of the GNCTU: A Police Spy's Report', *International Review of Social History*, 22 (1977), pp. 65-107

PROTHERO, I. J., 'Chartism in London', *Past and Present*, 44 (1969), pp. 76-105

_____, 'London Chartism and the Trades', *Economic History Review*, 2nd ser., 24 (1971), pp. 202-19

_____, 'William Benbow and the Concept of the "General Strike"', *Past and Present*, 63 (1974), pp. 132-71

_____, *Artisans and Politics in Early Nineteenth-Century London: John Gast and His Times* (Folkstone: Dawson, 1979)

_____, *Radical Artisans in England and France, 1830-1870* (Cambridge: Cambridge University Press, 1997)

PURVIS, M., 'Co-operative Retailing in England, 1835–1850: Developments Beyond Rochdale', *Northern History*, 22 (1986), pp. 198-215

PYE, N., *The Home Office and the Chartists 1838-48: Protest and Repression in the West Riding of Yorkshire* (Pontypool: Merlin Press, 2013)

RAISTRICK, A., *West Riding of Yorkshire* (London: Hodder and Stoughton, 1970)

RANDALL, A., *Before the Luddites: Custom, Community and Machinery in the English Woollen Industry, 1776-1809* (Cambridge, Cambridge University Press, 1991)

RANDALL, T., 'Chartist poetry and song', in O. Ashton, R. Fyson and S. Roberts (eds.), *The Chartist Legacy* (Woodbridge, Merlin Press, 1999), pp. 171-195

REDMONDS, G., *Surnames Around Huddersfield* (Huddersfield: Regent Printers, 1980)

RICHARDS, P., 'The State and Early Industrial Capitalism: The Case of the Handloom Weavers', *Past and Present*, 79 (1979), pp. 91-115

RICHARDSON, C., 'Irish Settlement in Mid-19th C. Bradford', *Yorkshire Bulletin for Economic and Social Research*, 20, 1 (1968), pp. 40-57

_____, 'The Irish in Victorian Bradford', *Bradford Antiquary*, ns., 45 (1971), pp. 294-316

RIMMER, W. G., 'Leeds Leather Industry in the nineteenth century', *Publications of the Thoresby Society*, 46 (1960), pp. 119-64

_____., 'Working Men's Cottages in Leeds, 1770-1840', *Publications of the Thoresby Society*, 46 (1961), pp. 165-199

_____, 'Industrial Profile of Leeds, 1740-1840', *Publications of the Thoresby Society*,

50 (1967), pp. 130-57

ROBERTS, M., *Political Movements in Urban Britain, 1832-1914* (Basingstoke: Palgrave Macmillan, 2009)

_____, 'Richard Oastler, Toryism, Radicalism and the limitations of Party, c.1807-1846', *Parliamentary History*, 37 (2018), pp. 250-273

_____, '"God Save the Paddock Flag": Anti-Poor Law and Chartist Banners, 1837-44', in J.A. Hargreaves (ed.), *The Charter Our Right! Huddersfield Chartism Reconsidered* (Huddersfield: Huddersfield Local History Society, 2018), pp. 39-62

ROBERTS, S. (ed.), *The People's Charter: Democratic Agitation in Early Victorian Britain* (London, Merlin Press, 2003)

_____ (ed.), *The Dignity of Chartism: Essays by Dorothy Thompson* (London: Verso, 2015)

_____, *Radical Politicians and Poets in Early Victorian Britain. The Voices of Six Chartist Leaders* (Lampeter: Edwin Mellen, 1993)

ROSE, M. E., 'The Anti-Poor Law Movement in the North of England', *Northern History*, I (1966), pp. 70-91

_____, 'The Anti-Poor Law Agitation', in J. T. Ward (ed.), *Popular Movements c. 1830-1850* (London: Macmillan, 1970), pp. 78-94

ROSE, S. O., *Limited Livelihoods: Gender and Class in Nineteenth-Century England* (London: Routledge, 1992)

ROYLE, E., *Victorian Infidels: The Origins of the British Secularist Movement, 1791-1866* (Manchester, Manchester University Press, 1974)

_____, *Chartism* (London: Longman, 1980)

_____, 'Owenism and the secularist tradition: The Huddersfield Secular Society and Sunday School', in M. Chase and I. Dyck (eds.), *Living and Learning: Essays in Honour of J. F. C. Harrison* (Aldershot, Scolar Press, 1996), pp. 199-217

_____, 'Chartists and Owenites – many parts but one body', *Labour History Review*, 65 (2000), pp. 2-21

_____ (ed.), *Power in the Land: the Ramsdens and their Huddersfield Estate, 1542-1920* (Huddersfield: Huddersfield University Press, 2020)

_____, 'Radicalism in the West Riding, 1790-1890', Huddersfield Local History Society, Annual Luddite Memorial Lecture 2021

RUBENSTEIN, D. (ed.), *People for the People: Radical Ideas and Personalities in British Social History* (London: Ithaca Press, 1973)

SALMON, P., *Electoral Reform at Work: Local Politics and National Parties, 1832-1841* (Woodbridge: Boydell Press, 2002)

SAMUEL, R., 'Workshop of the World: Steam Power and Hand Technology in Mid-Victorian Britain', *History Workshop Journal*, 3 (1977), pp. 6-72

SANDERS, J. R., 'Joshua Hobson: "One of Freedom's Boys", 1829-37', Unpublished BA thesis, University of Manchester, 1973

_____, 'Working-class movements in the West Riding textile district 1829 to 1839, with emphasis on local leadership and organisation', Unpublished PhD thesis, University of Manchester, 1984

_____, 'The Voice of the "Shoeless, Shirtless and Shameless": Community radicalism in the West Riding, 1829 to 1839', *Northern History*, 58 (2021), pp. 259-

281

————, 'John Douthwaite and "John Powlett": Trades' Unionism and Conflict in Early 1830s Yorkshire', *Labour History Review*, 86, 1 (2022), pp. 1-38

————, 'Out of Obscurity: Local Leadership and Cultural Wealth in the Radical Communities of the West Riding Textile District, 1825-40', *History Workshop Journal*, 94 (2022), pp. 1-23.

————, 'Turncoats and traitors, rogues and renegades: reviewing labour's lost leaders in reform era Yorkshire', *Social History*, 48, 3 (2023)

SANDERS, M., *The Poetry of Chartism: Aesthetics, Politics, History* (Cambridge and New York: Cambridge University Press, 2009)

SCATCHERD, N., *The History of Morley … etc.* (Leeds, 1830)

SCHWARZKOPF, J., *Women in the Chartist Movement* (London: Macmillan, 1991)

SCRIVEN, T., 'Activism and the Everyday: The Practices of Radical Working-Class Politics, 1830-1842', Unpublished PhD thesis, University of Manchester, 2012

————, *Popular Virtue: Continuity and Change in Radical Moral Politics, 1820-70* (Manchester: Manchester University Press, 2017)

————, 'Slavery and Abolition in Chartist Thought and Culture, 1838–1850', *Historical Journal* (2021), pp. 1-23

SCRUTON, W., 'The Great Strike of 1825', *Bradford Antiquary*, 1 (1880), pp. 67-73

————, *Bradford Fifty Years Ago: A Jubilee Memorial of the Bradford Corporation* (Bradford: G. F. Sewell, 1897)

————, *Pen and Pencil Pictures of Old Bradford* (Bradford: Thomas Brear, 1889)

SEARBY, P., *Coventry Politics in the Age of the Chartists* (Coventry: Coventry Historical Association, 1964)

SEWARD, D., 'The Wool Textile Industry, 1750-1960', in J. G. Jenkins (ed.), *The Wool Textile Industry in Great Britain* (London: Routledge and Kegan Paul, 1972), pp. 34-47

SIGSWORTH, E. M., *Black Dyke Mills: A History* (Liverpool: Liverpool University Press, 1958)

————, 'The Industrial Revolution', in M. W. Beresford and G. R. Jones (eds.), *Leeds and its Region* (Leeds: British Association for The Advancement of Science, 1967), pp. 146-55

SINGLETON, F., 'The Saddleworth Union, 1827-30', *Society for the Study of Labour History Bulletin*, 5 (1962), pp. 33-6

SMELSER, N. J., *Social Change in the Industrial Revolution* (London: Routledge and Kegan Paul, 1959)

SMITH, J., 'The Strike of 1825', in D. G. Wright and J. A. Jowitt (eds.), *Victorian Bradford. Essays in Honour of Jack Reynolds* (Bradford: City of Bradford Metropolitan Council, 1981), pp. 63-80

SMITH, W., *Morley, Ancient and Modern* (London: Longmans, Green and Co., 1886)

SOFFNER, R. N. 'Attitudes and Allegiances in the Unskilled North, 1830-50', *International Review of Social History*, 10 (1965), pp. 429-54

SPEIGHT, H., *Chronicles and Stories of Old Bingley* (London: Elliot Stock, 1898)

STANDING, G., *The Precariat: The New Dangerous Class* (London: Bloomsbury, 2011)

STEARNS, P. N. 'Patterns of Industrial Strike Activity in France during the July

Monarchy', *American Historical Review*, 70 (1964-5), pp. 371-94

STEARNS, P. N., 'Measuring the Evolution of Strike Movements', *International Review of Social History*, 19 (1974), pp. 1-27

STEDMAN JONES, G., 'England's First Proletariat', *New Left Review*, 90 (1975), pp. 35-69

_____, 'The Language of Chartism', in J. Epstein and D. Thompson (eds.), *The Chartist Experience: Studies in Working-Class Radicalism and Culture, 1830-1860* (London: Macmillan, 1982), pp. 3-58

_____, 'Rethinking Chartism', in G. Stedman Jones, *Languages of Class: Studies in English Working-Class History, 1832-1982* (Cambridge: Cambridge University Press, 1983), pp.90-178

SYKES, D. F. E., *Huddersfield and Its Vicinity* (Huddersfield: The Advertiser Press, 1898)

_____, *The History of the Colne Valley* (Slaithwaite, F. Walker, 1906)

SYKES, R., 'Popular Politics and Trade Unionism in South-East Lancashire, 1829-42', Unpublished PhD Thesis, University of Manchester, 1982.

_____, 'Early Chartism and Trade Unionism in South-East Lancashire', in J. A. Epstein and D. Thompson (eds.), *The Chartist Experience: Studies in Working-Class Radicalism and Culture, 1830-1860* (London: Macmillan, 1982), pp. 152-93

_____, 'Trade unionism and class consciousness: the "revolutionary" period of general unionism, 1829-1834', in J. Rule (ed.), *British Trade Unionism, 1750-1850: The Formative Years* (London: Longman, 1988), pp. 178-201

TAYLOR, M., 'Rethinking the Chartists: searching for synthesis in the historiography of Chartism', *Historical Journal*, 39, 2 (1996), pp. 479-95

TESTER, J., *History of the Commencement, Progress and Termination of the Bradford Contest… etc.* (Bradford, 1826)

THOMIS, M. I., *Politics and Society in Nottingham, 1783-1835* (Oxford: Blackwell, 1969)

THOMPSON, D. (WITH THOMPSON, E. P.), '"The Dignity of Chartism": Halifax as a Chartist centre', in S. Roberts (ed.), *The Dignity of Chartism: Essays by Dorothy Thompson* (London: Verso, 2015), pp. 73-124

THOMPSON, D., 'Chartism in Industrial Areas', *Amateur Historian*, 3 (1956-7), pp. 13-19

_____, 'Notes on Aspects of Chartist Leadership', *Society for the Study of Labour History Bulletin*, 15 (1967), pp. 28-33

_____, 'Chartism as a Historical Subject', *Society for the Study of Labour History Bulletin*, 20 (1970), pp. 10-18

_____ (ed.), *The Early Chartists* (London: Macmillan, 1971)

_____, 'Chartism, Success or Failure', in D. Rubenstein (ed.), *People for the People: Radical Ideas and Personalities in British Social History* (London: Ithaca Press, 1973)

_____, 'Ireland and the Irish in English Radicalism', in J. Epstein and D. Thompson (eds.), *The Chartist Experience: Studies in Working-class Radicalism and Culture, 1830-60* (London: Macmillan, 1982), pp. 120-51

_____, *The Chartists: Popular Politics in the Industrial Revolution* (London: Breviary Stuff, 2013 edn.)

_____, 'The Languages of Class', *Society for the Study of Labour History Bulletin*, 52, 1 (1987) pp. 54-7

THOMPSON, E. P., *The Making of the English Working Class* (Harmondsworth: Penguin, 1968 edn.)

_____, 'The Moral Economy of the English Crowd in the 18th Century', *Past and Present*, 50 (1971), pp. 76-136

_____, 'Patrician Society, Plebian Culture', *Journal of Social History*, 7 (1974), pp. 382-405

THOMPSON, F. M. L., 'Whigs and Liberals in the West-Riding, 1830-60', *English Historical Review*, 74 (1959), pp. 214-39

THORNES, R., 'Change and continuity in the Development of Co-operation, 1827-1844', in S. Yeo (ed.), *New Views of Co-operation* (London: Routledge, 1988), pp. 27-51

_____, 'The Origins of the Co-operative Movement in Huddersfield: the Life and Times of the 1st Huddersfield Co-operative Trading Association' in E. A. Hilary Haigh (ed.), *Huddersfield, A Most Handsome Town: Aspects of the History and Culture of a West Riding Town* (Huddersfield: Kirklees Cultural Services, 1992), pp. 171-88

TILLY, C., TILLY, L. AND TILLY, R., *The Rebellious Century, 1830-1930* (Cambridge, Mass.: Harvard University Press, 1975)

TREBLE, J. H., 'The Place of the Irish Catholics in the Social Life of the North of England', Unpublished PhD thesis, University of Leeds, 1968

_____, 'The Attitude of the Roman Catholic Church towards Trade Unions in the North of England, 1833-42', *Northern History*, V (1970), p. 93-113

TUCKETT, A., *The Blacksmiths' History: What Smithy Workers Gave Trade Unionism* (London: Lawrence and Wishart, 1974)

TUFNELL, E. C., *Character, Object and Effects of Trades' Unions; with some remarks on the law concerning them* (London: James Ridgway and Sons, 1834)

TURBERVILLE, A. S. AND BECKWITH, F., 'Leeds and Parliamentary Reform 1820-1832', *Publication of the Thoresby Society*, 41 (1954), pp. 1-88

TYLECOTE, M., *The Mechanics' Institutes of Lancashire and Yorkshire before 1851* (Manchester, Manchester University Press, 1957)

VERNON, J., *Politics and the People: A Study in English Political Culture, 1815-1867* (Cambridge: Cambridge University Press, 1993)

WALKER, J. W., *Wakefield, Its History and People* (Wakefield: West Yorkshire Print Co., 1934)

WALSH, D., *Making Angels in Marble, The Conservatives, the Early Industrial Working Class and Attempts at Political Incorporation* (London: Breviary Stuff, 2012)

WALTON, J. K. 'Revisiting the Rochdale Pioneers', *Northern History*, 80 (2015), pp. 215-45

WARD, J. T., 'M.T. Sadler', *University of Leeds Review*, 7 (1960)

_____, 'Matthew Balme, 1813-1884, Factory Reformer', *Bradford Antiquary*, 10, (1960), pp. 217-228

_____, 'Leeds and the Factory Reform Movement', *Publications of the Thoresby Society*, 46 (1961), pp. 87-118

_____, 'Bradford and Factory Reform', *Bradford Textile Society Journal*, (1961), pp. 41-52

_____, 'A Great Bradford Dispute', *Bradford Textile Society Journal*, (1961-2), pp. 117-31

_____, *The Factory Movement, 1830-1855* (London: Macmillan, 1962)

_____, 'Some Industrial Reformers', *Bradford Textile Society Journal*, (1962-3), pp. 125-6

_____, 'Squire Auty 1812-70', *Bradford Antiquary*, 11 (1964), pp. 104-123

_____, 'Two Pioneers in Industrial Reform', *Bradford Textile Society Journal*, (1964)

_____ (ed.), *Popular Movements c. 1830-1850* (London: Macmillan, 1970)

_____, *Chartism* (London: Batsford, 1973)

_____, 'Some Aspects of Working-class Conservatism in the 19th Century', in J. Butt and J. T. Ward (eds.), *Scottish Themes: essays in honour of Professor S. G. E. Lythe* (Edinburgh: Scottish Academic Press, 1976), pp. 141-7

_____, 'Richard Oastler on Politics and Factory Reform', *Nothern History*, 24 (1988), pp. 124-45

WARD, W. R., *Religion and Society in England, 1750-1850* (London: Batsford, 1972)

WEARMOUTH, R. F., *Methodism and the Working-Class Movements of England, 1800-1850* (1947)

_____, *Some Working-Class Movements of the Nineteenth Century* (London: Epworth Press, 1948).

_____, *Methodism and the Trade Unions* (London: Epworth Press, 1959)

WEAVER, S. A., *John Fielden and the Politics of Popular Radicalism, 1832-1847* (Oxford: Clarendon Press, 1987)

_____, 'The Political Ideology of Short-Time', in G. Cross (ed.), *Worktime and Industrialization: An International History* (Philadelphia: Temple University Press, 1988), pp. 77–103

_____, 'Richard Oastler', *Oxford Dictionary of National Biography*, (Oxford: Oxford University Press, 2004)

WEBB, S. AND WEBB, B., *The History of Trade Unionism* (London: Longmans, Green and Co., 1894)

WICKWAR, W. H., *The Struggle for the Freedom of the Press, 1819-1832* (London: Allen and Unwin, 1928)

WIENER, J. H., *The War of the Unstamped: The Movement to Repeal the British Newspaper Tax 1830-1836* (Ithaca, NY: Cornell University Press, 1969)

_____, *A Descriptive Finding List of Unstamped British Periodicals, 1830-36* (London: Bibliographical Society, 1970)

_____, 'The Working Class Press: Some Pre-Chartist Problems', *Society for the Study of Labour History Bulletin*, 25 (1972), pp. 26-7

_____, *Radicalism and Freethought in Nineteenth Century Britain: the Life of Richard Carlile* (Westport Connecticut: Greenwood Press, 1983)

WILD, M. T., 'An Historical Geography of the West Yorkshire Textile Industries to c.1850' Unpublished PhD thesis, University of Birmingham, 1972

_____, 'The Yorkshire wool textile industry', in J. G. Jenkins (ed.), *The Wool Textile Industry in Great Britain* (London: Routledge and Kegan Paul, 1972)

WILKINSON, R., AND PICKETT, K., *The Spirit Level: Why More Equal Societies Almost Always Do Better* (London, Penguin Books, 2009)

WILSON, A., 'Chartism', in J. T. Ward (ed.), *Popular Movements, c. 1830-1850* (London: Macmillan, 1970), pp. 116-134

WILSON, B., *The Struggles of an Old Chartist* (Halifax: John Nicholson, 1887)

WRIGHT, D. G., 'Politics and Opinion in Nineteenth Century Bradford, 1832-1880, with special reference to Parliamentary elections', Unpublished PhD thesis, University of Leeds, 1966

———, 'A Radical Borough: Parliamentary Politics in Bradford 1832-41', *Northern History*, 4 (1968), pp. 132-66

———, *Popular Radicalism: The Working-Class Experience, 1780-1880* (London: Routledge, 1988)

WRIGLEY, E. A., *Nineteenth Century Society* (Cambridge: Cambridge University Press, 1972)

YEO, E., 'Robert Owen and Radical Culture', in S. Pollard and J. Salt (eds.), *Robert Owen: Prophet of the Poor* (London: Macmillan, 1971), pp. 84-114

———, 'Christianity in Chartist Struggle, 1838-42', *Past and Present*, 91 (1981), pp. 109-39

YEO, S., 'Introductory: Rival Clusters of Potential: Ways of Seeing Co-operation', in S. Yeo (ed.), *New Views of Co-operation* (London: Routledge, 1988), pp. 1-9

———, (ed.), *New Views of Co-operation* (London: Routledge, 1988)

YOSSO, T. J., 'Whose culture has capital? A critical race theory discussion of Community Cultural Wealth', *Race Ethnicity and Education*, 8 (2005), pp. 69-91

Index

Simon Hannah, RADICAL LAMBETH 1979-1991

Ariel Hessayon (ed.), THE REFINER'S FIRE, *The Collected Works of TheaurauJohn Tany*

Catherine Howe, HALIFAX 1842, *A Year of Crisis*

Barry Reay, THE LAST RISING OF THE AGRICULTURAL LABOURERS, *Rural Life and Protest in Nineteenth-Century England*

Rachel Rogers, FRIENDS OF THE REVOLUTION, *The British Radical Community in Early Republican Paris 1792-1794*

Philip Ruff, A TOWERING FLAME, *The Life & Times of the Elusive Latvian Anarchist Peter the Painter*

Buchanan Sharp, IN CONTEMPT OF ALL AUTHORITY, *Rural Artisans and Riot in the West of England, 1586-1660*

Dorothy Thompson, THE CHARTISTS, *Popular Politics in the Industrial Revolution*

E. P. Thompson, WHIGS AND HUNTERS, *The Origin of the Black Act*

David Walsh, MAKING ANGELS IN MARBLE, *The Conservatives, the Early Industrial Working Class and Attempts at Political Incorporation*

David Walsh, THE SONS OF BELIAL, *Protest and Community Change in the North-West, 1740-1770*

Roger Wells, INSURRECTION, *The British Experience 1795-1803*

Roger Wells, WRETCHED FACES, *Famine in Wartime England 1793-1801*

David Worrall, RADICAL CULTURE, *Discourse, Resistance and Surveillance, 1790-1820*

For further information visit
www.breviarystuff.org.uk

Yorkshire Slavery +
abolitionists

P 152

- 247 -

Milton Keynes UK
Ingram Content Group UK Ltd.
UKHW010729190224
438095UK00003B/164

9 781916 158672